JOHN BELL, Ph.D. University of Illinois, is Professor of Economics at that university. Dr. Bell formerly taught at Syracuse University, Western Reserve University, and Temple University.

A HISTORY

of

ECONOMIC THOUGHT

By

JOHN FRED BELL

Professor of Economics
University of Illinois

THE RONALD PRESS COMPANY · NEW YORK

Library of Congress Catalog Card Number: 53-5712

To
RUTH

Preface

This volume traces the development of economic thought from antiquity to the present time. Designed primarily as a textbook for college courses, it seeks to give the student a proper understanding of the evolution of the significant economic doctrines, their content and methodology, their application and influence. It is the author's conviction that only by studying the great thinkers of the past can the student grasp fully the recurring, complex problems of economics and gain a fresh perspective for appraising current ideas and policies.

There is a definite need for a volume that provides a unified approach, a manageable organization, and breadth of coverage so that the diverse materials in the history of economic thought may be more easily summarized and integrated. Accordingly, the author has elected to include in this book only those thinkers whose ideas, insights, and teachings have had a substantial influence, directly or indirectly, on the main stream of economic thought. Attention is given to those factors of a political, social, and economic nature that provide the setting in which the ideas developed.

A chronological arrangement of individuals and schools has been followed in order to clarify the evolutionary process in theory and practice. The important works and the principal theories are taken up one by one, expounded and explained in detail, and related to their social and political background. Biographical sketches are given when pertinent. Interrelationships between the ideas of thinkers in different periods are consistently pointed out; and particular attention is paid to constructive criticisms of outstanding figures and doctrines by their contemporaries and successors.

Throughout the book, exposition, discussion, and interpretations are in terms of the fundamental questions and concepts with which economists deal. There is full discussion of the development of such important phases in economics as the growth of capitalism, international trade theory and policy, socioeconomic movements, welfare economics, and both macro- and micro-economics. But the strongest emphasis has been placed on the development of value and price analysis and distribution theory, since these topics have been historically the primary concerns of economists.

Together, the approach, the method, and the emphasis of this volume give the student the information necessary to show the development of economic thought without overloading him with unimportant details. The classics of economic literature have been quoted generously throughout, but the reader is reminded that there is no substitute for the study of the original works. The author's function is to introduce, not to indoctrinate. He has striven for balance and objectivity and has conscientiously tried to avoid favoring any one doctrine over another. The reader will see the foreshadowings of many doctrines (presumably new and different) in the writings of long ago. He will notice the similarities in the economic problems that have confronted mankind over the centuries. As they appear, these parallels and similarities are pointed out to serve as a warning against the hasty application of nostrums and quack remedies for economic disorders.

In the preparation of this volume the author is indebted to many persons. His first interests in the field of economic thought were stimulated by an eminent scholar and teacher, Professor Nathan Austin Weston (1868-1933), in whose seminars at the University of Illinois many hundreds of students had the thrill of association with a great classical mind. A great debt is due to my former students who have had access to the chapters for classroom use for several years; they ferreted out many errors and challenged the exposition. Valuable aid has been given by various members of the economics department of the University of Illinois: Professors Dwight P. Flanders, W. A. Neiswanger, and E. T. Weiler read the chapters which deal with their particular field of interest in theory and econometrics; Professor A. S. Hall assisted with the chapter on the Lausanne economists; Professors Charles W. Marberry and John W. Beall had a part in preparing the material on J. M. Keynes. Professor W. A. McConagha, Lawrence College, read critically most of the early chapters; and Mrs. Hilda R. Stice made editorial corrections. Any errors or shortcomings, however, are the author's alone.

Some of the materials were gathered on a sabbatical leave for study in Europe. Thanks are due to the librarians of several universities, notably Lausanne, Leyden, the London School of Economics, Oxford, and Cambridge, who made rare materials available. The economic collections at the Universities of Edinburgh, Glasgow, Belfast, and Dublin were opened unsparingly and personal interviews with many European scholars were highly rewarding.

J. F. BELL

Urbana, Illinois
February, 1953

Acknowledgments

The author wishes gratefully to acknowledge the permission to quote from the following publications:

ADDISON-WESLEY PRESS, INC.: Richard Clemence and Francis Doody, *The Schumpeterian System.* JOHN M. CLARK: J. B. Clark, *Distribution of Wealth.* J. A. COMMONS: J. R. Commons, *Institutional Economics* and *The Legal Foundations of Capitalism.* HARCOURT, BRACE AND COMPANY, INC.: J. M. Keynes, *Essays in Biography, The General Theory of Employment, Interest and Money* and *A Treatise on Money*; R. F. Harrod, *The Life of John Maynard Keynes.* HARVARD UNIVERSITY PRESS: A. E. Monroe, *Early Economic Thought,* and J. A. Schumpeter, *The Theory of Economic Development.* HENRY HOLT AND COMPANY, INC.: S. L. Levy, *Industrial Efficiency and Social Economy.* CHARLES H. KERR AND COMPANY: Karl Marx, *Capital* and *Value, Price and Profit.* THE MACMILLAN COMPANY: Alfred Marshall, *Principles of Economics*; Knut Wicksell, *Lectures on Political Economy.* NATIONAL BUREAU OF ECONOMIC RESEARCH, INC.: *29th Annual Report,* and W. C. Mitchell, *Business Cycles: The Problem and Its Setting.* OXFORD UNIVERSITY PRESS, INC.: Gustav Cassel, *On Quantitative Thinking in Economics.* PRENTICE-HALL, INC.: Allan G. Gruchy, *Modern Economic Thought.* ROYAL ECONOMIC SOCIETY: "John Maynard Keynes, 1883-1946," *Economic Journal,* Vol. LVII, No. 225. ST. MARTIN's PRESS, INC., THE MACMILLAN COMPANY OF CANADA, LTD., MACMILLAN AND COMPANY, LTD., OF LONDON: A. C. Pigou, *The Economics of Welfare* and *Memorials of Alfred Marshall.* UNIVERSITY OF CALIFORNIA PRESS: W. C. Mitchell, *Business Cycles.* UNIVERSITY OF CHICAGO PRESS: "Grundsätze," *American Journal of Sociology,* Vol. XXIX; R. G. Tugwell, "Notes on the Life of Simon Nelson Patten," *Journal of Political Economy,* Vol. XXXI, No. 2. VIKING PRESS, INC.: Thorstein Veblen, *The Place of Science in Modern Civilization.*

J. F. B.

Contents

ix

PART IV

CRITICS AND CRITICISMS OF CLASSICAL ECONOMICS

PART V

THE DEVELOPMENT OF MARGINAL UTILITY ECONOMICS

PART VI

THE DEVELOPMENT OF ECONOMICS IN THE UNITED STATES

PART VII

THE MAIN CURRENTS OF ECONOMIC THOUGHT IN THE TWENTIETH CENTURY

A History of Economic Thought

1

Introduction to the Study
of Economic Thought

The history of economic thought is a study of the heritage left by writers on economic subjects over many years. This heritage is the property of all students, for contributions have been made to it by writers and practitioners of every land. The earliest records describe the efforts of people to make a living, which, after all, constitutes the real subject matter of economics. The chronicles of these struggles reveal problems similar to, if not identical with, those which appear today. Nature did not endow all nations equally well with natural resources from which to satisfy their wants. The accounts relate how man has attempted to overcome scarcity, what principles were evolved to expedite trade and commerce, the barter or price mechanisms used in exchange, and the extremes to which man went to gain desired objectives. Probably few nations ever desired war for the mere sake of fighting, but now, as in earlier times, the desires of people for various things bring war. The history of economic thought, therefore, records some of the measures used by people in the struggle to gain economic satisfactions from nature's endowment.

The history of economic thought draws upon nearly every phase of human knowledge. The political annals and the economic history of peoples, since they deal with man's economic efforts in his political setting, provide its source materials. In addition, the prevailing philosophy, religion, sociology, culture, individual and national outlook, and the geography and the geopolitics of peoples are important determining factors in shaping the body of doctrines identified as economic thought. However complicated this development may appear, it is nevertheless as it should be. Nations and peoples do not evolve in any unilateral manner. Nor does the economic phase of their existence follow a single track. Practices of peoples preceded theorizing in the early history of economic thought. Early economic practices were those of a primitive economy. As the circumstances changed with time, the practices and the theories, if any, changed also. For example, the particular background of the early Middle Ages provided entirely adequate reasons for condemning interest-taking at that time. As the gradual revival of Europe brought concurrent changes in economic practices, there was a reversal of opinion and the taking of interest was made legal. What was true under given circumstances of time and place may not be true at some later time. Because of this fact alone, the student of economic thought must be tolerant of economic doctrines and dogmas which are no longer accepted and try to view them objectively by placing them in their proper setting. Final truth is, at least in economics, an elusive thing which must be sought in every element of human culture.

The student of economic thought must also possess considerable patience, as well as tolerance, in the pursuit of economic truths. One may read about economic practices long before there was any theorizing on the subject. Such theorizing as appeared bit by bit was a mixture of politics, logic, ethics, and moral philosophy. This is easily explained by the fact that for many years the economic aspect of man's endeavors was ranked far below the cultural aspects. Only within the past few hundred years has the individual been called an "economic man"; his other aliases are of much longer standing in the older disciplines. Efforts to find much economic material at the dawn of human history are not very rewarding. As ideas do begin to appear, a degree of patience is necessary to piece together the odds and ends which finally become the warp and weft of economic thought. Even though at times it resembles the pattern of a crazy quilt, eventually it assumes the shape of a body of thought deserving careful study.

The science of economics, in comparison with some other disciplines, is relatively young. It is difficult to determine accurately when interest in the subject of political economy—the original name of the science—began. Economic practices are as old as recorded history, but interest in them as a subject, science, or discipline is relatively recent. The English mercantilists in the seventeenth century wrote tracts and pamphlets on economic subjects more or less as a particular controversy struck their fancy. Also, in that century, the Germans developed a cameral science in which economic and political measures were blended for purposes of making a self-sufficient state. Chairs were endowed in certain German universities to teach this subject. Adam Smith's *Wealth of Nations*, in 1776, was the first comprehensive attempt to bring together materials representing economic practices. Smith combined his observations with descriptions of current economic practices to set forth a body of theoretical principles. This book became the starting point for subsequent publications of varying importance on political economy. It contained his views on political economy, some of which had been developed in his lectures at Glasgow College between 1750 and 1763. Another of the pioneers in the teaching of political economy in England was T. R. Malthus, who lectured (1805-1834) on that subject in Haileybury College. In 1825 the first chair of political economy in England was established at Oxford University. Even though the subject was taught early in the nineteenth century, there was no great interest in it, at least in universities, for by the end of the century there were no more than a half-dozen active chairs of political economy in the whole of England. That the development of the subject in all countries has been slow, relatively speaking, has been due to many factors but mainly to differences between theories as they were developed and actual economic practices. The present general interest in the subject of economics is traceable largely to advances in empirical knowledge in the subject and to relationships that have developed between government and both theoretical and applied economics.

Approaches to the Study of Economic Thought.—The subject matter of economic thought can be presented in at least three ways: first, a chronological presentation of materials as they were developed by writers and by "schools"; second, a straight-line development of concepts or ideas, with small reference to those who had a part in formulating the ideas; and third, a motivation approach which rationalizes economic ideas and motives for the purpose of explaining and justifying certain economic behavior. As will be shown, each approach has both advantages and disadvantages.

The chronological approach follows the traditional historical method and considers the writers, their ideas, and the "schools" as they appear. There is usually no dominant, unifying principle in this approach. This method permits the presentation of all factors believed to have influenced economic thought and attempts to provide the backdrop and setting for the ideas as they were finally developed. It is certain that writers in economics, from the very earliest tracts, have tended to mirror the strongest influences which prevailed at the time they wrote. There is no implication that all writers accepted the prevailing ideas, for many held views contrary to the accepted practices. In general, however, the theoretical issues and the applied problems were manifestations of current circumstances.

This approach, furthermore, enables one to see the development of economics on a broad front. Economics is the property of no special group; it is the product of many minds who have contributed over the years. Therefore, the student is put to the test of keeping in mind the broad time-and-space development of economic theories and institutions. Our present economic thought and institutions are made up of many tenuous threads which lead to early writers in many countries. Many of their contributions have endured and support Alfred Marshall's concept of the "principle of continuity," namely, that a strong nexus does exist with the past and that time periods and ideas blend into one another by "imperceptible gradations." The doctrines of economics have evolved at a painfully slow pace; when one scans this evolutionary process over the years, revolutionary flurries are seen as but a part of long-run, continuous growth.

The materials in the subsequent chapters are presented chronologically and on a broad front. Emphasis has been placed on the setting in which the ideas developed. This background is drawn, as time and space considerations permit, from economic and political history, sociology, religion, and the general cultural pattern of the various peoples; and it can be supplemented indefinitely.

The second approach is one that traces the evolution of concepts. The concept is traced as it developed, without any special emphasis upon the interdependence of thought or upon contributing causes and influences. This ideological approach has the advantage of showing a continuous development of one concept to present usage; the concept is given greater importance than any particular contributor or school. The approach may, of necessity, have to omit many influencing factors if they do not bear directly on the issue and it may also, to some extent, be repetitious of personalities. Few writers developed only one specific doctrine; the majority presented their views on many issues within the sphere of political economy. Yet it is true that some are remembered for specific contributions rather than for their general treatment of the subject. The chronological and the ideological approaches can be used in combination for greater thoroughness.

The third approach treats economics as but a phase of socioeconomic development in which economic forces are portrayed as struggles of conflicting interests. A materialistic interpretation is placed on economic motivation, and classes are identified and set forth in constant struggle with one another over economic resources and income. It has always been assumed in economics that man will attempt to maximize his gains and minimize his losses and that each individual seeks a larger gain in preference to a smaller one. In early classical writings a theory was held that wages can increase only at the expense of profits; the owners of these two factors, labor and capital, were described as engaging in sharp competition with one another for a larger share of the final product. If the landlord, who receives rent for the use of land, is added, each of the three competitors—landlord, capitalist, and laborer—was considered to be engaged in a relentless struggle to get a larger share for himself.

It must be admitted that the early writers, notably David Ricardo, identified this characteristic of the economy. It has been accepted and enlarged upon by Karl Marx and other socialist writers and provides a basis for the materialistic interpretation of history. While it cannot be denied that there always have been and always will be such struggles because of the unequal distribution of resources, they should be viewed as just one of the many characteristics of society. No one could have visualized the extent to which cooperation has become a part of man's existence at all levels in present-day society and thus tends to defeat the Marxian contentions. The doctrines of the class struggle are treated herein as a part of economic development.

The Scope of This Work.—The first materials presented are the economic practices of early peoples as recorded in the Bible. The accounts are fragmentary and therefore not conclusive; they are sufficiently accurate, however, to show that many present-day problems and practices were prevalent at that remote time. In economics, as in all branches of learning, one looks to the contributions of the great philosophers of ancient Greece. Aristotle in particular provided us with many concepts of modern economics. From the Romans we inherited laws, many of which deal with economic practices and provide elements of the legal framework of the state.

Next came the long stretch of years known as the Middle Ages, during which the Church was the predominant influence in temporal affairs. The concept of a just or fair price, rules against usury or interest-taking, and many trade practices can be traced to this period. More important was the rise of strong states. Moreover, modern capitalism has its roots in the practices which grew, more by accident than by design, from the planlessness of the Middle Ages.

As nations became stronger they engaged in trade practices afterward identified as mercantilism. These practices were designed to enhance their riches—a synonym for strength. The economic writings in this period of about one hundred and fifty years (1613-1767) were largely in defense of trade practices conceived in strongly nationalistic tones. Many of the mercantilistic doctrines have survived and are in current use.

The French physiocrats may be regarded as the first "school" of economists. Although they constituted a "school" for only a few years (c. 1755-1775), their influence on economic thought has been relatively great. Some writers [1] begin the study of economics with this group just as others [2] start with the mercantilists.

[1] Notably, Charles Gide and Charles Rist, A *History of Economic Doctrines* (1st French ed., 1909; 2d English ed., New York, 1948).
[2] Notably, W. A. Scott, The *Development of Economics* (New York, 1933).

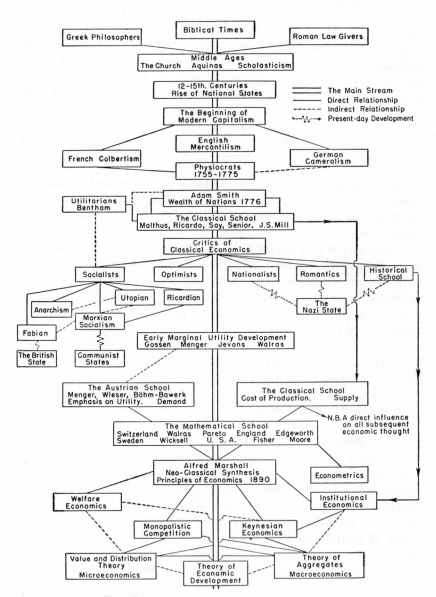

THE DEVELOPMENT OF ECONOMIC THOUGHT

As already stated, the first great work in political economy was Adam Smith's *Wealth of Nations,* after which many publications patterned largely on that book began to appear. In rapid order came the writings of David Ricardo, Thomas Robert Malthus, N. W. Senior, J. B. Say, J. S. Mill, and others, who together are grouped as the classical economists. Many of the specific theories developed by these men have long been a part of the accepted doctrines of economics. Not only have they formed the larger share of economic theory, but they have also evoked the largest amount of criticism of theories as well as practices.

Pure theory made its greatest advances as a result of the doctrines developed by a group at the University of Vienna, known as the "Austrian school," Jevons in England, and Léon Walras in Switzerland. The economics of Adam Smith and the classical group was largely objective or exchange economics of the market place, with emphasis on price. The former group stressed the subjective side, with emphasis on the want-satisfying power of a commodity. A new approach was thus afforded which placed the individual in the position of the final arbiter of value. Jevons and Walras first gave economics a mathematical expression, which has since been developed to high levels of perfection.

The greatest figure in economics at the close of the nineteenth century was Alfred Marshall, whose *Principles of Economics* (1890) was widely accepted. It set the pace for theory and was unchallenged, although modified, until the work of John Maynard Keynes appeared in 1936. Marshall taught the equilibrium of the forces of supply and demand and showed how time worked as an influencing factor. A great debt is owed to Marshall for placing economic theory and analysis on a plane higher than had previously been reached. His *Principles* was intended to be an account of the workings of capitalism with the ultimate objective of human betterment. A logical analysis of economic principles was made with a degree of finality which removed them from polemics, yet it avoided the pitfall of economic dogma.

Economics has had its share of criticism. In fact, that criticism has been at times extremely sharp and always voluminous. Some of the groups, notably the German historical school, made criticism of classical economics the common objective of their school. Socialist criticism likewise has assumed large proportions over the years. Of lesser importance were the nationalist and optimist critics in Europe and America. Criticism of economic doctrines has been looked upon as everyone's privilege and it has served the very useful purpose of testing the truth of the theories. The anvil has a peculiar way of wearing out the hammers; so also have economic truths weathered the storm of criticism.

The development of economics in the United States is treated in Part VI. A separate section on American economists presents the disadvantages of going back to early beginnings of economics, examining the controversies as they developed in this country, and fitting European economics into them. The advantages of treating the Americans as a group outweigh the disadvantages. For a time, at least, distinctly American issues were identifiable. By the end of the nineteenth century, however, the local flavor had disappeared and economics in America, like other sciences, became a universal discipline.

Part VII deals with the main currents of economic thought as they have developed in different countries in this century. The Marshallian analysis, as it was originally presented, is followed by the modifications which resulted from changes in the competitive assumptions. The Keynesian influence subsequent to 1936 is the note on which the main body of the book ends. An attempt has been made to present objectively this influence on both theory and policy. The main interest in Lord Keynes is in his influence and not in details of analysis. Current modifications of the Keynesian thesis are also noted. The trends in contemporary economic thought and the influence of government as a conditioning factor may be seen throughout the last three chapters.

PART I

The Beginnings of Economics

2

Economic Practices of Biblical Times

In dealing historically with economic thought, there has been no complete agreement on the scope of the subject matter or on the points of emphasis. Some authors give little or no attention to the practices of the biblical period as contributing to the development of economic thought. This is largely due to the lack of scientifically accurate data and to the possibility of different interpretations being placed on biblical teachings. Even though the amount of study and research that has been centered, over the centuries, on biblical history and interpretation exceeds by far that spent on any other materials, opinions remain far apart. The following discussion, by no means exhaustive, presents most of the significant economic practices of biblical times.[1] Throughout Part I of this book, the student of economics will decide how much or how little emphasis should be placed upon the early economic practices and their bearing upon the development of economic thought and institutions.

In Old Testament times, people engaged in many practices which have counterparts in modern capitalism. They engaged in some trade and commerce, created small surpluses, owned private property, practiced the division of labor, set up markets, used a money and price system, made profits, took losses, and so on. In general, their problems were the same as those of a more complex economy and differed mainly in degree. Human wants had to be satisfied and the materials to satisfy those wants were indeed scarce.

The persons who compiled the Old Testament and the New were not concerned primarily with matters which we would identify as economic. They were providing rules for behavior which were to guide men in their relationships with one another and ultimately to earn them

---

[1] "Biblical times" is here used to identify a period with which the materials of this chapter deal: only the persons and practices described in the Bible are included. This is not intended to be a complete historical development of that era. No attempt is made to include the prevailing practices of other peoples who lived at the same time.

life everlasting. The materials from which the economic topics of this
chapter are drawn are fragmentary and require interpretation and inference. The views of the writers are largely ethical and metaphysical
and refer to many types of society from the nomadic and patriarchal to
cities and kingdoms. Their subsequent influence on men's thoughts
and actions is of greatest significance. Even though these views may
appear primitive or unsophisticated to us, they have influenced men's
thinking and acting to a much greater degree than any other recorded
ideas and teachings.

The Period.—The Old and the New Testament cover a vast span of
years. While the period covered by the Old Testament is a controversial one, there is some agreement that it begins about 2500 B.C. and that
the Old Testament ends at about 150 B.C. The New Testament covers
about one hundred years from the birth of Christ. Some of the writings of the Old Testament were set down as early as the ninth century
B.C. Many of the dates are conjectural; however, the chronology of certain events is sufficiently well established to permit fairly accurate estimates of much of the history of the period. The sequence of events is
not always readily apparent, nor are unifying principles easily identified.
Allowing for inaccuracies in estimates of both the beginning and the
end of the biblical period, the fact remains that it covers one of the
longest spans in recorded history.

Certain economic practices were engaged in, many of which are similar to those found today. These practices were, in some cases, a matter
of conforming to applicable laws, and in other cases they were a result
of custom and tradition. Some of the most clearly defined economic
practices will be discussed at this point.

Property and Property Rights.—"Property" then, as now, had many
meanings. Likewise, possessions were an indication of affluence then,
as now. Wealth was measured in land, animals, slaves, pieces of silver,
talents, and precious metals.

One of the oldest forms of property was land. The "hunger for land"
has been a characteristic of peoples from earliest times, and land included all the resources above, on, and below the surface of the earth.
Since mankind in early times was dependent on land for its crops, herds,
and flocks, it is little wonder that the ownership or use of land was
important.

Originally there was no property in land, for the tribes were nomadic
and traveled over relatively wide areas. In time, however, peoples ceased
their wanderings and came into possession of small land holdings. The
Old Testament regarded the small landholders as the main source of

group strength, but wars and oppression repeatedly caused them to lose title to the land.

Permanent possession of the land was denounced by the writers of the Old Testament, the attitude being, "The earth is the Lord's, and the fulness thereof" (Psalms 24:1). The principle of hereditary owner- ship was strong in biblical times, hence the desire to keep title to the land within the family; if the ownership of land could be kept within the group, the alienation of the land to outsiders was thereby precluded. The sale of land was not permitted unless all members of the family agreed to the sale. In Leviticus (25:23) there is the verse: "The land shall not be sold for ever: for the land is mine; for ye are strangers and sojourners with me." If for any reason there should be a forced sale of land, the nearest kinsman had the first option to purchase it. An early example of this redemption practice is found in Jeremiah (32:6-15) where the purchase of a field is recorded "in the country of Benjamin" for "seventeen shekels of silver," which purchase was duly witnessed and sealed according to the law and custom.

Inheritance.—The laws of family inheritance were clearly outlined by Moses as they applied to degrees of relationship. The eldest son had first claim on inherited property, but if there was no son, then it went to the daughter. If no daughter, then the property went to the man's brothers, uncles, and so on, depending upon the degree of relationship. This statute of judgment, as the Lord commanded Moses (Num. 27:5-11), had the same intent as the purchase regulations referred to before, namely, to keep the social unit together. Probably this practice was a binding tie as strong as any other in unifying the tribes of Israel. Land was generally regarded not as individual property, but as clan or family property.

Agriculture the Favored Occupation.—Agriculture was the favored occupation, the main reason being that life itself was so dependent upon it. The pastoral peoples had flocks of sheep, goats, lambs, oxen, horses, and mules. Animals provided food, clothing, and shelter in a sense, as well as serving as beasts of burden. Agriculture became more important as peoples ceased their pastoral wanderings and took up per- manent abodes. This enabled them to grow grains such as millet, bar- ley, and wheat, and to plant orchards and vineyards. It was in Egypt that settled agriculture had first appeared with any degree of perma- nence.[2] Agriculture was the basic occupation of early peoples, and it has retained this importance until relatively recent times.

[2] See H. E. Barnes, *Economic History of the Western World* (New York, 1937), chap. i.

The Seventh Year.—The seventh or sabbatical year probably derived its numerical origin from the story of creation. It is recorded in Genesis (2:2) that "on the seventh day God ended his work which he had made; and he rested on the seventh day from all his work which he had made." The Old Testament peoples made many applications of this in their life.[3] The land was to lie fallow during the seventh year. The biblical rule, as recorded in Exodus (23:10-11), calls for six years of cultivation of the land "but the seventh year thou shalt let it rest and lie still." The law is restated with emphasis in Leviticus (25:4-17), which gives details for right behavior of peoples in both the seventh and the jubilee years. No sowing, harvesting, or storing was allowed; not even those food products which grew "of their own accord" could be gathered, "for it is a year of rest unto the land" (Lev. 25:5). However, "the increase thereof out of the field," i.e., from having lain fallow, was available for food.

The laws of the seventh year as applied to agriculture were probably nothing other than a necessary rule of agriculture for soil conservation. Since no definite year was set as the first, from which the rhythm of seven could be begun, it appears likely that different portions would lie fallow in different years. In all probability there was no food shortage of a general nature which could be attributed solely to lack of production for one year. One might ask what about the eighth and ninth years. Obviously more than a year would elapse before food was available. A probable answer is that the sixth year was to be exceptionally productive and furnish enough by bringing "forth fruit for three years" (Lev. 25:20-22).

The sabbatical principle was also applied to debts. "At the end of every seven years" the creditor was to grant a release to the debtor "to the end that there shall be no poor among you" (Deut. 15:1, 4). The probable meaning of the term "release" was a one-year moratorium on the debt with a return to the obligation after the seventh year. By using the same principle as the land's lying fallow, the basis of the indebtedness was to be allowed a year's rest, for fear the source of the payment might be destroyed. The Talmud (the body of Jewish civil and canonical law) interprets this to mean that the indebtedness should actually cease, which may have been the source of the Roman statute on debts and, later, of our statute of limitations.

Slaves were to be freed in the seventh year, provided they had served six years. This law, however, was intended to apply to Hebrews only

---

[3] It is difficult to say that the idea of the sabbatical year came from the story in Genesis. Some scholars believe that the setting aside of one day was a prehistoric practice or custom which was embodied later in the Book of Genesis. The best evidence supports the latter view.

(Exod. 21:2; Deut. 15:12-18). As a reward for six faithful years of service, the freed person was to be furnished "liberally out of thy flock, and out of thy floor, and out of thy winepress" (Deut. 15:14) as a symbol that "thou wast a bondman in the land of Egypt, and the Lord thy God redeemed thee" (Deut. 15:15). If a "brother that dwelleth by thee be waxen poor, and be sold unto thee" (Lev. 25:39-40), he was not to be treated as a slave but as a hired servant, and was to serve only until the jubilee year which ended his servitude.

The Jubilee Year.—According to Mosaic law the fiftieth year was to be a hallowed year; the people were admonished to "proclaim liberty throughout all the land unto all the inhabitants thereof" (Lev. 25:10). Every man was to return unto his possession (Lev. 25:13) and unto his family. In practice this would provide against alienation of the land and tend toward solidarity of the social structure. The jubilee year was reckoned on the basis of the number of seven sabbaths of years. Then "on the tenth day of the seventh month" (Lev. 25:9) the fiftieth or jubilee year began. An interesting price regulation was set up which required that anything sold be priced with relation to the number of years after the jubilee; that is, the greater the number of years after the jubilee, or away from the next jubilee year, the higher the price; the fewer the years, the lower the price (Lev. 25:16). Since this probably applied to land, it meant that a lease (since it could not be owned) was adjusted to the remoteness of the jubilee year.

Was the jubilee year kept or was it only a paper law? There is little, if any, real evidence that it was observed.[4] It is not mentioned in Deuteronomy, which presents a recapitulation of the laws previously given by Moses toward the end of his life, or by the later prophets, Isaiah and Micah. Biblical scholars believe that the jubilee year was purely an ideal scheme which was developed from the law of the seventh year or as an extreme development of the sabbatical idea. Historical evidence is lacking that the year of jubilee was ever observed in practice. Scholars also agree that the law was not observed after the Exile, which took place in the sixth century B.C. Even if it was ideal legislation, its social values lay in teaching personal liberty, restitution of property, and the simple life.

Trade and Commerce.—Most of the Old Testament peoples were engaged in agricultural pursuits, not trade and commerce. However, they sold or trafficked in some articles of which they had a surplus or in ar-

---

[4] References may be found in Ezekiel 46:17, also Ezekiel 7:12, 13, but the meaning is uncertain. Numbers 36:4 uses the term but does not show very convincingly the extent to which the practice was followed.

ticles which they desired. "He that withholdeth corn, the people shall curse him; but blessing shall be upon the head of him that selleth it" (Prov. 11:26).[5] The merchants who traveled with their wares were not Israelites, but traveling Canaanites and Philistines, who carried their merchandise on their backs and on pack animals as may still be seen in the Near East today. Phoenician traders were also engaged in trade and commerce over wider areas than any other peoples. The Hebrew wife, one of the earliest craftworkers,[6] would spin flax and wool, a part of which was sold to Canaanite or to Phoenician traders who would take it to distant lands. In the course of time, trade expanded and brought many social evils; it fell into the hands of a greedy aristocracy with consequent dishonesty which was denounced vigorously throughout both the Old and New Testaments.

Labor and Occupations.—Work was held in esteem among the Hebrews, hence one must conclude that occupations were considered honorable. The most important occupation mentioned is agriculture, which was virtually the basis of life itself. Trade and commerce, although always present to some extent, really began at a much later time after the Greeks and Romans appeared.[7] Certain occupations required skill, and the wares of the skilled craftsmen were sought after. The New Testament mentions many trades and occupations, and one may infer that all were regarded as honorable callings.[8]

Wages are first mentioned in Scripture as paid not in money but in kind by Laban to Jacob (Gen. 29:15-20; 30:32). Pharaoh's daughter promised to give the sister of Moses wages for nursing him (Exod. 2:9). A hired servant was to be paid promptly and adequately (Lev. 19:13; Deut. 24:14-15), for the hireling must not be oppressed in his wages (Jer. 22:13; Mal. 3:5).[9]

[5] See also Prov. 12:11; 13:23; 20:4; 24:27, 30-34; 27:23-27.

[6] Genesis 4:22 speaks of an early craftsman, Tubal-cain, "an instructer of every artificer in brass and iron." He was the counterpart of the mythical Vulcan of Roman times.

[7] Commerce flourished under King Solomon (965-926 B.C.) and brought great wealth (I Kings 10:14-29; II Chron. 9:13-27). Successful voyages were made by his fleet to lands as far away as India (I Kings 10:11, 22). For the protection and fostering of trade he built store cities, among them Palmyra in the desert midway between Damascus and the Euphrates River. Under him Israel attained its greatest wealth. However, his commercial gains were inadequate to support his luxurious expenditures, and the tax burdens were ruinous to the people.

[8] The most commonly named trades were those of the potter, fisher, shepherd, tentmaker, carpenter, and brickmaker. When the Temple was being built by King Solomon, there were not enough craftsmen, and they were imported from Tyre in Phoenicia.

[9] John the Baptist exhorted the soldiers who came to him to be content with their "wages" which included rations in addition to the usual pay (Luke 3:14). The

Another reason why wages and occupations are mentioned so infrequently was the predominance of slavery. The Mosaic law recognized the institution. Nowhere in the Old Testament or in the New Testament is slavery forbidden; various humane provisions are made for the status and treatment of slaves, but the practice is upheld. It may be pointed out, however, that the biblical teachings do instil principles which must prove fatal to a system based on inferiority in social rights among individuals. These points are brought out emphatically in the discussion of the Church in the period of the Middle Ages when Christianity denied such inferiority and declared the equality of man in the sight of God.

The practice of slavery was patriarchal in character, as was the entire society. The authority of the master over his slaves was similar to that of the father over his family. The master could not only buy or sell one of his own kinsmen, but also his daughter if he chose (Exod. 21:7). The slave could attain high position under certain circumstances: he could be adopted by his master; he could marry a free woman, hold property, and buy his freedom. His term of service was supposed to be six years (Exod. 21:1-11); yet the law of servitude was probably evaded generally. The prophet Jeremiah in the sixth century B.C. denounced the people bitterly for disobeying orders (Jer. 34:14), especially that in regard to freeing their Hebrew slaves. It appears, too, that servants who wished to remain with the master were branded with an awl thrust through the ear (Deut. 15:17; Exod. 21:6); however, no one can say how common this practice was. The treatment of slaves and servants was probably humane and generous, at least if the law was carried out to the letter (Deut. 15:13 ff.; Lev. 25:39-55). The slave was to be protected from hard taskmasters and his service was believed to be worth twice that of a hired servant (Deut. 15:18).

Public Relief and Loans.—Both the Old and the New Testament teach public responsibility for the fatherless, widows, and dependents. The laws provided that no unfair advantage be taken of another. In the harvest the corners of the field were to be left uncut and the gleanings were to remain on the ground. Not all the grapes were to be picked, but some were to be left for "the poor and stranger" (Lev. 19:9-10). The tithe which was levied was used to help the poor. Every third year the tithe of the increase of the land was to be stored up to be distributed to the "stranger, and the fatherless, and the widow, which are within thy gates" (Deut. 14:28, 29; also, 26:12-13). Charity loans (gifts) were encouraged, and to the poor or to their Israelite brothers no inter-

---

householder who engaged laborers in the parable promised them a denarius (17¢) per day (Matt. 20:2).

est was to be charged.[10] This admonition did not apply to those who were regarded as foreigners.[11] The foregoing rules emphasized the community responsibility which enhanced the patriarchal solidarity of the group. If a pledge was required to guarantee the loan, the law was careful in assuring that the pledge be not lost or destroyed. If the pledge should be a garment, it was to be returned to the owner before the evening (Exod. 22:26-27). No one was to take the upper or the nether millstone as a pledge, thus preventing the debtor and his family from grinding corn for their daily food (Deut. 24:6). All loans were to be canceled in the seventh year.

Taxation.—Taxes, in the present-day sense of a tax system, probably did not exist among the Hebrew tribes except during King Solomon's reign. No specific system of taxation was in use, for there was no monarchy or state as such to be maintained, so long as peoples remained nomadic and unsettled. Under Solomon we read of an Israelite corvée which was a labor service exacted from the laboring class especially for the construction of roads, bridges, and public improvements. This could well be true under King Solomon, for he was a great builder and used public works programs both to improve the kingdom and to keep the people occupied. The corvée, or labor service, and the many burdensome taxes were so vigorously resented that they became a cause for the downfall of the kingdom. The tithe was a levy, mostly in kind, which was used to support the poor and also the Levites who were not to be forsaken (Deut. 14:27). Later the Levites were not dependent on the generosity of the Israelites (Neh. 13:10-13) but were obliged to support themselves. The poll tax was a payment made by every male to maintain the Temple. This was often spoken of as tribute (Matt. 17:24) and fixed at one-half shekel, or about 32¢ (Exod. 30:11-16). Doubtless the tithes, tolls, tributes, customs, and other levies had the effect of a tax on the people, but taxation or tax systems in our modern sense of the term probably did not exist in ancient Israel.

The absence of a tax system applies only to the Hebrews when under their own rule and not when in subjugation to the Egyptian Pharaohs and the Persians. Then they had to pay levies and tributes to the imperial treasuries, for the Egyptians and Persians had highly centralized and efficient tax systems. The various levies were probably in-

---

[10] Exodus 22:25 reads "If thou lend money to any of my people that is poor by thee, thou shalt not be to him as an usurer, neither shalt thou lay upon him usury." See also Lev. 25:35-37.

[11] Deuteronomy 23:19 states "Thou shalt not lend upon usury to thy brother," and the following verse, "Unto a stranger thou mayest lend upon usury: but unto thy brother thou shalt not lend upon usury."

tended to be on the ability-to-pay principle (II Kings 23:35). The tithe
also implies ability to pay, whereas the poll tax was levied on all males
regardless of their wealth. The principle of equality, both economic
and social, was strong; yet in time there developed great inequalities in
wealth and worldly goods. Isaiah denounced his people whose land,
like that of the Philistines, is "full of silver and gold, nor is there any
end to their treasures" (Isa. 2:7). The conspicuous use of luxuries and
ornamentation in the form of jewels, earrings, and the like was denounced (Isa. 3:16-24), and national wantonness was decried (Amos
6:1-6).

Tribute.—"Tribute," a common biblical term, had many meanings.
It was often nothing more than a freewill offering made on festal days
or some religious occasion (Deut. 16:10), and in an amount corresponding to the blessing the person had received. Again, it meant a
gift to a lord or ruler as a means of buying protection or perhaps peace.
The Philistines once brought Jehoshaphat, the king of Judah, "presents,
and tribute silver"; and the Arabians brought him "flocks" (II Chron.
17:11-13). He "waxed great exceedingly," built castles and "cities of
store," and carried on "much business in the cities of Judah." Another
sense of the term was that of a fine or punishment, even to confiscation.
In the reign of the wicked Judaean king, Jehoiakim (c. 600 B.C.), heavy
tribute of "an hundred talents of silver, and a talent of gold" levied on
the land (II Kings 23:33-36) was turned over to Pharaoh Necho' of
Egypt. In other cases, tribute was a form of perpetual servitude or
bond service. This was exacted by King Solomon from some inhabitants who were not of the children of Israel (I Kings 9:21).

The Jews were frequently obliged to pay tribute to their priests, both
in money and in produce or kind (Num. 31:28-41), regardless of the
fruitfulness of the season. Nehemiah spoke of the heavy mortgages on
"our lands, vineyards and houses" (Neh. 5:3) and the debt incurred in
"borrowed money for the king's tribute," which was in addition to the
borrowings to purchase food. However, it appears that there were some
groups [12] exempt from "toll, tribute, or custom," a practice which has
been historically consistent through the ages. Certain groups have always been made to pay for the reasons aforementioned, while those
associated in some manner with a church or religious endeavor were
exempt.

In the New Testament, the payment of tribute or custom was a
requirement of many of the kings and rulers (Matt. 17:25). Under

[12] Ezra 7:24: "Also we certify you, that touching any of the priests and Levites,
singers, porters, Nethinims, or ministers of this house of God, it shall not be lawful
to impose toll, tribute, or custom upon them."

Roman rule, taxes were especially heavy to support the great empire. At this time the payments were mainly in coined money,[13] as the use of money in trade and commerce was general by then.

Commercial Regulations.—Commercial regulations for persons trading with one another were carefully worked out. Any form of deceit or dishonesty was denounced both in the sight of God and in the law codes of man (Amos 8:4-6). Weights and measures were to be standard (Deut. 25:13-15), not a larger one and a smaller one, and adulteration was forbidden.[14] Provisions were also made against speculation and monopoly when such acts would cause a rise in prices. This was especially true of food which could not be stored in times of famine. But this rule was not always adhered to. Joseph, who was made ruler of Egypt (possibly, c. 1739 B.C.), stored up food during seven rich years for the seven years of famine which were to follow (Gen. 41:46-57). Thereby he controlled the grain market for fourteen years and capitalized on the distress of Egypt and nearby lands to destroy the ownership of private property in Egypt. Commercial regulations among biblical peoples, however, were not so well worked out as they were under the Greeks and Romans, since trade was not engaged in to any great degree and regulations were not as necessary.

Usury.—Usury was strictly forbidden by the Mosaic laws. The term "usury" was applied to any payment for the use of something borrowed —not to excessive interest rates in the present-day meaning of the term. Furthermore, usury was not limited to a return on money loans as in our usage but implied "usury of money, usury of victuals, usury of any thing that is lent upon usury" (Deut. 23:19). This law applied only to Hebrews, for the following verse (Deut. 23:20) says, "unto a stranger thou mayest lend upon usury, but to thy brother thou shalt not lend upon usury." Usury was recognized as a burdensome payment (Neh. 5:10), and since loans were made mainly for charitable reasons, the lenders were told to expect no usury (interest) for their loans (Lev. 25:36-37). Praise was forthcoming to one who abided by these statutes and "executed true judgment between man and man" (Ezek. 18:7-9, 14-17).

In the New Testament the attitude is different. In one of the parables the servant who was afraid of losing the one talent and buried

---

[13] The familiar story of the tribute money of Caesar which was brought to Christ is told in Matthew 22:17-21. Paul advised the people to pay "tribute to whom tribute is due; custom to whom custom [is due]" in Romans 13:7.

[14] Hos. 12:7: "He is a merchant, the balances of deceit are in his hand: he loveth to oppress [deceive]." Lev. 19:35: "Ye shall do no unrighteousness in judgment, in meteyard, in weight, or in measure."

it was severely reprimanded for not putting the money in the hands of the exchangers, which would have made the principal grow with usury (Matt. 25:27). Yet Jesus was enraged at the money-changers in the Temple who bought and sold and made "the house of prayer . . . a den of thieves" (Matt. 21:13). His indignation, however, was caused by the defiling of the Temple rather than by the trading per se.[15]

Money.—Money was well known and its functions were well understood in Old Testament times.[16] Money, so-called, is not to be thought of as coined money, which came at a much later period and was introduced by the Persians.[17] The first money was probably in the form of bullion. The earliest struck coins, as distinguished from the more ancient bullion money mentioned in the Bible, are the Adarkon and Darkemon or "drams" (Ezra 8:27; Neh. 7:72) which were probably the Persian gold darics, first issued in the reign of Darius Hystaspes (521-485 B.C.). It is known that the daric (which weighed about 130 grams, equivalent to about £1 2s, or $5.34 computed on the $4.86 pound) was the standard gold coin until the time of Alexander the Great and circulated throughout the East.

The Jews, however, had no coins or stamped money of their own until a much later time. There is no evidence that the Jews possessed a native currency after the return from the Captivity (536 B.C.) until the time of Simon Maccabaeus (about 141 B.C.), who was granted authority by Antiochus VII to coin money with his own stamp. (I Macc. 15:6: "I give thee leave to coin money for thy country with thy own stamp.") The coins were shekels and half-shekels of silver or gold.[18] Before having their own coinage, the Jews paid tribute in or used the money of whatever nation happened to rule them at that time. Hence any reference to money in the Old Testament before 141 B.C. was in the form of either bullion money or the coinage of the Persians or Syrians.

[15] Money-changers served an important function in changing coins of different origins and denominations into money acceptable for Temple dues and for the purchases of sacrifices which were to be offered in the Temple. They set up their tables in the outer court of the Temple and charged excessive rates for exchanging the money offered by worshipers for "Temple coin."

[16] Any standard concordance will have well over 100 references to money in the Old Testament alone.

[17] The Lydians (Lydia is a part of modern Turkey on the Aegean Sea) are credited by some scholars with having originated the use of coined money. Modern historians and archaeologists date this achievement early in the seventh century B.C. See A. R. Burns, *Money and Monetary Policy in Early Times* (New York, 1927). Also, James Hastings, ed., *Dictionary of the Bible* (New York, 1921).

[18] The gerah (1/20 shekel) means "a grain or a bean." The rebah means "a quarter" and the bekah means "a half" shekel. The word shekel itself means "weight." The gold shekel weighed 224 grains with a value equivalent of about £2 or $9.90 (computed on the $4.86 pound). The gold shekel was the equivalent of fifteen silver shekels.

Precious metals were used from earliest times, more often in the shape of bullion, ingots, and perhaps rings.[19] In payment or in exchange they passed on a weight basis, in which the metal was weighed in a balance and valued by a system of weights adapted by the Jews from Persian and Assyrian methods. This accounts for the standard coins of ancient times having a weight equivalent; the stamping of coins was an innovation which began about 700 B.C. During the later days of the Old Testament and the beginning of the New Testament many new Greek and Roman coins came into use. The Greek drachma and the Roman denarius were silver, each having an exchange equivalent in terms of the other.[20] References in the Bible to money and money values should not be confused with purchasing power in the modern sense. Nor should one infer that any of the ancient peoples introduced a "money economy," so commonly referred to in present economic literature. When money was used first in the form of bullion, and later in the form of coined pieces, the weight was the fundamental thing in determining its exchange value. The stamp and name were conveniences in facilitating this exchange.

Summary.—The Bible is not an economic tract in any sense, nor was it ever so intended. In addition to its theological teachings, the Bible records the rise and fall of great kingdoms, wars, crop failures and famines, religious and political persecutions, migrations of peoples, riches and poverty, treaties, laws, economic practices, and so on. Cultural life seems to have followed the irregular pattern of economic life. For long years tribes and kingdoms would be happy and prosper; then their period of "dark ages" would set in with a possible "blackout" of the peoples and their culture, as for instance, the long gap between the Old and New Testaments.

It is futile to seek biblical analogies for all our modern economic phenomena. It is certain, however, that some of the characteristic attributes of capitalism existed in biblical times, e.g., private property, division of labor, money and exchange, trade and commerce. At first, the normal political organization, being tribal and nomadic with a patriarchal ruler, was not a type of society which readily lent itself to owning and amassing of wealth. As this form of society and community disintegrated and peoples became geographically fixed, the capitalistic possi-

[19] Professor Breasted says ring-money is the oldest currency known. J. H. Breasted, *A History of Egypt* (New York, 1919), p. 98.

[20] The denarius (penny) of Tiberius weighed 60 grams, equivalent to 17 cents. This is the "*d*" which means pence or penny in the English pound, shilling and pence system. The 30 pieces of silver paid for betraying Christ were probably Greek or Tyrian tetradrachms, equivalent to about $15.30. The wage of a field laborer in New Testament times was one penny (denarius, or about 17 cents) a day (Matt. 18:28).

bilities, such as the accumulation of wealth, commerce, and trade, increased. Then there arose a division between the rich and the poor. In time the extremes of wealth led to the usual pattern of luxury, reckless expenditures, costly wars, alienation of the land, misery of the so-called masses, and revolution in some form.

Much of the teaching of the compilers of the Scripture was by precept. There were detailed regulations for the performance of many specific acts. Some regulations seem to have been needlessly complex; they were drawn up to cover activities ranging from the planting and harvesting of crops, on the one hand, to a possible extreme, on the other, of precise instructions for trimming the hair and beard. Since the regulations or precepts were supposed to have divine origin, they took the form of positive or negative commands.

The moral side of economic relations was not omitted. There are strong admonitions against greed, pride, and arrogance; honesty in trade is insisted upon; there are strong exhortations to justice, mercy, charity, and beneficence in social relations. In some form or other, practically all these precepts have become a part of our present social, cultural, and economic pattern.

Some characteristics of the teachings of the prophets are a denunciation of change, a strong sympathy with the poorer classes, and an appeal for social justice. They regarded covetousness, greed, accumulation of wealth, rise of commercial classes, usurious practices, and conquest of lands and peoples as inequitable; they spoke vigorously against these social and economic changes and, especially, against idolatrous practices. They were unaware of the inadequacies of their own social structure, nor did they foresee the trend of their own economic and social institutions. There was a tendency, therefore, to be highly critical of human behavior irrespective of changing incentives; hence they talked and worked for restoration of former and supposedly better conditions. This characteristic is not confined to the writers of the Old and New Testament but is also to be found in the writings of the Greeks and Romans, and to some extent in the thought of the Middle Ages and the Church.

The economic teachings of the Bible, however fragmentary, have to be extracted from a complex mixture of theology, ethics, metaphysics, law, philosophy, and politics which appears with varying degrees of emphasis. Despite the heterogeneous origins of our economic practices and institutions, the fact remains that many of them may be traced to biblical origins. Even though few of the biblical rules are immediately applicable, they are, nevertheless, worth careful study.

3

Economic Thought and Practices
of the Greeks

Ancient Greece is recognized as the source of many of the finest things developed by man. In art, literature, sculpture, philosophy, and government, the Greeks attained levels of development rarely reached and probably never exceeded by a later people. Many ethnic groups lived at one time or another in Asia Minor and the Mediterranean basin but were conquered by stronger groups. As the ages went by, two powers, Greece and then Rome, survived to extend their influence. By the beginning of the Christian era Rome had conquered all by war and expanded its power over most of Europe. When Rome fell, after several hundred years of unification, ancient times came to an end and another era was ushered in.

In spite of the vast contributions made by the Greeks to almost every branch of human knowledge, they paid relatively little attention to political economy as a subject. No Greek treatise devoted solely to political economy has been preserved, nor is there evidence that such a work was ever written. Greek economics is bound up with ethics and political science. Nevertheless, a few observations on the life of the people may be helpful in providing a setting for some of the economic doctrines of the philosophers.[1]

The Greeks and the City-State

Asia Minor and southeastern Europe are the regions from which much of our present civilization and culture came. The most important area is the Aegean Sea with its many islands and peninsulas.

[1] A few helpful references are: Jules Toutain, *The Economic Life of the Ancient World* (New York, 1930), an excellent and authoritative study of ancient Greece and Rome; and J. H. Breasted, *Ancient Times* (Boston, 1944). M. L. W. Laistner, *Greek Economics* (New York, 1923), has translations of the pertinent passages from Greek writers.

This region was occupied by peoples known as Aegeans (originally from Asia Minor and Africa) when civilization dawned there about 3000 B.C., long before the Greeks occupied the region. Certain skills developed, such as metalcraft, pottery- and glass-making, and weaving, each of which created some surplus goods that entered into early commerce.

For many centuries the Greeks, like the Hebrews, were nomadic. Their society consisted of tribes or a loose grouping of families, and within the tribes there were many smaller groups of families known as brotherhoods. The tribes had councils of the older men whose responsibility it was to advise the tribal chief or king and to decide upon issues affecting the welfare of the entire group. Many of the decisions of these elders provided the beginnings of the political institutions of modern times.

As the nomadic peoples ceased their wanderings to settle and cultivate the land, villages were founded and private ownership of land became the practice. In time, the groups of villages grew into larger units or cities. This was a very important process in Greek political development, for the organized city was the Greek equivalent to the modern state. The city—known as the *polis*, or city-state—was a sovereign power in itself; it had its own laws, its own army, and its own gods. The citizen of such a state felt no loyalty to any other political unit, and to fulfil his duties as a citizen, he had to have a hand in the government. There were hundreds of city-states throughout Greece, on the islands of the Aegean area, and on the coast of Asia Minor, each with its own king. It was in these political units that Greek civilization flourished and around them grew the concept of the ideal political unit, as conceived by the philosophers. The stronger city-states grew in size and territory; for example, the city-state which occupied the Attic peninsula, an area about two thirds the size of Rhode Island, was called Athens and every resident—city dweller or farmer—was called an Athenian. The concept of the office of king never died out, although around 750 B.C. the Greeks overthrew many of their kings and the so-called nobles (aristocrats) became ascendant. The concept of the political city-state survived well into the Hellenistic Age.

Economic Expansion.—The Greeks expanded territorially to the east and west in the Mediterranean area. Greek merchants traded with all the nearby islands, Africa, Asia Minor, and as far west as Italy. In time, particularly between 800 B.C. and 600 B.C., Greek colonies were established on the shores of the Black Sea, as far west as France and Spain, in the Nile Delta, and in Libya in North Africa. The expansion of colonies and trade tended to make a Greek world of the entire Mediterranean region. The language, customs, and traditions bound the far-flung areas together and made a unity of peoples so compact that anyone not in the Greek sphere of influence was regarded as a "barbarian."

b) Colonial expansion was an important reason for the great development of trade and commerce in the seventh and sixth centuries B.C. While the items of commerce were limited in variety and amount, they were in demand in all areas accessible to the ships of the traders. Coinage was adopted for trading purposes in the seventh century B.C.; and wealth, formerly reckoned in lands and flocks, was now thought of in terms of money. Loans were made, the usual interest rate being about 18 per cent a year. Gradually a prosperous industrial and commercial middle class developed, which became prominent in the politics of the city-state. Likewise, as money became more plentiful, the rate of interest was lowered, and in Solon's day (c. 595 B.C.) the rate was 10 to 12 per cent.

c) Slavery was an accepted institution and in some city-states the number of slaves was nearly half of the total population. The majority of the slaves were of non-Hellenic origin; they were generally kidnapped peoples from the East and North and persons captured in war. Resident aliens as well as Greeks owned slaves for domestic and industrial labor; and in cities such as Athens, slavery became essential to the economic life of its citizens. In addition to slave labor, a wage-earning class grew up which was wholly dependent on earnings for its daily necessities.

Money was now a necessary and accepted institution in both private and public life. As the cost of government grew, taxes and customs became necessary. Of all the Greek cities, Athens had the largest income and expenditures. Most of the revenues came from tribute paid by the allies and dependent peoples, royalties from the silver mines of Attica which had been worked since the sixth century, indirect taxes, fees, fines, and rents from houses and lands. Athenians had no direct taxes, except a small poll tax levied on resident aliens.

d) As a result of many causes—among them a lack of leadership, a plague which took many lives, and war with Sparta and Corinth which was essentially a struggle for empire between democracy and oligarchy—the great city-state of Athens, which had achieved a higher level of civilization than any other Greek city, fell in 404 B.C. With her collapsed many of the finer elements of civilization and culture usually associated with ancient Greece. Sparta in turn fell in 371 B.C. and finally Thebes, in 362 B.C. The Greek city-states, which might have been welded into a strong federation, had crushed each other; and the Greek world, whose authority and civilization had been supreme for many years, became politically helpless.

The Development of Agriculture.—In the colonized areas and 3.
originally in Greece proper, agriculture was the chief industry and the
source of most of the basic commodities. The climatic conditions in
Greece, however, limited the products mainly to fruits and smaller
grains. The land was usually owned by the tiller, and ownership was
passed on through inheritance. But ownership and tillage of the land
were not always the same in the various states. In Laconia, some of
the cultivators were dependents of the ruling class, enjoying personal
liberty but no civic status. Many cultivators in other states were serfs
tied to the land, over whom the state had complete power of life and
death. In Crete agricultural labor was performed by bondsmen whose
condition was similar to that of the serfs. In areas such as Attica, where
there were many small farmers, the heavy duties and tithes exacted by
the landlords may have amounted to as much as five sixths of the total
produce; and failure to meet the payments could mean slavery for the
farmer and his family. This was especially true before Solon's reforms
in 594 B.C. In time, both the land and the cultivators were impoverished. Domestic animals were used, and the harvesting of the grains was
similar to practices which still prevail in the more backward places of
Europe and Asia. The varieties and productivity of crops reflected the
natural resources and also the method of land utilization of the various
colonized areas.

It is not within the scope of this work to present an economic history
of agriculture throughout the vast domain under Greek civilization, but
only enough to reveal a bit of the economic life. It is known, however,
that for many years the success of Greek agriculture, especially in Attica
and the Black Sea regions, was pronounced. In time, the cycle of
change brings disintegration and decay in agriculture as in other elements of national life. Agriculture, which was the basic industry in
Greece as in all the ancient states, declined and with its collapse the
whole social structure tended to disintegrate. In Greece, landowner- a)
ship later changed from small to large holdings and productivity decreased materially. In the Hellenistic period after 300 B.C., many landholders sold their property and families died out. There was a "dearth
of men" which led to concentrated ownership of the land that had
formerly been in small holdings. The big holdings, together with the
growing competition of foreign countries, "produced disastrous results
on the agrarian situation, and particularly on what remained of the
small landowners . . . The countrysides were deserted." ² Eventually
Greece proper suffered from agrarian pauperism and poverty, but in the
areas of Greek colonization in the eastern Mediterranean agriculture

² Gustave Glotz, *Ancient Greece at Work* (New York, 1926), p. 346.

flourished. These agricultural factors helped to transform the economic life of Greece and affected the economic development of the entire Mediterranean area.

Industry, the Division of Labor, and Trade.—The Greeks developed remarkable skills in many crafts. Metal-working was a fine art; building became classic in both style and construction. Textiles, furniture, leather, pottery, and embroidery were but a few of the better-developed industries. At first the products of these skills were traded with the Phoenicians, the "peddlers of the seas," who touched Grecian shores; later they formed a large part of the flourishing commerce of Greece. Division of labor or specialization was a very common industrial practice, which had been in use for centuries in ancient Egypt before Greece. In Greek history one finds many accounts of skills developed by craftsmen including carpenters, joiners, masons, carriers, ovenmen, stokers, grain crushers, wool carders, carpetmakers, cobblers, and so on.

Trade generally followed the water routes, although some roads were accessible. The Greeks built canals and opened and improved the seaports; the trade of the Mediterranean expanded into the Indian Ocean. Great entrepôts were developed, especially in the East, an area which was being developed rapidly. Corinth, Athens, Rhodes, and Miletus were leading ports, and Delos "offered every security to shipping and every convenience to trade. The anchorage was protected against the north wind by a strong breakwater. A mole divided it into two parts . . . All around stretched the commercial quarter with shops, workshops, bazaars and hostelries all heaped together . . . She organized the uninterrupted passage of slaves, grain, spices, etc." [3] The Greek cities were busy markets for goods from other cities in Greece, the East, Italy, and North Africa. For instance, Rhodes became exceedingly wealthy from transit commerce on which custom duties were levied. It has been reckoned that the revenues collected amounted to a net sum of a million drachmas every year.[4] When this great city was destroyed by an earthquake in 223 and 222 B.C., all the nearby princes and cities vied with one another in sending money and materials to aid in the restoration—a tribute to Grecian solidarity. When Athens fell (404 B.C.) and when Miletus was destroyed by the Persians, no such help was forthcoming, a fact which attests to the commercial esteem in which the city of Rhodes was held.

All commerce and trade had to pay customs and duties to the state. Duties were levied not only upon the goods that entered into export and import but also upon the manner of transport. Goods going in

---

[3] *Ibid.*, pp. 338-39.
[4] Toutain, *op. cit.*, p. 152.

and out of the gates of the towns were subject to a tax comparable to the French *octroi* of later date. Trading licenses were required of merchants, who were then taxed on sales. When tributes were levied, the total burden often became greater than the trade would stand.

It is probable that the trade and commerce of the Greek Mediterranean world was carried out on a greater scale than at any other period until modern times. It rested upon a money economy in which money, both metallic and paper, and credit instruments were in common use. There were both public and private banks which received deposits, established current accounts for their clients, issued letters of credit, and aided in business financing. Commercial companies with large capital were founded which actively engaged in far-flung trade. Most of this commercial greatness disappeared as a result of wars and internal strife and, finally, of Roman domination.

The Philosophers

Throughout the course of Greek history, there were many famous philosophers and schools of philosophy. Our concern here is with those whose writings include passages of economic interest. These writers made their contributions at a very turbulent period of Greek history. Greek national spirit waned after the Peloponnesian War (431-404 b.c.) and when Alexander the Great, a Macedonian, conquered Greece, the morale of the Greeks was broken; they lost their glorious ideals and decay set in. There was a pronounced tendency for the writers to look back upon the better days when Greek cities, notably Athens, were supreme; when there were leisure and culture; and when, in short, life was better than in their own time. Social discontent prevailed and the need for social reforms, as well as attempts toward that end, greatly influenced the concepts of the philosophers. They were actuated by motives very different from those which impelled the writers of the Bible. Nevertheless, the analysis made by the Greek philosophers of their contemporary society exceeded anything proposed by a biblical writer or by anyone else for hundreds of years after Greek civilization disappeared.

The writers considered here were erudite persons and made significant contributions to many phases of learning. However, it was their conception of the state and the functions and duties of its inhabitants that interested them most. They sought to attain the "good" life, one in which the individual through close participation in the life of the state would enjoy the greatest happiness. Therefore, it is in their views on ethics, politics, and statecraft that one finds their economic concepts.

Plato

Plato and the Republic.—The life of Plato coincided with the un-happy history of Athens after the death of Pericles (429 B.C.). The Peloponnesian War began in 431 B.C., four years before Plato's birth, and ended in 404 B.C. when Athens was captured by Sparta. The re-mainder of Plato's life was contemporary with the devastating wars among the Greek cities, for no one city held a balance of power after the fall of Athens.[5]

Plato's masterpiece is the *Republic*. In it appears a discussion con-cerning (1) justice, (2) the ideal state which shall realize justice, (3) the idea of the good, and (4) a criticism of the constitutions of states. It is written in dialogue form with Socrates, his great teacher, as one of the participants. In this manner, Plato was able to employ the Socratic method of questions and answers and also to provide a dramatic effect in idealizing his teacher, who usually has the final word. The work is Plato's crowning literary effort and the most complete statement of his mature views in formulating certain theoretical political conceptions of the ideal state.

Since the *polis* or city-state occupies a central position in the *Republic*, Plato explains its origin as follows:

A state arises, as I conceive, out of the needs of mankind; no one is self-sufficing, but all of us have many wants . . . Then as we have many wants, and many persons are needed to supply them, one takes a helper for one purpose and another for another; and when these helpers and partners are gathered together in one habitation, the body of the inhabitants is termed a state. . . . And they exchange with one another, and one gives, and another receives, under the idea that the exchange will be for their good. . . . The true creator [of the state] is necessity, who is the mother of our invention.[6]

Plato pictures the perfect society, not the perfect man, since the idea of perfection and happiness is not to be found in the individual but in

[5] Plato (427-347 B.C.) was born in Athens. While few particulars of his life are known, it is certain that he was well educated. When he was about twenty years old he became the favorite and constant pupil of Socrates. After the death of Socrates (399 B.C.), he traveled in Sicily, Italy, and North Africa. Then, ten years later, he returned to teach in the Athenian gymnasium known as the Academy. Apparently he taught without remuneration, having adequate income from his own private sources. Plato, an aristocrat, was opposed to democratic Athenian society, which was marred by the excesses of commercialism. His writings are in the form of dialogues in which Socrates always participates; they are, indeed, great classics in prose and composition. The works most important for their economic ideas are the *Laws* and the *Republic*.

[6] *Republic* ii. 369-70, in Benjamin Jowett (trans.), *The Dialogues of Plato* (New York, 1876), Vol. II, pp. 190-91.

the species. Happiness is for the whole of society, and the ideal of happiness can be reached only in the ideal state. The *Republic* is an attempt to show how justice, as a social virtue, can be attained. The state has but one real function, namely, to insure happiness to everyone through virtue, which means that justice will prevail. In his words, "I will tell you, I replied; justice, which is the subject of our inquiry, is, as you know, sometimes spoken of as a virtue of an individual, and sometimes as the virtue of a State." [7] Concerned with justice as provided by the state, Plato chose Sparta for his model. An aristocrat himself, he held the view that the state could best serve its purpose when ruled by a class trained to rule; he distrusted the political possibilities of a democracy. Only by an intelligently planned form of government could the state expect to exist.

The state, as Plato viewed it, should have classes. First, there is the working or peasant class whose great virtue is to be temperance; second, the warrior class to guard the state within and without, and whose virtue is courage; and the third and highest class are the philosophers or rulers who, by their insight, determine the laws of the state. Wisdom is the great virtue of the latter class. The highest justice is achieved when the classes have and exercise their proper ranks and functions. Ideally, then, all persons and classes may be provided for and a planned existence of the state made possible.

Turning next to some specific measures of economic significance, it is clear that Plato recognized the division of labor as a necessary means of production within a state. The basic wants for food, clothing, and shelter must be satisfied. In man's efforts to satisfy human wants, Plato points out that "there are diversities of natures among us which are adapted to different occupations." He observes that "better work will be done" when a workman has but one occupation, less spoilage when work is done at the right time.[8] However, when everyone specializes and is no longer self-sufficient, commercial organization becomes necessary.

Plato's concept of specialization and the division of labor reflected his observations of prevailing production methods. He was dealing with types of employment which were not a part of any particular economic system. The social aspects of the division of labor were not considered. His analysis, therefore, rests on what he regarded as the most likely means of satisfying human wants. Provision is made for husbandmen and for craftsmen, such as weavers and shoemakers, carpenters, and smiths. Exchange follows production and a merchant class is developed. Foreign traders and sailors are necessary in the exchange of

---

[7] *Ibid.*, p. 190.
[8] *Ibid.*, p. 191.

surplus products.   Lastly, there remain the slaves and hirelings, each serving an economic function in satisfying human wants.

Plato was not concerned with either the social or the economic aspects of the application of the division of labor.   He treated it merely as a logical economic necessity; he did not consider the long-run aspects of the principle, nor did he see that it served to perpetuate a caste system which had prevailed for many centuries.

The city-state of Plato's time was in a decline, and he was aware of the misery and suffering, class antagonisms, and political decadence that prevailed within it.   His ideal state, however, would be free from all the undesirable practices which then prevailed.   The rulers in his ideal state would constitute a group far above such base practices as economic exploitation.   They were to be guardians who would rule over artisans and warriors.   Members of this ruling class were to be educated from childhood in both philosophy and the arts of war, since they were to be protectors of the state.   They would be the "philosopher-kings," who, being free from the degrading pursuit of wealth, would devote their talents to the governing of the state by the rule of reason.

Plato's ideal state did not exist either in aristocratic Sparta or democratic Athens; both suffered from great internal conflicts and injustices bordering on tyranny.   The ideals of Plato never materialized, and the condition of the Greek states went from bad to worse until they fell to foreign invaders.   His unsuccessful attempt to recapture some of the glories of the past remained a theoretical blueprint.

Slavery.—The institution of slavery existed long before and long after Plato's day.   It may be assumed that since slavery existed before his time and was so common in Greece, Plato regarded it as a permanent factor in civilization.   In the *Laws* he points out the best kinds of slaves to have and the way in which they should be treated.   Even though he does not provide for slaves in his ideal city, we may infer that he does condone slavery, especially in agriculture, and regards it as an inevitable result of wars and luxury.   He seems to hold the view that foreigners conquered in war should become slaves; yet in the state described in the *Laws* the condition of the slave is not to be one of extreme hardship.[9] It should be remembered that in his time the laboring population included both slaves and freemen, yet his political philosophy prevented him from paying much heed to either group.   Plato also recognized that men and women were not born alike but have special powers fitting them for special tasks and that great differences also exist in native gifts

---

[9] *Laws* vi. 776-77.   The *Laws* was written in Plato's old age.   He was disappointed that his ideal scheme never succeeded; the *Laws* was therefore a revised version of the *Republic*—a sort of compromise between the unattainable ideal in the *Republic* and the political situation as it actually existed in historic Greece.

and endowments. Slavery, however, was not the fate of the less gifted, but mainly of those less fortunate in war.

Communism.—Plato's views on communism are found in the *Republic*, which sets forth his utopian ideas. They are significant not only in the description of his own ideal state but have been studied in connection with every scheme of social and political reform since they were written.

He proposed a complete communism for the guardians and possibly for the soldiers as well. The guardians were to have small houses, eat simple food, live as in a camp, and dine together in companies. They were not to have private property beyond a necessary minimum. Gold and silver were forbidden to them. They were not to be rich, since the purpose of the scheme was to provide for the good of the whole, not the happiness of any one class. He recognized that both riches and poverty were harmful, and so in his ideal state neither should exist.

Communism was also applied to the family. Friends, Plato said, should have all things in common, including women and children. He admitted that this presents some difficulties but not insurmountable ones. Girls and boys were to have the same education, and women were to have complete equality with men in all respects. "The same education which makes a man a good guardian will make a woman a good guardian, for their original nature is the same." He provided for eugenic principles to insure the "best" children, who would be educated at state expense to serve the state. This plan would insure community ownership of property or the absence of private property, promote harmony, and unite people in a common social interest. These measures, however extreme, were necessary if the "breed of guardians is to be kept pure." (Family life in classical Greece did not play an important part in the social organization of the community; wives had no civil status and the sole purpose of marriage was to continue the race.) Plato's views, in this respect, were strongly opposed by Aristotle, who stressed the importance of the family.

Provisions were made in Plato's scheme for not only quality but quantity of population. The state was to consist of 5,040 citizens, a number which would be held constant either by prizes to encourage population growth or, if a surplus should occur, by sending the extra persons to colonies. The relation of the individual to the state in Plato's ideal can profitably be studied by the student of state ideologies in our day, for the ideological analogies are most striking.

Wealth and Trade.—In addition to the foregoing points, which are outstanding, there are other items of economic interest in Plato's writings. His conception of production is closely related to his views on wealth. In the *Laws* [10] he praises the Cretan constitution for providing both spiritual and material blessings. The spiritual blessings are wisdom, temperance, justice, and courage. These are basic, for if a city possesses them the others will follow. The other or human blessings are health, beauty, strength, and wealth. He does not define wealth, and he uses it in a manner which carries two different meanings. One, outward goods and an excessive accumulation of them, is frowned upon. The other meaning treats wealth as a real necessity in human life when it is intelligently and moderately used and not acquired purely for the sake of accumulation. Wealth and intemperance seem to be treated as the same thing by Plato. He thinks it best for citizens of a good state to have neither poverty nor riches, for either extreme might tempt the citizen to sin and leads to excesses in the state.

In the *Laws* he speaks many times of a fixed limitation on personal wealth which no one is to exceed upon threat of severe penalties. He saw the possibility of expanding human wants but feared that luxury would result if they were greatly amplified. For the education of the guardians the wealth of the state would be drawn upon, not private wealth. A possible contradiction of terms appears from a statement in the *Laws*,[11] where he says it is not the object of the state to make itself as rich as possible. "Poverty results from increase of man's desires, not from diminution of his property." [12] The good man will have no wealth; however, if he does have any outward goods which may be called wealth, they will be "such as to be in harmony with his inward wealth and will be small in quantity and of a fixed and measurable amount." Plato held the ascetic view that one will be rich if he has few wants.

Most of Plato's views are speculative and applicable only in the ideal state and society, and he does make use of concrete examples. He recognizes that human frailty may lead men to forsake the ideal and accept the mundane. In the ideal state he had to make provision for exchange to be carried on, yet he states that the freeman should consider retail trade beneath him.[13] The craftsmen must be watched for fear they may charge their customers more than the true value of the goods. He does not define "true value" but he remarks that the craftsmen "themselves know perfectly well what it is." [14] Since there is no clear explanation of what he had in mind, it is probably safe to assume that he meant some roughly defined cost-of-production concept of value.

[10] *Laws* i. 631.
[11] *Laws* v. 742.
[12] *Laws* v. 736.

[13] *Laws* xi. 920; cf. v. 741.
[14] *Laws* xi. 921.

The Greek philosophers seem to have had strong prejudices against the artisan, even though his skill and his product are necessary in a state in which division of labor is practiced. Dr. Bonar thinks this may be explained by the fact that the artisan's work does not fit him for military service, partly because his labor is associated with that of slaves, and partly by the fact that many of the industrial arts were introduced by foreigners.[15] Plato, however, had a stronger prejudice against shopkeepers than against artisans, although admitting that the division of labor seems to require both as necessary evils. The very nature of the trade puts them under strong temptation when handling gold and silver.

Money-making as an end in itself is an unmixed evil. He condemns usury with great emphasis, the only exception being the case in which a customer does not promptly pay for work that has been duly executed to his order; thus he must pay interest after a certain time as well as the sum due.[16] Plato believed most of the abuses of money-making could be prevented by decreeing that gold and silver should never be privately owned and that the only currency should be token currency of small denomination. The guardians, of course, would possess neither precious metals nor private property.

In conclusion, it must be remembered that Plato's economics was a part of his ethics and politics and only incidental to his larger objective of creating an ideal and harmonious state. Although he left much unexplained and much which appears unreal, he did, nevertheless, present many original and challenging economic concepts, some of which have been incorporated into the general body of economic thought.

Aristotle

The most distinguished of Plato's pupils and the greatest scholar of antiquity was Aristotle.[17] He is regarded as the founder of many

---

[15] James Bonar, *Philosophy and Political Economy* (London, 1893), p. 21.

[16] *Laws* xi. 921.

[17] **Aristotle** (384-322 B.C.). At about the age of seventeen, Aristotle went to Athens to study with Plato; there he remained until his great teacher's death some twenty years later. He was invited by Philip of Macedonia to serve as tutor for his son, who later became Alexander the Great. After Alexander became king, Aristotle lived at the court as friend and counselor. When Alexander began his Asiatic campaign (334 B.C.), Aristotle returned to Athens and conducted a school in the Lyceum for twelve years before he was forced into exile by a prosecution for impiety. He died in Chalcis the following year. He left outstanding contributions in ethics, logic, metaphysics, politics, rhetoric, history, psychology, and the natural sciences. His writings show his respect for truth and scientific accuracy, even though his style is often uneven and obscure. He wrote no separate economic treatises, yet he was fully aware of the importance of economic relationships in life and discussed them in considerable detail. His ideas and teachings were used extensively by the Schoolmen, especially by Thomas Aquinas. Aristotle's ideas have influenced the development of economic thought both directly and indirectly.

sciences and also as the first analytical economist. His writings dealt with many subjects, and his work is characterized by careful, scientific observations and theoretical deductions. A scientist in search of facts, he showed extraordinary insight into society, being more of a realist than was his friend and teacher, Plato, in whose work the ethical interest was paramount. Aristotle's career "came at the end of the creative period in Greek thought, and after his death it was two thousand years before the world produced any philosopher who could be regarded as approximately his equal." [18] He was the personification of pure Greek learning.

Aristotle reasoned that people were more concerned with so-called rational activity and behavior than with happiness. Yet happiness was the highest good which man should aspire to attain and which can be attained only if the environment is favorable. Here, then, the political factor becomes very important. The state should be the epitome of the highest morals of the individual; it should also provide for him the fullest expression of his own moral attributes and thus bring about the greatest happiness. Every state should have a constitution which should provide for the greatest welfare of the people; the state should be devoted to the education of the people and to the development of the finest in human nature. Aristotle did not design an ideal state as did Plato. He was concerned only with pointing out the essentials necessary to the well-being of the state which, of course, he expects to be permanent and to function for the greatest happiness of all. The individual in Aristotle's state is subordinated, but not absorbed. In this respect he differed from Plato.

Most of Aristotle's views of economic interest are found in Book II of the *Politics* and in the *Nicomachaean Ethics*. Since he was concerned with the foundations and constitution of a state, he had examined the constitutions of over one hundred and fifty Greek city-states before presenting his own principles of politics and government. In his state he defended private property and strongly advocated scientific reforms in the use to which it is put. He opposed Plato's views on communism and the concept of community in property mainly because of the "lack of incentive" under such an arrangement.

Aristotle did not hold that all persons were equal. Citizens were either rulers or ruled. The rulers included the statesmen, the magistrates, the military class, and those in the priesthood. He had great confidence that as a man grew older, he would gain in wisdom; therefore, the young would be soldiers because of physical fitness, in middle life they would become statesmen and in their old age, priests. But not

[18] Bertrand Russell, A *History of Western Philosophy* (New York, 1945), p. 159.

all followed this route. Only those fitted to rule would attain these levels, whereas the ruled were the laborers, the craftsmen, and the agriculturalists. Aristotle reluctantly consented to slavery because he believed it to be a necessity, and he expressed strong desires for its reform. He held that from birth some were marked for subjection, others for ruling. Slaves should not be Greeks but peoples of inferior races, prisoners taken in war, and conquered peoples. The institution of slavery was justified only as a necessity.

General View of the State.—Aristotle, like Plato, begins his *Politics* with a discussion of the origin of the state, which he traces from the household. The state aims at the good and is the highest type of community. "Every state is a community of some good, and every community is established with a view to some good." [19] In the evolution of the state there was first the family; then several families combined to make a village; then several villages formed a state, provided that the combination was large enough to be self-sufficient. The state, although later in time than the family, was prior to it and even prior to the individual in authority; in the fully developed state, the whole is greater than the parts. The state is not a mere society banded together for simple exchange and protection; it rests on a broader concept which is to insure the good life: "The end of the state is the good life. . . . And the state is the union of families and villages in a perfect and self-sufficing life, by which we mean a happy and honorable life. . . . A political society exists for the sake of noble actions, not of mere companionship." That families organize into villages and villages into states is only natural and right. The state, or anything, "when fully developed we call its nature" and "to be self-sufficing is the end and the best." It is possible for Aristotle to contend logically that "it is evident that the state is a creation of nature, and that man is by nature a political animal." [20] After discussing the creation of the state, he examines the functions and practices of the individual and the household or family, and it is from this source that we learn his views on economics. While the smaller units within the state are important and necessary, the concept of the over-all state is foremost. Aristotle believed that the state should not exceed one hundred thousand persons in contrast with Plato's small community of 5,040.

Aristotle criticized Plato's ideal state on many grounds. First, he disagreed with his teacher on the extent to which the state should be-

[19] A translation of the pertinent passages in the *Politics* appears in M. L. W. Laistner (ed. and trans.), *Greek Economics* (New York, 1923), pp. 133 ff. See also A. E. Monroe (ed.), *Early Economic Thought* (Cambridge, 1924), chap. i, "Aristotle," pp. 1-29.

[20] Monroe, *op. cit.*, p. 5.

come an all-powerful unit. He objected to the abolition of the family and to the views on communism in general. Aristotle insisted that Plato's views on communism would lead to "anger against lazy people" and to general discord. Also, he regarded it contrary to certain feelings deeply rooted in human nature. He defended private property but he thought its use should be common, a view adopted by Plato in the *Laws*. Benevolence and charity are virtues which would be impossible without private property.

Aristotle neither believed in nor advocated equality. He would exclude cultivators of the soil, tradesmen, and mechanics from sharing in government; they would be the ruled. Monarchy, he thought, was better than aristocracy, but he offered only a qualified defense of democracy, which even though it may be faulty, tends to be the best form of government.

Economic Contributions.—Aristotle's main contributions to economics may be classified under three headings: (1) general economics, (2) exchange or value, and (3) money theory. He viewed the economy as divided into two parts: economy proper, or the science of household management, which is natural and proper since the state is made up of households; and the science of supply, which is concerned with the art of acquisition. The latter is the unnatural, artificial, wealth-getting activity which he called chrematistics.[21] His treatment of the concept of wealth could be regarded as classic. He says "wealth may be defined as a number of instruments to be used in a household or in a state." He does not regard it as having any great importance to the individual except for the purpose of realizing the "good life," confining its meaning to useful, material objects owned by man.

Value and Exchange.—In attempting to explain value Aristotle pointed out that of "everything which we possess there are two uses: both belonging to the thing as such, but not in the same manner, for one is the proper and the other the improper or secondary use of it. For example, a shoe is used for wear, and is used for exchange: both are uses of the shoe." [22] He clearly recognized the difference between value in use and value in exchange, or subjective and objective value as currently used.

However, the idea of value itself received little attention. Plato seemed to imply that value was a quality which was absolute and inher-

---

[21] *Chrematistike* is more accurately translated as "the science of supply" than as the "science of wealth." The word *oeconomia*, from which our word "economy" is derived, meant to a Greek the art or science of managing the household (or *oikos*). Laistner, *op. cit.*, p. viii.

[22] *Politics* ii. 1257. Laistner, *op. cit.*, pp. 149-50; Monroe, *op. cit.*, p. 16.

ent in a thing. Aristotle made value subjective, depending upon the usefulness of the commodity. Exchange rests upon man's wants: "In the truest and most real sense, this standard lies in wants, which is the basis of all associations among men." When an exchange is just, it rests upon equality of wants, not upon costs in a labor-cost sense. Man may exchange goods without being engaged in unnatural activity or in money-making. Aristotle seemed to regard value in exchange as existing apart from price, but he did not develop a theory of exchange. He saw that goods could have both value in use and value in exchange, but his views were not developed into a value theory as such. Many writers after Aristotle made use of the same illustration when developing a theory of value, for it was a cogent observation.

Aristotle opposed retail trade as such, for it made possible the gaining of wealth unnaturally. The natural way to get wealth is by skilful management of the house and land. The amount of wealth that can be earned in this way is limited, whereas the amount that can be earned by trade is unlimited. However, the worst form of gaining wealth unnaturally is usury. "The most hated sort, and with the greatest reason, is usury, which makes a gain out of money itself, and not from the natural objects of it. For money was intended to be used in exchange, but not to increase at interest . . . Of all modes of getting wealth this is the most unnatural." [23] The same views were recorded in biblical teachings and in the rules of the Church which prevailed until the end of the Middle Ages. The attitude toward usury represents the age-old conflict between the debtor and creditor groups, which took many forms.

Money and Its Uses.—Aristotle's views on money are found in both the *Politics* and the *Ethics*. His knowledge of money and its functions was very advanced and represented the best of his economics. Money came into use as a result of trade and commerce. He reasoned that the necessities of life were "not easily carried about, hence men agreed to employ in their dealings with each other something which was intrinsically useful and easily applicable to the purposes of life, for example, iron, silver and the like." He made this medium rest upon a mutual contract. Originally, money was valued by its weight and size, but in time a stamp was placed upon it to show its value.

In the *Ethics* he dealt with the functions of money: he found them to be a "sort of medium or mean," a store of value, and a "standard upon which the world agrees," for it makes all things commensurable as "the universal standard of measurement." He recognized that money, like other commodities, is subject to the same laws that influence value.

[23] *Politics* ii. 1258. Laistner, *op. cit.*, p. 154; Monroe, *op. cit.*, p. 20.

The value of money is not always the same, yet it "tends to have a more constant value than anything else."

It would be attributing too much to Aristotle to credit him with fully developed monetary theories, yet what he had to say was very accurate. He recognized the nature of trade and commerce and the necessity of money to expedite exchange. The real differences between wealth and welfare, money and wealth, were probably better understood and stated by him than by anyone for nearly fifteen hundred years afterward. Riches in coin could not be wealth if one could not get necessary food, as in the fable of King Midas. Indeed, many of Aristotle's views are completely modern.

Xenophon

The third writer whose fragmentary economic ideas should be included is Xenophon.[24] He produced a dialogue *Oeconomicus*, in which he showed a clear understanding of the meaning of wealth as something related to one's needs. Money is not wealth unless it serves a useful purpose in satisfying a need of its owner.

Xenophon was also concerned with Greek agriculture. His extreme praise of agriculture is comparable to that of the physiocrats in France in the eighteenth century. He regarded land and labor as the only agents of production; land, however, will not produce in abundance without "toil" or labor. In this same discussion he approached the law of diminishing returns in agriculture. He says "the landowners could all tell you how many teams and how many laborers are required for their estates. If anyone employs hands in excess of requirements, it is reckoned at a loss." [25]

It is in the essay on *The Ways and Means to Increase the Revenues of Athens* (c. 355 B.C.) that most of his economic views are found. He was concerned with finding a remedy for "the poverty of the common people." As the title indicates, the essay is in reality a study in public finance. How can the revenues be increased? He believed that foreign residents, *metics*, might provide a fruitful source of revenue through the increased trade they would bring; those foreigners who resided in Greece should not be taxed as a class and steps should be taken to

24 **Xenophon** (c. 440-355 B.C.) had been a pupil of Socrates and later a Greek general. His writings were not on the same level as those of Aristotle; however, he wrote some historical volumes, a philosophical romance, reminiscences of Socrates (*Memorabilia*), and other minor works.

25 Laistner, *op. cit.*, p. 16. See also Monroe, *op. cit.*, p. 39. The soil of Attica, which he praised, was extremely poor in antiquity: production of olives and grapes, for which the soil and climate were fitted, was far more important than the growing of grain crops, which would have afforded a larger food supply.

attract greater numbers of them to settle in Athens. The merchants especially were to be given special privileges and exemptions.

At one time the silver mines of Attica were productive but their productivity was declining. The silver mines had been worked since the sixth century B.C., but after the Persian wars they were developed extensively. The mines were owned by the state but leased to private citizens, who worked them with slave labor. He recommended that more persons be employed in production and thus implied the law of increasing returns. He said "we should send with confidence as many workmen as possible into the silver mines, and should with confidence continue our operations in them, fully trusting that the silver ore is not going to fail, and that silver will never lose its value." [26] Elsewhere he expressed the view that an excess of entrepreneurs would lead to cheapness. But not so with silver. By advocating that great numbers of slaves should be procured and put to work in the mines, he implied that silver mining would never be subject to diminishing returns. Having witnessed the devastating wars of Greece, he strongly advocated that peace be maintained, for only then could Athens enjoy increased revenues and flourish. He also understood and advocated division of labor as necessary for more efficient production.[27]

Summary.—While it is true that there is some unreality in Plato's and Aristotle's philosophies, nevertheless they set up objectives which, if attained, would recapture and establish man in conditions vastly better than those that prevailed in their day. The teachings of the philosophers on certain points had, in the opinion of some who followed, the impact of laws. Aristotle came nearer than anyone else in antiquity to developing a distinct science of economics.

The teachings of the Greek philosophers, and especially Aristotle, appear again in the church doctrines of the Middle Ages. Their views of an economic nature were blended with biblical doctrines and incorporated in canon law, which served as a guide to individuals in their commercial relations with one another. The philosophers' concepts of the origin and the necessity of the state entered into political doctrines for centuries. And one must consider the state in its origin and its functions, for in it capitalism, with all its shades of meaning, rules, regulations, and so on, had its genesis. Even though only a relatively simple economic society existed at this early period, the philosophers anticipated many of the problems that were to arise in a more complex time, and wrote about them with great discernment.

[26] Monroe, *op. cit.*, p. 40.
[27] See *Cyropoedia*, viii. ii, 5-6, in the Loeb Classical Library translation, for a description of the division of labor in the kitchen of the King of Persia. This passage is quoted by Karl Marx in *Capital* (Chicago, 1908), Vol. I, p. 402 n.

Inasmuch as Aristotle came nearest to developing a consistent set of economic doctrines they may be briefly summarized. In the first place, Aristotle used a metaphysical concept of the natural or the part nature plays in the state, in the domestic economy, and in true wealth which has an ethical relationship to the satisfaction of human wants. While he identified what is natural, he differentiated as unnatural many human endeavors which lead to mere accumulation; this reflects his acute distinction between value in use and value in exchange.

The idea of justice looms large with Aristotle, as with Plato. Justice is not attained when the end of economic activity is gain in itself. His views on money and value are clear; money he considered a medium for making exchange possible; because of this view of the function of money, he was obliged to condemn usury or interest. Aristotle did not understand the nature and functions of capital. Exchange was barren because it was an interchange of equivalent values. Value was explained as a subjective thing even though he recognized that, under certain conditions, an item may have value in exchange. His concept of value (a subjective one) was largely a result of the fact that everyone in society has a demand for the services of one another; thus, demand is a common tie which characterizes society. The subjective element, as developed by Aristotle, prevailed for many years until the cost theories were developed. In general, Aristotle's views may be regarded as correct when viewed in their own setting.

4

Rome and Roman Contributions

The total contribution of the Romans to Western thought was small compared with that of Greece. The Greeks who enriched civilization with their accomplishments in literature, sculpture, philosophy, political institutions, science, and art had few counterparts in Rome. The history of Rome is largely one of conquest and struggle which for a time engulfed almost all of the world then known. At one time or another Rome held the entire Mediterranean area including Asia Minor and North Africa, Gaul (modern France), Spain, parts of central Europe extending to the Danube River, and Britain as far north as Scotland.

Roman leaders were essentially engaged in more active pursuits than the Greeks. They were warriors and statesmen and empire builders. In time, most of Rome's great edifices fell at the hands of enemies both within and without. Her political excesses brought about the decline of her institutions; her agriculture and commerce declined; slavery and absentee-landlordism further affected production and poverty; revolution and turmoil spread. The Empire had extended itself so far over Europe and Asia that it could no longer be held together. Historians generally agree that the fall of Rome was in process for several hundred years before the Empire actually succumbed in A.D. 476.

Our greater cultural heritages are of Greek origin, yet Roman contributions should not be minimized. A people who had the capability to set up first a great republic, later a world empire, and to hold it together for so many years must have had great qualities. The two hundred years of peace (*Pax Romana*) and prosperity under the emperors (c. 31 B.C. to A.D. 180) were the best of all antiquity, not only for the Romans, but for all peoples "except Greece, which was deserted and almost depopulated and Palestine which was ruined by bloody insurrections and still bloodier repressions." [1] The impact of some of the contributions of the Romans was even greater than those of the Greeks. That the Roman viewpoint was cosmopolitan to a greater degree than

[1] Jules Toutain, *Economic Life of the Ancient World* (New York, 1930), p. 256.

45

that of the Greeks was due, in large part, to their world conquests. The Greeks at the peak of their colonization did expand over a great geographical area, but comparatively speaking they did not approach the Romans in the extent of their influence or in their years of power as a nation.

Economic Life of the Romans.—A complete account of the economic life of the Romans would cover a period which extends from the early people, who endured the most primitive existence, to include the many nationalities who shared in the complex, large-scale problems of a world empire. Such a story is not within the scope of this work, but a few of the high points are given. Likewise, it is extremely difficult to generalize on subjects pertaining to Rome and Roman achievements, for the history covers a span of more than a thousand years. During this period there were several hundred years of Rome as a city-state, next as a republic, and last as a world empire. Her fortunes were both good and bad; she had many wars and conquests but in one interval enjoyed two hundred years of peace. The problem is to extract the items of economic interest from the vast mass of materials which are available.

One of the earliest economic policies adopted by expanding Rome was that of agricultural development. The gains from this policy were not confined to an increase in foodstuffs alone. In addition, it made available a body of hardy men who could be called upon to bear arms in defense of the state. The Romans, like all early peoples, were largely dependent upon agriculture. The expansion of agriculture was one of the factors which brought Rome to dominant leadership within Italy.

The policy of commercial expansion also brought in great gains, but it led the city into conflict with other peoples outside Italy, especially with Carthage, a rivalry which culminated in the Punic Wars. The merchant classes, growing in numbers and power, looked with envy on the trade and commerce of every one else, especially the Carthaginians. Competitive trade led first to commercial treaties but eventually to war. In other words, the desire for trade and commerce was strong and the encroachment of anyone upon Roman trading prerogatives was resisted.

As Rome expanded, the expenses of government mounted. Taxes were increased, finally to such an extent that they became ruinous to the citizens. As a result, the loot and booty of conquest looked all the more desirable, and Rome began to build her empire.

The functions of money were known and clearly understood. Money-lenders were everywhere present who enriched themselves from high interest rates. The merchant class that engaged in extensive coastwise and foreign trade had to have banks to handle the business. In these banks the wealthy merchant classes met "to transact financial business, and here large companies were formed for the collection of taxes and for taking government contracts to build roads and bridges or to erect public buildings. Shares in such companies were daily sold, and a business like that of a modern stock exchange developed in the Forum." [2]

In time the personal accumulations of wealth became extremely great and the gulf between the wealthier and the poorer groups became wider. In "conspicuous consumption" the rich Romans exceeded anything recorded for ancient potentates. In the beauty and grandeur of temples, forums, arches, and the general adornment of her edifices and cities, Rome had no rival.

While great extremes of wealth were to be found mainly in the cities, the large rural estates were also growing. There has always been a certain respectability attached to ownership of land which, to the Romans, was a semisocial justification for their private wealth, no matter how ill-gotten. Many of the peasants or small landholders lost their lives fighting in Rome's wars of conquest, and others lost their original holdings because of inability to pay taxes. In the depopulation and destruction of the countryside, the wealthy class—many of them nobles—came into possession of landholdings, large at first and eventually even larger. These were known as the latifundia, later to be decried as an enemy to the "glory that was Rome." Also the small farm operators could not compete with the operators of great estates who used slave labor extensively; the fall of grain prices resulting from slave labor production and the cheap imported grain from Africa, Sicily, and Egypt ruined the small peasant producer. The small farms almost disappeared as they did in Greece because of the land and labor practices of the greedy wealthy classes.

The decline of agriculture, especially small farming, is regarded as the most important reason for the fall of Rome. The over-all results add up to just one thing, namely, not enough food for the people. The land was so heavily taxed that small landholders could not operate. They would enter into agreements with the large landholders to become *coloni*, an arrangement which bound them by law to the land they worked. Any change of ownership of the land carried with it a transfer of the *coloni*. While not actually slaves, they were not free to leave the land and all incentive was lost. Other people left the land and went to the cities for public relief—evidence that many of the farmers did not even have enough food for themselves.

The great landlords of the latifundia were, like most of the small farmers, very unproductive agriculturists. Various methods were tried to restore land tenure to smaller holders and increase production but without success. The work of the writers on agriculture came too late.

[2] J. H. Breasted, *Ancient Times* (2d ed.; Boston, 1944), p. 630.

The population pressure on the food supply, which was so significant in bringing about the fall of Rome, is but a well-known page from history. Rome had made great strides in commerce and trade, industry, transportation, banking, and so on, but none of these compensated for the failure of agriculture. The prime importance of agriculture in the history of all peoples must never be overlooked.

Slavery.—Slavery was a necessary institution. The larger landowners, particularly in Italy and Sicily, could not work their estates without slaves. Probably no people was so successful in supplying the slave market as were the Romans. From the Punic Wars onward—the first one began in 264 B.C., the third one ended more than a hundred years later—the Roman conquests had brought to Italy numberless captives of war from Spain, Greece, Carthage, and Asia Minor. The Adriatic coast was a source of thousands of slaves. A large and lucrative traffic in these poor unfortunates developed, and slave piracy was very common. The island of Delos, lying near Athens, was reported to be the largest of slave markets. The incredible number of 10,000 slaves was supposed to have been sold in a single day in this market alone.[3] The Roman armies while engaged in conquest and territorial expansion took vast numbers of slaves; the subjugation of Greece and Macedonia alone netted over a million. While the Romans were not unwilling to enslave any captive, the Greeks were the ones most highly prized for their various skills. The many years of brutal treatment of slaves brought on revolts which were really bloody revolutions. In time the poorer farming classes or freed men who were reduced to serfdom and the slaves became a social class hostile to the rich and propertied class. Excesses in the treatment of slaves, together with the dangerous political aspect of such a large class, demanded reform measures. A complete set of laws to govern ownership, treatment, and sale of slaves was finally developed.

Some General Economic Advances.—A great unevenness appears in the political fortunes and development of Rome. Excesses and abuses, as well as peace and progress, are in her chronicles. With the establishment of the Empire the economic side of the heavy and planless methods of taxation in previous years was superseded by relatively scientific methods of property assessments, based on the valuation of the property in each province. The ruler could then determine how much tax could be collected from each province. Augustus, the first and the greatest of the emperors who ruled from 31 B.C. to A.D. 14, developed a fairly scientific method of a direct tax on land and one on personal property

[3] Jules Toutain, *op. cit.*, p. 232.

in addition to customs duties. He had complete control of the funds collected, which were put to use in building roads, bridges, aqueducts, and public buildings.

Business ventures were common inasmuch as the government under the leadership of Augustus was orderly. Private capital was available for loans at as little as 4 per cent. Internal commerce and communication grew rapidly. Excellent roads and bridges made commercial intercourse faster and surer. It is estimated that the speed of travel and communication was fully as high as that attained in Europe and America before the advent of the railroad. Sea-borne commerce was extensive. Grain ships plied regularly between Rome and Alexandria. Good harbors, docks, and lighthouses aided shipping. Rivers of central Europe carried goods as did the caravans which connected less accessible areas. Products of the Orient such as Egyptian papyrus, linen, spices, rugs, rich embroideries, fine glassware and pottery, metal products, grain, oil, and wine were a few of the items of trade.

In the first two centuries A.D. the trade within and between the areas of the Empire increased. Law prevailed and exchange was carried out in an orderly manner. The government encouraged economic activity in the form of public works, draining of swamps, building of roads and bridges, working of mines and quarries, improvement of harbors and shipping, and encouragement of industry and trade. The transactions were carried on under the law. For two centuries, save for relatively brief interruptions, economic gains were made which, for some nations, have never been equaled.

Likewise, in this period many cities had sprung up, some of which endured, in name at least, until today. They became powerful, self-ruling units which developed their own economies. Local industries developed within them; crafts and skills devoted to certain distinctive products made many cities famous. Iron and metal products, various textiles, especially wool, pottery products, and luxury goods of many types, entered east and west trade. The strong guild spirit, which appeared even in the early centuries of the Christian era, developed along lines of specialization by freemen and had many mutual benefits. Most of the production remained in the handicraft stage and was carried on in the homes. A wage payment was part of the system. Coinage and banking facilitated trading, and improved transportation by land and by sea hastened the exchanges. In all, one may view the early beginnings of the ordinary commercial elements of capitalism. The changes instituted in subsequent centuries are indeed pronounced; nevertheless capitalism's beginnings are clearly apparent when the Empire was at its height. Cities and states as well as individuals grew in wealth; specialization, commercial expansion, new raw materials, and world markets reached levels relatively higher than ever before known. But decline in the political unity of the Empire let loose the forces which ultimately brought about the downfall of the whole structure. Not all the economic gains were lost, but for many hundreds of years the level of economic activity was at a very low ebb.

Some Economic Characteristics.—Throughout the centuries of Roman hegemony there developed many economic institutions and practices. The practices are better known than the theories, if any, that supported them. It is known that the expenditures of various rulers were great and the taxes were ruinous. Likewise, great amounts of wealth were brought to Rome from her many conquests; there were many rich citizens—rich in landholdings and in private wealth as well. The supply of and the demand for the many items in use in a great state created problems of supply and of price. Many commercial and industrial regulations were introduced; even though the Romans believed in private property and had many laws dealing with it, the state did interfere, even to extremes. It regulated occupations, fixed prices of grain and other commodities, and passed laws prohibiting export of grains and precious metals. Quality of goods was inspected; standard weights and measures were employed, largely for the purpose of preventing fraud. While these measures were very likely beneficial to the merchant and the consumer, the great frauds and graft practiced by public officials were most reprehensible. The regulations indicated a need for state control over certain economic activities. Practical rather than theoretical considerations determined the nature of the regulations. Some specific considerations follow.

Money and Interest.—The functions of money in trade and commerce were well known. Early trade was carried on by barter methods, but about the middle of the fourth century B.C. the state introduced official coinage. Greece had long used coins for exchange purposes, but the Romans were late in adopting money in trading relations. The first Roman coins were bronze and silver. This bimetallic system brought difficulties, mainly in the fluctuation of the cost of the ingredient metal, copper, and led to a new coinage system in 269 B.C. At that time the silver unit known as the denarius was adopted, with fractional coins in both silver and copper. The new coinage stimulated sales and purchases not only at home but in foreign trade as well. The money-changers and banks could then accept current Greek coins in exchange. In fact, Toutain notes that "there were even financial crises, created by the much more active circulation of coin." [4] Roman bankers made great

_____
[4] Toutain, *op. cit.*, p. 224.

profit on loans at interest.[5] The borrowers were cities, sovereigns, those
engaged in business ventures, ambitious young noblemen, such as
Caesar and Antony, who needed funds for their political careers. The
rates of interest varied, depending upon the risk. Impoverished sovereigns paid the highest rates, for the risk was obviously greater. The loan
capital which became such a vital part of Roman economic life had its
origin in the spoils taken from conquered peoples; booty of conquest,
tribute collected by the victorious ruler, and the unscrupulous exactions
of the publicans (tax collectors and also money-lenders), as well as the
profits of the bankers, provided the funds.

The profit motive was strong and many of those who engaged in business enterprise were successful in amassing great wealth. Interest-taking
was opposed in earlier periods of Roman history for reasons similar to
those advanced by the Greek writers. The Laws of the Twelve Tables
(450 B.C.) condemned usury (used in the sense of excessive charges) but
fixed the interest rate. With the growth of wealth, borrowing and lending became a common practice. The interest rate in Rome on loans of
low risk was from 4 to 8 per cent, but in the provinces it might be 10
or 12 times as much. The *Institutes* of Justinian set the legal rate at
4 to 8 per cent, according to the type of the loan.

Ideas on Value.—Little or no attention appears to have been given to
value theory as such in Roman writings. The Romans were less concerned than the Greek writers with speculative ideas. The vast amount
of trade and commerce, together with the money and price system that
prevailed, would imply rather clearly defined value and price ideas, but
no such concepts are to be found. Price seems to have been determined
by the prevailing supply and demand factors of the market. In time a
concept of *verum pretium* developed, which meant a true or just price.
It is probable that this was a cost-of-production idea which included a
profit. Diocletian, in one of his edicts in A.D. 301, attempted to fix the
true price at what it cost to produce the article. The *justum pretium*
concept of the Middle Ages also carried the same implications. The
concepts were in reality indefinable and unenforcible in practice, but
they do indicate some consideration of the ethical issues of value. The
legalistic thinking is reflected in the principle of *caveat emptor* (let the
buyer beware), which held that the buyer had no recourse unless fraud
and misrepresentation occurred. Even though Rome had many commercial regulations at one time or another, even to regulation of the

---

[5] Breasted, *op. cit.*, pp. 629-30, states, "During the Hannibalistic Wars (217-201
B.C.) banks first appeared in Rome, occupying a line of booths on each side of the
Forum." Business resembling that of a modern stock exchange developed in the
Forum.

prices of grains, oils, and other commodities, speculations on value and price theories were absent.

The Writers on Agriculture.—The best known writers on agriculture were Pliny, Cato, Varro, Columella, and Palladius. They were primarily interested in improving the agricultural methods and reforming land ownership and holdings. The land reforms attempted by Caius and Tiberius Gracchus in the years 133-123 B.C., which were devised to break up the large landed estates known as latifundia, were defeated by the landowners. The rich landholders gradually forced small owners of adjoining property to dispose of their holdings to them; in accomplishing this objective, all sorts of treachery were used. The big estates were worked by slave labor, which completely supplanted free labor on the land. Pliny the Elder (A.D. 23-79) says, in a much quoted passage, that the latifundia destroyed Italy: "Latifundia perdidere Italiam." [6] No doubt there remained small holdings in the less desirable areas, but only fragments were left. Slavery and large holdings appear to have been complementary evils.

Cato (234-149 B.C.), as well as other writers, produced semitechnical treatises based largely on his own observations, with a large element of reflection on what had prevailed in earlier days. He praised small farms and denounced the large ones. He thought an estate should consist of 150 acres (240 jugera) of olive groves and 62 acres (100 jugera) of vineyards, which would be a medium-sized holding. Varro (116-27 B.C.), who wrote a *De Re Rustica* (37 B.C.), was trying to advise both large and small landholders on what crops should be grown and on stock-breeding. The writers all advocated a "back to the land" movement as a means of counteracting the increasing poverty of the masses and the certain impoverishment of the state. They also complained that land was being given over to olive and wine production, whereas the production of grains, especially wheat, was rapidly declining. Famines resulted and grave disorders arose in many of the provinces. Measures were taken by the state to correct this situation, but they were generally ineffective.

Columella devoted most of the thirteen Books in his *De Re Rustica* to wine and olive growing, livestock, bees, and gardens, but neglected emphasizing grain crops. A writer of the fourth century, Palladius, author of another *De Re Rustica*, also emphasizes wine, olive, fruit, and livestock production rather than grain crops, which are mentioned only incidentally. There must have been severe shortages of grains for much of the period of the Empire. The emperors were always concerned with keeping adequate food in the city of Rome, reflecting, no

[6] Pliny, *Natural History* xviii. 7.

doubt, their own desire for popularity and for safety. Therefore they prohibited, at various times, the corn of Egypt to be exported to any place but Rome; and the harvests from the imperial estates in Sicily, Africa, Spain, and Gaul were reserved for the Roman population.

The landownership, which led to great transformations in the rural economy, had marked social consequences. The countryside was deserted by most of the small landholders and free laborers who crowded into the towns, especially into Rome. This swelled the number of plebeians and added to an already dangerous populace made up of practically every nationality. They became an unruly group, which constantly demanded more and more from the state. Rome was no longer the capital of an agricultural state, with some balance between the landowners and the urban population, but a state in which the masses were dispossessed of property and dependent on such industry, trade, and commerce as the city could provide. In the end the masses hastened the downfall of the city.

Roman Law.—The Roman Empire as a political entity passed away centuries ago, but Roman law through its influence still remains a world force. In its modernized form, Roman law has become the law of more than three fourths of the civilized globe.[7] The development and the impact of Roman law are of especial significance to the student of economic thought. Few persons realize how many of our daily activities rest upon legal sanction. The institutions of capitalism rest upon legal foundations. The state is a legal, political concept. All its sovereign acts rest upon law. The details of the full import of law to economic practices would require a volume in itself.

It is a well-known fact that the Romans were lawmakers. The imperial codes of law represent the work of some of the greatest legal minds the world has ever known. Roman law was dominant because of its equity and universal adaptability; it was just, logical, fair, humane, and thoroughly practical. It was the Roman genius for statesmanship, political organization, and universal law that constitutes her greatest contribution to mankind.

[7] Roman law, in its modern form and modified only by local customary laws and statutes, is the basis of the law of Italy, France, Spain, Portugal, Switzerland, Belgium, Holland, Germany, pre-Communistic Jugoslavia, Czechoslavakia, the Balkan states and China, Greece, Scandinavian countries, Turkey, Egypt, Abyssinia, Mauritius, the South African colonies, Ceylon, Sumatra, Java, the Philippines, and Japan. In the Western Hemisphere, the civil law obtains in Quebec, Louisiana, Mexico, and all the countries of Central and South America and the West Indies, including Cuba and Puerto Rico. W. L. Burdick, *Principles of Roman Law and Their Relation to Modern Law* (Rochester, N. Y., 1938), pp. 7, 8. English common law is the law of England and of most of the English-speaking areas, including the United States.

Roman law was developed by an evolutionary process over several centuries. From the founding of Rome (c. 753 B.C.) to the death of Justinian (A.D. 565) more than thirteen centuries elapsed. During that time, Rome experienced many changes in government, and her laws were likewise changed. The laws of all countries and of all peoples, even including the storied immutability of the laws of the ancient Medes and Persians, change from century to century and even from generation to generation. Each age in Roman history left its impress upon her laws.

The Twelve Tables (codified in 450 B.C.) mark the real beginning of Roman law. The Roman jurists considered them the foundation of all law. In style they were brief, terse, and imperative. They were a collection of legal principles covering the general outlines of the law, engraved on metal tablets and set up in the Forum. Cicero described them as a "summary of all that is excellent."

The jus civile was developed by the Romans (450 to 336 B.C.) as a law for Roman citizens only. The student of Roman history must be impressed by the extraordinary degree to which the fortunes of the Republic were affected by the presence of foreigners on her soil. "The foreign element in the commonwealth determined the whole course of its history, which, at all stages, is little more than a narrative of conflicts between a stubborn nationality and an alien population." [8] The Roman citizens always believed themselves united in blood kinship and resented any claim by foreigners to equality of privilege as a usurpation of their birthright. In the minds of the jurists the exclusion of foreigners from the protection of civil laws was justifiable, just as they were justifiably excluded from citizenship under the constitution. The jus civile reflected Roman customs; it was law for Roman citizens only.

But the foreign element in Rome grew apace with Rome's rise and created many national problems. It developed from small minorities into large groups who always constituted a threat to the equilibrium of society. If for no other reason than self-preservation alone, the Romans were obliged to devise methods of adjusting the rights and duties of foreigners who might otherwise resort to armed strife. Furthermore, Rome was engaged in trade and commerce and foreigners were always in contact with Romans in trading ventures. The Roman jurists refused to settle disputes as they arose under Roman civil law, nor would they degrade themselves by applying the law of the particular state from which a foreign litigant came. They were, therefore, obliged

8 Henry J. S. Maine, Ancient Law (London, 1871), p. 28.

to evolve a set of laws which would cover such cases. This led to the enactment of laws known as *jus gentium*—"laws common to all nations."

The *jus gentium* was an expedient set up (336 to 31 B.C.) for the purpose of selecting the rules of law common to Rome and to the different Italian communities. It was a political necessity. It had in it the common ingredients of old Italian customs. If particular practices were observed as a common characteristic of a large number of separate races, it was set down as a part of the law applicable to foreigners in their relations with the Romans, or a *jus gentium*. Thus it was a collection of rules and principles determined by observation to be common to the institutions which prevailed among the various tribes. It was a broader and more comprehensive law than *jus civile*, but it should not be interpreted as being the same as what we now call international law.

The next great event in the evolution of the development of Roman law came late in Roman history. The Emperor Justinian, who reigned from A.D. 527 to 565, ordered a consolidation of all existing law into a concise and compact form, known as the *Code*, along with various commentaries. The work, which constituted the entire body of the civil law, is known as the *Corpus Juris Civilis*, a term not used by Justinian but by European writers centuries later.

After the establishment of civil law, several hundred years elapsed in which it was greatly modified. As the Church grew and began to assume temporal powers, it set up its own laws. It blended civil law with canon law; the latter became the supreme law, supplanting civil law. Canon law is a system of law that was developed for the government and regulation of the Christian or Roman Church. Canon law means the law laid down by ecclesiastical councils and by epistles and decrees of the head of the Church. Following the pattern of the Justinian compilation, an attempt was made in 1114 by Ivo, Bishop of Chartres, to bring together the great mass of church and ecclesiastical laws accumulated during the centuries, and the task was completed by the monk Gratian in 1150. This work is now known as the *Corpus Juris Canonici*. While the Canon law is based largely on civil law, it departs therefrom in many important respects, especially in laws governing offenses and matters of procedure. The *Corpus Juris Canonici* became the basis of English ecclesiastical law, but it never made much headway against the English common law as the law of the land.

The influence of Roman law upon English common law, hence upon our own, is controversial. Some students have vigorously asserted that English common law is not at all indebted to Roman law, while others hold the opposite view. The fact that many principles of English law are similar to or identical with principles found in Roman law does not convince all students that the former was borrowed or copied from the latter. Equally good legal authorities may be quoted on both sides. Certainly there were periods in the development of English law when Roman influence was pronounced. The twelfth and thirteenth centuries have been called the "Roman epoch in English legal history." Writings of this period, both lay and professional, show that the spirit of Roman law prevailed almost everywhere. The courts cited it with approval and it was taught in the schools of learning.[9] It seems certain that, despite the assertions of some English writers that English common law is an indigenous product, the development of many of its principles was materially influenced by the Roman law.

Since law plays such a significant part in the development of society (and vice versa), it may be well to note a few of the laws specifically applicable to the development of a capitalistic society. The Roman laws of contract and of private property were explicit. Our modern maritime law may be traced to Roman codes. The law of persons covered rights of freemen and slaves, citizens and aliens; it included family law and the disposal of property. The Roman law recognized natural persons and juristic or artificial persons. From this recognition the rules and regulations on corporations, which recognize rights and privileges of an artificial person, have been developed. Blackstone, the great English jurist, who ordinarily could find little to admire in Roman law, even went so far as to give the credit of inventing the corporation form of enterprise wholly to the Romans.[10]

The Roman law of obligations was clearly defined and all-inclusive. The laws of succession show great mastery of the problems which arise in that field. The laws as to public wrongs are nearly standard in contemporary legal practice. The idea of a jury may be traceable to Roman procedure, and under Roman law there was no presumption of guilt. As under English law, guilt had to be established by the prosecutor. This brief review should serve to emphasize the importance of Roman law, in fact all law, to the development of economic thought and institutions. It is one of the curious facts of history that Rome, with her appalling record of warfare and bloodshed, gave to mankind one of the world's two great systems of jurisprudence. Law was Rome's most lasting contribution to civilization.

Economic Downfall of the Ancient World.—Attention should be given to the economic factors in the downfall of Rome, for with her ended the greatness of the ancient world. Political and economic causes for the downfall of Rome are almost inseparable. Economic

[9] Burdick, *op. cit.*, p. 74.
[10] Blackstone, *Commentaries* (London, 1809), Vol. I, chap. xviii, p. 486.

prosperity depended in large measure on secure frontiers with order and peace prevailing within them, political unity, a well-developed agricultural, industrial, and commercial organization, stable wages and prices, individual enterprise, and a measure of freedom. Indeed, the same elements which we today regard as essential to economic prosperity were essential in Roman times. Before the end of the second century the same symptoms of decay were appearing in Rome which had been evident in Greece even earlier. Conditions grew much worse in the third century. Frontiers were crossed by barbarian hordes who greedily plundered and laid waste the richest lands of the Empire. They also came by sea and from every direction; not only was the outer circumference attacked and ravaged but no part of the Roman world escaped.

Anarchy prevailed within. Riots and insurrections broke out in the cities and in the country. Brigandage and vandalism were practiced aimlessly and needlessly for the malicious pleasure of destruction. The moral unity of society was damaged by persecution of the Christians. Production declined in basic industries. High prices, money shortages, depopulation, and general ruin threatened the whole economic fabric and finally broke it completely. The countryside and farms were abandoned; land fell to waste. Taxation was unscientific and inadequate for the state treasury. Public and private wealth vanished as its source was destroyed.

Efforts, sometimes heroic, were made to reverse the economic trends, but with little success. Penalties of death did not bring production of foodstuffs nor did reorganization of finance and reformation of coinage correct the erratic price system. The reforms of Aurelian, Diocletian, Constantine, and finally Julian represented an enormous advance compared with the anarchy of the third century but they came too late. Diocletian, who tried very drastic measures as reforms, perhaps hastened the end. He preferred to live in Asia Minor rather than in Italy, and to delegate the ruling of the western half of the Empire to an associate emperor. He therefore created an even larger governmental organization which had to be paid and supported. The taxes were increased until the citizens could no longer pay. The scarcity of coin forced payment in produce, and Rome thereby sank to an oriental "payment in kind" taxation a thousand years old. Taxation simply ruined everyone. The farming class was destroyed by the land policy and the business class was ruined by taxation. Diocletian forbade farmers to leave the land and workmen to change occupations. Wages and prices were fixed by the state; craftsmen, retailers, grain dealers—in fact everyone was watched by the state in the minutest dealings. The Roman government was regulating every phase of the citizen's life. He was but a cog in the vast machinery of government which was gradually stifling all the fine qualities which had once made a Roman a noble type of citizen. Freedom and initiative were sacrificed and an oriental despotism put in its place. The damage to the whole national fiber lay much too deep to be repaired by makeshift reforms, no matter how well meant.

At the end of the fourth and the beginning of the fifth century, the barbarians poured in over the Danube and hastened the end. They found wealth in the provinces, in the villas of the latifundia, and in many of the cities, but these were the impoverished remains of an economic prosperity which had been steadily declining for nearly two hundred years, for lack of peace, security, and liberty.

The economic life of the ancient world passed through a very instructive evolution. At first the economic activities were domestic in form and on a small scale. At the end the whole economy became highly complex and was finally ruined by the tyranny and corruption of the public authorities. The end of a great empire was hastened by the failure of those in authority to realize the depressing influence of the absence of liberty and the prevalence of injustice. The Greek ideal of justice, once written so explicitly in Roman law, was no longer an actuality. The deep-seated destructive forces were more powerful than any ruler could combat. There was no preventing the end of the greatest empire of ancient times.

Summary.—Rome was culturally parasitic on Greece. Nevertheless, the contributions in law and government made by Rome have no equal. The Romans taught men the unifying principle of a single government and a single civilization, the full impact of which is appreciated in modern times. They were builders on a scale rivaling the Pharaohs, but many of their edifices and what they symbolized, like those of the Pharaohs, crumbled. Some Roman rulers made heroic efforts on many occasions to reform the structure of the state but the reforms had little permanent, lasting effect. Rome fell, and with her went many of the worth-while institutions which had made her great. Yet no scientific discoveries, no new or original philosophical systems, no original thinking on economic matters was left to posterity by the Romans. She did build roads, bridges, aqueducts, and monuments, and systematized and codified laws. New logistics in warfare and great armies were distinctly Roman. Anyone familiar with the ruins of the ancient temples, forums, and the like which stand in Rome today is duly impressed with the mute testimony to a great capital city. But internal decay coupled with insurmountable external problems brought her fall. The Romans excelled the Greeks only in military tactics and social cohesion. These too, lost their power and the great entity—Rome—which stood for a thousand years became largely a matter of history.

It was from her ruins that Christianity rose. The Hebrew prophets told of the coming of the Messiah, who, according to the Scripture, would establish a kingdom of God on earth. It befell what remained of Rome to become the center from which Christianity spread throughout the world. Christianity, long a revolutionary movement in the Roman world, was legally recognized in A.D. 311. The decree was maintained by the first of the emperors to embrace Christianity, Constantine, who resided then at his new capital, Constantinople, in Asia Minor. In time there developed two distinct branches of the Christian Church: the Eastern (Greek) Church with headquarters in Constantinople, and the Western (Latin) Church at Rome. Thus, even though Rome lost a type of glory and greatness, she probably gained a greater one in helping create the most revolutionary movement of antiquity or of all history, Christianity.

5

The Middle Ages and the Schoolmen:
St. Thomas Aquinas, Nicholas Oresme

The Middle Ages cover a span of roughly one thousand years. Scholars disagree on the dates, but the period known as the Middle Ages is generally regarded as extending from the fall of Rome in A.D. 476 to about 1500. The exact beginning or end is not especially significant for our purposes. What happened within this long stretch of years is, on the contrary, very important.

In the Middle Ages there was an amalgamation of the cultures of many peoples. Culture strains and patterns of the borderlands of Europe and the Near East were blended with those of the Mediterranean basin. By the end of the fourth century, uncivilized or barbarian peoples began to migrate into the declining Roman Empire. With the disintegration of Rome the path was open to all peoples. During the fifth and sixth centuries, Vandals, Visigoths, Ostrogoths, Franks, and Teutons or Germans settled in the western part, and in the next two centuries, Islam conquered the entire southern half of the ancient world and closed the Mediterranean to the Christians of the west. Only parts of the former empire were not overrun and retained a sort of independence. In the five centuries which followed the fall of Rome a great fusion of peoples took place. The Teutons, Celts, Franks, Romans and others formed a great amalgam in the debris of the Roman Empire. In time, these peoples were associated with land areas which later became the states of western Europe. Wars, migrations, absorption of conquered peoples, economic and political necessity—all contributed to the mixtures which gradually took on characteristics that identified the amalgamations with certain geographical areas and later with the several states and nations. During this long span of years some groups prospered and grew into strong nations. Others made little progress or in some instances retrogressed; later these were absorbed by the stronger states.

The End of the Roman Empire and the Rise of Christianity.—The great Roman Empire affords one of the best examples of the fate that may befall a state. The reasons for her growth and subsequent decline and fall are many; some of them were set forth in the preceding chapter. In addition to the decline in agriculture, which was only one economic factor, there were many others of a social and political nature. Population was declining; moral and social turpitude was pronounced. Graft and corruption degraded the citizenry to a level which destroyed the high distinction of being a Roman citizen. Business declined, coinage was debased, the supply of precious metals was inadequate, prices were uncertain, and economic chaos prevailed. Political anarchy was rampant within the Empire, and the barbarians from the north, who attacked and burned many a city and laid waste the countryside, were unopposed by the Roman armies. History records the victories of the barbarians. Those emperors who were relatively effective provided temporary stability, but they could not check the ebb tide which was sweeping away the Empire and much of its greatness. Five hundred years after the reign of the great emperor Augustus, Rome had become a matter of history.

Christianity arose in the downfall of Rome. After many years of ruthless persecution of the Christians, the teachings of Christianity prevailed and were legalized by a decree in A.D. 311. This victory, however, did not become final for many years. As men learned of the new teachings, Christianity grew in strength and influence and spread over the whole of Europe in one form or another. Churches and monasteries were established and became powerful. The Church proved to be the greatest agency in perpetuating culture, spreading learning, and developing statesmanship. In time, the bishops of the Church assumed temporal as well as secular powers.

The teachings of the Church and Christianity were revolutionary. Jesus taught the dignity of man; he condemned slavery and emphasized human brotherhood. He denounced the accumulation of riches and the exploitation of the less fortunate. These teachings were in sharp contrast to those of the Greek philosophers, who favored slavery and frowned upon the dignity of labor and occupations. The Christian influence gave life a purpose. Service to God and to fellowmen would assure one of a better life hereafter. A life patterned on the Beatitudes (Matt. 5:1-12) would remove from man the base, pugnacious, and selfish characteristics which led to conflict. Theoretically the world could be one of peaceful, harmonious development based on Christ's concept of a kingdom of righteousness. The inspiration, hopes, promises, and rewards offered by the Christian faith gave mankind a new orientation. The failure to realize these promises was believed to be due to man's sin and stubbornness.

The history of the growth of Christianity as a great power and influence in the European world is a long and detailed story which cannot be told here. The Church was a civilizing influence and served both as a vehicle and as an agency for the spread of culture, art, and practically all learning. Besides, it was a great landlord which owned and operated the largest, and usually the best, lands under cultivation. The monasteries became centers of learning as well as centers of economic control over wide areas. They were, in many places, the nuclei around which towns and cities grew. Many of the monasteries were built on mountain peaks or high places, thus affording better protection to themselves and to the towns which grew up about them. Such agriculture as was carried on was done by the laborers who dwelt in the towns and went out to the fields. Many of the beautiful churches which grace European cities stand as monuments to the fine art and craftsmanship of the period.

The events of greatest economic interest in the period will be considered in connection with such topics as the feudal system, the growth of towns, the crafts and guilds, the state and emergence of capitalism, and the teachings of the Schoolmen.

Feudalism and the Growth of States.—In the evolutionary changes that came in the Middle Ages it appears that by the eighth century western Europe had reverted to an agricultural economy. Land was the source of food supply and the chief form of wealth. Everyone, from the lord to the serf, lived directly or indirectly on products of the soil. Practically all elements of the state depended on the land; revenues, armies, and food products were land-produced. Soldiers came from the serfs and officials from the large landholders. Under such conditions the center of authority rested with the landholders and no longer in a sovereign who headed a state.

Feudalism, which appeared in western Europe in the course of the ninth century, was a return of society to a rural existence. The landlords tended to be a lawless group and became independent of the kings. It was the time of the founding of the great estates. Such holdings had existed in the Roman Empire and also in other early states such as Gaul and Germany. However, the great landed estates and their dependents in the Middle Ages brought significant economic and social changes with far-reaching consequences. The units were mostly self-sufficing, and trade and commerce were reduced to insignificance. A student of medieval history, Pirenne, remarks that "western Europe, from the ninth century onwards, appears in the light of an essentially rural society, in which exchange and the movement of goods had sunk to the lowest possible ebb. The merchant class had disappeared."[1] In time, however, these self-sufficient feudal units began to trade with others, and markets began to develop in some areas.

It was the dependence of the people on the landed proprietor that made him a small-scale sovereign. The landlord became more and more the actual ruler of the people because the kings could not control the landlords. Finally, the lords became practically independent rulers who made their own laws; in this manner the feudal system became a substitute for government, providing a degree of law and order. Eventually feudalism declined and strong states arose. However, despite its many undesirable characteristics, it did save western Europe from anarchy and in so doing established a basis for the development of modern government.

The Towns and Town Economy.—It has been pointed out that in ancient Greece and early Rome the town or city played a paramount part in the political life of society. The state was identical with the city. The political theories of the ancients centered around what they significantly called the city-state. In medieval times the towns were destined to play important roles in the development of the modern state; it was through them that the economic influence of trade and commerce had significant effects on rulers and forms of government.

Towns and cities grew throughout Europe. Many were walled for protection. (The English word "town" originally meant an enclosure.) They were to some extent self-sufficing with highly developed skills and crafts, merchants, and a rather well-developed business and trading activity. The inhabitants were frequently impeded in their commercial activities by an overlord or bishop in whose jurisdiction they happened to reside. In the eighth century the bishops, whose cathedrals were usually located in a town, were given complete sovereignty over the people and their lands. When trade practically disappeared in the ninth century, the last traces of independent city life, with its self-governing bodies, vanished and the towns came under the complete control of the bishops. The inhabitants were more or less directly dependent on the Church, and the bishops held both temporal and spiritual powers.[2] In the tenth, eleventh, and twelfth centuries there was an almost constant struggle between the populace and the overlord or bishop for privileges and even for independence or separate political

[1] Henri Pirenne, *Economic and Social History of Medieval Europe* (New York, 1937), p. 12.
[2] See Henri Pirenne, *Medieval Cities* (Princeton, N. J., 1926), chap. iii, "City Origins."

entities. During the same time, towns developed around the castles of feudal lords and wherever particular occupational skills and natural resources could be found.

By the early eighth century the invasions of Islam changed European life. The Mediterranean, formerly a Roman lake, now became a Moslem sea which carried the invaders to the Atlantic. The presence of the Moslems in the Mediterranean area tended to give greater importance to the inland areas of continental Europe where the cities grew and where the overland trade routes became of vital importance. By the end of that century the Mediterranean was virtually closed to trade and the economic position of western Europe reached its lowest ebb. The tenth century was one of peace and slow recovery, relatively speaking. The feudal system, which practically displaced the weak monarchies, was already established. Peace permitted a growth and expansion of economic activity which amounted to a revival of commerce. But the real revival of commerce came in the eleventh and twelfth centuries, when great cities arose as powerful trading centers for both sea-borne and overland traffic.

The Crusades (the first began in 1096), which were organized for the purpose of breaking the hold of Islam on Europe, restoring Christianity, and regaining the Holy Land, had significant economic consequences. The religious and political results of the Crusades were ephemeral. However, Islam was driven from the Mediterranean, and the Christian West and the East could trade again. Trade and commerce benefited greatly from the Crusades in that new markets were opened and new commodities were introduced. The Crusades also helped to break the grip of feudal lords, many of whom lost their lives in the conquests. The crusading lord would frequently be obliged to borrow from towns in exchange for privileges, which helped to free the towns; and later the towns helped the kings against the lords. The rise in the cost of living during the Crusades tended to impoverish the fighting group, but to enrich others. These and many other factors were great determining forces in shaping the course of events and institutions in western Europe in succeeding years.

In the evolutionary process, town economy developed and attained high levels of achievement. The towns became great producing and trading centers not only locally, but in some instances they attained international fame. Despite the hazards of transport, merchants took their goods to the towns; thus there arose the medieval markets and fairs. Merchants and customers met for trading purposes under the walls of the manorial castle or of the monastery or church, where they would be protected from marauders. For protection the merchants were willing to pay sums which amounted to substantial revenues. Likewise, special rules and laws were made which regulated trade and exchange, credit and money lending.

The merchandise for sale was, in most instances, produced by craftsmen who had formed themselves into guilds for the purpose of regulating their own industries. The merchants also formed guilds for economic self-defense, which became monopolies with considerable power. Division of labor characterized both production and sale of goods. The trading was carried on with relative efficiency by means of money and credit instruments and crude bookkeeping systems. The markets, which generally dealt in products produced and sold locally, were held at regular intervals. The fairs, which were held less frequently, were on a larger scale and attracted wares and professional traders from distant lands. This was especially true of the great Champagne country fairs of the twelfth and thirteenth centuries. Some markets and fairs were held on days having religious significance, but generally they were held at times which reflected the crops or the seasons. All manufactured as well as agricultural products were trafficked in; thus the products for which different cities were famous were sold throughout Europe on a scale which permitted further development of the industry.

Money and credit instruments were in common use, loans were made, bills of exchange were used in trade, and profits were received from the transactions. The Church opposed usury to the end of the Middle Ages, but in business practice money was loaned at interest. The moral issues in the usury question aligned the churchmen on one side and business practice on the other. In any event, loans were made and the borrower agreed to pay back a sum greater than he had received, the difference being known as usury or interest. The rates varied with the risk. "In general the rate of interest varied between 10 and 16 per cent. Sometimes it fell as low as 5 per cent, or rose as high as 24 per cent and even more." [3]

In summary, the growth of towns and the feudal system in the medieval period preceded the beginnings of the modern state; also trade and commerce grew from small-scale markets to world-wide enterprises.

The Emergence of Capitalism.—Few, if any, vestiges of medieval economic institutions remain to this day; however, modern capitalism has its roots in this period. Barter economy ended and a money and price economy was firmly established. The ownership of tools of production became divorced from the use of the tools. The wage system came to be the rule, and production began to be centered in large

[3] Pirenne, *Economic and Social History of Medieval Europe,* p. 130.

corporate groups of complex structure, which held the economic destinies of many individuals.

The pricing of goods presented problems in that the profit motive was strong, yet justice as a religious concept was implied in setting prices. The Church prescribed rules which were intended to guarantee justice for both buyer and seller. The principle was deeply ingrained in religious practices and the *justum pretium* concept of the third and fourth centuries. The theory was that goods should sell at prices which would approximately cover their cost of production. Since the labor expended represented the most important element in the cost of production, the just price was a derivative of the doctrine of fair wages. Fair wages rested largely upon the concept of a wage sufficient to maintain the worker in his own social class, which, if done, answered the demands of justice and fairness.

In some instances wages and prices were arbitrarily fixed either by town or by ecclesiastical authority. Apparently no great reliance was placed on freedom of competition as a regulator of prices or values. Measures were drawn up to forestall speculation, the cornering of the market supply, and other monopolistic practices. Regulations on weights and measures, trade practices, debts, methods of payment, and the like grew apace in an effort to govern men in their dealings with one another. One should not assume that these well-intended efforts were completely successful. The profit motive could not be eliminated and, despite its excesses, it did bring about a great expansion of trade and contribute to a fuller life for many.

The State and Its Economic Functions.—The struggle between the popes and the kings over who should rule the state is well known. But the City of God, like the ideal state depicted by Plato and Aristotle, was far from being realized anywhere in Europe. The states that grew out of feudalism, and survived, rested primarily on their military strength. Later, the political theories of Machiavelli provided a rationalization of the use of force by the state to ensure its survival.

The matters of especial interest here are the economic practices and functions of the state. The state was to provide protection, care for the poor, sustain the population, build and maintain roads, provide a standard system of weights and measures, coin money, and provide certain legal safeguards. It was the duty as well as the prerogative of the ruler to provide adequate coinage and maintain its value—a difficult assignment. The state was entitled to levy taxes, and for a time tax revenues were regarded as a private income belonging to the ruler, who was not obligated to use them in any manner other than as he chose. There was no scientific tax system of money payments, and often payment was made in kind, as had been done in earlier times. The taxes were unscientifically levied and always burdensome, even to the extent of confiscation. Public administration was corrupt and inefficient. Money and coinage systems were unstable; dishonesty and fraud in weights and measures were common. Finally, as economic life grew more complex, it also became more chaotic; order was not restored completely until strong states were established toward the close of the medieval period.

One must keep in mind the over-all importance of the state in the study of economic development. By the end of the Middle Ages the modern state was practically a *fait accompli*. It was essential to individual existence and, conversely, the state had to depend upon its citizenry for its own existence. As a rule, the prosperity of one was tantamount to that of the other. The modern state was, in a very real sense, responsible for the forces that made possible the growth of a bourgeois society and its capitalistic trappings. The state became autonomous and began to promote endeavors which made capitalism possible. The state preceded capitalism. It found capitalism useful and necessary in procuring money to accomplish its ends; in turn, those engaged in capitalistic endeavors had to depend on the state to protect them. Each was complementary to the other.

The Economic Significance of the Middle Ages.—The ten centuries of the Middle Ages had many noteworthy elements. One of the most significant was the emergence of definite national characteristics and traditions of the great peoples of Europe: Italian, German, French, Spanish, and English. They became established in definite geographical areas and experienced many of the same economic, political, social and religious problems. Each passed through a feudalistic period which saw the development of crude institutions in an attempt to rise above barbarism. About A.D. 1000 urbanization began with the subsequent advance of culture, self-government, and economic enterprise. Progress was uneven, slow, and frequently at great sacrifice; yet it was made.

The outstanding factors responsible for the progress of the Middle Ages, as has been pointed out, were both political and religious, namely, feudalism, the growth of the town economy, and the influence of the Church. Economic advances, though significant, were adjuncts of or incidental to the larger movements. Cultural advances were embodied in the religion and philosophy which we know as Christianity. The Church, dating back to Roman times, provided the one unchallenged and dominating agency to carry on the religious teachings, while the Christian religion, which provided the body of firmly held beliefs, became the unifying spiritual bond of the period. The Church and the

Christian religion provide the keystone and the arch which are indispensable in evaluating the medieval period.

The early Middle Ages were characterized by primitive economic wants and primitive means of satisfying them. After trade began to revive about A.D. 1000, the economic significance of the period becomes immensely important in the development of economics. Trade fostered industry and together they provided the impetus to economic growth and expansion. This led to world discovery and market expansion and finally to inevitable conflict. Modern capitalism began in the late Middle Ages and with it came the rise of capitalistic society. National economy replaced domestic economy, and more emphasis was placed on commerce and manufacturing rather than upon agriculture alone. Labor emerged from slavery and serfdom to a free status dependent upon a wage system.

Many of the centuries-old religious teachings and practices gave way before the inevitable growth of a capitalistic economy. The practices of interest-taking were stronger than the theories against it, and the concept of a just price, based on production costs in a narrow sense, now included a profit. The emphasis ceased to be on the ascetic approach to wants, and greater happiness was found in satisfying wants than in stifling them. With the Reformation came liberalization of religious dogma, and the Church could no longer stand in the way of the growth of commerce and trade. Concessions were made by the Church but it could not abandon its basic principles. The Church and religion finally became something apart from another phase of thought built essentially upon wealth-getting activities. Economic practices tended to carve their own path through a tangled maze of theology, ethical teachings, and legal concepts of justice so as to lay the foundations for independent economic analysis and economic thought.

The Awakening of Medieval Minds—Learning, Literature, and Art.— During the period of the Crusades, while trade and town life were emerging, there was also a mental awakening. The demand for learning led to the founding of universities where attempts were made to broaden the body of knowledge and to inquire more deeply into theological and philosophical questions inherited from ancient times. Great progress in learning was made during the twelfth and thirteenth centuries; religious and historical writings and heroic poems appeared, most of them written in Latin, as well as other literature in the vernacular. Beautiful edifices, mostly churches, were built in a new style of art which we call Gothic.

The earliest instruction at the close of the eleventh and the beginning of the twelfth century was in theology, which was designed to educate persons for service in the Church. In addition, there was an interest in law. At Bologna, in northern Italy, a school was established for the purpose of studying the Justinian Codes. Likewise, in Paris students assembled from many lands to study the few subjects then available. Other universities (the name originally meant "all who belonged" to an association or guild, and was later applied only to schools of higher learning) were established in Heidelberg, Oxford, Cambridge, and other medieval cities.

In time the scope of offerings was expanded to include not only theology but law, medicine, and the liberal arts. Of the four, main fields, theology was the most highly developed. Law was next, and still remains as one of the strongest subjects offered in many European universities. A few universities became famous in medicine, but most of them taught the liberal arts. These were the cultural subjects long known as the seven liberal arts, which were divided into two parts: the *trivium* of grammar, rhetoric, and dialectic (deductive logic); and the *quadrivium* of arithmetic, music, geometry, and astronomy.

Interest in these subjects grew and there were many famous teachers and many books were written. The dialectic method of reasoning (or deductive logic) was the most highly developed of the liberal arts. The Schoolmen of the twelfth and thirteenth centuries relied upon it heavily in developing their system of theology and philosophy. They accepted certain principles as true and, using these as premises, they arrived at conclusions which were valid if the premises upon which they rested were true. Thomas Aquinas, the greatest of the Schoolmen, was a master of this method.

Scholasticism.—The Church and Christianity served as the one powerful, unifying principle in society throughout the Middle Ages. Christianity had been institutionalized in the Church and accepted generally. While many of the popes were not leaders and did not always adhere to their own teachings, the underlying power of the Church was ever present. The Church had its "Dark Ages" and periods in which it appears to have lost ground, but it managed to survive even though states rose and fell. Just as the year 1000 may be considered as marking the lowest depth to which western European civilization sank, so the Church also experienced a great ebb in its power and influence about this time, which was followed by ecclesiastical reform in the eleventh and twelfth centuries.

The greatest advance of a thousand years came in the twelfth century with the rise of the cities, the Crusades, and the growth of Scholasticism. In this period, the Crusades came to a rather inglorious end; the cities achieved a great measure of independence; and Scholasticism reached its highest development. The first two achievements have been discussed; the growth of Scholasticism is of great importance in tracing theoretical issues. Scholasticism, which began early in the twelfth century, represents an orthodoxy in theology and an acceptance of the newly discovered Greek and Moslem philosophy and science, especially Aristotle's; it reconciles faith and reason and organizes all knowledge under theology, the supreme authority. The Scholastics, or Schoolmen, used a dialectic method and syllogistic reasoning to present their doctrines. In economics, they codified temporal laws and rules which were guides for men in their trading relations for many centuries.

St. Thomas Aquinas.[4]—St. Thomas Aquinas is regarded as the greatest of the Scholastics. In his *Summa Theologica* is a systematic attempt to reconcile theological dogma with actual conditions in economic life. He considers how worldly economic problems should be determined by citing biblical teachings and canonical dogma, to which he applies the principles of Aristotle. From these three sources an answer is drawn which represents the highest and final authority. The rules or precepts so derived were to serve as standards in guiding mankind in right living.[5]

Thomas Aquinas agrees with Aristotle that the holding of private property is not contrary to natural law; also, that production under private ownership is to be desired rather than under communism of property, and that peace and order are better preserved under private

[4] St. Thomas Aquinas (c. 1225-1274) was the son of the Count of Aquino whose castle, in the kingdom of Naples, was close to the famous Monte Cassino, the original Benedictine monastery (founded about 520), where his education began. He attended the University of Naples for six years, then he became a Dominican and went to Cologne to study under Albertus Magnus, who was the leading Aristotelian philosopher of the time. After a time in Cologne and Paris he returned to Naples in 1259; there he spent the remainder of his life except for three years, 1269-1272. During these three years he was in Paris where the Dominicans, on account of their Aristotelianism, were in trouble with the university authorities over a matter of theology. Aquinas is responsible for adapting Aristotle's philosophy to Christian doctrine. He was made a Doctor of Philosophy at the Sorbonne and gained great fame as a teacher and lecturer. He lectured at seats of learning in London, Paris, Rome, Boulogne, and Naples. He wrote as many as sixty works, the most important being his *Summa Contra Gentiles*, written during the years 1259-1264, which is an attempt to establish the truth of the Christian religion, and his *Summa Theologica*. The latter work contains his ideas of economic interest. The book was written in Latin. Even though it purports to be an exposition of theology and Christian philosophy, it is in reality a systematic summary of the knowledge and best teachings of the time. Aquinas's teachings are held in highest esteem by Catholic educators and his principles have been accepted as standard since a rescript of 1879 by Pope Leo XIII. Aquinas is not only of historical interest but a living influence. He was canonized in 1323.

[5] A. E. Monroe (ed.), *Early Economic Thought* (Cambridge, Mass., 1924), pp. 53-77, for selected translations from the *Summa Theologica*.

ownership. Wealth is good only if it leads to a virtuous life. Trade, although not good or natural, is permissible if it is used to maintain the household or for the benefit of the country. Justice exists when goods are exchanged at equal values. Value is regarded as inherent in the merchandise or goods, and just price reflects the customary price, which again implies justice. He seems to hold a vague cost-of-production theory of exchange value, which has an ethical meaning. Trade and exchange were carried on extensively at the time, a fact which the churchmen disliked but could not abolish. If the price of goods was a just price, then trade was morally almost justifiable, especially if it contributed to the common good and insured equal advantage to both parties. In fact, it may be said that Aquinas and the churchmen in general were not in sympathy with many of the economic practices they saw going on about them, but they could do little to change them to their liking. They then attempted to make the practices as respectable as possible by setting rules of a moral and ethical nature to apply to economic practice.

For example, a seller was always bound to bring notice to a buyer of any defects in his wares in so far as he knew them. And "trading for the sake of trading was a shameful thing because it promotes the love of lucre, which knows no limits. Lucre should not be sought after for its own sake but for some good end." [6] The rules were drawn up mainly for the purpose of avoiding fraud in trading practices, since fraud and usury were sins committed against commutative justice. Trading could become licit and honest when engaged in for some good end, such as that which would contribute to the public benefit.

One of the "vulgar" trade practices against which we have biblical and Aristotelian admonition was usury. It will be recalled that about A.D. 325 usury was forbidden to the clergy only, but by the end of the twelfth century it was forbidden to the laity. It was declared absolutely illegal in 1311 at the Council of Vienna. Aquinas invoked his authorities—the Scriptures, the philosophers, and Church dogma—to which he added his own arguments to condemn usury, mainly because a payment in excess of the loan itself took advantage of the borrowing poor and because money was held to be barren. Lending at interest was considered, in fact, one of the worst forms of exchange and the most unjust, for it was an act of injustice in itself. The function of capital was either misunderstood or not clearly understood, and the borrowers were usually the poor and needy. Opportunities for profitable investment were few.

---

[6] *Summa Theologica* ii. ii, chap. 25, q. 77, 3 and 4.

The Church was frequently in a paradoxical position with reference to money, loans, interest, and profits. It was a large landholder and the recipient of considerable sums of money and of goods and crops as payments in kind. The Church made loans as well as outright gifts. Not all the loans were to needy persons for consumption purposes. The Church, as a large landholder, was obliged to assume many of the functions of an individual capitalist. Later, it needed an interest income to help keep the institution going. Late in the Middle Ages the large banking houses (e.g., the Fuggers) were closely associated with the Church at Rome. In time, the Church and the public laws were more concerned with regulation of interest rates than with the prohibition of interest. Decrees fixing maximum rates of interest which could be charged were common toward the end of the Middle Ages, and the Church was obliged to change its views on interest-taking. Economic practices had made the teachings of a thousand years ridiculously impractical. The medieval ideas on money could not exist with the growth of a money economy. The preachments against usury were rooted in a social organization quite different from that which existed toward the end of the Middle Ages. The compact social unit of tribe, clan, or family and later the guilds implied a personal, fraternal unit, which was quite different from the impersonal relationships existing under the state and an emergent capitalism. So long as the personal relationships existed it was more logical that interest or usury be condemned. With the impersonal relationships which came with the growth of a money economy, the arguments formerly used became unrealistic.

Wages, as well as interest or usury, claimed the attention of Aquinas and the Church. The Christian principle prevailed that "the laborer is worthy of his hire" (Luke 10:7; I Tim. 5:18). Prompt payment of wages was demanded by the Old Testament statement that the laborer was to be paid by sundown (Deut. 24:14-15; Lev. 19:13). Again, the amount of the wage rested upon the concept of justice, i.e., upon the amount necessary to enable the worker to maintain his standard of living. St. Thomas Aquinas recognized that the just wage was a component part of the cost of production and therefore a determinant of price.

The wage system grew with capitalism. The earliest records show that although wages were paid for services rendered, a widespread wage system did not exist at the time of Aquinas and was only in its infancy in the fourteenth century. It was not until the ownership of the means of production changed from the small individual producer to concentrated ownership of capital that the wage system really began. Wages were paid by the Church to the craftsmen who constructed the magnificent churches and cathedrals. However, much of the labor was donated by the workers as a service to the Church and to God. While the beginnings of the wage system and the absentee ownership of means of production date from this medieval period, St. Thomas Aquinas and the Church really had little to do with either their development or their regulation.

Nicholas Oresme.—Nicholas Oresme,[7] the distinguished French churchman, held some very advanced economic ideas, especially on money, which show a detachment not found in the writings of other churchmen.

He begins the *Traictie* with a detailed account of the origin of money in which he follows Aristotle's reasoning. He shows how men trafficked in goods by barter methods without money. "But since many difficulties and disputes arose among them under this method of exchanging things, clever men devised an easier way—the making of money, an instrument for measuring and exchanging one with another . . ."[8] He follows this with a careful discussion of the materials from which money should be made, namely, gold and silver, since they possess the requirements for a good money. He advocates a bimetallic standard with a mint ratio between the two determined by the normal market value of the two metals. He clearly understands that the value of the metals for money use is derived from the value of the metals as commodities. He would give to the prince (i.e., the state) the right to coin money, but the coined money should not be owned by him since "money belongs to the community and its individual members." Therefore, the cost of coinage should be "the expense of the community," since money belongs to the community. He vigorously denounces anyone, prince or citizen, who debases or alters the proportion, weight, or material of money. It was a common practice to make a gain by

[7] **Nicholas Oresme** (1320-1382), Bishop of Lisieux, was born in or near Caen, France, and educated in Paris. He served as grandmaster of the College of Navarre and later he became dean of Rouen. In 1377 he was made Bishop of Lisieux, which post he held until his death. He had wide training in many subjects. He investigated the existing planetary theories and set forth his own as well. In this respect he was a precursor of Copernicus. He translated the works of Aristotle into French from Latin and wrote on theological subjects and mathematics. His celebrated work, *Traictie de la Première Invention des Monnoies*, was written around 1360. (There is some question about the originality of the work. Some hold that Buridan [1300-1358] provided the ideas which Oresme developed.) It does, however, summarize Scholastic thought and discusses economic matters with considerable objectivity. Oresme translated the work from Latin into French at the request of King Charles V, one of his early pupils. The discussion of money shows very advanced thinking.

[8] A. E. Monroe, *op. cit.*, p. 81. See this source for selected translated chapters of the *Traictie*.

debasing currency and this gain, Oresme says, is "worse than usury." He is anxious that money serve one of its proper functions, namely, to protect the user. He says (in Chapter 13) that "according to the opinion of Hugues,[9] money is derived from *moneo*, since it warns us against fraud or deception in its metal or weight." Any debasement was both dishonest and unnatural and it was also a hidden tax on the people and a cause of the flight of money. In this he anticipated Gresham's law. All things considered, Oresme's ideas on money were far in advance of his time.

Summary.—The Middle Ages were characterized by the growth of institutions and a dearth of theoretical refinements in economic thought. Although there were considerable contributions to art, literature, philosophy, logic, and science, the Greek creations of earlier centuries were not improved upon. The evolutionary development of society from feudal relationships into strong national states was the greatest single event in the temporal sense, and the rise of the Christian Church was the crowning event in the spiritual sense. Many—in fact most—of the institutions of capitalism began in this period, largely as the result of the trial-and-error method and completely devoid of any plan. Semblances of law and order came in time and legalized many of the practices, which were really nothing other than the ordinary expediencies.

The Church, once all-powerful in both spiritual and temporal affairs, lost its control over the states but expanded its efforts in the religious sphere. The Reformation, in turn, brought great changes in religious practices and the Renaissance revolutionized the cultural aspects of European life. Change was the common characteristic of the later Middle Ages; some change was evolutionary, some revolutionary. The stronger institutions and practices, like the stronger states, survived; the others disappeared. The growth of commerce and trade forced the Church to codify rules for trading relations. Gradually the rules, like most institutions, went through changes which amounted to a surrender of power to regulate all trade and commerce. By the end of the medieval period, strong states had arisen; new concepts of economic life appeared which led ultimately to the ardent nationalism which prevailed in every European state. The stage is therefore set for a study of the policies of mercantilism.

---

[9] Hugues de St. Cher (Hugo à S. Caro), an early biblical scholar who died in 1263. The division of the books of the Bible into chapters is ascribed to him.

PART II

The Beginnings of Modern Theoretical and Applied Economics

6

English Mercantilism

Some of the economic changes which came at the end of the Middle Ages were related in the previous chapter. The old trappings of feudalism were gradually discarded and new, strong states arose. The metaphysical concept of a "natural" economy and the Scholastic teachings were discarded. The church and state controversy abated with each recognizing its own sphere of influence and enjoying supremacy therein. No longer were efforts made to stop trade and commerce on moral and religious grounds; on the contrary, the highest premium was placed on economic activity, for the rewards of trade and commerce provided the sinews of national greatness. A body of economic thought known as mercantilism was developed in association with the emergence of the modern state and the changing economic practices. (See table on page 78.)

The study of mercantilism, then, is intended to provide an account of the ways and means whereby the state has sought to control economic life in the interest of political and national strength and independence; this endeavor, by virtue of the importance attached to the maintenance of a favorable money balance in foreign trade, has been called the "mercantile system" or "mercantilism." In investigating the subject one must examine: (1) the aims of political and national power; (2) the ideas which were believed to provide the true foundations of that power; and (3) the methods adopted by the state for the promotion and regulation of commerce, industry, and agriculture. Although the aims and methods were practically the same in all European states, differences in traditions and in geographical features or natural resources produced differences in emphasis among the states.

Neither the term "mercantilism" nor "mercantile system" adequately describes or even suggests the nature of the vast and complex theory and practice which it is used to designate. The practices never assumed the coherence of a system. They were at times nothing more than tendencies and opportunistic expedients. Yet mercantilism, as followed in each state, held the same general aim, which was to make a strong,

77

THE RISE OF EUROPEAN STATES AND ECONOMIC MEASURES DESIGNED TO CONTRIBUTE TO THE GROWTH OF THE STATE

II—ECONOMIC MEASURES.

I—RULING HOUSES.

Timeline headings: 1400 | 1500 | 1600 | 1700 | 1800

ENGLAND

I — x 1485 Tudor Period   1603 x   x 1603   Stuarts   1714 x   1649-1660, x Commonwealth   x 1714 House of Windsor (Before 1917, House of Hanover) . Present

II — x 1500   Importation of Precious Metals   Rise in Prices throughout Europe   x 1550 Bullionism   x C. 1650   x 1651   1675 x   Mercantilism   Navigation Acts   x 1776   1776 x C. 1776 Indus'l Rev'n   Free Trade   C. 1860 x   American Revolution

FRANCE

I — x 1461   1589 x   x 1589   Valois   Bourbons   1792-1804 First Republic   179? x   1804-1814 Napoleon I

II — x 1664-1687 x   Colbertism   1775 x   Mercantilism   x 1756-1778 x   Physiocracy   x C. 1785 Industrial Rev'n C. 1875 x

GERMANY

I — x 1499   Electors of Brandenburg   State of Prussia, House of Hohenzollern   1701 x   x 1701   Kings of Prussia   1871 x   1871-1918 x   German Empire

II — x C. 1550   Cameralism   Period of greatest influence   C. 1750 x   Less influence   x   x C. 1836 Ind'l Rev'n C. 1870 x

AUSTRIA

I — x 1526   House of Hapsburg   1867   1918   x 1867   Austria-Hungary Dual Monarchy   1918

II — x C. 1550   Cameralism   Period of greatest influence   C. 1770 x   x

78

independent state. In this respect a striking family resemblance may be identified. The emphasis on ways to attain the end varied in different countries, but all states sought positions of greatness and security in a period when insecurity prevailed.

Even though the adjective "mercantile" has often been challenged as unsatisfactory, no better term has been found. It has been called a "commercial system," or a "restrictive system," which stresses a negative aspect of the policy; to call it "Colbertism" after one of its famous practitioners obscures the scope and significance of the movement.[1] Mercantilism is a régime of economic nationalism. In historic annals it is one phase of the history of modern civilization from the point of view of the economic and political evolution of modern states. It is associated with the growth of nationalism, national self-consciousness and egoism. Mercantilism implies strength and power for both offensive and defensive action, to be employed in pursuing both "hot" and "cold" wars. In every instance where conflicts arose and where issues were settled, the economic aspects followed characteristic mercantilist lines. One may use the term "system" provided that it does not imply a rigid body of theories and practices.

Difficulty with the choice of a name is but one of the controversial issues connected with the subject. Differences of opinion arise as to what nation first practiced mercantilistic policies; the extent to which the policies prevailed and the end results attained in different countries; whether certain rulers, statesmen, and writers were mercantilists; whether or not the system led to war or peace; and whether or not, in the light of the outcome, the system was to be praised or condemned. These controversies must not be regarded as of historic interest only, for indeed similar issues confront nations at present just as they did in the mercantilist period of roughly one hundred and fifty years from 1613 to 1767.[2] Every European nation at one time or another followed mercantilistic practices either from choice or necessity. Whatever the policies employed—mercantilistic or free trade—they reflected the prevailing economic philosophy of the time.

[1] It was Adam Smith who brought the term "mercantile system" into use, although he used the term indifferently as a system of commerce, the commercial system, or the mercantile system. See *Wealth of Nations* (Ed. Edwin Cannan; 2 vols., London, 1904), Book IV, chap. i, entitled "Of the Principle of the Commercial or Mercantile System," I, 395, 401.

[2] The length of the mercantilistic period depends on the date one accepts as the beginning. If the bullionists are included with the mercantilists, then the period covers the years from 1550 to about 1767 or 1776. If Serra's tract (1613) is taken as the beginning, then the period is considerably shorter. The last mercantilist work was Steuart's *Principles of Political Economy* in 1767. The end of the period is marked by the publication of the *Wealth of Nations* in 1776.

Mercantilistic Practices of the Ancients.—England in the sixteenth and seventeenth centuries provides the best example of a European state in which mercantilistic practices reached full flower. But before taking up the main topic of this chapter, a brief look at the measures employed in some earlier states will be rewarding. Mercantilistic or semi-mercantilistic explanations have been offered for many of the practices in early Greece, Rome, and Carthage. It is certain that money played an important part in the economy of ancient societies. Likewise, precious metals, coined or uncoined, were regarded as a desirable form of wealth and as such had an effect upon public policy. The concept of a strong, self-sufficing state was familiar, and the extent of the state's control over economic political and social activity of the individual is well known. Paternal control, while extensive, was not confined solely to economic measures, nor did political strength rest so much upon economic bases as it did in later centuries elsewhere in Europe. But expansion of trade and commercial monopoly were high among the causes for state rivalries and conflict in classical antiquity. It is probable that Carthage surpassed any ancient state whose policy, both in peace and war, was dominated by commercial or mercantile ambition. To win and exploit markets and peoples was one of her main objectives; her colonial areas were subordinated to home interests.

Rome expanded over Europe as the greatest power of the ancient world—but though her conquests brought economic gains, commercial expansion was not the sole motive; her world domination rested on motives other than purely economic. Shortages of bullion became a problem in the late years of the Empire. There was a tremendous drain of precious metals to the East to pay for imports which were not offset by exports; however, this was but one of the many causes for the decline of Roman greatness. The mercantilistic practices of antiquity were undoubtedly destructive in their ultimate effects; but the loss of liberty and independence, the extreme regimentation under paternalistic states, the endless wars which destroyed nations and laid waste civilizations, tend to obscure those measures which, in the light of more recent history, fit sharply into a commercial pattern. However, many of the underlying elements have a close kinship to traditional mercantilistic practices: the differences are more in emphasis than in kind.

Some Influencing Factors in the Rise of Modern Mercantilism.— In the Middle Ages many factors were at work which shaped the course of nations in modern history. The Romans had shown what could be accomplished by a centrally unified, strong state. The Church was a unit with its central power and its authority stood unchallenged. Object lessons in government were provided by both ancient Rome and the Church with the result that many forms of political units evolved. At various times governing units in the form of communes, city-states, and feudal lordships prevailed before the national state appeared. The economic units were first the household, then the manor, the village community, the town, and the league of cities. Gradually, and quite unlike anything in the ancient world, strong centralized states emerged, which developed specialized economic measures, money and credit, commercial institutions, and practices designed to make the state self-sufficient.

The teachings of the Church were generally opposed to many of the practices of the growing states. The Church taught a world unity, not a narrow nationalism; it condemned usury; it opposed any gain without labor. However, the Church was put in the anomalous position of condemning something which it indirectly encouraged. The Crusades were given the blessing of the Church; their results scored greater economic than religious gains in expanding the whole breadth of commerce and the money economy. They prepared men's thoughts for international commercialism, as is borne out by the liberal trade relations developed in the twelfth and thirteenth centuries.

The canonical doctrines, many of which were developed before the growth of strong centralized states, were changed and adapted to conditions as they actually were, with a view to regulating the practices rather than forbidding them. The Church both taught and practiced cooperation and interdependence of peoples. This also was a characteristic of the relationships which developed along craft lines, town systems, and other community-of-interest endeavors: local groups found common ties—a practice later carried out on a national scale. Yet, in the Middle Ages town economics had become exclusive and, in a sense, set a pattern for exclusive national economics. Urban interests were protected by various monopolistic measures designed for craftsmen, merchants, markets, or other common interests. Regulations as to price and quality, tolls and customs, called for external barriers as well as internal trade measures. The measures were designed to protect home industry and keep a favorable trade balance for the city itself. This practice was especially noticeable in such areas as Germany, which had a very weak central authority but many strong cities that grew in wealth and power.

In time, the power of a central government was extended over both the feudal and the municipal elements; the territorial area was enlarged mainly by might, and laws were gradually developed along distinctly nationalistic lines. Furthermore, the Renaissance and the Reformation had much to do with the secular development of the modern state.[3]

Some states were successful in developing colonial empires which influenced their policies in many ways. The discovery of America gave Spain an advantage over her neighbors of a huge colonial empire and a great supply of precious metals necessary for the burgeoning economy of Western Europe in the sixteenth and seventeenth centuries. This period was marked by a growth of commerce with an expanding money economy and by a concurrent decline in the supply of precious metals for the support of the economy. These factors had much to do with debasement of coinage and with stimulating exploration in pursuit of gold, which, in turn, influenced the relations among states. Since the general belief was that one could gain in trade only at the expense of another, the prohibition of the export of the precious metals was only a crude expedient for conserving the nation's supply.

The balance-of-trade doctrine was an accepted policy as early as the latter half of the fourteenth century and was generally practiced: as commerce grew, a philosophy was accepted which made the procurement of precious metals the proper motive of foreign trade. Spain alone could procure the metals directly from her colonial mines; other states were obliged to use the indirect measures of favorable trade balances. The desire for treasure was common to all; only the means of its procurement varied with nations. Jealousies and rivalries leading to wars were bound to follow. Money actually did provide the sinews of war; with money, the needed soldiers and materials for war could be obtained. Spain, unable to keep the bullion she received from America, lost it to the trading nations of Europe, notably England and Holland. It seemed obvious, therefore, that a carefully controlled and regulated foreign trade policy which assured a sale of more goods than were bought would guarantee a strong state. Money circulating within a realm was held to add nothing to the wealth of the state. Thus, it was an accepted rule that a nation could obtain the wealth it needed by measures which successfully regulated the balance of its trade. Not only would the state be made strong externally, but internally her industries would flourish.

Some General Aspects of Mercantilism.—In each nation, economic, political, cultural, and even religious factors had roles in shaping mercantilist policies. Toward the end of the fifteenth century states were growing in strength and aspiring for power as nations. The oceans ceased to be barriers and the desire for colonies was widespread. In

---

[3] See J. N. Figgis, *Cambridge Modern History* (New York, 1934), Vol. III, pp. 736 ff.; also, A. F. Pollard, *History of England* (New York, 1912), pp. 94 ff.

order to hold colonial areas and to exploit their resources, a nation had to be strong. To facilitate commerce, a money economy with banking and credit institutions was in process of development. The profit motive was universal. Competition was a natural complement of the expansion of trade and commerce. There followed the dramatic struggles for power in wars and conquest. The ultra-nationalistic policies tended to make every state the enemy of every other and no advantage could be yielded to another.

The measures designed to regulate and control economic endeavor are well known. The mercantilists made the following assumptions; they were the means to make a strong national state:

1. Precious metals were the most desirable form of national wealth.
2. If a nation did not possess natural sources of precious metals, the chief way to get them was by trade.
3. In order to accumulate precious metals, the trade balance must be favorable: an excess of exports over imports.
4. Colonies could be useful both as a market for exports and as sources of supply for raw materials, even precious metals.
5. Colonies could only be feeders to the mother country: manufacturing was forbidden in the colonies for fear of spoiling the market of the mother country and exhausting the supply of raw materials. All colonial trade should be a monopoly of the mother country.

They were significant in shaping the life and future greatness of nations. The German scholar, Gustav Schmoller, who was one of the first writers on the subject, remarked that mercantilism "at its very core is nothing other than state-formation (*Staatsbildung*) but not state-formation in itself but simultaneously the building up of the state and the economic system, state-formation in the modern sense of the word, to make the community that forms the state into an economic society and to give it increased importance." [4] The Swedish scholar, Eli Heckscher, accepted the same general objective as the dominant force but broadened its meaning. He identified a series of economic policies which were concurrent with the transition from medievalism to capitalism and were designed to bring about national unification. Many practices were deep-rooted in medievalism and in fact were "unintentional planlessness." [5]

---

[4] Gustav Schmoller, "Das Merkantilsystem in seiner historischen Bedeutung," *Jahrbuch für Gesetzgebung, Verwaltung und Volkswissenschaft im Deutscher Reich* (Leipzig, 1884). Vol. I, pp. 15-63. See also Schmoller's *The Mercantile System*, in the series, "Economic Classics," ed., W. J. Ashley (London, 1896).

[5] Eli Heckscher, *Mercantilism* (2 vols., New York, 1935), Vol. I, p. 40.

National unification in western Europe continued to 1870; however, mercantilism is considered here in its more common definition of economic measures to enhance national power in the period of commercial capitalism, before the Industrial Revolution radically changed economic life. The policies differed somewhat in emphasis from one nation to another but not in their one objective, namely, national strength and greatness. The earliest writer [6] to advocate thoroughgoing mercantilistic policy is usually regarded to be Antonio Serra (c. 1580-1650) who wrote a tract in 1613 entitled *A Brief Treatise on the Causes Which Can Make Gold and Silver Plentiful in Kingdoms Where There Are No Mines.*[7] The last systematic treatise on mercantilism was Sir James Steuart's *Inquiry Into the Principles of Political Economy* (1767). In the intervening years many persons contributed their ideas on the general policies in the form of tracts and pamphlets of varying length and importance. Complete agreement on ways and means of accomplishing the desired ends was lacking, but the general objectives were not in dispute. The writers "offered a variegated fabric of economic ideas, unsound and inartistic as an entity, but containing much that was sound and worth preserving." [8]

Bullionists and Bullionism.—The term "bullionists" has been used to distinguish a group of early seventeenth-century writers who represent the first and perhaps the crudest of the group characterized as mercantilists. They had in mind a common objective, which was how to increase the stock of bullion. To accomplish this, they favored restrictions on the import of luxury items, a government exchanger who would keep exchange rates at par, a close regulation and control of foreign exchange dealings, and lastly a prohibition of the export of bullion. The purpose of the regulations was to secure and to keep a surplus of bullion from each transaction. If this could be done, the state would not only be strong but the prince would be relieved of the necessity of debasing the coinage, which was then a common practice. The influence of precious metals on the level of prices and the true gains from foreign trade were not understood. These early writers could not see that the bullion used to procure foreign wares might possibly bring a greater gain from the transactions. Strong opposition to the export of bullion arose in England after an East India Company ship carrying a large shipment of bullion was wrecked in 1613. This brought strong rejoin-

---

[6] Machiavelli (1469-1527), in his writings on political theory, advocated measures now identified as mercantilistic, as did also Jean Bodin (1530-1596) in France.

[7] See A. E. Monroe (ed.), *Early Economic Thought* (Cambridge, Mass., 1924), chap. vii, pp. 145-67, for a translation of significant extracts.

[8] E. A. J. Johnson, *Predecessors of Adam Smith* (New York, 1937), p. 3.

ders by persons who argued that export of bullion was necessary for trade.[9]

The leading English spokesman of the bullionist theory was Gerald de Malynes (c. 1586-1641), an English merchant who wrote several tracts;[10] a part of one work was devoted to an argument with Edward Misselden (fl. 1608-1654) over trade and exchange regulations.[11] Malynes centered his arguments around the need for supervision and control of the exchange which, if uncontrolled, would lead to dangerous social consequences. While many of his views were basically correct and advanced, he tended to defend them with archaic, medieval arguments.[12] Misselden, on the other hand, wanted to promote policies that would insure a favorable balance of trade, and the way to do this was to "make our Importations lesse, and our Exportations more."[13] To accomplish this he favored a limitation of imports and of the consumption of foreign luxury items by restrictive tariffs, and measures to overcome idleness and poverty by providing employment in industries that would decrease England's dependence on foreign nations. While at first opposed to any export of bullion, he changed his views and later defended the chartered companies which exported bullion for the purpose of procuring goods abroad.[14]

Significant differences are not great between these early writers and the later mercantilists. Except in their views on the export of bullion, the bullionists held many views essentially the same as those propounded by the later mercantilists. In the reasoning of the latter the export of bullion was generally accepted as necessary for a flourishing trade.

Some Leading English Mercantilists and Their Theories.—England under the régime of Elizabeth (1558-1603) and in the subsequent reigns of the Stuarts had many years of growth and expansion. Scotland and Ireland were brought into integrated relations with England; her

[9] Notably, Dudley Digges, a director in the Company, who wrote the *Defense of Trade* (1615) and defended the export of bullion, and by Thomas Mun in *A Discourse of Trade from England into the East-Indies* (1621).

[10] *A Treatise on the Canker of England's Commonwealth* (London, 1601); *The Maintenance of Trade* (London, 1622); and *Centre of the Circle of Commerce* (London, 1623).

[11] Misselden's first tract was *Free Trade or The Means to Make Trade Flourish* (London, 1622), in which he defended the policies of bullionism. When attacked by Malynes, he replied in the *Circle of Commerce* (London, 1623), where he reversed his views and defended the export of bullion. Viner attributes to Misselden the first appearance in print of the term "balance of trade." (See *Journal of Political Economy*, XXXVIII, 257.)

[12] See E. A. J. Johnson, *op. cit.*, chap. iii, "Malynes, the Dogmatist," pp. 41-54.

[13] *Circle of Commerce*, p. 134.

[14] See Johnson, *op. cit.*, chap. iv, "Misselden, The Critic."

Parliament became more assertive; and the nation engaged in wars with Holland and France and established her colonial system. Mercantilist theory and literature form a significant part of the many circumstances and events of this period. The functions of government were expanding at increasingly higher costs. Influx of metals from the New World had caused sharp price rises in the Old. Revenues failed to keep pace with expenditures, and for most of the sixteenth and seventeenth centuries the crown was almost constantly in financial embarrassment. Trade and commerce were recognized as absolutely essential to the state, but controversies arose over the merits of "free" versus "regulated" trade. The "free traders" objected to the concessions held by companies or merchants who enjoyed the sole right of trade with specific foreign ports. They did not disapprove of barriers to trade erected against the foreigner but only resented the grants which limited trade to a few privileged merchants. They wanted the removal of restrictions that throttled the expansion of trade and argued that greater benefits would result from a growth of trade. They pointed to Holland as a good example of freedom in trade and to its success in winning markets at England's expense. The "free traders" never succeeded in passing laws in their behalf or in breaking the monopolies granted to concerns under the "regulated" principle. It is certain, however, that in many cases the monopolies or semimonopolies were not economically productive. It was but a part of the prevailing practices of the time to regulate trade, both import and export, to close ports to certain traffic, to regulate production, apprenticeship, competition, and so on in an endless list.

As has been noted, the purpose of English mercantilistic policy was to regulate trade with other countries so as to secure and preserve a favorable balance for the homeland. It was in this nationalistic atmosphere that Thomas Mun's *Englands Treasure by Forraign Trade, or, the Balance of Our Forraign Trade is The Rule of Our Treasure*, appeared. Thomas Mun (1571-1641) had been a London merchant and a director of the East India Company; he was several times appointed to the standing committee on trade which later became the Board of Trade. An influential person in his lifetime, he set down his views in the above-named tract in the years 1622-28, and upon publication in 1664 they were quickly accepted as the gospel of both financial and commercial policy. Adam Smith held that Mun's views became the fundamental economic policy not only of England but of other European states at that time.

While Mun's ideas epitomized the best of mercantilistic theory and practice, many of them, especially the balance-of-trade doctrine, are traceable to the fourteenth century, long before Mun. Throughout the seventeenth century to the middle of the eighteenth, pamphlets and tracts appeared in great numbers. However, no one writer may be said to have set forth a systematic development of the aim and methods of a national economy in which mercantilism's balance of trade, bullion restrictions, and the like form only a part. The over-all policies, directed as they were at self-sufficiency and national strength in both peace and war, have to be extracted from fragmentary tracts produced by persons not always in agreement with one another, and from records of national policies and practices. Mun is the best representative of the writers whose tracts and pamphlets appeared over the years.

In his most important work, *Englands Treasure by Forraign Trade*, Mun, like nearly all mercantilists, identified wealth with money. He sought to increase the amount of money in the nation by securing a favorable balance in the export of goods, not by restrictions on bullion export. He argues that, "the ordinary means therefore to increase our wealth and treasure is by Forraign Trade, wherein we must ever observe this rule: to sell more to strangers yearly than we consume of theirs in Value." [15] He pointed out that the only way a nation without mines can increase its supply of gold and silver is by exporting more goods than are imported. In order to accomplish this, he set forth twelve "particular ways to increase the exportation of our commodities and to decrease the consumption of forraign wares." To this end the main measures which he advocated were sumptuary laws to restrain the consumption of foreign luxuries, a higher price for English goods for which there is no other source of supply, shipping in British ships exclusively, and the encouragement of the fishing industry. He visualized England as a great entrepôt which would profit by import and export of goods. A heavy duty should be placed upon goods imported for home consumption but only moderate duties upon exports.

His arguments are directed toward the accumulation of treasure. Foreign trade must be instrumental in laying up treasure which, when "managed to advantage, will become a great summe of money, able to make a long defence, which may end or divert the war." Treasure is "the sinews of war," yet only because it "doth provide, unite and move the power of men, victuals, and munition where and when the cause doth require." Mun shows his awareness of the importance of non-commodity items in computing the "balance of our Forraign Trade" by pointing out that merchants' gain from shipping, insurance, freight charges, remittances, travelers' expenses, merchants' commissions, and goods lost at sea should be added or subtracted in computing the total balance.

[15] *Englands Treasure by Forraign Trade* (London, 1664); reprint in J. R. McCulloch (ed.), *Early English Tracts on Commerce* (London, 1856), pp. 134 ff.

In addition to Mun's ideas on mercantilism, it is possible to identify passages in his writings which imply a quantity theory of money, and a value theory. He implies a policy of "what the traffic will bear" for prices on sales abroad, but at home prices should not be so high as to discourage business. He observes that high prices in the home country, which would result from a large amount of money, would affect the balance of trade adversely. On the other hand, he believes that a small amount of money in domestic circulation would make prices low. His ideas, like those of other writers, led him to fear the loss of bullion and to center his emphasis upon accumulating it. These men never fully understood the relationship of price levels which existed between their own nation and the nations with whom they traded, nor did they develop a theory of international prices. Mun looks upon taxes as "a rubble of oppressions," which makes the sovereign rich and the people poor; he admits, however, that they are necessary, especially for national defense. He believes the prince could draw into his treasure so much money that "the life of lands and arts must fail and fall to the ruin both of the publick and private wealth." Also he held that the prince is "esteemed no less powerful by having many rich and well affected subjects" than by possessing much treasure in his coffers, a possible result of burdensome taxation.

The scope and organization of Mun's ideas, together with their logical force, make him the outstanding spokesman for mercantilism.[16] He succeeded more than any other mercantilist writer in establishing for posterity the belief that "the Balance of our Forraign Trade is the Rule of our Treasure."

That Mun had a keen insight into the true nature of trade and commerce is seen in another of his writings. The East India Company had been granted the privilege of exporting £30,000 in bullion on each voyage, provided that it imported the same amount within six months. A charge had been made that this privilege was draining the country of specie, because the Company exported bullion and imported Indian goods exceeding in value its export of English goods. Mun answered this charge with A Discourse of Trade from England to the East Indies (1621) in which he defended the practice and argued that it was to England's advantage, since useful commodities were brought in which could be purchased elsewhere only at higher cost. The re-export of these goods further netted England a profit; thus the net result was an inflow, not an outflow, of specie. He brought countercharges that the economic evils resulted from manipulations of the exchange and excessive consumption of foreign goods.

[16] See E. A. J. Johnson, op. cit., chap. v, "Mun, the Strategist," for a comprehensive treatment.

Certain other mercantilistic writers followed the same general line of reasoning as Mun. A few gave more attention to some specific economic problem than to general policies. Sir Thomas Culpeper (1578-1662) [17] was primarily concerned with ways and means of lowering the interest rate and held that the passing of a law lowering the rate in England would bring to England the same prosperity the Hollanders enjoyed. The economist and politician Charles Davenant (1656-1714) [18] despite his liberalism, subscribed to the mercantilistic doctrines of his time. He favored careful restrictions on import trade and reduced costs of production for English-made products. Like others, he believed that a large population fully employed at wages near subsistence levels was a certain way of increasing national wealth. Davenant was ahead of his contemporaries in his comprehension of the use and functions of money; he held that the value of money, like that of all other commodities, is determined by its "want or scarcity" and that "gold and silver are often a surfeiting diet to a Nation" if not turned to proper uses. Spain was the example cited to prove this point. He, like Sir William Petty, was interested in statistics, or political arithmetic, which he defined as "the art of reasoning by figures upon things relating to the government."

The philosopher John Locke (1632-1704) [19] showed great profundity and breadth in his general economic concepts but adhered to the common economic fallacy of the times, namely, that excess commodity balances must be counteracted by movement of specie. He had a good understanding of the quantity theory of money; therefore, he would not accept the older doctrines which held that there was something absolute and unchanging in the value of money. By insisting that "intrinsic value is not natural but is only the opinion of men consenting to it," he introduced a subjective element in money. [20]   Locke argued that "the value of money in respect of those [other articles] depends only on the plenty or scarcity of money in proportion to the plenty or scarcity of those things" (p. 44). The importance of velocity of circulation is shown when he points out that the amount of money needed to support trade "depends not barely on the quantity of money, but on the quickness of its circulation" (p. 47). His ideas on money are advanced, and those on international trade are even better in

[17] *A Tract against the High Rate of Usurie* (London, 1621; 3d ed.; 1641). He advocated lowering the interest rates as a means of bringing national prosperity.
[18] Author of *Essay on East Indian Trade* (London, 1696) and *Essay on the Probable Means of Making People Gainers in the Balance of Trade* (London, 1699).
[19] Although primarily a philosopher, he supported the main tenets of mercantilism. His principal economic doctrines are contained in *Consequences of the Lowering of Interest and Raising the Value of Money* (London, 1692).
[20] *Consequences of the Lowering of Interest*, p. 30.

explaining the economic bases for trade,[21] yet he reverts to a vehement balance-of-trade position and deplores an unfavorable trade balance as certain to lead to national ruin.

To Sir James Steuart (1712-1780) falls the doubtful honor of being the "last of the mercantilists." He was not only the last but possibly the ablest of the eighteenth century writers before Smith. His two-volume work, An Inquiry into the Principles of Political Economy, published in 1767, was a systematic study, yet it attracted little attention. In style it was ponderous, and in reasoning not altogether sound. The book was published nine years before the Wealth of Nations, yet Smith ignored it. This fact helped the book along its way to obscurity. He was, however, the first English writer to use the term "political economy."

Steuart's Principles is divided into five books: Population and Agriculture; Trade and Industry; Money and Coin; Credits and Debts; Taxes. The subjects are treated with a considerable degree of thoroughness and understanding but the mercantile pattern pervades his thoughts. His belief in the potentialities of capable statesmen reflected his own frustrated ambitions. A staunch nationalist despite his own political difficulties and exile, his nationalistic prejudices added to his economic errors. He, like the rest of the Stuarts, is of only limited historic interest.

Liberal Mercantilists.—The writers now to be considered were generally more liberal in their views than those previously named. They were just as ardent nationalists as any, but on issues involving ways and means to make the state self-sufficient their views were more advanced. They apparently understood the true nature of trade and commerce, the function of money, and generally did not support the view that the gain in trade of one state meant a loss of trade for another.

The first of this group is Sir William Petty.[22] His wide experience, together with the influence of his learned friends and associates, gave

21 J. W. Angell in The Theory of International Prices (Cambridge, Mass., 1926), states, "he [Locke] presents the first outline that I have discovered of a theory of international prices" (p. 19).

22 Sir William Petty (1623-1687) has been called by some the founder of political economy. He had a career which took him from poverty to riches, as a sailor, clothier, professor of anatomy, physician, professor of music, surveyor, landlord, and man of affairs. After the Irish rebellion he was sent to survey the lands which were forfeited by the rebels. He spent most of his years after 1666 managing his Irish estates, writing on economic subjects, and advocating administrative reforms. He was interested in reducing political and economic matters to "terms of number, weight, and measure" which he succeeded in doing to a marked degree in his Discourses on Political Arithmetic (London, 1690). His work rightly earns for him the title of "founder of statistical method." Other writings of his are A Treatise of Taxes and Contributions (1662), Political Anatomy of Ireland (1672), and Quantulumcunque Concerning Money (1682).

to his work a freshness and originality unequaled for a hundred years. All Petty's writings show his interest in scientific analysis and its practical application to specific problems. While it can not be said that he arranged his topics systematically or that he presented a complete body of political economy, he did, nevertheless, set forth advanced ideas in the general field.

Unlike Mun, who began his analysis with an assumption of national affluence, Petty approached his problem by an analysis of the principles of scientific taxation, and from this he developed his theory of national wealth. Like Mun, he agreed that taxation is inevitable. He saw in taxation a means of enriching or of impoverishing a state: the money collected could be used to stimulate trade and industry and thus improve the riches of the state if wisely spent. In the *Treatise* appear his views on the role of capital, a doctrine of population, a rent theory, a value theory, his ideas on money, and some ideas on production.

His theory of government implies complete state sovereignty. It is the responsibility of the state to maintain the well-being of its subjects; for this purpose it must have adequate revenues. Reasons for high taxes are the unwillingness of some to pay their taxes and the extravagance of the ruler. Wars and government extravagance may also cause heavy expenditures. He objects to the government's supporting a large list of supernumeraries, some of whom would at times be idle. To care for them he proposed a public works program in mining, forestry, manufacturing, or public construction. He held to the benefit theory of taxation; "Men," he writes, "should contribute to the Publick Charge according to the share and interest they have in Publick Peace; that is, according to their Estates or Riches." [23] He believed that taxes are not harmful provided the revenue collected is not spent on foreign commodities.

Since Petty worked on the Down Survey in Ireland he knew a great deal about land, rents, taxes, and problems of land valuation; however, his knowledge did not always aid him in being clearly articulate on such matters. He objected to setting aside lands from which the sovereign would draw his revenue, contending that the total revenue of the state, regardless of origin, should be levied upon to provide the King's income. Land on which a tax was levied would sell at a price less the amount of the tax. Leases would be lower by the amount of the tax, with the result that some landlords would lose and some gain. He was indecisive in his reasoning concerning the relationship of "the mysterious nature of" rents to prices and land values. It is certain that he saw the differential surplus element in rent, and also that he held rent to be

[23] *Treatise*, in C. H. Hull (ed.), *The Economic Writings of Sir William Petty* (2 vols., Cambridge, 1899), Vol. I, p. 91.

price-determined although he recognized the reciprocal influence of rents on price.

Petty's value theory must be "extracted" from his discussions on wealth. He emphasizes both land and labor as sources of wealth: "Labour is the Father and active principle of Wealth, as Lands are the Mother." [24] In discussing the value of gold as a measure of things, he states that "all things ought to be valued by two natural Denominations, which is Land and Labour." At another place he speaks of the "Wealth, Stock or Provision of the Nation"; he regarded wealth as "being the effect of past labour." [25] He refers to the advantages of the division of labor,[26] as is illustrated in making a watch. He points out the advantages of improvement in production and ultimately carries his reasoning to the growth of large towns, which specialize in certain products. The wages of labor are implied to be at subsistence level. He states that "a law that appoints such Wages . . . should allow the Labourer but just wherewithal to live; for if you allow double then he works but half so much as he could have done, and otherwise would; which is a loss to the Publick of the fruit of so much Labour." [27] In these quotations may be found ideas similar to those of Ricardo and Marx, which are taken up in later chapters.

His value theory, therefore, appears to be a surplus labor theory. He found that both land and labor created a surplus. But the fact that the productive power of labor (people) is more important than land and capital combined is the reason for his mercantilistic desire to increase the population. "Fewness of people, is real poverty; and a Nation wherein are eight millions of people, are more than twice as rich as the same scope of Land wherein are but four." [28]

Petty's ideas on usury (interest) follow a simple pattern. If the borrower must repay the loan whenever the lender calls for it, no interest should be charged. If one loans "upon condition that he may not demand it back until a certain time to come . . . he certainly may take a compensation for this inconvenience which he admits against himself." [29] He related the rate of interest to the rent of land by a capitalization process applied to rent, making the return to land when capitalized the determinant of interest. He admitted that this is not entirely satisfactory as a theory; and since the security behind loans varies in every lending venture, it would be futile to set any legal limits on interest rates. Likewise, he opposed all efforts to fix exchange rates by law. He strongly objected to prohibitions on the export of bullion, which he viewed as being both futile and unwise.

---

24 *Ibid.*, Vol. I, p. 68.
25 "Verbum Sapienti," *ibid.*, Vol. I, p. 110.
26 *Economic Writings*, Vol. II, pp. 473-74.

27 *Treatise, ibid.*, Vol. I, p. 87.
28 *Ibid.*, Vol. I, p. 34.
29 *Ibid.*, Vol. I, p. 47.

He believed that customs, laws, and duties should be used for regulating trade and consumption, not for revenue. Export duties should be kept low in order to eliminate smuggling and should not discourage export. Import duties should be selective and apply in place of sumptuary laws. Raw materials which England needed in her industries should be "gently dealt with."

On the subject of money [30] he reasoned that it is needed only to facilitate trade and industry and that, while under some conditions a nation could have too little, under other conditions it could have too much. The duty of maintaining the value of money was the responsibility of the state. Export of coin was useless, since the state could melt it down if it had too much. If there were too little money, a bank should be established which could "double the effect of our Coined Money." Although he showed a clear grasp of the velocity of circulation of money, he did not, however, give any attention to the relationship of money to prices.

Sir William Petty, like other writers of the period, was concerned with ways and means of making government policy contribute to England's prosperity. He could not avoid the acceptance of most of the basic principles of mercantilism. However, the basic premises and the scope and method of his reasoning, his knowledge of economic structure, and his powers of observation made him distinctly outstanding and more liberal than many other writers. His works are not entirely systematic, nor do they present a complete economic philosophy, but they do set forth numerous ideas which attest to his originality and lend support to the assertion that he deserves to be considered one of the founders of classical economics.

Sir Dudley North (1641-1691) followed Petty in advocating free trade in strongest terms.[31] In his *Discourses on Trade* (1691) he argues for free trade and especially criticized the British policy of restrictions on commerce with France. He sees no difference between foreign trade and domestic trade and maintains that the former could not exist without the latter. All trade which is profitable to the trader is also profitable to the public. Government restrictions, however, injure the public, although possibly they do benefit a few traders. He envisioned the

---

[30] *Quantulumcunque Concerning Money* (1682) is a brief treatise but it contains some of his best ideas in money matters. *Economic Writings*, Vol. I, pp. 437-38.

[31] North wrote one small tract, published in the year of his death. The full title is *Discourses upon Trade: Principally Directed to the Cases of the Interest, Coynage, Clipping, Increase of Money* (1691), and it is reprinted in J. R. McCulloch (ed.), *Early English Tracts on Commerce* (London, 1856). He rejects many of the most fundamental mercantilistic doctrines, but his ideas were soon forgotten and his tract was not reprinted until 1822.

whole world as an economic unit without trade barriers, a condition which he hoped could be brought about.

Money, like any other commodity, may exist in excess; therefore he has no desire to encourage the state to lay up treasure. The amount of bullion needed by the state will automatically adjust itself; if there is an oversupply, it will depreciate in value for monetary uses, be melted, and exported as a commodity in spite of legal restrictions. "Silver and gold, like other commodities, have their ebbing and flowings." [32] Low interest rates are the result of a large number of lenders in relation to the number of borrowers. Hence, legal restrictions on interest rates are unnecessary. His other ideas on money are not especially pertinent here.

Sir Josiah Child (1630-1699) deserves brief attention.[33] He, like North, argued for low interest rates as a cause of national prosperity. He advocated free trade, except with the East Indies. His A New Discourse of Trade (1775) represented the views of a practical businessman rather than an economist or a philosopher, and his works contribute relatively little to this body of economic thought.

Hume, A Transitional Thinker.—The Scottish philosopher, David Hume (1711-1776), must be included as one who had considerable influence in bringing an end to mercantilistic thought. His views on economic issues are so original and cogent that he might have been a great economist had he not been a greater philosopher. Only his views on mercantilism and related topics will be mentioned here; [34] his other economic ideas will be discussed with those of Adam Smith.

Hume was a free trader yet at times he repeated mercantilistic errors. In urging the development of trade and commerce, Hume, like many other writers, naïvely praised merchants as "one of the useful races of men in the whole society." He remarks that "merchants . . . beget industry by serving as canals to convey it through every corner of the state. . . . Without commerce, the state must consist chiefly of landed gentry, whose prodigality and expense make a continual demand for borrowing; and of peasants, who have no sums to supply that demand." [35]

[32] J. R. McCulloch, ed., op. cit., p. 527.

[33] Author of Discourse of Trade (London, 1690; new ed., A New Discourse of Trade, London, 1775). He was the wealthiest man in England in his time and his interest was centered in finance and foreign trade.

[34] Political Discourses (Edinburgh, 1752) contains most of his economic ideas. The essays (or discourses) "Of Money," "Of Interest," "Of Commerce," and "Of the Balance of Trade," are the most important of the twelve.

[35] "Of Interest," ibid., pp. 67-71 passim. Adam Smith held a very different view: he pointed out that their monopolies were often antisocial. Wealth of Nations, Book I, pp. 424, 426-27, 457-58.

One of the greatest contributions of Hume is his theory of international trade, which is substantially the doctrine of Ricardo and J. S.
Mill. He applied a quantity theory of money to international trade
and held that the balance-of-trade theory was wrong in that excessive
trade balances would cause an increase in the supply of specie in a
country, which in turn would affect the level of domestic prices and,
therefore, the volume of export or import of merchandise trafficked
in between nations. The relationships thus established between the
prices of commodities of trading nations would automatically regulate
specie flow, and the trade balance of any country could not long remain
favorable or unfavorable.[36]

Hume saw that the level of prices and the amount of money were
related, but he did not connect national wealth closely with the amount
of money and commerce of a nation. He says, "Men and commodities
are the real strength of any community." [37]   Money is not "the great
wheel of circulation," as Adam Smith called it; it is only a lubricating
oil. Money represents goods in exchange, and its value represents a
relationship between its amount and the amount of goods it would
command. Its value is a "fictitious one"; therefore, the amount of
money in circulation would affect the price of goods.

His theory thus provided a permanent relationship between prices
and the quantity of money. He did not advocate a fixed quantity of
money, since he was aware of both the good and bad effects of the
import of bullion. He admitted, however, that beneficial effects might
accrue to industry if the supply of money were increased and an increase in the volume of trade resulted.

Like others, Hume saw the automatic working of economic forces
as being of more importance than artificial state regulation. He was
interested in low interest rates but for reasons of state welfare, not for
the purpose of aiding anyone to borrow at low rates. "High interest
arises from three circumstances: a great demand for borrowing; little
riches to supply that demand; and great profits arising from commerce:
and these circumstances are clear proof of the small advance of commerce and industry, not the scarcity of gold and silver." [38] He reasoned
that low interest rates arise from the three opposite circumstances. In
the final analysis, therefore, the amount of industry and commerce, not
the quantity of gold and silver, was the responsible factor influencing

[36] See Jacob Viner, *Canada's Balance of International Indebtedness* (Cambridge,
Mass., 1924), for pre-Ricardian international trade theories. Also Hume, "Of the
Balance of Trade," *op. cit.*
[37] "Of Interest," *op. cit.*, p. 40
[38] "Of Interest," *op. cit.* p. 64.

the rate of interest. But this was only the short-run result; in the long run, an increase in home industry leads to more production, lower profits, and lower interest rates. These factors tend to equate production costs in foreign countries or even cause the production costs of home industry to fall below those in foreign countries. When this comes about, "a nation may lose most of its foreign trade and yet continue a great and powerful people." [39]

Hume favored extensive commerce with other nations. He believed, as a free trader, that the best interests of the nation demanded free exchange with other countries. This policy was economically necessary for England, as Hume shrewdly saw. While he did not entirely emancipate himself from all the vestiges of mercantilism, he did show marked liberalism and opposition to mercantilistic tenets. He praised foreign trade but doubted the benefits of a favorable balance of trade. His liberal outlook is shown in the following quotation which could not have come from any of his predecessors, "I shall therefore venture to acknowledge that, not only as a man, but as a British subject, I pray for the flourishing commerce of Germany, Spain, Italy and even France itself. I am at least certain that Great Britain, and all of those nations, would flourish more, did their sovereigns and ministers adopt such enlarged and benevolent sentiments towards each other.[40]

Many contradictions appear in Hume's doctrines, for he accepted many of the mercantilistic doctrines but favored a free-trade policy. The long- and short-run effects of the influx of specie on domestic prices were analyzed with clarity. First, inflow inflates prices; this in turn stimulates production and encourages new industries to develop; the state becomes less dependent upon foreign goods. Internally, the new level of production provides more employment, more savings, lower profits, and lower interest rates. In the long run, this is bound to bring about a situation in which the nation enjoys a greater degree of self-sufficiency and independence and becomes powerful even with a loss in her foreign trade. In many respects Hume departs from accepted traditional theories and resembles a transitional writer whose advanced doctrines anticipate Smith and others.[41]

[39] "Of Commerce," op. cit., p. 17.
[40] "Of the Jealousy of Trade," in Essays Moral, Political and Literary, eds. T. H. Green and T. H. Grose (London, 1875), Vol. I, p. 348.
[41] E. A. J. Johnson, in Predecessors of Adam Smith (New York, 1937), very appropriately treats Hume as a synthesist. "Hume's economic theory represents a logical reconciliation of divergent doctrinal ingredients. To the extent that Hume incorporated earlier ideas into his economic thought, he fused these ideas into a tentative system" (p. 181). Consult the same work for additional writers of mercantilism.

Summary and Evaluation.—In a brief sketch of mercantilism only the high points can be presented. It should be regarded as but a phase in the development of the states of Europe, and studied as such. It is not something separate and apart from the whole sweep of forces—political, economic, social, and religious—that had significant influences in shaping the course of events leading to the growth or decline of nations. It should be recalled that this span of years from 1613 to 1776 (Serra to Smith) was filled with wars brought about by many causes, but primarily by commercial conflict of one kind or another.

England, particularly in the period of Elizabeth (1558-1603), presents the best case study of mercantilism, and English writers were the most articulate on this subject. In subsequent years, which were times of great colonial expansion, mercantilist policies were on a much extended scale to include foreign and colonial relations as well as the control of internal industry. National ego asserted itself in practically every phase of external and internal life. The English Navigation Acts which restricted and regulated trade were typical measures which could not, at the time of their enactment, have been seen as causes which would lead to revolution and loss of the most valuable unit of the British colonial empire. But the American revolution itself was only a phase of the evolution of the times. The simple measures of the early stages of mercantilism had become very complex and quite inapplicable and unworkable in late eighteenth-century Europe. Mercantilist writers always put forward as the cardinal aim of public policy the good of the state and the need of subordinating the interests of the individual to the good of the community. Yet behind their arguments in both theory and policy, their ostensible aim was commonly modified and colored by the selfish interests of persons, corporations, chartered groups, and classes. Indeed, in the light of the diverse theories, one must wonder how the nation ever could arrive at decisions which would contribute effectively to that elusive concept known as national welfare.

It can easily be argued that the main foundations of mercantilism had been almost completely undermined before Adam Smith put the finishing touches to its demise in his *Wealth of Nations*. He argued that the well-being of the nation could best be enhanced when individuals were allowed to pursue their private interests unchecked rather than when monopolies and restrictions prevailed. The true nature of trade and the use and purpose of bullion were revealed: true wealth was shown to be not money, but what money was worth. The vigor of Smith's attack is well known and the subsequent change in national policy attests to the accuracy and acceptance of his views. He reshaped the course of both theory and practice thereafter.

The foregoing treatment of the leading writers and their ideas should impress the student with the absence of general agreement on many fundamentals. There is no such thing as a mercantile system, per se, nor is there a "school" of thought in the generally accepted meaning of the term; there is no real master and disciples. Smith, who leaned heavily upon Mun for a statement of mercantilistic principles, does not regard them as a body of arguments and conclusions carefully worked out by thoughtful writers motivated by a desire for truth, but rather as a scheme for a commercial policy or a "system of commerce," as he calls it, adopted by different governments largely upon the advice of interested merchants and traders. Smith regards mercantilism as a collection of maxims of businessmen who are primarily interested in trade benefits to themselves and have little concern as to how the system benefits the nation. His assessment seems inconsistent in view of some of the measures adopted by the government—measures which could hardly have been initiated merely for the benefit of some merchants and manufacturers. The fundamentals, such as they were, provided the bases for national commercial policies for two centuries. This fact alone would place the motives of mercantilist writers on a much higher objective level than indicated by Smith.

It appears logical to conclude that the policies of the government in attempting to increase the supply of precious metals rested upon a survival-of-the-fittest idea that treasure could be used for expansion and consolidation of national strength, by warlike or peaceful methods as the occasion demanded.

All the measures designed to gain this objective were therefore consistent. Exports and imports should be carefully watched to make certain who is the short-run monetary gainer. The desire for large population rested upon both economic and military grounds. It meant cheap labor, lower production costs, larger consumer demand, and—by no means last—soldiers. When states developed a national consciousness, they became less interested in other states and more interested in their own welfare; how could there be such things as mutual gains in trade and commerce?

Criticisms of mercantilism, from Smith onward, have been voluminous. The absurdities and nonsense of mercantilist generalizations are well known—at least to academic students, if not to politicians and statesmen. The error in emphasizing the value of amassing precious metals is still with us. The failure to emphasize, let alone even to mention, agriculture shows a lack of knowledge of a well-balanced economy. Despite its innate errors and the criticisms leveled against it, mercantilism still prevails in some degree through the world. Economic literature is enriched by men's attempts to point out errors in what was believed to be true. Yet mercantilistic "errors" still plague us. One who wished to do so could easily produce a book of considerable dimensions on "modern mercantilism." National ego has never been especially pacifistic, and close cooperation between states in the interest of a world economy is a worthy goal for nations.

7

French and German Mercantilism: Colbertism and Cameralism

French Writers and Practitioners

French mercantilism shows many of the same elements as English thought, which was presented in the previous chapter. While not the same in every respect, the mercantilistic concepts in the two countries were similar enough that the ideas which prevailed in France may be regarded as supplementing those in England. French mercantilism—often called Colbertism, a term which is entirely too narrow—was probably not as aggressive as the British yet just as nationalistic in its undercurrents. In general, French mercantilism upheld the doctrine of the desirability of possessing precious metals as the best form of wealth and gave attention to ways and means of increasing the supply. When the underlying theories were challenged, the criticisms were much the same as those advanced by the English critics. For the most part, the French critics denied the supremacy of the precious metals, urged that exports of bullion should not be prohibited, and encouraged a favorable balance of exports. Other interests, notably those of agriculture and industry, were regarded as of equal significance with commerce in the welfare of the state. Finally, toward the end of the period, the restrictive measures became unpopular and were overthrown.

Figuratively speaking, France, like England, was on the banks of a stream which was flowing with gold and silver from the New World. The great influx of precious metals between 1500 and 1700 brought about price increases amounting to as much as several hundred percent. Spain brought the precious metals to Europe but could not keep them. They were lost to England, France, Holland, and, to a lesser extent, Germany. France took part in the free-for-all race for precious metals largely because everyone else was doing it. Many French writers, like many of the early English mercantilists, never could quite comprehend the relationships between money and prices within the country or their relationship to foreign trade and the flow of bullion. Some—especially Sully and Montchrétien—held ideas on restricting the export of bullion similar to those of the English bullionists, whereas others had a more enlightened viewpoint on the export of money and of commodities in general.

At least in its early stages, French mercantilism was an attempt to nationalize many elements of medievalism. The guilds in Europe were medieval institutions which frequently stood in the way of effective state regulation and were, therefore, opposed by the state. The fact that the guilds always tended to benefit the towns at the expense of the country was inconsistent with national objectives. In France, however, edicts of 1581, 1597, and 1672 made guilds compulsory throughout the nation. The first edict, passed in 1581 under the rule of King Henry III (1574-1589), was only one of the many senseless measures which had religious as well as economic implications. The edict of 1597 was a measure of Henry IV (1589-1610) to help restore industry and commerce, which had been laid waste by civil wars. Henry introduced reforms (largely conceived by Sully, his chief minister) which aided the French economy materially; they included reforms in the collection and disbursement of taxes, the building of roads and canals, and the special encouragement of better methods in agriculture. The King was not interested in developing extensive manufacturing, declaring that the crafts "did not produce men fit for soldier work." He did, however, encourage silk culture, textiles, and glass manufacturing, industries whose products had been imported from Italy.[1] The edict of 1673 was under Colbert's administration, which presently will be considered. While it is questionable that the edicts, especially the first two, served any useful economic purpose, they did help to perpetuate the medieval heritage.

Jean Bodin and Antoine de Montchrétien.—The writings of the French political and social philosopher, Jean Bodin (1530-1596), were pioneering in economic as well as social science. France, like other countries, had been plagued by high and rising prices. The explanation for the high prices was generally couched in mercantilistic terms; remedies, so-called, such as the prohibition of bullion export, tariffs, sumptuary laws, and price-fixing measures were instituted. Debasement of coinage further aggravated the situation. Malestroit, the comptroller of the mint, had presented an argument that the rise in prices was due to the lower intrinsic value of the debased coinage. To this Bodin

---

[1] A. Dubois, *Précis de l'histoire des doctrines économiques* (Paris, 1903), pp. 103-5, discusses the industries of French cities in the period before Colbert.

Bodin

replied [2] that the rise in prices was due to an abundance of gold and silver, not to the debasement of the currency, the rise being greatest in Spain and Italy, which had received the greatest amounts of precious metals. His arguments were clear and forceful; he showed that an increase in the quantity of gold and silver makes their value fall, just as an abundance of anything affects its value. However, he did not recognize the importance of the velocity of circulation of money. Bodin further argued that extravagance and waste, scarcity of goods, and monopolistic practices had affected prices but that their influence was much less than that of the increased supply of gold and silver. He showed further antimercantilistic insight in pointing out the advantages of free trade between states.

One of the very earliest French writers on mercantilism was Montchrétien (c. 1575-1621). His ideas are found in his *Traicté*,[3] published in 1615; thus it ranks in time along with the work of Serra, the Italian, published in 1613. The pamphlet sets forth mercantilistic principles designed to strengthen France. He treats national wealth as the product of the labor of the citizens of a state, not its stock of gold and silver. However, he believed that none of the bullion stock should be exported. Industry should be fostered by the state, and artisans in wool, silk, leather, and glass-making crafts should be encouraged. Foreign artisans should be excluded from such crafts. He advocates heavy duties on exports of French raw materials, and prohibition of the import of manufactured articles. His work is not as scientific as some of its counterparts in England, but it is an interesting expression of early French views on mercantilism. His economic observations on his times are of great historic value.[4]

Jean Baptiste Colbert.—The foremost "practitioner" of mercantilism was Colbert, the minister of finance under Louis XIV.[5] He was a thoroughgoing mercantilist in advocating complete state authority over all measures which would make the state a self-sufficient power. The policies of Colbert were very nationalistic and pragmatic, and in many

[2] Jean Bodin, *Réponses aux paradoxes du sieur de Malestroit* (Paris, 1566 and 1578).

[3] Antoine de Montchrétien, *Traicté de l'oeconomie politique* (Rouen, 1615). This was probably the first time that the term "political economy" was used.

[4] The *Traicté* was ". . . the longest, the most complete, and the best written treatise on economic matters which had up to that time appeared in France, and perhaps in Europe." Charles W. Cole, *Colbert and a Century of French Mercantilism* (2 vols.; New York, 1939), Vol. I, p. 84.

[5] Jean Baptiste Colbert (1619-1683) was minister of finance from 1661 to 1683 under Louis XIV. He had marked talents as an organizer and public administrator. While not a writer on economics as such, Colbert's views on mercantilism can be extracted from his voluminous edicts, orders, official memoranda, etc.

respects narrower than English policies. He stood for absolute power of the state to control and regulate all economic activity. Therefore, he brought the regulatory functions of the guilds under state control, he opposed trade restrictions between the provinces, and controlled the export of grain, partly because of his desire to maintain an abundant and cheap food supply for the industrial population—another genuine mercantilistic policy. Internal commerce was encouraged by building roads and canals.

His views on industry were likewise narrow and nationalistic. He desired to free France from dependence on foreign manufacturers. The purchase of iron, porcelain, laces, woven goods, and other articles from nearby states disturbed him. To overcome this dependence, he induced craftsmen to immigrate to France. He offered bounties to encourage domestic production, especially of those things which required skill to produce. Privileged manufacturers were free from statutory regulations and supervision of the guilds. His administration was responsible for the state purchase and operation of the famous Gobelin works, which became a great training center for skilled textile craftsmen.

As minister of finance, Colbert built both a merchant marine and a navy. Shipping facilities were improved in order to facilitate the movement of goods, and he granted bounties to French shippers and shipbuilders. He promoted successful trading companies and expanded the French colonial empire, reserving colonial trade as a French monopoly. So far as Colbert's theory was concerned, he believed that the only way of building up his own country was to take something away from another.

Colbert's views on money were also thoroughly mercantilistic. He held that "manufacturers will produce returns in money, which is the single aim of commerce and the only means of increasing the power of the state." Nevertheless, his well-intended efforts brought only limited results. The larger aims tended to be lost sight of and all his measures became manifestations of absolute authority by the state.[6]

"Colbertism" is a synonym for mercantilism in its narrow sense. Yet we do not find him interested or engaged in the doctrinaire controversies nor the fine (although often erroneous) theories spun by the Englishmen. There is no economic analysis of long-run or short-run policies; his were the policies of an economic dictator who had the power of the state behind him to enforce his orders. Even though Colbert played a part through his patronage and the awarding of pensions in establishing the intellectual supremacy of France, he contributed little to the sum of human knowledge in his own field of

[6] See Charles W. Cole, *op. cit.*; see also Pierre Clément, *Histoire de la vie et de l'administration de Colbert* (Paris, 1846).

economics. The main reason why Colbert is of interest to us is his applied economics—not his theories, and we have his counterpart in some of the Germans and Austrians who were also in a position to apply mercantilistic policies in their states.

John Law and Richard Cantillon.—In the eighteenth century the influence of English mercantilism became more noticeable in France. "Between 1749 and 1760 the works of a considerable number of the English writers such as Petty, Gee, Tucker, Child, and others were translated into French." [7] The chief controversy in France centered about precious metals, money, prices, export and import trade, much the same as in England, but there was complete agreement on the desirability of building up the power of the state.

Another practitioner and, at the same time, a theorist was the Scottish-born financier John Law (1671-1729), who found political haven in France. He was influenced by English writings and by the general economic conditions of Europe and France at the end of the seventeenth and the beginning of the eighteenth centuries. Law was a mercantilist who possessed more insight into economic relationships than most of his predecessors. He admitted that land, population, and natural and industrial production are essential to national wealth, but these elements depend upon "commerce and commerce depends on specie"—which is gold and silver. He conceived the idea of substituting paper money for specie, secured by the value of the nation's land and to be put into circulation by a bank. His theory was that an increase in money stimulates an increase in economic activity which, in turn, would offset any price increase because of an increase in goods. His plan was adopted by the French government in 1716 and lasted four years; it failed then because of the overexpansion of money, and Law was obliged to leave France. Although he was best known for his efforts to apply his pet schemes, he showed excellent insight into the workings of money and prices.

Another writer, French by temporary adoption, was the Englishman, Richard Cantillon (1680-1734), who had advanced and original ideas on economic matters. An unusually keen student and observer, he surpassed most of his contemporaries in his analysis of both theoretical and applied economic problems. Cantillon was not concerned with the numerous ideas and controversies usually associated with mercantilism. He was interested in national wealth, exchange, and foreign trade.[8] He contends that land and labor—not currency (metal

[7] J. W. Angell, *Theory of International Prices* (Cambridge, Mass., 1926), p. 211.
[8] Richard Cantillon, *Essai sur la nature du commerce en général* (written about 1730 and published in 1755).

or paper)—are the true measure of wealth of a state. Value (especially exchange value) depends upon land (which provides the raw material) and labor. He applies this idea to international trade and arrives at the conclusion that a country should export commodities that are as little as possible the unworked products of the soil; and conversely, the country should import articles that are as much as possible products of the soil, i.e., raw materials. The net balance of such imports would constitute a "favorable balance of trade." [9] National strength (including population) and prosperity rest upon this trade balance.

Cantillon shows a clear knowledge of the quantity theory of money, which he attempts to reconcile with his balance-of-trade theory. He reasons that an increase of precious metals from mines may be basically bad for an economy in that they are often drained off to pay for imports for which inflated prices have been paid. However, if an increase in precious metals is due to a favorable trade balance, entirely different results will follow. This is mercantilistic doctrine in that he thought an abundance of precious metals should be the effect of a favorable trade balance. He knew that an influx of precious metals into a country would raise prices and lead to an *unfavorable* balance of trade. But he was mainly concerned with the time lag between the time when prices began to rise and the point at which the trade balance turned unfavorable. As was also noted earlier, his concept of "balance" was a balance of imports of products of the soil.

Cantillon thus arrived at the mercantilistic conclusion that the favorable balance of trade will bring in precious metals which are desirable as an evidence of national prosperity and, to some extent, its cause. He believed the converse to be just as true—an unfavorable balance of trade would drain off precious metals and bring about national depression. But he was more concerned that the nation enjoy prosperity than that it accumulate a store of precious metals.

Other writers engaged in the balance-of-trade controversy, but by the middle of the eighteenth century the trade theories had become pretty well accepted on the basis of Hume's reasoning (see Chapter 6, p. 95). Cantillon's work, even though advanced, probably exerted little if any influence upon contemporary French economic thought, but he himself is known to have been conversant with Law, the minister of finance, while his money and land-bank schemes were being tried out. That they disagreed on the money scheme is known from the fact that Law ordered Cantillon to accept his plan or to leave France, which he did, not doubting Law's political power. Internal decadence fol-

[9] See Cantillon, *op. cit.*, pp. 297-307; Dubois, *op. cit.*, pp. 242-44; A. E. Monroe (ed.), *Early Economic Thought* (Cambridge, Mass., 1924), chap. xi.

lowed by economic and political bankruptcy submerged French economic theories for some time. We next hear of France under physiocracy in Chapter 8.

Summary of French Mercantilism.—French mercantilism, like English, was a product of the times. The persons who wrote on economic
subjects from which French mercantilistic ideas are derived were not
capitalists, merchants, or nobles as many English writers were. In
general, they defy "occupational" classification, although some were
statesmen and some were philosophers. They were neither so numerous nor such voluminous writers as were the English and the Germans.
Except for the emphasis on population, the underlying fundamentals
were just as much French as English, for the basic objectives were the
same in both countries. The points of agreement and disagreement on
ways to achieve the end were approximately the same in both countries.
Under Colbert, applied mercantilism was carried to extremes, farther
than it ever was in England. The measures soon became burdensome
and set the stage for a strong reaction against the practices. They
should, however, be viewed in a much broader perspective than merely
as the edicts of Colbert.

German Mercantilism or Cameralism

Cameralism is the German and Austrian conception of mercantilism.
It is a term applied to the whole body of political and economic practices of absolute monarchy in the states of Germany and Austria during
some three hundred years.

The origin of the term is of some interest. In the Middle Ages the
royal treasure was stored in the *Kammer* (from Latin *camera* or chamber). In time the *Kammer* became associated with, or synonymous with,
royal property, treasure, and income as well as systematized government
procedure. Since the welfare of the king was the welfare of the state,
the science dealing with state finances became known as *Kameralwissenschaft*. During most of the period of cameralism, every element which
could be of significance in *Staatsbildung*, or state-formation, was employed. Political policies, tax measures, regulatory laws, technical measures dealing with production, sale, and distribution of goods, as well as
general economic policies were incorporated in the broad sweep of
cameralism.

Many of the measures were for self-defense, but all were directed
toward the same end as mercantilism, viz., building up the power of
the state. The citizens were trained in the duties of public servants and

were expected to contribute to state welfare through taxation. University chairs were subsidized for the purpose of teaching the principles. While the practices changed in minor respects toward the end of the period, the fundamentals held for nearly three hundred years.

The Background of Cameralism.—The foundations of cameralism, like those of mercantilism, lie deep in the medieval period. While England and France were taking form as unified states, the many small principalities of Germany were struggling with one another in futile efforts to attain supremacy within Germany. The states were small and constituted separate political, legal, and economic units. Consolidation of the units into larger and stronger states was a long process in which many rulers participated. It was in the interest of permanent state consolidation that most of the practices of cameralism grew. Laws were directed toward the centralizing of financial administration as well as the administration of all those measures in which a completely paternalistic state was concerned. This, in effect, was cameralism.

Cameralism in Germany and Austria was predicated on particular theories of the state. The period following the Reformation was filled with barren theological controversies. The Thirty Years' War reduced the states to lower economic, political, and even cultural levels. So long as independent principalities existed, there could be no spirit of larger nationalism. At this juncture the political philosopher Pufendorf (1632-1694) appeared as "the first representative of rationalistic thought and of modern enlightenment in Germany."[10] He developed the concept of natural law, which he worked into an elaborate system of political philosophy. He held that civil society was established by voluntary contract. Society as a whole entered into a compact in establishing its state and selecting its ruler. The sovereignty thus established was not entirely absolute, but it was absolute or supreme in the sense that there was no higher human authority and no law to which it was subject. States and individuals must conform to the law of reason as interpreted by sane and intelligent men. Pufendorf's theory reconciled the benevolent despotism of German states with the spirit of individual freedom by allowing supremacy to the sovereignty of the state but at the same time denying to it absolutely complete control over the lives and activities of the citizens.

The theory of natural rights, as applied, meant that individual freedom was expressed by a union of individual wills in the social compact. The ruler's authority rested upon inalienable powers delegated to him, and his position as benevolent ruler was secure. This concept became

[10] R. G. Gettell, *History of Political Thought* (New York, 1924), p. 233.

the theoretical basis for paternalism of the ruler; likewise, the theory would not tolerate interference by any group which might stand between the ruler and the people. It justified the ending of the power of the craft guilds which stood between ruler and ruled. It also justified state intervention in the life of the people and provided a *Kameralwissenschaft* which attempted to systematize the ever-increasing number of the state's tasks and responsibilities.

In a very real sense, therefore, cameralism was a theory or practice not of economics but of politics. Economic conditions and purposes did, however, share heavily in the adaptation of cameralistic principles. It is probable that cameralism produced no fundamental theoretical issues in economics. It was primarily a theory and a technique of government which, of necessity, dealt with certain economic problems in an applied though narrow sense.

The purposes or objectives of the state dominated everything and everybody. The cameralists, as teachers and writers on the subject, were servants of the state as were the persons attached to the bureaus of government. Cameralism rested upon the fundamental assumption of the power of collective interests, or the subordination of individual interests to those of the community or state. This concept of the relationship of the state to the individual, which resembles the relationship between a drill sergeant and a raw recruit, does not fit into our concepts either of freedom or of state function. Yet this is what prevailed for almost three hundred years and was indeed a most important conditioning factor affecting subsequent German development.

Cameralist Writers and Writings.—The leading cameralistic writers may be divided into two groups, each of which represents a phase of cameralism. The earlier group consists of those writers who emphasize the political aspects and possibilities of the state, which border on absolutism. They include Seckendorff, Becher, and Hornick, each of whom will be treated separately. In the second group are those who are more concerned with systematizing the numerous functions of the state and providing a justification for its actions. In this latter group are von Justi, Darjes, and von Sonnenfels. Each writer differs from the other significantly. Becher is concerned with the internal political and economic relationships of states. Hornick is interested in ways and means of making a greater Austria. Specific economic recommendations characterize the second group. From this heterogeneous group we shall attempt to extract their economic policies, but with an awareness of the political setting in which they are found and in which they are intended to function.

The works of the cameralists have been neglected.[11] The tradition of both the English and the American scholar of necessity focuses attention on mercantilism, especially on its practical side. It affected the national economy of both countries for many years. On the theoretical side it provided theories which have occupied the economists' attention for several hundred years. It forced a sort of internationalism which has characterized both political and economic theories. Cameralism, on the other hand, suffered from isolation and provincialism. It was a type of economics which applied to a closed economy, both semifeudal and semicapitalistic. While it definitely lacked the scope of mercantilism, it is characterized by an effective and efficient even though, as we may view it, narrow series of measures of far-reaching significance.

Seventeenth-Century Writers: Seckendorff, Becher, and Hornick.— The first writer to be considered is Ludwig von Seckendorff (1626-1692), author of *Der Teutsche Fürsten Staat* (1655) and *Der Christen Staat* (1685). He was the exponent of the type of German state found in the middle of the seventeenth century, which was at least a quasi-absolute state. Seckendorff was a leader in giving rationalizations for the power and efficiency of the state. Small regards him and his works as establishing a landmark, "the Adam Smith of Cameralism." [12]

To achieve the ends of the state Seckendorff favors an increase in population, and he suggests ways of caring for it, both physically and morally. No subject should lack the means of support. The surplus or special products of the country shall be carefully managed in order to secure in exchange the useful and necessary products from other countries. To accomplish this, Seckendorff proposes twelve measures, the most important ones of which are a good education of the youth; special attention to goods which are most necessary such as products of the field, grazing, forestry, and of iron, spinning, weaving and wool trades; ordinances regulating prices; abolition of usury; regulation of weights and measures; passage of certain sumptuary laws; curtailed use

[11] Several studies have been made of the cameralists, each with a different emphasis. Students generally depend on Roscher for an economic interpretation of cameralism: Wilhelm Roscher, *Geschichte der National-ökonomik in Deutschland* (Munich, 1874), pp. 228-35. Zielenziger tried to distinguish between mercantilism and cameralism: Kurt Zielenziger, *Die alten deutschen Kameralisten* ("Beitrage zur Geschichte der National-ökonomik," No. 2, Jena, 1914). Professor Small in an excellent study which is accessible to most students treated them as political scientists: A. W. Small, *The Cameralists* (Chicago, 1909). The author of the article on cameralism in the *Encyclopaedia of the Social Sciences*, Louise Sommer, is concerned with cameralism and mercantilism as systems: see also Louise Sommer, *Die österreichischen Kameralisten in Dogmen geschlichtlicher Darstellung* (2 vols.; Vienna, 1920-25). For additional references see "Cameralism," *Encyclopaedia of the Social Sciences* (New York, 1933).
[12] A. W. Small, *The Cameralists*, p. 69.

of foreign wares in clothing and food; suppression of parasitic occupations such as gamblers, fakirs, etc. His views on government restrictions were liberal and moderate. He opposed the monopolies of the guilds and favored the encouragement of foreign purchases of domestic products. The government should "maintain the zeal" of persons engaged in especially advantageous occupations and at all times protect the people against fraud.[13]

These measures are like mercantilistic ones in some respects. There is no emphasis on treasure, yet Seckendorff, like the others, is concerned that the supply of money be adequate. There is a degree of practicality in his recommendations, which were intended generally to bring immediate results. Theoretical implications are of minor concern to him, and he never overlooks the importance of the state in executing his proposals.

In a similar manner Johann Joachim Becher (1625-1685) emphasizes cameralistic elements. His most important cameralistic work was his *Political Discourse* [14] in which he gives an outline account of the state of trade in Germany. He recognizes that traders, artisans, and peasants make up the bulk of the population which should be under one administration, to aid these groups in increasing their numbers. Government policy should also aid in promoting consumption and sale of goods by these three groups. Becher expresses his views on foreign trade vigorously: "Trade in foreign goods, when the same could be produced at home, makes for the destruction of the community. Instead of favoring men who enrich themselves by bringing in foreign goods, we ought to deal with them as the meanest criminals. On the other hand, those merchants by whom the state gains in money and sustenance are, next to nature, the nursing-mother that makes the desert bloom." [15] The enemies of the three classes named above are first *Monopolium*, which checks the population; next, *Polypolium*, which limits their means of support; and third, *Propolium*, which divides the community. Each tends to destroy the state. The first implies that population will be restricted if denied opportunity to work, a practice which had been charged against the guilds. The evils of *Polypolium* result from an unrestricted supply of workers and artisans in excess of labor demands. Everyone is at liberty to earn his living as he may, which means that people rob one another of work "by which traders and wholesalers keep the artisans in constant poverty and toil." He probably uses the term *Propolium* in the sense of monopoly, or a corner in the market.

---

[13] *Der Teutsche Fürsten Staaten*, chap. viii; see also Small, *op. cit.*, p. 90.
[14] *Politischer Discurs von den eigentlichen Ursachen des Auf- und Abnehmens der Städte, Länder und Republicken* (Frankfort, 1668).
[15] *Discurs*, pp. 106 ff. See also Small, *op. cit.*, p. 128.

Becher urged the encouragement of foreign trade by state-sponsored and state-regulated trading companies as devices by means of which the evils of monopoly and of *Polypolium* might be avoided. The trade with foreigners would be encouraged by selling cheap and good wares to the foreigner and thereby securing treasure or money from abroad. To guarantee cheap wares good workmen and good materials were needed, as well as cheap food, which could be assured by low import duties and preferential treatment. All trade, he reasoned, must be based on a stable currency and a strong bank. A state board of commerce should supervise money, banks, and state factories. He favored taxes which should fall upon the rich rather than upon the poor, but no taxes should hinder economic development. His principles in general are mercantilistic, and for their application they need a quasi-absolute state. His policies exerted considerable influence upon the Austrian government of his day. Becher was, indeed, one of the most distinguished of the cameralists.

The last of the earlier group was Philip Wilhelm von Hornick [16] (1638-1712), an Austrian by birth and in sentiment. He lived during the terrible war years of 1680-1684 when Germany and Austria were engaged in conflict with the French in the west and the Turks in the east. This fact materially affected his political views and embittered him against France in particular. The work which presents his cameralistic principles, *Oesterreich über Alles, Wann es nur will*, appeared in 1684. In the book he undertook to formulate a policy which would restore Austria to a place above all other countries and make her self-sufficient. He attempted to prove that Austria, more than any other European state, possessed the natural resources to make her independent.

Hornick did not make the mistake of identifying the possession of money with wealth. He writes, "The power and excellence of a land is its surplus of gold, silver and all other things necessary or convenient for its subsistence, and so far as possible derived from its own means, without dependence upon others." A land that had only gold and silver would be rich, to be sure. However, since gold and silver can neither feed nor clothe people, a land that has all other things except gold and silver is somewhat more independent. But he holds that gold and silver are essential to the life of commerce.

Among the best known of Hornick's cameralistic proposals are his "nine chief rules of public economy," which make up his "merchants or Cameral primer." The rules were widely read by others and exerted

---

[16] Sometimes written Hornigk, Horneck, or Hornig.

considerable influence on Austrian commercial policy. They follow in an abbreviated form.[17]

First. The country's soil properties should be thoroughly investigated. Every form of plant should be experimented with to see whether it can be grown. Above all, no expense should be spared to discover any silver or gold.

Second. All products of a nation which cannot be used in their natural state should be worked up within the country. Payment for manufacturing generally exceeds by many fold the value of raw materials.

Third. In order to make the first two rules effective, attention should be given to the population; it should be as large as the country can support. The population should be kept from idleness and encouraged to engage in remunerative employment.

Fourth. Gold and silver should not be exported for any purpose, but always kept in circulation. Hoarding is forbidden.

Fifth. So far as possible, consumption should be confined to home-produced goods.

Sixth. Should import of foreign goods be necessary, they should be exchanged for domestic wares and not paid for by gold or silver.

Seventh. If foreign goods must be imported, they should be imported in the raw state and worked up within the country, thus earning the wages of manufacture there.

Eighth. Every effort should be made to sell superfluous goods to foreigners in manufactured form for gold and silver.

Ninth. No imports of goods should be permitted if there is already a sufficient supply of tolerable quality at home, even if they could be bought cheaper abroad. Two dollars spent for a product within the country is better for the country than one dollar spent abroad for an item which is imported.

Hornick thought these rules were perfectly obvious and reasonable, just as he thought the exclusion of imports would be easy and simple. In the discussion supporting his points he resorts to logic, ridicule, derision, mockery, and even propaganda to prove his point that Austria could excel all other countries if she would but decide to do so.

The responsibility for making the program work rests with the government, whose task it is to assure quality of wares, check any wantonness, exclude luxury items, encourage craftsmen, inspect merchandise, erect halls and warehouses, and encourage foreign craftsmen from

[17] See A. E. Monroe, *op. cit.*, chap. x, pp. 223-43, for a full translation of the nine rules and other parts of von Hornick's book.

abroad by prizes and special privileges. While all the measures are necessary and essential, the real problem is not the balance of trade with its concurrent economic rules, but the balance of political power. He believed that the economic fortunes of Austria, which were at a low ebb industrially, could be made to surpass those of other nations; hence the title of the book, *Austria Over All, If Only She Will.* 1684

Eighteenth-Century Cameralists. Justi.—The second classification of Cameralists includes those writers who believed the numerous state functions could be classified and justified. The most distinguished representative of this group, as well as one of the most distinguished of the eighteenth-century cameralists, was Johannes Heinrich von Justi (1717-1771). He was trained in jurisprudence and became a professor of cameral sciences at Vienna; later he was administrator of mines under Frederick the Great. He was a voluminous writer. In his writings he incorporated many cameralistic ideas of his predecessors; by correlating the different ideas, his systematic presentation of them makes his work outstanding.[18] His bulky works represent a summary or epitome of cameralistic doctrines up to that time. In his *Staatswirtschaft* he includes practically everything that had been said by other writers and adds his own thoughts with the result that we have a most compendious document—a *"summa cameralisma."*

He starts his epitome by showing that the sciences dedicated to the government of the state are the economic or cameralistic sciences. What economics attempts to do in connection with the goods of private persons, the governmental sciences aim to do for all the means of supporting the state. Cameralism is necessarily administrative in nature, with the ultimate aim of common happiness. "All the administrative transactions of a state must be so ordered that by means of them the happiness of the same [i.e., the state] shall be promoted." To him, this was the "first and universal principle of all economic and Cameralistic sciences." [19] He supports the theory of enlightened despotism and state intervention but his real contribution lies in his efforts to keep cameral science or economics (*Kameralwissenschaft*) separated from general administration of the state (*Polizeiwissenschaft*).

Only a few of the cameralistic teachings of Justi are presented here; they include the usual assumptions of the desirability of gold and silver and an increase in population, which he assumes cannot overtax the food supply since it assures an increase in sustenance. He is especially

---

[18] His main contributions are *Staatswirtschaft; oder, systematische Abhandlung aller oekonomischen und Cameralwissenschaften* (2 vols.; Leipzig, 1775), *Grundsätze der Polizeiwissenschaft* (Berlin, 1756) and *System des Finanzwesens* (Halle, 1766).
[19] Small, *op. cit.*, p. 319.

anxious to encourage an increase in the immigration of rich foreigners who would bring treasure with them. Tax exemption, subsidies, and special building credit facilities should be used to encourage the foreigners to come to Germany. Foreign commerce can increase the wealth of the land if it brings in more gold and silver than it takes out. It is incomparably more profitable for the state than domestic trade. Banks and an adequate supply of stable money are necessary to facilitate trade. The importation of luxury items should be discouraged. The government must assume responsibility for the quality of wares by promulgating rules of inspection and standards to insure both quality and quantity. If companies are organized to engage in trade they should have adequate capital, even if funds must be borrowed abroad. Adequate money and credit facilities for small artisans and craftsmen should be provided. Goods for export must not be burdened with heavy duties, but the export of raw materials must be prohibited or heavily taxed.

One of Justi's contributions is his systematization of tax rules. He gives a great deal of attention to taxation under which he discusses contributions, taxes, imposts, taxes on immovable goods, personal taxation, taxes on occupations, the right of a sovereign to impose special taxes, and means of collecting taxes. His famous rules of taxation are presented in an abbreviated form as follows: [20]

The first rule requires that the subjects be able to pay the taxes with "willing and happy hearts, and at their own initiative."

The second rule is that taxes must not interfere with reasonable freedom of human conduct or credit of merchants, nor oppress industry and commerce.

The third rule says that taxes must be levied with righteous equality. They should not be prejudicial to the welfare of the state or to its subjects.

The fourth requires that taxes be sure, fixed, and levied upon objects from which the tax can be promptly and certainly collected and not be subject to fraud and concealment.

The fifth rule requires that taxes be based on objects which will limit the number of collectors' offices and officials.

The sixth and last rule is that payments must be made as easy as possible and payable at convenient times.

In addition to his ideas on taxes and on cameralism in general, Justi gives at least some attention to agriculture, which he views as necessary to a flourishing state. Land which is wisely used and has a flourishing,

[20] *System des Finanzwesen*, Book II, pp. 309 ff. See also A. E. Monroe, *Early Economic Thought* (Cambridge, Mass., 1924), pp. 379-99.

sustaining system of trade and industry never can have too many inhabitants. The government must see to it that land is in the hands of those
who will live on it and cultivate it. Rural population would be increased if peasants were granted proprietary tenure.

Many of Justi's ideas on cameralism may be found in his *Finanz*
Schriften.[21] This work is a collection of miscellaneous ideas which
cover practically the whole range of cameralistic activity. If one has
the ability, patience, and time to peruse the three volumes and assort
the cameralistic ideas from the many other things, he would be rewarded with some choice bits of cameralism. Justi says: "There is no
other way whereby people can become rich than through commerce"
(I, 175); as to population, he writes: "The more populous a state the
more prosperous will be its food industries (*Nahrung*) and trade (*Ge-*
werbe) and the more active will be the circulation of money" (I, 199).
The high esteem with which he regards population is shown in the
following quotation: "If one should ask me whether the chief consideration of a genuine and wise Cameralist to which, according to the
general principle of the happiness of the state, his chief care must be
directed and back to which he must refer in all measures and operations,
could be expressed with a single word and concept, I would without a
moment's hesitation cry out the word POPULATION. Yes, truly,
POPULATION must be the chief interest of all his measures" (III,
379).

Justi's ponderous works draw in extensive detail a complete blueprint
for making a great state. While he is not always consistent in his arguments, nor always right, he does formulate the most well-rounded and
complete rules on cameralism yet produced. He comes close to setting
forth a complete body of rules for cameralistic procedure and for the
quasi-absolute state.

J. G. Darjes.—Another cameralist who gained great fame both as a
teacher and adviser was Joachim Georg Darjes (1714-1791).[22] He was
a leader in reorganizing and transforming the loose principles of the
early cameralists into an administrative science which could be presented academically and used to train men for government service. He
held to the usual cameralistic theory that the state was justified, in order

[21] Johann Heinrich Gottlob von Justi, *Gesammelte Politische und Finanzschriften*
über Wichtige Gegenstände der Staatskunst, der Kreigswissenschaften und des
Cameral- und Finanzwesens (3 vols.; Leipzig, 1761).

[22] Darjes was a professor at Jena and, upon the invitation of Frederick the Great,
went (1763) as a professor of cameral science to Frankfurt a. Oder, where he later
founded the Königliche Gelehrte Gesellschaft (Royal Academy). In 1772 he became director of the university and professor of law. His work *Erste Gründe der*
Cameral-Wissenschaften was published in 1756, almost ninety years after Becher's
pioneering work, *Political Discourses*, appeared in 1668.

to guard its own best interests, in intervening in the affairs of the people. He believed that state officials should be especially trained in handling the revenues and capital (*Fond*) [23] of the state in order to insure the general happiness of the people. While he is primarily interested in the prince's revenues, he sets up an important premise in pointing out that "the first case of those interested in increasing princely revenues must be to discover how the yearly income of the subjects may be increased. Accordingly a prince is rich when he has rich and skillful subjects." [24] This sets the pattern for his book. Cameralistic teachings and practices should be directed toward ways of increasing the yearly income of the people. Accordingly, there must be no hindrances to the efforts of people to increase their income but the state must aid in leading them to the "necessary occupation." The citizens' zeal for labor must be awakened and directed into productive channels.

If these measures work out as they should, there need be no fear of a large population. A dense population would increase the food supply, increase the trade—hence the income of the prince—and aid in national defense. A dense population engaged in productive employment is a source of wealth to the state. Darjes places a broad interpretation on his use of the term *Kameralwissenschaft*.

The third part of his work contains his thoughts on *Polizeiwissenschaft*. In this part he maintains that the "state is beautiful and its well-being is assured if its subjects have a flourishing means of subsistence." In accomplishing this he is concerned not only with the increase but with the welfare of the population, the establishment of schools and universities, incitement of subjects to labor, state activity in preserving the health of its subjects, beauty of the country, promotion of security, care for the poor, etc. He is also concerned with details of agriculture and cattle raising and detailed accounts of the fabrication of certain goods.

Darjes' work was a splendid expression of cameralism. In many respects his *First Principles* shows a comprehension of economic relationships superior to anything which appeared before the *Wealth of Nations*. He is more direct and forceful than most of the cameralists and shows marked abilities in establishing a positive science. One student believes "no single writer in the Cameralistic succession gives a brief account of the scope and purpose of their discipline which better reflects the genius of the whole movement." [25]

[23] *Fond*, or capital of the princely revenues, is the riches of the state and its subjects.
[24] *Erste Gründe*, p. 27.
[25] Small, *op. cit.*, p. 272.

J. von Sonnenfels, a Neocameralist.—The last of the second group to be considered is Joseph von Sonnenfels (1733-1817). Like some others in the cameralistic group, he served as professor of *Finanz und Polizeiwissenschaft* at Vienna in 1763. He was a sort of neocameralist in that he challenged in a guarded and indirect manner many of the quasi-absolutist assumptions which characterize the state. He placed greater emphasis on individual rights than any of his predecessors, even advocating state care for the sick, penal reforms, and opposition to capital punishment. While holding to the quasi-absolutist concept of the state, he would make the state responsible for the general improvement of the lot of the people by guaranteeing at least a minimum of subsistence to all who would work. He became adviser to Maria Theresa, Joseph II, and Leopold II, and in this capacity had much to do with shaping the economic and political policies of Austria. Roscher says, "For more than two generations Austrian national economy was dominated by Joseph von Sonnenfels." [26]

He was a mercantilist in his thinking, yet he went much farther than most of his predecessors in the scope of his ideas. His single, three-volume work [27] contains his main mercantilistic ideas. Sonnenfels upholds the theory of enlightened absolutism of the state; nevertheless he reckons with individual welfare in a very real sense. He runs true to cameralistic theory in advocating a large population as a protective or defense measure, as an aid to agriculture and industry, and as a means of insuring state revenue. To this end he advocated the development of industries that would employ many people and favored small land-holdings and restrictions on the guilds. Likewise, he believed that if imports were limited to raw materials and exports of finished products encouraged, the welfare of the people would be bettered. He was, in a sense, a tax liberal if not a reformer. He vigorously opposed tax exemptions for nobility and clergy, holding to the view that it was the obligation of everyone to share in the expenses of government. He thought indirect taxation was best for Austria.

Sonnenfels used the welfare principle to justify foreign trade. He held that the revenues so received could be used to increase employment and thereby contribute to national welfare, and the state had the responsibility of enacting measures to this end. On money he held enlightened views. Money should serve not only as an exchange medium but as a factor in production if properly used. He opposed usury laws and proposed that the interest rate be low to encourage capital expan-

---

[26] *Geschichte der National-ökonomik in Deutschland* (Munich, 1874), pp. 533-52.
[27] *Grundsätze der Policey, Handlung, und Finanz* (2 vols., Vienna, 1765-67; 3 vols., 1819-22).

sion. He understood credit and advocated that the banks should serve as grantors of credit as well as handle money.

Sonnenfels had a very comprehensive grasp of economic problems and relationships. He did not, however, treat the economic problems either as systematically as or with the understanding of Adam Smith. He was a follower of Justi, but he went farther than Justi in narrowing the issues to specific cases and then applying attempted solutions to them; in his capacity as a state functionary he could do so. (Because he outlived the other cameralists he had an opportunity to observe a very different world from that of his predecessors.) The mercantile world of Mun and Petty, Seckendorff and Becher, had been greatly changed under the blows of Hume and Smith and other critics of monopolistic practices. Realignments had taken place among nations as a result of wars and subsequent settlements. World trade and the importance of colonial empires had long since passed the theoretical stage, and at the end of the eighteenth century world trade and colonial empires were assuming a relatively stable pattern. Sonnenfels had ample opportunity to observe the great changes in his and other countries, a fact which tended to liberalize and modernize his thinking.[28]

Summary and Evaluation of Cameralism.—Neither time nor space permits a detailed inquiry into the writings of all the writers listed as cameralists. It is believed, however, that enough has been presented to give a clear picture of what cameralism was and what it stood for in the German states.

→ The student must see cameralism as a series of proposals devised first, to help the quasi-absolutist states recover from the ravages of endless wars; second, to bring about a self-sufficiency which would be beneficial both to the people and the state. The civic and economic problems were treated as one, and both were bound up in the mystical unity of the prince and the people. This concept of state was a char-

---

[28] There were other cameralists in addition to the list treated in this chapter. The more important ones were:

Wilhelm Freyherr von Schröder (1640-1688), adviser to Emperor Leopold I of Austria. He ranks with Becher and Hornick in his influence on Austrian cameralistic policy. His principal work on cameralism was *Fürstliche Schatz-und Rent-Kammer* (1686).

Justus Christoph Dithmar (1677-1737), first professor of cameralistic science at Frankfort a. Oder. Author of *Einleitung in die öckonomischen Polizei- und Cameralwissenschaften* (1731). He founded the first magazine devoted to economics, *Ökonomische Fama*. Ten issues were published, beginning in 1729.

Georg Heinrich Zincke (1692-1768) was also a teacher of cameralism. He wrote *Cameraliste-Bibliothek* (1751-52), which was the first systematic bibliography on cameralism. He also edited the first periodical devoted exclusively to Cameralistic problems, viz., *Leipziger Sammlungen von wirthschafftlichen, Policey- Cammer- und Finantz-Sachen*. He was a prolific writer of textbooks and manuals on cameralism.

acteristic of the period and has more or less remained as a German concept of state until the present.

Cameralism should not be regarded as a philosophy. It was an ← administrative technology. It was a complement to a political or governmental technique in which short-run benefits received greater consideration than long-run policies. While there were many economic points on which there appeared to be complete agreement, they were points not in economic theory but in economic practices. The ideas were not economic generalizations in the sense of the generalizations which the nineteenth-century economists developed. They saw few, if any, long-run economic implications in their practices, which were mainly domestic. International aspects of theory or practice did not concern them, chiefly because cameralism began as a means to help the ruler attain efficient administration of the state, and it always bore that rather limited characteristic.

On the practical side cameralism was effective. Schmoller points out numerous practical results.[29] For 250 years, for instance, the rulers regulated labor, industry, trade and commerce, encouraged skilled craftsmen to migrate to Germany, built industries in many cities, regulated money and credit, encouraged or forbade export trade as they chose, and so on. There can be no doubt that these practices were of inestimably marked value in developing Germany and Austria and in influencing the whole fabric of economic and political activities well into the nineteenth century.

Mercantilism and Cameralism Compared.—Throughout this chapter German cameralism has been identified with mercantilism, and rightly so. This is because the two "isms" were basically concerned with the same objective. Each represented somewhat fantastic views on wealth and treasure, with the margin of error being much greater on the part of the English mercantilists. The mercantilists placed more stress on the possession of precious metals in the belief that treasure could accomplish any objective. The cameralists (especially Justi) regarded precious metals as essential to fiscal needs, an oil for the machinery of state.

Both groups believed in state regulation, with the cameralists outdoing the mercantilists on this score. This is largely traceable to the theories of state which prevailed in the two countries. Both stressed tariffs on imports and bounties on some exports. Both stressed international rivalry, but in rather different degrees of internationalism. England was a carrying nation with far-flung colonies; since she was

[29] Gustav Schmoller, *Die deutschen Kleingewerbe im 19. Jahrhundert* (Halle, 1870).

an island nation, carrying trade was essential to her life. On the other hand, the many German states and Austria were contiguous with other European states, and to them foreign trade might be nothing other than crossing a state line. Each, however, enjoyed the luxury of commercial rivalry.

Both the mercantilists and the cameralists praised dense population in much the same way as agriculture was praised by the Greek and Roman writers. Indeed, population was regarded as a natural resource similar to agricultural land or minerals. Population could be made a productive agent in wealth-getting. The cameralists, in so far as they were concerned with agriculture at all, held that the lands were undercultivated, therefore underpopulated. The British saw in a large population a source of labor for low-cost production as well as a market for goods. The Germans could see no threat to their state from an increase in population and there really was none at that time.

The student must be impressed with the difference between the writings of the two groups. The English writers wrote tracts and discourses, not ponderous volumes covering every minute phase and regulation as they saw them. The typical German capacity of classification, enumeration, and subdivision is most striking when compared with the absence of such detail in many of the English writings. It may well be that the total pages of Justi's writings would be more (the three volumes of his *Finanzschriften* alone contain some 2,000 pages) than those of all the British writers on mercantilism together. The German writers come much nearer to giving us a homogeneous body of thought; if points of difference among the Germans may be identified as they have been in this chapter, it can scarcely be regarded as disagreement at all, whereas the British disagreed on many basic fundamentals in both theory and practice. The cameralists identified individual and state welfare, but the English did not believe them identical.

Additional points of similarity and dissimilarity could be pointed out; they are, however, the less important ones. Each scheme served a useful purpose in its time, and they should be viewed by the student as two of the most interesting examples of economic thought.

8

The Physiocrats and Their Doctrines

The first scientific school of economics developed in France about the middle of the eighteenth century as a result of intolerable political and economic conditions caused by many years of war and extravagance. The events of hundreds of years set the stage for the brief act known as physiocracy, which, short-lived as it was, left an indelible imprint on men's thought and actions thereafter. The "act" lasted for only about twenty years—1756 to 1778. In these few years a group of men wrote on a theme which minimized regulatory controls and maximized freedom. They believed there was a natural order which prevailed over all man's activities; the problem was to discover the natural order and then to conform to it; hence, the origin of the term "physiocracy" which means the "rule of nature." [1]

The Background of Physiocracy.—A complete description of the background of physiocracy would be, in reality, a political and social history of France. Therefore only a few of the most significant facts which led to the reform movement known as physiocracy can be presented.

In the previous chapter some of the efforts which were designed to keep France in the forefront with other mercantilistic states of Europe were explained. The measures of Colbert under Louis XIV and the schemes of Law had run their course. The monarchy was on the wane. The seventy-two-year reign of Louis XIV (1643-1715) had been marked by wars and extravagance with too few years of prosperity. His successor, Louis XV, ruled for fifty-nine years (1715-1774). The reigns of these two absolute monarchs covered a wide and most significant span of the world's history. Wars were waged with monotonous regularity, national boundaries were changed, colonies were won and lost. Finally, when national boundaries became more or less fixed, the conquests for colonial empire became the main *casus belli*. France lost great ele-

[1] The term "physiocracy" was first used by Du Pont de Nemours who wrote a book entitled *Physiocratie, ou constitution essentielle du gouvernment le plus avantageux au genre humain* (Paris, 1768).

121

ments of her colonial empire (such as Canada and India) and signed humiliating peace treaties. Practically everything she did as a nation contributed to her debts and insolvency. The ground was indeed fertile for the growth of ideas which promised relief from intolerable conditions.

There were few significant improvements over the years in public policy, but social, political, and intellectual changes were taking place which radiated from France throughout all Europe. These changes finally passed from theory to action and produced one of the greatest political explosions the world has seen—the French Revolution.

While progress in colonial growth and industrial and commercial expansion was being made in England, France continued to be primarily agricultural. By the middle of the eighteenth century France possessed the largest areas of fertile and productive land of western Europe. Agriculture was the leading occupation and the main source of royal revenue; yet, because the peasants were heavily burdened by taxation they were not prosperous.

The taxes were numerous and of long standing. The chief direct tax was the *taille*. In the south of France this tax was levied on lands and houses, but in other parts of the country it was levied upon the presumed fortune or wealth of the taxpayer, whatever its origin. It was arbitrarily imposed and had no rational basis for assessment. It fell upon the peasants, craftsmen, and bourgeoisie only; the nobles and clergy were exempt. It has been roughly estimated that the *taille* took as much as 50 percent of the entire earnings of the nonprivileged classes. The collection of taxes was "farmed out" to persons who paid the King a lump sum for the privilege of collecting them. In their effort to make a profit from collection of taxes they used many practices similar to those of the "publicans" of ancient Rome, who were denounced in the New Testament.

The *gabelle*, or salt monopoly, was one of the most grievous taxes. Every subject above the age of seven was legally obliged to purchase at least seven pounds of salt annually which could be used only for cooking or at the table. A heavy fine was imposed if this salt was used to preserve provisions. Agents were employed to apprehend anyone using contraband salt, which could easily be identified because of the inferiority of the government-monopolized salt. This tax was an important cause of hatred for all laws.

The *aides* were petty taxes levied upon commodities when manufactured, again when sold to the first handler, then when in transit and at every halting place in transit, and finally when they passed to the retailer. The tax frequently amounted to nearly as much as the price of the article. There was no uniformity in either the *aides* or the *gabelle* as they were levied.

The *traites* were customs duties levied on commodities passing between France and other countries and between certain provinces within France. Some of the duties were for protection to French industries, but most of them were for revenue. The most important of the *traites* was the one on grain. These duties, when applied, were in addition to seignorial and other taxes. Colbert remarked that goods in transit from the north of France to Spain paid four kinds of customs in addition to the other duties. The effect was that little export took place.

Both the nobles and the clergy were exempt from most taxes, the former allegedly paying to the King their blood, and the latter their prayers. These two groups, comprising about 600,000 in a total population of 25,000,000, were much more fortunate than the vast majority of the people. Approximately one fifth of the total land of France was owned by the clergy but in some provinces they held as much as two thirds. Besides the tithe, the "feudal rights" which the Church enjoyed brought a total revenue running into millions of dollars.[2]

In addition to the foregoing taxes, a peasant was charged for the use of roads and bridges and for the use of the local gristmill. His crops were ravaged by pigeons kept by the lord, and his growing grains ruined by the huntsmen. He was liable to a *corvée royale*, a payment in personal labor usually in the form of work on public roads, which was made a general obligation in 1738.

The craft guilds continued their medieval practices and claimed a membership reckoned at two and a half million, or roughly one tenth of the population. They held monopolistic advantages which tended to ruin competition and stifle initiative and production throughout the period. They were never really abolished by any governmental reforms; only the Revolution broke their grip.

The peasants, who were the backbone of France, had little chance to make the agricultural lands very productive. Nearly nine tenths of the population, or more than twenty-one million persons, lived by agriculture. About one million were legally serfs, whereas the remainder were considered "free." Of the total, only about five hundred thousand actually owned land. Most peasants worked for subsistence and a small wage. Some were *métayers*, who farmed land assigned to them by the owner on crop shares; they also shared in paying taxes which were enormous. Still others farmed small areas on which they paid a perpetual rent, in addition to their feudal dues. These were the unlucky

---

[2] It is estimated that the total revenues of the French Church amounted to $100,000,000 per year in 1789, or nearly one half as much as the total revenues of the state. W. S. Davis, *A History of France* (Boston, 1919), p. 257.

cens payers—probably the most unfortunate of all the peasants. The net result of all these levies was that the King, the priest, and the lord took around 75 percent of the total income of the average peasant.

There can be little doubt that this unhappy state of the vast majority of the population contributed greatly to the demands for reform. National extravagance increased the financial burdens upon the population; costly wars took a heavy toll in population and further increased the debts. The industry and commerce of France added little to national income, and over the years regulation, protection, and restriction of industry lost favor and finally became objects of attack. The policy of fostering manufacturing and trade, restricting markets, and granting special privileges at the expense of agriculture proved wrong. Agriculture in England during the eighteenth century was going through a revolution; it was regarded as the most efficient and progressive in Europe, and a significant cause for England's prosperity. This fact was known to many French writers and became a reason for breaking the prestige of mercantilism and concentrating their attention on agriculture.

Precursors of Physiocracy.—The reactions against the abuses in France were mild at first, both in criticism and in proposed reforms. Criticism of governmental practices under absolute monarchy was dangerous. One of the first to call attention to the deplorable conditions which prevailed and to suggest reforms was Pierre le Pesant Boisguillebert (1646-1714), whose primary concern was to reform the economic and fiscal system of Louis XIV. He pointed out [3] the misery of the people and the abuses in taxation. He urged reforms by use of direct instead of indirect taxes: he proposed that the *taille* be reformed and the *aides* and internal customs be replaced with a direct hearth tax. In *Le factum* he advocated a tax of one tenth of all incomes.[4] He regarded a supply of necessary goods as wealth. He favored bounties on the export of wheat and prohibition of the import of wheat. His proposals were to protect the agrarian interests; yet he saw a common purpose and harmony in the economy which would benefit everyone. For his liberal views he was rewarded with exile and disgrace.

Another keen observer who knew intimately the plight of the French citizen was Marshal Vauban (1633-1707), a great soldier under Louis XIV. In his long military career he had an opportunity to observe how wars and economic deterioration had brought about the plight of the

---

[3] *Détail de la France* (Rouen, 1696) and *Le factum de la France* (Paris, 1707) both published anonymously. They may be found in E. Daire, *Economistes financiers du XVIII siècle* (Paris, 1843).

[4] A. Dubois, *Précis de l'histoire des doctrines économiques* (Paris, 1903), pp. 309-13.

citizenry in all sections of the country. He wrote in 1707 his *Projet d'une dixme Royale* [5] in which he proposed to substitute a tithe upon all the classes and all kinds of revenue for the many other taxes then in force. This theory rested upon a conviction that all men were obligated to contribute to the support of the King in proportion to their income and industry. This meant, then, that every tax exemption was an abuse and an injustice.

Vauban's specific tax plan called for the abolition of all existing taxes except the import and export duties and the establishment of four "funds." The first was the "royal tenth," a tax in kind upon the gross produce of the soil at the rate of 5 percent. This was expected to produce about one half of the necessary revenues. Next was a tax on house rents, wages, government salaries, and commercial and industrial profits, ranging from 5 to 10 percent. Third, a universal but low salt tax. Finally, a sort of excise tax on tobacco, drinks, coffee, tea, and other minor revenue products. No sooner had these proposals, which appeared logical and simple, been made than the anger of the bureaucrats and the privileged classes was aroused: the former feared the loss of employment and the latter disliked being taxed with all others. Vauban "stigmatized luxury, privilege, public debts, and the farming of taxes; extolled labor, agriculture, and equality before the law." [6] He, like Boisguillebert, was denounced and dishonored. His book was suppressed but the ideas lived and had their part in attempted reforms which came later.

The Irish-born English banker, Richard Cantillon,[7] had a large part in providing original ideas not only for the physiocrats but for Adam Smith. Cantillon had banking houses in the principal cities of Europe and made a great fortune by speculation during Law's bank scheme in France. His work, *Essai sur la nature du commerce en général,* was published in 1755, twenty-one years after his death. The manuscript was known in France long before its publication, and the Marquis of Mirabeau, who had a copy, made the ideas of Cantillon the basis of much of the economics in his *L'Ami des Hommes* (1756), which had very great influence in the years before the Revolution. Cantillon's *Essai* furnished the physiocrats with many ideas which they put to use. Ideas of his which the physiocrats used dealt primarily with wealth, which he regarded as consisting of the comforts and conveniences of life, and land, which is the source of the materials from which wealth is drawn. "Land is the material, and labor is the form of all com-

[5] This work may also be found in E. Daire, *Economistes financiers du XVIII Siècle.*

[6] Henry Higgs, *The Physiocrats* (London, 1897), p. 13.

[7] Cf. Chapter 7, pp. 104-5.

modities and merchandise: and since those who work must necessarily live on the products of the land it seems as if we could find a relation between the value of labor and that of the produce of land." [8]

Mirabeau used the same idea when he wrote, "Like him [Cantillon] and so many others, I had reasoned as follows: Wealth is the fruit of the earth for the use of man. The labor of man alone has the power to increase it, hence the more men there are, the more labor there will be: and the more labor there is, the more wealth there will be." [9] Furthermore, "The multiplication of men is called population: the increase of the products of the earth is called agriculture. These two principles are intimately bound together." [10] Agriculture was the source of food for human beings and upon it depended the population and welfare of the country; thus, agriculture was of foremost importance. The work of Mirabeau, which was essentially that of Cantillon, attracted the attention of those who are regarded as founders of physiocracy. Cantillon, therefore, both directly and indirectly provided many of the ideas of physiocracy.

François Quesnay.—The real founder of the physiocratic school was François Quesnay.[11] His whole plan was built upon a concept of natural order. This meant that nature, antecedent to all human institutions, was the model to which mankind and all social classes should conform. The natural order was a providential plan, universal in its

---

[8] R. Cantillon, *Essai sur la nature du commerce en général* in A. E. Monroe, *Early Economic Thought* (Cambridge, Mass., 1924), p. 251.

[9] Georges Weulersse, *Le Mouvement physiocratique en France* (Paris, 1910), I, 54.

[10] *L'Ami des Hommes* (Paris, 1756), p. 13.

[11] François Quesnay (1694-1774) was born of peasant stock and spent the first seventeen years of his life on a farm near Paris. His education was gained largely by self-tutoring; at the age of twenty-five he had qualified as a surgeon. Because of defective eyesight he turned from surgery to medicine and gained sufficient reputation in that field to secure an appointment (1749) as court physician to Madame de Pompadour, and later to Louis XV. His first publications were in the field of medicine: *Observations sur les effets de la saignée* (1730), in which he opposed bleeding to cure ills; *Essay physique sur l'économie animale* (1736); *Traité de la suppuration* (1749); and *Traité des fièvres continues* (1753). These works show his great faith in the healing power of nature. His convictions on the powers of nature plus his knowledge of the circulation of the blood (discovered by Harvey in 1616), together with his early farm experience, materially influenced his thinking and writing. His first economic writings, published in the *Grande Encyclopédie*, were entitled "Fermiers" (Vol. VI, 1756) and "Grains" (Vol. VII, 1757), both over the signature of his son. He felt that his official position restrained him from taking a public stand on governmental matters. His crowning work, *Tableau Oeconomique* (1758) was published when he was sixty-four years of age. His last work, which is a further development of the *Tableau*, was *Maximes générales du Gouvernement économique d'un Royaume agricole* (1760). His writings were not numerous but his influence was disproportionately great. His followers who composed the physiocratic school were: Mirabeau the Elder, who was his first convert (1757); in the next decade, he

scope, and faultless; it implies duties as well as rights, order, and system. Man's duty therefore is to embrace the obvious rules of nature, which will afford him the fullest self-expression and happiness. This is also his natural right. When men violate the laws of the social order, which are equally natural, they destroy themselves; when they conform to the natural order, they secure the greatest benefits.

The natural order could, therefore, be applied to the relation of the state to trade and industry. Production and distribution of goods should be in accord with the fixed laws of nature and not interfered with by government restrictions. In the natural order everything was perfect and its laws were the will of God; this is in contrast with the "positive order"—such as prevailed in the government of France—which was imperfect and unnatural. The government, a necessary evil, should protect life, liberty, and the property of the individual; but the individual, knowing his own interests best, would act in conformity with the laws of nature.

The rights of the individual were to be protected by an absolute state, but its absolutism would be tempered by enlightened public opinion which would prevent infractions of the natural laws. This provided the inspiration for Quesnay's reply to the Dauphin, who complained of the difficulties of being a King. "I do not see," said Quesnay, "that it is so troublesome." "What then would you do if you were King?" "Nothing," Quesnay replied. "Then who would govern?" To this Quesnay replied, "The law!" [12] This law was the law that divinely and automatically guides mankind and supersedes all positive law. The concept of natural law furnished the basis for the theory which lies behind the famous motto, "laissez faire, laissez passer." [13]

was joined by Du Pont de Nemours (1763); Mercier de la Rivière (1767), Turgot, Badeau, Le Trosne, and others of minor importance. To Quesnay, however, belongs the major share of the honor of establishing the first school of economics.

In their day the group was known as "les économistes." Du Pont's book, *Physiocratie, ou constitution essentielle du gouvernment le plus avantageux au genre humain* (1768), gave the later name, "Physiocracy," which means the "rule of nature," to the group. When the term "economist," used in a generic sense, became common writers dropped the older designation and began using the term "physiocrats" to identify Quesnay and his followers.

[12] Higgs, *op. cit.*, p. 45.

[13] Du Pont attributes the origin of the maxim to Gournay. Turgot, in his *Elogé de Gournay*, attributes the famous maxim to Le Gendre, a merchant who attended a deputation to Colbert about 1680 to protest against excessive state regulation of industry and pleaded for liberty of action in the phrase "Laissez-nous faire." Oncken thinks the credit should go to the Marquis d'Argenson, who employed the term in his *Mémoires* as early as 1736. The entire phrase is "Laissez faire et laissez passer: le monde va de lui-même." See Oncken, *Die Maxime Laissez-faire* (Berne, 1886); Higgs, *op. cit.*, p. 67; C. Gide and C. Rist, *History of Economic Doctrines* (New York, 1915), p. 11, note.

It appears very paradoxical that the state could be an absolute monarchy and still follow a "hands off" policy as the scheme required.

Agriculture and the Net Product.—The physiocrats made land the most important agent in production. Labor, when applied to land, was capable of producing a surplus or "net product." No other industry such as commerce, transportation, or manufacturing could produce a surplus and was, therefore, regarded as "sterile." But Quesnay held the view that commerce, as a mere branch of agriculture, could be considered as a source of wealth. Only agriculture (probably including mining and fishing and raw material production in general) brings in a return greater than the amount expended and leaves a surplus or clear net gain, which is no other man's loss.[14] To Quesnay the farmer was not a manual laborer but the entrepreneur who employed, organized, and directed agricultural production. Agriculture, therefore, should be the chief concern not only of the farmer-entrepreneur but of the entire nation. It was to the best national interest that agriculture be encouraged and promoted, hence, all obstructions should be removed. There should be free export of grains and raw materials. Good prices should prevail to encourage further cultivation, which would provide more food, thus aiding to increase and support the population that would assure a market for the produce of the basic industry, agriculture. Since no other endeavor but agriculture would yield a net product the whole economy and civilization itself were dependent upon it. Du Pont made the extreme statement that "the prosperity of mankind is bound up with a maximum net product." [15]

The sterile classes are those not engaged in raw material production but who draw their incomes from the productive classes. The manufacturer does nothing but give new form to materials extracted from the earth; the value which he adds in manufacture represents only the quantity of materials used in putting the product in final form. Those engaged in commerce do no more than transfer already existing wealth; the gains or profits made by the trading classes are but an appropriation of that which rightfully belongs to the nation and should therefore be as small as possible. The manufacturer, the merchant, and those in the professions render "useful" services but as a group they are "sterile." Their incomes are drawn from the surplus earned by agriculture (under the guidance of the farmer-entrepreneur) and not from any income which they themselves create. This unfair and erroneous position drew sharp criticisms, but Gide and Rist say, "the Physiocrats had the good sense to try to give an explanation of this unfortunate

14 "Grains," *Grande Encyclopédie*, VII, 820.
15 Du Pont, *De l'origine et des progrès d'une science nouvelle* (Paris, 1768), p. 346.

term [sterile class], which threatened to discredit their system altogether, and which seemed unfair to apply to a whole class that had done more than any other towards enriching the nation." [16]

Physiocratic Ideas on Trade.—Since trade and commerce loomed so large in the mercantilistic doctrines which the physiocrats opposed, some attention should be given to the physiocrats' ideas on trade. Basically, they held that all exchange, foreign or domestic, was unproductive, for it was but an exchange of equal values. This was in sharp contrast to the concept of the mercantilists, who held that trade and commerce were the only means of increasing the wealth of the nation. Yet the physiocrats were obliged to admit that some foreign trade in raw materials was a necessary evil.

The physiocrats were, by direct and indirect statements, critical of the methods used by European governments in dealing with trade and commerce, and even industry. The policies of Colbert, which may have had temporary value, were abused, discredited, and condemned by the physiocrats. Yet it is paradoxical that, in condemning legislative restrictions and the illusory benefits of trade, the physiocrats should become champions of free trade. They did not admit that nations could gain by free exchange of goods, yet the philosophy of laissez faire demands free trade. Gide and Rist explain the physiocrats' position as follows: "It is a noteworthy fact that they are to be regarded as the founders of Free Trade, not because of any desire to favor trade as such, but because their attitude towards it was one of disdainful laissez faire." [17] In order to be consistent they had to favor both domestic and foreign free trade. The abolition of restrictions would naturally lead to free trade.

The *Tableau économique*.—The physiocratic conception of the circulation of wealth or goods was presented schematically in the *Tableau économique*.[18] Starting with the assumption that the annual average net disposable income of landed proprietors which they receive as rent for one year is $2,000 (dollars are used in place of livres as appears in the *Tableau*), the sum would be distributed as follows:

[16] *Op. cit.*, p. 14.
[17] *Ibid.*, p. 29.
[18] The *Tableau* was prepared by Quesnay and copies were privately printed in the palace at Versailles in 1758. It was believed lost until 1890, when a copy was found among the manuscripts of Mirabeau in the National Archives in Paris, and it was reproduced by the British Economic Association in 1894. The *Tableau* has been reproduced in Oncken's *Geschichte der Nationalökonomie*, Vol. I, p. 394. The Oncken reproduction appears in A. Gray, *The Development of Economic Doctrines* (New York, 1931), p. 107. A verbal description probably gives the best explanation of the *Tableau*.

1) $1,000 would go back to the farmers who supply the means of subsistence and the other $1,000 would go to trade and industry for purchases.

2) The $1,000 which went to the farmers would be used "productively," thus creating $2,000, one half of which is a reproduction of the original $1,000 which goes back to the landowners, and the other half ($1,000), a 100 per cent profit, goes to the agriculturalists.

3) Of the $1,000 now in the hands of the agriculturalists, $500 is consumed by them and $500 goes to industry for the purchase of products.

4) The $500 which goes to industry, being a sterile expenditure (mainly for wages), is not doubled but is reproduced.

5) Of the $500 now in the hands of industry one half ($250) goes to buy industrial products for consumption by the industrialists themselves and the other half ($250) they spend for agricultural products.

6) The $250 now in the hands of the agriculturalists will again double itself; one half ($250) will go to the landowners, and the remainder ($250) will again be halved as before—one part going to industry and the other back to agriculture.

This process goes on until the amounts passing to each group become negligible. The amount spent by the landowners ($1,000, which is the net surplus to agriculture) on purchases from the industrialists would take the same pattern as that spent by the agriculturalists on purchases from the industrialists. The process could be repeated over an indefinite period of time with the same results—a net surplus to agriculture. The *Tableau* is based upon an assumption that each group will spend one half of what it receives upon the other two groups.[19] Should they not spend this amount, then the net disposable income for all would decline. If they expended more than one half, the proper shares would not be returned to perpetuate production. The former would make for a progressive decrease in the wealth of the state, and the latter would seriously menace it. The exact balance of expenditures was absolutely necessary.[20]

---

[19] They were (1) the productive class consisting entirely of agriculturalists; (2) a proprietary class to whom the net product is paid; (3) the sterile (unproductive) class of merchants and manufacturers, servants, and members of professions. Strictly speaking there is a fourth class of wage-earners, but they claim little notice.

[20] Quesnay cites eight obstacles which prevent the working of the balance and bring about the decay of an agricultural nation:
1) Bad forms of taxation, bearing upon the capital of cultivators
2) Excessive costs of collection of taxes
3) Excessive luxury of decoration
4) Excessive expense in litigation
5) Lack of export trade in raw materials
   (*Footnote continued on next page*)

It should be noted that the proprietary or landowner class was held in highest esteem, since private property was one of the fundamental bases on which the natural order rested. This class was really the dispenser of wealth. The physiocrats justified the private ownership of land on the basis of the original cost of clearing or draining the land. Because of this expenditure of labor and capital the proprietary class had a real part in making land usable, and thus they acquired a prior and superior right even above the real cultivators of the land. They are, therefore, entitled to the entire net product, but it also falls upon them to bear the whole burden of taxation.

The persons who cultivate the soil were regarded as the only truly productive class. They cooperate with nature, but it is really nature that produces wealth. This class ranks above the artisans who do nothing more than earn subsistence but create no surplus. Nor does the merchant, manufacturer, professional man, or domestic servant create any surplus. It follows then, that members of the unproductive classes are maintained by the cultivation of the land.

The *Tableau* rests upon assumptions which are highly unreal. In fact, the assumptions are more mystifying than the mechanics of the table itself. The category of sterile groups is as arbitrary as are the assumptions of how much any group purchases from another. The *Tableau* does, however, show that Quesnay had a comprehensive view of the interrelationships of different economic groups in society. He applied the biological fact of the circulation of the blood to the economic system in his attempt to show that wealth could freely circulate in a system if unobstructed by artificial barriers.

Regardless of the qualifications and the peculiarities of the scheme, the physiocrats were interested in maximizing the rate of increase in their national wealth. The prosperity of the country, they believed, depended (1) upon the size of the disposable revenue, or surplus over production costs, which was yielded by agriculture and (2) upon the proportion of this net revenue which was annually converted into capital. Since agriculture was the only employment that yielded a net product, the welfare of the entire nation depended upon it. The value of the net product was computed not only upon the physical productivity of the land, but also on the market value of the physical product. Thus the higher the price of the grain the greater would be the net product. Emphasis was therefore placed on raising the prices of commodities so that they bring a *bon prix* to the producer. A good price

6) Lack of freedom in (*a*) internal trade in raw materials, and (*b*) cultivation
7) Personal harassing of the country people
8) Lack of return of the annual *product net* to the category of productive expenses
See Higgs, *op. cit.*, pp. 40-41.

would thus increase the net product and national prosperity. Freedom of trade was the first step in the direction of raising prices.

The second aspect dealt with investment and consumption of net revenue, for this was of greatest importance. In this connection they developed their *théorie du luxe* which dealt with expenditures. The most desirable expenditure was a reinvestment of funds into agriculture, which was regarded as a productive capital outlay. However, expenditures which dissipated the net product and thus deprived agriculture of capital were basically wrong. Excessive spending on consumption goods was, in general, contrary to the best interests of the economy; however, if agriculture was flourishing then some money might be so used after the capital reinvestment had been made. If agriculture was in a depressed state, then the fund should go only to improvement of the land, and anyone who spends on consumption in the form of luxury, display, or extravagance, commits a crime against the state.

These rather arbitrary rules were developed by Baudeau in 1767 [21] for the purpose of explaining what was productive and what was unproductive expenditure of the net product. The doctrine led some to contend that the physiocrats supported an underconsumption theory. Such views were held by Malthus, Sismondi, James Mill, and other writers of the nineteenth century,[22] but with little justification.

The Physiocratic Theory of Taxation. Since taxation was in effect a national "scourge" on the French economy, the physiocrats were concerned with its reform. They wished to simplify the taxes and at the same time put the burden on those who had the ability to pay. They did not advocate abolition of taxes, but they believed that generous tax funds could and would be available under their scheme.

The tax scheme is rather intricately tied up with the three groups— the landlord, the farmer, and the artisan—the net product, and the state. Since the state has responsibilities which require funds, then the funds must come from the *produit net,* for according to the physiocrats there is no other source from which the funds could come. Taxes levied on any base other than the net product would affect the sources which create wealth and ultimately destroy them. If taxes were levied upon the farmers, or cultivator class, they would not get the full amount due them (according to the *Tableau*) and the succeeding product would be diminished; this in turn would impoverish the other classes, or the farmers would pay less to the proprietary class whose income is, in reality, the net product. If taxes were levied on the artisan (or sterile)

---

[21] Abbé Baudeau, *Principes de la science morale et politique sur le luxe et les loix somptuaires* (1767), pp. 14-32.
[22] See R. L. Meek, "Physiocracy and the Early Theories of Under-consumption," *Economica* (August, 1951), pp. 229-69.

classes, they in turn would buy less from the cultivators—thus diminishing the amount the cultivators had to spend—or cause an increase in prices of products they have to sell; taxes levied on either of these classes would ultimately shift the tax back to the proprietary class.

The proprietary class, however, would be able to pay the taxes for it was to them alone that the net product, the only truly dispensable wealth, flowed. They enjoyed the protection of the state and were indeed held in high esteem, primarily because of the significance attached to the ownership of land. The proprietary owner was regarded as a co-owner with the state or sovereign of the land he cultivated; the proprietor of the land made the original improvements in the land necessary to bring it into cultivation. The state, in turn, did its part in protecting the owner of the private property and in building roads, bridges, and the like which were essential to agriculture. The interests of the state (or sovereign) and the people were the same. There was no desire on the part of the physiocrats to rob the proprietary class (or the landed gentry) of their incomes. The physiocrats desired to protect the capital investment in the original land which took the form of preparing the soil for cultivation or improving the land. In fact, they sought to make land ownership and cultivation more attractive. They had no fear of overpopulation on the land, for nature, which had limited the amount of land, would also limit the number of landowners.

The physiocrats arrived at the conclusion that the net product should and could provide the necessary revenues; hence, they proposed the *impôt unique* or single tax on the true net product. They held that the misery of the nation was due to great inequalities in the burden of taxation; this would be rectified by abolition of all taxation except the single tax levied upon the products of land, a tax which should not exceed one third (Baudeau estimated 30 per cent) of the net product. The single tax appeared adequate to them to meet all fiscal needs; it was simple, direct, inexpensive to collect, and above all a really burdenless tax. They were sure that under their enlightened plan the economy would prosper, the net product would increase, and the tax return would grow proportionately. They expected the extravagances of the state to diminish and the needs of the state to be adjusted to the revenues, not vice versa. The actual results will be discussed later in an evaluation of physiocracy.

Other Members of the School. The first convert and, in fact, a co-developer of physiocratic doctrines was Mirabeau the Elder. His first work, *L'ami des hommes*, contained basic economic ideas which were later incorporated into physiocracy, but the book is not, strictly speaking, a work on physiocracy.[23]   However, his *La Théorie de l'impôt* (Paris(?), 1760) and *La Philosophie rurale* (Paris, 1763) are physiocratic tracts. The former was a severe attack upon the administration of national finances, especially upon the parasitic tax collectors.   He advocated simple, direct, and lighter taxes, as well as a reduction in the salt tax. He also attacked the right of the King to collect taxes from his subjects without their consent and, by inference, really challenged the right of the King to rule.   He aroused the anger of the tax-collecting interests (the farmers-general), who denounced him and his book; they were the ones responsible for sending Mirabeau into prison for a brief time and into exile from Paris to his country home at Bignon.

La Philosophie rurale can be considered the most complete statement of physiocratic principles.   It is probable that Quesnay inspired the work and wrote at least a part of it.   Mirabeau wrote many other works,[24] some of which were published anonymously or under the pseudonym of L.D.H. (L'Ami des Hommes).   Through his numerous writings he spread physiocratic doctrines more extensively than any other person.

One of Mirabeau's early converts to physiocracy was Du Pont de Nemours, who joined the ranks in 1763.[25]   He contributed little to the general principles of physiocracy but as a propagandist of the doctrines his contributions were great.   One of his tracts provided the name for

[23] In Part I of the book he argued for an increase in small peasant farms; in Part IV he presented "l'Explication du Tableau économique," or an exposition of its workings.

[24] Notably, *Les Economiques* (2 vols., Amsterdam, 1769-71); and *Lettres Economiques* (Paris(?), 1770).

[25] Pierre Samuel du Pont de Nemours (1739-1817) was born in Paris and died near Wilmington, Delaware.   He had an active public life, having served as member of the States-General and as president of the National Assembly.   He was an aide to Turgot during the latter's brief period in office (1774-1776).   He helped negotiate with the English commissioner recognition of the independence of the United States (1782) and to prepare a treaty of commerce with Great Britain (1786).   He also served as councillor of state and commissionary-general of commerce.   He sided with the King (1792) and was obliged to go into hiding.   Finally he was arrested and imprisoned, barely missing execution on the guillotine.   After the republican triumph in 1797 his house was sacked by a mob; in 1799 he migrated to the United States, where he remained until 1802.   While he was here, Thomas Jefferson asked him to prepare a plan for national education; the report, published in 1800, was entitled *Sur l'éducation nationale dans les Etats-Unis d'Amérique.*   The report was not used; however, many of his own as well as physiocratic ideas influenced early American statesmen.   He returned to France in 1802 and in 1814 he became secretary to the provisional government under Louis XVIII.   He came back to America in 1815 upon the return of Napoleon and took up his residence near the Swedish settlement at Wilmington, Delaware.   He is the founder of the Du Pont family which has made a powder mill grow into a great industrial empire.   For an excellent biography see G. Schelle, *Du Pont de Nemours et l'école physiocratique* (Paris, 1888).

the school. He presented a clear statement of physiocratic doctrines in his *De l'origine et des progrès d'une science nouvelle* (Paris, 1768). During the brief years of his association with Quesnay and physiocracy he devoted his efforts to popularizing and bringing about an appreciation of the principles; in this he met considerable success.

Another person sometimes considered a cofounder of the school was Gournay (1712-1759). He translated and popularized the reading of certain English works, notably those of Child (*A New Discourse of Trade*) and Cantillon (*Essay on the Nature of Commerce in General*). Gournay was a liberal who directed his arguments against the industrial regulations of mercantilism. He pleaded for freedom from medieval and bureaucratic practices and urged acceptance of the new philosophy —"laissez faire, laissez passer." He recognized the importance of industry and commerce as well as of agriculture. In this he differed from Quesnay. He did, however, give attention to scientific methods in agriculture and did much to encourage it. While he believed in the removal of regulations, he was not as ardent a free trader as the other physiocrats; he favored free trade within the state but held that protection might be necessary to defend domestic enterprise from foreign competition. His contribution was to the general cause of economic freedom and reform more than to specific physiocratic doctrines.

Another person of great importance was Robert Jacques Turgot (1727-1781) who, as a statesman, had an opportunity to apply some of the physiocratic doctrines. His first economic tract was a criticism of Law's paper money scheme. From 1761 to 1774 he was *intendant* of the poverty-stricken city of Limoges, where he introduced reforms that gained him a reputation and later an appointment (1774-1776) as comptroller-general of France under Louis XVI. His local reforms included improvement in tax collection and abolition of the corvée on roads; he had the work done by hired workmen who were paid from general taxes. He facilitated the grain trade and introduced freedom of enterprise as well as educational and charitable reforms.

In his capacity as comptroller-general he applied his reforms to all of France with considerable success despite much opposition. He succeeded in curing, for a brief time at least, some of the long-standing abuses and excesses. Special privileges of the gilds and monopolies were abandoned. He eliminated the corvée everywhere and introduced measures permitting the free circulation of grain throughout France, despite the resistance of Parliament and the privileged groups. He tried to get taxes levied uniformly on all groups—a method which, he held, would be more fruitful than any increase in taxes on a few.

Turgot's reforms were short-lived; he was dismissed in 1776 after serving less than two years; his reform measures were revoked as soon as he was dismissed. Had he been given an opportunity to effectuate his reforms, they might have prevented bankruptcy of the *ancien régime*.

His greatest contribution to economic literature was his *Réflexions sur la formation et la distribution des richesses*, published first in *Ephémérides* in 1769-70 and later in book form in 1776.[26] This work ranks him along with Quesnay as a scientific expositor of the principles of political economy. Cossa says, "This work states in clear and taking form the common doctrines of the Physiocrats, but it also marks a step forward in the history of our science, since Turgot achieved in it a complete separation of economics from jurisprudence. It therefore deserves to be entered in red-letter, as the first scientific treatise on social economics."[27] Professor Ingram says, "The treatise, which contains a surprising amount of matter in proportion to its length, must always retain a place among the classics of the science."[28]

The *Réflexions* consists of short, numbered sections in which Turgot presents the fundamentals of political economy as conceived by the physiocrats. In addition he discusses land and its productivity, money and capital in industry and enterprise, the influence of the rate of interest, the circulation of money, and so on.[29]

Turgot cannot be regarded as a true physiocrat. He never was quite willing to accept the *produit net* as a return to land alone or to admit that all classes except farmers were sterile producers. Although he may be regarded as a disciple of Quesnay, he was not a member of the school, which he referred to contemptuously as a "sect." Mirabeau never regarded him as an ardent disciple of the school.[30]

Value and Distribution Theories.—Despite their interest in securing a good price for their agricultural products, the physiocrats showed little interest in a value concept. Turgot showed some interest in value which hinged, in reality, on utility. In comparing two goods he pointed

[26] English translation as *Reflections on the Formation and the Distribution of Riches*, "Economic Classics," ed. by W. J. Ashley (New York, 1898).

[27] L. Cossa, *Introduction to the Study of Political Economy* (London, 1893), p. 264.

[28] J. K. Ingram, *History of Political Economy* (London, 1923), p. 67.

[29] A. E. Monroe, *Early Economic Thought*, presents selected sections from the *Réflexions* in chap. xv.

[30] Other physiocrats of more or less importance were: Mercier de la Rivière (1720-1794), who wrote an important treatise, *L'Ordre naturel et essentiel des sociétés politiques* (1767). His work was an attempt to create a philosophy of the state which rested upon nature's plan. The welfare of all was bound up in the plan of nature; therefore the discovery and application of the laws or plan would bring happiness to áll. Abbé Baudeau (1730-1792) and Le Trosne (1728-1780) both contributed to the general cause of physiocracy, viz., a new social order based upon natural laws, freedom of trade, and reform in general.

out that values were not fixed but changed from one moment to another, depending upon need. Exchange resulted from the different position of the consumer in relation to the availability of commodities. Turgot came near to expressing a utility theory of value, but his attention, like that of the other physiocrats, was occupied with production. They did, however, see the difference between value in use (*usuelle*) and value in exchange (*vénale*), but price and value were treated as one, for as Quesnay said, "What is called value is price." They were concerned with exchange value yet they did not explain it. Presumably, goods were exchanged at equal value, each commodity being the measure of value of the one for which it exchanged. Value was not inherent in goods but it reflected a quantitative market ratio. The products of agriculture were presumed to sell at a *bon prix* but the products of industry were to sell at a *bon marché*, or, agricultural products were to bring a good selling price but products of industry were to be sold at a cheap price to the consumer. Quesnay held a concept of price based upon the expenses of production set by competition, which he called *prix fondamental*, but what composed production cost or what constituted competition was not explained. He also implies a supply and demand relationship when he refers to the competition of buyers' and sellers' influence on *prix courant* or market price. Traces may also be found of a natural price. None of the ideas are sufficiently well developed to permit a claim to any theory of value.

The physiocrats regarded rent as a "providential surplus" accruing to the landowners. Their scheme provided a larger return from labor when applied to land, than in any other employment; the return, however, went to the owners of land. Labor received its wage—a subsistence payment—and the surplus created by labor when applied to land was held to be owed to the land (and the landowners) and not to labor in the form of a wage. The *Tableau* provided for restoration of the original capital to which is added the subsistence wages, and the remaining surplus was rent. (No provision was made for a deficit.)

Turgot implies a differential surplus theory when he says,

the competition of rich entrepreneurs in agriculture establishes the current price of leases in proportion to the fertility of the land and the price at which its produce sells, always according to the estimates which the farmers make of all their expenses and the profit they should make on their advances; they can pay the Proprietor only the surplus.

But when competition between them is very keen, they pay him all their surplus, the Proprietor leasing his land only to the one who offers the highest rent.[31]

---

[31] *Reflections on the Formation and the Distribution of Riches*, sec. lxiii, p. 56.

He treats the return to land as comparable with the rate of return obtainable on other capital investments. Any return above this rate goes to the owner of land as rent, which in turn depends upon the competition for leases. The entrepreneur (or farmer) could not afford to pay more than the surplus. He held that a surplus would accrue only to land; neither labor nor capital created a surplus.

Capital and interest per se did not receive any significant treatment by the school. Turgot, although not a "member in good standing," showed a comprehensive understanding of capital and interest. In his *Reflections* he regards capital as being as necessary for enterprise as labor and skill; money he considers "a principal means for saving small gains, accumulating profits, and becoming rich . . ." It is not the quantity of money but the quantity of capital which affects interest rates. Capital included commodities not required for immediate consumption or money which could be used in the purchase of commodities. The rate of interest then depended upon the "relation between the demand of the borrowers and the offer of the lenders: this relation depends principally upon the quantity of movable riches accumulated, by the saving of revenues and annual products to form capitals, whether these capitals exist in money or any other kind of property having a value in commerce." The supply-demand relationship is emphasized by the statement, "It is these accumulated savings that are offered to borrowers, and the more there are of them the lower is the rate of interest, at least if the number of borrowers is not augmented in proportion." [32]   The capacity of the people to increase the amount of capital and thereby bring about a fall in interest rate was due to the fact that the "spirit of economy has been more general than the spirit of luxury" over Europe, a tendency which he approved. Turgot also believed that some loans should yield a higher interest rate than others, because of risk; yet despite the difference in yields on various investments, the rates tended toward a kind of equilibrium level.

In general the theories were suggestive of later developments, but not sufficiently developed to endure. Their development was incidental to the larger objectives of physiocracy.

Critics of Physiocracy.—The physiocrats reached the peak of their influence about 1767, after which a decline caused by many factors set in. In the first place, the whole concept of the *produit net* as a cure-all for the ills of French taxation was not accepted. The group depended upon rather active propaganda to enlist popular support, but their

---

[32] *Ibid.*, sec. lxxx. pp. 78-79

periodicals were short-lived.[32] The reforms which the physiocrats proposed were unpopular with many groups and so they never succeeded in gaining a wide following. Their ideas of the state, which provided for absolute monarchy, were most unpopular in the face of the rising tide of liberal political thought. The bourgeoisie disliked the plan, for they saw in it heavier rather than lighter taxes. The manufacturing and commercial interests disliked the lower role assigned to them. A crop failure in the summer of 1776, after an edict providing for free grain trade with foreign countries, was almost disastrous. The people put the blame for the rise in the price of grain upon the edict rather than upon the crop failure, and the physiocrats were the ones accused of passing the edict. Turgot was the only one among the physiocrats in a position to initiate the reforms, and his efforts during his less than two years in office were not lasting.

In the meantime, strong antiphysiocratic influences were at work. The physiocratic ideas were severely attacked by François de Forbonnais (1722-1800), who wrote *Elémens du commerce* (2 vols., 1754; 3d ed., 1767); this contains a severe criticism of the *Tableau économique* and the articles "Fermiers" and "Grains." He denies that trade and industry are sterile, doubts the validity of the *produit net* and the value of *impôt unique*, and objects to free trade. His ideas are sane and moderate. Like the physiocrats he objected to exemptions and special privileges, especially in taxation. He attacked court extravagance and recommended a graduated tax on land as being more reasonable than attempting to make it bear the entire burden. He retained a strong mercantilistic taint in defending a favorable balance of trade but advocated a limited amount of state regulation. His attitude toward the physiocrats is shown in the following: "Metaphysicians," he wrote, "intoxicated with their subtleties, are too hasty in claiming haughtily that the world can be governed by syllogisms. That is what we call in our day seeing things on a big scale. . . . The exalted imagination finally bends the exactitude of the facts under the yoke of abstractions which are more hollow than profound." [34]

Another very severe critic was the Abbé de Mably (1709-1785), who ridiculed the whole plan (*Doutes sur la théorie de l'impôt*, 1761), espe-

---

[32] The physiocrats relied upon a periodical to spread their views. They issued a *Journal de l'Agriculture* and later the *Ephémérides*. The *Journal* was their organ from September, 1765, to November, 1766; then in January, 1767, the *Ephémérides* supplanted it as the organ of the school; it was discontinued in September, 1772. In later years (1775-1783) attempts were made to revive the journals but with little success. See M. J. Wasserman and J. D. Tate, "The Citizens Ephémérides of the Physiocrats," *Quarterly Journal of Economics*, LXV (August, 1951), pp. 439-43.

[34] G. Weulersse, *Le mouvement physiocratique en France* (Paris, 1910), I, 151-52.

cially that China should provide any prototype for the schemes of physiocracy. (The Emperor of China was considered the sovereign who best represented the ideal physiocratic ruler.)

The school was attacked by Voltaire (1694-1774), whose criticism of the natural order and the single tax was very sharp. He changed his ideas somewhat in later years, partly because of his friendship and admiration for Turgot; however, he never embraced the entire teachings of the school, nor did he ever hold anything but deep hatred for Mirabeau, whom he regarded as a scoundrel and charged with "breathing a leper on the human race." [35]

The Abbé Galiani (1728-1787), a secretary to the Neapolitan embassy at Versailles, made the theories of the physiocrats appear dull and ridiculous.[36] He denied that land was the sole source of wealth. He showed that economic measures which were successful in England or Holland would not necessarily succeed in France. To prove his points he used the historical method effectively, showing great comprehension of the economies of the states of Europe. He attacked the excessive abstractions of the physiocrats as lacking all elements of reality when applied. His dialogues were very popular and evoked a storm of both praise and criticism. The physiocrats were so disturbed that they called upon their best journalistic talent to answer the attack; this was done by Du Pont, Baudeau, and de la Rivière. The government commissioned Morellet to reply to the Galiani arguments,[37] but he had little success. Galiani's arguments were devastating and logical and, above all, readable. His opposition to physiocracy was purely on reasonable and logical grounds. Probably no other critic did more harm to the physiocratic movement than the Abbé. He showed a comprehension of economic relationship hardly equalled by any writer up to that time.[38]

The Practical Significance of the Physiocrats.—The influence of the physiocrats is difficult to evaluate, mainly because it was more indirect

[35] See Louis de Loménie, *Les Mirabeau* (Paris, 1889), Vol. II, p. 266 n. For his excellent discussions of physiocracy see pp. 198-226 and 243-349.

[36] Galiani wrote *Dialogues sur le commerce des blés* (London, 1770), which was translated from the Italian by Diderot. He was a very witty writer who saw in physiocratic writings nothing but absurdity. He proposed that his own monument bear a Latin inscription stating that he had "wiped out the economists, who were sending the nation to sleep." He was in France only ten years, 1759 to 1769.

[37] *Réfutation* (London, 1770).

[38] Other critics of physiocracy whose blows were more or less effective were Graslin (1727-1790), whose criticism of the *impôt unique* was very sharp; and Necker (1732-1804), a bitter opponent of Turgot and his successor as director-general of finance. He shows his neomercantilistic thought in his *Eloge de Jean Baptiste Colbert* (Paris, 1773). His antiphysiocratic convictions were recorded in his work *Sur la législation et le commerce des grains* (Paris, 1775). The physiocrats always regarded him as a formidable adversary.

than direct. The ideas were not applied by Turgot, the only minister who might have made some application of them.[39] It is likewise doubtful whether he, or anyone, could have applied them in view of the rising tide of revolt against absolutism in government, which was the form of government the physiocrats deemed essential to their scheme. It appears that no one except the tax collectors objected to tax reform, yet the physiocrats could reform taxes only by a complete adoption of their scheme, which was never done.

The indirect influence of the physiocrats is significant. They showed the interdependence of all groups in an economic society. The comparison of the flow of wealth within the economic system to the circulation of blood in the anatomy showed a dynamic concept of society. Using the same analogy, if money or wealth should flow out of the country with no inflow to compensate the loss, the state and society would suffer lasting damage. The laissez-faire philosophy was but a phase of popular revolt against tyranny applied to the economic system. The political laissez faire led to the overthrow of the monarchy and to the French Revolution. Many of the reforms advocated by the physiocrats were effected by the Revolution, but it would be a mistake to regard physiocracy as more than one of many factors that brought about the Revolution.

The general spirit of freedom which physiocracy breathed continued in other writers. Smith was influenced both by the men and their writings,[40] as were other classical economists, especially Malthus and Mill. Early American economists and statesmen, notably Franklin and Jefferson, were familiar with the school and its teachings. In France, however, physiocracy never attained much popular influence.

The physiocrats had some followers outside France. The Margrave of Baden, Carl Friedrich (1728-1811), joined the ranks and applied some of the theories in three cities of his duchy with questionable success. Gustavus III, King of Sweden, was interested in the scheme. The Grand Duke of Tuscany, Leopold III, afterwards Emperor of Austria, carried out some of the reforms. Stanislas of Poland, Charles III of Spain, Emperor Joseph II of Austria, and Catherine, Empress of Russia, all showed more or less interest in the scheme. They, like France, were looking for an easy way out of their troubles and at least showed a hopeful interest in the physiocratic schemes. The court at Versailles (especially the ladies) adopted physiocracy in that they even went so far

---

[39] See G. Weulersse, Les physiocrates sous le ministère Turgot (Paris, 192–).

[40] Smith would have dedicated the Wealth of Nations to Quesnay had the latter not died (1774) before the publication of the book. See Gide and Rist, History of Economic Doctrines, p. 3.

as to adopt peasant attire for a time at least. But more than court livery was required. As Gide and Rist say, "It may be that its [the court's] curiosity was aroused by that terse saying which Quesnay wrote at the head of the *Tableau économique: '*Pauvres paysans, pauvre royaume: pauvre royaume, pauvre roi!' " [41] Anything to help a losing cause!

An Evaluation of Physiocracy.—To contemporaries, physiocracy, like so many untried principles, meant all things to some and nothing to others. The same reaction is true to this day. Mirabeau could praise the *Tableau économique*, on which the scheme was built, as a discovery ranking along with the great discoveries of writing and money; yet to Galiani the whole thing was a ridiculous absurdity. Rousseau charged the physiocrats with supporting despotism; however, Voltaire held the scheme to be clear and easily comprehensible. Socialists, notably Proudhon, held it to be utopian, especially in tax reform, while Blanc saw in the advocacy of private property a trace of bourgeois individualism. Smith said the "system with all its imperfections is perhaps the nearest approximation to the truth that has yet been published upon the subject of political economy, and is, upon that account, well worth consideration of every man who wishes to examine with attention the principles of that very important science." [42] An interesting point of view is shown by a contemporary student,[43] who contends that they created a "complex system of socio-political thought to meet the agricultural problem of eighteenth century France and to serve the interest of a new class of commoner landowners." He believes that "their system of thought was not the product of 'pure' or even 'academic' reasoning but of class interest, which they conscientiously regarded as the interest of the nation as a whole." Each student of physiocracy may therefore enjoy the harmonious concert of a perfectly planned and well-ordered nature, or he may raise his blood pressure in pointing out the errors, false assumptions, and impracticalities of the school.

The fact remains, however, that the physiocrats founded the first school of political economy. Their errors were basic in that they assumed an entire system could be built upon a philosophy deduced from metaphysical "natural" laws which would lead to self-interest and bring about a harmonious development in economic life. The fundamental

---

[41] *Op. cit.*, p. 5.

[42] *Wealth of Nations*, ed. Edwin Cannan (2 vols., London, 1904), Bk. IV, chap. ix, p. 642.

[43] Norman J. Ware, "The Physiocrats: A Study in Economic Rationalization," *American Economic Review*, XXI, No. 4 (December, 1931).

notion that agriculture alone was productive was just as erroneous as the mercantilistic notion that commerce alone could make a nation prosperous. The *impôt unique* was not a single tax on land at all, but a tax upon surplus agricultural products. Could such a tax have been identified and taken by the state it would have relieved the burden which fell so heavily on the landed classes and the peasantry. The physiocrats can never be excused by even the mildest critic for identifying certain groups as unproductive or sterile. Nor can it be easily explained how they argued so vigorously for freedom yet defended absolute monarchy, special privileges, corporations, and certain monopolies.

The physiocrats did not understand the part played by money in a price structure. They understood money as a medium in exchanges but they did not appreciate its dynamic effects on prices. They held to none of the mercantilistic doctrines of precious metals and favorable trade balances, since they made the soil the source of wealth.

Their interest in the welfare of the masses may be challanged: they had to have a *bon prix* for the products of agriculture. It was pointed out that on one occasion the combination of a crop failure and an edict of Turgot brought about high bread prices and rioting. Quesnay, the leader of the school, said, "It is a great inconvenience to accustom the common people to buying wheat at too low a price; they become less laborious, they obtain bread at little cost, and become lazy and arrogant. Farmers have difficulty finding laborers and domestic servants, consequently they are very badly served in the abundant years." [44]   One of Quesnay's famous dicta in *Maximes* (XIX) reads, "One should not believe that the cheapness of agricultural products is profitable to the masses."

It is true that agriculture in France received some impetus from the physiocrats, especially from Turgot. The peasants shared in these and a few other of the reforms. Viewed in the light of the great political, economic, and social changes that came from the Revolution, they appear small indeed. Yet, objectively, the physiocrats were committed to bring about not only economic but also political and social reforms. Their program called for political action with a definite role assigned to the state. Their economics omitted many fundamentals.

It is possible to read into the numerous works of the physiocrats other ideas sacred to the folklore of economics, but the ideas were incidental to the larger objectives. It is perhaps more accurate to credit them with the systematization of ideas (however inaccurate), the

[44] "Grains," *Grande Encyclopédie*, VII, p. 302; see also E. Daire, *Physiocrates* (Paris, 1846).

development of the concept of free competition, and the recognition of the complete interdependence of all elements in an economy. These contributions were lasting; most of the other so-called contributions were of short duration. Their noble efforts in establishing economics as a science were completely eclipsed by Adam Smith's *Wealth of Nations.*

PART III

The Development of Classical Economics

9

Adam Smith and the Beginning
of Classical Tradition

The generic term "classical economics" has been applied to the body of doctrines developed in England by Adam Smith, Thomas Robert Malthus, David Ricardo, James Mill, John Stuart Mill, and J. E. Cairnes, whose work (1874) closed the classical epoch. (See p. 148.) Smith is commonly referred to as "founder of the classical school," because of the treatment of ideas contained in his great work *An Inquiry into the Nature and Causes of the Wealth of Nations*, published in 1776. Classical economics was an indigenous English product; however, it was not confined to its original locale—the British Isles. For example, in France, Jean Baptiste Say popularized and improved upon the general work in *Traité d'économie politique*, published in 1803. Classical economic doctrines [1] dominated the economic thought of the entire civilized world in the first half of the nineteenth century. In more or less modified form they still exercise influence upon economic thinking. The classical teachings have been rejected by some groups, modified and criticized by others. Some have used parts of the classical doctrines as foundations on which to build their theoretical edifices; others have used them as a base for critical departure and then proceeded to formulate their own theories.

In a sense the classical economists did not possess the characteristics of a school as did the physiocrats. Higgs identified the physiocrats as "an alliance of persons, a community of ideas, an acknowledged authority, and a combination in purpose, which banded them into a

---

[1] Karl Marx was the originator of the term "classical economics." "The analysis of commodities according to their two-fold aspect of use value and exchange value by which the former is reduced to work or deliberate productive activity; and the latter, to labor time or homogeneous social labor, is the result of a century and a half of critical study by the Classical school of political economy which dates from William Petty in England and Boisguillebert in France and closes with Ricardo in the former country and Sismondi in the latter." Karl Marx, *A Contribution to the Critique of Political Economy*, trans. N. J. Stone (Chicago, 1904), p. 56.

THE CLASSICAL SCHOOL

Timeline scale (top): 1700 — 1720 — 1740 — 1760 — 1780 — 1800 — 1820 — 1840 — 1860 — 1880

Predecessors

1670

x 1704
Bernard de Mandeville
Fable of the Bees
1731

1730
Richard Cantillon
x 1734
Essay on the Nature of Commerce in General (publ. 1755)

1694
François Quesnay
Tableau économique
1758   1766-9   1774
x   x   x
1727
Turgot
Réflexions
1781
x

1694
Francis Hutcheson
x 1746
Introduction to Moral Philosophy   A System of Moral Philosophy (1755)
1742
x   1752

1711
David Hume
x
Political Discourses
1776

Developers

1723
Adam Smith
x
1776
Wealth of Nations
1790

1748
Jeremy Bentham
Essayist, Utilitarian philosopher
1832

1766
An Essay on Population
1798
x
1820
x T. R. Malthus
1834
x
Principles of Political Economy

1772
David Ricardo
x 1823
On the Principles of Political Economy and Taxation
1817

1773
James Mill
x 1821
Elements of Political Economy
1836

1767
J. B. Say
x 1803
Traité d'économie politique
1832

Disciples

1790
N. W. Senior
x 1836
An Outline of Political Economy
1864

1806
John Stuart Mill
x 1848
Principles of Political Economy
1873

1820
John E. Cairnes
1874 1875
x
Some Leading Principles of Political Economy Newly Expounded
1863

1833
Henry Fawcett
x
1884
Manual of Political Economy

148

society apart." [2] This description appropriately characterizes the physiocrats as a "school" and, by definition, the only school of economists
that ever did exist. These criteria cannot be applied to the so-called
classical economists. Yet it is commonplace to speak of the "classical
school"—a term which carries with it the accepted meaning of a group
of writers whose thought is patterned on principles contained in Smith's
Wealth of Nations. His ideas provided the impetus for subsequent inquiries into all phases of economic life. And in most respects, the principles developed by the classical economists have furnished a point of
departure for all economics ever since 1776.

The Background of Classical Economics.—Classical economics was
not, like physiocracy, a product of desperation, born of a troubled and
disordered national economy. By accepted standards of evaluation,
England in the eighteenth century was economically far ahead of any
other European state. Her political position and her form of government were relatively secure, her colonial empire appeared to be permanent, her markets were lucrative, and her sources of raw materials
were adequate. The early practices of mercantilism had paid off very
well, and by the last quarter of the century that system was rapidly
giving way to more liberal views and practices. At least four of the
basic institutions of modern capitalism were firmly established; notably,
the corporation as a form of doing business, the capitalistic proprietor,
the wage system, and the commercial bank. The English had been
particularly successful in both the organization and management of
business; then, as improved technology in production came along, their
supremacy was virtually assured. The technological advances, notably
in textile manufacturing and metallurgical industries, together with the
application of water and steam power revolutionized production and
ushered in the era characterized as the Industrial Revolution.[3]

In agriculture there were marked improvements. The increase in
population, with the resulting pressure upon the food supply, hastened
the conversion of land from small tracts to large holdings, especially
in the last four decades of the century. This tended to establish a concentration of land in the hands of a few, the landlord class (against
whom Smith and Ricardo directed some sharp blows), to depopulate
the countryside, and to increase in the industrial cities the number of
those who became the wage-earning class. The land policy was not

---

[2] *The Physiocrats* (London, 1897), p. 3.
[3] The term was probably first used by Jerome Blanqui in 1837. Engels and Marx
also used it in 1845. Arnold Toynbee, the English economic historian, put the term
into academic circulation. For a splendid discussion of the era, see Herbert Heaton's
article, "Industrial Revolution" in the *Encyclopaedia of the Social Sciences* (New
York, 1933), VIII, 3-12.

wholly bad, for it permitted revolutionary improvements in both quantity and quality of grains and animals which may indeed be regarded as the beginning of modern scientific agriculture.

Commercial developments contributed to larger export and import trade. The increased demand for goods put heavy pressure upon the methods of production and hastened the technological advances. England's foreign trade made great strides in the eighteenth century.[4] In these hundred years the exclusive trading companies lost their commercial advantages, but the trade volume continued to increase. London, once the center of foreign trade, encountered competition from other ports such as Liverpool, Bristol, Edinburgh, and Glasgow. English ships enjoyed exclusive trade privileges with India and America and with all other British colonies. Many articles were re-exported from England to markets all over the world. There appeared to be no limit to which English trade and commerce could be expanded, except for the restraining measures which the English themselves placed on their own commerce. It was against these practices that Smith loudly protested, but not soon enough to prevent the war for independence in the English colonies in America.

These great economic changes were observed by Smith, for many of them occurred in his lifetime. However, greater changes, especially in technological methods of industrial production, took place after his day. Other English classical economists, notably Malthus (1766-1834) and Ricardo (1772-1823), lived during a period of even greater changes not only in the economic but in the political world as well. John Stuart Mill (1806-1873) wrote in 1848 the last of the books strictly patterned on traditional classical economic lines; by that time the Industrial Revolution in England had practically run its course. The span of years from 1776 to 1848 was indeed an eventful one. National states and political economy took definite forms which, aside from normal modifications, prevail to this day.

Adam Smith—The Formative Years, 1723-1751.—One who occupies a place in the development of a science as important as that of Adam Smith in economics deserves more than a brief biographical sketch. The following discussion, while by no means exhaustive, highlights the points of particular significance.

The formative years of Adam Smith's life, which for the present purpose are regarded as having ended in 1751 when he went to Glasgow as a teacher, are treated in some detail because a rather full account of this period of his career is essential to an understanding and interpretation

---

[4] The tonnage clearing her customs in 1800 amounted to 1,924,000 tons, compared with 311,000 tons in 1700.

of his writings. Some have said that there was nothing unusual in his life but this is not true; a man as important as Smith should be examined with some care in an effort to understand the circumstances of his education, what stimulated his efforts, his experiences, his associates, and all that had a bearing upon the great creative work which he produced. The significant influences after 1752 are interwoven with his experiences and writings.

Adam Smith [5] was born in 1723 at Kirkcaldy, Scotland, then a town of about 1,500 population on the north side of the Firth of Forth. His father, Adam Smith, was a man of some means, having held a number of appointive posts, including that of collector of customs at Kirkcaldy. The father died three months before his son and namesake was born; the mother, a talented woman, was left with the responsibility of his upbringing; her influence on her son was most pronounced throughout his life.

Kirkcaldy, though little more than a village, had considerable commerce and shipping: there were collieries and salt beds nearby, and the town had a nailery in which some division of labor was used in production. (Smith's observations of the nail-making process may have provided the ideas for his famous account of the division of labor illustrated in the manufacture of pins.) His mother's family were landholders in Fifeshire, and his frequent visits to relatives in the country may have awakened the interest in agriculture which is seen throughout his work. Thus the locale did bring to the youth something of the nature and influence of trade, commerce, and agriculture.[6]

His early education was obtained in the local schools, where he showed marked ability. By the age of fourteen he was sufficiently advanced in classics and mathematics to be sent to Glasgow College with a view to obtaining a Snell exhibition (or scholarship) at Balliol College, Oxford, as a means of preparing for the ministry.[7] From 1737 to 1740

[5] The materials used in presenting Adam Smith's life are taken primarily from the biography by John Rae, *Life of Adam Smith* (London, 1895); Dugald Stewart's *Biographical Memoirs of Adam Smith, LL.D.*, and his "Account of the Life and Writings of Adam Smith, LL.D." in Adam Smith, *Essays on Philosophical Subjects* (Dublin, 1795); R. B. Haldane's *Life of Adam Smith* (London, 1887); James Bonar, *A Catalogue of the Library of Adam Smith* (London, 1932); and the recent excellent work by W. R. Scott, *Adam Smith as Student and Professor* (Glasgow, 1937). Also H. C. Macpherson, *Adam Smith* ("Famous Scots Series," London, 1899).

[6] The present city of Kirkcaldy (pronounced "Kirk-cawdie"), of 50,000 inhabitants, has taken adequate measures to preserve the memory of its famous son. A metal plaque marks the birthplace. The Museum and Art Gallery houses some Smith relics as well as first editions of his books. The Adam Smith Hall is a center of cultural activities.

[7] Smith was one of five recipients of the Snell exhibition, which went to high-ranking students who planned to enter the ministry of the Episcopal Church of Scotland. The funds (£40 per student) were provided originally by a former Glasgow

he was a student in Glasgow College and he graduated with the M.A. degree; it was during these years that he came into contact with some fine scholars and teachers, including Francis Hutcheson, whose influence on Smith's thinking was pronounced and whose teachings were largely responsible for Smith's interest in economic subjects.

Smith left Scotland for Oxford in 1740, riding the four hundred miles on horseback. He told a friend many years afterwards that he was struck from the moment he crossed the border with the richness of the English countryside and the great superiority of England's agriculture over that of Scotland. This observation may have influenced him in selecting the title of his great book.

He remained at Balliol College, Oxford, from 1740 until 1746, and earned a B.A. degree in 1744. His days in Oxford were not pleasant, nor was the instruction he received adequate. "His residence there fell in a time when learning lay under a long and almost total eclipse." [8] The six years were spent in study of many subjects and languages in the well-equipped library of the College. He was especially interested in the Greek and Latin classics, having forsaken his interest in mathematics, the subject which he had favored in Glasgow. Smith, like other students from Scotland, was unpopular in the English school and continually complained of the treatment accorded them. (England and Scotland had been united only since 1707, and the old antagonisms had not entirely subsided.) He also complained of bad health and an affliction of "inveterate scurvy and shaking of the head" which he tried to cure by drinking tar-water as recommended by Bishop Berkeley. When he left Oxford, he left for good; he never showed any interest in the university,[9] nor did Oxford show any interest in him even when he became a most distinguished alumnus; she did not offer him the ordinary honor of a doctor's degree. His LL.D. was conferred by Glasgow in 1762.

Upon Smith's return to Kirkcaldy he stayed at home with his mother for two years until autumn, 1748, without any regular employment. In

---

student. By the terms of the will the holders were bound under penalty of £500 "to enter holy orders and return to serve the Church in Scotland." The purpose of the founder was frustrated when the Church of Scotland became Presbyterian. Efforts were made in the courts to make the students conform to the doctrines of the Church of England but to no avail. There is no evidence to prove that Smith was ever ecclesiastically minded. It is probable that his aspiration to occupy a pulpit was a family-inspired, artificial daydream. Among the devout peasantry of Scotland there used to exist one all-absorbing desire, that of seeing the clever son of the family "wag his head in the poopit."

[8] Rae, *op. cit.*, p. 20.

[9] See *Wealth of Nations*, ed. Edwin Cannan (2 vols., London, 1904), Book V, chap. i, part iii, art. 2, "Of the Expence of the Institutions for the Education of Youth" for his views on Oxford where "the greater part of the public professors have, for these many years, given up altogether even the pretense of teaching."

the winter of 1748-1749 he delivered public lectures on English literature in Edinburgh, probably before the Philosophical Society in a college building; the lectures were successful and were continued for three
successive winters. For at least one winter (1750-1751) he gave lectures
on economics in which he advocated commercial liberty, as Hutcheson
had taught him.

Smith's Edinburgh lectures bore fruit. He was named professor of
logic in Glasgow in January, 1751, and thus began a teaching career that
lasted for thirteen years.[10] Logic included rhetoric and belles-lettres;
and when he received the chair of moral philosophy in 1752, he also
lectured on jurisprudence and politics.[11]

His lectures were popular and were attended by sons of the Scottish
aristocracy and by young men preparing for the Presbyterian ministry.
About one third of the number were Irish students, who for religious
reasons were unwelcome in their own universities. His lectures were
also attended by sons of rich Glasgow merchants, who in turn discussed
his ideas with others engaged in business. As a result, the thirteen years
of his teachings practically converted the city to his doctrine of free
trade. The doctrines which he developed in his lectures in Glasgow in
1752 and 1753, and later incorporated in the *Wealth of Nations*, antedated the publication of Cantillon's *Essai* (1755) and Quesnay's tracts.

Factors Influencing Adam Smith: Glasgow and Francis Hutcheson.—
Adam Smith, like everyone, was subject to certain influences, some of
which markedly shaped the nature of his interest and the trend of his
thinking. No attempt is made to include all the influences or to weight
them for importance. Grave injustice, too, may be committed by engaging in the quibbling pastime of sorting out and weighting the "influences" which might be interpreted as detracting from Smith's originality. He had great teachers at the impressionable stage of his life;
he had erudite friends and associates; his environment was always challenging; his own intellectual curiosity took him into the classics and
the best learning then extant. Travel and observation added to his
stature. But finally, his own creative ability which enabled him to
amalgamate the influences is indeed outstanding. What appear to be
the most significant factors which influenced Smith in both his life and
his writings are traceable to his years in Glasgow, first as a student and
later as a professor.

[10] Long afterwards he referred to this period as "by far the most useful and therefore as by far the happiest and most honourable period of my life."

[11] His salary as professor was about £170 per year, which was a very respectable
income. There were three to four hundred students in Glasgow College in Smith's
time; he had eighty to ninety in his public classes and twenty in the private class.

The influence of Glasgow College was an important factor. Like the city in which it was situated, it was on the upswing. In contrast with Oxford, which was then in a stage of deep decadence, Glasgow was very much alive. Many of the teachers were exceptional, the library was excellent, and the intellectual life of the college was stimulating. Liberal and progressive views made the college outstanding.[12]

Smith's contact with Glasgow College falls into two periods: the first one covering his student years, 1737-1740; the second, his career as a teacher, 1751-1764.[13] In the first period the greatest influence was that of his teacher, Francis Hutcheson, whom he held in highest respect, later referring to him as "the never-to-be-forgotten Hutcheson." Hutcheson was professor of moral philosophy and, in a very real sense, Smith's intellectual father. He was a liberal thinker of original power and an unrivaled academic lecturer.

Hutcheson was a deeply religious man yet not in full sympathy with much of the prevailing theological dogma. The subject of moral philosophy was to him not a revealed religion but a study of human nature. He was deeply concerned with the "rights of man" and on these rights, and in line with eighteenth-century philosophy, he built his concepts of moral philosophy, politics, jurisprudence, and political economy. His views were admittedly metaphysical rather than scientific. It was his belief that truth could be discovered by reason, not by revelation, that nature was beneficent, and that human interests were harmonious when left to justice and liberty. In accordance with this belief the best interests of the individual could be reached by each respecting another's rights; an enlightened self-interest would lead to universal social harmony. Hutcheson coined the famous phrase "the greatest happiness to the greatest number," which characterized his outlook on religion, politics, and political economy. The affinity between the philosophy of Hutcheson and the conceptions which underlie Smith's two works is apparent. The rationalist philosophy of the teacher overcame the traditional orthodoxy which had led Smith first in the direction of the Church; it led him to adopt the newer philosophy with its humanitarian outlook which placed the individual in an entirely new setting. Hutche-

---

[12] The physical plant of the original college was quite adequate for the time. As the city of Glasgow grew the original site became less desirable as a location; in 1866 ground was broken for a new physical plant in a section known as Gilmorehill, a high spot overlooking the city. Some of the fine old portions of the original college have been preserved and built into the new. Today, the university library has the greatest quantity of Smith's papers and letters. It also owns the splendid libraries which once belonged to Dr. James Bonar, William Smart, and W. R. Scott.

[13] W. R. Scott in *Adam Smith as Student and Professor* covers these two periods in great detail.

son clearly shaped the course of Smith's thinking and left an indelible stamp upon his writings.

Hutcheson had well-developed ideas on economic subjects which were presented in his lectures on jurisprudence.[14] He had a clear grasp of such matters as value, interest, and money: he held none of the mercantilist fallacies on precious metals. "His remarks on Value contain what reads like a first draft of Smith's famous passage on Value in use and value in exchange."[15] He taught a doctrine of freedom of industry to which Smith, as a student, was introduced long before physiocracy appeared. Hutcheson was "an earnest and devoted teacher [whose] largest influence as an economic thinker was exerted through his two great pupils, David Hume and Adam Smith."[16]

The second period at Glasgow covers Smith's thirteen years as a teacher from 1751 to 1764. He was successful as a teacher and lecturer, but more important is the fact that it was here that he wrote the _Theory of Moral Sentiments_ (1759) and shaped the materials which afterwards became the _Wealth of Nations_. The first work established his reputation as a philosopher and eventually led to his being invited to travel as a tutor to a young Scottish nobleman, the Duke of Buccleuch, on an extended visit to the Continent. In addition to his duties as a teacher he served the college in many administrative capacities. Gray remarks that "Adam Smith in fact ran the University during the thirteen years he was there."[17] It was with considerable reluctance that he resigned his position in order to travel. He had hoped that David Hume might become his successor, but Hume's liberal views, together with his atheism, precluded his appointment and Smith was succeeded by one Thomas Reid from King's College, Aberdeen.

The city of Glasgow also afforded Smith the opportunity to see thriving and growing enterprise. Its population was about 23,000; it was expanding from a provincial to a commercial capital. Navigation on the Clyde was improved and Glasgow ships were engaged in extensive hauling, especially of tobacco from Virginia and the West Indies. Glasgow products (silks, leather, iron, etc.) found their way into every market in the world. Banks were established to handle the financing of shipments. Smith saw Glasgow in a period of great commercial enterprise

[14] See W. R. Scott's _Francis Hutcheson_ (Cambridge, 1900), chap. iv, and chap. xi; also Leechman's _Life of Hutcheson_, p. 34. Hutcheson's _Introduction to Moral Philosophy_ was published in Latin in 1742; the English translation appeared in 1747. The more formal _System of Moral Philosophy_ was published posthumously in 1755.

[15] Rae, _op. cit._, p. 14.

[16] J. H. Hollander, "The Dawn of Science," chap. i, in _Adam Smith 1776-1926_ (Chicago, 1928), p. 11.

[17] Sir Alexander Gray, _Adam Smith_ (The Historical Association, General Series, G. 10; London, 1948), p. 5.

and expansion, and it proved to be an excellent observation point. His observations, one may conclude, led him to believe that the thing most needed to assure further growth and expansion was nothing other than freedom of opportunity. "Glasgow belonged to him: it was his laboratory and its merchants were his teachers." [18] The city likewise acknowledged the influence of Smith and made him an "honorary burgess of the city, or as the formula went, a burgess, *gratis*." [19]

While Smith was a professor at Glasgow College he was intimate with James Watt, who was given haven "as instrument maker to the university" because the Glasgow trade union would not allow him to open a workshop in the city. Smith was greatly interested in Watt's experiments with steam which ultimately led to his invention of the steam engine.[20] Watt was a true scientist in his field; he applied known scientific facts concerning heat and steam to industrial use. He deserves to be regarded as the founder of scientific industrial technology. Watt entered into a partnership with Matthew Boulton and succeeded in introducing steam engines into all kinds of industrial uses.[21] It is a strange and interesting coincidence that these two men, working at the same time and under the same roof, each produced a work, Smith in theoretical and applied economics and Watt in the application of power to industry, that revolutionized both economic thought and production methods throughout the world.[22]

Smith's Friendship with David Hume.—The person who exercised the greatest influence on Smith in his adult years was his close friend, David Hume (1711-1776). Their friendship began early (probably when Smith was nearing the end of his term in Glasgow College in 1740) and lasted until Hume's death. Each had the greatest respect for the opinions of

[18] Gray, *op. cit.*, p. 5.

[19] Scott, *op. cit.*, pp. 81-82.

[20] Watt obtained his first patent in 1769; his first steam engine was not technically perfected until 1774.

[21] A. P. Usher, *A History of Mechanical Inventions* (New York, 1929), chap. ii; also pp. 314-18; and Paul Mantoux, *The Industrial Revolution in the Eighteenth Century* (New York, 1927), pp. 326-29.

[22] Many of Watt's working models and an original engine are preserved in the Hunterian Museum, which is a part of the University of Glasgow. It is an interesting fact that the original college was bought by the City of Glasgow Union Railway Company. Within a few years the old college gateway bore the legend, "Entrance to Passenger Station." The melancholy circumstance that the steam engine should destroy the scene of Watt's labors was the concluding theme of an editorial in the *Glasgow Herald* of May 3, 1870: "Deep-brooding Watt, sitting in his academic shop, studying great physical powers, evoked from his brain the very spirit . . . which is about to lay the walls of his student's cell in ruins. It is to the railway that the University is about to yield up its ancient dwelling place, and, in a few months, there will sweep over the spot where the great philosopher sat the very spirit which he was then chaining to the car of civilization."

the other. Richard Haldane describes the relationship very well. "They lived, sometimes together and always in constant communication, for a quarter of a century. The chief difference between them was the difference of the directions which they respectively gave to the great currents of thought in the world; the origins of these directions lay very close together. Whether Hume could have been but for Smith, we cannot now say; but we know that, but for Hume, Smith could never have been." [23]

Hume was a philosopher, logician, historian, and lastly an economist. Smith's philosophy was influenced directly by Hutcheson and indirectly by Hume. The religious views of Hutcheson were deeply implanted in Smith; both were Deists whose ethical views were in harmony with the tenets of Deism. Hume, on the other hand, was a disintegrating force, a severe critic, of both ethical and metaphysical concepts. John Locke had attempted to build a philosophy which made experience the source of ideas and knowledge. He denied that man is endowed with innate moral principles and innate knowledge, although he acknowledged a first cause which had a deistic basis. Hume attacked the premises and substituted for causation the principle of association which, under his skilful analysis, led to agnosticism. Hume's purpose was to deduce the laws of individual well-being from human nature shorn of theological trappings. In this respect Hume could (and perhaps should) be regarded as the first utilitarian. Hutcheson would not support Hume's views; he firmly believed that man was endowed with a moral sense which could distinguish right from wrong. Smith was exposed to the philosophical views of Hutcheson before he came in contact with those of Hume. The first impressions of his teacher were in conflict with the devastating logic of his friend Hume. In his more mature years when he was called upon to record his own views, he discarded the moral sense concepts of his teacher and the association concept of his friend and substituted his own. He set himself to show that sympathy was the root of all moral life and of ethical judgments. This is the concept on which his first work, the *Theory of Moral Sentiments*, rests.

The volume, as a philosophic treatise or as a work on ethics, is of small value but as a literary contribution it ranks very high. Its conceptual foundation is no more secure than those it sought to supplant, nor is the concept as simple as Smith believed it to be. It was just as metaphysical as were the concepts of Hutcheson and Hume; there was no more reason to believe that man was born with innate feelings of sympathy than with a refined moral sense. Yet the book was widely accepted and the author generally acclaimed as a philosopher. Hume,

[23] *Life of Adam Smith* (London, 1887), p. 19.

therefore, had no small part in shaping the first of the works of Adam Smith.

The *Theory of Moral Sentiments* is of especial interest because it, like the *Wealth of Nations*, was but one of the subjects Smith planned to develop. His lectures on moral philosophy at Glasgow were divided into four parts; natural theology was first; then ethics, which he expanded into the *Theory of Moral Sentiments*; the third dealt with that aspect of morality which relates to justice and jurisprudence; the fourth part of the lectures was devoted to "those political regulations which are founded, not upon the principle of *justice,* but that of *expediency,* and which are calculated to increase the riches, the power, and the prosperity of the state." [24] This part ultimately became the *Wealth of Nations*. His notes on the two undeveloped topics may have been burned with his other manuscripts shortly before his death.[25]

Hume's views on economics are found in a small volume entitled *Political Discourses,* published in 1752. In this work are essays on the subject of money, interest, commerce, balance of trade, taxes, and public credit, which he treats with great ability and penetration. His arguments against mercantilistic practices were discussed in Chapter 6, pp. 94 *et sqq.* He views the scope of economics as an inquiry into the nature of commerce and riches and their effect on the greatness of the state and the happiness of individuals. The wealth of nations is explained as follows: "our passions are the only causes of labour, and labour (which includes mental and physical exertions) is the means of purchasing from nature all the wealth of the world." Agriculture provides the necessities first, but in a civilized state agriculture and manufacturing are mutually necessary to each other, and trade and commerce grow up with them. He does not support the physiocratic overemphasis of agriculture. Likewise he never overemphasizes the accumulation of money and wealth as did the mercantilists. "Men and commodities are the real strength of any community . . . Money is nothing but the representation of labour and commodities and serves only as a method of rating and estimating them." [26] Further on, he speaks of the value

[24] Reported by a student named John Millar who attended the lectures when they were first delivered in 1751-1752. See Dugald Stewart in his "Account of the Life and Writings of Adam Smith, LL.D.," read before the Royal Society of Edinburgh in 1793 and published in Adam Smith's posthumous *Essays on Philosophical Subjects* (Dublin, 1795), p. xviii. See Rae, *op. cit.*, pp. 53-55.

[25] The two works are intimately related, though not in mutual contradiction as had been claimed by critics. In the first work, Smith used sympathy to characterize man's actions; in the later one, he held that self-interest governed man's actions exclusively. They are not contradictory in their fundamental premises but supplemental parts of the general outline as presented in his lectures at Glasgow College. For further discussion of this issue see Gray, *op. cit.*, pp. 12-18.

[26] "Of Money," *Political Discourses* (London, 1752), pp. 46-58 *passim.*

of money as "being a fictitious one arising from the agreement and convention of men." [27] He draws upon his utilitarian ethics to prove that the happiness of a people is not affected by the great or small quantity of money in use, nor is foreign trade essential to happiness or national prosperity. Hume has no clear statement of a value theory; in fact, he does not deal exhaustively with economic theories. However, he treats certain economic subjects with brilliance. He sets forth a theory of international trade which became the basis of later doctrines as developed by David Ricardo and J. S. Mill. His ideas on the quantity theory of money (see Chapter 6) are far advanced. Hume protests against the prevailing view that the rate of interest was dependent upon the quantity of money: he holds the important factors to be the demand and supply of capital or loan funds and the rate of profit. Both the rate of interest and the amount of profit reflect the stage of development reached by the commerce of a nation.

In general, Hume agreed with the principles developed by Smith on all points except the part played by rent in price determination. Smith, although uncertain in his own mind, held that rent was price-determining. After the *Wealth of Nations* was published Hume wrote to Smith, "If you were here at my fireside, I should dispute some of your principles. I cannot think that the rent of farms makes any part of the price of the produce, but that the price is determined altogether by the quantity and the demand." [28] Hume was essentially a philosopher and a historian. His great learning and his judgment were both respected and drawn upon by Smith, but the basic pattern of Smith's writings and the development of the ideas were his own work.[29]

In addition to Hutcheson and Hume one other writer and predecessor who exerted some influence on Smith should be mentioned, namely, Bernard de Mandeville. He was not an economist or a philosopher but a doctor with considerable philosophical talent. In 1704 he published a small poem of 400 lines entitled, "The Grumbling Hive, or Knaves Turn'd Honest," which was expanded and republished in 1714 under the title of *The Fable of the Bees, or Private Vices Public Benefits.*[30] The book caused a sensation and was finally seized by order of the

[27] "Of Interest," *ibid.*, p. 63.

[28] From a letter of April 1, 1776, reprinted in Rae, *op. cit.*, p. 286.

[29] Quite unintentionally Smith created a furor, especially among the theologians, by a letter which he wrote describing the death of his friend Hume in which he said, "Upon the whole, I have always considered him, both in his lifetime and since his death, as approaching as nearly to the idea of a perfectly wise and virtuous man as probably the nature of human frailty will permit." *Letter* from Adam Smith, LL.D., to William Strahan, Esq., dated August 26, 1776, and reprinted in David Hume, *The History of England* (London, 1803), Vol. I, p. 14.

[30] See S. H. Patterson, *Readings in the History of Economic Thought* (New York, 1932), pp. 7 ff.

government. The fundamental ideas were that civilization is the outcome of the vices of mankind, not of its virtues. The author contended that the desire for well-being, comfort, luxury, and all the pleasures of life arises from our natural wants—a sort of apology for the natural man and a criticism of the virtuous.

Smith criticized *The Fable of the Bees* in his *Theory of Moral Sentiments.* He objected to regarding tastes and desires as vices and declared that "it is the great fallacy of Dr. Mandeville's book to represent every passion as wholly vicious." Smith objected not only to Mandeville's premises but "to the ingenious sophistry of his reasoning" and the "ambiguity of language." He admitted that Dr. Mandeville's system "which once made so much noise in the world" might not be entirely untrue. In all fairness he added, "But how destructive soever this system may appear, it could never have imposed upon so. great a number of persons, nor occasioned so general an alarm among those who are the friends of better principles, had it not in some respects bordered upon the truth." [31] However, it may be said that Mandeville may have impressed upon Smith the truth that expenditures generate incomes and that every member of an economic society is mutually dependent upon every other member. This is really the cornerstone of the *Wealth of Nations.*

Clubs and Travel.—Still another significant influence on Smith's life was provided by the clubs to which he belonged both in Glasgow and in Edinburgh. "Clubs in the eighteenth century sense, where congenial spirits met once a week and combined chicken-broth with discussion on trade and fine arts." [32] Many were informal social clubs, whereas others were literary in character. It is probable that Smith lectured before the Philosophical Society in Edinburgh, of which he was a member. In Glasgow he belonged to a Political Economy Club founded by Andrew Cochrane who was "acknowledged to have been Glasgow's greatest provost [mayor] and who was an extensive merchant." It was Cochrane who first recognized Smith's economic ability and, according to Scott, "furnished Smith with many of the facts and some of the ideas which, eventually, found a place in the *Wealth of Nations.*" [33] Smith was one of the founders of the Select Society organized in Edinburgh in 1754, which discussed economic questions. [34] He belonged to the Oyster

[31] *Theory of Moral Sentiments* (2 vols., London, 1759), Part VII, chap. iv, "Of Licentious Systems," II, 98-105.

[32] Gray, *op. cit.*, p. 5.

[33] Scott, *op. cit.*, p. 81.

[34] The patriotic spirit which led to the founding of the Select Society prompted the starting of a magazine, *The Edinburgh Review*, in 1755. It lasted only one year mainly because it was too liberal. A new magazine with the same title began publication in 1803.

Club in Edinburgh and was also an original member of the Poker Club, founded in 1762. This club, contrary to what the name might imply, was originally founded to agitate for a Scottish militia and had among its members many leading Scots. It is probable that these several clubs had a part in shaping the views of Smith; they provided a sounding board for many shades of opinion among the leaders of Scotland.

While in Glasgow Smith published in 1759 his first book, *Theory of Moral Sentiments*, which received wide acclaim and placed him in the first rank of contemporary writers.[35] The substance of the book, as shown earlier in this chapter, had been given in his lectures at Glasgow College; it was a series of essays in support of the doctrine that moral approbation and disapprobation were expressions of "sympathy" with the feelings of an imaginary and impartial spectator. He might have rested upon the laurels he earned by this one publication, but his interests were rapidly turning toward jurisprudence and political economy. It was largely as a result of the popularity earned by this publication and of his general acclaim as a scholar that he was invited by Charles Townshend (Chancellor of the Exchequer and of tea-duty fame) to travel with his stepson, the Duke of Buccleuch, on the Continent.

The invitation to travel with the young Duke was accompanied by an offer of £300 a year and traveling expenses and, at the end of the tutorship, a pension in the same amount for life. This compensation was twice his Glasgow income. The stipend, together with the opportunities of travel, was so tempting that Smith resigned his professorship and spent the next two and one-half years abroad from February, 1764, to November, 1766. On the Continent Smith and his pupil spent most of their time in Toulouse and Paris. It was in Toulouse that Smith began to write. He says in a letter to Hume, dated July 5, 1764, "I have begun to write a book in order to pass away the time." This was incorrectly believed to be the outline of what later became the *Wealth of Nations*.[36] In Geneva he met Voltaire, whom he always

---

[35] The very first of Smith's writings to appear in print were two anonymous items which appeared in the two issues of *The Edinburgh Review*, founded in 1755. The first was a review of *A Dictionary of the English Language* by Samuel Johnson which appeared in the first number (January to July, 1755); in the second number (July, 1755, to January, 1756) he contributed a "Letter" of suggestions to the authors for the improvement of the *Review*, on comprehensive and original lines. The "Letter" gives a key to Smith's political creed; he did not support the Tory views of his friend Hume. Likewise he made it clear that he supported political as well as industrial liberty and held stronger republican than monarchial views.

[36] It was long believed that Smith was referring to what later became the *Wealth of Nations*, but this appears to be wrong. Professor Scott found, along with the 1763 manuscript draft of the *Wealth of Nations*, a draft of a book on the Funds upon which Townshend and Adam Smith were working. It is Scott's opinion that Smith was referring to his part of the joint work. Townshend died in 1767 and the work was never completed. W. R. Scott, *Studies Relating to Adam Smith*

greatly admired. In December, 1765, he went back to Paris, where he met Turgot, Diderot, Morellet, D'Alembert, Condillac, Necker, Du Pont, Quesnay, and many other influential persons. He returned to England in November, 1766. Smith's stay in France was an invaluable education: it supplied him with materials and a wealth of illustrations drawn from personal observations which he so capably wove into his writings.

Upon his arrival in England, he stopped in London for about six months to supervise the printing of the third edition of his *Theory of Moral Sentiments*. He then returned to Kirkcaldy, where he remained for most of the next eleven years; during this time he completed the *Wealth of Nations*. It is probable that the first draft of the manuscript was finished by 1770, but he kept revising it for six years more. In the spring of 1773 he went to London for the purpose of doing more work on the manuscript and finding a publisher. It appears that much of the book was rewritten and chapters were added during his three years in London, where it was published in 1776.

Adam Smith had, upon the publication of the *Wealth of Nations*, fulfilled a promise made in 1759 in the concluding paragraph of Volume I of the *Theory of Moral Sentiments* to "give an account of the general principles of law and government, and of the different revolutions they have undergone in the different ages and periods of society, not only in what concerns police, revenue and arms, and whatever else is the object of law." Years later, in the preface to the sixth edition of *Theory of Moral Sentiments* he wrote, "In the *Inquiry Concerning the Nature and Causes of the Wealth of Nations,* I have partly executed this promise: at least so far as concerns police, revenue and arms." He spent twelve years in writing the book, but many of the ideas had been developed by him over another twelve-year period. The lectures he delivered in Edinburgh in the winter of 1750-1751 were amplified and expanded in his years in Glasgow and delivered under the title, "Lectures on Justice, Police, Revenue and Arms." [37]

The Influence of the Physiocrats.—The influence of the physiocrats on Smith's writing has been a point of controversy among students of

During the Last Fifty Years, Proceedings of the British Academy (London, 1940), XXVI, 23.

[37] These Glasgow lectures, reported by a student in 1763, were edited with an introduction and notes by Edwin Cannan in 1896. The original copy is in the possession of the Library of the University of Glasgow. They attest the originality of Smith's thinking on ideas later developed in the *Wealth of Nations.* Professor Scott's discovery (1935) of an early draft of a manuscript prepared before Smith went to the Continent proves that the work was started about 1763. See W. R. Scott, *Adam Smith as Student and Professor* (Glasgow, 1937). All evidence uncovered by many careful researchers indicates that Smith's ideas were independently developed.

economic thought. The tendency has been to attribute to the physiocrats a very considerable influence in shaping his thinking, especially
on freedom and self-interest. It is known that while in Paris Smith
often met and visited with Turgot, whom he admired greatly. Turgot's
Formation and Distribution of Wealth was written in 1766 but published three years later in the official physiocratic journal and mouth-
piece, *Ephémérides*. It is reasonably certain that Smith discussed the
work with the author. Thorold Rogers thinks the influence of Turgot's
reasoning on Smith is easily perceptible. Leon Say contends that
Turgot owed much of his philosophy to Smith, and Smith owed much
of his economics to Turgot. It is also known that Smith was on friendly
terms with Dr. Quesnay in Paris and Versailles, but it is not correct to
regard Smith as a "disciple" of Quesnay as does Du Pont, who frequently was given to exaggeration. While in Paris, Smith had entree
to the best of intellectual society, which included the leading physiocrats and statesmen. Since physiocracy was "the rage" at that time, it
is natural to assume that much of the conversation covered this general
subject. Physiocracy reached its peak in organization and influence
about 1767; it waned from that date onward and by 1776 its demise
was complete.

Smith referred to physiocracy as the "system . . . nearest to the truth
that has yet been published on the subject of political economy," [38] yet
he built his own system of political economy, a system much nearer
reality than physiocracy. Since Professor Cannan has identified and
accepted as authentic the manuscript copy of a student's notes of
"Lectures on Justice, Police, Revenue, and Arms," delivered by Smith
at Glasgow, opinion has tended to minimize the influence of the physiocrats and recognize the complete independence of Smith's ideas. The
opinion has been reinforced by Scott's discovery of the early draft of
the *Wealth of Nations*. The catalogue of Smith's personal library as it
was in 1781 shows a few French books that he brought back from
France, mainly gifts from his friends.[39] Since some French publica-

[38] *Wealth of Nations* (Cannan, ed.), Book IV, chap. ix, p. 642.

[39] Smith's library, as catalogued by Dr. James Bonar for the Royal Economic Society in 1894 (2d ed., London, 1932), is exceedingly useful not only for the list of
books but for additional items in "Smith-lore." A large portion (The Bannerman
Collection) of the library is in Glasgow University; some (The Cunningham Collection) is in Queen's College, Belfast. About three hundred volumes were bought by
a Professor I. Nitobe in 1920 and sent to the Imperial University, Tokyo. A complete list of the books in the Tokyo Library is now available in *The Catalogue of
Adam Smith's Library*, edited by Tadao Yanaihara (Tokyo, 1951). Other items from
the library are in the possession of sundry collectors in many places. There are about
eleven hundred books or pamphlets and twenty-two hundred volumes in the complete catalogue. Some of the additional volumes not listed in the Bonar catalogue
are now in the Hutzler collection of economic classics at The Johns Hopkins Uni-

tions (notably the *Encyclopédie*, which contained Quesnay's article, "Fermiers") were in the library of Glasgow College when Smith was there, it is reasonably certain that he read them.

It is necessary to distinguish between the French influence in general and the physiocratic influence in particular. It is more probable that Smith was influenced by the French political philosophers who were advocating natural liberty than by the physiocrats or their specific teachings. He knew something about France and French political philosophy from his own observations and study and from his friend Hume, who had spent many years there. Smith knew the writings of Cantillon either from the latter's book, which was in his own library, or from extracts from it which appeared in Postlethwayt's *Dictionary of Trade and Commerce*. But his work at Glasgow was certainly not shaped by the physiocrats; and in writing the *Wealth of Nations* he was influenced rather by the general trend of enlightened political opinion which prevailed in France, by the teachings of Grotius to which he was introduced by his teacher, Francis Hutcheson, at Glasgow, and by the naturalism of the eighteenth century.

The Years After the Publication of the *Wealth of Nations*.—The success of the *Wealth of Nations* was instantaneous. By 1790, the year of Smith's death, the book had gone through five English editions (1776, 1779, 1784, 1786, and 1789; no changes were made in the text after the third edition) and had been translated into several foreign languages. Hume praised the book, saying, "It has depth, and solidity, and acuteness, and is so much illustrated by curious facts, that it must at last take the public attention." It claimed the attention of the public and of statesmen like Pitt and Fox. Buckle declared that it was "in its ultimate results probably the most important book ever written, and certainly the most valuable contribution ever made by a single man towards establishing the principles on which government should be based." [40] Pultney said in 1797 that Smith would persuade the then living generation and would govern the next.[41] A greater tribute than these words is the rank and importance attached to the work by students for nearly two centuries.

The last years of Smith's life were spent in or near Edinburgh, with an occasional trip to London. He was appointed commissioner of cus-

---

versity. See *Economic History*, IV, No. 15 (February, 1940), p. 326. The Kress Library of the Harvard Graduate School of Business has the largest collection of "Smithiana" in this country.

[40] *History of Civilization in England*, ed. J. R. Robertson (London, 1857-1861), p. 122.

[41] *Parliamentary History*, XXXIII, 778.

toms in Scotland (a peculiar post for the sponsor of free-trade doctrines) in January, 1778, which paid him £600 a year. In addition to this he retained his £300 annuity from the Duke of Buccleuch.[42] The combined income enabled him to live in considerable affluence for the remainder of his life. His work afforded valuable business experience and provided some illustrations which were incorporated in the third edition. The years in the customs office were, in reality, fruitless so far as benefits to posterity were concerned in that he had no time to devote to his promised work on law and government. Dugald Stewart, Smith's biographer, wrote, "Now that his career is closed, it is impossible to reflect on the time they [his years as a customs officer] consumed without lamenting that it had not been employed in labors more profitable to the world and more equal to his mind." He enjoyed the "Sunday suppers" which he gave when he established his residence in Panmure House in the Canongate, Edinburgh; the suppers were attended by the most distinguished academicians of the city and some professional men. Stewart was one of the constant attendants.

Smith was greatly honored by his own Glasgow College, which appointed him Lord Rector in 1787. This award "gave him great satisfaction" and served as the crowning distinction to the one who had brought highest honors to his alma mater. The revision of his *Theory of Moral Sentiments* was his last work. The book had passed through five editions without revision, and he wished to make numerous changes in the context; he did this in 1790 even though he was suffering from severe illness. It was Smith's desire that his unfinished manuscripts and papers be destroyed; therefore in the week before his death he had sixteen volumes of manuscript burned.[43]

His passing, July 17, 1790, claimed little attention. Rae quotes from a letter by Sir Samuel Romilly in which he says, "I have been surprised, and, I own, a little indignant to observe how little impression his death has made here. Scarce any notice has been taken of it, while for about a year together after the death of Dr. Johnson nothing was to be heard of but panegyrics of him—lives, letters, anecdotes. . . ." Dugald Stewart's account of the life and writings of Smith read before the Royal Society of Edinburgh in 1793 was the first sustained attempt to do justice to the memory and genius of this great thinker. Others since then have presented thorough delineations of the personality of Smith in every aspect except the social side, which has been neglected.

[42] On receiving the appointment of collector of customs he expressed a desire to resign the annuity which he had from the Duke. The Duke replied by saying that Smith seemed more concerned about his own honor than about his patron's, and the annuity was continued until Smith's death.

[43] Rae, *op. cit.*, p. 434.

There are many phases of Adam Smith's genius which remain unmentioned in the foregoing pages; but perhaps enough has been said to highlight the outstanding influences and characteristics of the man and his legacy. When viewed as a man, without the halo of his writings, he was one of simple habits whose life had never been greatly disturbed by any economic adversity; this fact may, to some extent, account for his benignant disposition. He was notoriously absent-minded yet capable of sustained concentration. Composition was admittedly slow and laborious for him. He was uncompromising in his firm beliefs—a hard-headed Scot. He favored free trade but deliberately enumerated the exceptions to the doctrine. He was optimistic in outlook and supported a harmony of all interests yet recognized that there would be clashes of interests under certain conditions. Strange as it may seem, Smith was never an economic theorist in a strict sense, for he held that every problem would have to be decided on the facts surrounding each case. He was not an advocate of unbridled laissez faire, for he acknowledged a variety of spheres of state activity, but each case would have to rest on its own merits. He was a solitary thinker, out of touch with the theological views of his countrymen and somewhat alone in pioneering the frontiers of economics.

Enough for his life. "Great geniuses," says Emerson in *Representative Men*, "have the shortest biographies. . . . They lived in their writings." The course charted by Adam Smith through the maze which has since become political economy, is the subject of the next chapter, the *Wealth of Nations*.

10

The *Wealth of Nations*

Method of Analysis and Presentation.—Much controversy has arisen as to whether the method used by Smith in his great work was inductive or deductive. The issue is important not only in helping to understand how he arrived at his conclusions in this—the first and most important work [1] in economics—but also because his method and his conclusions were vigorously attacked by later writers, notably the historical school in Germany.

Smith generally used the deductive method. He tended to derive his particular points from universal propositions which, to the best of his knowledge, were established. He worked with known, universal facts of human nature and the characteristics of material objects, which provide the premises from which he drew his conclusions. Doubt may be expressed as to where the conclusions may lead, but the methodology is right. More subject to criticism are his semimetaphysical a priori assumptions concerning a natural order, which he regards as universally beneficent. The assumptions that nature has made provision for both individual and social well-being by creating within the individual a motivating principle which prompts every man to better his condition; [2] that the individual, aiming only at his private gain, is led by "an invisible hand" to promote public good; that human institutions which interfere with this principle in the name of public interest defeat their own end; that when restraining measures are taken away, natural liberty will re-establish itself—these assumptions are open to severe criticism. It is at least charitable to allow Smith the philosophical excursion and at-

---

[1] All references used hereafter refer to the two-volume edition by Edwin Cannan which is a reprint of the fifth edition of *An Inquiry into the Nature and Causes of the Wealth of Nations* (2 vols., London, 1904). The fifth was the last edition published before Smith's death. Every student of economics owes to himself the privilege of reading the *Wealth of Nations* in its original entirety.

[2] "It is not from the benevolence of the butcher, the brewer, or the baker, that we expect our dinner, but from their regard to their own interest." *Wealth of Nations*, Vol. I, p. 16.

tribute it to the influence of physiocratic teachings and eighteenth-century philosophy.

The essential difference between the deductive and inductive method is that in deduction we reason *from* principles; in induction we reason *to* principles. Deduction proceeds from a greater to a smaller; induction passes from the particular to the general. Deductive method descends from the abstract to the concrete, whereas in reasoning inductively we rise from the concrete to the abstract. Smith used both methods, but he used deduction to a much greater degree. The deductive thinker may use premises borrowed from antiquity, or notions which prevail in contemporary society, or premises which result from his own peculiar economic, political, or social organization. From the premises, the principles or laws are derived. Smith used this method generally but not to the exclusion of inductive reasoning, for the methods are, in reality, complementary.

The methods employed by Smith are not so abstract as those employed by some later economists. Smith was a keen observer of contemporary economic affairs, who wrote about a mercantile world in which he lived. He continually emphasized the facts and their significance instead of drawing conclusions from abstract principles by elaborate reasoning alone. He was always concerned with the realities of life. He recognized the importance of the desire for wealth as being innate, but he did not make wealth the foundation for a system of political economy. The center of his system is the individual who, Smith assumes, will follow his own interests exclusively, or at least what he deems to be his own interests. In the *Wealth of Nations* he considers man as necessarily selfish, whereas in the *Theory of Moral Sentiments* he regards man as naturally sympathetic and hence investigates the sympathetic part of human nature. Thus he removes from political economy any association with one country and any partisanship and makes his principles applicable to everyone.

Scope of the Work.—The *Wealth of Nations* was intended by its author to be a complete social philosophy. In many respects this objective was accomplished; however, only the parts dealing with economics are remembered. He was not motivated by patriotism, as were the physiocrats, nor by philanthropy; but, as a philosopher, he was essentially interested in finding the truth and applying it. The scope of the study was intended to include political philosophy as well as economics. In Book IV, Smith discusses "Systems of Political Œconomy" in a narrower sense; he says in the introduction to that part, "Political œconomy, considered as a branch of the science of a statesman or legislator, proposes two distinct objects: first, to provide a plentiful revenue or subsistence for the people, or more properly to enable them to provide such a revenue or subsistence for themselves; and secondly, to supply the state or commonwealth with a revenue sufficient for the public services." [3] He then proceeds to criticize this narrower point of view as exemplified by the mercantile and the physiocratic system (he calls the latter the agricultural system). He refers to the physiocrats as a "sect" whose works "treat not only of what is properly called Political Œconomy, or of the nature and causes of the wealth of nations, but of every other branch of the system of civil government." [4] This quotation indicates that Smith intended the title of his book to be the equivalent of the term "political economy." [5]

But the work is much more than a book on political economy dealing with domestic and international economic problems; it is a comprehensive philosophical work which deals in problems of human welfare, ethics, economics, and jurisprudence. Smith drew from the current knowledge of the entire civilized world and presented an analysis of economic practices and relationships as he saw them. The work is not faultless. However, in pioneering a new science it is without a peer.

The *Wealth of Nations.*—The *Wealth of Nations* consists of an introduction of three pages in which the author states the plan of the work, five books, and a short appendix. The first two books present his "economics"; the third book, in which he discusses the "progress of opulence in different nations," deals with the history of agriculture and the rise and progress of cities and towns after the fall of the Roman Empire and with the effect of the commerce of manufacturing towns upon the agriculture of the country areas. Book IV is a critical examination and refutation of the mercantile and agricultural (physiocratic) systems. The fifth and last book deals with revenues and expenditures, principles of taxation, and state interference. The complete treatise really contains four different basic materials: first, a disquisition on general economic principles; then, a refutation of contemporary economic heresies; next, a historical account of politico-economic institu-

[3] *Wealth of Nations*, Vol. I, p. 395.
[4] *Ibid.*, Vol. II, p. 176.
[5] It was pointed out (Chapter 6, p. 90) that Sir James Steuart was the first English writer to use the term "political economy" in his book entitled *An Inquiry into the Principles of Political Economy* (1767), but apparently Smith ignored it. An interesting speculation appears in W. R. Scott, *Adam Smith as Student and Professor* (Glasgow, 1937, p. 323), on the possibility that Smith might have borrowed the phrase "Wealth of Nations" from Dryden or Johnson. Lines in the verses of Dryden to "the Duchess of York on the memorable victory gained by the Duke against the Hollanders, June 3, 1665," read: "Those, yet uncertain on whose sails to blow, These, where the wealth of nations ought to flow." In Johnson's *Rambler* the phrase also occurs: "To be poor, in the epick language is not only to command the wealth of nations, nor to have fleets and armies in pay."

tions; and lastly a treatment of practical and applied economic principles.

In the Introduction, Smith gives the keynote of the book. It reads as follows:

The annual labour of every nation is the fund which originally supplies it with all the necessaries and conveniences of life which it annually consumes, and which consist always either in the immediate produce of that labour, or in what is purchased with that produce from other nations.

According therefore, as this produce, or what is purchased with it, bears a greater or smaller proportion to the number of those who are to consume it, the nation will be better or worse supplied with all the necessaries and conveniences for which it has occasion.

But this proportion must in every nation be regulated by two different circumstances; first by the skill, dexterity, and judgement with which its labour is generally applied; and secondly, by the proportion between the number of those who are employed in useful labour, and that of those who are not so employed. Whatever be the soil, climate, or extent of territory of any particular nation, the abundance or scantiness of its annual supply must, in that particular situation, depend upon those two circumstances.[6]

The first sentence of the quotation, which places the emphasis on labor, was not intended to minimize the part played either by natural resources or by capital in production. He recognizes the limitation of natural resources and the unlimited creative capacity of labor. This is a statement apparently intended by Smith to set him and his ideas apart from the two previous groups, the mercantilists and the physiocrats. It will be recalled that the mercantilists emphasized precious metals as the most desirable form of wealth, whereas the physiocrats built their system on the proposition that land alone is productive and that the wealth of a nation increases only as the net product from agriculture increases. Smith saw that, assuming limitations of natural resources, the true source of wealth was in human activity.

The Division of Labor.—In Book I, Smith treats "Of the Causes of Improvement in the productive Powers of Labor, and of the Order according to which its Produce is naturally distributed among the different Ranks of the People," and examines labor as the source of the wealth of nations. In this book he deals with production, exchange, and distribution of goods. The first chapter, entitled "Of the Division of Labour"—probably the most famous chapter in the entire treatise— presents his view that the production of wealth can be brought about by effective organization and utilization of labor. He explains the advantages of the division of labor in terms now familiar to most

---

[6] *Wealth of Nations,* Vol. I, p. 1.

students of economics: greater dexterity of the workman; saving of time commonly lost in passing from one sort of work to another; and, last, stimulation to the invention of machinery which enables one man to accomplish the work of many. He uses the pin manufacturing industry to provide his examples.

In Chapter II the author practically asks how this useful division originates. He recognizes the separation of different trades and employments as well as a separation of individual processes within each trade. He believes that

This division of labour . . . is not originally the effect of any human wisdom, which foresees and intends that general opulence to which it gives occasion. It is the necessary, though very slow and gradual, consequence of a certain propensity in human nature which has in view no such extensive utility; the propensity to truck, barter, and exchange one thing for another. Whether this propensity be one of those original principles in human nature, of which no further account can be given; or whether, as seems more probable, it be the necessary consequence of the faculties of reason and speech, it belongs not to our present subject to enquire.[7]

He does not say to which it belongs, but he does add, "It is common to all men," and therefore deeply rooted in human nature. He recognizes that in civilized society man "stands at all times in need of the co-operation and assistance of great multitudes."

Limitations to the Division of Labor.—The significance Smith attaches to the division of labor leads to the inquiry, How far can it be carried? He considers it to be limited only by what he calls the extent of the market, which is, in turn, limited by the nature of the occupation and by the facilities with which commerce is carried on. This point he develops by a lengthy discussion of the means by which commerce was carried on by many nations at various times in history; he recognizes the inability to dispose of the surplus created by the division of labor as the factor which limits the extent to which division may be developed. Mankind, possessing many talents, will use their talents according to their own best interests and disposition "to truck, barter, and exchange" in such manner that "every man may purchase whatever part of the produce of other men's talents he has occasion for."

This leads him to a consideration in Chapter IV "Of the Origin and Use of Money." The difficulties of bartering the surplus which results from the division of labor are discussed. He gives examples of many commodities that have been used since ancient times in effecting exchange. He finally arrives at the conclusion that "money has become

7 *Ibid.*, Vol. I, p. 15.

in all civilized nations the universal instrument of commerce, by the intervention of which goods of all kinds are bought and sold, or exchanged for one another."

At this point Smith attempts to ascertain the rules which determine the basis on which the exchange takes place—or the nature of *value*. He finds that value has two different meanings, sometimes expressing utility (or the want-satisfying power possessed by the commodity—not a marginal but a total utility concept) and "sometimes the power of purchasing other goods which the possession of that object conveys": in other words, value in *use*, subjective value, and value in *exchange*, objective value.[8] He illustrates his point by showing that some things (e.g., water) have great value in use but little value in exchange, whereas others (e.g., diamonds) have great exchange value but little use value. Smith then sets a pattern for the ideas he wishes to develop in the next three chapters. He states that he wishes to investigate the principles which regulate the exchangeable value of commodities by finding out: first, what is the real measure of this exchangeable value or the real price of commodities; next, what are the components of real price; and last, what are the forces responsible for prices being higher or lower at certain times than at others. Then, after asking the reader to be patient and attentive, he launches into a discussion of the analysis and explanation of exchange value.

Value Analysis.—Smith gives a clue to the analysis presented in Chapter V the title of which reads, in part, "the real and nominal Price of Commodities, or of their Price in Labour, and their Price in Money." He believes that the real measure of the purchasing power of anything is not its price in money, but the quantity of labor which it will enable the purchaser to command. "Labour, therefore, is the real measure of the exchangeable value of all commodities" (*Wealth of Nations*, I, 32). From the seller's point of view, the article he sells derives its great or small value, according to the power of the equivalent he receives to purchase labor. From the buyer's point of view, the commodity he buys is of great or little value, depending on the labor it saves him or the labor of others which it purchases. Smith, therefore, makes labor the measure of value. He also makes labor the original cause of all value:

Labour was the first price, the original purchase-money that was paid for all things. It was not by gold or by silver, but by labour, that all the wealth of the world was originally purchased: and its value, to those who possess it,

[8] *Ibid.*, Vol. I, p. 30. See Chapter 3, p. 40, for the same idea as developed by Aristotle.

and who want to exchange it for some new productions, is precisely equal to the quantity of labour which it can enable them to purchase or command.[9]

He clearly makes labor alone the ultimate and real standard by which the value of all commodities can at all times and in all places be compared and estimated. Labor is the real price; money is only the nominal price of commodities. He admits the difficulty of ascertaining the proportion between two different quantities of labor: there may be differences in time spent in production, differences in skill, hardship, ingenuity, and so on. No accurate measure can be commonly applied, but the rate of exchange is adjusted "by the higgling and bargaining of the market, according to that sort of rough equality which, though not exact, is sufficient for carrying on the business of common life" (I, 33).

But this explanation of value in terms of labor is applicable "In that early and rude state of society which precedes both the accumulation of stock and the appropriation of land . . ."; it is only in such a society that "the proportion between the quantities of labour . . . seems to be the only circumstance which can afford any rule for exchanging them [objects] for one another" (I, 49). But as soon as "stock" (used in the sense of capital goods) has accumulated "in the hands of particular persons . . . something must be given for the profits of the undertaker of the work who hazards his stock in this adventure" (I, 50).

Smith does not regard profits as merely wages of "inspection and direction" or, in modern usage, wages of management, but as an interest return on capital. "In the price of commodities, therefore, the profits of stock constitute a component part altogether different from the wages of labour, and regulated by quite different principles" (I, 51). Thus, "In this state of things [advanced society], the whole produce of labour does not always belong to the labourer," but it must be shared with the owner of the capital which employs the laborer.

At this stage in the development of his inquiry, Smith introduces another claimant, the landlord. "As soon as the land of any country has all become private property, the landlords, like all other men, love to reap where they have not sowed, and demand a rent even for its natural produce" (I, 51). Thus he accounts for three elements in price —wages, interest, and rent. He says, "In every improved society, all the three enter more or less, as component parts, into the price of the far greater part of commodities" (I, 52). The inaccuracy of this deduction will be discussed later in the text.

Smith now finds (in Chapter VII) that in every society or neighborhood there are ordinary or average rates of wages, profits, and rent

[9] Vol. I, pp. 32-33. See also David Hume, "Of Commerce," *Political Discourses* (1752), p. 12: "Everything in the world is purchased by labour."

which may be called the natural rates at the time and place in which they commonly prevail. These rates are determined by the circumstances of the society or community. "When the price of a commodity is neither more nor less than is sufficient to pay the rent of the land, the wages of the labour, and the profits of the stock employed in raising, preparing, and bringing it to market, according to their natural rates, the commodity is then sold for what may be called its natural price" (I, 57). But, "The actual price at which any commodity is commonly sold is called its market price. It may be either above, or below, or exactly the same with its natural price" (I, 58). The market price of a commodity is regulated by the proportion between the quantity which is actually brought to the market and the demand of those who are willing to pay the natural price for the commodity. Under competition the market price constantly tends toward natural price as a center. At this point in his analysis, Smith puts great faith in the regulatory functions of competition both on the demand side (which he calls effectual demand) and on the amount of goods offered. He recognizes that sometimes conditions may prevail which keep the market price of commodities "a good deal above the natural price" (I, 62) for a long time. For the contrary, he argues that the market price "can seldom continue long below" its natural price, assuming "perfect liberty," for forces would be set to work which would soon raise the market price to the natural price. Monopoly would naturally disturb the working relationships of competition, since a monopolistic price "is the highest which can be got" (I, 63) but, "The natural price, or the price of free competition . . . is the lowest which the sellers can commonly afford to take."

This brings the inquiry to the point where Smith finds it necessary to investigate how natural price varies with the natural rate of each of the component parts, wages, profit, and rent, and what causes variations. He recognizes that wages, profit, and rent are elements both of income and price. This he does in the four chapters, VIII-XI, and it is here that we find Smith's ideas on distribution. It may be observed that neither his chapters on value nor those on distribution add much, if anything, to the discussion of division of labor, the importance of which he makes the subject of the first book. Likewise, it is generally believed that these chapters on distribution were added after his association with the physiocrats: in many respects they are less well developed and less acceptable than his value theory.

The Wages of Labor.—Smith again refers to the "original state of things" which precedes both the landlord and the capitalist and asserts that the "whole produce of labour belongs to the labourer" (I, 66).

However, in contemporary society with its private property, the land-lord, toward whom he manifests dislike throughout the book, "demands a share of almost all the produce which the labourer can either raise or collect from it [the land]. His rent makes the first deduction from the produce of the labour which is employed upon the land" (I, 67). Next, the capitalist lays claim to a return for the employment of his "stock." "This profit makes a second deduction from the produce of the labour which is employed upon land" (I, 67). This explanation implies a loose "residual claimant" theory of wages, which is indeed but one of the many wage theories to be found in the chapter.

Next he maintains that wages depend upon the contract usually made between the parties, in which "The workmen desire to get as much, the masters to give as little as possible" (I, 68), each having the privilege of combining, the one group to raise wages and the other to lower them. He goes into considerable detail concerning the factors which may be employed by both parties in arriving at a wage which hints at both a "bargain theory" of wages and an explanation dependent upon demand and the supply of labor. Smith holds that, in bargaining for a wage, the "masters must generally have the advantage," but that there is a level below which it is impossible to reduce wages; wages must at least be "sufficient to maintain" the laborer. Indeed, the rate must be some-what more; "otherwise it would be impossible for him to bring up a family, and the race of workmen would not last beyond the first gen-eration" (I, 69, 70). The excess wages above this rate depend upon the circumstances of the country and the consequent demand for labor —wages being high when national wealth is increasing, low when it is declining.

A "wages fund" theory is suggested by the following passage: "The demand for those who live by wages, it is evident, cannot increase but in proportion to the increase of the funds which are destined for the payment of wages" (I, 70-71). These funds consist of the employers' revenue surplus over their own subsistence and any "stock" in excess of what is necessary for their own employment. He ties high or rising wages to increasing national wealth.

Then follow several pages discussing wages in different sections of the world and an admirable exposition of the causes for wage inequali-ties. Smith's friendly attitude toward the laboring class is evident. He holds that whatever improves the circumstances of the greater part of society is beneficial to all. "No society can surely be flourishing and happy, of which the far greater part of the members are poor and miser-able. It is but equity, besides, that they who feed, cloath and lodge the whole body of the people, should have such a share of the produce of their own labour as to be themselves tolerably well fed, cloathed and lodged" (I, 80).

Smith is also concerned with the possible rise of conditions where population exerts heavy pressure on the means of subsistence—a consideration which is the foundation of the Malthusian principle. He believed that the tendency for population to press upon the means of subsistence would be true of a stationary society, but it would not be applicable to England or Scotland in his time.

There are the hints or suggestions of several different wage theories, but the one Smith seems to have held roughly approximates a productivity theory.

He saw that the portion of the produce of labor which goes to wage payments is not a fixed proportion but one dependent upon a variety of causes and circumstances, which relate to the status and subsequent general changes in the society. The wages paid, the increasing or decreasing national wealth, the growth or decline of population, the amount taken by other agents in production, the good and the bad years, the cost of provisions, and so on, are all important determining factors of the rate of wages.

The Rent of Land.—In Chapter VI Smith treats rent as one of the component parts of price. The laborer must "give up to the landlord a portion of what his labour either collects or produces. This portion, or, what comes to the same thing, the price of this portion, constitutes the rent of land, and in the price of the greater part of commodities makes a third component part" (I, 51). In a subsequent paragraph he states, "All the three [wages, profit, and rent] enter more or less, as component parts, into the price of the far greater part of commodities" (I, 52).

The author shifts his position in Chapter XI, "Of the Rent of Land," when he makes rent a differential.

Rent . . . enters into the composition of the price of commodities in a different way from wages and profit. High or low wages and profit are the causes of high or low price; high or low rent is the effect of it. It is because high or low wages and profit must be paid, in order to bring a particular commodity to market, that its price is high or low. But it is because its price is high or low; a great deal more, or very little more, or no more, than what is sufficient to pay those wages and profit, that it affords a high rent, or a low rent, or no rent at all (I, 147).

In other words, rent does not enter into price determination at all; it is not a cause but a result of price. The differential surplus idea is present when he shows that no rent will be paid at all if the produce of the land only recompenses the landlord for the stock laid out in improvement of the land. Fertility and situation are both factors affecting the rent of land. Since the landlord is a monopolist, he is in a position to take all above the minimum which is necessary to insure that the land will be used. The fundamentals of the Ricardian differential surplus theory are set forth by Smith, even though inaccurately.[10]

Profits and Interest.—It has been pointed out that Smith generally regards "profits of stock" as interest on capital, although at times he seems to regard profits as a surplus. He recognizes that there is a difference in the effect a rise or fall in profits of stock and wages of labor have on the wealth of society even though the originating causes are the same. "The increase of stocks, which raises wages, tends to lower profit" (I, 89). He explains that "when the stocks of many rich merchants are turned into the same trade, their mutual competition naturally tends to lower its profit." The forces which determine profits "are regulated altogether by the value of the stock employed and are greater or smaller in proportion to the extent of this stock" (I, 50). The rate of profits is difficult to ascertain and varies from year to year—and almost from hour to hour. He concludes that high profits tend to raise the price of work much more than do high wages. An increase in wages means an increase in the cost of certain stages in manufacture, but an increase in profits will amplify and increase the price far more than a similar increase in wages. He arrives at a conclusion that "as the usual market rate of interest varies in any country, we may be assured that the ordinary profits of stock must vary with it, must sink when it sinks, and rise as it rises. The progress of interest, therefore, may lead us to form some notion of the progress of profit" (I, 90). He employs the idea of a minimum interest rate, as he did for wages, which, though not well worked out, seems fairly certain. "The lowest ordinary rate of interest must . . . be something more than sufficient to compensate the occasional losses to which lending, even with tolerable prudence, is exposed" (I, 98). Smith is fairly consistent in regarding "profits" as a return upon capital or "what can be made by the use of capital." Interest, then, appears to be a part of profits, a payment made by a borrower for the use of capital.

The materials of Chapter X, in which the author presents a long discussion of wages and profit in different employments of labor and stock, are of little help in explaining profits or interest. The materials are indeed a digression from his general theme. In fact, it is Cannan's opinion that both the chapter and its details were suggested by Cantillon's *Essai*. The lengthy digression into the field of distribution (about four

---

[10] Roll thinks, "In some respects Smith's analysis was even superior to that of Ricardo." *History of Economic Thought* (New York, 1939), p. 175.

fifths of the first book), when he is, presumably, setting forth his ideas on value, is one of the inexplainable excursions of the author. However, some of his greatest contributions are found in these chapters. In Book II he again discusses the subject of production which was introduced in the first book.

In Book I Smith made "stock" one of the three factors in production. In Book II he points out that the division of labor is limited by the amount of accumulated stock which must "in the nature of things, be previous to the division of labour"; and this accumulation is necessary "for carrying on this great improvement in the productive powers of labour" (I, 259). His ultimate objective in the book is to point up the importance of capital in setting the machinery of production into operation, the function of the entrepreneur in employing both labor and capital in production, and the means by which capital is created. He regards capital as the agency for setting the great productive capacity of labor in motion. In advanced as compared with primitive society, capital supplies labor with its tools, materials, machines, food, and so on, as well as with opportunity to use them.

In Chapter I he treats "stock" (1) as a means of affording its owner revenue, which he terms capital, and (2), as that destined for immediate consumption (I, 261). Thus, according to the manner in which capital brings an income to its owner, he classified it into "fixed" and "circulating" capital. Fixed capital yields "a revenue or profit without changing masters" and consists of "useful machines and instruments of trade, . . . profitable buildings which are the means of procuring a revenue, . . . improvements of land," and "the useful abilities of all the inhabitants or members of the society" (I, 264). Circulating capital is that which yields a revenue "only by circulating or changing masters." It consists of money; the stock of provisions which are in the possession of the butcher, the grazier, the farmer, etc., who expect to derive a profit from the sale of the provisions; raw materials of manufacture; partly manufactured goods; and finally, completely manufactured goods "not yet disposed of or distributed to the proper customers" (I, 265). He emphasizes the necessity of both kinds of capital to society, which in turn must provide security for its employment.

In his long second chapter on money, "the great wheel of circulation" (I, 275), he makes an important distinction between "gross and net revenue" of society. Gross revenue of

. . . all the inhabitants of a great country, comprehends the whole annual produce of their land and labour: the neat [net] revenue, what remains free to them after deducting the expence of maintaining, first, their fixed; and secondly, their circulating capital; or what, without encroaching upon their capital, they can place in their stock reserved for immediate consumption, or spend upon their subsistence, conveniencies, and amusements. Their real wealth too is in proportion not to their gross, but to their neat [net] revenue (I, 270).

The objective of society should be to maximize the net revenue, an idea which is reminiscent of the physiocratic concern with the *produit net* in agriculture. Money, though it makes "a very valuable part of the capital, makes no part of the revenue of the society to which it belongs" (I, 275). Money serves only to circulate the capital (provisions, materials, and finished work) of any society.[11]

In Chapter III, which deals with the accumulation of capital, Smith makes his untenable distinction between productive and unproductive labor. The former, such as the work performed by a manufacturer, produces a value; the latter, however useful, adds nothing to value. Under this grouping Smith puts "menial servants, . . . the sovereign . . . with all the officers both of justice and war, . . . the whole army and navy," also "churchmen, lawyers, physicians, men of letters of all kinds; players, buffoons, musicians, opera-singers, opera-dancers, etc." (I, 314). Both productive and unproductive laborers are, however, maintained by the annual produce of the land and labor of the country.

His remarks on what determines the size of the capital fund of a country are significant. Capital is the result of saving. "Capitals are increased by parsimony, and diminished by prodigality and misconduct" (I, 320). Whenever a person saves he adds to this capital. Saving, which increases the capital fund, "puts into motion an additional quantity of industry, which gives an additional value to the annual produce" (I, 320). The frugal man is a social benefactor, whereas the prodigal tends to "impoverish his country." It is of great importance, therefore, that capital be diligently employed and not wasted.

Smith is interested in the quantity of money which a country may have and may need. He recognizes that the quantity of money must increase as "the value of its annual produce increases." The more goods there are to circulate, the more money is required to circulate them. Gold and silver serve as aids in bringing this about, and any increase in them is a result and "not the cause, of the public prosperity" (I, 323). The emphasis that Smith places on the increase and the use of capital in augmenting the wealth of the nation is indeed a real contribution to economics.

In the fourth chapter, "Of stock lent at interest," the author discusses interest and interest rates. He criticizes (I, 335-36) those who held the

[11] Vol. I, p. 279. The remainder of the chapter deals with banks and banking, Law's scheme, kinds of money, etc., both historically and analytically.

rate of interest to be dependent upon the amount of money in circulation (this point had been refuted by Hume) rather than upon the demand and supply of capital. He opposes the prohibition of interest, a regulation that tended to increase the "evil of usury." He favors a legal rate of interest but hedges his views by arguing that the legal "rate ought to be somewhat above the lowest market price rate . . . but ought not to be much above the lowest market rate" (I, 338). However, "No law can reduce the common rate of interest below the lowest ordinary market rate at the time when that law is made" (I, 339). Apparently he was undecided both as to the desirability of legal rates of interest and as to the level of the rates if fixed by law.

Smith is concerned in Chapter V with the "different Employment of Capitals," and with the quantity of productive labor that would be put into motion by a fixed amount of capital. He considers the problem as applied to cultivation of land, mines, or fisheries; next to manufacturing; then to wholesale merchandising; and lastly to retailing. The persons whose capital is employed in any of these four ways are productive laborers, but "no equal capital puts into motion a greater quantity of productive labour than that of the farmer." Moreover, "In agriculture too nature labours along with man; and though her labour costs no expence, its produce has its value, as well as that of the most expensive workmen" (I, 343).

He shows that the country which does not have sufficient capital to put these three business activities in motion has "not arrived at that degree of opulence" to which it is entitled nor will it be able to increase the revenue of all the inhabitants of the country. He considers foreign trade and the transportation of exports in ships of the mother country, colonies, and other countries. He holds that capital employed in home trade will generally "give encouragement and support to a greater quantity of productive labour in that country, and increase the value of its annual produce more than an equal capital employed in the foreign trade" (I, 351). Since the "great object of the political œconomy of every country is to increase the riches and power of that country" it ought to "give no preference nor superior encouragement to the foreign trade of consumption above the home trade" (I, 351). He believes that neither foreign trade nor domestic trade should be permitted to "force nor to allure" more capital into either than would naturally be forthcoming. Smith strongly advocates the sale of the exportable surplus of a country, for without this export "a part of the productive labour of the country must cease, and the value of the annual produce diminish" (I, 352). When foreign imports exceed home consumption they should be re-exported; this point he illustrates by the trade of different nations, and by the British trade with the American colonies in his day.

Historical and Applied Economics.—In Book III, Smith is concerned with "the Progress of Opulence in different Nations." In this book the author draws upon history, and sketches the development of agriculture and industry in Europe from the fall of the Roman Empire. In this short book (of only four chapters) he deals with causes which have developed or retarded the growth of national opulence or wealth. He points out that in many nations the policy had not been "according to the natural course of things," which calls for the greater part of the capital of every growing society "to be directed first to agriculture, then manufacturing, and last of all to foreign commerce" (I, 359).

The fourth book is an elaborate and exhaustive polemic against what he calls "Systems of Political Œconomy." His attack on mercantilism relegated it, as a system, to the economic scrapheap and materially influenced subsequent economic legislation. He also criticized physiocracy which he called the agricultural system, but not as severely. Even though mercantilism in England was already in its decline when he wrote, it was the logical force of his arguments against it that undermined the last traces of mercantilism as a national economic policy. After disposing of the fallacy which made precious metals the most desirable form of wealth, he attacks "the two great engines" (I, 416) which were supposed to enrich the nation—restraints upon importation, and encouragement to exportation.

In Chapter II, Smith attacks the restraints upon imports of goods that can be produced at home. He opposes special privilege and trade monopoly and is especially bitter in denouncing the doctrines of protection. He emphasizes the unduly high cost to society of maintaining the monopolies. "The general industry of the society never can exceed what the capital of the society can employ" (I, 419), nor can any regulation of commerce increase the quantity of industry beyond what its capital can maintain. He enlists his powerful self-interest doctrine and points out that the individual continually exerts himself to find most advantageous employment both for himself and his capital and thereby brings the greatest benefits to himself and society. The individual

. . . neither intends to promote the public interest, nor knows how much he is promoting it. By preferring the support of domestic to that of foreign industry, he intends only his own security; and by directing that industry in such a manner as its produce may be of greatest value, he intends only his own gain, and he is in this, as in many other cases, led by an invisible hand to promote an end which was no part of his intention. . . . By pursuing his own interest he frequently promotes that of the society more effectually than when he really intends to promote it. I have never known much good done by those who affected to trade for the public good (I, 421).

This expresses Smith's individualism very well. It is not a dogmatic statement but an observation from his own knowledge of men, resulting from his varied experience. He naïvely believed that, as a general rule, everything would be best managed when people were left as much as possible to their own devices.

The Effects of Governmental Restraints.—Smith's dislike for monopolies is well known. He applies irrefutable logic in denouncing them as uneconomical, hence unjustifiable.

To give the monopoly of the home-market to the produce of domestic industry, in any particular art or manufacture, is in some measure to direct private people in what manner they ought to employ their capitals, and must, in almost all cases, be either a useless or a hurtful regulation. If the produce of domestic can be brought there as cheap as that of foreign industry, the regulation is evidently useless. If it cannot, it must generally be hurtful (I, 421).

He believes it is foolish for either an individual or a nation to make a commodity if a foreign country can make it cheaper; it would be better to buy it with a commodity which the home nation has an advantage in producing.

It was argued by protectionists that their policy would aid in acquiring a particular manufacture which in time would be able to turn out products as cheaply as or more cheaply than the foreign country. To this Smith replies, "But though the industry of the society may thus be carried with advantage into a particular channel sooner than it could have been otherwise, it will by no means follow that the sum total, either of its industry, or of its revenue, can ever be augmented by any such regulation" (I, 423). He also points out that the natural advantages which some nations have are so great that to struggle against them would be vain, and that it is likewise absurd to struggle against smaller advantages "whether the advantages . . . be natural or acquired." He continues this same argument at some length, with special application to illustrations drawn from England and Scotland.

Smith says that there are "two cases in which it will generally be advantageous to lay some burden upon foreign, for the encouragement of domestic industry." The first case is when "some particular sort of industry is necessary for the defence of the country" (I, 427). "The second case, in which it will generally be advantageous to lay some burden upon foreign for the encouragement of domestic industry, is when some tax is imposed at home upon the produce of the latter. In this case it seems reasonable that an equal tax should be imposed upon the like produce of the former" (I, 429). There are two other possible exceptions which he allows: he holds that importation of goods should be free except when a "foreign nation restrains by high duties or prohibi-tions the importation of some of our manufactures into their country. Revenge in this case generally dictates retaliation, and that we should impose the like duties and prohibitions upon the importation of some or all of their manufactures into ours. Nations accordingly seldom fail to retaliate in this manner" (I, 431-32). He cites the French as having used this device, but with none too beneficial results. The second ex-ception is not so extreme: in cases when duties have been in force he believes that "freedom of trade should be restored only by slow grada-tions, and with a good deal of reserve and circumspection" (I, 433). This is because of the disorder that might be caused by a sudden removal of the import duty in that cheaper foreign goods would be poured into the home market with consequent loss of employment and means of subsistence.

Smith carries further his arguments on the main points in Chapter III. After a "Digression concerning Banks of Deposits," particularly that of Amsterdam, he returns to his favorite topic of "how unnecessary it is to lay extraordinary restraints upon the importation of goods from those countries with which the balance of trade is supposed to be dis-advantageous." He presents a summary statement which clearly ex-presses his views.

Nothing, however, can be more absurd than this whole doctrine of the balance of trade, upon which, not only these restraints, but almost all the other regulations of commerce are founded. When two places trade with one another, this doctrine supposes that if the balance be even, neither of them either loses or gains; but if it leans in any degree to one side, that one of them loses, and the other gains in proportion to its declension from the exact equilibrium. Both suppositions are false. A trade which is forced by means of bounties and monopolies, may be, and commonly is, disadvan-tageous to the country in whose favor it is meant to be established. . . . But that trade which, without force or constraint, is naturally and regularly carried on between any two places, is always advantageous, though not always equally so, to both (I, 453).

In Book IV, Smith continues to denounce mercantilistic practices and finishes his arguments in Chapter VIII entitled, "Conclusion of the Mercantile system." [12] The author cites many examples of commodities which enter into export or import trade as a result of mercantilistic policies and regulations. He says the motive of the policies—to extend home manufacturing—was laudable but "not by their own improve-ment, but by the depression of those of all our neighbours, and by put-ting an end, as much as possible, to the troublesome competition of

[12] This chapter was added in the 3d edition.

such odious and disagreeable rivals" (II, 159). This shortsighted policy overlooks the consumer and, for general welfare, is untenable.

Consumption is the sole end and purpose of all production; and the interest of the producer ought to be attended to, only so far as it may be necessary for promoting that of the consumer. The maxim is so perfectly self-evident that it would be absurd to attempt to prove it. But in the mercantile system, the interest of the consumer is almost constantly sacrificed to that of the producer; and it seems to consider production, and not consumption, as the ultimate end and object of all industry and commerce (II, 159).

This emphasis upon consumption is in sharp contrast to the emphasis on production which appeared in most economic literature up to Smith's time. The pressing problem was always to increase production of all goods, which was never adequate to meet the demand. Even though this idea of favoring the consumer was probably borrowed from the physiocrats, it is to Smith's credit that he recognized and emphasized it. Consumption stands at the head of the economic system of all nations at all times; however, this fact is sometimes not fully realized.

His criticism of physiocracy, which is generally more charitable than that accorded to mercantilism, is found in Chapter IX, entitled "Of the Agricultural Systems, or of those Systems of Political Œconomy which represent the Produce of Land as either the sole or the principal Source of the Revenue and Wealth of every Country." He agrees with the physiocrats in their criticism of certain of the practices which were mercantilistic, such as monopolies, favorable commercial treaties, drawbacks, embargoes, bounties, high tariffs, and the like. He especially agrees with the principles of physiocracy in emphasizing the superior production of the extractive industries. He reasons that it is possible for nations to enjoy some degree of prosperity in spite of hurtful regulations which they may impose upon themselves. This, he believes, is true even under physiocracy.

He says that the "capital error of this system [physiocracy] seems to lie in its representing the class of artificers, manufacturers and merchants, as altogether barren and unproductive" (II, 172). After showing the errors in this position he admits that "this system, however, with all its imperfections is perhaps the nearest approximation to the truth that has yet been published upon the subject of political œconomy" (II, 176). Even though Smith acknowledges the truth of some of the physiocratic principles and makes use of them, the independent originality and scope of his general knowledge of economic interdependence and interrelationships rank him far ahead of any of the physiocrats.

The fifth and last book deals with the "Revenue of the Sovereign or Commonwealth." In accordance with Smith's system of natural liberty, the sovereign has three responsibilities: first, the duty "of protecting the society from the violence and invasion of other independent societies"; next, the duty "of protecting, as far as possible, every member of society from the injustice or oppression of every other member of it, or the duty of establishing an exact administration of justice"; and last, the duty of erecting and maintaining certain public works and public institutions, which could not be profitably erected and maintained by any individual or small number of individuals. In this book, therefore, he attempts to identify certain duties of the state, and then explain how to secure the necessary revenues to perform them. He explains first what are the necessary expenses of the state and which of them ought to be defrayed by general contributions of the entire society and which by certain members only. Next he discusses the various methods by which the contributions can be levied; and last, the circumstances under which a public debt should be incurred.

After a typical Smithian digression into the education of youth and religious instruction, he comes to the well-known principles of taxation frequently referred to as "Smith's Canons of Taxation." He sets forth his canons as maxims which apply to taxes in general. The first is, "The subjects of every state ought to contribute towards the support of the government, as nearly as possible, in proportion to their respective abilities." This is often referred to as the "ability to pay" principle or "equality" principle. Second, "The tax which each individual is bound to pay ought to be certain, and not arbitrary." Third, "Every tax ought to be levied at the time, or in the manner, in which it is most likely to be convenient for the contributor to pay it." Fourth, "Every tax ought to be so contrived as both to take out and to keep out of the pockets of the people as little as possible, over and above what it brings into the public treasury of the state" (II, 310-11). He shows considerable favor toward taxing rent (a land tax), rather than wages or profits; this position shows his dislike for the landlord class and a sympathetic leaning toward physiocratic doctrines. He admits that a land tax would be contrary to this first canon (mainly because of different valuations on land), and also that a tithe is equally objectionable. Except that a land tax is not in conformity with the first canon, it is theoretically unobjectionable. He regards rent as the most suitable subject for taxation and the only one which would not discourage industry. He ends the *Wealth of Nations* by a rather lengthy discussion of historical factors that have been of importance to England and her colonial policies over the previous hundred years.

Summary and Estimate.—The foregoing analysis follows the order of presentation of materials in the *Wealth of Nations*. Little attempt was made to be critical in giving an exposition of the materials. Since the subjects of value and distribution are of greatest interest and importance in economics, a brief critical estimate of Smith's treatment of these two subjects follows.

Smith was concerned with several problems in this attempt to explain value. They may be put in the form of at least three questions. What is it that determines value? What is the best measure of value? What determines the ratio at which goods are exchanged?

His argument is that in the "early and rude state of society" where it took twice as long to catch a deer as a beaver, then one deer was worth two beavers; in this society the "whole produce" of labor belonged to the laborer. The cost or sacrifice involved would determine the value of the product. But in a society such as he found about him, "stock" (capital) had been accumulated and land had been appropriated and the whole produce of labor no longer belonged to the laborer; the owners of the other two agents (land and stock) must also receive a normal rate of return. Now the problem of the best measure of the value of a commodity produced under these conditions arises; he warns that the value of gold and of silver will fall as the supply increases, but the "equal quantities of labour will . . . be purchased more nearly with equal quantities of corn, the substance of the labourer (or the real price of labour), than with equal quantities of gold and silver, or perhaps any other commodity." However, he finally decides that the price of corn may fluctuate greatly and will therefore command different amounts of labor. His final conclusion is that "labour, therefore, it appears evidently, is the only universal as well as the only accurate measure of value, or the only standard by which we can compare the values of different commodities at all times and in all places" (I, 38).

Smith makes a strong case to show that the division of labor leads to a surplus which must be exchanged. The ratio at which the surplus exchanges in advanced society is thus the real determinant of both individual and national prosperity. The production of goods and the theory of value are therefore interdependent. The value problem which he really wishes to resolve in this connection is: What determines the ratio at which goods are exchanged?

It has been pointed out that Smith refers to utility, or "value in use." He presents the paradox between value in exchange and value in use as illustrated by diamonds and water; with that his interest in utility practically ends.[13] He does not regard utility as a prerequisite of value

[13] The so-called economic paradox had been developed by his teacher Hutcheson (A *System of Moral Philosophy*, Vol. II, pp. 53-54), by John Law (*Money and Trade*

and naturally, therefore, dismisses it as a factor in determining exchange value. Smith and his followers compared only the total utility of the objects: as Hubert Phillips remarked, "Smith, the wily bird, had never heard of marginal utility." For some reason he did not compare the exchange ratio of individual units but the whole amount of the two commodities: the paradox therefore could not be resolved. One cannot find in his references to value in use and value in exchange an explanation of value.

When Smith shifts to the "real price of commodities, or their price in labour, and their price in money," labor is again made both the source and the measure of value. The ratio at which goods exchange becomes a labor-cost explanation in which the cost of goods purchased is equated against the cost of goods produced in terms of the labor-cost of each. This, in turn, calls for a common unit which would make it possible to equate the two costs. In attempting to accomplish this, he encounters the impossible task of creating a unit of labor which embraces time (time spent), hardship (different degrees of hardship endured), and ingenuity exercised—elements which he admits are "not easy" to measure (I, 33). He says, "Labour is the real measure of the exchangeable value of all commodities. . . . Equal quantities of labour at all times and places, are of equal value to the labourer." [14] This leaves Smith's theory of value dependent upon the labor cost of production or the supply side, since the utility or demand aspects are ignored.

Because he made labor both the source and the measure of value, he was in difficulty with his labor theory from the start. In a complex society labor had to be paid a wage by the owner of capital (stock);

Considered, 1705, chap. i), and by John Locke (_Considerations of the Lowering of Interest and Raising the Value of Money_, 1698, p. 41). Locke wrote, "What more useful or necessary things are there to the well-being of men than air and water? And yet these generally have no price at all, because their quantity is immensely greater than their vent in most places of the earth. But as soon as ever water comes anywhere to be reduced into any proportion to its consumption, it begins presently to have a price and is sometimes sold dearer than wine. Hence it is that the best and most useful things are commonly the cheapest, because though their consumption be great, yet the bounty of providence has made their production large and suitable to it." Joseph Harris wrote, "Water is of great use and yet ordinarily of little or no value because in most places water flows spontaneously in such great plenty as not to be withheld within the limits of private property; but all may have enough without other expense than that of bringing or conducting it. . . . On the other hand, diamonds being very scarce, have upon that account a great value, though they are but of little use." (_Essay upon Money and Coins_, 2 vols., London, 1757-58, p. 5.)

[14] Vol. I, p. 31. J. K. Ingram says, "This sentence, which on close examination, will be found to have no intelligible sense, affords a good example of the way in which metaphysical modes of thought obscure economic ideas." Both the phrases "quantity of value" and "of equal value" have no accurate meanings, in Smith's or anyone's language. _History of Political Economy_ (London, 1893), p. 92 n.

the owner of land, the third factor, also demanded a return. Smith reckoned that wages must be paid to the laborer and that the rate of wages would vary in amount. The differences in wages, as between occupations, he believed, were due to: (1) the agreeableness of employment, (2) the difficulty of learning a skill, (3) the degree of constancy of employment, (4) the relative trust imposed upon the workman, and (5) the probability of success (Book I, Chap. X, Part I). These were treated in the sense of a disutility or cost incurred in obtaining money wages. This explanation makes costs of production rest upon money costs. He includes the rent of land and the profits on stock along with the wages of labor in arriving at the cost of production and hence at the natural price of a commodity.

Smith's theory of value is therefore a two-sided labor-cost and a labor-command theory: the former holds that the value of an object is determined by the quantity of labor required to produce it; the latter makes the value of a commodity depend upon the amount of labor which can be purchased with it. Many statements appear in the early part of Chapter V in Book I which provide evidence that he held two separate theories, but he failed to distinguish between them.[15] In general, then, Smith's theory of value was not a single but a twofold concept, yet it was commonly referred to as a "cost-of-production" theory, which emphasizes the supply or production of goods, and goods reflect their labor-cost. Other classical economists, notably Ricardo and McCulloch, tried to recast Smith's explanation but with little success. It will be shown in a subsequent chapter that Ricardo used the labor-cost explanation as the basis for his own theory of value. Karl Marx and other socialists found in the theory what they wanted and needed to prove that labor was the sole source of value and that the workers should receive all they produce.[16] It was many years before the utility concept was developed by the Austrians in the 1870's and 1880's, and still later that the relationships between the functions of the factors of production were understood and all the supply and demand factors were synthesized by Alfred Marshall.

Smith's contributions to a theory of value are more confusing than enlightening. Errors, inaccuracies, and contradictions plague his statements. It is possible that Smith did not regard an explanation of value as of first importance, for his treatment of this subject suffers by comparison with some others. Yet it is Smith who is mainly responsible

15 Von Wieser suggested that Smith intended the labor-cost theory to apply only in primitive societies and the labor-command theory to apply in advanced society. Smith, however, did not use them in that manner.

16 For a detailed discussion see Paul H. Douglas, "Smith's Theory of Value and Distribution," chap. iv in *Adam Smith: 1776-1926* (Chicago, 1928).

for both the original truth and error of the classical value theory. The elements of truth, namely, that labor-cost is one factor and that the supply side is indispensable, are admitted. That labor should be regarded as the cause and source of all value is the gravest of errors, yet on this premise rests much of the value theory of the socialist doctrines. In the development of economic thought it is important that each be known and recognized.

In developing theories of distribution Smith met with somewhat better success. He recognized that land, capital, and labor cooperate in producing the national fund of wealth. Successful cooperation of the three factors depended upon the fundamental condition of liberty, which would insure fullest use of the factors and provide the greatest happiness to all. The owners of the factors would receive returns for the use or services, but he was uncertain about the exact amount each would receive and therefore of the part attributable to each factor in the final cost of production.

Smith was not certain just what part rent played in price determination. He treats rent as a monopoly, as a differential advantage (surplus), and as a bounty of nature. Rent accrues to the landlord who owns the title to private property in land, using land in its widest sense. Even though Hume argued with him that rent did not enter into price (cf. Chapter 9, p. 159), Smith still treated it as a factor in the cost of production, hence affecting the price of goods. It has been shown (cf. p. 176) that Smith also treated rent as a differential surplus and as a result of price in a manner anticipating the Ricardian doctrine. He did not, however, have a clear concept of marginal or no-rent land to help him in his analysis. Despite his uncertainty as to the relationship between rent and price, he did come near to an acceptable differential-surplus theory. His emphasis, however, was upon rent as a component part of price.

Smith makes profits, along with wages and rent, the original sources of exchange value. Much confusion arises over the meaning he attaches to both profits and interest. He refers to profit on stock, which he defines as that part of the value which the capitalist appropriates after wages are paid. He then attempts to explain the rates of profit and of interest as varying inversely with the amount of capital; the size of the profits accruing to the owner of capital depends upon the size of the total stock of capital employed. The less capital employed, the higher the return to its owner, but an increase in the amount of capital "tends to lower its profit" (I, 89). He admits that a rate of profits can hardly be identified because it will vary with time, place, and nature of the business. Likewise, he adds little to clarity when he says that interest on money provides a clue to the rate of profits and, by implication, that the rate of interest is determined by the rate of profits.

Smith believed that wages and profits varied in opposite directions. An increase in the demand for labor will raise wages, but an increase in stock (capital) will increase competition and lower profits. Only in new countries would one find both high wages and high profits. He set limits between which both wages and profits would fluctuate but both would reflect "a supply of and a demand for" relationship; he believed both would tend to fall to lower limits with the progress of society.

It requires very little imagination to read into Smith's analysis all the elements necessary for a doctrine of class struggle or class conflict. The landlords, who "love to reap where they never sowed" through the legal rights to private property in land, including natural resources, demand the rent return; the capitalists, who own the tools of production, demand their return for the use of equipment with which the worker must labor in order to obtain a wage. Smith points out that each seeks a larger return, which the other resents and resists giving up. While Smith did not make class conflict a fundamental premise of his work, he was aware of its presence and recognized it as a characteristic of social change.

Many of the views expressed in the *Wealth of Nations* bore fruit. Governments made concessions which paved the way for free trade. Pitt, whose economic views were advanced, made sympathetic reference to the *Wealth of Nations* in the House of Commons in 1792; tariff reforms followed in England and elsewhere. The "Manchester School" of Cobden and Bright attempted to put the Smithian principles into practice and bring about complete free trade. It was on the subject of laissez faire in general, and free trade in particular, that Smith's arguments were most cogent and probably had the most telling results.

Smith believed that nature provided the key to a harmonious world in industry, commerce, and agriculture. It was self-interest, which, when directed by liberty and justice, would bring about the fullest rewards for all: freedom, self-interest, and sympathy, when combined, would assure mankind of the greatest happiness. The idealistic assumptions rested upon convictions which appear unrealistic in that too much reliance is placed in the infallibility of man's judgment. It is hardly likely that Smith, or anyone else, would have foreseen the excesses of unbridled competition which practically ceased to function as an automatic regulating force, nor can the invisible hand be entrusted with all the specific responsibilities which Smith accorded to it. Somewhere between unrestrained competition and completely regulated governmental activity is the area in which Smith believed the economy should operate.

Finally, it must be admitted that Smith did not develop a consistent theory of either value or distribution. In fact, it may be argued that such was not his intention; he had promised to write a complete social philosophy, which was a much larger assignment. Even though he was one of the master minds of the eighteenth century and a dominating influence in the next, his work was hardly a complete social philosophy.

Academic excavators have come up with traces of ideas from many sources of which Smith may have made some use. But it was Adam Smith alone who combined the materials which became the body of political economy and set the pattern for the development of the science for the next hundred and fifty years. Scientific learning is advanced by trial and error methods. As a scientist and as a methodologist, Smith "builded better than he knew"; post-Smithians to this day continue to place new stones on the cairn so certainly begun by the wise Scotsman in his *Wealth of Nations.*

11

Thomas Robert Malthus

The Industrial Revolution and Population.—The last quarter of the eighteenth century should be examined for the background to the issues raised and discussed by the so-called classical economists. It was shown in Chapter 9, p. 149, that Adam Smith lived and wrote in a significant period in which great changes were taking place. However, far greater changes came after 1776. Smith lived in the period known as the Industrial Revolution but he was not fully aware of its scope and influence. Certainly, in spite of all his perspicacity and foresight, he could not have foreseen the developments which came so rapidly in the next few decades.

The years between the two great works of the two foremost classical economists, Smith and Ricardo—the period 1776-1817—were years of revolution in more than the political world. The English were involved in two wars: first with the American colonies (1775-1781); and next the long struggle with revolutionary France and Napoleon, which ended in 1815. In the meantime the great changes now called the Industrial Revolution were producing results in England with which neither the government nor the economy was prepared to cope. Improved technological methods, better means of transportation, an expansion of bank and credit facilities, mass production of goods by new forms of business organization and absentee capitalism, growth of urban population, improved agriculture—these were but a few of the many significant changes which occurred. The factory system, the consequence of the revolution in production, carried with it evils which no one could have foreseen. Had Smith known what evils the system would bring to society, he might have been less enthusiastic for free enterprise and more willing to defend, rather than to denounce, the institutions which gave a modicum of protection to labor.

Concurrent with the growth of the new industrial system, the "social question" with all of its ramifications was demanding public attention. Socialism, although of much earlier origin, became more vocal in calling attention to the conditions of the working class and promising better things. The government, too, was confronted with the aggravated problem of caring for the poor, many of whom had been reduced to their present state by the industrial system. The urbanization of the population resulting from the factory system materially changed the ways and standards of living of the people. Unemployment became a pressing problem for Parliament and local government as well, which required more taxes to care for the increasing numbers of the poor. State and individual alike were plagued with the great and frequent price changes, especially in the prices of grain and other food products. The reasons for price fluctuation were many and varied, but wars, which always interrupt production and commerce, archaic laws, monopoly privileges, the abandonment of farms, and the dependence of people on a fluctuating wage income were the most significant causes. Indeed, the economic forces at work in this span of approximately forty years created a most decisive period in the history of modern capitalism.

Population has been a subject of interest and speculation since Plato proposed his ideal city-state of 5,040 inhabitants. The tendency has been for peoples to follow the Scriptural admonition to "be fruitful and multiply, replenish the earth." Deficiencies in hands to do useful work or to swell the ranks of armies were frequently made up by resort to slavery. So long as soldiers and laborers were needed, governments could not be unmindful that a large population was a necessary and useful resource. The mercantilists and the cameralists favored dense population.[1] The physiocrats likewise saw a great natural asset in an increasing population. Adam Smith was interested in a large population but was also concerned that the people enjoy a degree of prosperity: "No society can surely be flourishing and happy, of which the far greater part of the members are poor and miserable" (*Wealth of Nations*, ed. Cannan, Bk. I, chap. viii, p. 80).

Malthus and His Times.—It befell a hitherto unknown English clergyman, Thomas Robert Malthus, to focus the attention of the world upon the problem of population. He did it not as a reformer, nor as a proponent of any new freedom for the laboring class, but quite by "accident" in defense of a conservative governmental policy.

Thomas Robert Malthus (1766-1834) came from a distinguished family of considerable means and learning.[2] His father, Daniel Malthus,

[1] For instance, the mercantilist Petty said, "Fewness of people is real poverty," and the cameralist Justi stated, "Population must be the chief interest of the wise Cameralist." Cf. Chapters 6 and 7.
[2] For a detailed biography, see James Bonar, *Malthus and His Work* (London, 1885; new ed., New York, 1924); and the charming sketch by J. M. Keynes in his *Essays in Biography* (New York, 1933), pp. 95-150.

a country gentleman and lawyer by profession, was a friend of Hume and Rousseau. Although the father was educated at Oxford, he sent his son to Cambridge (Jesus College) in 1784. There he took prizes in Greek, Latin, and mathematics and graduated in 1788. In 1791 he received the M.A. degree. He entered the ministry of the Church of England upon graduation and at the age of thirty-one took charge of a parish. Malthus suffered from a speech difficulty described as "not only a low voice but a very great impediment in his utterance"; biographers indicate, however, that it was no serious handicap.

His first essay was not on population. Instead, it was a criticism of Pitt's administration entitled, "The Crisis, a View of the Recent Interesting State of Great Britain by a Friend to the Constitution," which was written in 1796 but not published. There appeared in 1798 an anonymous publication entitled, An Essay on the Principle of Population, as it affects the future improvement of Society: with remarks on the speculations of Mr. Godwin, M. Condorcet, and other writers, of which Malthus was generally known to be the author. In subsequent revisions he acknowledged his authorship.

The Essay took form as a result of an argument between Malthus and his father over a publication by William Godwin entitled, An Enquiry Concerning Political Justice and its Influence on General Virtue and Happiness (1793; 2d ed., 1796). In 1797 Godwin, himself a quondam parson, novelist, politician, and quasi-anarchist, published a new book, The Enquirer, in which many of his former ideas were reproduced but with new emphasis.[3] Godwin's thesis was, in short, that human reason and scientific advancement would lead to the perfectibility of man. He believed that men would listen to reason and truth, abandon their present laws, and form a society without any laws or government at all. All government, even at best, is an evil.[4] Every man will do that which is right as he sees it. The evils of society are due to faulty distribution of goods, not to inadequate production. Godwin furthermore believed that if we had equal division of goods and of the labor used in making them, our wants could be satisfied with

[3] **William Godwin** (1756-1836) was a controversial figure. His chief work, An Enquiry Concerning Political Justice (1793) was written as an answer to Burke's Reflections (1790). His writings were found useful in support of both anarchist and socialist theories. For two excellent biographies see Kegan Paul, Life of Wm. Godwin (2 vols.; Boston, 1876), and Ford K. Brown, The Life of William Godwin (London, 1926). See also Alexander Gray, The Socialist Tradition (New York, 1946), chap. v.

[4] Godwin quotes (Political Justice, Book II, chap. i, p. 79) Thomas Paine as follows: "Society and government are different in themselves, and have different origins. Society is produced by our wants, and government by our wickedness. Society is in every state a blessing; a government even in its best state is but a necessary evil." (Common Sense, p. 1.)

half an hour's work a day by each laborer. Reason would prevail to such an extent that man would become so full of energy that he would need no sleep, and so full of life that he would not die. Marriage and reproduction would cease and man would be immortal. There would be no crimes, no war, no administration of justice, hence no government. Besides this "there would be neither disease, anguish, melancholy, nor resentment. Every man will seek with ineffable ardor the good of all." [5]

This was a dream world which people had been hearing about for five years when Malthus awakened them with his anonymous publication. Daniel Malthus, for argument's sake, had defended the Godwin thesis, whereas the son opposed it mainly on grounds of the inadequacy of human reason and on the limitations of resources.

A second publication which is referred to in the subtitle of the *Essay* was written in France by Condorcet, a political prisoner awaiting execution on the guillotine. His work, *Esquisse d'un tableau historique des progrès de l'esprit humain* (Paris, 1795), expressed the same hope and confidence in human reason and science as affecting human welfare that characterized Godwin's *Political Justice*. No doubt both utopian schemes were of hopeful interest to people who suffered from the factory system in loss of employment and income, higher prices, and a multitude of economic disorders.

Malthus revised his *Essay*, with significant changes, in 1803 after travel and observation in Germany, the Scandinavian countries, France, and Switzerland. In 1805, Malthus was appointed professor of history and political economy (perhaps the first professorship of political economy) at the newly founded East India College at Haileybury, England, a position he held for the remainder of his life. He married in 1804 and became the father of three children. His work at Haileybury College was pleasant and especially significant in training young men for service in India. While there, he made extensive revisions in the subsequent editions of the *Essay* [6] and wrote his *Political Economy* (1820, a second edition appearing posthumously in 1836). His interest in contemporary controversial subjects is shown in his more important pamphlets.[7]

Malthus helped found the Political Economy Club in 1821 and the Royal Statistical Society in 1834. The now famous friendship between Malthus and Ricardo began in 1811 and lasted until the latter's death in

---

[5] *Political Justice*, Bk. VIII, chap. ix, p. 528.

[6] *Essay*, 2d ed., 1803; 2 vols., 3d ed., 1806; 4th ed., 1807; 5th ed., 1817; 6th ed., 1826; 7th ed., 1872.

[7] *High Price of Provisions* (1800), *Letter to Whitbread on the Poor Laws* (1813), *Observations on the Effects of the Corn Laws* (1814), *Nature and Progress of Rent* (1815), *Grounds of an Opinion of the Policy of Restricting the Importation of Foreign Corn* (1815), *Measure of Value* (1823).

1823. Their economic ideas were discussed on frequent visits to each other's homes and in letters which are now classics in economic literature.[8] Malthus deserves a much greater place in classical economy than that afforded him by the *Essay on Population*, as will be shown in the following pages.

Essay on the Principle of Population.—Malthus says in Chapter I (p. 7 of the first edition, 1798), "I have read some of the speculations on the perfectibility of man and of society, with great pleasure. I have been warmed and delighted with the enchanting picture which they hold forth. I ardently wish for such happy improvements." He cannot, however, allow the wish to be father to the thought and says that he sees "great and unconquerable difficulties in the way to them," although "nothing would give me greater pleasure than to see them completely removed." But, in reality, he calls upon his reading public (French as well as English society) to distrust the speculations completely. There is no evidence extant to prove the points of either Godwin or Condorcet. Therefore, he begins his work by calling attention to two postulates: first, food is necessary to the existence of man; second, the passion between the sexes is inevitable and will remain as it has in the past. Civilization has not weakened or abolished the passion of sex, and food is always necessary for human beings brought into the world. Since the power of increasing the population is greater than the power of the earth to produce subsistence for man, dire consequences may follow. The growth in population is rapid and easy and, when unchecked, increases in a geometrical ratio. The increase in the food supply is, by comparison, slow and toilsome and takes place at an arithmetic ratio. When population grows beyond food supply, vice and misery will cut down its numbers.[9] Malthus believes the inequality between the power of a population to increase and the production of food to be so great and such an immutable natural law that he "could see no way by which man can escape from the weight of this law which pervades all animated nature" (p. 16). This is his answer to Godwin's claim that man could achieve by the power of reason a status of perfectibility.

Malthus illustrates the relative rates of growth of population and food by reference to the United States, "where the means of subsistence have been more ample, the manners of the people more pure, and consequently the checks to early marriage fewer, than in any of the modern

---

[8] The letters from Ricardo to Malthus were discovered by Dr. James Bonar and published in 1887. *Letters of Ricardo to Malthus, 1810-1823* (Oxford, 1887).

[9] Malthus regards a family of six children as being a normal one. Of the six, two will die before reaching a marriageable age or will remain unmarried; the remaining four will presumably become parents.

states of Europe, the population has been found to double itself every twenty-five years" (p. 20). He makes this observation a rule and says "that population, when unchecked, goes on doubling itself every twenty-five years or increases in a geometrical ratio" (p. 21). But means of subsistence could only continue to increase in the arithmetic ratio of 1, 2, 3, 4, etc.

Malthus continues in the remaining nineteen chapters to refute the Godwin thesis and further to support his own contentions by introducing some ideas concerning Smith's emphasis on the relationship between wealth and the funds for the maintenance of labor. His comments are largely his own deductions without the aid of statistical data or extensive research. The main fault of this method, however, was not incompleteness of materials but wrong emphasis. His subject was controversial and revolutionary. The spectacular element and the novelty of the idea tended to receive the emphasis and other truths, equally important, were not emphasized. The two basic postulates, namely, the desire for food and the desire for marriage, were made coordinate, which is an invalid assumption. It is true that mankind cannot live without food, but the second postulate is in no sense coordinate with the first. Marriage may be postponed until adulthood and even longer; some persons never marry for religious reasons or otherwise. Malthus realized he had drawn erroneous conclusions and corrected them in the second edition after five years of foreign travel and research.

In the second edition, entitled *An Essay on the Principle of Population, or a View of its Past and Present Effects on Human Happiness* (1803), Malthus changed his arguments materially. He says in the preface that the first edition of 1798 "was written on the spur of the occasion and from the few materials which were then within my reach in a country situation." He is much more moderate in his view in the second edition and is inclined to speak of tendencies rather than absolutes. To the preventive and positive checks of the first edition, he has added a third check which he calls "moral restraint." The preventive check is peculiar to man and arises from his superior reasoning faculties which enable him to calculate consequences. The positive checks cut down existing population and increase the death rate. Moral restraint he regarded as a form of preventive check. By this he means "abstinence from marriage followed by no irregularities." He intended, by means of the third check, to ease the severity implied in the first two checks.

Malthus regards the dire consequences of his premises as inevitable.

Of the positive checks, those which appear to arise unavoidably from the laws of nature may be called exclusively misery; and those which we obviously bring upon ourselves, such as wars, excesses, and many others which would be in our power to avoid, are of a mixed nature. They are brought upon us by vice, and their consequences are misery. In every country some of these checks are, with more or less force, in constant operation; yet, notwithstanding their general prevalence, there are few states in which there is not a constant effort in the population to increase beyond the means of subsistence. This constant effort as constantly tends to subject the lower classes of society to distress, and to prevent any great permanent melioration of their condition.[10]

Malthus offers evidence to prove that the checks have operated in the past and that they were operating in most nations, savage and civilized, in his day. He thereby refuted the arguments of those who advocated, for any reason whatsoever, large populations. The emphasis now was shifted to limitations of population for reasons of greater social good.

An Evaluation of the *Essay*.—A complete evaluation of all phases— economic, political and social—of the *Essay* hardly falls within the scope of this study. However, the student should know more about the so-called Malthusian theory than that population increases in a geometric ratio and food only arithmetically—which, lamentably enough, is sometimes all that it means to most students. Behind the contentions of the *Essay* lies a certain sincere utilitarianism and humanism which cannot be doubted. The Poor Laws which were in operation in his time, although well-intended, were in reality adding to the misery and suffering of those whose lot they were intended to alleviate. He writes, "The Poor-laws of England were undoubtedly instituted for the most benevolent purpose, but there is great reason to think that they have not succeeded in their intention." [11] But he adds, "I feel little doubt in my own mind, that if the poor-laws had never existed, though there might have been a few more instances of very severe distress, yet the aggregate mass of happiness among the common people would have been much greater than it is at present." [12] In the first essay he spoke not only against Pitt's Poor Bill but against all legal relief. Malthus does not contend that the poor should not be aided, but he does object to relief as an illusory thing which relieves suffering at the cost of creating more. This is what he had in mind in the famous passage which states that there is no *right* to relief; man may find that at "Nature's mighty feast there is no vacant cover for him. She tells him to be gone, and will quickly execute her orders, if he does not work

[10] *Essay* (2d ed., 1803), Bk. I, chap. ii, pp. 90-91.
[11] *Essay* (1798), Bk. I, chap. v, p. 91.
[12] *Ibid.*, p. 94.

upon the compassion of some of her guests." [13]   The English Poor Laws practically conceded the right of everyone to have poor relief, but Malthus opposed this as basically wrong. The laws tended to encourage the recipients to do nothing for themselves but to depend upon society to do everything for them. They tended to relieve individual suffering at the cost of making the suffering general. With the certainty of state or parish assistance, the laws tended to encourage, or at least not to discourage, marriage. There followed a likely increase in population with no increase in food supply—a consequence which Malthus dreaded. He was sincere in trying to get to the causes of misery and suffering. On the strength of his natural biological assumption, together with nature's limitations, he found a situation which could not be cured by the Poor Laws of England. They stood condemned by experience.

It may be doubted whether the theory of population belongs to the subject matter of economics at all. Although Malthus devoted much study to primitive society—and in that field of sociology must be regarded as a pioneer—he was not primarily a sociologist. His studies and research, even though they led to immature opinions, produced the mixture of economics, sociology, and political philosophy known as the theory of population. Although he does not expressly mention the law of diminishing returns he was aware of its workings: it had been accurately phrased by Turgot and known to many economists. Malthus made particular use of the law in his work An Inquiry into the Nature and Progress of Rent (1815).

In a very real sense, the Essay was a reaction to the optimism of Smith in the Wealth of Nations. Malthus believed that Smith had put too much emphasis upon the production of wealth and not enough upon its distribution. He agreed with Godwin that his own Essay was a study of the nature and causes of the poverty of nations. It took the electric shock provided in his essay to bring about the English Poor Law reforms of 1834. The educational process so necessary for reform was a long and tedious one, harsh, yet effective.

Criticisms of Malthus and the population theory were voluminous. His ideas were attacked by persons in nearly every walk of life: the clergy, politicians, journalists, philosophers, and others criticized or denounced the theory as heretical. Some supported the doctrines in principle and, like the Quarterly Review, admitted that "it was much easier to disbelieve Mr. Malthus than to refute him." [14]   Some, notably

[13] Essay (2d ed., 1803), Bk. IV, chap. vi, p. 531. This passage was omitted in subsequent editions.
[14] See James Bonar, Malthus and his Work, Bk. IV, for detailed discussion of many critics and criticisms. See also "Malthus on Population" in Quarterly Review (London), XVII (July, 1817), p. 396.

Ricardo and other classical economists, made the theory the buttress of their wage and rent theories. Marx severely criticized the theory, yet at the same time used parts of it to prove his contentions that wages would always be low.

In a sense, the low wages which prevailed in Mathus' day could be blamed upon the habits of the poor. "The poor are themselves the cause of their own poverty." [15]   It was up to the people themselves, not the capitalistic institutions such as they were, to improve the lot of the poor: they had to make the choice between bread or celibacy. Charitable institutions, whether sponsored by the state or by the parish, tended to perpetuate the evil of overpopulation. The doctrine of Malthus is a strong appeal to personal responsibility in improving one's own lot. "He would make men strong in will, to subdue their animal wants to their notion of personal good and personal goodness, which, he believed, could never fail to develop into the common good and goodness for all." [16]

Critics have been tireless in pointing out that his economic predictions have been disproved by facts; the population of England and Scotland when he wrote was about ten and one-half millions: it has since increased to more than forty millions, but the wealth and means of subsistence have increased much more than fourfold. While it is true that population has increased in some countries at a rate which put heavy pressures on the means of subsistence, the pressure has not been so great as to bring all the dire consequences promised in the *Essay*. Misery and suffering have, indeed, been the bitter cup of many nations since the days of Malthus, but the one great cause has been war. Man's apparent desire to wage war, together with his ingenious techniques for doing so, have cut the population of some nations to an extent which threatens the labor supply, hence national production. Both long and short run problems are created which affect the future strength and greatness of the nation. Population trends in most European nations before World War II were tapering off if not falling. Indeed some nations are confronted with the danger of race suicide, not overpopulation. Likewise it is true that even in the best years the food supply has kept only a little ahead of population; since every nation is more or less dependent upon imported food products, the great disturbances caused by wars have aggravated the situation and tended to make the pressure of population on food a very real thing.

Although Malthus' reasonings were based upon imperfect observations and inadequate data, he did economics a useful service in placing

[15] *Essay* (7th ed., London, 1872), p. 405.
[16] Bonar, *op. cit.*, p. 398.

population and its importance high in economic reasoning. Pressure of population on subsistence—or the man-land ratio—has led to migrations of people and subsequent industrial development: it has changed or modified culture patterns of many lands, and in most instances for the better. Modern techniques in agricultural and industrial production, improved distribution, and all the myriad of things which mankind has developed to improve his situation, could not have been foreseen by Malthus or anyone. The consequences which he thought threatened mankind have been postponed if not forestalled, yet the general truth of the theory remains irrefutable as a broad statement of a tendency.

The *Principles of Political Economy.*—It was pointed out that the *Essay* went through several revisions and that, in addition to the revisions, Malthus took part in contemporary economic controversies by publishing a series of pamphlets in support of his views. In 1820 his *Principles of Political Economy Considered with a View to Their Practical Application* appeared. Malthus set forth in this 592-page book of seven chapters his views which represent a refutation of the teachings of Smith, an answer to the arguments of Ricardo, and his opinions of contemporary issues in politics and economic practices. Ricardo's *Principles of Political Economy and Taxation* came out in 1817. Malthus and Ricardo had been intimate friends for many years and many of their ideas had been freely discussed and exchanged prior to their publication. It is impossible therefore to disassociate these two men, even though they were in substantial disagreement on important issues.

Malthus, like Ricardo, begins his book with references to Adam Smith, and in doing so he also shows that perhaps the "original scripture" might be open to doubt or at least susceptible to other interpretation. Each disputant held to his own course and convictions on points of both theoretical intepretation and public policy and thus was unknowingly bidding for leadership among economists. The issues were fairly joined and patiently fought out. Ricardo enlisted in his ranks the leading economic thinkers of the time, including James Mill, McCulloch, Senior, and many others, whereas Malthus had but one competent ally in Sismondi. He had insufficient aid even to keep the battle active, let alone win it over the devastating arguments of Ricardo. Even when Ricardian theories lost their grip later under the poundings of F. A. Walker, Cliffe Leslie, Thornton, and others, the theories of Malthus had no recuperative powers. Malthus will probably always be remembered for the *Essay on Population* rather than for his *Principles of Political Economy* or for his attempts to construct sane political measures.

In form his *Principles* [17] is forbidding: each chapter consists of what amounts to an essay on a subject often not clearly related to the chapter heading. He maintains that man, not wealth, is the proper subject of political economy. He believes that man, like the soil he cultivates, is "so variable" that "the science of political economy bears a nearer resemblance to the science of morals and polities than to that of mathematics" (p. 2). He complains of the tendency of some writers to commit errors in their attempt to "simplify and generalize" and of their "unwillingness to acknowledge the operation of more causes than one in the production of particular effects" (p. 6). Likewise, he believes that premature generalization is a common fault of some of the principal writers on political economy, who fail "to bring their theories to the test of experience" (p. 10). He says the first business is "to account for things as they are; and till our theories will do this, they ought not to be the ground of any practical conclusion" (p. 11). Malthus was a better observer than analyst; in contrast to Ricardo he was inclined to generalize too little.

After the discussion of wealth, he turns in Chapter 2 to "the nature and causes of value" and identifies three kinds of value:

1. Value in use; which may be defined as the intrinsic utility of an object
2. Nominal value in exchange; which may be defined as the value of commodities in the precious metals
3. Real value in exchange; which may be defined as the power of an object to command in exchange the necessaries and conveniences of life, including labor

He says the distinctions in the different kinds of value are "in the main those of Adam Smith; though . . . he has not been sufficiently careful to keep them always separate" (p. 62).

In his value analysis he clearly sees the relationships between demand, supply, and price: "When prices are said to be determined by demand and supply, it is not meant that they are determined either by the demand alone or the supply alone, but by their relation to each other" (p. 65). In analyzing the way in which cost of production affects value in regulating the supply of commodities, he recognizes that "labor cost has a powerful effect upon prices" (p. 78), yet at the time of the actual exchange of the commodities "no circumstance affects it but the rela-

[17] All references are to the 1820 edition of the *Principles*, unless otherwise indicated. No significant changes appear in the 1836 edition.

tion of the supply to the demand." Since "all objects of human desire are obtained by the instrumentality of human exertion" it is necessary that labor be so remunerated in the value of objects given in exchange that the supply of the goods will be adequate, that goods will be supplied continually, and that there must be adequate materials as well as food for the laborer. These conditions must be met by every society in order that the greater number of its wants may be satisfied. The price of the commodities entering into exchange is therefore made up of "that which pays the labourer employed in its production; that which pays the profits of capital . . . and that which pays the rent of land . . . the price of each of these component parts being determined exactly by the same causes as those which determine the price of the whole" (p. 83). This price was called by Adam Smith the "natural price," but Malthus prefers to call it the "necessary price" because it more nearly expressed the importance of supply. He adds, "It will be the price necessary, in the actual circumstances of society, to bring the commodity regularly to the market" (p. 83). (This is similar to Alfred Marshall's "supply price" concept which will be taken up in a later chapter.)

Malthus disagrees with both Smith and Ricardo, who tend to regard labor as the sole measure of value. He contends that in a "very early period, profits will be found an important part of the cost and consequently to enter largely with the question of exchangeable value as a necessary condition of supply" (p. 86). He quotes the passage from Smith which states that rent "enters into the composition of the price of commodities in a different way from wages and profit" (*Wealth of Nations*, I, 145-46). Smith tends to make rent a cause, not a result, of price. But Malthus regards "the cost of the great mass of commodities as resolvable into wages, profits and rent," the amount of each depending upon the specific commodity under consideration.

Much of the discussion on value is given to arguing against the theories of Smith and Ricardo and an effort to refute them. His overall conception of value is, in many respects, superior to those of his predecessors, yet so much attention is given to answering certain points in their theories that he fails to offer a distinct theory of his own. Even though he clearly emphasizes the interdependence of supply and demand, he does not lead very far away from the labor cost theory of value.

The Rent Doctrines of Malthus.—One of the problems of greatest concern at the turn of the nineteenth century was the rising price of foods, especially grains. The problem created both political and economic controversies, into which Malthus and Ricardo and many others entered. Since the price of grain was thought to be closely related to the large profits which landlords were making, the rent doctrines of the classical economists were developed in reference to these controversies.

For nearly a hundred years from 1711 to 1794 a quarter of wheat (8 bu.) sold at around 60s. After 1795 it rose so fast in price that it reached 177s. by 1801; the rise continued over the years and in the five years (1808-1813) the price was never less than 96s. per quarter. Strangely enough, grain prices rose in spite of improved methods in agriculture as well as an increase in acreage. In an effort to alleviate the situation caused by rising grain prices, the Corn Laws, enacted in 1815, subjected foreign wheat to high duties when the price of English wheat fell below 50s. per quarter. From 1795 to 1802 the price averaged over 50s. per quarter, and importation of grains was almost free. Agricultural interests forced a rise in the base price to 63s. before duties were applied, but the price of grain continued to rise and the import of grain was as free as before. Free import of grain was therefore not a factor in grain prices. Malthus prepared several articles (or pamphlets) on the controversy and it is to them, as well as to Chapter III of his *Principles of Political Economy*, that we must look to find his ideas on rent.[18]

Malthus was a protectionist, but in 1814 in his pamphlet, *Observations on the effects of the Corn Laws and of a rise or fall in the Price of Corn on the agricultural and general wealth of the country*, he presented an impartial exposition and comparison of both the advantages and disadvantages of free trade but emphasized that a restriction upon imports would raise the price of corn. In fact, he held that England should import some of her corn and not attempt to grow it all at home. High grain or food prices were beginning to bring political unrest: wages were forced upward by rising food prices, a tendency which employers resented. The landlord was therefore identified as the guilty one responsible for all the trouble because he raised the price of rents to the tenant who, in turn, raised the price of the products he produced on which the wage earner depended for food. Since both the landlord and the tenant were in a "conspiracy" to keep up corn prices, how could wages be kept down? The Corn Laws were under constant debate, for both domestic and foreign issues were involved. All the discussions of rent by both Malthus and Ricardo have a close bearing upon the Corn Laws of the time.

Malthus was probably the first in England to expound the rent doctrine clearly. A contemporary of Adam Smith, Dr. James Anderson, an agricultural economist and farmer, had ideas very similar to those

[18] See Edwin Cannan, *A History of Theories of Production and Distribution* (London, 1903), pp. 148-52.

of Malthus but they did not command attention. Anderson wrote in 1777 in *Observations on the means of exciting a Spirit National Industry* that rent was a premium for cultivating the more fertile soils. He says:

> In every country there are various soils, which are endued with different degrees of fertility; and hence it must happen that the farmer who cultivates the most fertile of these can afford to bring his corn to market at a much lower price than others who cultivate poorer fields. But if the corn that grows on these fertile spots is not sufficient fully to supply the market alone, the price will naturally be raised in that market to such a height as to indemnify others for the expense of cultivating poorer soils. The farmer, however, who cultivates the rich spots will be able to sell his corn at the same rate in the market with those who occupy poorer fields; he will, therefore, receive much more than the "intrinsic" value for the corn he rears. Many persons will, therefore, be desirous of obtaining possession of these fertile fields, and will be content to give a certain premium for an exclusive privilege to cultivate them; which will be greater or smaller according to the more or less fertility of the soil. It is this premium which constitutes what we now call "rent," a medium by means of which the expense of cultivating soils of very different degrees of fertility may be reduced to a perfect equality.

He later wrote that "rent is in fact a simple and ingenious contrivance for equalizing the profits to be drawn from the fields of different degrees of fertility." In answer to the question, "Why is rent paid?" he says, "Rent is paid for all land for which it is paid, because such land is more fertile than the worst land which, at the prices prevailing, it is profitable to cultivate." Dr. Ingram comments,[19] "This volume [*Observations*] can hardly have escaped Smith's notice," yet Smith never changed his views on rent.

Anderson was aware that his ideas were not the accepted ones and that they would probably be unpopular; however, he wrote, "It will be said that the price to the farmer is so high only on account of the high rents and avaricious extortions of proprietors. Lower your rents and the farmer will be able to afford his grain cheaper to the consumers." But he refutes this conclusively and points out that "it is not, however, the rent of the land that determines the price of its produce, but it is the price of that produce which determines the rent of the land." Later in the same discussion he adds, "The lowering of rents alone could never have the effect of rendering the grain cheaper." [20] Malthus knew of Anderson's rent theories and made some application of them in his

---

[19] J. K. Ingram, *History of Political Economy* (1923), p. 125. See also Jacob Hollander, "Adam Smith and James Anderson," *Annals of the American Academy*, II, No. 3 (1896), pp. 461-64.

[20] *An Inquiry into the Nature of the Corn Laws* (1777), pp. 3, 7; reprinted in *Scarce and Valuable Economic Tracts*, ed. J. R. McCulloch (London, 1859), pp. 321-25.

explanation. Nearly a half century elapsed before this doctrine became an essential part of economic theory as a result of the independent work of Malthus and West.

Sir Edward West, a contemporary of Malthus, in a pamphlet, *Essay on the Application of Capital to Land* (1815), entered into the rent controversy. He treats the causes which determine rent and emphasizes the diminishing returns of land as the important factor; he says, "It is the diminishing rate of return upon additional portions of capital bestowed upon land that regulates, and almost solely, causes rent" (p. 49). He sees the differential of rent arising when pressures force second-grade land into cultivation. "When in the progress of improvement new land is brought into cultivation recourse is necessarily had to poor land, or to that at least which is second in quality to what is already cultivated" (p. 9). He pointed out different gradations between richest and poorest land and maintained that the best land would be cultivated first. He believed that the farmer got only the return for the use of his stock and his labor on the land and from the grain, which is raised at the greatest expense. Any additional return went to the landlord "in the shape of rent." [21]

Malthus and West formulated the so-called classical rent theory. Ricardo recognized the accuracy of their explanation and embodied their ideas into his system of distribution; he added little to the doctrine, per se.

Malthus' explanation of rent is clear and concise, if one has the endurance to ferret it out of the pamphlets and the *Principles of Political Economy*. He identifies a portion of the earnings or income of both landlord and proprietor as having an origin and character different from those of other incomes, namely, an excess yielded over and above the costs of production and the current rate of profits. Whatever produce remains after the outlay of the cultivator has been restored, together with the current rate of profits, is rent. The reasons given by Malthus for the appearance of rent were:

1. Land produces more than sufficient produce to maintain the cultivators or producers; in other words, there is fertility of the soil.
2. The peculiarity of agricultural land which makes demand for land increase with the supply of it, or "to raise up a number of demanders (population) in proportion to the quantity of necessities produced."

[21] P. 50. For additional references on the general subject of rent and diminishing returns, see Edwin Cannan, *op. cit.*, pp. 147-82, 310-20; and Edmund Whittaker, *A History of Economic Ideas* (New York, 1940), chap. 10.

3. The comparative scarcity of fertile land, either natural or artificial. When it becomes necessary to use the produce of the
inferior land, it will be cultivated at a price of the product which
repays its cost and repays ordinary profits to the farmer. Naturally that which is cost to the farmer in this case will pay
much more to the owner of superior land, and this is economic
rent. The pressure of the population forces the use of inferior
soils or more intensive use of all soils. In the absence of new
technology (other things remaining the same) this third reason
is the law of diminishing returns (pp. 139-40).

He further emphasizes the fact that rent is a result of price in the
statement, "There is no just reason to believe that if the landlords were
to give the whole of their rents to their tenants, corn would be more
plentiful and cheaper" (p. 201).

The Wages of Labor.—In Malthus' time the wage level was rising; the
wage system was already firmly entrenched. The theory of population
incorporated a principle of subsistence wages. This theory became the
basis of the so-called Ricardian theory of wages, but Ricardo hedged his
views by asserting that the standard of subsistence was not a fixed thing
but a matter of custom or habit. This was Ricardo's idea prior to his
writing in 1817. Malthus had by 1820 abandoned any subsistence
theory of wages. Thus, his ideas on wages are of interest, for did he
not provide in his writings on population the determining element in
the wage theory of classical economy and subsequent socialist theory?
Malthus starts out by defining the wages of labor as "the remuneration of the labourer for his personal exertions. They may be divided,
like the price of commodities, into real and nominal. The real wages
of labour consist of their value, estimated in the necessaries, conveniences, and luxuries of life. The nominal wages of labour consist of their
value, estimated in money" (p. 240). He believes that the money wages
of labor are determined by demand and supply; assuming periods when
"money may be supposed to maintain nearly the same value, the variations in the wages of labour may be said to be regulated by the variations
in the demand compared with the supply of labour" (p. 241). This
principle is the regulator for commodities not only temporarily but
permanently.

Malthus is sharp in his disagreement with Ricardo's definition of the
natural price of labor as being "that price which is necessary to enable
the labourers one with another to subsist; and to perpetuate their race,
without either increase or diminution." [22] Malthus argues, "This price

[22] David Ricardo, *Principles of Political Economy and Taxation*, ed. E. C. K.
Gonner (London, 1908), chap. v, p. 70.

I should really be disposed to call a most unnatural price; because in a natural state of things, that is, without great impediments to the progress of wealth and population, such a price could not occur for hundreds of years" (p. 247). Instead, Malthus contends that the "natural or necessary" price of labor should be defined as "that price which, in the actual circumstances of society, is necessary to occasion an average supply of labourers, sufficient to meet the average demand" (p. 247). He probably means by this the actual wages paid in an average or normal production year.

There is no suggestion of a rigid level of wages based either upon the amount necessary to maintain a physical subsistence level or upon the "habits of the people in respect to their food, clothing and lodging" (p. 248). He writes,

If the habits of the people were to remain fixed, the power of marrying early and of supporting a large family would depend upon the rate at which the resources of the country and the demand for labour were increasing. And if the resources of the country were to remain fixed, the comforts of the lower classes of society would depend upon their habits, or the amount of those necessities and conveniences, without which they would not consent to keep up their numbers. It rarely happens that either of them remain fixed for any great length of time together (p. 248).

Influencing factors are "physical causes of climate and soil"; moral causes are due "to a variety of circumstances." Likewise, he points out that the habits of the people are generally affected by the amount of wages received: this argument is directed against the subsistence theory.

When the resources of a country are rapidly increasing, and the labourer commands a large portion of necessaries, it is to be expected that if he has the opportunity of exchanging his superfluous food for conveniences and comforts, he will acquire a taste for these conveniences and his habits will be formed accordingly. On the other hand, it generally happens that, when the resources of a country become nearly stationary, such habits, if they ever have existed, are found to give way; and, before the population comes to a stop, the standard of comfort is essentially lowered (pp. 248-49).

Wages and subsistence were related to each other but not to other things.

A wage-fund theory might be "read into" some of Malthus' statements. The theory that wages were high or low, depending upon the great or small amount of circulating capital and that they can only be increased in proportion to the increase in circulating capital (p. 261), appears to indicate this view. He did not, however, advocate a wage-fund theory per se, but applied the supply and demand interrelationship throughout the chapter.

Malthus did not support any theory which would advocate low wages. It was commonly maintained by manufacturing interests of the time that it was to the interest of the nation to have low wages, cheap food, and a large population. He refers to this as a "distressing and disheartening cry of the master manufacturers and merchants." Moreover, "If a country can only be rich by running a successful race for low wages, I should be disposed to say at once, perish such riches" (p. 236). In discussing the progress of wealth in Chapter VII, he writes, "It is most desirable that the labouring classes should be well paid, for a much more important reason than any that can relate to wealth; namely, the happiness of the great mass of society" (p. 472). He commented that competition between workers would fail to bring wages up: he expected that such "a degree of prudence" would prevail among them "as to keep their wages permanently high, than that they should not enter into competition with each other in working" (p. 474). There were no trade unions at this time (as we know them), and the responsibility of improving their lot depended upon the workers themselves.

The Returns to Capital.—Even though Smith spoke of the profits of stock, Malthus refines the term and contends that "stock" is not so appropriate an expression as capital.

Stock is a general term, and may be defined to be all the material possessions of a country, or all its actual wealth, whatever may be its destination; while capital is that particular form of these possessions, or of this accumulated wealth, which is destined to be employed with a view to profit . . . it may be useful to recollect that all stock is not properly speaking capital, though all capital is stock (p. 293).

He treats profits of capital as the difference between the value of the "advances" necessary to produce the commodity and the value of the commodity when produced. The rate of profits depends, therefore, on the proportion between the advances and the final value of the product. One of the largest items affecting the "advances" is the wages of labor, and this item is in turn regulated by "the quantity of necessities of life actually awarded to the labourer" (p. 297). Since the quantity of necessities is a variable, we cannot suppose such a thing as a "natural or constant price of labour" for it all depends on "the progress of capital and revenue, and the demand for labour compared with the supply" (p. 297).

Malthus regards profits as a remuneration of capital just as wages are the remuneration of labor. "It is not quite correct, as Adam Smith does, to consider the profits as a deduction from the produce of labour."

Profits are a remuneration to the capitalist and "estimated exactly in the same way as the contribution of the labourer" (p. 81). Labor can produce more with the aid of capital; each shares in the final product in proportion to the amount used. Capital does not get all of the amount produced any more than labor does; each gets only a part of the total productivity. Malthus does not show why the capitalist shares in production or, in other words, why interest must be paid.

One of the fundamentals which Ricardo tried to establish was the theory that the natural tendency of profits was to fall; he held "that in all countries, and at all times, profits depend on the quantity of labour requisite to provide necessaries for the labourers, on that land or with that capital which yields no rent." He says again, "It has been my endeavor to show throughout this work, that the rate of profits can never be increased but by a fall in wages." [23]

Malthus never would accept this conclusion; "It is merely a truism to say that if the value of commodities be divided between labour and profits, the greater is the share taken by one, the less will be left for the other; or in other words, that profits fall as labour rises, or rise as labour falls" (p. 310). He explains the relationship by "recourse to the great principles of demand and supply, or to the very principle of competition brought forward by Adam Smith, which Mr. Ricardo expressly rejects" (pp. 310-11). A deficiency in the supply of capital is the only explanation of permanently high profits, which deficiency would vary from nation to nation and over different periods of time. Profits as he sees them "depend upon prices of commodities, and upon the cause which determines these prices, namely the supply compared with the demand" (p. 334). His views on profits, though somewhat deficient, represent an understanding of broad causal relationships. He definitely does not hold the theory that one of the factors, e.g., profits, can rise only at the expense of another. His last paragraph of discussion on profits sums up his own thoughts when he states that, "No theory of profits therefore can approach toward correctness, which attempts to get rid of the principle of demand and supply and competition" (p. 336).

Malthus' Theory of Economic Development.—The last chapter (VII) of the *Principles of Political Economy*, which takes up one third of the book, is given to a discussion of "The Immediate Causes of the Progress of Wealth." In this he is concerned with the causes which check the progress of wealth in nations even though the powers of production remain practically undiminished. He pointed out in the *Essay on the Principles of Population*, causes which tend to keep the population of a country at a level more or less set by actual food supplies. Now he

[23] D. Ricardo, *op. cit.*, pp. 105, 112.

is interested to find out what affects the supplies, hence, the wealth of a nation and its general well-being. He wants to know what are the most effective and immediate stimulants which may be used to increase national wealth.

First he considers an increase in population as a stimulus to the continued increase in wealth but points out that this cannot be a basic cause unless the demand for the labor keeps pace with the supply of labor. A mere increase in population alone cannot increase wealth. He believes that there must be a continued increase in capital; this may be achieved by adding to it from the annual revenue. Fertile soil also adds to national wealth by supplying raw materials and food products. New inventions likewise contribute to the supply of goods for both domestic use and export. He takes a summary view that the powers of production must be united with the means of production to insure a continued increase in wealth. Much of the long chapter is given to argument with Smith and Ricardo on issues for which they stood. He draws heavily upon practices in other lands and from England's own experiences to bolster his arguments. The author gives so much attention to detail in the sections of the chapter that the real issues are obscured.

The Question of General Overproduction.—The question of whether or not it was possible to have a general overproduction of goods, or a general market glut, was argued by Malthus, Ricardo, and J. B. Say. Say contended that an increased or diminished demand for a commodity depended on an increased or diminished supply of that commodity. He argued with James Mill and Ricardo that there could never be general or universal market gluts.[24] This became the famous "Say's Law" which is discussed in Chapter 14. Goods (Say used the term "products") were always meant to be exchanged for goods; hence production (amount supplied) is the sole source of effective demand. Should there be an excess supply of an article it is only because it has outrun the total demand for it in one of two ways: "either because it has been produced in excessive abundance, or because the production of other commodities has fallen short." [25]

Malthus argued that goods were not always exchanged for goods and that the doctrine was "utterly unfounded." He held that commodities are frequently exchanged for labor or personal services. He further argued that Say committed a grave error in treating "commodities as mathematical figures" instead of "articles of consumption" which, after all, owe their character to the human wants that they satisfy.[26] Malthus,

[24] J. B. Say, A *Treatise on Political Economy*, trans. C. R. Prinsep (Philadelphia, 1865), Bk. I, chap. xv, pp. 132-40.
[25] *Ibid.*, p. 135.
[26] Malthus, *Political Economy*, p. 355.

like Ricardo, accepted Smith's dictum that the division of labor is limited only by the extent of the market. Thus, an extension of the division of labor would cause an overproduction or market glut. Malthus contended that this situation might happen in a great many cases as well as in a few. Only in the production of food would Malthus admit that there could not be an overproduction, while Ricardo argued that only in this case was there any likelihood of a glut.[27] Ricardo's argument rests upon the insatiability of human wants, which he assumes to be fully developed wants; no allowance is made for potential undeveloped wants. Malthus, on the other hand, believed that the undeveloped potential wants of the population would insure against overproduction rather than subscribing to the direct production-consumption formula of Say and other "very able writers."

But Malthus, despite his best efforts, lost the argument and "Say's Law" was adopted by Ricardo and became a bulwark in classical theory.[28] The tendency has been to refer to the Malthus treatment as an underconsumption theory, a technical term which he did not use. On this point he remarks, "It has also been said that there is never an indisposition to consume, that the indisposition is to produce" (*Principles*, 1836 ed., p. 322). He explains that some groups of producers, notably manufacturers, employ their capital for production, and they have no disposition to consume all of what they produce; further, if it were not for the fact that in every country there are those who are "indisposed to consume to the value of what they produce," there could be no increase in national capital. He held that there must be expenditures to encourage commerce and general economic activity, yet a "state could be ruined by extravagance. . . . All that is contended for is, that no nation can possibly grow rich by an accumulation of capital arising from a permanent diminution of consumption; because such accumulation being beyond what is wanted in order to supply the effectual demand for produce, a part of it would very soon lose both its use and its value, and cease to possess the character of wealth." [29] Malthus was striving to establish a balance of the factors responsible for the "progress of wealth" and development of the economy. His analysis proved that overproduction or a general market glut was possible, yet the issue was not a pressing one and his arguments did not supplant the Say-Ricardo thesis.[30]

[27] Ricardo, *op. cit.*, pp. 275-76.
[28] Cf. J. M. Keynes, *General Theory* (New York, 1936), p. 32.
[29] *Principles*, 1836 ed., pp. 326-27; 1820 ed., pp. 369-70.
[30] See David Ricardo, *Notes on Malthus' "Principles of Political Economy"* (London, 1928), pp. 163-67.

An Evaluation of Malthus as an Economist.—The economic theories held by Malthus were not identical with those of Ricardo and his followers, yet they are generally grouped with the classical doctrines. The ruling orthodox doctrines for nearly all the first half of the nineteenth century were those which stemmed directly from Ricardo and indirectly from Smith.

Malthus is treated by most writers as a classical economist and rightly so. As a writer and teacher he ranks with the earliest, but as an expounder of original theory and doctrine he does not rank nearly so high as Smith or Ricardo. Most students associate Malthus with the population theory and let him have whatever glory may be attached to it and put little or no emphasis upon his contributions as a writer on distinctly economic subjects. The foregoing pages are intended to show some of his important economic ideas.

Malthus was a more polished scholar than Ricardo and should have been able to produce clearer statements of principles. Furthermore, he had the benefit of a complete knowledge of Ricardo's theories and views before he began to write. Unfortunately, he continued his argument in a way that excluded an immediate and decisive contribution to economic thought.

Malthus entered the controversies of his day with alacrity and showed keenness of observation and effective reasoning. His views on the rent controversy provided the fundamentals of Ricardo's rent doctrine. The emphasis Malthus put upon supply and demand as coordinates always at work under competition as the price-determining factors of the productive agents was an advance in economic reasoning. Neither supply nor demand was analyzed effectively, but their interdependence was emphasized. One might correctly argue that Malthus did not produce a well-rounded work on political economy. His sins of omission are indeed great. Theories of trade, exchange, money and credit, and the like are not developed. Only a limited knowledge of the impact of the industrial changes in his times is indicated and many of the contemporary issues are unmentioned. Nevertheless, no scholar was more anxious than Malthus to find the truth on the issues with which he dealt. It is to his credit that he emphasized man before wealth and wealth only as related to man's well-being. Had other economists placed greater emphasis upon man than upon wealth, not only might economic science have taken a different course but perhaps the world might have been a better place in which to live. In any event, Malthus should not be charged with the full responsibility for making political economy a "dismal science" with all its forebodings of the disasters which would overtake mankind. He called a halt to the loose thinking that nature was a great and sure provider. He had a boundless faith in man's ability and willingness to find the truth, which he himself pursued with vigor. Perhaps in time Malthus' contribution to political economy will rank, as James Bonar has placed it, second in time and honor to Adam Smith's and at least equal to Ricardo's contribution to general theory. But opinions of long standing are hard to break; doubtless Malthus will be remembered solely for his work on population and Ricardo will continue to hold his rank for contributions to original theory, especially in the field of distribution.

12

David Ricardo, the Developer
of Classical Tradition

The name of David Ricardo has long been pre-eminent in economics.
A great share of economic theory stems from the work of this man,
who became a most distinguished economist more by accident than
by design. Whereas Adam Smith ranged over a broad field of economic
subject matter, it was Ricardo who erected the landmarks of economics
which, for so many years, have provided the bearings for reckoning the
course of classical economic theory. Ricardo became the acknowledged
leader not only of his contemporaries but of economists for nearly a
century. He attained eminence equal to that of Smith, if not greater,
yet these two men were vastly different from one another in method
of analysis, scope of reasoning, and objectives. Students of economics
often fail to appreciate the extent to which Ricardo furnished both
warp and weft of current economics. Our purpose is to examine the
origin and development of what is so commonly known as "Ricardian
economics."

His Life and Times.—David Ricardo (1772-1823) was born in London,
the third child of a Jewish immigrant of Spanish descent who came
from Holland, and who later became a prosperous member of the
Stock Exchange. Young Ricardo went to school in London until he
was twelve, when he was sent to school in Holland for two years for
a commercial education. In 1786, at the age of fourteen, he entered
his father's business, where he soon learned the intricacies of brokerage
in the Exchange. He was brought up in the tenets of strict orthodoxy
and in comfortable material circumstances but in considerable seclusion.
Evidences of reaction to rigid conformity were shown at an early age.
However, when at the age of twenty-one he married a Quakeress, Miss
Priscilla Anne Wilkinson, and embraced Christianity, a rupture came
between father and son with the result that young Ricardo was put
completely on his own. He then entered the trading floor of the Ex-

change on his own account with the financial backing of other members of the Exchange. He showed exceptional capacity in trading and by the age of twenty-six had amassed a large fortune: in less than ten years of active trading he had acquired a fortune estimated at about £2,000,000. He began to retire from the Exchange in 1814. Meanwhile, he maintained his interest in academic subjects and studied mathematics, chemistry, and science and became one of the original members of the Geological Society. In 1814 he moved to a country estate, Gatcomb Park, in Gloucestershire, where he spent the remainder of his days.

Ricardo's first acquaintance with the *Wealth of Nations* came in 1799; the book stimulated him more than the other sciences and led him to thinking and writing on economic subjects. In 1819 he entered politics as a member of the House of Commons. He bought his seat in Parliament as a representative of Portarlington, an Irish pocket borough, commonly known as a "rotten borough." His interest in politics and parliamentary issues was keen; he participated freely in the controversial issues of the day such as resumption of specie payment, bank reform, tax proposals, national debt retirement, Robert Owen's schemes, savings banks, and projects for popular education.

Ricardo enjoyed the friendship and intellectual stimulation of James Mill, J. R. McCulloch, J. B. Say, and Malthus on matters of more or less theoretical and academic nature, and with Trower in the field of banking and finance.[1] He was one of the founders along with Malthus, of the Political Economy Club of London, in 1821, which did so much to establish the classical doctrine.

Even though Ricardo, in comparison with Smith and Malthus, possessed little formal education, he was an exceptionally keen thinker. "Fewer men possessed in a higher degree than Mr. Ricardo, the talent of speaking and conversing with clearness and facility on the abstrusest topics." [2] He never engaged in controversial issues without thoughtful deliberation, and when he spoke or wrote his ideas were well developed. In Parliament his speeches were noted for their elegance of diction and devastating logic.

As a member of Parliament, Ricardo stood for Parliamentary reform, universal suffrage, and the secret ballot; he held liberal views on reforming the Bank of England, currency, agriculture, poor relief, tariff and

---

[1] See James Bonar and J. H. Hollander (eds.), *Letters of David Ricardo to Hutches Trower and Others, 1811-1823* (Oxford, 1899). Trower was a member of the Stock Exchange and, like Ricardo, a shareholder in the Bank of England. He was a man of many business interests, active in politics and bank reform, and a keen writer and observer. The *Letters* shed important light upon Ricardo's thinking.

[2] J. R. McCulloch (ed.), *The Works of Ricardo* (London, 1852), p. xxx. The first volume contains "Memoir," a brief account of Ricardo's life, pp. xv-xxxiii.

free trade, freedom of the press, free speech, reduction of the national debt by levies on capital, and repeal of duties on grain. Many of the reforms he advocated would surely have been costly to him as a rich man; he was, as Professor W. C. Mitchell has said, a "millionaire radical." Never a party politician, he strove for the common good and for the rights and liberties of all classes.

Ricardo died in 1823, in his fifty-second year. During his lifetime he was most generous with his wealth, having contributed heavily to charity and maintained two almshouses at his own expense. His once large estate had dwindled to £700,000 at his death, largely because of his generous gifts. He left a widow, three sons, and four daughters. McCulloch gives an interesting characterization as follows:

No man was ever more thoroughly free from every species of artifice and pretension; more sincere, plain and unassuming. He was particularly fond of assembling intelligent men around him, and in conversing in the most unrestrained manner on all topics of interest, but more especially on those connected with his favorite science. On these as on all occasions, he readily gave way to others, and never displayed the least impatience to speak; but when he did speak, the solidity of his judgement, his candor, and his extraordinary talent for resolving a question into its elements, and for setting the most difficult and complicated subjects in the most striking point of view, arrested the attention of everyone, and delighted all who heard him. He never entered into an argument, whether in public or private, for the sake of displaying ingenuity, of baffling an opponent, or of gaining a victory. The discovery of truth was his exclusive object.[3]

Ricardo's Writings.—For purposes of clarity and emphasis Ricardo's writings will be treated under two groupings: first, the minor pamphlets which represent his ideas on controversial issues; second, his work on principles of political economy. This is done with an awareness of the timing of the pamphlets in relation to the *Principles,* and at the sacrifice of complete chronological sequence. It seems expedient, however, to treat the principles as a basic unit and his other minor articles or pamphlets as, in a sense, supplemental material.

Ricardo's minor writings fall under two general headings: those dealing with money and financial subjects, and those dealing with agricultural subject matter. Since some of his minor writings are among the best things he wrote, they deserve attention not only as evidence of his advanced, liberal ideas on the issues, but also as exhibits of his style and method of analysis.

Ricardo's style and method of analysis almost defy classification. Adam Smith was shown (cf. Chapter 10, pp. 167 ff.) to have used the

---

[3] McCulloch, "Memoir," p. xxx.

deductive method rather generally and had the faculty of simple and concrete presentation of materials; since Ricardo was in a sense a follower of Smith, one might expect him to use somewhat similar methods. But this is not true. One of the very interesting anomalies of the two men is that Smith, well-trained through formal education and travel but without business experience, wrote in a style and applied a method of deduction from observed facts which he intended "all the world of educated people" to read. Ricardo, on the other hand, without much formal education but a highly successful businessman, wrote with an abstractness that challenged the best minds to comprehend. He sets up hypotheses and makes assumptions many of which are overstrained and incorrect. He tends to move in a world of abstractions. Some of his assumptions are arbitrarily chosen; yet from them he reasons deductively and arrives at his conclusions. In some of his minor writings, however, he is much less abstract and more inductive than his critics give him credit for. He uses loose phraseology, faulty arrangement of materials, and at times loses the sequence of thoughts. Criticism of his method has been voluminous. Senior called him "the most incorrect writer who ever attained philosophical eminence." Yet with all his faults in composition the fundamentals of his theories are clearly discernible. Generally speaking, his errors are the results of confused meaning in the use of ordinary terminology and specific application to illustrations which he devised. Little is to be gained in fault-finding; however faulty their expression, the contributions of Ricardo far outweigh his faults.

Ricardo's monetary and financial pamphlets deserve first consideration. He wrote them in terms indicating complete and authoritative acquaintance with the subject matter. His first printed work was "The High Price of Bullion, a Proof of the Depreciation of Bank Notes," a series of letters which appeared in the *Morning Chronicle* in the fall of 1809. They stimulated considerable discussion and encouraged Ricardo to expand his theories into a tract bearing the same title, which was published in 1810 and went through four editions, the fourth being the best. This tract had an important bearing upon the so-called "Bullion Controversy," which was then raging on matters concerning banking and currency. Ricardo showed conclusively that both redundancy and deficiency in circulating media were relative terms. The value of money —not whether it consisted of gold or silver coins or convertible paper money—was the important issue. Before the value of any money could be arrived at, an agreement had to be reached on what was to be standard money and what the bank notes were to represent. These issues, as well as the power of the Bank of England to regulate the supply and other questions regarding exchange rates, were skilfully handled; they were incorporated substantially as he presented them in the report of the Bullion Committee in 1810. This fact gave Ricardo great prestige. The controversy brought forth a statement by a prominent merchant, Mr. Bosanquet, entitled *Practical Observations,* which was at complete variance with the Committee's report. Ricardo completely destroyed the arguments of Bosanquet in his *Reply to Mr. Bosanquet's Practical Observations on the Report of the Bullion Committee,* published in 1811, which McCulloch characterizes as "one of the best essays that has appeared on any disputed question of Political Economy." [4]

Ricardo's next monetary tract appeared in 1816 and was entitled *Proposals for an Economical and Secure Currency, with Observations on the Profits of the Bank of England.* In this tract he discussed whether or not the Bank was obliged to pay its notes in specie upon demand and what the public should receive in return from public deposits with the Bank.

The first point was the most significant one. Here he proposed that, instead of being payable in coins, bank notes be made payable in bars of gold bullion of the standard weight and purity. This plan would check overissue, prevent gold from getting into circulation, save expense of coinage, wear and tear, and so on. He opposed the excessive profits made by the Bank of England from the monopoly it enjoyed and from its use of public funds: he proposed that the directors of the Bank make liberal concessions to the government from its extra and unusual profits.

The materials dealing with agriculture reflect Ricardo's interest and participation in the contemporary Corn Laws controversy. Those discussions were most important from 1813 to 1815. In the latter year Ricardo wrote a significant pamphlet relating to agriculture, namely, *The Influence of a Low Price of Corn on the Profits of Stock* and in 1822 another entitled, *On Protection to Agriculture.* Both essays deal with protection against free trade in grain; he favored gradual repeal of corn duties except for a small duty which would be just sufficient to compensate for certain taxes incident to the cultivation of the land. It was generally argued that high duties on corn meant an increase in rent at the expense of profits. In other words, any increase in the price of raw produce forced wages up and profits down. Ricardo showed that savings came from profits and that a low rate of profits would affect savings and capital accumulation, which were so sorely needed for the development of industries. He favored obtaining corn from as many sources as were available. He held that distress in agriculture, as in all other industry, could be due to monetary problems and that

[4] McCulloch, "Memoir," p. xx.

taxation affects other industries as well as agriculture. He showed that agriculture had no greater grievance than any other industry and that no special claims could be advanced in its behalf. Ricardo's tract *On Protection to Agriculture* (1822) is regarded by McCulloch as "the best of all his pamphlets." He adds, "Had Mr. Ricardo never written anything else, this pamphlet would have placed him in the first rank of political economists." [5] After his death in 1823 a pamphlet entitled *Plans for the Establishment of a National Bank* (1824) and *Notes on Malthus' Principles of Political Economy* were published. The latter was in defense of his own theories against the criticism of Malthus. One other pamphlet completes the list: *Essay on the Funding System,* which is of little or no interest now. [6]

Principles of Political Economy and Taxation.—Ricardo is best known for his *On the Principles of Political Economy and Taxation,* published in 1817. Many of the ideas that appeared in his minor works or in pamphlets are incorporated in this book on principles, which established him as the greatest representative of classical political economy. He was a follower of Smith, yet he carried many of the doctrines to points of greater refinement than Smith. Ricardo did not have the educational background of Smith; as a result, his works lack the polish and finesse of the *Wealth of Nations.* There is no attempt in Ricardo's *Principles* to present a complete social philosophy as Smith tried to do. Ricardo made distribution the chief problem in economic theory, a narrower objective than Smith's, yet a most important one. The practical problem, as he saw it, was whether the power of the state should be used to maintain high incomes for the tenants and landlords, or whether the import duties should be reduced for the purpose of safeguarding the incomes (and profits) of the manufacturers and merchants. Specifically, then, what determines the proportions of national dividend (or income) which goes to labor, landlords, and capitalists?

The problems of distribution were not purely academic. On the contrary, they were very real and stemmed from English political and economic conditions of the time. England was in the midst of reconstruction problems following the Napoleonic Wars. Specie payment had been suspended, prices had advanced sharply, taxes were excessive, and a four billion dollar national debt confronted the nation. Manu-

[5] McCulloch, "Memoir," p. xxix.
[6] It does not fall within the scope of this book to present the full particulars of these pamphlets. See David Ricardo, *Economic Essays,* ed. by E. C. K. Gonner (London, 1923) for a complete list of his essays. Also *The Works of David Ricardo,* ed. J. R. McCulloch (London, 1852). Burt Franklin and G. Legman, *David Ricardo and Ricardian Theory, A Bibliographical Checklist* (New York, 1949), contains a complete list of Ricardo's writings, works about him, and Ricardian theory.

facturing had made rapid strides despite the wars, and the tendency was to make the manufacturers and merchants, whose profits had been great, bear the burden of taxes and loans. The factory system, with its higher wage rates and by drawing population to industrial centers, created both economic and social problems; the increase in population made the nation dependent upon the import of food despite improved agricultural methods at home. There was a tendency for the capitalistic groups (merchants and manufacturers) to seek political unity and power, and for the laboring groups to combine and become vocal. The Tory government was in power and resisted reform, thereby encouraging what it most feared. Parliament wavered between pressure groups and passed laws often antithetical to public interest. The landed interests feared the import of grain would ruin their prices; therefore, they advocated raising the duties on grain. The towns and industrial districts representing the wage earners protested any measure which would increase their living cost. The reasoning was that high food prices forced high wages, and high wages meant high prices, less business, and ruinously low profits. Low profits in turn would affect capital expansion, hence employment, and so on. The controversy ultimately became a bitter struggle between the two identifiable classes of landlords and capitalists. Labor, being without leadership in Parliament, did not participate directly in the struggle.[7]

It was into this economic and political setting that Ricardo plunged and gave the full strength of his keen mind to salvaging something from the muddied intellectual waters. He worked fast. The issues were most pressing and reform was imperative. This pressure accounts, to some extent, for the lack of accuracy which may be found in his work. He could not afford the luxury of ten or more leisurely years in composition such as Smith enjoyed. Errors crept in: lack of sequence, organization, and system plague the reader; rigorous deduction from questionable assumptions, hypothetical rather than historical illustrations are his forte. Abstraction seems to have been an obsession with him. However, despite the sharp contrast between his methods and those of Smith, Ricardo was essentially a concrete thinker whose theorizing rested upon the contemporary world as he knew it.[8]

It is probable that he did not want to write a book. James Mill was the one who was most urgent in persuading Ricardo to undertake the work.[9] His thoughts on various important subjects were combined and

---

[7] William Smart, *Economic Annals of the Nineteenth Century* (London, 1910-17), I, 450-57, presents an interesting account of the Corn Law debates.

[8] See S. N. Patten, "The Interpretation of Ricardo," *Quarterly Journal of Economics*, VII, April, 1893, pp. 26-31.

[9] J. S. Mill, *Autobiography*, p. 23.

sent to the press before they were completely finished. The book, there-fore, lacks system. Even in the second edition (1819) and the third (1821) he added chapters to the work but made no attempt to recast it.[10] Some chapters, notably those on taxation and the one on ma-chinery, logically belong elsewhere in the book than where they now appear. Many of the later chapters are mainly investigations related to general principles as set forth earlier in the book. Professor E. C. K. Gonner in his "Introductory Essay" to the *Principles* shows a rearrange-ment of the chapters by subject matter and logical relationship; the book thus rearranged is much more presentable. Let us, however, look at the *Principles* as Ricardo left them, remembering that he was not enter-ing a prize essay contest.

The book really deals with two major topics; first, the determination of value, wages, profits and rents; second, the effects of the many meth-ods of taxation. For purposes of logical presentation Ricardo's theory will be discussed under the following topics: (1) value theory; (2) rent, wages, and profits; (3) foreign trade; and (4) taxation.

In the preface to his *Principles of Political Economy and Taxation* [11] Ricardo begins by saying, "The produce of the earth—all that is derived from its surface by the united application of labour, machinery and capital, is divided among three classes of the community; namely, the proprietor of the land, the owner of the stock or capital necessary for its cultivation, and the labourers by whose industry it is cultivated." The proportions or shares which the three classes receive are rent, profits, and wages. "To determine the laws which regulate this distribution is the principal problem in political economy . . ." He gives to Mal-thus and West the credit for developing the "true doctrine of rent" and admits that "much as the science has been improved by the writings of Turgot, Steuart, Smith, Say, Sismondi and others, they afford very little satisfactory information respecting the rational course of rent, profit, and wages." Thus he accepts a differential rent doctrine (as de-veloped by Malthus, West, and possibly Anderson), the principle of diminishing returns, and the population theory of Malthus, and uses them as necessary equipment in his work.

Value Theory.—Ricardo begins his chapter on value—the longest in the book—by quoting from Adam Smith that passage (cf. *Wealth of*

10 It is probable that James Mill advised against any revision of principles, for he wished to convey a sense of positiveness to the work. Ricardo says in a letter to Trower, "Indeed, he advises me not to notice any of the attacks which have been made upon me, in my third edition." *Letters of David Ricardo to Hutches Trower and Others,* p. 141.

11 All textual references hereafter are to the edition by E. C. K. Gonner (London, 1908), a reprint of the third edition in 1821 of the *Principles.*

Nations, Book I, chap. iv) referring to the two uses of the term value: value in use and value in exchange. He uses air and water as examples of useful, even indispensable, goods; gold, on the contrary, though of little use as compared with air and water will exchange for great quantities of other goods. And he adds, "Utility then is not the measure of exchangeable value, although it is absolutely essential to it," and "Possessing utility, commodities derive their exchangeable value from two sources: from their scarcity, and from the quantity of labour required to obtain them" (pp. 5, 6). He allows for exceptions in some commodities, such as "rare statues and pictures, scarce books and coins, wines of a peculiar quality" whose "value is wholly independent of the quantity of labour originally necessary to produce them" and is owing to scarcity. "No labour can increase the quantity of such goods, and therefore their value can not be lowered by an increased supply." He insists that these commodities form a very small part of the mass of articles daily exchanged in the market but that the "greatest part of those goods which are the objects of desire are produced by labour; and may be multiplied . . . almost without any assignable limit, if we are disposed to bestow the labour necessary to obtain them" (p. 6). In general he is concerned with commodities which can be "increased in quantity by the exertion of human industry, and on the production of which competition operates without restraint" (p. 7). He is interested in the explanation of the value of what we would identify as freely reproducible goods, from the point of view of the producer, or seller, rather than the buyer of goods. His concept of natural value rests upon perfect competition with no restrictions upon the supply of goods.

Ricardo quotes the *Wealth of Nations* (Book I, chap. v) in proof of his contention that goods exchange for each other in proportion to the amount of labor required to obtain them. He admits difficulty in "comparing an hour's or a day's labour, in one employment, with the same duration of labour in another" (p. 15). But he thinks that the relationship "comes soon to be adjusted in the market with sufficient precision for all practical purposes, and depends much on the comparative skill of the labourer, and intensity of the labour performed." Once a scale of precision is established, it "is liable to little variation." He points out the error in Smith's reasoning that sometimes labor purchases a greater and sometimes a smaller quantity of goods, but "it is their value which varies, not that of the labour which produces them." He concludes, "it is the comparative quantity of commodities which labour will produce, that determines their present or past relative value, and not the comparative quantities of commodities, which are given to the labourer in exchange for his labour" (p. 11). In other words, the value of commodities is measured by "embodied labour" and not by what it will "command" in exchange.

The meaning of "labor" is not exactly clear. It is composed of persons with different degrees of skill and qualities; likewise, it may be directly or indirectly employed, the latter term referring to the labor required in creating tools or implements or capital employed in final production. He also recognizes problems in attempting to compare past labor, already expended, with present labor. He never resolved these issues to his complete satisfaction.

Ricardo's theory of value went through at least three identifiable stages.[12] The mental anguish he endured in trying to arrive at a satisfactory theory reflects the controversies of his day involving Smith's theory, those of contemporary writers and critics, and his own analysis. In each of the three editions, this struggle is apparent and he never felt he had stated his thoughts in final form. Strangely enough, his attempt at an explanation of value in the 1817 edition of his *Principles* was more for the purpose of proving "the compatibility of a rise in wages, with a fall in prices" (*Principles*, 1817 ed., p. 42) than an exposition of a theory of value. In other words, he attempted to prove the proposition that higher wages do not necessarily mean higher prices.

The familiar postulate of "embodied labor" of Smithian derivation was that so long as the relative value of commodities was measured by this "embodied labor," only an increase in the amount of labor necessary to produce them could increase their value, and, conversely, only a decrease in the amount of labor would lower their value. Therefore, a general rise or fall in wages would bring no change in prices. Smith's problem was to establish labor (embodied labor) as a universal measure of value, which would then prove that prices did not necessarily rise or fall as wages rose or fell. But this applied in "a rude state of society," a condition which changed when private ownership and use of land and capital prevailed. Labor ceased to be the sole measure of value. Rent of land and profits now became a part of price, and the real price of commodities changed with every change in the rate of wages, rate of profits, and the rent of land; or so Adam Smith would have one believe.

Ricardo dissented. Rent of land did not enter into price in any society. The rate of wages and the amount of profits were the important factors in value and price. Production was carried on by labor with the aid of fixed and circulating capital to which wages and profits (interest) were paid. Any change in the amounts of either of the factors used in production, or in the amounts paid to either, would affect the

    [12] See J. H. Hollander, "The Development of Ricardo's Theory of Value," *Quarterly Journal of Economics*, XVIII (August, 1904).

relative values of each in terms of the other. Prices would therefore be affected by changes in an inverse relationship. "Every rise in wages, or, which is the same thing, every fall in profits, would lower the relative value of those commodities which were produced with a capital of a durable nature, and would proportionately elevate those which were produced with capital more perishable. A fall in wages would have precisely the contrary effect" (p. 33). This statement implies that the value of money remains unchanged.

Ricardo used money as an expression of "embodied value." He admits that "money being a variable commodity, the rise in wages will be frequently occasioned by a fall in the value of money. A rise in wages from this cause will, indeed, be invariably accompanied by a rise in the price of commodities; but in such cases it will be found that labour and all commodities have not varied in regard to each other, and that the variation has been confined to money" (p. 40). In the same section he repeats, "A rise in wages, from an alteration in the value of money, produces a general effect on price, and for that reason it produces no real effect on profits." He makes many references to prove his doctrine of the absence of any direct relationship between wages and prices.[13]

Criticisms of Ricardo's "embodied labour" explanation of value came from a number of sources.[14] Ricardo complained to McCulloch that he had distinctly stated that the quantity of labor was not the sole regulator of value when capital of unequal durability was employed.[15] He says in another letter to McCulloch,

I am more convinced than ever that the great regulator of value is the quantity of labour required to produce the commodity valued. There are many modifications which must be admitted into this doctrine, from the circumstances of the unequal times that commodities require to be brought to the market, but this does not invalidate the doctrine itself. I am not satisfied with the explanation which I have given of the principles which

[13] In chap. vii, p. 112, he writes, "It has been my endeavour to show throughout this work, that the rate of profits can never be increased but by a fall in wages, and that there can be no permanent fall of wages but in consequence of a fall in the necessities on which wages are expended." He adds, ". . . every diminution in the wages of labour raises profits but produces no effect on the price of commodities."

[14] Torrens criticized it in the *Edinburgh Magazine and Literary Miscellany*, October, 1818, in an article, "Strictures on Mr. Ricardo's Doctrine respecting Exchangeable Value." McCulloch defended Ricardo in the same magazine. Malthus gave an entire section (chap. ii, sec. iv) in his *Principles of Political Economy* to an effective criticism of the adequacy "Of the Labour which a commodity has cost, considered as a Measure of Exchangeable Value."

[15] *Letters of David Ricardo to James Ramsey McCulloch, 1816-1823* (New York, 1895), p. 15.

regulate value. I wish a more able pen would undertake it. The fault is not in the adequacy of the doctrine to account for all difficulties, but in the adequacy of him who has attempted to explain it.[16]

The criticism of Malthus in his *Principles of Political Economy* (p. 104) forced Ricardo to give further attention to the theory. McCulloch was his defender, yet it was to McCulloch that he wrote in May, 1820, "After the best consideration that I can give to the subject, I think that there are two causes which occasion variations in the relative value of commodities: 1st, the relative quantity of labour required to produce them; 2nd, the relative times that must elapse before the result of such labour can be brought to the market." [17] Here, Ricardo brings in a time element as coordinate with the quantity of labor; this apparently is but another element in his already confused attempts to arrive at an explanation. He admits to McCulloch again that

It must be confessed that this subject of value is encompassed with difficulties. I shall be very glad if you succeed in unravelling them, and establish for us a measure of value which shall not be liable to the objections which have been brought against all those hitherto proposed. I sometimes think that if I were to write the chapter on value again which is my book, I should acknowledge that the relative value of commodities was regulated by two causes instead of one, namely, by the relative quantity of labour necessary to produce the commodities in question, and by the rate of profit for the time that the capital remained dormant and until the commodities were brought to the market. Perhaps I should find the difficulties nearly as great in this view of the subject as in that which I have adopted.[18]

In the last edition of the *Principles*, Ricardo emphasizes that "embodied labour" is the most practicable measure of value and that gold is the most acceptable monetary medium for expressing value. He is not so anxious to refute the charge that higher wages are the cause of higher prices, yet he keeps pressing the relationship of wages and profits, "The proportion which might be paid for wages, is of utmost importance in the question of profits; for it must at once be seen, that profits would be high or low *exactly in proportion* as wages were low or high but it could not in the least affect the relative value . . ." of the commodity in question.[19]

Ricardo never felt that he had a satisfactory theory of value, and he continued to maintain that an invariable measure of value was unattainable but that one must make the "best choice among confessedly imperfect measures" (*Letters . . . to McCulloch*, p. 177). He says, "There

16 *Ibid.*, pp. 47, 48.
17 *Ibid.*, p. 65.
18 *Ibid.*, pp. 71, 72.
19 *Principles*, chap. i, sec. iii, p. 21; italics supplied.

has never been, and I think there never will be, any perfect measure of value" (*Ibid.*, p. 173). He indicated, however, that the great mass of commodities were produced by labor and capital rather than by either alone. Money, which compounded the two factors, wages and profits, was more serviceable for practical purposes than labor alone (embodied labor) or profits alone.

What, then, is his theory of value? His concern was with exchange value or the extent to which one commodity will command another in exchange. He believed that a ratio will exist which will show whether the amount of one commodity which may be gotten in exchange will be due to a change in its value or a change in the value of the commodity for which it exchanges. This is not a cost of production theory. He does not call cost of production the cause of value,[20] but he does make the foundation of his theory rest upon cost, a coordinate wages and profits cost. Even though he says in the Preface that the "produce of the earth" is divided into three parts, rents, profits, and wages, and divided among the three classes, he never again makes them coordinate. Wages and profits are all that he includes in his cost of production explanation. He often contrasts wages and profits or rent and profits, but never rent and wages. Wages are a cost of production and he sometimes treats profits as a surplus. When he considers the distribution of the surplus, he contrasts rent and profits; but rents grow at the expense of profits, since an increase or growth of population again raises the price of food. These he believed to be true relationships in his day.

His theory is neither a labor theory nor a quantity of labor theory of value. He struggled with the problem of discrepancies between value and price. He realized that value was not always identical with market price and that an average rate of profits must be forthcoming to the owner of capital in order to induce investment. The lack of precise meaning has enabled some to see in Ricardo's work nothing but a cost of production theory and to set it up as a strictly labor cost theory.

Rent Theory.—Ricardo defines rent as "that portion of the produce of the earth, which is paid to the landlord for the use of the original and indestructible powers of the soil" (*Principles*, chap. ii). The definition was not accurate or true, as he applied it. Rent is paid only for "powers" of the land which exceed those in the land just worth cultivating; "powers" are indeed destructible: powers—in the sense of fertility—can be either created or destroyed. His contribution to rent theory is the well-known differential surplus theory, not his definition.

[20] See *Principles*: "In early stages of society, the exchangeable value of these commodities . . . depends almost exclusively on the comparative quantity of labour expended on each." P. 7, also p. 14.

In his discussion of rent, he has the same difficulty as he had in discussing value—an uncertainty as to what he meant. The first uncertainty is found in the definition of "payment." In Chapter II ("On Rent") he means a crop-rent or commodity-rent. In Chapter XXIV ("The Doctrine of Adam Smith Concerning the Rent of Land") he uses money-rent in attempting to prove that the landlord's interest in securing higher rent is opposed to the community interest. In Chapter XXXII ("Mr. Malthus' Opinions on Rent") he defends the people against the landlord class, the group championed by Malthus. Malthus regarded rent as an addition to national wealth, whereas Ricardo held it to be only a transfer of value from one person to another; "Rent then is a creation of value, but not a creation of wealth; it adds nothing to the resources of a country, it does not enable it to maintain fleets and armies . . ." (p. 394). Here, then, he had to regard rent as a money return not a commodity-rent. It was pointed out (cf. Chapter 10, p. 189) that Smith looked upon the landlord as a monopolist and rent as a monopoly return. On this point also Ricardo is uncertain, at times treating it as a monopoly payment and then again as a competitive return. He presents the latter view in his Chapter II. Another uncertainty was in regard to the treatment of the rent return as a pure land-rent or as a return to capital and land when used conjointly.

It should be remembered that Ricardo was interested in profits; rents and profits were always contrasted, because they varied inversely. As margins of cultivation are contracted, rents in the form of differential surpluses decline, and vice versa; assuming continued population pressure on food supply, rents and prices go up because of declining profits and because of expanded margins of cultivation which bring in land of higher cost. Should the Corn Laws be amended to permit importation of corn, Ricardo believed that it would not only mean lower rents and lower prices but higher profits and higher margins of cultivation. Thus the interests of the receivers of rents (landlords) were antithetical to the interests of capitalists and manufacturers. As a free trader he supported the removal of the Corn Law duties which were beneficial to all non-agricultural classes but detrimental to the landlords. Ricardo saw well enough that all of society would lose, because of a smaller national product, a fact which presented him with a dilemma. He avoided it, in a sense, by taking the point of view of national welfare and adhering to money rent—a monetary value of the surplus.

It was pointed out that Malthus was credited by Ricardo with developing the rent theory. But the two men arrived at different conclusions. Malthus wanted to prove that the high price of food was not due to monopoly in landownership or to the Corn Laws but resulted from national social progress. An increasing population required more food which could be produced only by cultivation of inferior land; this cultivation meant higher production costs and subsequently higher food prices. Prices had to be sufficiently high to allow farmers their usual profits even on the inferior lands; in fact, national progress and prosperity were at stake. The high price of food therefore was a result of population pressure and not of the Corn Laws. A retention of the Corn Laws would encourage farmers to improve production methods and create surpluses out of which rents would be paid. Thus Malthus became a protectionist and defended the Corn Laws as important contributing factors in building national wealth.

Ricardo differed with Malthus' conclusion. Since he held that rent was not an element in national wealth [21] but, as he says, "a creation of value," he could draw a theoretical conclusion which was universally applicable and not the result of a narrow political expedient such as the Corn Laws. He could build his case on a universal principle that as food prices rose profits would fall. Since national prosperity depended upon profits, which were mainly of industrial origin, rather than upon high rents, which were of agricultural origin, the importance of the two factors is at once apparent. One must look to wages and profits and not to rents as the most important factors in the national economy.

Specifically, then, Ricardo argues that "The most fertile, and the most favourably situated land will be the first cultivated." The produce raised on this land will get its value "by the total quantity of labour necessary . . . to produce it and bring it to market." When inferior grades of land are cultivated, the "exchangeable value of raw produce will rise, because of the labour required to produce it" (p. 49). This exchangeable value is "always regulated" not by the "less quantity of labour" required for production under "circumstances most highly favourable" but by a "greater quantity of labour" required for production "under most unfavourable circumstances" (p. 50).

The reason then why raw produce rises in comparative value, is because more labour is employed on the last portion obtained, and not because a rent is paid to the landlord. The value of corn is regulated by the quantity of labour bestowed on its production on that quality of land, or with that portion of capital, which pays no rent. Corn is not high because a rent is paid, but a rent is paid because corn is high; and it has been justly observed, that no reduction would take place in the price of corn, although landlords should forego the whole of their rent. Such a measure would only enable some farmers to live like gentlemen, but would not diminish the quantity

[21] "The rise of rent is always the effect of the increasing wealth of the country, and of the difficulty of providing food for its augmented population. It is a symptom, but never a cause of wealth" (p. 54).

of labour necessary to raise raw produce on the least productive land in cultivation (pp. 50, 51).

Smith spoke of rent as a bounty of nature; he wrote, "nature labours along with man and though her labour costs no expense its produce has its value, as well as that of the most expensive workman." But Ricardo argues that "the labour of nature is paid, not because she does much but because she does little. In proportion as she becomes niggardly in her gifts, she exacts a greater price for her work. Where she is munificently beneficent, she always works gratis" (p. 53).

Ricardo emphasizes the rent-price relationship—which principle he insists is "of utmost importance to the science of political economy"— that rent is a result of price. He says the "corn which is produced by the greatest quantity of labour is the regulator of the price of corn; and rent does not and cannot enter in the least degree as a component part of its price" (p. 55). In pricing other commodities their value (or price) is, like that of corn, "regulated by the productiveness of the portion of capital last employed on the land and paying no rent: and therefore rent is not a component part of the price of commodities" (p. 55). There can be little doubt that Ricardo won the argument. Land cultivated at the margin yields no surplus but on all lands above the margin a surplus appears which affords an "unearned increment" [22] to the owner of the land and an income properly subject to taxation. The tax would fall wholly on the landlord, who is unable to shift it to anyone else. The tax would only take a certain amount from the landlord and transfer it to the state.

In Chapter III Ricardo discusses the "Rent of Mines." Adam Smith had spoken of the rent of forests, quarries and mines. In the concrete cases which Smith uses, he refers to the payments not as fixed annual sums but in percentages of produce extracted. Smith treats wages, profit, and rent as component parts of price. The payments for the materials removed or "destroyed" are neither wages nor profits; accordingly he was obliged to regard the payment as rent.

Ricardo was confronted with a serious problem of definition of terms, for certainly mineral resources are destructible. Quarry products and minerals are not replaced, and timber cut by wasteful methods may never be replaced by man or nature. Here a difference in landlordism arises. A landlord may normally expect some care in land utilization and a continuous income or rent ("annual value"). The owner of a quarry or mine, however, takes part (possibly all) of the capital value of the estate in extracting the commodity, rather than receiving an in-

[22] J. S. Mill's term, *Principles of Political Economy* (5th ed., New York, 1864), Bk. V, chap. ii, par. 5, p. 411.

come over a period of time from it. Ricardo says, "Mines as well as land, generally pay a rent to their owner" (p. 62). If mines were all "equally fertile" they would yield no rent. He applies the same reasoning to mines as he applied to land: granting ordinary profits on stock necessary to carry on the undertaking, "the return for capital from the poorest mine paying no rent, would regulate the rent of all the other productive mines." He holds that since the "principle is precisely the same as that which we have laid down respecting land" there is no need to expand on it.

His inconsistency probably rests upon a land-rent caused by diminishing returns. He could not use the same reasoning for mine-rent. He discusses gold and silver mines in America and refers to the fall in value of the metals "attributed to the improvements in the mode of working the mines" (p. 64), thus implying an increasing return. In any event his reasoning on land-rent as a differential still remains, and it was left for Alfred Marshall to resolve the dilemma by applying the term "royalty" to the payment for the products of the extractive industries.[23]

Wage Theory.—Ricardo's wage theory is commonly referred to as a subsistence theory. This theory—if indeed it may be called a theory— was not original with him. Some of the early mercantilists held ideas that may be regarded as explaining wages on a subsistence basis. Smith accepted a subsistence theory along with other theories.[24] The physiocrats put forward a kind of subsistence explanation by maintaining that the cultivators of land got only enough for their maintenance, the difference in production going to the landowners. It is likely that the statements of such writers were only observations of tendencies and not theoretical explanations or justifications for wages being at certain levels. The wage system was like Topsy, "it just growed"; labor was not vocal for many years, and wages tended to be as low as the least sum a worker could afford to take and keep himself and family alive. It was generally held that wages must be low in order to keep production cost low, thus making possible competition with other low-cost producing areas. Ricardo's observations contain an admixture of his theorizing on general economics, from which come some truth and considerable error.

---

[23] See E. A. Cannan, *Review of Economic Theory*, chap. viii, "Decay of the Ricardian Theories of Rent." Critics of the rent theory have been numerous: H. C. Carey in America; Torrens and Samuel Read, English contemporaries; von Thünen in Germany.

[24] Thos. Mun, *Englands Treasure by Forraign Trade*, p. 154. John Locke, *Some Considerations of the Lowering of Interest and Raising the Value of Money*, in *Works of John Locke*, Vol. V, p. 57. Adam Smith, *Wealth of Nations*, Bk. I, chap. i; cf. Chapter 10, p. 174 *supra*.

He begins his Chapter V, "On Wages," with the oft-quoted passage that "Labour, like all other things which are purchased and sold, and which may be increased or diminished in quantity, has its natural price and its market price. The natural price of labour is that price which is necessary to enable the labourers, one with another, to subsist and to perpetuate their race, without either increase or diminution" (p. 70). By natural price he means a long-run tendency, whereas the market price refers to varying conditions in the labor market at a given time. He then qualifies his statement that the "natural price" is not a definite sum but depends upon custom or habit of the worker and varies from time to time and in different countries (p. 74).

The power of the labourer to support himself, and the family which may be necessary to keep up the number of labourers, does not depend on the quantity of money which he may receive for wages, but on the quantity of food, necessaries, and conveniences become essential to him from habit, which that money will purchase. The natural price of labour, therefore, depends on the price of the food, necessaries, and conveniences required for the support of the labourer and his family. With a rise in the price of food and necessaries, the natural price of labour will rise; with the fall in their price, the natural price of labour will fall (p. 70).

The market price may deviate from the natural price as it does for commodities, but the tendency is to conform to it. "When the market price of labour exceeds the natural price, the condition of the labourer is flourishing and happy"; when the market price of labour is below the natural price, "the condition of the labourers is most wretched: then poverty deprives them of those comforts which custom renders absolute necessaries" (p. 71). If the market price of labor exceeds the natural price, the laborers get greater enjoyments of life and "rear a healthy and numerous family." However, the encouragement of high wages leads to "increase in population," thereby increasing the number of laborers, and wages fall again to their natural price, or even below it. Then when wages are so very low it is only "after privations have reduced their numbers, or the demand for labour has increased, that the market price of labour will rise to its natural price, and the labourers will have moderate comforts which the natural rate of wages will afford." [25]

The natural wage of Ricardo's theory will tend to keep population at its existing level, and no higher. It is not an average of high and low market rates, but a minimum below which market rates may not fall for any length of time although they may exceed it for an indefinite

---

[25] P. 72. Cantillon had somewhat the same idea on the importance of habit in wage determination. *Essay on the Nature of Commerce in General*, pp. 65-67.

period. The pessimism attributed to Ricardo in regard to future wage
rates came from his belief that the market rates of wages, even though
under some circumstances they might be above the natural rate, always
had the tendency to sink to the natural rate. He never argued that
rates must be low, nor did he say that they must approximate a bare
subsistence for the worker; he believed low wages to be a long-run
tendency, resting for the most part on the Malthusian principle of
population growth.

Ricardo held the view that wages and profits together constituted
cost of production and that the relationship between the two was inverse. Since these two shares taken together gave him a market price,
a decrease in one n.eant an increase in the other, and vice versa. But
a rise and fall in the shares each received meant a rise or fall in the
ratios or proportions which went to each share, not in the absolute
amounts. Also, he held that profits might increase without a decrease
in wages, because of improved modes of production, or for other reasons.
(See chap. i, sec. vii, pp. 41, 42.) "When wages rise it is generally because the increase of wealth and capital have occasioned a new demand
for labour, which will infallibly be attended with an increased production of commodities" (p. 81). He held that the only remedies to alleviate the pressure of the population, with its concurrent low wage,
misery, and suffering, were either a reduction of people (an unlikely
possibility) or a rapid accumulation of capital. These would vary considerably, depending upon the country, the amount of fertile land, the
nature of the people, and their capacity for accumulating capital.

Ricardo was not interested in high wages from the standpoint of any
benefits that might accrue to a wage earner. He saw in high wages a
manifestation of the higher costs of articles which the laborer consumed.
The employer received no compensation for higher wages in the form
of increased productivity, efficiency, and the like; their only meaning
for him was a fall of profits. It is probably true that Ricardo had no
interest in the wage earner per se, yet he comments that "The friends
of humanity cannot but wish that in all countries the labouring classes
should have a taste for comforts and enjoyments, and that they should
be stimulated by all legal means in their exertions to procure them.
There can be no better security against superabundant population"
(p. 77). In the same chapter he says in very certain terms that the
Poor Laws are to blame for perpetuating a bad condition and that the
poor must "have some regard on their part . . . to regulate their numbers" (p. 84). There can be only one remedy for the Poor Laws, and
that is their abolition. This, then, would be getting at one of the
basic factors affecting the supply of labor in relation to demand in so
far as wages are regulated by these forces.

Ricardo's ideas on wages, as on many other topics, are susceptible to other interpretations. He spoke of the tendency for the natural rate of wages to approach subsistence level, which in turn depended upon Malthusian assumptions. Some have made this tendency, as he called it, into a wage theory, more or less to suit their own needs. Thus, the German socialist, Ferdinand Lassalle, read into it the "Iron Law of Wages" (das eherne Lohngesetz) and made it a theory useful in radical doctrine to show the pessimistic outlook for all labor.[26] The theories of economic harmony of Quesnay and Adam Smith were no longer tenable.

Likewise it may be rightfully maintained that Ricardo accepted a wages-fund theory. Adam Smith and James Mill held such a theory, and Ricardo was greatly influenced by both men. Ricardo regards the demand for workers (or labor) at any time to be a fixed magnitude, dependent on and determined by the amount of necessities or commodities devoted to the payment of wages. Only on the basis of an increase of these items (which we may call a wages-fund) can there be an increase in wages. He makes the "fund" rest on real, not nominal, wages. He says, "The quantity of necessities to be allotted to the labourer depends upon the comparative demand and supply of labour, money being only the medium in which the quantity is expressed; and as neither of these is altered, the real reward of the labourer will not alter" (p. 146). He expressed the same idea in his correspondence with Malthus by saying that "the rise in wages would be in proportion to the increase in quantity of commodities produced." Ricardo always maintained that wages were only indirectly affected by the efficiency or productivity of labor; therefore a productivity theory could not be attributed to him. While he had accepted a wages-fund theory in principle,[27] the credit or discredit for the theory is generally given to John Stuart Mill, whereas the theory that the tendency of wages to approach a subsistence level is one for which Ricardo must answer.

Profits.—His profits theory, like his wage theory, is a mixture of error and achievement. His wage theory is a long-run subsistence theory re-

[26] Lassalle's statement reads: "The limitation of the average wages of labor to the necessities of life requisite among a people, according to custom, for the prolongation of the existence of the individual and for the perpetuation of the species—this is the iron and cruel law which controls the wages of labor under the relations of today." L. Brentano, *The Relation of Labor to the Law of Today* (New York, 1897), p. 163. Colonel Robert Torrens in his *Essay on the External Corn Trade* (London, 1815) says approximately the same thing, "The natural price . . . consists in such a quantity of the necessaries and comforts of life . . . as are necessary to support the labourer, and to enable him to rear such a family as may preserve in the market an undiminished supply of labour" (p. 62).

[27] See F. W. Taussig, *Wages and Capital* (New York, 1896), chap. ix.

lated to the real cost of commodities (food) "essential to him [the laborer] from habit," which commodities, for their values, depend on a labor-cost theory. Labor, therefore, being a definite element in cost of production was inversely related to profits. "Whatever increases wages, necessarily reduces profits" (p. 96). In this statement he was recording an economic fact of his day: cultivation was being extended to poorer soils, food costs were rising, as were rents while profits were declining.

Ricardo defined capital, in the chapter "On Wages," as "that part of the wealth of a country which is employed in production, and consists of food, clothing, tools, raw materials, machinery, etc., necessary to give effect to labour" (p. 72). His treatment of profits is really what we would identify as interest and entrepreneurial returns, but the two are not distinguished. The rate of interest is dependent upon the rate of profits that capital can make. He says, "The high profits on capital employed in producing that commodity, will naturally attract capital to that trade; and as soon as the requisite funds are supplied, and the quantity of the commodity is duly increased, its price will fall, and profits of the trade will conform to the general level" (p. 97). Thus he recognizes the power of competition to reduce profits to what he calls the "general level." But an inequality of profits may prevail which will cause capital to shift from "one employment" to another. Profits may fall in one industry but not in another, and extraordinary stimulus may be given at times to other employment. Regardless of exceptions, however, they "by no means invalidate the theory, that profits depend on high or low wages, wages on the price of necessities, and the price of necessities chiefly on the price of food" (p. 97). What Ricardo virtually says is that of the total product wages have the first claim, that the owner of capital takes what is left.

Another pessimistic element is his contention that "the natural tendency of profits is to fall." For reasons already given, higher labor costs are involved in producing more food. But the tendency of falling profits "is happily checked at repeated intervals by the improvements in machinery . . . discoveries in agriculture which enable us to relinquish a portion of labour before required, and therefore to lower the price of the prime necessary of the labourer" (p. 99). That profits are necessary is shown by his contention that "the farmer and manufacturer can no more live without profit than the labourer without wages. Their motive for accumulation will diminish with every diminution of profit, and will cease altogether when their profits are so low as not to afford them an adequate compensation for their trouble, and the risk which they must necessarily encounter in employing their capital productively" (p. 101).

After many pages he concludes that "in all countries, and at all times, profits depend on the quantity of labour requisite to provide the necessaries for the labourer, on that land and with that capital which yields no rent" (p. 105). Hence we must look to the margin of cultivation. The least productive land yields only enough to pay wages to labor and interest to capital employed in its cultivation. There is no rent. The product of the land then regulates the amount of wages and profits, and in turn the amount each receives depends on the real cost of necessities to the laborer.[28]

Ricardo never could escape from the dilemma in which he found himself; his assumptions were at fault, as were also his conclusions. Profits are not dependent upon wages but, like wages, are independently determined by many forces.

Foreign Trade.—Ricardo's contribution to foreign trade theory was the formulation of the principle of comparative costs. He was concerned with an explanation of the ratios at which commodities exchange in international trade. In internal trade the exchange tended to be fixed or governed by the *absolute* differences in cost; however, between countries there was no mobility of capital or labor and a theory of exchange based on absolute costs would not hold. Ricardo held that it was the *comparative* difference in costs that determined the rates of exchange. If one country can produce two commodities at a lower cost than another country but the advantage of producing one commodity is not so great as that of the other, it will pay the country to import the first commodity and to export the other in payment. The ratios of exchange between the two countries are therefore limited by the ratios of costs between the two countries. The costs are measured in terms of labor, as formerly explained.

It will be recalled that Ricardo favored perfect freedom of trade as "beneficial to a country as it increases the amount and variety of objects on which revenue may be expended . . . affords by the abundance and cheapness of commodities, incentives for saving . . . accumulation of capital, has no tendency to raise the profits of stock unless the commodities imported be of that description on which wages of labour are expended" (p. 113).

Ricardo was thoroughly familiar with the behavior of the exchange from his experience as a trader. He illustrates the comparative cost doctrine with English cloth and Portuguese wine to bring out his cost

[28] One of the most precise statements of the relations between profits and wages is found in chap. vii, "On Foreign Trade": "Profits, it cannot be too often repeated, depend on wages: not on nominal, but real, wages: not on the number of pounds that may be annually paid to the labourer, but on the number of days' work necessary to obtain those pounds" (p. 124).

principle for trading purposes. He points out that money plays a highly important part in trade: the diminution of money in a country (say Portugal) and its accumulation in another (say England) will "produce such a state of prices" that foreign trade between the two countries will cease. All commodities are affected by changes in the "state of prices" (price level) in such a manner that one nation may find its prices excessively high, thus becoming a "sellers' market" or excessively low and a "buyers' market." In time a new distribution of the precious metals takes place, restoring the former trade relationships. However, many artificial practices may interfere with the distribution of metals and thus affect price levels and trade.

Many details and involvements are omitted in this treatment, but enough has been presented to show that he clearly understood the theory and practice of the exchanges and to provide the theoretical "equilibrium" foundation for classical foreign trade doctrines.[29]

Taxation.—Almost one third of the *Principles* is devoted to taxation, in accordance with the title of the book. Even though a great deal of attention is given to many types of taxes, this part of the book is, from the standpoint of theory, least satisfactory. Ricardo is inclined to treat all taxes as special cases and therefore does not develop general principles or general classifications of taxes. He seems to treat the same form of taxation in different ways under different headings. Taxes on rents are discussed under three different titles ("Taxes on Rent," chap. x; "Land Tax," chap. xii; "Taxes on Houses," chap. xiv) and taxes on raw produce in at least four different ways. He fails to establish any exact principles on the incidence of taxation and how taxes affect prices, who bears the burden, and so on. All too often he merely recounts English tax practices and popular attitudes which, when mixed with unscientifically developed principles, nearly defy scientific arrangement.

In Chapter VIII, dealing with taxes in general, Ricardo begins by pointing out that when the annual production of a country exceeds its annual consumption, it increases its capital. Capital may be increased by increased production and diminished by unproductive consumption. It is very important, therefore, that "national capital" be unimpaired. If consumption is diminished as a result of the levying of taxes, then taxes will fall upon revenue, and capital will not be impaired; but if there is no increased production, the taxes will fall on capital and will "impair the funds allotted to productive consumption" (p. 132). All taxes, he holds, interfere with capital accumulation. "There are no

<hr />

[29] See J. W. Angell, *The Theory of International Prices* (Cambridge, Mass., 1926), chaps. ii, iv, xiv.

taxes which have not the tendency to lessen the power to accumulate. All taxes must either fall on capital or revenue" (p. 133). This, then, is one of his fundamental propositions: taxes should be so levied as to fall upon revenue, not capital. "It should be the policy of governments . . . never to levy taxes as will inevitably fall on capital; since by so doing, they impair the funds for the maintenance of labour, and thereby diminish the future production of the country" (p. 134). He held that taxes may be levied on rents, on prices, and on profits. Wages are automatically exempt, for they can stand no reduction, assuming that they are at their permanent (natural) level.

A tax on rent, he says, would affect rent only: "it would fall wholly on the landlords and could not be shifted to any class of consumers" (chap. viii, p. 154). But this statement applies only to economic rent which arises because of the characteristics of land. However, land generally requires some capital in the form of "buildings and fixtures . . . which form strictly a part of the stock of the farm." Rent (economic) is paid to the landlord "for the use of the land only." The additional sum which is paid him under the name of rent "is for the use of the buildings, etc., and is really the profits of the landlord's stock." A tax on this part of the capital equipment does not fall upon the landlord or the farmer, but on the consumer of raw produce. Thus, he distinguishes two elements: a tax on economic rent which is borne by the landlord, and a tax on the physical equipment or capital which is passed on to the consumer of the produce of the land.

He holds that any tax on raw produce which may be imposed upon the cultivator, whether it be in the form of land tax, tithes, or a tax on the produce when obtained, would increase the cost of production, and would therefore raise the price of raw produce to the consumer. Ricardo reasons that these taxes would be passed on, because the producer (farmer or cultivator) would not accept a profit return lower than the general level of profits; if the producer withdrew from production it would affect the supply of commodities, force prices of raw materials up, and restore the general level of profits. He says, "A tax on the produce of land . . . would raise the price of raw produce by a sum equal to the tax, and would therefore fall on each consumer in proportion to his consumption and . . . it would raise the wages of labour and lower profits" (p. 141). He goes on to say, "The probable effect of a tax on raw produce, would be to raise the price of raw produce, and of all commodities in which raw produce entered, but not in any degree proportioned to the tax" (p. 151). Any tax which would increase costs, hence prices, of home products would not necessarily discourage exports, since it would produce the same effect as an alteration in the value of money; the higher prices in the home country would limit sales but not purchases. In time, money would be exported, and the value of the money remaining within the home country thus made greater; this would gradually and automatically restore the balance in export and import of the commodities.

Tithes are a "tax upon the gross produce of the land and, like the taxes on raw produce, fall wholly on the consumer. They raise the price of the raw produce" (p. 157). Likewise "a land tax will fall wholly upon landlords" (p. 161). But if the tax is levied according to acreage of the land, without regard to fertility, it will cause a rise in price of the produce and fall on the consumer.

In discussing taxes on profits (chap. xv) he presents conflicting theories. Taxes levied on luxuries are borne by the consumer, but taxes on necessities do not affect the amount consumed. Taxes levied on the profits of a manufacturer would tend to reduce his profits below the general level and "he would quit his trade." A tax on the profits of the farmer would raise the price of corn and the same would be true of a tax on the profits of a clothier; if the profits of all trades were taxed, the price on goods would rise. He never departs from the thesis that "taxes on raw produce, tithes, taxes on wages, and on the necessities of labour" (p. 196) will raise wages (through prices) and reduce profits. The full impact of a tax on any one base will not react in exactly the same degree on prices, hence on profits; but the general effect will be the same: higher wages—lower profits.

Enough of Ricardo's ideas on taxation have been presented to show that he was inclined to make a special case out of each tax and that he arrived at no basic principles or laws. Likewise, his emphasis was upon the temporary effects of a tax—the ultimate effects were overlooked. He did not offer laws, as did Smith, nor did he generalize in his tax discussions as he did in his discussions of value and profits. He was, in a real sense, straying from the field with which he was best acquainted, namely, money and prices.[30]

Summary and Evaluation.—An evaluation of Ricardo is admittedly a difficult task. He means all things to some persons but something less to others. Like all original theorists he had both followers and critics. The *Principles*, which appeared in 1817, provided the doctrines which enlisted his supporters and also furnished the basis for the attack by his critics. The supporters were few, the critics, many. In the first few years after 1817 only James Mill and James Ramsey McCulloch were in

---

[30] S. N. Patten suggests that he "lacked a Malthus to stir him up to his best thinking." "The Interpretation of Ricardo," *Quarterly Journal of Economics*, VII, April, 1893, p. 20.

the Ricardian camp.[31]   Among the many critics the best-known names
were Malthus, Lord Lauderdale, Torrens, West, Thompson, Young, the
agricultural economist, and Sismondi.[32]   The critics far outnumbered
the followers but Ricardo had as his master promoter, James Mill, who
was most effective in propagating the Ricardian "faith."

For a few years after the *Principles* appeared, Ricardo's system was
referred to as the "New Political Economy," and its supporters as the
"New School." [33]   For numerous reasons, however, the New School
identification did not survive although the principles did.   Checkland
remarks that "from then on the adjective 'New' began rapidly to disappear and the Ricardian system soon became synonymous with political economy.   In a space of something less than ten years a system had
emerged from fragments and had assumed the stamp of orthodoxy." [34]

The two men most responsible for promoting Ricardian doctrines
and for keeping them alive were Mill and McCulloch.   Mill, whose
own book, *Elements of Political Economy* (1821), was intended as a
"school-book of Political Economy," was cast in the Ricardian mould
and avoided only a few of the Ricardian errors.   McCulloch, a close
friend of Ricardo, Malthus, and James Mill, never deviated from the
Ricardian tenets.[35]   He was a very prolific writer and editor who deserves great credit as a popularizer of political economy in the two
decades after 1817.   On the other hand, "McCulloch is probably responsible for the annihilation of more constructive economic thinking
than any other political economist." [36]   This was because of his successful popularizing of the new political economy, with all its faults.
The critics, although numerous, were less persistent and less vocal, and
their efforts were lost.   Ricardian economics became orthodox economics.

The peak of its acceptance was reached within the decade after
Ricardo's death in 1823.   Thereafter, McCulloch still was his staunch
defender but, in general, the fundamental Ricardian concepts lost

---

[31] James Mill wrote to McCulloch at the time of Ricardo's death in 1823 that
they were his "two and only genuine disciples."   Alexander Bain, *James Mill: A
Biography* (London, 1882), p. 11.

[32] See S. G. Checkland, "The Propagation of Ricardian Economics in England,"
Economica, New Series XV-XVI (February, 1949), pp. 41-52.

[33] In an article written by McCulloch for the Supplement to the *Encyclopaedia
Britannica* in 1821 the title and the system were accepted and discussed as such.

[34] *Op. cit.*, p. 41.

[35] In a sympathetic book review he referred to the *Principles* as "one harmonious,
consistent, and beautiful system." (*Edinburgh Review*, June, 1818, p. 87.)   In this
review McCulloch made a very deliberate effort to give "an accurate exposition" of
the principles of political economy as developed by Ricardo who "has done more
for its improvement than any other writer, with perhaps the single exception of
Dr. Smith."

[36] Checkland, *op. cit.*, p. 49.

ground rapidly. There are many reasons for the decline, among which the following appear to be most significant. Ricardo held rigorously to his original doctrines as set out in the first edition of the *Principles* and in the two subsequent editions made no changes (probably on James Mill's advice) even though criticism was abundant and known to him. Some of his doctrines had been adopted by so-called radicals and used to show the defects in the capitalistic system. Then, too, other theories were definitely wrong, as was proved by empirical facts. His errors were not in faulty observations but in limiting the assumptions. One of Ricardo's basic theories was that the tendency of profits was to fall. Smith had discussed the same issue and ascribed the fall of profits to the accumulation of capital. But Ricardo held that "There cannot, then, be accumulated in a country any amount of capital which cannot be employed productively, until wages rise so high in consequence of the rise of necessities, and so little consequently remains for the profits of stock, that the motive for accumulation ceases" (p. 274). In this connection he also cited J. B. Say and the famous "Say's Law" (discussed in a subsequent chapter) to refute Smith; he said, "Mr. Say has, however, most satisfactorily shown that there is no amount of capital which may not be employed in a country, because demand is only limited by production."

Ricardo used this argument in defense of his basic premise that a rise in wages would affect profits inversely, and vice versa. Production was tied in with wages and wages with his labor theory of value; therefore he used Say's Law to defend the basic premise of the relationship of profits and wages. Malthus had argued that profits might fall as a result of accumulation of capital and a market glut would occur because of a failure of effective demand. Ricardo found in Say's Law an effective rebuttal and an answer to the market glut contention of Malthus. No such thing could happen, for demand would create its own supply and there could be no failure of effective demand. Furthermore, it was vital to the whole of Ricardian theory that his explanation of the relationship between wages and profits remain true; for if it could be shown that profits were affected by any factor other than wages, the whole theoretical edifice would collapse. He was more or less obliged, in defending his own theories, not only to use but also to defend Say's Law, even as a short-run tendency.

It has been pointed out that England was making rapid industrial progress, also that labor was becoming vocal. Under the critical blows of lesser economists, points hitherto neglected or submerged were coming to light. So-called radical writers were "making capital" of certain parts of Ricardian theory. Some of Ricardo's principles were thus being used to cast doubt upon the entire capitalistic system. It was finally recognized that the interests of the landlords were not antithetical to society and that profits could be employed for social betterment as well as for personal gain. In addition, his pessimistic outlook did not fit in with human experience. "The early reaction against Ricardo . . . was in large measure due to the widespread feeling that important elements of his system set limits to the prospects of human progress under capitalism, and therefore could not possibly be true." [37]

The labor theory of value, which became the most useful of tools to the socialists, was one of the first of the Ricardian theories to be discarded. Samuel Read noted as early as 1829 "the almost universal rejection of labour as the standard by later political economists." [38] Only McCulloch defended Ricardo's theories of value and rent but admitted that the theory of profits was defective.

The Political Economy Club,[39] which afforded its members an opportunity for discussion of political and economic subjects, discussed Ricardo's doctrines on at least two occasions. The members proposed questions for discussion on many issues. In the proceedings of the Political Economy Club,[40] it is recorded that early in 1831 Colonel Torrens proposed the question, "What improvements have been affected in the science of Political Economy since the publication of Mr. Ricardo's great work; and are any of the principles first advanced in that work now acknowledged to be correct?" The question was debated at two meetings. Mallet reports that Colonel Torrens "held all the great principles of Ricardo's work had been successively abandoned, and that his theories of Value, Rent and Profits were now generally acknowledged to have been erroneous." Mallet then refers to certain persons who had successfully criticized particular theories, adding that "Tooke also thought that Ricardo was wrong in his theory of Value . . . McCulloch stood up vigorously for Value as well as Rent, and paid very high compliments to Ricardo, whom he still considered as right in most points, and at all events as having done the greatest service to the science. . . ." [41] In reporting further discussions, the diarist records that "it was generally admitted that Ricardo is a bad and obscure writer,

[37] R. L. Meek, "The Decline of Ricardian Economics," *Economica*, February, 1950, p. 57.

[38] *Political Economy: An Inquiry into the Natural Grounds of Right* (Edinburgh, 1829), p. 203.

[39] The Club was founded in London in 1821. Among the twenty persons appearing on the original list of members are Thomas Tooke, David Ricardo, Rev. T. R. Malthus, James Mill, J. R. McCulloch, and Col. Robert Torrens.

[40] *Political Economy Club, Centenary Volume* (London, 1921), pp. 35, 36. This volume also contains the diaries of Mr. J. L. Mallet, an original member of the Club. They present enlightening views of the discussions from 1823 to May, 1837. The first one gives an intimate picture of Ricardo in the form of a laudatory essay.

[41] *Ibid.*, pp. 223, 224.

using the terms in different senses; but that the principles are in the main right." He adds, "Neither his Theories of Value, nor his Theories of Rent and Profits are correct, according to the very terms of his proposition; but they are right in principle." The Club members were critical of Ricardo's failure to take into account the progress of society. Mallet says, "One of the errors of Ricardo seems to have been to follow up Malthus' principles of population to unwarrantable conclusions." He reports that social improvement, such as bettering of the condition of people, and the growth of capital have resulted in a condition which made Ricardo's "conclusions all wrong."

It is certain that many, perhaps even most, of Ricardo's theories were discarded within the two decades after their appearance. Not only were they pessimistic in outlook with no promise of betterment, but they tended even to challenge the plans of the Almighty.[42] The population principle of Malthus was the popular target of scholars, who disproved it—at least to their own satisfaction. Industrial progress was confuting the inverse relationship between wages and profits and it was becoming apparent that these two factors could actually increase together. The labor theory was attacked on all sides and new value theories with emphasis on demand and cost of production began to be advanced by Longfield, Senior, Whately, and others subsequently to be discussed. John Stuart Mill in 1848 came near to presenting a demand and supply analysis of value but he could not quite break free from earlier traditions. At least he adopted Senior's abstinence theory of capital. "Ricardo's system, in short, was purged of most of its more obviously disharmonious elements, particularly those which might have been used to suggest that there was a real conflict of economic interest between social classes under capitalism or that progress under capitalism might be limited for some other reason." [43]

It will be shown in subsequent chapters that although some of Ricardo's theories were wholly acceptable to some writers, others were subjected to vigorous criticism. This was true in both England and America. Ricardo's economics was the favorite point of critical attack by early American writers such as Raymond, List, Carey, and others. In England, Mill's *Principles*, done in more optimistic overtones, provided the accepted doctrines until Marshall's *Principles of Economics* appeared in 1890. Yet despite all efforts, deliberate or otherwise, to dislodge it, Ricardian economics proved to have great staying proper-

[42] See J. S. Reynolds, *Practical Observations on Mr. Ricardo's Principles of Political Economy and Taxation* (London, 1822). "It would not be difficult to trace Mr. Ricardo's theory to consequences inconsistent with the goodness of Providence, and to the scheme of Divine government" (p. 15).

[43] Meek, *op. cit.*, p. 62.

ties.   J. M. Keynes commented,[44] when referring to the failure of
Malthus to establish his contention that effective demand could be
deficient or excessive and the disappearance of this idea from economic
literature, that "Ricardo conquered England as completely as the Holy
Inquisition conquered Spain."   He further admitted, "The complete-
ness of the Ricardian victory is something of a curiosity and mystery."

The name of David Ricardo remains almost a synonym for classical
economics.   He has been praised as the author of the finest elements in
classical tradition and blamed for its errors and shortcomings.   Both
liberal and radical writers have found in his writings exactly what they
wanted to support many of their theories.   Others deny the interpretations made by the radicals and claim him as the bulwark of capitalism.
Still others have devoted their efforts to understanding and improving
upon his theories.

That his work is not so complete as one would like it to be is
apparent from the foregoing pages.   His range of topics is narrow.   He
has no treatment of production as such, nor of consumption.   Even
contemporary economic institutions are not mentioned or are inade-
quately treated.   He shows little knowledge of or, at least, gives little
recognition to the work of other economists, and he does not comprehend the impact of the Industrial Revolution and general economic
advances of his time.

Ricardo's errors were both of omission and of commission.   His treatment of many subjects must be regarded as inadequate.   His value
theory is admittedly incomplete and confused and no improvement
over that of Smith.   The rent theory, although basically correct when
applied to the supply side of the analysis, is deficient on the demand
side.   He failed to see that the same differentials which were used to
explain rent may be found in wage payments to labor and in interest
returns to capital.   Interest, in the form of a return to capital, and
profits—an income above costs—are nowhere clearly distinguished.
While his greatest contribution was to distribution theory, he left
much to be desired.

Ricardo made short work of Smith's harmony of interests.   Laissez
faire could not be relied upon; this observation could readily be made
in view of many excesses which developed as a result of unbridled competition.   He recognized the great significance of price in the operations of the whole economy.   He regarded the businessman, in the
sense of the producer, as the center of economic activity around whom
the problems of price and distribution theory revolve.   Yet it may be

[44] *General Theory,* p. 32.

correctly said that his outlook on economic behavior was as unrealistic as his outlook on the future of mankind was pessimistic.

Ricardo influenced the national economy both directly and indirectly. His ideas on money and currency, bank policy, national finance and taxation, international trade practices, tariffs, and exchange regulations were of great significance in shaping policy matters in England. Despite his proclivities toward excessive deduction, his contributions to political economy were indeed great—and very important in methodological development.[45]   He will always be regarded as the master of deduction in economics.

[45] Students of Ricardo may look forward to a complete edition of Ricardo's work in nine volumes entitled, *The Works and Correspondence of David Ricardo,* edited by Piero Sraffa and M. H. Dobb of Cambridge University.   This definitive work, now published, was not available when this chapter was written.

13

The Disciples of Classical Economics:
N. W. Senior, J. S. Mill, and J. E. Cairnes

The fundamentals propounded by Smith, Malthus, and Ricardo compose the body of doctrines commonly identified as classical economics. They are the high priests of the temple. The persons considered in this chapter are disciples. In general they found the teaching to their liking; they showed little or no disposition to question it or, as skepticism became common, to revise the doctrine in the light of the burning edifice, or to make plans for a new one. This work befell others more iconoclastically minded.

It is interesting to observe how tenaciously the original doctrines were defended even in the face of the severest criticisms and despite the fact that some of them were nearly a hundred years old. Certain fundamentals in classical doctrine were as true in Cairnes' day as when Smith and Ricardo formulated them, but others had to be modified. Great changes had taken place throughout the world. Although the classical disciples acknowledged some of the changes, they did not allow them to affect the fundamentals they had inherited.

Senior, Mill, and Cairnes are considered chronologically and in proportion to their influence in the development of economic thought. Senior is directly tied to Smith, Malthus, Ricardo, and Say (Smith's defender of the faith in France), and Mill admits his indebtedness to the same predecessors as well as others. Cairnes defends all by vigorously following Mill. After their work, classical tradition becomes of historic interest; its best elements become a part of a larger synthesis.

Nassau William Senior

The greatest English economist after Ricardo and before John Stuart Mill was Nassau William Senior.[1] He was orthodox in supporting the

[1] **Nassau William Senior (1790-1864)**, born in the third generation of an English family of Spanish origin, was educated at Magdalen College, Oxford, from which he

classical tradition yet he made several distinct contributions. In recent years, after the publication of two volumes of materials hitherto unknown,[2] much more attention has been given him in recognition of his original and mature thought.

Unlike certain other writers, notably Adam Smith and John Stuart Mill, Senior did not take as his goal the construction of a complete social philosophy but set relatively narrow limits to what he regarded as the scope of political economy. This he defines as "an outline of the Science which treats of the Nature, the Production, and the Distribution of Wealth," and he followed the general outline of Ricardian economics and the Malthusian population theory. Yet his knowledge of practical affairs prevented his being as dogmatic on economic doctrines as McCulloch and James Mill, except in his application of the population theory to English poor laws. He was familiar with and influenced by certain German and French writers, notably J. B. Say. He was, therefore, receptive to criticisms of orthodox doctrines and sufficiently flexible to adopt what he believed to be the best: in this respect he became a harmonizer of the orthodox and the new developments.

Senior's Economics: Value Theory.—Senior's theoretical economics is found mainly in his book *Political Economy (1850)*, first published

---

graduated with a B.A. in 1812 and an M.A. in 1815. He studied law and was admitted to the bar in 1819. Senior abandoned a career in law because he was physically handicapped and entered upon the study of political economy. In 1825, when the Chair of Political Economy was founded by Henry Drummond at Oxford (the first in an English university), Senior was chosen for the professorship, a position which he held for five years. (The rules of the appointment limited the professorship to five years.) He occupied the same Chair from 1847 to 1852. During these years he wrote and lectured on money and methodology and contributed to contemporary periodicals. For a brief time he was Professor at Kings College, London. He was Master in Chancery from 1836 to 1855 and served on the following Royal Commissions: Poor Laws (1832), Factory Conditions (1837), Hand Loom Weavers (1841), Irish Poor Laws (1844) and National Education (1857). He travelled abroad extensively and met most of the great men of his day. His contemporaries knew him as a reformer rather than as an economist, mainly because he championed the cause of health, housing, and education. This fact accounts for an impression held by scholars for many years that his economic theory carried a strong class bias. Recent investigations have not only disproved this but have established Senior as a brilliant and original thinker. The best works on Senior are Marian Bowley, *Nassau Senior and Classical Economics* (London 1937), which is a sympathetic treatment of his theoretical views; and S. Leon Levy's *Nassau W. Senior, The Prophet of Modern Capitalism* (Boston, 1943), which gives much hitherto unpublished material on his life. An authoritative biography has been promised by Senior's granddaughter, Mrs. St. Loe Strachey, written from materials now in the possession of her family.

[2] Most of the credit for reexamination of Senior and for restoring him to his rightful place belongs to Miss Bowley and to S. Leon Levy, who found and published many of the Senior manuscripts in *Industrial Efficiency and Social Economy* (2 vols., New York, 1928).

as an article, "An Outline of the Science of Political Economy," in the
Encyclopedia Metropolitana in 1836. In this work he makes wealth
the center of the science; he defines wealth as those things "which
are susceptible of exchange . . . or those things which have Value."
Wealth consists of those things which possess relative scarcity, transferability, and utility, the last of which attributes he defines as "directly
or indirectly productive of pleasure or preventive of pain." [3] He recognizes the extent to which utility was used by certain economists (notably
Malthus and Say) as a necessary constituent of value, which is not an
intrinsic quality in useful things but merely expresses their relationships
"to the pains and pleasures of mankind." But he says that in determining value the limitation of supply (or relative scarcity) is of greater
importance than utility. Transferability is used to mean that "all or
some portion of its powers of giving pleasure, or preventing pain, are
capable of being transferred, either absolutely or for a period" (p. 8).
Senior brings diminishing utility into his definition by showing that

. . . our desires do not aim so much at quantity as at diversity. Not only
are there limits to the pleasure which commodities of any given class can
afford, but the pleasure diminishes in a rapidly increasing ratio long before
those limits are reached. Two articles of the same kind will seldom afford
twice the pleasure of one, and still less will ten give five times the pleasure
of two. In proportion, therefore, as any article is abundant the number of
those who are provided with it, and do not wish, or wish but little, to increase their provision, is likely to be great; and so far as they are concerned,
the additional supply loses all, or nearly all, its utility (pp. 11-12).

Senior's treatment of value was original in some respects. He made
utility of greater importance in value theory than did Ricardo or his
own contemporaries, but he did not develop a subjective theory of
value. Although utility is not accorded a prominent place in his value
theory, Jevons regarded him as one of the many prophets of the marginal
utility theory. Under the subject of exchange in the section on the
distribution of wealth Senior again returns to the matter of value and
contends that "comparative limitation of supply, or . . . comparative
scarcity, though not sufficient to constitute value, is by far its most important element; utility, or, in other words, demand being mainly dependent on it" (p. 96). Supply, in turn, is dependent upon "human
Labor and Abstinence and the spontaneous agency of Nature." Then
he explains the obstacles which limit the supply of all that is produced
and concludes that "supply is limited by cost of production" (p. 97).
Cost of production is the most important factor in Senior's value
theory. He maintains that Ricardo's theory, which makes the labor

[3] *Political Economy* (London, 1850), p. 6.

embodied in a commodity the source and measure of its value, is wrong; he objects to Ricardo's explanation mainly on the grounds that scarcity is the general cause of value, whereas labor cost is only a secondary cause with limited applicability. Senior also uses a definition of cost of production (p. 101) based upon the aggregate amount of the labor and abstinence (a term subsequently used in the sense of capital) necessary to continue the production of goods. Capital is made coordinate with labor in production. Under free competition "cost of production is the regulator of price," but he does not mean to use cost of production "as a point to which price is attached, but as a center of oscillation which it is always endeavoring to approach" (p. 102). He differs from Ricardo in holding that the price of a good must equal the sum of labor and abstinence in its required production or "a price equal to the amount of wages and profits which must be paid to induce the producers to continue their exertions" (p. 102). Following the Ricardian analysis, he did not treat land as a separate factor in production; and since rent does not enter into cost of production, it is irrelevant to price determination.

Senior's theory made production costs reducible to and comparable in money terms. Cost of production, however, was not the final cause of price but only the "regulator." He stressed the influence of demand or utility in price determination to a greater degree than any other previous writer who employed the terms. But the importance of demand as related to cost of production in fixing prices depends upon the degree of monopoly in the production of the commodity. He identified five different circumstances of production which affect the price of commodities:

1. Absence of all monopoly—all persons being capable of producing with equal advantage

2. A monopoly under which the monopolist has not the exclusive power of producing but [has] exclusive facilities as a producer, which may be employed indefinitely with equal or increasing advantage

3. A monopoly under which the monopolist is the only producer and cannot increase the amount of his produce

4. A monopoly under which the monopolist is the only producer and can increase indefinitely, with equal advantage, the amount of his produce

5. A monopoly under which the monopolist is not the only producer but has peculiar facilities which diminish and ultimately disappear as he increases the amount of his produce (p. 111).

These cases are intended to show the relationship of value to cost of production. No general rules can be applied to cases 2, 3, and 4, except that while there may be no upper limit to the price which may be charged, the cost of production tends to set a lower limit. In case 5, production may be carried on under conditions in which the supply of the factors is definitely limited, such as land which is subject to diminishing returns. This is what gives rise to rent of land. Here, commodities are produced under what he calls "unequal competition or qualified monopoly." Any increase in production results in a proportional increase in cost which "has a constant tendency to coincide with the cost of production of that portion which is continued to be produced at the greatest expense" (p. 115) or the high cost margin in the Ricardian sense. Anyone producing at a lower cost would receive a surplus or rent.

Distribution Theories.—Senior's problem in distribution was to explain not only the cost of the factors of production but also the value of the final product of the factors. In his *Political Economy* (p. 101), he states that the price of commodities "represents the aggregate amount of the labor and abstinence necessary to continue their production." Therefore if the price of commodities should either rise or fall, the remuneration of labor and of abstinence would likewise rise or fall. In time prices tend to equalize at the cost of production level, and the returns to the factors likewise tend to equal their costs. The explanation is a generalization which is applicable to all factors of production. In his Oxford lectures of 1847-1852 he was more explicit in his meaning and emphasis: he included land in his capital concept by contending that it was impossible to distinguish between land and capital in production, since capital loses its mobility when invested in durable goods. It is the immobility of land rather than its absolute limitation that makes it distinct from other factors.[4]

His wage theory is not clear. In so far as it was a theory, it shows traces of a productivity theory in line with Say's analysis. Actually, it was a wages-fund theory substantially the same as that expressed by Smith and Ricardo. He says, in discussing the cause of the rate of wages, that wages depend "on the extent of the fund for the maintenance of labourers, compared with the number of labourers to be maintained" (p. 153). He recognizes the difference between real wages, in the form of commodities to be used by the laborers, and money wages. Yet he was unable to accomplish a reconciliation between a wage theory

---

[4] This view was not unknown in England, but it was admittedly due to the influence of the German economist, Hermann, that Senior's views were somewhat modified in the lectures.

based upon productivity of labor and his concept of the productivity of capital. One must conclude that he has no theory of wages per se but makes wages entirely dependent upon his theory of capital.[5]

Senior's abstinence theory of interest is the contribution for which he is best known. "It has long been recognized as the most complete of the classical theories, and under various names has become incorporated in the general corpus of economic theory." [6] He supplemented Ricardo's ideas by introducing a third factor in production. Human labor and natural agents (land and the like) were considered primary agents; the secondary agent, or third factor, was termed "abstinence." He held that since the two primary agents were inadequate to produce the necessities of existence, a third instrument of production was necessary—viz., abstinence: "a term by which we express the conduct of a person who either abstains from the unproductive use of what he can command, or designedly prefers the production of remote to that of immediate results" (p. 58). Furthermore, "by the word Abstinence, we wish to express that agent, distinct from Labour and the agency of nature, the concurrence of which is necessary to the existence of capital, and which stands in the same relation to Profit as Labour does to Wages." The result of combining the three factors is that "Wealth may be indefinitely increased by using their Products as a means of further Production." (p. 59). In other words, capital results from the combination of factors.

Senior deliberately prefers the term "abstinence" and avoids the term "capital" on the grounds that capital "is not a simple productive instrument: it is in most cases the result of all three productive instruments combined. Some natural agent must have afforded the material, some delay of enjoyment must in general have reserved it from unproductive use, and some labour must in general have been employed to prepare and preserve it" (p. 59). Capital is neither land nor labor or even their combination, but it is an intermediate product resulting from the current application of the factors to provide for the future by postponing present consumption.

This intermediate product—which we prefer to call capital—is highly productive in making roundabout methods of production possible, yet Senior never definitely identified capital as consisting of tools, machinery, buildings, etc. The superiority of the roundabout methods of production accounts for the demand for capital. The creation of capital —or the supply of capital—depends upon a definite, present, and painful sacrifice which will be undertaken only with the prospect of a reward.

[5] For a detailed treatment see Marian Bowley, *op. cit.*, chap. v, "The Theory of Wages."
[6] Bowley, *op. cit.*, p. 137.

He says, in discussing the proportionate amounts of profit and wages, that "Profits and Wages differ in almost all respects from Rent. They are each subject to a maximum and minimum. They are subject to a minimum because each of them is the result of a sacrifice. It may be difficult to say what is the minimum with respect to profit, but it is clear that every capitalist, as a motive to abstain from the immediate and unproductive enjoyment of his capital, must require some remuneration exceeding the lowest that is conceivable" (pp. 139-40). He does not make clear why people prefer present to future goods nor does he explain the determinants of abstinence, although the theory of time preference may be read into his discussion. He makes the real cost of saving, which he calls abstinence, the important factor on the supply side of capital.

In Senior's opinion, errors in Ricardo's and Smith's treatment of cost of production could· have been avoided "with the assistance of the term 'abstinence' or of some equivalent expression" (p. 98). Ricardo recognized that interest must be paid on capital used in production. He treated capital as stored-up or past labor, the cost of which when added to current labor costs in production constituted total labor costs. Since the interest paid for the use of this capital was probably never very closely related to the cost of producing capital, Ricardo was obliged to admit that goods were not exchanged for other goods in exact proportion to their labor costs. Adam Smith and Malthus included profits as elements in the cost of production. James Mill held almost the same view. Colonel Torrens regarded profits as a surplus over cost of production. Senior believed that these conflicting views could have been avoided had the writers· understood the importance of abstinence ir production.

It is difficult to share Senior's conviction on this point. At times he is none too certain just what he should include in cost of production of either capital or commodities. He clearly makes cost of production the "sum of labor and abstinence necessary to production" (p. 101) and treats each as a sacrifice necessary to obtain goods for the satisfaction of wants. Profits and wages are equally value determinants. Nevertheless, Senior probably does not intend to imply that value is determined solely by cost of production but only that such cost is one of the elements determining value.

Senior's theory of capital and interest was not a finished product as treated either in his *Political Economy* or in his Oxford lectures of 1847-1852. He never explained the rate of interest on fixed capital, nor were motives for saving and the sacrifice of saving closely related. However, he coined a magic term "abstinence" which was used by J. S. Mill and many others in explaining cost of production and, indirectly, in explaining value. The term has had a long, and in some respects, useful career in value theory, especially in the camp of the English economists.[7]

Money and International Trade.—The subjects of money and banking, as well as trade, were pressing contemporary issues in Senior's time. Likewise, the classical heritage of money and trade theories involved controversial subjects of both theoretical and applied economics in most discussions of the period.

Senior treats money as a commodity in which credit is crystallized, thus becoming "a mere substitute for credit." He cites commodities that have been used by various peoples as money and adds that the commodities are money "only so long as it is received merely for the purpose of being again given in exchange."[8] He can see no other meaning for money than that of a substitute for credit, even in the very first use of money. When, in the advance of society, barter becomes impossible, money becomes the universal medium of exchange, the universal measure of value, and finally an expression of value which makes future payments possible. These are the functions requisite of any money.

The ideal qualities for money require, first, a commodity that is valuable—that is, "capable of affording gratification and limited in supply" and uniform in quality. Certain physical properties of divisibility, portableness, durability, and steadiness of value are also necessary. Only gold and silver fit these requirements. The state should coin the money. Paper money could theoretically be kept at a nominal value even though intrinsically valueless if it were received for payment of taxes and its quantity closely related to foreign exchange rates. He adds, however, that "the power to issue inconvertible paper has never been granted or assumed without being sooner or later abused."[9]

Senior makes a rather critical analysis of the quantity theory of money as presented by Torrens, Ricardo, and especially James Mill. Senior's criticisms rest upon two objections: first, Mill had not included monetary theory in economic analysis, thereby failing in an examination of the forces which determine the value of money; second, the value of money is determined by the same principles as the value of any commodity, and therefore the quantity theory is not a factor in international

[7] W. S. Jevons, *The Theory of Political Economy* (3d ed.; London, 1871), pp. 232-34. Alfred Marshall in *Principles of Economics* (London, 1890), Bk. IV, chap. vii, paragraphs 8, 9 uses the term "waiting."

[8] See "The Nature of Money," *Three Lectures on the Value of Money* (1840); available in London School of Economics, Reprints of Scarce Tracts in Economics and Political Science, No. 4 (London, 1931).

[9] S. Leon Levy, ed., *Industrial Efficiency and Social Economy* (New York, 1928), Vol. II, p. 54.

price levels. Senior contends that velocity or, as he calls it, rapidity of circulation, is not a determinant in the value of money. He argues that the quantity of money held depends upon the money value of incomes and "the average proportion of the value of his income which each individual habitually keeps by him in money." The demand for money therefore would rest on the factors affecting the value of incomes, which would reflect credit and the confidence of both the individual and state. The supply depends upon labor and abstinence cost. Thus Senior writes,

. . . my principal object . . . has been to show that the value of money, insofar as it is decided by intrinsic causes, does not depend permanently on the quantity of it possessed by a given community; or on the rapidity of circulation; or on the prevalence of exchanges; or on the use of barter and credit; or, in short, on any cause whatever excepting *the cost of its production*. Other causes may operate for a time; but their influence wears away as the existing stock of the precious metals within the country accommodates itself to the wants of the inhabitants.[10]

This constant-cost condition appears within a country, but he adds that

. . . the whole commercial world may be considered as one community, using gold and silver as money; and ascertaining the value of other commodities by comparing their cost of production with the cost of obtaining gold and silver. And though many causes may alter the quantity of the precious metals possessed by any single nation, nothing will permanently alter their value, so far as that value depends on intrinsic causes, unless it affect the cost at which they are obtained.[11]

The criticism contains the unreality of constant costs in producing precious metals as well as overemphasizing cost of production. By omitting the importance of the velocity of the circulating media he makes his whole criticism vulnerable and ineffective. Aside from his specific treatment of the properties of money, his discussion is of questionable value.

Senior treated domestic and international trade as similar and assumed complete immobility of the factors among trading areas. He made little contribution to the Ricardian analysis except in a discussion of changes in prices and incomes rather than in comparative costs.

Senior's Contribution.—It is somewhat difficult to evaluate Senior's contribution to economic thought and thereby assign him a proper position with either the great or the near-great. His more or less delib-

[10] *Ibid.*, p. 90.
[11] *Ibid.*

erate objective was to reconcile the theories of Ricardo and Say. In this he attained considerable success; but even more important are his own ideas. There was a rigidity in his work, for he treated economics as a purely deductive science in which his four fundamental propositions provided the sole source of all economic truth.[12] To him, his conclusions are not hypothetical deductions but facts. He had a broad learning gained by formal education and travel which he drew upon for his materials. He enjoyed great prestige professionally and as a public servant. In a sense, therefore, he was entitled to a certainty of conviction.

Despite this, Senior never developed a following or exerted an influence comparable to J. S. Mill. As a harmonizer of classical tradition with contemporary developments, Mill excelled. In actual accomplishments in the general field of social reform, Senior excelled. He advised the government on important social problems; notably, Poor Law Reform of 1834, Factory Acts of 1837, and Handloom Weavers in 1841. In each case, he showed that he was not a defender of laissez faire but advocated government interference so long as such interference did not jeopardize the working of economic laws. His views on reform problems drew the attention (and criticism) of his contemporaries away from his work in economics and account for his being thought of as a social reformer rather than as an economist.[13]

The extent to which Senior contributed to utility analysis depends largely upon one's sympathetic willingness to impute meaning to his treatment. He made utility, limitation of supply, and transferability the three factors on which value depended, but he always held the limitation of supply to be the most important element. But price, or final value, rested upon both supply and demand. He recognized the relative utility of different objects to different persons and the difficulty

---

[12] They are:

1. That every man desires to obtain Wealth with as little sacrifice as possible.
2. That the Population of the world, or in other words, the number of persons inhabiting it, is limited only by moral or physical evil, or by fear of a deficiency of those articles of wealth which the habits of the individuals of each class of its inhabitants lead them to require.
3. That the powers of Labour, and of the other instruments which produce wealth, may be indefinitely increased by using their Products as the means of further Production.
4. That, agricultural skill remaining the same, additional Labour employed on the land within a given district produces in general a less proportionate return, or, in other words, that though, with every increase of the labour bestowed, the aggregate return is increased, the increase of the return is not in proportion to the increase of the labour.

Political Economy, p. 26.

[13] Bowley, *op. cit.*, discusses this phase of Senior's work in Part II, "Problems of Social Policy."

of measuring it; he also recognized elements of marginal utility theory and diminishing marginal utility but did little to develop the ideas. His contribution to their early development was much less than that of Craig, Lloyd, or Longfield who are subsequently discussed. His value theory rested upon the factors limiting the supply of goods—the subjective costs of the workers' sacrifices and the abstinence of the capitalists. Even though he strayed from the fold in explaining value theory, he still belongs in the ranks of classical economists.

John Stuart Mill

The best known disciple of the classical tradition was John Stuart Mill (1806-1873). Some prefer to place him along with Smith, Malthus, and Ricardo in the front ranks of classicism. Yet if one uses original economic contributions as a criterion, John Stuart Mill deserves a place of lesser importance. He was a disciple of "the masters" and as such excelled all others. He was trained, even steeped, in the thought and tradition of pure classical economy. In his writings on the principles of economics he attempted to achieve the standard of perfection in theoretical refinement and in orderly presentation, and he met with marked success in the endeavor. For many years his *Principles* was the standard textbook. It was a synthesis of the best in classical economics, presented in an orderly, scientific arrangement and with an assurance of finality. Mill's influence in perpetuating the so-called classical tradition can scarcely be overemphasized. It was only the criticisms of classical economy in general (notably those of the socialists and the historical school), and the developments in marginal analysis which came toward the end of the century, that reduced Mills' work to negligible importance. In modern economic analysis, classical economics is no more or no less important than if John Stuart Mill had not written his *Principles of Political Economy* in 1848.

John Stuart Mill's early education and his associations were very important determining factors in shaping all his work.[14] Indeed, they are so important that they deserve more than passing mention. Perhaps few persons have been subjected to so many significant ideas and have had contact with so many important personages as John Stuart Mill. His father indoctrinated him with Ricardo's political economy and Malthus' doctrine of population. His philosophy was Bentham's

[14] The best sources dealing with his life are his own *Autobiography* (1873), edited by H. J. Laski with introduction (London, 1924); and Dr. Alexander Bains' two works; *James Mill: A Biography* (London. 7882) and *J. S. Mill: A Criticism* (London, 1882). An excellent brief treatment is W. L. Courtney's *Life of John Stuart Mill* (London, 1889).

utilitarianism; his psychology was that of his father. In later years the French Saint-Simonians taught him "the limited and temporal value of the old political economy"; De Tocqueville helped to make him democratically minded; and Auguste Comte and Positivism influenced his sociology. Mill's reading and his direct contacts with intellectual developments which occurred before and during his lifetime were almost limitless. While it is true that he was unable to digest all the ideas to which he was subjected, thus affecting his ability to make up his own mind, he was, nevertheless, one of the most erudite of men.

James Mill (1773-1836), the father of John Stuart Mill, was of Scottish extraction and had obtained his education at Edinburgh University. He went to London in 1802 to make his home, and it was there that John Stuart and the eight other children were born. The father's interest was centered in his eldest son, John Stuart, whom he educated along a pattern of his own design. The father had very fixed ideas not only as to mental discipline, but also as to what his son ought to know, and proceeded to instil them in the son in a manner reminiscent of medieval torture, a method which is frequently referred to as an educational experiment.

In his *Autobiography* Mill tells of his learning Greek at the age of three and Latin in his eighth year, by which time he had read many Greek classics. He also read many books on history and literature, studied mathematics, and served as tutor to his younger sisters and brothers. The youth discussed what he read with his father as they took daily walks over the countryside. In this way he developed a critical attitude toward what he read as well as methods of logical inquiry. In the year 1817 he corrected the proof sheets of his father's best known work, *History of British India.* James Mill had been at work on this book for eleven years, and it contributed greatly to the son's education. After the publication of the book, the author received an appointment to the East India Company offices, which made the family income less precarious.

Mill says that in 1819 his father took him "through a complete course in political economy." Ricardo's book ("which would never have been published or written but for the entreaty and strong encouragement of my father") came out in 1817 and this book, together with Adam Smith's *Wealth of Nations*, provided the essentials. On their walks, the father would expatiate on the subjects of political economy. The son would present a written account of the materials on the day following the lectures. In this manner the outline and notes were prepared which James Mill used to write his own *Elements of Political Economy* (1821). The book was in large measure the work of the son.

Mill's fourteenth year was spent in France. For a few days he was in Paris where he met J. B. Say, the political economist. Afterward he went to Toulouse, where he resided with the family of Sir Samuel Bentham, brother of Jeremy Bentham. His time in France was spent mainly in rigorous study of the classics, botany, mathematics, and the French language, with some travel. He developed a great liking, which he held throughout his life, for France and French institutions. He returned to England in 1821 and for two years studied history, philosophy, literary composition, and law. In May, 1823, he was appointed junior clerk in the Examiner's Office of the East India Company, thus ending what might have been a career in law. Few persons of his time had a wider experience in the responsible application of the principles of government.[15] After his service with the East India Company, he devoted his time to research and writing. He represented Westminster in Parliament from 1865 to 1868. In politics Mill was a liberal; even though he represented a conservative constituency he was always aligned with reforms which embraced such issues as the perennial Irish land question, greater representation of the working classes, woman's suffrage, and so on. He was not re-elected when the Conservatives returned to power; his constituency found him to be more of a philosopher than a politician. Although Mill's speeches in Parliament were on a very high moral level, oratory was not his forte. Mill was not fluent; his speeches were labored, and, as Gladstone remarked about his oratory, "physically, it came as from a statue."

In 1830 Mill met a Mrs. Taylor whose effect on all his work was pronounced. She influenced his thinking on women's rights, social progress, liberty, and style, rather than his scientific theories. Yet he credited her with the best of his writings. He remarks in his *Autobiography* that "all my published writings were as much her work as mine"; he believed her excellence of mind and heart were "unparalleled in any human being he had known or heard of." They were married in 1851 and until her death in 1858 they wrote and traveled together. Both Mill and his wife are buried in Avignon in the south of France.

Mill's Writings On Economics.—Mill wrote on many subjects during his lifetime; however, only the works on political economy will be considered here.[16] Mill is best known for his *Principles of Political Econ-*

---

[15] Clerks received no salary, only a gratuity, and for three years he received £30 a year. He was not made head examiner until 1856, at a salary of £2,000 a year. When the enterprise was taken over by the Crown in 1858, Mill was retired on an annual pension of £1,500.

[16] In addition to numerous articles which he contributed to contemporary magazines such as the *London and Westminster Review, Examiner, Tait's Magazine, Travellers,* and so on, his main writings are: *Essays on Unsettled Questions in Political Economy* (London, 1844); *A System of Logic* (London, 1843); *On Liberty*

omy, with some of their Applications to Social Philosophy, which was published in two volumes at London in 1848. He had been a student of political economy from his early years, when his father led him through the works of Ricardo, Malthus, and Smith. In this manner he became well acquainted with the accepted masterpieces of economics and especially with his father's interpretation of them. As a result John Stuart Mill's economics remained largely those of his father to the end of his life. Some have regarded Mill as a disciple of Ricardo, though not exactly a servile follower. He believed it was his responsibility to justify Ricardo's "superior lights" to the world and to apply the Ricardian principles; but in addition, his object, as he tells us, was to exhibit economic phenomena in relation to the most advanced conceptions of his time on the general philosophy of society—a deficiency of former works on political economy. He sought to present a complete social philosophy for the nineteenth century as Smith had done for the eighteenth. As has been said, Mill set out to write an up-to-date Adam Smith but instead he wrote a readable Ricardo. Yet he departs from the Ricardian path on many occasions, although seldom from the fundamentals and their interpretation as propounded by James Mill. As Ashley remarks, "After reading through the first three Books of the son's *Principles* of 1848, one has but to turn to the father's *Elements* of 1821 to realize that . . . the main conclusions, as well as the method of reasoning, are the same in the two treatises." [17]   But there are other ingredients than Ricardo, classical economy, and James Mill in his political economy. Bentham and the philosophical radicals of the time, the physiocrats, Coleridge, the Saint-Simonians, Comte and the Positivists, Tocqueville, his wife—all influenced and colored his thought.[18]

Since Mill was greatly influenced by so many, his eclecticism is easily explained. He was receptive to that which he conceived to be the best in the intellectual development of his time and sought to weave it into

---

(London, 1859); *Dissertations and Discussions, Political, Philosophical and Historical* (4 vols., London, 1859-75); *Considerations on Representative Government* (London, 1861); *The Subjection of Women* (London, 1869); *Three Essays on Religion* (London, 1874); *Autobiography* (London, 1873).

[17] *Principles of Political Economy,* ed. W. J. Ashley (2 vols., London, 1909), p. viii. All references hereafter are to this edition.

[18] Mill recognized Coleridge as a leader of "the European reaction against the philosophy of the eighteenth century" (*Autobiography,* p. 128) and its Benthamite tendencies. However, he sought to make Benthamism and Coleridge's insights complementary bodies of truth in two articles published in *London and Westminster Review,* in 1838 and 1840. These are reprinted in *Dissertations and Discussions,* Vol. II, p. 5 ff., and Vol. III, p. 300 ff. What Mill learned from Coleridge was the historical point of view in its relation to politics and the inadequacy and final abandonment of laissez faire. He had no use for Coleridge as an economist, saying he was an "ardent driveller, and it would have been well for his reputation if he had never meddled with the subject."

his own thinking. This led to inconsistencies from which he could not escape. He was a firm believer in capitalism, yet he showed strong convictions on social reform with "Fabian" socialist tendencies. He always held to the principle of free competition and individual liberty as expounded by his father. Yet he wrote,

If the choice were to be made between Communism with all its chances, and the present [1852] state of society with all its sufferings and injustices; if the institution of private property necessarily carried with it as a consequence, that the produce of labour should be appropriated as we now see it, almost in an inverse ratio to the labour—the largest portions to those who have never worked at all, the next largest to those whose work is almost nominal, and so in a descending scale, the remuneration dwindling as the work grows harder and more disagreeable, until the most fatiguing and exhausting body labour cannot count with certainty on being able to earn even the necessities of life; if this or Communism were the alternative, all the difficulties, great or small, of Communism would be but as dust in the balance (*Principles*, Bk. II, chap. i, p. 208).

Mill never hesitated to criticize established institutions; at times he showed almost emotional zeal for social reform, yet he would not abandon the fundamentals of capitalism and accepted political practices. Despite his vacillations on many issues, he wrote his *Principles* with a positiveness "as one expounding an established system." His own explanations carried a finality and conviction that defied challenge.

The *Principles of Political Economy*, when considered analytically along with the works of Smith, Malthus, and Ricardo, will be shown to have distinct merit. It surpasses any prior work in arrangement of materials—its five books are: Production, Distribution, Exchange, Influence of the Progress of Society on Production and Distribution, The Influence of the Government. Unlike his father's *Elements*, his work does not have a section on consumption. Mill had the problem not only of presenting the "latest developments which have been made in the theory of the subject" of political economy, but also, under the promptings of Comte, of outlining a complete and comprehensive social science. Political economy was but a division of a much larger science. In his *Essays on Some Unsettled Questions of Political Economy* (1844), he defines political economy, "and the definition seems to be complete," as follows: "The science which traces the laws of such of the phenomena of society as arise from the combined operations of mankind for the production of wealth, in so far as those phenomena are not modified by the pursuit of any other object" (Essay V, "On the Definition of Political Economy," p. 141).

But in 1848 Mill envisioned political economy as a much more comprehensive subject. He was sincerely concerned with the applications of some of the principles of political economy to social philosophy. He felt he had accomplished this in his *Principles*; as he says in the *Auto-biography*, "It was, from the first, continually cited and referred to as an authority, because it was not a book merely of abstract science, but also of application, and treated Political Economy not as a thing by itself, but as a fragment of a greater whole; a branch of Social Philosophy, so interlinked with all other branches, that its conclusions, even in its own peculiar province, are only true conditionally, subject to interference and counteraction from causes not directly within its scope" (Laski edition, p. 200).

This broader point of view is emphasized in Book II on distribution. Mill holds that "the laws and conditions of the Production of Wealth partake of the character of physical truths. There is nothing optional or arbitrary in them" (p. 199), but "it is not so with the Distribution of Wealth. That is a matter of human institutions solely. The things once there, mankind, individually or collectively, can do with them as they like . . . In the social state . . . any disposal whatever of them can only take place by the consent of society . . . The distribution of wealth, therefore, depends on the laws of custom or society" (p. 200). He considers custom along with competition as agencies which determine the distribution of wealth under the social institution of private property. He was critical of "political economists generally and English political economists," especially, for stressing the forces of competition as a relatively modern regulating element. Fixed customs, historically speaking, have had pronounced influence upon all transactions. "Custom is the most powerful protector of the weak against the strong; their sole protector where there are no laws or government adequate to the purpose" (p. 243). Moreover, he recognizes both competition and custom as regulators of price in modern society. In this view, Mill breaks with the past. He sees basic differences between the laws of production and those of distribution; the former resting on "physical truths" and the latter "are partly of human institutions."

The *Principles of Political Economy*.—While it is true that Mill added little to economic theory, the recasting of the work of his predecessors and the orderly presentation of materials together with contemporary illustrations made his book the accepted principles of political economy during most of the second half of the nineteenth century.

He begins his discussion of production by setting up two requisites, labor and appropriate natural objects. Labor is either physical or mental. Appropriate natural objects are those which "exist or grow up spontaneously, of a kind suited to the supply of human wants." Nature

supplies both raw materials and inherent powers or attributes. Both
labor and nature join in the production of goods; neither can be identified as the sole producer nor can one claim to give more assistance in
production than the other. However, in production some labor is
applied directly and some indirectly. He identifies labor as directly
productive in extractive industry; in making of tools and implements
for the assistance of labor; in the protection of industrial structures,
such as buildings, warehouses, manufactories, and docks; in making
things already in existence accessible to those who desire their use; and
lastly, in mental labor such as that of inventors.

Three kinds of utilities are produced by labor: first, utilities fixed and
embodied in outward objects; labor is employed in investing external
material things with properties which render them serviceable to human beings (or form utility, in modern usage). Next, utilities fixed and
embodied in human beings; the labor in this case is employed in con-
ferring on human beings qualities which render them serviceable to
themselves and others (a category in which he puts the services of professional men). And lastly, utilities not fixed or embodied in any object
but consisting of a mere service rendered (this includes the labor of a
musician, actor, legislator, army and navy, agents of government, and
so on). Here Mill perpetuates the Smithian tradition of unproductive
labor. "Productive labour means labour productive of wealth" (chap. iii,
p. 45). "Unproductive labour . . . will be understood [as] labour which
does not terminate in the creation of material wealth . . . which does
not render the community or the world at large, richer in material
products, but poorer by all that is consumed by the labourers while so
employed" (p. 49). He struggles with shades of meaning of each term
for several pages, then applies the same reasoning to productive and unproductive consumption. "Whoever contributes nothing directly or
indirectly to production, is an unproductive consumer. The only productive consumers are productive labourers" (p. 51). Mill failed to
grasp the interdependence of all groups and the fact that his concept
of wealth was both narrow and inaccurate, an error which affected the
entire edifice of his theory.

In addition to labor and natural agents—the primary requisites of
production—he makes capital, which he calls "previously accumulated
stock of the produce of labour," a third factor. Without capital, production could not be carried "beyond the rude and scanty beginnings
of primitive industry" (chap. iv, p. 54). He emphasizes that money is
not capital nor does it "perform any part of the office of capital." In
production "capital affords the shelter, protection, tools and materials
which the work requires, and to feed and otherwise maintain the labourers during the process." He recognizes the importance of capital

in the productive process by pointing out that "industry is limited by capital." This is the first of the four theorems respecting capital. He admits that capital may be temporarily unemployed, during which time it does not set any industry in motion. He contends, too, that "every increase in capital gives, or is capable of giving, additional employment to industry; and this without assignable limit" (p. 66). Capital is created by saving (second theorem), but he means that even though capital is a result of saving it is consumed—used in productive consumption (third theorem). The fourth theorem is that which "supports and employs productive labour, is the capital expended in setting it to work." It is the demand for commodities that determines "in what particular branch of production the labour and capital shall be employed; it determines the *direction* of the labour . . . the demand for labour is constituted by the wages which precede the production, and not by the demand which may exist for the commodities resulting from the production" (pp. 63-81 *passim*).

Mill recognizes a paradox in his theory in that it includes under consumption not only that capital which is spent but that which is saved. He sees a perpetual consumption and reproduction process which, even though it may suffer temporary interruptions, is necessary in an economy. He points out, however, that capital applied in industry needs periodic renewal. He recognizes both fixed capital—which "persists in durable form and permits returns over a period of some duration" and circulating capital—which performs the "whole of its office in production in which it is engaged by a single use." Mill believes that it is very important that fixed capital does not increase at the expense of circulating capital; allowing it to do so might be prejudicial to the best interests of the laboring groups. He admits that labor may suffer temporarily as a result of the introduction of machinery yet (in the long run) "there is probably no country whose fixed capital increases in a ratio more than proportional to its circulating" (p. 97).

Mill summarizes his book on production by setting forth in Chapters X-XIII his "economic laws": the law of the increase of labor rests upon the principles laid down by Malthus and is the important factor in the supply of labor. Capital—a result of saving and "of abstinence from present consumption"—depends upon "the amount of the fund from which saving can be made, and the strength of the dispositions which prompt it" (p. 163). In order that production increase it is necessary for capital to increase, thus rendering production "susceptible of an increase without any assignable bounds" (p. 175). Land, however, is "not susceptible to indefinite increase, . . . the produce of the land, *ceteris paribus,* increases in a diminishing ratio to the increase of labour employed" (p. 181). As was pointed out earlier, the laws "partake of the character of physical truths. There is nothing arbitrary or optional in them. We cannot alter the ultimate properties either of matter or mind, but can only employ those properties more or less successfully, to bring about the events in which we are all interested (p. 200).

Distribution Theories.—The first ten chapters of Book II on distribution are devoted to property and land reform. In Chapter XI ("Of Wages"), Mill turns to the "threefold division of the produce among labourers, landlords, and capitalists." Wages, he contends, are regulated either by competition or by custom but "depend mainly upon the demand and supply of labour" or "on the proportion between population and capital" (p. 343). Most students of economics will always associate John Stuart Mill with the so-called wages-fund theory, which he states as follows:

Wages not only depend upon the relative amount of capital and population, but cannot, under the rule of competition, be affected by anything else. Wages (meaning, of course, the general rate) cannot rise, but by an increase of the aggregate funds employed in hiring labourers, or a diminution in the number of competitors for hire; nor fall, except either by a diminution of the funds devoted to paying labour, or by an increase in the number of labourers to be paid (pp. 343-44).

The essence of the wages-fund theory is that the available stock of capital furnished the fund from which wages were paid and that when this fund was paid out there was no more. Should the fund be large enough to pay labor in excess of the subsistence standard, the rise in wages would bring an increase in population and thus force down wages. This theory was suggested by Adam Smith (*Wealth of Nations*, Book I, chap. viii) and adopted by Ricardo (see *Works of David Ricardo*, p. 51). The fact that both Malthus and James Mill subscribed to the wages-fund theory made that theory practically standard from the standpoint of accepted authority.

The wages-fund theory had an important practical application. Labor was agitating for wage increases and this theory could be used to show that its demands were futile. It was a simple arithmetical process of division with the fixed dividend as the fund. Should the divisor be increased, the workers would get less; or if one group got an increase, it would be at the expense of another group. The only way out of the dilemma of how to increase wages was either to increase the size of the fund or to decrease the number of persons among whom it was to be divided. Even though Mill did not believe labor unions could assist the working class as a whole, he was not unfriendly to trade unions and labor reform. This latter attitude was no doubt a factor in helping him to change his views on the theory when he made his famous recantation in the *Fortnightly Review* (May and June, 1869).

The wages-fund theory had been attacked by a number of critics in England and elsewhere.[19] But in 1869 W. T. Thornton (1830-1880) published a book, *On Labor*, in which he stated that wages were paid out of capital in the hands of the employers, but he argued that the amount of the employers' resources devoted to the payment of wages was a matter of their decision. Mill reviewed the book in the *Fortnightly Review*; he admitted the force of the argument but decided that the results of the discussion were "not yet ripe for incorporation in a general treatise on Political Economy" (Preface to the seventh edition, 1871). He did not rewrite his chapter on wages after his recantation; the last edition of his *Principles* carries only a footnote calling attention to Thornton's criticism. It may well be contended that Mill never did adhere to a rigid wages-fund theory. It was never carefully analyzed nor were the consequences of such a theory understood.[20]

Mill next turns to the share of the capitalist—"the profits of capital or stock" (Bk. II, chap. xv). The profits of the capitalist, "according to Mr. Senior's well-chosen expression," are properly "the remuneration of abstinence"; they are his reward for abstaining from consumption of this capital for his own uses. Mill is not able to separate profits from interest; however, he says, "the rate of profit generally exceeds the rate of interest" (p. 406). Gross profits from capital must pay to those who supply the funds for production a reward for abstinence, an indemnity for risk, and a reward of superintendence. A return to capital is a minimum which, although it may vary in time and place, is a necessary reward. Then, assuming no monopoly, there is a tendency of profits to seek a general level even though they may, like the "vacillations of the pendulum," sometimes be below and sometimes above the general level. The real cause of profits, however, is the fact "that labour produces more than is required for its support."

The two elements on which the gains of the capitalist depend are the productive power of labor and the amount of the productivity required for supporting the laborers engaged in the enterprise. The rate of profit depends upon the share paid to labor, not on the amount of the product to be shared. Thus, Mill arrives at Ricardo's conclusion and admits "that the rate of profits depends on wages; rising as wages fall, and falling as wages rise" (p. 419). Ricardo's meaning, Mill insists, was that profits "depend on the *cost of labour*." Under this cost, Mill includes all the elements that enter into productive efficiency; labor cost

[19] Notably, Senior, F. A. Walker, Brentano, and Francis Longe.
[20] See F. W. Taussig's *Wages and Capital* (New York, 1896) for support of the theory, but in a different form.

may be high when wages are low and vice versa because of cheap but inefficient labor and so on. The cost of food enters in, for under some circumstances low wages may buy much food or the converse may be true that the wages, even though high, may buy little food. He sees a close relationship between wages and profits but he never quite disentangles the maze of ideas of other writers, the political implications, and his own urge for social reform. At any rate, the discussion is a marked improvement over that of Ricardo.

Mill adds little to the Ricardian analysis of rent. He holds that rent is the result of a monopoly in the ownership of land. Land is limited in quality and quantity, ranging from that which is highly productive to that which is so poor it yields no rent. The main proposition he seeks to prove is that the "rent of land consists of the excess of its return above the return of the worst land in cultivation, or to the capital employed in the least advantageous circumstances" (chap. xvi, pp. 427-28). He makes no mention of causes which produce variations in rent, but asserts that it is a payment for "superior power" over that of other areas for which no rent is paid. He follows Ricardo in holding that "rent does not really form any part of the expenses of production, or of the advances to the capitalist" (p. 433). Aside from a few quite relevant illustrations and a refutation of H. C. Carey's ideas on rent, there is less worth-while material in this chapter than in any of the chapters on distribution.

Value Theory.—Book III, "Exchange," contains more economic materials than any other of the five. In this book of twenty-four chapters he treats the important topics of value, money and credit, currency regulation, international values, the rate of interest, foreign exchanges, and other topics. However, only his ideas on value, international trade, and international values will be discussed here.

Mill is fully aware of the importance of the explanation of value when he says, "The subject on which we are now about to enter fills so important and conspicuous a position in political economy that in the apprehension of some thinkers its boundaries confound themselves with those of the science itself" (p. 435). He is anxious therefore, that the limits of his explanation be clearly defined. He says there is an ambiguity in the use of the term "Value"; in one sense it signifies usefulness and in another the power of purchasing, or value in use and value in exchange. The sense in which Mill uses the term is always that of value in exchange. He objects to the use of value and price as synonymous terms as was done by earlier writers, and defines price as the value of a thing in relation to money: "the quantity of money for which a thing will exchange," or "its value in money." Value, or the exchange value of a thing, is "its general power of purchasing: the command which its possession gives over purchaseable commodities in general" (p. 437). The money value, or price, represents the general exchange value or purchasing power. He then emphasizes that there may be such a thing as a general rise in prices (in terms of money). But there can be no such a thing as a general rise in values. One commodity can only rise in value by exchanging for a greater quantity of another, in which case the latter would exchange for less of the first commodity. He points out that "all things cannot rise relatively to one another. If one-half of the commodities in the market rise in exchange value, the very terms imply a fall of the other half" (p. 439).

In order for a good to have value in exchange, it must have some use, or, as Mill writes, "it must conduce to some purpose: satisfy some desire" and "there must be some difficulty of attainment" (p. 442). This, then, becomes the important problem of supply. Goods are classified into three groups; first, according as their supply is "absolutely limited in quantity such as ancient sculptures and pictures." The value of these goods is determined solely by supply and demand. Next those commodities "of which the supply may be indefinitely increased without increase in cost"; in this case value is determined by supply and demand and cost of production: the former determining their market value or their fluctuation about a natural or "long-run" value; the latter being responsible for determining the natural or "long-run" value. Last, "those commodities susceptible of indefinite multiplication but not without increase in cost." Here again, value is determined by demand and supply, and the cost of production "in the most unfavorable existing circumstances." At any given time demand and supply which exist in a given market situation determine market value: the forces of demand and supply then tend to cause an oscillation about natural value, just as the surface of the sea, although ruffled by storms, waves, and tides, tends to a natural level.

Mill follows Ricardo closely in his explanation of cost of production except for his emphasis on entrepreneurial outlay in the form of wages, profits (the return for abstinence), and taxes, which he includes in cost of production (chap. iv, "Ultimate Analysis of Cost of Production"). He considered the expenses incurred in production by the entrepreneur to be of greater importance than the quantity of labor alone in determining the exchange ratio of goods. He was convinced (following Senior) that value or price must be adequate to cover production costs in the long run. Value (or price) at any particular time is the result of supply and demand and is always that which is necessary to create a market for the existing supply. "But unless that value is sufficient to repay the Cost of Production, and to afford, besides, the ordinary expectation of profit, the commodity will not continue to be produced" (p. 451). Losses may be incurred on capital already invested and may continue for a considerable time, but the losses cannot be borne indefinitely. Under such conditions no new capital will be invested and old capital may be withdrawn. "The cost of production, together with ordinary profit, may therefore be called the *necessary* price, or value, of all things made by labour and capital" (*Ibid.*).

But Mill was not consistent here. He shifted from the subjective labor and abstinence, or *real costs*, of Ricardo and Senior to *money costs* or remuneration paid to laborers and suppliers of capital. He objects to the "maxim laid down by some of the best political economists, that wages do not enter into value" (p. 461). Relative wages do enter into value, but *general wages* do not affect value. He believes that if all wages rose or fell equally, relative values would be unchanged. But the entrepreneurial reward, profit, must be considered. The suppliers of capital demand a profit return which is commensurate with capital's part in production. Profits, then, "as well as wages, enter into the cost of production which determines the value of the produce" (p. 462). But since value is relative, it is only relative wages and relative profits that are significant. Mill was aware that there are permanent differences in both wages and profits and that they do influence market values. He did not see that these permanent differences have little or no connection with the relative amounts of labor and abstinence which they call forth. Rent, which he discusses "in its relation to value" (chap. v), is Ricardo's view restated, namely, that it forms no part of the cost of production.

Mill's value theory remains a subjective exchange theory. Even though he, like his predecessors, referred to utility and made demand coordinate with supply, he did not materially improve upon the theory's meaning and application. Cost of production he sometimes coordinates with supply and demand, but seems to imply that it is cost of production working on the supply side that determines value. His theory is not a labor-cost theory: it is much more comprehensive. He regarded competition as establishing market value which in the long run would closely approximate a natural value. Despite his assurance that "happily there is nothing in the laws of value which remains [in 1848] for the present or any future writer to clear up: the theory of the subject is complete" (p. 436), he did not have the final word. It remained for others to analyze the forces underlying both demand and supply and present a theory which, even now, is not a closed issue.

Theories of International Trade.—Mill's contribution to international trade theory is significant. He expanded the original theories of Smith and Ricardo, but he attempted to establish a more exact *a priori* means of determining the international exchange ratios by means of his "Equation of International Demand."   Mill first expressed his views on the subject in his *Essays on Some Unsettled Questions of Political Economy* in 1829 and 1830. He propounded the same doctrine in the *Essays* as he later did in the *Principles* in 1848. He points out (following Ricardo) that the advantage of exchange between nations comes from being able to obtain, with a given amount of labor and capital, a greater amount of commodities. One gains when he can purchase more goods, with a given amount of capital and labor, than could have been produced at home with equivalent capital and labor.

To render the importation of an article more advantageous than its production, it is not necessary that the foreign country should be able to produce it with less labour and capital than ourselves. We may even have a positive advantage in its production: but, if we are so far favored by circumstances as to have a still greater positive advantage in the production of some article which is in demand in the foreign country, we may be able to obtain a greater return to our labour and capital by employing none of it in producing the article in which our advantage is least, but devoting it all to the production of that in which our advantage is greatest, and giving this to the foreign country in exchange for the other. It is not the difference in the *absolute* cost of production which determines the interchange, but the difference in the *comparative* cost.[21]

He illustrates the principle with Swedish iron and English cottons and points out that

. . . it may be to our advantage to procure iron from Sweden in exchange for cottons, even though the mines of England as well as her manufactories should be more productive than those of Sweden; for if we have the advantage of one-half in cottons, and only the advantage of a quarter in iron, and could sell our cottons to Sweden at the price which Sweden must pay for them if she produced them herself, we should obtain our iron with an advantage of one-half as well as our cottons. We may often, by trading with foreigners, obtain their commodities at a smaller expense of labour and capital than they cost to the foreigners themselves. The bargain is still advantageous to the foreigner, because the commodity which he receives in exchange, though it has cost us less, would have cost him more (p. 576).

In other words, goods are not exchanged between countries on the ratio of their costs of production, but on a reciprocal demand in such

[21] *Essays.* p. 2.   Also quoted in *Principles*, p. 576.

a way that the quantity of the article which a country imports is exactly compensated for by the amount it exports. He explains the balance thus: "the 'produce of a country exchanges for the produce of other countries, at such values as are required in order that the whole of her exports may exactly pay for the whole of her imports" (pp. 592-93). He calls this the "Law of International Values" and says it is "but an extension of the more general law of Value, which we have called the Equation of Supply and Demand" (*Ibid.*). This is his doctrine of demand and supply as applied to international trade. He abandons cost of production as a means of comparing values of goods entering into international trade. Labor and capital do not easily cross national boundaries; in fact, they possess only limited mobility within a state. He therefore adopts a measure which will express the value of the imported article in terms of the value of the exported article which must be given in exchange for it.[22] Since "all trade is in reality barter," the law of international values does not depend on a comparison of production costs but upon the law of demand and supply. The prices of the goods will adjust themselves under competition, in such manner that the amounts demanded by the trading countries will automatically balance.

The theory, although incomplete and possibly oversimplified, did represent an improvement over that developed by Ricardo. It provided a means of judging the intensity of foreign demand and making it possible for a nation to drive a hard bargain. The self-regulatory element under competition proved unworkable, for nations would not permit competition to work. Even Mill, with his faithful adherence to free trade doctrines and his strong denunciation of protection, would justify protection of new or "infant" industries. With all its imperfections and vulnerable aspects, the theory afforded a point of departure for later work in the general field of international economics.[23]

Monetary Theories and Market Situations.—In the subsequent chapters of Book III Mill discusses money, currency, banking, and distribution of the precious metals. He insists that trade between nations tends toward "an equilibrium between exports and imports whether money is employed or not; . . . in other words the Equation of International Demand, under a money system as well as under a barter system, is the law of international trade" (p. 621).

[22] "The value of a thing in any place depends on the cost of its acquisition in that place; which, in the case of an imported article, means the cost of production of the thing which is exported to pay for it" (p. 583).

[23] See James W. Angell, *The Theory of International Prices* (Cambridge, Mass., 1926), chap. 4.

Some attention should be given to competition between countries in the same market (chap. xxv) or commercial rivalry which leads to underselling. He believed that

Nations may, like individual dealers, be competitors, with opposite interests, in the markets of some commodities, while in others they are in the more fortunate relation of reciprocal customers. The benefit of commerce does not consist, as it was once thought to do, in the commodities sold; but, since the commodities sold are the means of obtaining those which are bought, a nation would be cut off from the real advantages of commerce, the imports, if it could not induce other nations to take any of its commodities in exchange; and in proportion as the competition of other countries compels it to offer its commodities on cheaper terms, on pain of not selling them at all, the imports which it obtains by its foreign trade are produced at a greater cost (p. 678).

In the final analysis,

. . . one country could only undersell another in a given market, to the extent of entirely expelling her from it on two conditions. In the first place, she must have greater advantage than a second country in the production of the article exported by both; meaning by a greater advantage (as has been already so fully explained) not absolutely, but in comparison with other commodities; and in the second place, such must be her relation with the customer country in respect to the demand for each other's products, and such consequent state of international values, as to give away to the customer country more than the whole advantage possessed by the rival country; otherwise the rival will still be able to hold her ground in the market (p. 679).

English producers should not be disturbed that a competitior, "at some particular time" may undersell them. If this should occur, there would follow a redistribution of the precious metals, a change (fall) in the level of prices resulting from the diminution of her exports, and a readjustment of all the forces again restoring the former balance. A significant point of emphasis is that the real burden of the loss of export trade does not fall upon the exporters, but upon those who consume the imported commodities. Low wages in one country may permit it to undersell a competitor, but only when they prevail in certain industries, not generally or in all branches of industry. "General low wages never caused any country to undersell its rivals, nor did general high wages ever hinder it from doing so" (p. 684). This is a strong argument for those supporting free trade.

The Influence of the Progress of Society on Production and Distribution.—In Book IV, which bears this title, are found some of Mill's most challenging ideas; they form a theory of economic development. He

deals with a dynamic as opposed to a static society. His explanation of
the nature and the consequences of change in a dynamic society as it
advances shows his knowledge of the interdependence of the many
social forces. Some of his economic views are those generally held by
Ricardo, but the over-all concept, or "oneness" of society, is a result of
Comte's influence.

Among the elements which characterize progressive economic advances in civilized nations he lists "a progress in wealth; an advancement of what is called material prosperity," "increase in production
and in population," "the growth of man's power over nature," "knowledge of the properties and laws of physical objects" and the "skill
requisite for executing the most delicate processes of the application
of science to practical uses." He also lists "increase of the security of
person and property . . . against violence and rapacity of one another
. . . against arbitrary exercise of the power of government." On the
production side he lists the "improvement in the business capacities of
the general mass of mankind," mankind's "greater capacity of united
action," and "the capacity of cooperation which led to the formation
of the joint-stock companies" and "associations of workpeople either for
production or to buy goods for their common consumption" (Bk. IV,
chap. i, pp. 695-99 *passim*).

The result of these changes has been an increase in wealth and in
population in civilized countries. Improved production methods have
tended to diminish the cost of producing manufactured commodities,
but in agriculture "increased production takes place at a greater cost."
He makes a comparison of manufacturing and extractive industries
and summarizes their tendencies as follows:

The tendency, then, being to a perpetual increase of productive power
of labour in manufactures, while in agriculture and mining there is a conflict between the two tendencies, the one towards an increase in productive
power, the other towards a diminution of it, the cost of production being
lessened by every improvement in the process, and augmented by every addition to population; it follows that the exchange values of manufactured
articles, compared with the products of agriculture and of mines, have, as
population and industry advance, a certain and decided tendency to fall.
Money being a product of mines, it may also be laid down as a rule, that
manufactured articles tend, as society advances, to fall in money price
(p. 703).

He points out that whether agricultural prices increase in absolute
as well as comparative costs of production depends on the "conflict of
two antagonistic agencies, increase in population, and improvement in
agricultural skill." He thinks that "in most states of society" both are

nearly stationary or increase very slowly and "the cost of production of food is nearly stationary." When a society is advancing in wealth, "population increases faster than agricultural skill, and food consequently tends to become more costly" (pp. 703-4).

Next, Mill is concerned with the manner in which prices of commodities fluctuate in a progressing society. He says, "there can be no doubt that the tendency has been to decrease them." Improved communication and transportation and "speculative merchants" have tended to reduce price fluctuations. He praises the speculation as serving a very useful economic function for society in leveling out price variations due to seasonality, and so on.

In Chapter III of Book IV, Mill traces the "influence of the progress of industry and population on rents, profits and wages." He regards the characteristic features of industrial progress as increase of capital, increase in population, and improvements in production. He then arrives at his conclusions by assuming a change in one while the other two remain stationary. For example, suppose population increases while capital and the "arts of production" remain stationary. Wages will fall; the status of the capitalist is improved, for "with the same capital he can purchase more labour, and obtain more produce. His rate of profit is increased."

Next he assumes that capital increases and population remains stationary. Real wages of labor would then rise: "Since the cost of production of the things consumed by the labourer is not diminished, this rise in wages implies an equivalent increase in the cost of labour and diminution of profits" (p. 713). The same causes will bring a rise in rents, assuming that laborers use all or part of the increase in wages for increasing their consumption. Should both capital and population increase with the arts remaining stationary, food costs will rise, as will agricultural prices, and "rents will rise both in quantity of produce and in cost"; money wages will also rise. Since the capitalist is unable to improve his status by changing his investment, he must lose in profits. The "tendency of an increase of capital and population is to add to rent at the expense of profits"; but rent does not gain all that profits lose, for part must go to increased expenses of production resulting from an increase in the supply of agricultural products.

He summarizes the long and rather involved treatment as follows:

... the economical progress of a society constituted of landlords, capitalists, and labourers tends to the progressive enrichment of the landlord class; while the cost of the labourer's subsistence tends on the whole to increase and profits to fall. Agricultural improvements are a counteracting force to the two last effects; but the first ... is ultimately in a high degree promoted by these improvements; and the increase of population tends to transfer all the benefits derived from agricultural improvements to the landlords alone (p. 724).

. It is interesting that Mill, with all his erudition, should continue to perpetuate these fallacies—a heritage from his predecessors.

Mill next points out in Chapter IV that early writers on industry and commerce recognized "the tendency of profits to fall as society advances." Adam Smith's opinion was that profits fall as a result of competition of capital which lowers prices, but Mill objects to this theory as being "incorrect in fact, as well as unsound in principle." Mill holds that "there is at every time and place some particular rate of profit, which is the lowest that will induce the people of that country and time to accumulate savings, and to employ those savings productively." But the rate varies according to circumstances. One is "the strength of the effective desire of accumulation"—a weighing of future interests against present. The other is "the degree of security of capital engaged in industrial operations" (p. 728).

On the first point he insists that "a state of general insecurity" would affect the disposition to save and the general risk involved. He points out, however, that, for reasons largely personal, there would be some saving, e.g., a reserve for sickness or a means of leisure, even if capital yielded no profit. Likewise some may find no motive for saving "for the mere purpose of growing richer or of leaving others better off than themselves." These are exceptional cases, however. The dynamics of society, which tends to reduce risk for both the economic present and future, tends "to diminish the amount of profit which people absolutely require as an inducement to save and accumulate." Therefore, the percentage rate of interest tends to be much lower than in earlier times. He then arrives (p. 731) at the "fundamental proposition which this chapter is intended to inculcate." It is this:

. . . when a country has long possessed a large population, and a large net income to make savings from, and when, therefore, the means have long existed of making a great annual addition to capital; (the country not having, like America [in 1848], a large reserve of fertile land still unused;) it is one of the characteristics of such a country, that the rate of profit is habitually within, as it were, a hand's breadth of the minimum, and the country therefore on the verge of the stationary state.

By minimum rate of profits, he means the lowest rate that will induce people to save for productive purposes: by stationary state he means a country in which a minimum has been reached and "no further increase of capital can for the present take place."

The counteracting circumstances which will keep a nation "a hand's breadth from the minimum" are first, "the waste of capital in periods of over-trading and speculation" and the "commercial revulsions" which follow. The "improvements in production" followed by "obtaining cheap commodities from foreign countries" and lastly the "perpetual overflow of capital into colonies or foreign countries, to seek higher profits than can be obtained at home."

Mill saw strong counter-influences which tended to offset the major economic movements. The tendency of profits, he thought, was to be reduced to a minimum, and crises tended to dissipate the volume of capital for investment. However, the desire for capital accumulation still remains, as do also the risks. He fears neither the long-run effects of these tendencies nor the effects of the introduction of machinery on the laboring class. New capital in the form of machinery would increase the productivity of labor, enlarge the funds from which savings were made, and finally enlarge the funds from which labor was paid.

He raises the question: To what point is society tending by industrial progress? To this he replies that "the increase of wealth is not bound-less" and at the end of "the progressive state lies the stationary state." He states emphatically that "the richest and most prosperous countries would very soon attain the stationary state, if no further improvement were made in the productive arts, and if there were a suspension of the overflow of capital from those countries into the uncultivated or ill-cultivated regions of the earth" (p. 746). Mill held the opinion that the stationary state might be an improvement over the present one. He makes the following rather startling statement:

I am inclined to believe that it would be, on the whole, a very consider-able improvement on our present condition. I confess I am not charmed with the ideal of life held out by these who think that the normal state of human beings is that of struggling to get on; that the trampling, crushing, elbowing, and treading on each other's heels, which form the existing type of social life, are the most desirable lot of human kind, or anything but the disagreeable symptoms of one of the phases of industrial progress . . . The best state for human nature is that in which, while no one is poor, no one desires to be richer, nor has any reason to fear being thrust back by the ef-forts of others to push themselves forward (pp. 748-49).

It appears that his idealism got the better of him. He believed that there would be human improvement in the stationary state with "all kinds of mental culture, moral and social progress; as much room for the Art of Living and much more likelihood of its being improved, when minds ceased to be engrossed by the art of getting on" (p. 751). He believed that better distribution of goods rather than greater production of wealth should be the objective of civilized countries.

The Role of Government in Economic Life.—Book V of the *Principles* deals with the influence of Government. Here he describes the necessary and the optional functions of government and makes many exceptions to the laissez-faire principle in government. Chapters II-VII, dealing with taxation, add little to tax theory; however, he does discuss general principles as well as specific taxes. His general treatment is very similar to that found in Ricardo's work. The remaining chapters deal with topics which were pressing issues of his day but fall within the general framework of governmental influence. They have little of interest in them.

Summary and Evaluation.—John Stuart Mill's niche in the development of economic thought was not earned by his contribution of original ideas. Indeed, it is very doubtful whether he even came very close to accurately restating the doctrines of Smith, Malthus, and Ricardo. Yet Mill deserves to be classed with the near-great, if not with the great. A contemporary writer has said of Mill, "No one in the history of economics was more celebrated, even sometime after his death . . . and no one has faded more completely." [24] This is very true. Once or twice a year the works of John Stuart Mill will be dusted off for re-examination by the student in logic, government, sociology, or economics, or possibly by someone researching in socialist literature. After a cursory examination, the student has at least a partial awareness that the work, while significant, is not the epitome of all things great.

Mill was an expositor with a strong bias for giving advice. He had opinions on practically everything and would express them with finality on the least provocation. More than that, he had firm convictions in most instances, but a careful reading will show the conflict between the traditional doctrinaire background and the progressive, liberal thought of the period in which he wrote. *Principles of Political Economy* was *the* textbook for nearly fifty years. It still is a masterpiece of exposition, smoothly written with a high moral tone, and based on the conviction that political economy is indeed a science deserving the best talents of statesmen and students alike. He saw the realities of the economic world; he was interested in logical consistency and a philosophical basis for economic science and made quick work of the "natural law" and "natural rights" heritage. He did, however, retain most of the a priori assumptions of his predecessors, notably, that self-interest motivates man in his economic affairs and that this motivation is best for general

24 E. Heimann, *History of Economic Doctrines* (New York, 1945), p. 119.

welfare. Mill was a firm believer in individual motivation and generally objected to restrictions or interferences. He had great faith in the ③
laissez-faire philosophy, with utility as the ultimate test. His utilitarianism was the standard for evaluating actions both of the individual and
of the state. Only when the greatest good to the greatest number
could be served was any interference on the part of the government or
anyone else warranted. Smith's laissez faire was more absolute than
that of Mill; the latter allowed considerable flexibility, even admitting
at times that the judgment of the individual should be overruled by
law (Bk. V, chap. xi, pp. 963-66).

Even though Mill accepted the Malthusian population principle his
belief was that man could, by a gradual educational process, surmount ④
the forces which tended to weigh him down and thus retard society.
He therefore deserves, along with Smith, to be classed as an optimist.
His social institutions could, and in their time would, be improved by
society itself. This would come as a part of social betterment on a
wide front in which all groups would share. He visualized (Book IV,
Chapter VII, "On the Probable Future of the Working Class") a plan
of producers' cooperation which would virtually dispense with the wage
system, the employees becoming their own managers and sharing the
income, "collectively owning the capital with which they carry on their
operations, and working under managers elected and removable by
themselves" (p. 773). It is certain that Mill had socialist leanings, even
utopian hopes, but the full impact of his socialism on the British liberal
movement is an indeterminable quantity.[25]

The liberal social views of Mill were often at variance with the economic fundamentals in which he believed. He held that competition ⑤
would automatically equalize wages and profits and would be aided in
so doing by tax measures; this idea contrasts his views on cooperation
and socialism, and his extreme view on communism. He lived at a
time when the present was breaking radically with the past, yet he could
not make a complete transition in his own thought. Even though a
liberal, a parliamentarian, and, in a restricted sense, a politician, he was
not really in touch with the liberal movement and its leaders except
from the "book" approach. The full import of Saint-Simonianism and
the French Revolution was never quite fully understood by Mill. Nor
did he foresee the full significance of utilitarianism as it might be applied under a liberal government which theoretically could demand
that many established economic institutions—notably the corporate
form of enterprise—be directed to make their decisions in behalf of

[25] Sidney Webb takes the view that socialism in England owes its whole existence
to Mill. *Fabian Tract*, No. 15, p. 11. See also Webb, *Socialism in England* (Baltimore, 1895), p. 19 *et seq.*

the thousands of people they serve by producing goods or services, rather than the few who own the shares of stock. Theoretically, Mill's philosophy leads to production for use and not production for profit. So with a *pax vobiscum* we leave Mill at his retreat in Avignon, fully aware that most students say either too much or too little about him, and turn to other disciples of the classical tradition.

John Elliot Cairnes

The last significant defender of the faith of the English classical tradition was John Elliot Cairnes.[26] Mill had restated the classical teaching and put it in its most attractive form. Cairnes became the ablest disciple and interpreter of Mill, much as Say was for Adam Smith. Although he was not always in complete agreement with Mill, he regarded himself as Mill's disciple [27] and as an orthodox classical economist with strong preference for the deductive method. He accepted laissez faire as a safe and practical rule of conduct. As to the fundamentals, he was as much a classical economist as any of the school. Marshall feared that Cairnes's attempt to amend and, in a real sense, defend classical economic doctrines would aid in overthrowing them. Cairnes held the narrow conception that wealth alone constituted the subject matter of economics. He defined political economy as "the science which investigates the laws of production and distribution of wealth, which result from the principles of human nature as they operate under the actual circumstances of the external world." [28] The laws of the science of political economy are "First, the desire for physical well-being implanted in man, and for wealth as the means of obtaining it, and, as a consequence of this in conjunction with other mental

[26] J. E. Cairnes (1824-1875) was educated at Trinity College, Dublin, from which he graduated in 1848. He studied law and was a member of the Irish bar, but disliking the practice of law, he began to read political economy. He competed for the Whately professorship of political economy at Dublin and won a five-year appointment in 1856. In accordance with the requirements of the appointment his first set of lectures was published in 1857 under the title, *The Character and Logical Method of Political Economy* (London, 1857; 2d ed., 1875). He next served (1861-1866) as professor at Queens College, Galway, and subsequently (1866-1872) as professor at University College, London. In 1862 he wrote a defense of the northern states in the issue over slavery entitled, *Slave Power*. His ideas on educational policy, money and prices, and the ever-present Irish land question may be found in his *Political Essays* (London, 1873) and in his *Essays in Political Economy Theoretical and Applied* (London, 1873). His chief work was *Some Leading Principles of Political Economy Newly Expounded* (London, 1874), which earned him a wide reputation. Upon the death of Mill in 1873, Cairnes was generally regarded as the foremost living economist. He died at an early age, 51, as a result of a hunting accident.

[27] The first edition of *Slave Power* was dedicated to J. S. Mill.

[28] *The Character and Logical Method of Political Economy*, Lecture III, p. 73.

attributes, the desire to obtain wealth at the least possible sacrifice; secondly, the principles of population as derived from the physiological character of man and his mental propensities; and thirdly, the physical qualities of the natural agents, more especially land, on which human industry is exercised." [29]   He believed that these laws expressed the phenomena of wealth as certainly as "Chemistry does for the phenomena of the functions of organic life."   Hence political economy was not concerned with solving social and moral problems.   So much for what Cairnes believed on scope and method.

Cairnes is best known as an economist for his work, *Some Leading Principles of Political Economy Newly Expounded,* which appeared in 1874, two years after he resigned his University College appointment. It was an attempt to "recast" and "strengthen, in some degree, and add consistence to that fabric" built by Smith, Malthus, Ricardo, and Mill, thereby better fitting it to "endure the strain of modern criticism."

Value and Price Theory.—The book discusses value, labor and capital, and international trade.   Value he defines as "expressing the ratio in which commodities in open market are exchanged against each other" (*Some Leading Principles,* p. 11).   He objects to Jevons's attempt to substitute "ratio of exchange" for "value," preferring the classical meaning which expresses a relationship of commodities in exchange.   He uses the identical three circumstances essential to the existence of value as used by Senior—utility, difficulty of attainment, and transferableness. Demand and supply he treats as aggregates.   In a simple barter economy, supply would consist of the commodities offered in exchange for other commodities and demand would have exactly the same meaning. "Each commodity would be in turn supply and demand" (p. 24).   But when a medium of exchange is introduced it represents general purchasing power; since all transactions are conducted through this medium, it is "impossible to distinguish Demand and Supply."   He makes "Demand and Supply strictly analogous conceptions" (p. 25).   In other words, he objects to the use of Demand and Supply as independent economic forces.   Producers are also consumers, and "any diminution in general supply would be exactly balanced by a corresponding diminution in general demand" (p. 33).   Cairnes then sets up his "fundamental law of Demand and Supply" as follows: "The Supply of a commodity always tends to adapt itself to the Demand at the normal price" (p. 41).

Under normal value analysis (chap. iii), he carefully analyses the cost of production influence on price.   After summarizing Mill's theory, he dissents from it as unsound and confusing.   To him, cost of production means "the sacrifices incurred by man in productive industry" (p. 49)

[29] *Ibid.*

rather than expenses of production. He strongly emphasizes that cost of production means "sacrifice" and not a reward for skill. In his explanation, cost of production as a determinant of normal value depends upon free competition in which capital and labor move freely from one employment to another or to higher rewards. Obstacles to free movement of the factors affect his cost doctrine to the extent that it would probably not work at all. He found such obstacles in both international and domestic trade.

It is in conjunction with obstacles to free competition that he introduces his "non-competing" groups, a concept which has been extremely useful. He gives "in rough outline the form which industrial organization . . . tends to assume." His explanation of the "layers" of industrial society follows:

What we find, in effect, is, not a whole population competing indiscriminately for all occupations, but a series of industrial layers, superposed on one another, within each of which the various candidates for employment possess a real and effective power of selection, while those occupying the several strata are, for all purposes of effective competition, practically isolated from each other. We may perhaps venture to arrange them in some such order as this: first, at the bottom of the scale there would be the large group of unskilled or nearly unskilled laborers, comprising agricultural laborers, laborers engaged in miscellaneous occupations in towns, or acting in attendance on skilled labor. Secondly, there would be the artisan group, comprising skilled laborers of the secondary order, carpenters, joiners, smiths, masons, shoe-makers, tailors, hatters, etc., etc., with whom might be included the very large class of small retail dealers, whose means and position place them within the reach of the same industrial opportunities as the class of artisans. The third layer would contain producers and dealers of a higher order, whose work would demand qualifications only obtainable by persons of substantial means and fair educational opportunities—for example, civil and mechanical engineers, chemists, opticians, watch-makers, and others of the same industrial grade, in which might also find a place the superior class of retail tradesmen; while above these there would be a fourth, comprising persons still more favorably circumstanced, whose ampler means would give them still a wider choice. This last group would contain members of the learned professions, as well as persons engaged in the various careers of science and art, and in the higher branches of mercantile business (pp. 66, 67).

Labor tends to move freely within the groups or layers of industrial society and the "principle of cost of production controls" or holds within the groups. However, there is no such freedom of movement among the groups, and normal exchange value does not rest upon cost of production but upon what he calls "reciprocal dealings" which govern "normal value in the absence of competition." The demand of each of the groups for the products of the other groups will enable each group to pay for the products of the other groups offered in exchange. In other words, there is a "reciprocal demand" in J. S. Mill's sense (p. 89). Cairnes speaks of reciprocal demand as "merely a duplicate of supply and demand regarded in its full significance" but supply and demand, in relation to prices, are "merely proximate agencies governing the fluctuations of the market, but themselves controlled by forces lying deeper in the economy of production" (p. 91). Cost of production and reciprocal demand each "furnish a center about which market values gravitate" (p. 93). Cost of production is directly related to the individual commodity under consideration, whereas reciprocal demand is applied to "the average fluctuation of a considerable aggregate of commodities" (p. 93). When applied to the normal value of goods produced, it means that cost of production governs the value within a group, whereas reciprocal demand determines the average relative level of prices among the groups. Reciprocal demand tends to be more stable and equitable in the long run. Cairnes made a sincere attempt to explain normal value in detail by using and improving upon Mill's concept. He carried his explanation further than Mill, but he fell short of analyzing the cost of production concept with the same thoroughness as he did the sacrifice concept. On the basis of the original assumptions and explanations the discussion in the succeeding chapters of Part I is of little value.

Labor and International Trade.—The second part, "Labor and Capital," is a defense of the wages-fund doctrine which Mill himself appears to have abandoned (cf. p. 265) and which Longe, Thornton, and others had severely criticized. In defending the wages-fund, Cairnes gave what is probably its best analysis and presentation.

In conjunction with his defense of the wages-fund theory he drives his hardest blows against the rising power of trade unions. His strong views have been responsible for his being considered as an uncompromising opponent of unionism. He admits that strong trade unions may temporarily raise the rate of wages "beyond the level determined by the economic conditions prevailing in the country" (p. 218) but are "powerless to effect a permanent increase" beyond what the economic conditions will warrant. He holds, following classical tradition, that trade unions might "for the moment raise wages at the expense of profits" but in the long run would result in just the opposite effect on wages. The action of the trade union would increase the risks on investment and thereby raise the minimum rate of profit; "in proportion as it did so, it would narrow the field for the employment of capital in the country" (p. 223). This would tend to diminish the supply of the wages-fund, and unless there was a reduction in the number of laborers, the general rate of wages would fall. The general tenor of the discussions would indicate that Cairnes was unalterably opposed to trade unions. However, his opposition was directed against anything that interfered with the free working of competition; he did not oppose trade unionism per se.

Cairnes deals with international trade in Part III. It is mainly an exposition of Ricardo's condition of trade and of Mill's theory of international values, to which he adds a balance of debts. He supported free-trade principles. In his discussion of free trade and protection (Chapter IV) he argues at length against the typical protectionist argument of the "inability" of Americans to compete against the "pauper labor" of Europe. He objects to the attitude of American enterprise toward free trade which would "turn natural laws to their best account." High import duties, which had characterized the American commercial policy "since 1861" was but an "attempt to override the laws of nature" (p. 388). His economic arguments were much stronger than his political arguments: he conceded the need for diversification of industry and to some extent admitted the need of tariffs to protect the "infant industry" so-called. His statements reflect a point of view rather than a deep conviction.

Cairnes's work is developed at some length, for it is the last important work of the old classical English school. Unfortunately, he was blind to the significant developments of his time. The past was ever too much with him.[30]

[30] See T. E. Cliffe Leslie, *Essays in Political and Moral Philosophy* (Dublin, 1879), chaps. xii and xvi for a discussion of Cairnes and his work.

14

The Influence of Classical Economics
in France and Germany

Not all the defenders and developers of classical doctrines were English. The influence of the doctrines on economic thinking and economic policy was far-reaching. They had, within limits, a universal applicability. Through adaptations of both theory and practice or to provide destructive criticism of prevailing policies, classical economics became everyone's property. Refinements, elaboration, systematization, and interpretation became everyone's privilege. In this, the French and German writers had a relatively large share. For the most part, their work went beyond a mere popularization of the work of Smith, Malthus, and Ricardo; some made distinct contributions in addition to cogent criticisms.

Jean Baptiste Say

The rise of political economy in England was concurrent with its decline in France. The contribution of physiocracy, if indeed it may be so honored, was eclipsed by Smith's work, *The Wealth of Nations*, which was translated into French in 1779.[1] The popularization of this work and the final destruction of the remains of mercantilism (or Colbertism) and physiocracy were undertaken by Jean Baptiste Say. He was the founder and the most eminent of the French classical school and probably the most pre-eminent of Smith's disciples on the continent. His *Traité d'économie politique* (*Treatise on Political Economy*, 1803) did more to popularize Smith's work than any other book.[2]

[1] The first French translation was by Blavet in the *Journal de l'Agriculture, du Commerce, des Finances, et des Arts*, 1779-80. The later translation by Count Germain Garnier is considered the standard one.
[2] Jean Baptiste Say (1767-1832) was born in Lyons, of a Protestant family that had fled from France after the revocation of the Edict of Nantes, but returned in the eighteenth century. He intended to enter business and went to England where he worked in a business house, later returning to France where he went into a life assurance office. He was a soldier and, as a statesman, he served in the

In a sense his *Political Economy* was patterned after the *Wealth of Nations*, but actually it was a great improvement on the masterpiece. He recognized—sometimes exaggerated—Smith's faults and proceeded to rearrange the ideas, improve the form, style, and readability of the book and in so doing gave Smith's ideas and his own a wide reading. It was for many years the standard economics text in American institutions of higher learning. He did more than popularize Smith. His own contributions place him in the front ranks. The student has to read only a few of his short chapters to appreciate the clear and orderly presentation of the materials.

In the "Introduction" Say tells us that "political economy . . . makes known the nature of wealth; from the knowledge of its nature deduces the means of its creation, unfolds the order of its distribution, and the phenomena attending its destruction."[3] He viewed the science as purely theoretical and descriptive, resting upon "a few fundamental principles and a great number of corollaries or conclusions drawn from these principles" (p. xxvi). He complains that "the work of Dr. Smith is a succession of demonstrations, which has elevated many propositions to the rank of indisputable principles, and plunged a still greater number into that imaginary gulph, into which extravagant hypotheses and vague opinions for a certain period struggle, before being forever swallowed up" (p. xxix). He further criticizes Smith on "the plan of the work," with presenting "obscure and indistinct notions," with being "deficient in perspicuity," and for presenting a work which "almost throughout is destitute of method" and fails to develop "his fundamental principles . . . in the chapters assigned to their development" (p. xliii). Say then

Tribunate in 1799, from which he was later dismissed by Napoleon. He next became a cotton-spinning mill proprietor for about ten years. His *Treatise on Political Economy* appeared in 1803. Because he would not retract certain statements on government finance which were displeasing to the government, the book was not revised until 1814. Say was sent in 1814 by a more friendly government to study the economic condition of Great Britain. The result of his observations appeared in a tract, *De l'Angleterre et des Anglais*. A chair of industrial economy was founded for him in 1819 at the Conservatoire des Arts et Métiers. In 1830 he became professor of political economy at the Collège de France, a position he held until his death. Five editions of his *Traité* were published in his lifetime, in 1803, 1814, 1817, 1819, and 1826. A sixth edition was edited by his eldest son in 1846 and a seventh edition by A. Clement (Paris, 1861). The work was translated into English by C. R. Prinsep (Boston, 1821) from the fourth edition. In addition to his *Treatise* he published A *Catechism of Political Economy* (1817) and A *Complete Course in Political Economy* (6 vols., 1828-1829), a work which enlarged upon his previous writings. His life span covered the significant years in French history of the Revolution, the Napoleonic era, the Restoration, and the Revolution of 1830. See E. Teilhac, *L'Oeuvre économique de Jean-Baptiste Say* (Paris, 1927) for an excellent treatment of his life and writings.

[3] *Treatise on Political Economy*, trans. C. R. Prinsep (Boston, 1821), p. xviii.

addresses himself to the "useful task" of "unfolding the manner in which wealth is produced, distributed and consumed" (p. xlv).

This gives the pattern of his book, the production, distribution, and consumption of wealth—a pattern which has become a standard arrangement in most textbooks on economic principles.[4]   He defines production as "the creation, not of matter, but of utility."   Wealth can exist only "where there are things possessed of real and intrinsic value" (p. 61).   "There is no actual possession of wealth without a creation or augmentation of utility" (p. 63).   Say recognizes the nature and importance of capital and land in production.   In land (natural agents), he recognizes the physical attributes of productivity, in the broadest sense, which work along with capital (tools, implements, raw materials) and labor in production, or the creation of utility.   He disagrees sharply with Smith, who drew "a false conclusion that all values represent pre-exerted human labor or industry, either recent or remote; or, in other words, that wealth is nothing more than labor accumulated; from which position he [Smith] infers a second consequence equally erroneous, viz., that labor is the sole measure of wealth, or of value produced" (p. 76).   Say rejects Smith's distinction between productive and unproductive labor.   He recognizes both the advantages and the disadvantages of the division of labor, whereas Smith emphasized the former and tended to disregard the latter.

Say held that capital was formed by "the process of saving; in other words, of reemploying in production more products created than have been consumed in their creation" (p. 111).   The process is slow, for it takes time and labor to produce in excess of what is consumed during the saving process.   But capital, when finally created and amassed in some amount, "is a powerful engine consigned to the use of man alone" (p. 117).   He adds that "there is no assignable limit to the capital he [man] may accumulate with the aid of time, industry, and frugality" (p. 118).   Say regards manufacturing equally as important as agriculture, whereas Smith had emphasized agriculture and commerce.

One of the concepts for which Say is best known is the theory of the markets (*la théorie des débouchés*), often called "Say's Law."[5]   The theory is that goods and services are bought with other goods and services.   Money "performs but a momentary function" in effecting the exchange of commodities or services.   He holds that the very production of goods creates a demand for other goods; in effect, goods are purchasing power, or supply is potential demand.   He remarks "a product is no sooner created, than it, from that instant, affords a market for other

---

[4] The plan of arrangement might have been borrowed from Turgot's *Réfléxions*.
[5] Bk. I, chap. xv, "Of the Demand or Market for Products."

products to the full extent of its own value. . . . The creation of one product immediately opens a vent for other products" (p. 134). It follows then, from his premises, that there can be no such thing as a market glut—in other words, overproduction is impossible. If there is an excess in the amount of certain goods, it is because the production of other goods has fallen short; overproduction in one commodity would be cured by increased production in another, which would then become the market for the excess of the first. Malthus and Sismondi, on the contrary, held that there could be overproduction or a market glut.[6]

Say draws three conclusions from his theory. First, the more numerous the producers and the more extensive the market, the more profitable the market is to the producers, for price rises with the demand. Next, he draws the conclusion that "each individual is interested in the general prosperity of all, and that the success of one branch of industry promotes that of all others" (p. 137). He argues that there is no point to classifying people into consumers and producers, for everyone is both. In national life it is likewise incorrect to "divide nations into agricultural, manufacturing, and commercial . . . for the success of a people in agriculture is a stimulus to manufacturing and commercial prosperity" (p. 138), and vice versa. A nation surrounded by rich nations is "sure to profit by their opulence." The third conclusion is the essence of free trade doctrine; no injury can come to "the internal or national industry and production" by importing from abroad; "nothing can be bought from strangers, except with native products, which find vent in this external traffic" (p. 139). The net result is, therefore, that "the encouragement of mere consumption is no benefit to commerce; for the difficulty lies in supplying the means, not in stimulating the desire of consumption; and we have seen that production alone, furnishes those means. Thus it is the aim of good government to stimulate production, of bad government to encourage consumption" (p. 139).

Value and Distribution Theory.—In Book II, "Of the Distribution of Wealth," he attempts to "analyze the nature of value, the object of distribution . . ." and "to ascertain the laws, which regulate the distribution of value . . ." It has been pointed out that Say places greater emphasis upon utility than his contemporaries or predecessors and that he breaks with the labor theory of value. But his analysis falls short of developing a new theory of value, or an equilibrium analysis. Say criticizes Smith for his labor-cost theory and argues that industrial costs, which include rent and profits, determine value; but he adds that "the

---

[6] See *Letters to Mr. Malthus* (Paris, 1820), pp. 294-95. English translation in the *Pamphleteer*, XVII, No. 34 (London, 1821). Malthus held that only food could not be overproduced. Cf. Chapter 11, p. 211.

desire of an object, and consequently its value, originates in its utility"
(p. 287). He distinguishes between supply and stock, the former being
the amount of a commodity which the owners are "disposed to part
with for an equivalent" and not merely "what is actually on sale at the
time" (p. 289), the latter referring to the amount in existence. His
treatment of the interrelationships of demand and supply is not always
distinct, but in the analogy which follows he shows a clear understanding of the interrelationships of supply, demand, and price:

Demand and Supply are the opposite extremes of the beam, whence depend the scales of dearness or cheapness: the price is the point of equilibrium, where the momentum of the one ceases, and that of the other begins.
This is the meaning of the assertion, that, at a given time and place, the
price of a commodity rises in proportion to the increase of the demand and
the decrease of the supply, and vice versa; or in other words, that the rise
in price is in direct ratio to the demand, and inverse ratio to the supply
(p. 290).

Say was groping for an equilibrium theory. Indeed, if one is careful to include some statements and exclude others, several theories may
be identified. The value discussion is not clearly a utility treatment,
nor is it the classical analysis. Ricardo, in Chapter XX in his *On the
Principles of Political Economy and Taxation*, severely criticizes Say and
identifies twelve quotations which he could not "reconcile." No important French economist after Say held to the Ricardian cost theory
of value. Despite Say's inconsistencies, he made considerable progress
in emphasizing with clarity the interdependence of the forces of supply
and demand in price determination.

Say criticized "Smith and most of the English writers" for combining "profit derivable from the employment of capital" and "profit of the
industry," or interest on capital with the returns to "the Master-agent,
or Adventurer in Industry" (pp. 354-55). He identifies the *entrepreneur*
as the one who assumes the risk of combining the factors of land, labor,
and capital in production.[7] He defines explicitly the functions of the
entrepreneur and describes his qualifications (pp. 329-32). Say thus provides the fourth factor in production and makes possible an analysis of
distribution superior to that of any of his predecessors, an analysis which
gives a separate identity for interest and for profit.

Consumption Theory.—In Book III, "On the Consumption of
Wealth," Say considers consumption and public finance. Consumption has to be examined in its relationship with public revenues. The
interest of the state in consumption is just as important and natural as

---

[7] Teilhac, *op. cit.*, chap. iii.

its interest in trade or manufacturing. The state, like the individual, consumes an "aggregate of values within a year" whether produced at home or imported. Total national consumption he divides into public consumption and private consumption, the former being a state problem and the latter an individual problem. He considers the effects of all kinds of taxation, holding that "taxation in no way contributes to national wealth" but that it "deprives the producer of a product" (p. 447); he maintains that since a tax deprives the payer of a product which to him is "either a means of personal gratification or a means of reproduction, the lighter the tax is, the less must be the privation" (p. 449). Extreme taxation has the lamentable effect of impoverishing the individual without enriching the state. No one could challenge the accuracy of this view when applied to the France of his day. His views on taxation are tied up with his views on consumption and lack the generalizations such as Smith drew in his "canons of taxation." (Cf. Chapter 10, p. 185.)

Say's contributions are significant. He had neither the originality of Smith nor the brilliance of Ricardo, but in exposition he excelled both. His conception of political economy was that of a pure science resting not upon the work of man but on the very nature of things, which makes it and its laws universal. He treated political economy as an inductive, theoretical, and descriptive science. The economist must remain a "passive spectator"; he must not give advice.[8] That he had greater faith in laissez faire than any predecessor is difficult to understand in the light of his own experience and knowledge of French politics. This extreme view is about the only thing he salvaged from physiocracy.

His point of view which was at one time individual and social at another, hence his final conclusions, caused him trouble and brought much criticism of his theories. Ricardo found many points to criticize (see the index of any edition of Ricardo for a list of criticisms) and rightly so. Say tended to be confused in his analysis because of an uncertainty in his point of view. At times he considered cost as an entrepreneurial outlay and wealth as exchangeable goods, but the three major divisions of the book—production, distribution, and consumption—are treated from a social point of view.

Notwithstanding his faults, Say's contribution to economic thought has probably not been properly recognized. He wished to be regarded as the outstanding economist of the age—not a modest ambition, but no more egotistical than what J. S. Mill cut out for himself. Say did more in directing French doctrines away from medieval tradition and

[8] See *Letters to Mr. Malthus*, p. 314.

metaphysics than any other economist. He was generally faithful in interpreting Smith [9] but he never hesitated to accentuate some points and reinterpret others. He could draw upon Turgot and Condillac to improve upon Smith; he was keen in his observations of the progress of the Industrial Revolution, and could apply actual illustrations to support his points. He did not, however, have a profound knowledge of history or statistics to bolster his analysis. Finally, it may be said that he was not attempting to write a complete social philosophy but only to make the fundamentals of Smith available to Frenchmen. In this he more than succeeded; in fact, he helped make classical doctrines available to the entire world.[10]

Jean Charles Sismondi and Charles Dunoyer

Another Frenchman, Jean Charles L. Sismonde de Sismondi (1773-1842), deserves mention here. On the basis of his later writings he belongs in the socialist group more than with the supporters of classical tradition. But his first work, *De la richesse commerciale* (*Commercial Wealth*, 1803), was based strictly on the principles of Adam Smith. Later he regarded the principles as inadequate and in need of modification. In his two-volume work, *Nouveaux principes d'économie politique, ou de la richesse dans ses rapports avec la population* (*New Principles of Political Economy, or of Wealth and its Relation to Population*, 1819; 2d ed., 1827), he breaks with orthodoxy and the views of Smith on the method of political economy and the relation of government and business. He borrowed Aristotle's term "chrematistics" and applied it to the teachings of classical economics with the criticism that it dealt too much with means of increasing material wealth and not enough with human welfare. Wealth, he thought, should be devoted

---

[9] "I revere Adam Smith—he is my master. At the commencement of my career in Political Economy, whilst yet tottering, and driven on the one hand by the Doctors of the Balance of Trade, and on the other by the Doctors of the Net Proceeds, I stumbled at every step, he showed me the right road. Leaning upon his *Wealth of Nations*, which at the same time discovers to us the wealth of his genius, I learned to go alone. Now I no longer belong to any school . . . I am only under the subjection of the decrees of eternal Reason, and I am not afraid to say so. Adam Smith has not embraced the whole of the phenomenon of the production and consumption of wealth, but he has done so much that we ought to feel grateful to him. Thanks to him, the most vague, the most obscure of sciences will soon become the most precise, and that which of all others will leave the fewest points unexplained." *Letters to Mr. Malthus*, p. 305. Say once wished to visit the room where Adam Smith lectured on Moral Philosophy in Glasgow University. Upon the fulfillment of his wish he was moved to exclaim, "Lord, now let thy servant depart in peace." *University of Glasgow Through Five Centuries, 1451-1951*, p. 22.

[10] The student is referred to Charles Gide and Charles Rist, *A History of Economic Doctrines* (New York, 1948), pp. 118-33, for an interesting treatment of their famous compatriot.

to the improvement of human welfare. He disagreed sharply with Smith on the doctrine of laissez faire. He held that laissez faire was largely responsible for the fact that the rich were getting richer and the poor growing more miserable. The answer was strong government intervention; he held the state responsible for more than the maintenance of peace—the state should make certain that all classes of society shared in social progress.

Sismondi agreed with the general principles of the classical economists; he disagreed with their ultimate aim and method. Well-being should be the aim of everyone, and only a better distribution of the products for consumption can bring happiness to a people. He saw the rapid advances in machine production which were displacing men; mechanization he held to be undesirable unless society provided employment elsewhere for the displaced workers. He disagreed with Smith in holding that individual interests are essentially those of society; this opinion rested upon his observations of the extent to which unevenness in the ownership of property resulted in inequalities. He did not condemn the ownership of private property or the accumulation of riches, but only the evils which result therefrom.

His acute observations led him to discuss the causes of crises which were a necessary concomitant to the accumulation of wealth by some and the poverty of others. Insufficient revenues to buy the products of industry brings a decline in prices with subsequent unemployment, panic, and, finally, a crisis. This theory was subsequently borrowed by Marx and used to explain the inevitability of crises in a capitalistic system.

Sismondi could not completely disentangle his own thoughts; they were a mixture of Smith's fundamentals and his own brand of liberalism. He missed being either a defender of the Smith-Say tradition or an apostle of socialism. His views were often paradoxical and his proposed remedies impractical. Yet he challenged the views of his predecessors, whom he characterized as the "Orthodox School," and ultimately forced a revaluation of the fundamentals. In this he rendered a distinct service in being one of the first critics of classical doctrines. His influence in spreading classical doctrines—either by criticism or by support—was not comparable with that of Say. (Sismondi will be reexamined with the early critics of capitalism, in Chapter 17.)

In contrast to the pessimism of Sismondi, the French journalist and economist, Charles Dunoyer (1786-1862),[11] outdid both Smith and Say

---

[11] See René Adenot, *Les Idées économiques et politiques du Charles Dunoyer* (Toulouse, 1907).

in his optimistic views of the economy. His ideas were presented in a three-volume work, *De la liberté du travail* (1845), wherein he develops the view that labor is the only productive factor. Value is but a measure of the exchange of commodities on the basis of amount of services stored in them: all value, then, is due to human activity. Nature labors gratuitously along with man in production, hence, land-rent is not a production cost but only a form of interest on capital invested in land. Land-rents per se he completely disavows.

In his work he shows a tendency to make economics an all-embracing social subject which deals with all social forces. However, in his treatment he keeps within the framework of accepted political and economic ideas. He emphasizes both material and immaterial wealth, the latter being in the form of services rendered.

He was an extreme believer in laissez faire. The term "Liberté" in the title of his book is intended to refer to any measure or measures which would increase the efficiency of labor. This would be accomplished by the spontaneous efforts of labor itself in developing foresight and improving its own efficiency and thereby improving all social conditions. He held extreme views on the part played by the government in improving social conditions—namely, that its actions were repressive, not constructive or directive. The government must become a mere subsidiary to industry. The laboring class, he held, was responsible for its own ills and would remain in a state of bondage regardless of any interference.

According to Dunoyer, the principal causes of poverty are that the upper classes have dispossessed the mass of the people and kept them in servitude for centuries. Crushing taxes, laws which prevented the workers from deriving the best possible advantage from their labor, and the institutions of society have contributed to this servitude. But he adds

. . . the condition of the lower classes does not alone proceed from the wrongs the higher part of society may have been guilty of toward them; it has also its root in their especial vices, their apathy, their heedlessness, and their ignorance of the causes which make the price of labor rise or fall. Their distress is at least as much their own fault as that of the classes that may be accused of having oppressed them; and, if society should be reestablished on more equitable bases, if the strong should abstain from every sort of domination over the weak, I do not doubt that there would still be developed a more or less numerous class of miserable beings at the bottom of society.[12]

[12] *De la liberté du travail*, Vol. I, p. 404.

The Malthusian principle of population was held to apply to the population-subsistence ratio, which was beyond the scope of state controls. Dunoyer was defending existing institutions and practices against contemporary criticisms.

There is not much in the work of Dunoyer which would, we believe, make Smith proud to have him in his camp. He was a follower of Smith but asserted much independence. Even Smith would not have defended his extreme views of laissez faire nor have supported him in his outlook for labor. Dunoyer maintained the Say tradition in abstaining from giving advice: he said, "Je n'impose rien; je ne propose même rien; j'expose." ("I impose nothing; I propose nothing; I expose.") It is doubtful whether his arguments could be thus interpreted. Despite Dunoyer's interesting views and a smattering of contributions, it is likely that Say will always be regarded as the greatest French expositor of classical doctrines.

The German Writers: Nebenius, Rau, von Thünen, and von Hermann

English classical economics never gained the foothold in Germany that it did in France. Chairs of cameral science had been established in the leading German universities (cf. Chapter 7, p. 108), and the teaching continued along the well-established lines of state-building. Weighty tomes were written by Germans trained largely in jurisprudence and political science. Theoretical abstractions, such as Smith and Ricardo formulated, are not found in the early German writings. By the middle of the nineteenth century the classical doctrines were more or less generally accepted everywhere—in academic circles and in formation of state policy. However, Germany came near providing an exception. Indeed, it could be argued that classical economics, except for certain elements, was always alien to German scholarship. This is more nearly true in Germany proper, for the Austrians were much more flexible and receptive to "alien" thought. The German tendency all too frequently was negative and expressed as an "it does not apply" attitude without an explanation of what does apply. No lament is herewith expressed that the Germans did not accept classical tradition with the enthusiasm of Say. It is to be regretted, rather, that theory suffered from this attitude, despite the great array of men whose names belong in the list of German economists.

It is doubtful that any German writer could be classed as a strict adherent of classical English economics. There were those whose criticism (discussed in a later chapter) of classical economics made them distinctly anticlassical. An irreconcilable difference in the basic philosophies of the English and German thinkers tended to keep them apart: the former held a philosophy of the laissez faire function of the state, the latter never could assent to such a concept. Therefore, many English deductions were unacceptable in Germany. In English theory, and in practice as well, the atomistic concept of the "rugged individual" was opposed to the German concept of an organic, all-important, paternalistic state. Briefly, the German setting was not conducive to English deductive economics.

The classical economics of Smith and Ricardo exerted little influence in Germany for many years. The *Wealth of Nations* was translated into German by Johann Friedrich Schiller shortly after its publication. The next (and better) translation was made in 1794 by Christian Garve.[13] Roscher says that Smith made little impression in Germany at first. The book reviews of the *Wealth of Nations* generally praised its composition but were unfriendly to its contents.[14] His work was not known by Frederick the Great (reigned 1740-1786), or at least exerted no influence upon him. Emperor Joseph II of Austria (reigned 1780-1790), a liberal, took no notice of the book. Karl Friedrich of Baden was trying to make physiocracy work in his province and was apparently uninterested. Those early German writers of the first quarter of the nineteenth century who had any knowledge of Smith at all did little more than mention him. Studies of the specific influence of Smith on early German economics, which was overwhelmingly cameralist, have not been made and indeed could not be made without a tremendous amount of research; it appears that the reward is not worth the effort.[15]

It is possible to find in the works of German writers points of agreement and disagreement with Smith. Some of the points were cogent while others were in error. Few supported Smith in laissez faire, hence they could not support a free-trade policy; the exceptions were notably

[13] Other translations by Garve were made in 1799 and in 1810. See W. Roscher, *Geschichte der Wissenschaften in Deutschland* (1874), p. 603.

[14] For example, "He has yet had no influence whatever on the change of economic doctrine in our country." *Göttingische Gelehrte Anzeigen*, November 29, 1794, p. 1901.

[15] Carl W. Hasek in *The Introduction of Adam Smith's Doctrines into Germany* (New York, 1925) points out that the University of Göttingen was more friendly to Adam Smith's doctrines than any other German university. He lists Georg Sartorius (1765-1828), August Leuder (1760-1819) and Christian Kraus (1753-1807) as being the three most ardent economist supporters of Smith. He also lists von Stein, von Schön, Dohna, Altenstein and Hardenberg as social and economic reformers who showed some admiration for Smith but he adds, "There is no evidence, however, that Hardenberg was at any time directly influenced in his views by study of Adam Smith's work and the same conclusion is apparently here of Dohna and Altenstein" (p. 146). It is probable however that some reforms in the Prussian state by 1811 may have gotten some impetus from Smith's work.

Hufeland (c. 1760-1817) and Lotz (1770-1838). Nebenius (1785-1857), a civil servant, wrote a cameralistic tract *Der Oeffentliche Credit* (*Public Credit*) in 1820, called by Roscher the greatest economic monograph in Germany. It is an excellent treatment of money and credit, public debts, and capital, in the best cameral form, but his reference to Smith is to disagree on elements of state regulation. He, like Smith, talked of productive and unproductive labor and also confused the parts played by wages, rent, and profits in distribution. His connection with Smith is indeed obscure.

In many respects the greatest contribution was made by Karl Heinrich Rau.[16] He was more adept in thorough presentation than he was in original thinking. His *Lehrbuch* is encyclopedic and exhaustive: its more than two thousand pages cover a wide range of topics and subtopics with much statistical documentation. In the scope of the work he is rivaled only by von Justi, the Austrian cameralist. Rau pioneered the separation of the theoretical and the practical aspects of political economy which has become a common practice. In breadth of topic and in detail of historical treatment, his work outstrips the *Wealth of Nations* by far. Many of the principles of classical economics are effectively blended with the indispensable cameralistic treatment, but the book remains essentially a typical textbook of *Kameralwissenschaft*. The practices of cameralism far outweigh theory except in the first volume, which treats of the theory of wealth. In this he speaks of value in use and value in exchange, abstract and concrete value in use. He made the same error as Smith in viewing some labor as unproductive, notably personal services. He held this view despite Say's attempt to recast it. It was Say who gave us the "entrepreneur," but Rau gave us the "wages of management" (*Unternehmergewinn*) concept.

His practical views on public finance were outstanding attempts to relate taxes to their effect upon industrial production and general economic welfare. In some respects the nature of his research and presentation of materials fitted him into the historical school; however, the scope of his work and his interest in applied economic problems differentiated

[16] **Karl Heinrich Rau** (1792-1870) studied at Erlangen, where in 1818 he became a professor. In 1822 he was made professor of political economy at Heidelberg, which post he held for nearly fifty years. He also served in the Baden legislature for a brief time. He wrote the standard text for use in universities and for candidates training for civil administration positions. The book, *Lehrbuch der Politischen Oekonomie* (*Textbook of Political Economy*), was published in three volumes (1826-1837); the first one dealt with the theory of wealth, the second with economic policy, and the third with problems of public finance. The close relationship between these topics and cameralism is apparent. He showed keen insight into practical problems, and his ability to use his materials, both statistical and historical, together with a sagacity in judgment, earned for his work a pre-eminence unequaled by any other German economist for at least a half century.

him from the historical school, which came into prominence some fifty years later. Rau comes nearer to making use of Smithian technique than any of his compatriots.

The last German considered here is Johann Heinrich von Thünen (1780-1850), author of an original and unique work, *Der Isolierte Staat* (*The Isolated State*), published in 1826. In most respects he should be regarded as an agricultural economist, although he held advanced ideas on many economic subjects. He was the first writer to give attention to theoretical considerations of the location of agriculture and industry. He frequently used the theories of Smith and Ricardo as points of departure for his own theories or for direct criticism; however, he said repeatedly that he regarded Smith as his teacher in economics. The value theory of Smith and Ricardo, resting as it did upon labor cost, he regarded as inadequate. This theory, which was generally held by German writers and many others as well, was criticized not only because of its inherent defects, but also because it was a "dangerous" theory in a rapidly industrializing world where capital was becoming more and more important. Any theory which made labor the sole or even the main creator of value might be interpreted as antithetical to growing capitalism.

Von Thünen explained wages and interest in terms far removed from the classical pattern. In fact, his explanation was in terms of a marginal concept almost as perfect as that advanced by the Austrians fifty years later. He saw the difference between the utility of the first and last expenditures for an item by pointing out that the expenditure on the last item must not exceed its returns. The rate of interest was determined by the last-used unit of capital. The Ricardian explanation of wages was "revolting." He was interested in a wage payment which had a welfare or humanitarian element in it. Therefore he opposed Ricardo's subsistence wage or the "iron law" as Lassalle called it. In general his theory was a marginal productivity theory; wages tend to equal the product of the last worker employed. He saw a relationship between wages and interest rate; a low interest rate which would assure the accumulation of capital would be advantageous to the worker and thereby increase total wages.

Von Thünen believed his most important contribution was his doctrine of natural or just wages. He held that wages to those who produce consumers' goods must equal the wages of those who produce capital goods or the wages of subsistence producers and capital producers must be equal. His concept of natural wage is expressed by the formula $\sqrt{ap}$. He holds that the natural wage depends on the cost of the necessities for the maintenance of the laborer (a) and the value of the product of his labor (p) expressed either in kind or in money. The implication of the formula is that natural wages would rise with an increase in the product. The theory has been shown to be mathematically erroneous (by Knapp, Knies, and Brentano of the historical school), and as a theory of natural wage it has long been rejected. Von Thünen thought so well of the theory that he ordered it to be engraved on his tombstone.

Based upon his observations of agriculture, he developed independently a differential rent concept very similar to Ricardo's. However, his deductions rest more upon the importance of location than upon a natural fertility explanation as used by Ricardo. Von Thünen's ideas on distribution were far in advance of Ricardo's and indeed anticipate the best of later marginal analysis.

Originally he followed Smith in defending free trade. But under the impact of nationalism he reversed his former position and became an advocate of protective tariff on grounds similar to cameral teachings and similar to those held by List. (See Chapter 15.) In general, Smith's doctrines of free trade held until the formation of the Customs Union (*Zollverein*) in 1834, when the states in the Union agreed to moderate ad valorem rates on internal trade, but to erect general tariff barriers against external trade.

There can be no doubt about the advanced and original thinking of von Thünen. His work was so far in advance of that of his contemporaries that little attention was given to it for many years. Now he is examined and credited with very original ideas in marginal productivity analysis, for pioneering work in scientific agriculture, and for his theories on the location of industry. He rightly merits a front-rank position with the leading German economists. Economics in the broader sense was carried by von Thünen far beyond the limits set by followers of classical tradition, yet his contemporaries lacked the perspicacity to appreciate this fact.

The German economist and statistician Friedrich Benedikt Wilhelm von Hermann (1795-1868) has been compared with Ricardo in originality. His book *Staatswissenschaftliche Untersuchungen* (*Investigations in Political Economy*, 1832) was an exceedingly important work for many years. The work is a critical analysis of classical theories. His usual method was to quote from Smith, then present his own ideas on the subject under consideration. He does not follow laissez faire doctrines which, when applied to the individual, frequently brings the latter's interests into conflict with public welfare. He cannot see how the individual's best interests will provide the best program for a state or national economy. This attitude is in line with that held by most

German writers, who view the objectives of the state as having a definite purpose which cannot be achieved by any "invisible hand" philosophy.

Summary and Evaluation

The foregoing discussion gives an idea of the extent of the influence of Adam Smith and classical economics on the leading thinkers of Germany and France. The influence is less clearly defined when one leaves England and France. The degree of acceptance is closely related to the extent to which liberal thought and liberal policies prevailed in the various nations. The pattern of German thinking had been set by the cameralists, and it had succeeded in no small degree in achieving its desired objective. Why, then, should alien theories be brought in which, if strictly applied, would have undone much that had been achieved? The French, on the other hand, were in a position to gain more than the Germans by an application of classical fundamentals. Their geographical position, their colonial interests, their desire for greater diversification of economic interests were more comparable with the British. They were not as insular as the Germans but not as cosmopolitan as the English; English theory and practice could promise more opulence, and indeed it did bring more to France than to Germany.

The indirect influence of classical economics on Continental economic thought is difficult to evaluate. There were some who admittedly followed classical theory but reserved the right to accept or reject what they chose. Not always were the choices right, for classical errors were perpetuated by some while classical truths were held inapplicable by others. It is certain, however, that classical economics offered a new challenge to those interested in writing on economic affairs as well as to practitioners. The influence both direct and indirect on France was far greater than in Germany, where *Kameralwissenschaft* was deeply rooted. As time elapsed, new theories and emphasis were to supplement and even to supplant classical economics.

PART IV

Critics and Criticisms
of Classical Economics

15

The Nationalist and the Optimist Criticism

The Nationalist Critics

Classical economic doctrines spread throughout the entire world. However, this does not mean that they were universally accepted. Criticism of method and content, of interpretation and emphasis, and of scope and objectives began shortly after Smith's *Wealth of Nations* was published. Indeed, Hume, his great friend and, in a sense, collaborator, expressed great disappointment that Smith retained his own views on rent and price, which were contrary to Hume's explanation. The friendly interpretation of Say was not always free from criticism. Criticism is only a normal expectancy. Many of the criticisms were germane, others were futile. Some rested upon broad objective principles, others upon doctrinaire interpretations. In any event, the net results have been generally beneficial and productive.

One of the most common criticisms was directed at the underlying philosophy of classical economics. It was a philosophy of individualism with a hedonistic bias; it emphasized materialism and omitted ethical considerations. The laissez faire philosophy would remove government interference and make individual self-interest the guiding force for both individual and social well-being. The "economic man" was a consumer and a producer of goods but his citizenship was lost. The teachings of classical economics tended toward cosmopolitanism; strictly applied, the individual might be, like Diogenes, "a citizen of the world." But the dissenters contended that individual and national interests might be at variance, instead of being in complete harmony. Changing conditions had made the survival of the individual dependent upon the survival of the state. The state afforded the fullest expression of the powers of the individual, and national welfare expressed individual welfare. Besides, certain theories of classical economics were definitely pessimistic in their outlook. Little hope could be derived from a strict application of the teachings, especially in the realm of human betterment. The outlook was gloomy and foreboding. Finally, some critics saw no possible hope for improvement under the prevailing system and its fundamental tenets; hence they not only became critics of the economic and social order, but planned a new one.

In the succeeding chapters of Part IV the leading individual critics and critical groups or schools are discussed. Some critics got in their blows on Smith's work only, before Ricardo, Malthus, Mill, and others had firmly established the classical tradition. These critics were unaware of the size of the giant they were attacking; in fact, the critical attacks of some were virtually unknown for many years.[1] Others made frontal attacks and became known as schools—e.g., the historical school. The critics did not belong to any one country nor did they come in an exact chronological sequence, which accounts for the widely scattered attacks, first on individual members, and later, on classical economics as a body of thought.

The nationalists believed that classical economics failed to recognize the importance of national or state elements in economic life. They attacked the laissez-faire, free-trade, individualistic teachings of classical economists and favored the building of strong states. National wealth to them was not the sum total of individual wealth as the classical economists believed. The nationalists put the nation ahead of the individual and made his wealth dependent upon the well-being and power of the state. According to their theory, the welfare of the individual and the welfare of the state were not identical; indeed, they sometimes were in conflict. The nationalists held that economic phenomena and economic behavior should be viewed from the national viewpoint, which was in direct conflict with the cosmopolitan, individualistic teachings of the classical economists.

Lauderdale on Public and Private Wealth.—One of the earliest English critics was Lord Lauderdale, whose work *An Inquiry into the Nature and Origin of Public Wealth* appeared as early as 1804.[2] Since this antedated the works of Ricardo and Mill, it was aimed directly at Smith and his followers. Lauderdale's book was mild in its criticism as com-

---

[1] See E. R. A. Seligman, "Some Neglected British Economists." *The Economic Journal*, XIII, 1903.

[2] James Maitland (1759-1838) was the eighth Earl of Lauderdale. He studied law at Glasgow and Edinburgh and became an advocate. In Glasgow he studied under Dugald Stewart, who succeeded Adam Smith as professor of political economy. He was a member of the House of Commons from 1781 to 1788. On his father's death in 1789, he inherited his title and seat in the House of Lords. He served on government missions, his most notable service being in France, when he had a part in drafting treaties made during the French Revolution. His interest in political economy was always great; his works in the field were monographs, of which *An Inquiry into the Nature and Origin of Public Wealth* (Edinburgh, 1804) is the best known. A second edition of the work appeared in 1819 with few significant changes; the first is cited in the following pages.

pared with others which followed. It was more argumentative than critical, setting forth his own interpretation of certain issues.

Lauderdale criticizes Smith and his predecessors for faulty conceptions which led to erroneous conclusions. The mercantilists, and physiocrats as well, were guilty of "conceiving Wealth and Money to be synonymous," which led to faulty legislation. He objects to the error, which he says is the same in "all languages," of considering "private riches . . . as a portion of national wealth. . . . The sum total of the riches of those who form the community is thus regarded as necessarily conveying an accurate statement of the wealth of a nation" (p. 6). But, "Public wealth ought not to be considered as merely representing the sum of individual riches" (p. 7). Two chapters are devoted to an explanation of the relation of public wealth and individual riches. In the first chapter he considers value, "the possession of which alone qualifies anything to form a portion of individual riches" (p. 8). Here he vigorously criticizes Smith, who "has struggled most to establish the opinion that labor may be considered as an accurate measure of value" (p. 23), his own theory being that "value cannot be expressed but by a comparison of two commodities" (p. 24).

Next Lauderdale distinguishes between public wealth and private wealth: the former he defines as "to consist of all that man desires, as useful or delightful to him," and private wealth or individual riches "to consist of all that man desires as useful or delightful to him; which exists in a degree of scarcity" (pp. 57, 58). Scarcity is the distinguishing attribute between public and private wealth. Thus, he makes scarcity a fundamental characteristic of private wealth and essential to value, which is the measure of private wealth. Value is a result of supply and demand relationship: "the value of everything is so completely dependent upon the proportion betwixt the demand for it and the quantity of it" (p. 15). When either supply or demand increases or decreases relative to the other, value responds in a similar manner. He contends that private wealth or riches change as their supply and demand relationships change, whereas public wealth is dependent solely on its supply. The relationship between public and private wealth is inverse: "in proportion as the riches of individuals are increased by an augmentation of the value of a commodity, the wealth of the society is generally diminished; and in proportion as the mass of individual riches is diminished, by the diminution of the value of any commodity, its opulence is generally increased" (p. 49).

Lauderdale is critical of Smith's classification of labor into productive and unproductive groups; he argues that the important point at issue is not the "nature of labor" but "the use subsequently made of the commodity on which it was bestowed" (p. 145). He concludes that it is "impossible to contend, that the labor of the manufacturer and artist, or even the labor of that class whose services perish at the moment, are not, as well as that of husbandmen, to be considered as productive of wealth" (pp. 147-48).

Another point of criticism centers around parsimony or savings as the chief means of increasing public wealth.[3] This is a fallacy which, "if persisted in, must infallibly ruin the country that adopts or preserves it" (p. 201). Smith's argument was that increasing private wealth by parsimony or savings is the most active means of augmenting public wealth. Lauderdale argues that capital is, like labor, an active factor in production; in fact, "capital supplants a portion of labor which would otherwise be performed by the hand of man." He contends that parsimony "does not augment opulence; it only changes the direction in which the labor of a community is exerted" (p. 210). But, parsimony in reality means that a forgoing of consumption by the consumer, in turn, has its bad effects on society. Thus, "the wealth of a society never can be increased by a system of continual parsimony, this abstinence from expenditure in consumable commodities, and consequent accumulation, may evidently be highly injurious to its progress" (p. 215).

Lauderdale was convinced that the supply of capital should be adjusted to the needs of the country. Too much emphasis upon parsimony or saving (as Smith would have it) would lead to an overproduction of capital. He held that labor and capital supplemented one another. The real challenge then was to find new uses for both labor and capital which would be productive. He understood well that the nature of the distribution of goods in a community reacts on the production of goods:

. . . the distribution of wealth in all societies must ultimately regenerate the formation of wealth. . . . The distribution of wealth not only regulates and decides the channels in which the industry of every country is embarked, and, of course, the articles of production of which it excels; but a proper distribution of wealth insures the increase of opulence, by sustaining a regular progressive demand in the home market, and still more effectually, by affording to those whose habits are likely to create a desire of supplanting labour, the power of executing it (pp. 314, 349, 350).

The surest way to increase national wealth is to make public expenditures, and the quickest way to decrease it is to accumulate a large sinking fund. He sees clearly the relation between saving and consumption and emphasizes the importance of consumption; he points out that capital "accumulates" and consumption must be maintained, otherwise there will be an overproduction due to underconsumption. Lauderdale may

[3] Cf. Chapter 10, page 179; *Wealth of Nations*, Vol. I, p. 44.

be regarded as the first to propound this theory, which has recently been used in explaining business cycles.[4]

From the foregoing analysis it is at once apparent that Lauderdale was, as an individual critic of Smith's doctrines, both keen and original. He was not criticizing Smith's theories for the same purpose as the thoroughgoing nationalists did subsequently, but because he believed the premises Smith used were wrong and therefore dangerous in forming national policy. His criticisms were those of a realist, not of a romanticist as were many of the strictly nationalistic critics.

Lauderdale shows original thinking in his views on making capital coordinate with labor and land in production. He went too far in expressing fear of the overproduction of capital, and his conception would overequip a nation in relation to its capacity to consume. He enlists the aid of both predecessors and contemporaries; he quotes from the physiocrats, Hume, Locke, Petty, and others. His work, although not of notable significance in his own country, greatly influenced the early American economist Daniel Raymond and a French economist, Ganilh,[5] who likewise influenced Raymond. The translation of Lauderdale's work was also to some extent influential upon other French economists and especially upon the German economist Hermann.

The German Romantics.—The movement which followed in Germany is known as the "romantic movement"; it embraced art and literature as well as social thought. Romanticism drew upon the teachings of Kant (1724-1804), who emphasized moral law and moral self-determination. The state exists to secure freedom, not for the happiness of those who make the state. Liberty, equality, and happiness are secured only by the state or the collective will. Man is made for society, not society for man. Fichte (1762-1814) contributed an even larger share to the movement. In his essay *The Dignity of Man* (1794), he puts the ego (man) in the center of all philosophy. Therefore his criticism of Adam Smith for making wealth the objective of human endeavor was most acute. Following rather closely the Kantian teachings he taught that the state is natural and its laws are but expressions of the true rights of nature realized. Persons are not "atoms" but members of a social union, which means a people "united into one body completely in accord with itself and uniformly developed." The existing states were but "strange combinations formed by senseless accident" but his true state will be a combination of free wills striving for moral perfection in which every citizen is supporting and supported by the state.

[4] For an excellent treatment see "Lauderdale's Oversaving Theory," by Professor F. A. Fetter in the *American Economic Review*, XXXV, No. 3 (June, 1945).

[5] See J. A. Blanqui, *History of Political Economy in Europe* (American trans., 1880), p. 489.

Fichte's state permits private property and it is the duty of the state to protect the individual property owner. Therefore the state should be closed commercially; otherwise competition, which will lead to anarchy, will defeat the purpose. This, then, does not permit free trade between states, a fundamental of classical economics. Fichte's state would be an autarchy. His teachings were, to a considerable degree, the antithesis of the political views resulting from English economic liberalism and the political liberalism of the French Revolution. The Germans were apprehensive of the liberal views then at large which could undermine their political and social structure.

The German philosophers, Kant and Fichte, provided an *Aufklärung* or enlightenment in a very real sense. It may be maintained that Fichte provided the philosophical impetus for the German socialism and that later his doctrines were used effectively by the Nazis in developing their concept of a totalitarian state. Fichte's metaphysical principles were later used by Hegel in developing his dialectic, which was used by Marx, in turn, in explaining dialectic materialism. Romantic nationalism in Germany was not merely the product of a few original thinkers but one which represented a synthesis of philosophy, medieval practices, and a reaction to a rising tide of liberalism. In final form it was an indigenous German product, although a few of its elements were borrowed from writers of other nations.

The leading economic theorist of the German romantics was Adam Müller,[6] whose teachings are of interest not only in the historical development of economic thought but in affording a spiritual godfather for the ideology of Nazism. His criticisms were sweeping. Müller attacked Fichte [7] and his unrealities and defended Smith and his pro-

---

[6] **Adam Müller** (1779-1829), born to a Prussian Protestant family in Berlin, studied law and theology in Göttingen, and subsequently held political appointments in Berlin. Through the politician Gentz he became acquainted with Metternich, the reactionary Austrian minister, who appointed Müller to important political positions in the treasury (1813) and later as consul-general at Leipzig (1818-1827), and as observer at various international congresses. In Austria he embraced Catholicism (1805), thus providing a religious element which he wove into his teachings. His best known writings are Von der Idee des Staats (*On the Idea of the State*, Dresden, 1809); Die Elemente der Staatskunst (*The Elements of Politics*, 3 vols.; Berlin, 1809); Die Theorie der Staatshaushaltung (*The Theory of State Finance*, Vienna, 1812); Versuch einer neuen Theorie des Geldes (*An Essay on a New Theory of Money*, Leipzig, 1816). In Dresden he delivered and published a series of lectures entitled Vorlesungen über die Deutsche Wissenschaft und Literatur (*Lectures on German Science and Literature*, Dresden, 1809). His work is a strange mixture of medievalism, romantic nationalism, mysticism, Catholicism, and practical politics.

[7] In his critical review of Fichte's Der Geschlossene Handelstaat (1800), Müller defends Smith and praises his insight and realism, the lack of which he charges to Fichte. He held Smith in high regard but attacked German followers who had attempted to apply Smith's generalizations to Germany.

gressive, liberal views, which, however, he soon repudiated in becoming a stark reactionary.

Müller held that the state was an organism: the individuals could not be thought of outside the framework of the state. The state is continuous with past and future generations. The real wealth of a nation is not the sum of the private wealth of its citizens but its national, moral, and intellectual elements. This concept is in strong contrast to Smith's ideal of laissez faire, which would give self-interest full freedom in developing wealth and private property. Müller saw that this philosophy would clash with the idea of nationality and the totalitarian concept. He idealized the Middle Ages and would like to have seen their conditions restored. He contended that people had idealized wealth and luxury. This attitude, together with the application of Roman laws, especially those of property and contract, had led them astray. If the feudal economy could be restored all peoples would enjoy greater happiness and be bound together in bonds of unity.

Müller's religious convictions strongly influence his views. He criticized Smith for emphasizing material things and self-interest and excluding moral and spiritual values. He held, for example, that the farmer should not labor because of his own self-interest but first of all for God's sake and for the love of work, next for the gross product, and last for the net product. The factors of production are nature, man, and the past—not land, labor, and capital. In the "past" factor he includes both physical and spiritual capital, the latter being the aspect neglected by writers on economics. These factors all collaborate in production but in different proportions, depending upon the good produced, whether an agricultural or an industrial product. His value theory, if indeed he has one, is an organic theory in which a thing to be useful and have value must be related to civil society or have social utility. He sets up this sort of theory in place of Smith's labor theory, which he rejects completely.

His theory of money is of interest in its conception. It was but another tie that, like the state, bound the people together. He viewed money as an expression of the oneness of the people, for it made economic oneness a reality. He denied the intrinsic worth of metal money and objected to its use because it could be used by other nations, whereas paper money, a product of the issuing state, tied men closely into the state. Only paper money could be national. This theory supported the issuance of inconvertible paper money in Austria by Metternich with whom he was associated.

Müller exerted little influence in his day—and, one may add, little since his day, unless one wishes to credit him with totalitarian concepts. Spann, whose treatment of Müller is extremely sympathetic, says he "was the greatest political economist in his own day." [8]   He adds that "even in our own day Müller continues to be undervalued."   An evaluation of Müller therefore depends largely upon the point of view of the one making the evaluation.   He was a reactionary who glorified the Middle Ages and proposed a return to that way of life.   He disliked change and proposed to insulate the economy against all foreign infiltrations.   His economics is a combination of classical criticism and mysticism.   His original ideas were never systematized nor carried to their final conclusions.   The writings of his later years are reminiscent of the old Roman writers who lamented the passing of the "good old days."   However, Müller would recall and restore them in place of what prevailed in his day.

His emphasis upon the cultural ties with the past was drawn upon by List and the historical school.   The believers in the totalitarian state and autarchy owe a great debt to him.   Little did he realize how his doctrines would be re-examined and found to provide a rationalization for the Nazi state.

Friedrich List, Ardent Nationalist.—Friedrich List was another critic of classical economics, a nationalist but not a romanticist.   Indeed List's realism makes him the direct antithesis of Adam Müller and he is by far the best known of the nationalists.[9]   List, like other critics of classical

---

[8] Othmar Spann, *The History of Economics* (New York, 1930), p. 167.

[9] **Friedrich List** (1789-1846) was born in Würtemberg, where he obtained his early schooling.   At the age of seventeen he was appointed to a clerkship in the Würtemberg bureaucracy in the city of Tübingen.   While there he attended lectures in the University of Tübingen.   His first known writing was an essay in which he urged local officials really to learn something about local government, pointing out that no such subject was taught in the University.   His arguments were so convincing that he was appointed to the newly created chair of administration and politics in Tübingen.   His ideas were liberal and too far advanced for the government, which would tolerate no reforms however modest.   He was ousted from the position; and thenceforth throughout his life he was at cross purposes with entrenched bureaucracy. Finally he had to flee from Germany.

He was sentenced to prison for ten months for his liberal ideas but escaped to Paris where he met General Lafayette, who urged him to go to America with him. He went to England instead, then to Switzerland, and finally back to Germany, where he was captured and imprisoned for nine months, then given his freedom and a passport to America with orders to leave the country in three days.   He sailed for New York in 1825.

List traveled with Lafayette during the latter's stay in this country. He finally settled on a farm near Harrisburg, Pennsylvania, but shortly thereafter moved to Reading, where he became editor of the *Readinger Adler* (*Reading Eagle*).   He discovered an outcropping of anthracite coal, which proved to be an exceedingly rich vein.   He then became concerned with getting the coal to the Philadelphia market and was one of the sponsors of canals and finally of the railroad which is now the Reading Railroad.

He took a most active part in the early protectionist movement and was largely responsible for developing the early tariff policies of the nation.   For many years

economics, opposed those elements which tended either to break down the concept of a strong national state or to destroy nationality. He denied that the individual good is identical with the national good. A nation is a unity formed by its language, manners, culture, its historical background and, finally, by its constitution or accepted government. This national unity comes first and in it is bound up the well-being of the individual, who must subordinate all his interests to the state and thereby strengthen its unity or nationality. Holding these fundamental beliefs, he was obliged to deny general free-trade doctrines which led to cosmopolitanism and away from nationalism. Thus far, his ideas are similar to those of Müller's, and indeed they might well be, for the men were friends.

From here on, however, the two part company. List was more of a realist. He had seen other economies in action in France, England, Switzerland, and America. Each economy, he believed, had to develop along the lines best adapted to its own resources, culture, and so on. He would not deny that England's development was correct for her economy, but he would deny that the same economic methods were applicable to Germany. Thus, he advocated a national pattern developed along lines best adapted to the national interests of the state. Smith held such a view on another level: he regarded the best interests of the individual as conducive to the best interests of the state. The world, however, was made up of many nations, the national interests of which were not always harmonious. The free trade which List does ad-

his influence was foremost in economic thinking in this country. He remained in America from 1825 to 1830, when he returned to Germany, first as consul to Hamburg (in which capacity he never served) and later as consul to Leipzig and Stuttgart. The Germans never forgot and never forgave him (while he lived) for his early liberalism. Despite his arduous labors for German unification and for removing customs barriers, building of German railroads, and other similar reforms, they never really trusted him. He committed suicide while in the Tyrol where he had gone for a rest.

He wrote his best known work, *Das nationale System der politischen Oekonomie, der internationale Handel, die Handels politik und der deutsche Zollverein* (1841; Eng. trans. by Lloyd, 1885, as *The National System of Political Economy*), while exiled in Paris (1837-1840). This work sets forth his views on a national economy. His editorials in the *Adler* and the magazines of the day set forth his strong views on protectionism.

He was greatly honored by Germany after his death. Jena awarded him an honorary doctor's degree; monuments were erected to him; streets and schools also bore his name. The greatest recognition of his work was the *Deutsche Friedrich List Gesellschaft*, founded in Heidelberg in 1925 for the purpose of encouraging the study of Friedrich List. It sponsored the publication of the ten volumes, *Friedrich List Werke*, which bring together all his works. The Nazi government made use of many of List's teachings. See Margaret E. Hirst, *Life of Friedrich List and Selections from his writings* (London, 1909); Ludwig Hausser, *Friedrich List's Leben* (1850); J. F. Bell, "Friedrich List, Champion of Industrial Democracy," *Pennsylvania Magazine of History and Biography*, January, 1942.

vocate he calls a "cosmopolitical" free trade, or world-wide free trade.[10]
If all nations were in a union or in a confederation as a guaranty of
perpetual peace, the principle of international free trade would be justified. But since no such union obtains, nations must use in their trade
relations other tactics designed to build up their own economy and
defend their very existence. List asserts that this is as it should be
according to "the nature of things" and is founded "on the lessons of
history and on the requirements of the nations. It offers the means of
placing theory in accord with practice and makes political economy
comprehensible by every educated mind." The economics of the classical group, in contrast, was "founded on bottomless cosmopoliticalism
. . . scholastic bombast, contradictions and utterly false terminology."
List further says, "I would indicate, as the distinguishing characteristic
of my system, NATIONALITY. On the nature of *nationality*, as the
intermediate interest between those of *individualism* and of *entire humanity*, my whole structure is based" (p. xliii).

Next in importance to his discussion of nationality are his views on
capital and the powers of production in producing national wealth.
Smith included in his concept of fixed capital both the natural and the
acquired abilities of the inhabitants. However, later usage limited
capital to material things. The wealth of nations, then, depended upon
individual accumulation of natural things. List emphasizes that the
"*power of producing wealth* is infinitely more important than *wealth
itself*" (p. 109). He emphasizes the organization of the productive
forces of society over mere accumulation of wealth and states that "all
the discoveries, inventions, improvements, perfections and exertions of
all generations which have lived before us . . . form the *mental capital
of the present human race*" (p. 113). This is what is responsible for
developing wealth within a nation; a much broader concept than "mere
bodily labor."

List drew upon "the teachings of history" to generalize that "nations
have to pass through the following stages of development: original barbarism, pastoral condition, agricultural condition, agricultural-manufac-
turing condition and agricultural-manufacturing-commercial condition"

---

[10] List, in a chapter entitled "Political and Cosmopolitical Economy" (*The
National System of Political Economy*, Bk. II, chap. xi), complains that Smith and
Say give a wrong meaning to the term "political economy." True political or
national economy "teaches how a nation in the present state of the world and its
own special national relations can maintain and improve its economical conditions";
cosmopolitical economy "originates in the assumption that all nations of the earth
form but one society living in a perpetual state of peace"; it is an economy of
the whole human race.

(p. 143).   England provided the best example of the transition of a state through the stages, but in view of their resources not all countries could accomplish this.   Nations with adequate resources should aim at the highest stage.   List strongly advocated a balance among agriculture, manufacturing, and commerce; since they did not rise and develop concurrently, it behooved the state to bring about the necessary balance. Clearly, this could not be done under a laissez-faire policy, which he summarily rejected.

The protectionist policies of List are one of the features that make him outstanding.   He is frequently referred to as the "father of American protectionism."   His influence in securing early protectionist legislation in the United States is well known.   For several years (1825-1830) he was the leader in the movement for protecting American industry from competition with goods produced abroad.   In his desire to bring about the diversification of agriculture, manufacturing, and commerce he advocated measures which he believed would guarantee this result. When final results had been obtained, his national policy would be changed.   He reasoned that a nation advanced in agriculture but retarded in manufacturing can "improve its social conditions" by an exchange of agricultural produce for manufactured goods, and vice versa. However, it is not a desirable state of affairs for a nation to develop solely an agricultural or manufacturing economy.   He says that, in order to bring about a balance of agriculture and manufacturing, nations which

. . . possess all the necessary mental and material conditions and means for establishing a manufacturing power of their own, and of thereby attaining the highest degree of civilization, and development of material prosperity and political power, but which are retarded in their progress by the competition of a foreign manufacturing Power which is already farther advanced than their own—only in such nations are commercial restrictions justifiable for the purpose of establishing and protecting their own manufacturing power; and even in them it is justifiable only until that manufacturing power is strong enough no longer to have any reason to fear foreign competition, and thenceforth only so far as may be necessary for protecting the inland manufacturing power in its very roots (p. 144).

He adds, "it is not necessary that all branches of industry should be protected to the same degree."   He would protect the industries whose products "belong to the category of the first necessities of life, and consequently are of the greatest importance as regards their total value as well as regards national independence" (p. 145).   He regards cotton, woolen, and linen manufacture, or industries in which "machinery does a greater part of the work" as industries that need protection. In modern tariff parlance they are called "infant industries." [11]

But List does not advocate protection as a permanent policy. He emphasizes the danger that progress will be checked and national decadence will follow if this policy is continued after a nation has attained its full, balanced development. From that point on, he emphasizes free trade as a positive virtue. List admits that the adoption of a protectionist policy will be costly to a nation. He says a nation "must sacrifice and give up a measure of material prosperity in order to gain culture, skill and powers of united production, it must sacrifice some present advantages in order to insure to itself future ones" (p. 117). He shows that protective duties would at first increase the price of manufactured goods, but it is just as true that in time the nation will develop its own manufacturing power and be able to "produce the goods more cheaply at home than the price at which they can be imported from foreign parts" (p. 117). It should be noted that his policies are applicable to industry only, for in agriculture he advocates free trade, admitting that he is "quite in accord with the prevailing theory." The reason was that he had in mind the economies of Germany and America, which were predominantly agricultural and developed to a relatively advanced state; agriculture would benefit from well-developed industry; food would be cheaper, and industry would get cheaper raw materials. It was the status of manufacturing and industry that he would like to see advanced.

It should be observed that the specific formulae of List are but means to accomplish an end—that end being a development of the productive power and strength of a nation to the level of the strongest nation. In his time England had come nearest to achieving this desired end. In his fifth stage (agricultural-manufacturing-commercial development) all nations would adopt free trade but this would require time; until this fifth stage was reached protection seemed most expedient. Ultimately, though, protection would be abandoned for free trade.

List's doctrines were approximately the same when applied to Germany and to America. Each area was agricultural and—in a comparative sense—backward. Germany suffered from interstate competition and trade barriers and lacked a unifying spirit, whereas the American states were completely federated. There was no problem of expanding the area of America, but for Germany List visualized a German Union (including Holland) that would extend from the North and Baltic Seas

[11] He complains, "The doctrine was taught from a hundred professional chairs, that nations could only attain to wealth and power by means of universal free trade" (p. 312).

to the Mediterranean.[12]   For both states he advocated a vigorous expansion of all manufacturers and commerce.   The Germans did establish a customs union (*Zollverein*) in 1834 and ended the petty tariff nuisances between states.   Roads were built, as he had urged, which not only carried the goods but broke the bars of state isolation.   Above all stood his great desire to make a strong German state as the only means of developing the country's own latent powers and the only way of competing with the stronger state—Britain.   He pleads with the Germans, saying, "From day to day it is necessary that the governments and the peoples of Germany should be more convinced that national unity is the rock on which the edifice of their welfare, their honor, their power, their present security and existence, and their future greatness must be founded" (p. 324).

In practical results List's work accomplished a great deal. His works focused much attention on political economy and materially influenced industrial policy.   As a theorist List is not comparable with Smith or Ricardo.   "The prevailing school" or "the popular school," as he liked to refer to the teachings of Smith and Ricardo, did not fare too badly from his criticisms of classical economics.   Many of his criticisms rested upon a false interpretation, whereas other points were criticized as inapplicable to a given economy (say American or German), scarcely a valid criticism.   There was always an admixture of demagogue, liberal, social and political reformer, and eighteenth-century mercantilist and propagandist in his make-up.   The work he turned out, therefore, could hardly be expected to be a finished scientific production in theoretical economics or a complete social philosophy.   By going back into the remote past to examine the social and economic evaluation of peoples he did lend greatest impetus to a movement in Germany known as the historical school.

Daniel Raymond: the First American Economist.—It is of more than passing interest to us that the first systematic treatise on political economy to be published in America should be, in large part, a criticism of the then prevailing body of economic thought.   But its author Daniel Raymond,[13] a Baltimore lawyer, in writing *Thoughts on Political Econ-*

---

[12] List vigorously objected to the fact that Germans had "humbled themselves to the position of hewers of wood and drawers of water for the Britons."   He also objected to the fact that the Germans had been "barred for half a generation [from the use of] Germany's greatest river [Rhine] by means of contemptible verbal squabbles" (p. 312).

[13] Daniel Raymond (1786-1849) was born and reared in Connecticut but practiced law in Baltimore, Maryland.   His law practice was not enough to occupy his time and talents, and so he turned to writing in the field of economics and on questions of public interest at the time.   He says, "The public has not seen fit to give me constant employment in my profession, otherwise this book [*Thoughts on Po-*

omy (1820) offered more than criticisms: his work was a fairly comprehensive treatise dealing with the general topics of wealth, value, the mercantile system, monopolies, corporations, taxation, debt, slavery, and so on. He remarked in the preface that "the only American book that has the semblance of a treatise on political economy is Hamilton's Report . . . yet in these Reports he does not profess to treat of political economy generally, but only of detached parts of it." Raymond did not profess that his work was a "general treatise on political economy." He says, "All the merit I can claim for it . . . is that of having made a humble effort to break loose from the fetters of foreign authority —from foreign theories and systems of political economy." [14]

Despite his expressed desire to break away from foreign systems, it is doubtful that he accomplished his objective. His slants at Adam Smith and J. B. Say were not entirely devastating, nor was his knowledge of European economic literature broad enough to afford other important areas of criticism. His work, therefore, turned out to be an expression of opinion on vexing contemporary issues rather than an effective criticism of foreign doctrine. In treating the domestic and contemporary issues he irritated about as many as he won to his side. His book had a very limited distribution and its contemporary influence was probably small.

Raymond held a strange mixture of doctrines. He opposed the philosophy of rugged individualism and laissez faire and favored government interference and protective tariffs; he opposed monopolies and all forms of corporations; he distrusted the regulation of banks and the issuing of paper money and vigorously denounced slavery on economic, as well as moral and religious, grounds. These were issues of great significance at the time and his thoughts on them reflect a firm conviction independently arrived at as an ardent American nationalist. He was not, therefore, primarily concerned with criticisms of the *Wealth of Nations*. Since he dealt with many of the same topics as Smith, his treatment of them naturally might be expected to be similar or even critical. Raymond, as a realist, was first of all more concerned

litical Economy] had never been written. I had read musty law books till I was tired. Idleness was irksome, and I sought relief in putting on paper some of my thoughts on political economy." He also wrote on the slavery question, reflecting his strong New England belief in complete abolition. He was an ardent protectionist. Mathew Carey, the onetime leader of the protectionists in Philadelphia, was so impressed with the orthodoxy of Raymond's protectionist theories that he offered $500 toward a professorship at the University of Maryland on condition that Raymond be appointed. He never accepted the appointment. Raymond's *Thoughts on Political Economy* was the first comprehensive economic treatise published in the United States.

[14] P. v. All references are to the first edition in 1820 of *Thoughts on Political Economy*, unless otherwise indicated.

with the American political issues and their economic implications than he was with showing that Smith's ideas were alien to local issues. Yet of necessity their paths crossed, for indeed it was Smith who laid out the original paths.   Careful reading of Raymond's *Thoughts on Political Economy* leads one to agree with Teilhac that "the similarities that may exist between his theory and that of the Physiocrats, Ganilh, Smith, Say, Malthus, Ricardo or Lauderdale are, by and large, co-incidence rather than direct borrowings." [15]   Despite the fact that the book was never popular it passed through four editions without significant change of views or content.[16]

Raymond's Economics.—The familiar controversy over the definition of national wealth and of what it consists is of great importance in Raymond's economics.   He contends that all previous writers had made the mistake of "the confounding of national with individual wealth, than which no two things can be more different or distinct." [17] He believes that national wealth is not the sum total of individual wealth; indeed, it may not even consist of the same ingredients, nor may an increase in wealth of a citizen be regarded as an increase in national wealth.   He cites the slave trade to prove that individual interests might be "perpetually at variance with national interests." The error commonly made by those who treat national and individual wealth as one is found in the mistake of making the nation the same as the individual or person: a nation cannot, he maintains, be likened to an individual who has faculties, whereas a nation is but a "huge artificial being composed of millions of natural beings" (p. 36).   National wealth he defines then as "a capacity for acquiring the necessities and comforts of life. . . . This capacity for acquiring by labor the necessities and comforts of life for all its citizens, is as high a degree of national wealth, as any nation ever did, or can ever hope to attain" (p. 37).   He places great confidence in the labor and industry of a people who really create "the stock of national wealth."   He says, "Labour then, is the cause, and the only cause which produces national wealth" (p. 87).   After criticizing Smith and Lauderdale for their "errors in confounding of national with individual wealth," he makes a rather fruitless comparison of agricultural and manufacturing labor.

The objective of his long diatribe on wealth is to discover whether or not private wealth (and what creates it) has been confused with

[15] Ernest Teilhac, *Pioneers of American Economic Thought in the Nineteenth Century,* trans. E. A. J. Johnson (New York, 1936), p. 37.
[16] 1823, 1836, 1840.   See Charles P. Neill, *Daniel Raymond: An Early Chapter in the History of Economic Thought in the United States,* Johns Hopkins University Studies, Fifteenth Series, VI (June, 1897), pp. 21-28.
[17] *Thoughts on Political Economy,* p. 26.

national wealth, which he developed into an almost meaningless concept. The individual who owns land, property, or capital may obtain "a quantity of necessities" without his own labor; obviously, a nation cannot do this. Basically, however, individual wealth, no matter what form it may take, is a result of labor. The purpose of analyzing public and private wealth is to inquire into the basic origins and meanings of each and then to examine how the flow of each may be affected by legislation which, under certain circumstances, may bring private and public interests at variance with one another. He follows Lord Lauderdale in pointing out that public and private wealth must be distinguished, but he has a very different purpose in mind and his definitions are by no means the same. The two writers were confronted by different conditions, and each had different objectives in mind: Raymond was more concerned with national problems, whereas Lauderdale was concerned with criticising Smith.

After establishing what he believes are important differences between national and private wealth, he examines the most important economic institutions of the time as factors affecting wealth. Here his nationalistic convictions are shown in clear relief. The subjects of value, rent, wages, interest, and profits do not concern him greatly, for they are matters affecting the individual economy not national issues.

Raymond's discussion of national issues reflects both the general thinking of the time and his own prejudices. His personal views on some specific issues were not advanced but reactionary. He wrote at a time when the national bank and the regulation of all banks were unsettled issues. His dislike for "money corporations" is seen in such strong statements as follows: "The object of a money corporation is to give to the members artificial power, which they would not otherwise possess, or to exempt them from some liability, to which they would be subject, but for the act of incorporation. The very object then of the act of incorporation is to produce inequality, either in rights, or in the division of property. Prima facie, therefore, all money corporations are detrimental to national wealth. They are always created for the benefit of the rich, and never for the poor" (p. 427). An incorporated banking company therefore is not good: like every money corporation, it is "injurious to national wealth and ought to be looked upon by those who have no money, with jealousy and suspicion. They are . . . engines of power, contrived by the rich, for the purpose of increasing their already too great ascendancy, and calculated to destroy the natural equality among men, which God has ordained, and which no government has a right to lend its power in destroying" (p. 429).

Raymond did not regard all corporations as enemies of the national economy. He admits that corporations for building roads and canals and for making permanent improvements were beneficial to the country. Banks, he said, rendered important services, but constantly posed a threat to the nation if allowed to issue paper money. Only gold and silver should be used as money; however, if paper money had to be used it should be issued by the government, not by a bank.

In defending a strong protective tariff he admitted that it created many paradoxes. "If an individual or a nation can buy an article cheaper than it can make it, they had better buy than make it, as a general rule" (p. 360). In order to keep the entire labor force constantly employed he advocated giving "national industry a monopoly of the home market" (p. 376). He recognized the disorder caused by the great influx of British goods after the War of 1812 and firmly believed that a protective tariff was necessary if we did not want our labor "reduced to the necessity of working as hard and living as poor as the English laborers." He recognized that tariffs would have to be revised from time to time and forecast that the revisions would be upward. Tariffs should be lowest on imported goods which are not produced domestically and highest on goods produced by industries employing the greatest number of laborers.

Raymond's arguments on the tariff are not especially incisive as might be expected from one writing at this critical stage in economic history. The strong anti-slavery views of Raymond alienated many who might have supported him on other issues.

Summary and Evaluation of Raymond.—Since Raymond wrote the first systematic treatise to be published in this country, American scholars are somewhat inclined toward a charitable evaluation of his work. He admits his limitations in attempting to engage in controversy with Smith and others whose works were widely known. While he dared grapple with Smith on many issues, he did not write merely for the purpose of answering Smith. Nor was he anti-British, as Cossa claims.[18] He had read enough of the works then available to know the general tenor of the prevailing doctrines, and this gave him the framework both for criticism and for expressing his own views. His work, however, is a reflection of his own environment and its problems rather than a formal, critical reply to Smith or anyone. There is a prevailing sympathy for the poor induced more by an impression of the failure in the availability and development of the natural resources of the country than for any other reason. He wished to see a strong nation with full employment of resources and labor. If contemporary doctrines or legislative practices did not bring this about, it was because of reasons which

[18] L. Cossa, *Introduction to the Study of Political Economy* (London, 1893), p. 465.

were susceptible to change and correction. He had a strong conviction that work was the surest way to wealth. Thus work and the boundless natural resources of this country could make it great. On this point he was in strong opposition to Smith, who held "that parsimony, and not industry, is the immediate cause of the increase of capital. Industry, indeed, provides the subject which parsimony accumulates. But whatever industry might acquire, if parsimony did not save and store up, the capital would never be the greater" (*Wealth of Nations*, p. 321). Thus, although Raymond agrees with Lauderdale, who severely criticizes Smith on the issue, his arguments differ from those of Lauderdale. Raymond held firmly to the view that the capacity to produce goods was the real source of national wealth rather than a stock of goods at any given time. The mere accumulation of national wealth whether by saving or by "parsimony . . . is radically unsound" (p. 51).

Raymond's work is difficult to evaluate. There is no logical sequence in topics nor is there any balance between the greater and the lesser issues. The details of the issues are generally well developed, but as already indicated, criticisms of Smith and others frequently interfere with his own ideas on the same issues. In some places his work has a juristic flavor; in others it reflects a deep religious conviction. Throughout, however, there is a deep sincerity and a genuine desire to bring about a clearer understanding of pressing national issues. The work, however, good or bad, is distinctly an indigenous product.

The Optimists

The nationalists were seen to be a group of men who objected to and criticized the methods and assumptions of classical writers, especially Adam Smith. National greatness was a desirable objective for Smith, and the best way of achieving it was of utmost importance. But national wealth and welfare, although of first consideration, might be in conflict with that of individuals. Since classical economists emphasized this individualistic point of view, the results of their doctrine would not be basically good for the nation; or so said the nationalist critics.

The next critics to attack the citadel of classical economics and economists—especially Ricardo and Malthus—were known as the optimists. The American Henry C. Carey and the Frenchman Frederic Bastiat best present the tenets of optimism. Both men were familiar with the writings of Smith, Ricardo, Malthus, and J. B. Say. For Carey, Ricardo and Malthus afforded adequate grounds for criticism, but Bastiat found Say more to his dislike. While each writer found many things in classical doctrines with which he was in complete disagreement, it is probable that their economic environments influenced their views more than anything else, especially in the case of Carey. Both critics wrote with a deep conviction of the truth of what they presented rather than from a desire merely to criticize.

Henry C. Carey's works appeared over the span of years 1835-1859 when this country was making rapid strides: population was increasing; land was cheap and abundant; wages were relatively high, prices relatively low; roads, canals, and railways were being built; technological improvements were many; peace and plenty prevailed. While everything may not have been perfect, certainly the gloomy forebodings of Ricardo and Malthus could not apply to this flourishing young nation. The contrast between America and Europe, especially when seen through the eyes of one not constitutionally friendly to Europe, was indeed great. Here the economy clearly promised to be built upon abundance, whereas scarcity constantly plagued European states. Optimism characterized this dynamic young nation, which really had nothing to fear.

Conditions in France were somewhat improved in Bastiat's time. Although that country was deficient in many of the elements found in the American scene, she had a better social and political outlook than ever before; persistent wars had subsided, thus allowing an opportunity for internal development. Bastiat's optimism clearly rested upon what he believed could be accomplished with what the French had to work with, plus an intelligence capable of overcoming natural deficiencies. His belief in finding in his own people the "touchstone" for converting his country's natural resources into greatness characterizes his optimistic hopes. One cannot find any reason to quarrel with his objective. With this brief background of the men we turn to their writings.

Henry C. Carey.—The work of Henry C. Carey [19] covers a range of subjects on which his ideas show breadth rather than depth. The treat-

---

[19] **Henry Charles Carey** (1793-1879), "the first American economist," was born in Philadelphia. His father, Mathew Carey, was an Irish political exile whose views of the British were never friendly. The father established a publishing and bookselling business, which afforded the son his greatest educational opportunities, for his formal education never went beyond the local schools. He took over the business while a young man of twenty-four and soon made a considerable fortune, which enabled him to retire from the business at the age of forty-two. He devoted the remainder of his life to writing in the field of social sciences. He made trips to Europe in 1825, 1857, and 1859; there he met certain notables, among them J. S. Mill. He was a prolific author, having written 13 volumes and three thousand pages of pamphlet materials, and even a greater amount contributed to newspapers. He was widely read in many fields, including history, sociology, mathematics, physics, psychology, philosophy, biology, and chemistry. Carey, like J. S. Mill, was ready and willing to write and offer advice on pressing issues of the day. The best known of Carey's works are: *Essay on the Rate of Wage* (3 vols., Philadelphia, 1835); *The*

ment of subject matter was intended to be exhaustive. For example, in his *Principles of Political Economy*, Volume I has the title *Laws of the Production and Distribution of Wealth*; in Volume II he considers the causes which retard the increase in the production of wealth and improvement in the physical and moral conditions of man; and in Volume III he deals with the causes which retard the increase in the numbers of mankind and, finally, the causes which retard improvement in the political conditions of man. Carey encompasses even more in his three-volume work, *Principles of Social Science* (1858-59). Social science, he contends, "treats of man in his efforts for the maintenance and improvement of his condition." He defines it to be "the science of the laws which govern man in his efforts to secure for himself the highest individuality, and the greatest power of association with his fellowmen" (I, 63). He regards social science as the most concrete and the most difficult of all sciences. In this, as in his belief in the need of integration of the social sciences, he follows Comte. He draws heavily upon both history and geography for illustrations and comparisons which he uses profusely. Throughout his work he emphasizes human happiness as the thing of greatest importance. The classical emphasis upon wealth and its accumulation pales when compared with the near-divine scope of social science, in which man is placed as the center of all things good by a Creator whose plan surmounts all things human.

Carey's economics was a mixture of criticism and his own views, neither of which was always consistent. He professed great admiration for Adam Smith, but on Malthus and Ricardo he heaped scorn and criticism. His early ideas on trade made him an ardent free-trader, but later he became just as ardent a protectionist.[20] His ideas on specific economic theories follow.

On value he develops a cost-of-reproduction theory: "The cause of the existence in the human mind of the idea of value . . . is simply our estimate of the resistance to be overcome, before we can enter upon the possession of the thing desired" (*Principles of Social Science*, I, 148). The value of a thing then increases or decreases as the resistances increase or diminish. As nature is forced to labor more and more with man there follows a steady diminution in the cost of reproduction. He uses the cost of reproduction to explain all value, from the vocal powers of Jenny Lind to the value of fine specimens of glass. He asks, "To

---

Principles of Political Economy (3 vols., Philadelphia, 1837-40); *The Past, the Present and the Future* (Philadelphia, 1843); *The Harmony of Interests* (Philadelphia, 1850); *The Principles of Social Science* (Philadelphia, 1858-59); *The Unity of Law as Exhibited in the Relation of Physical, Social, Mental and Moral Science* (Philadelphia, 1872).

[20] His break with classical tradition first appears in his *The Past, the Present and the Future* (1848).

what extent are they valued? To that of the cost of reproduction, and no more; and that tends to decline with every step in the growth of population and wealth" (*ibid.*, p. 174). He recognizes utility but treats it as a "useful capability of all matter" (*ibid.*, p. 178). "The utility of things is the *measure of man's power over nature*—and this grows with the power of combination among men. Their value, on the other hand, is the *measure of nature's power over man*—and this declines with the growth of the power of combination. Thus the two move in opposite directions and are always found existing in inverse ratio to each other." (*Ibid.*, p. 179; Carey's italics.)

Carey uses this ratio idea to explain exchange on a reciprocity basis. He makes trade in commodities rest on the cost of reproduction of the commodity at the present; no one would give more for a commodity than its present reproduction cost regardless of what it cost at some remote time. This meant that cost (and values) would always be declining since man's power over nature was always increasing—and the two in combination (man and nature) were the source of all value.

He does not apply his cost of reproduction theory to labor. He regarded labor and capital as equal claimants to the wealth they produced. Land being treated as another commodity, there is no place for the landlord as a claimant since he is regarded as a capitalist. He says that "the value of land is a consequence of the improvement which labor has affected upon it and it constitutes an important item of wealth," yet its value represents but a small portion of its cost. No problems could arise over the distribution of wealth, for under his scheme there would exist "a perfect harmony of interests of the various portions of society . . . neither [labor nor capital] profits at the expense of the other . . . Both are equally interested in every measure looking to the maintenance of peace . . . the most perfect development of individuality, and the largest and most unrestricted commerce with their fellow-men." (Vol. III, 120.)

Carey rejects the Ricardian rent theory. Ricardo, it will be recalled, held that the best soils were cultivated first. But Carey argues that the first settlers always are found on the most barren soil. He says, "Mr. Ricardo's . . . theory must be abandoned as wholly destitute of foundation . . . everywhere, in both ancient and modern times, cultivation has commenced on the poorer soils—and that it has been with the growth of population and wealth alone that man has been enabled to subdue to cultivation the richer ones. . . ." (Vol. I, 107.) He attempts to prove his contention with illustrations of land use in many of the states and in foreign lands. He concludes his meticulous arguments by asserting that "the work of cultivation having everywhere been commenced upon the sides of the hills where the soil is the poorest and where the natural advantages of situation are least" (I, 138). Thus he contends that history everywhere contradicts Ricardo's assumptions, thereby making his conclusions wrong. Man is dominant over nature and nature serves the purposes of man. In his harmonious scheme of things, "Population and wealth tend to increase and cultivation tends toward the more fertile soils, when man is allowed to obey those instincts of his nature which prompt him to seek association with his fellow-men" (I, 139).

The population theory of Malthus has no place in Carey's good world. He denies the premises of Malthus and holds that the arithmetic and geometric ratios of food and population are absurd and ridiculous. He argues that such a tendency is inconsistent with the plans of the Creator. He refutes Malthus by arguing that "we find, throughout nature, a constant tendency towards the perfect adaptation of the earth to the wants of a growing population" (Vol. III, p. 319). In support of this he offers one of his most farfetched arguments: "with increase in numbers of mankind, the lower animals tend to diminish in their numbers, and gradually disappear—vegetable products tending, as steadily, to increase in quantity. Were it otherwise, the earth would become less and less fitted for man's residence—carbonic acid being more and more produced, and the air declining in its powers for the maintenance of human life. Increase in vegetable life tends, on the contrary, to promote the decomposition of that acid—thereby increasing the supply of the oxygen required for maintenance of animal life, while diminution in the composition of animal food is attended by decreases in the quantity of oxygen required for human purposes" (*Ibid.*).

This curious argument is at least original with Carey. It is consistent with his belief in the harmonious relationships of all things. More men and women would produce more carbonic acid, which would create a greater supply in the vegetable world: mankind and the "vegetable world" each supplying the other with a perpetual meal ticket—an easy, even though illogical, answer to the population question.

Carey was indeed an optimist. He held consistently to a statement he made in the preface of an earlier book that "this volume now offered to the public is designed to demonstrate that existence of a simple and beautiful law of nature, governing man in all his efforts for the maintenance and improvement of his condition, a law so powerful and universal that escape from it is impossible, but which, nevertheless, has heretofore remained unnoticed." [21] In order to be true to his text he had to deny all doctrines not in accord with his own beliefs of a com-

21 *The Past, the Present and the Future,* p. v.

plete harmony between the forces of nature and man. Surrounded as he was with undeveloped and limitless natural resources, few of the issues that troubled Smith, Ricardo, or Malthus were problems in Carey's day or at any foreseeable time. There was no reason for being anything but an optimist.

Carey's contribution to economics has proved to be meager, despite his great output of materials. He failed to develop any lasting theories and, likewise, failed to develop any school of thought. He stood for an ardent protectionist policy for America (discussed in Chapter 21), which view was upheld by many. Supporters of the policy of protection were in no greater debt to Carey than to List, Hamilton, Raymond, and others. Carey advocated a balance in the development of agriculture, commerce, and industry. Like List, he did not want to see this country become a stupid, uninteresting, and barbarous country devoted solely to feeding Europe. Only a balanced development would make it possible for the products of each to find markets. In this respect his views were sound. However, his denial of the law of diminishing returns, his scorn of both the Ricardian rent theory and the population theory of Malthus, his untenable theory of value, his treatment of labor and capital as the only factors of production, and his identification of land with capital and rent with interest, all leave grave doubts whether he understood theoretical analysis at all. He was so obsessed with the desire to discredit Ricardo and Malthus that, at times, his ideas become almost counter-propagandistic in nature.

Carey was held in high esteem abroad. He made friends and contacts there, and scholars, notably the Germans, found in his attack on English economists a binding tie with their own thinking. He preached a nationalist (not romantic nationalist in the Adam Müller sense) gospel very similar to German thinking. His books were translated into several languages and quoted by Mill and many others. He greatly influenced Bastiat in France, as will be shown shortly. In Philadelphia, his "Carey's Vespers" afforded a sounding board for discussion of national issues, especially the tariff. (The "Carey Vespers" were the counterpart in the "Ricardo breakfasts" and the "Sunday suppers" of Adam Smith.) Carey had some followers among early American economists—notably E. Peshine Smith, Wm. Ellis Thompson, Stephen Colwell, and Charles Nordhoff—but he founded no "school," unless the followers of protectionist doctrine are regarded as a school, in which case Carey's influence cannot be identified.

Frédéric Bastiat.—Another writer classed as an optimist on the basis of his views on a harmonious universe was the Frenchman, Frédéric

Bastiat.[22]   Like Carey, Bastiat finds Adam Smith's theories more to his liking whereas Ricardo and Malthus, he felt, presented fundamental errors.   Bastiat did not attack either Ricardo or Malthus with anything like the vigor shown by Carey.   For Bastiat, "the subject of political economy is man."   Men alone have the faculty of working together, exchanging their services with all the involved combinations to which that procedure gives rise.   This, then, is what explains the origin and delimits economics, which he defines as, "Every effort, capable of satisfying, on condition of a return, the wants of a person other than the man who makes the effort, and consequently the want and satisfactions

[22] Frédéric Bastiat (1801-1850) was born near Bayonne and lived the larger part of his life as a gentleman farmer on an estate which he inherited.   His fluency in English, Italian, and Spanish enabled him to become familiar with literature of other countries.   In 1824 he became interested in the writings of Smith and Say and was actively interested in the English free trade measures and in the efforts of Cobden and Bright and others of the Manchester School in their attempts to repeal the Corn Laws and establish laissez faire.   In time he organized a Free Trade Association in Bordeaux and attempted to organize a similar group in Paris.   He was active in popularizing the Manchester movement in France.   He became secretary to a commission and edited a weekly journal which became their publicity organ.   He was a deputy in the Constituent Assembly in 1848 but his health prevented effective work, except in his constant war against the socialists and communists let loose by the Revolution.

He was a clever and brilliant writer.   His use of fable and satire when applied to the numerous government regulations made them appear ridiculous.   Although he was not a profound economist, he was both a popularizer and a propagandist for certain economic theories.   The economic principles which he singled out for emphasis were stressed with almost fanatical zeal and devotion.   His facile pen and his voice, as long as he could use it, served to spread his convictions.   He suffered from an incurable malady of the throat and lungs which caused his death in his forty-ninth year.

Most of his writings were crowded into the last six years of his life.   He contributed articles to the *Journal des Economistes*, the *Journal des Débats*, and the *Libre Exchange*.   His most important work, *Harmonies of Political Economy (Harmonies économiques)*, the first volume of which was published posthumously in 1850, was left unfinished.   (Some of the chapters appeared in the *Journal des Économistes* as early as 1848.)   The first series of his *Sophisms of Protection* appeared in 1845 and the second series in 1848.   His *Essays in Political Economy*, a small volume of some 230 pages, contains some of his most clever essays—notably "The Broken Window," "The Disbanding of Troops," and others.   The oft-cited "Petition from the Candlemakers against Competition by the Sun" appears in his *Sophisms of Production*.

Considerable controversy once raged over the issue of whether or not his work was a plagiarism of that of H. C. Carey.   In the year 1850, when Carey's *Harmony of Interests* came out, he wrote a letter to the *Journal des Economistes* in which he accused Bastiat of plagiarism.   The accused, already on the point of death, defended himself in the same *Journal*.   Bastiat admitted he had read Carey's work but added that he did not mention the fact because of the uncomplimentary remarks therein about France.   Some have upheld Carey's charge; others regard it as a literary coincidence resulting from a common inspiration of the two men.   See E. Teilhac, *Pioneers of American Political Thought in the Nineteenth Century*, pp. 100-13.   For Bastiat's works see *Oeuvres Complètes*, ed. by P. Paillottet with biography by R. de Fontenay (7 vols., 1st ed., Paris, 1855; 2d ed., Paris, 1862-64).

relative to this species of effort, constitutes the domain of Political Economy." [23] He says on the next page that "Political Economy may again be defined *the theory of exchange*. . . . Value consists in the comparative appreciation of reciprocal *services* and Political Economy again may be defined *the theory of value*."

Bastiat's theory of value is confused and somewhat lost in his own terminology. He recognizes its importance when he says "the theory of value is to Political Economy what numeration is to arithmetic" (p. 131). He uses the terms "utility" and "value" loosely but recognizes that a good may have utility without having value (e.g., atmospheric air) and that utility is the foundation of value. He does not hold to a labor-cost (or labor performed) theory but to a labor-*saved* theory— saved to the person who receives the service, and service to Bastiat is the essence of value. Thus, "Value is the appreciation of services exchanged. . . . principle of value is always in the services and not in the utility of which these services are the vehicle" (p. 167). He uses the term "services" to include all the terms used by economists with whom he was familiar,[24] such as utility, scarcity, cost of production, and labor; he adds, "Thus I hope to satisfy economists of all shades of opinion." [25]

Bastiat's distribution theories, if indeed they may be so designated, were bound up in his all-embracing harmonies. Capital, he says, is composed of materials, provisions, and instruments. The owners of capital would be paid only for its value, which means services rendered in creating that capital, or costs (pains) created in producing the capital and pains saved to the user. Consisting as it does of "commodities or products," it does not have an independent existence. The person who lends or transfers capital deprives himself of immediate satisfactions and foregoes productive opportunities himself; he therefore renders a service for which he is entitled to a return. The remuneration Bastiat calls interest, which is but a term applicable to "that supreme law of society, *service for service*" (p. 201). Interest is a legitimate payment for capital which will fall in rate as capital becomes more abundant. However, the sum total of interest, like the sum total of capital, will continually increase. This fact rests upon "an unassailable principle" that "in pro-

[23] *Harmonies of Political Economy*, translated from the 3d French edition by P. J. Sterling (2d ed., Edinburgh, 1880), p. 72. Subsequent references are from this source.

[24] He quotes from Smith, Say, Senior, Storch, Ricardo, Proudhon, and the physiocrats.

[25] P. 169. While Bastiat's use of "service" is of little use in our concept of value theory, it is of great use in general economic literature. We have the problem of evaluating "goods and services"; we speak of "productive and unproductive" services, and so on. Perhaps, we should credit Bastiat with popularizing the term.

portion to the increase of Capital the absolute share of the total product falling to the capitalist is augmented and his relative share is diminished" (p. 212). "The more abundant capital becomes, the more interest falls" (p. 213), but he has no fear that the rate of interest will sink to zero. (Annihilation, as he calls it.)

His explanation of rent of land was never fully developed. He quotes brief passages from Smith and Ricardo but he never clearly understood nor refuted them. In this respect he is much inferior to Carey, who meticulously challenged every step in Ricardo's theories. Bastiat nowhere refutes either the differential surplus or the monopolistic theory of rent. His explanation, following a standard pattern, makes rent a return for past services. Since the value of present services is less than that of past services, rents would tend to decline. It appears that Bastiat realized that his explanation of rent presented numerous discords in his harmonies, but he did not live to disentangle the problem.[26]

Bastiat's optimism is evident in his discussion of wages. Since he believed the interest rate would become lower, more wages would be available for labor. Labor and capital jointly create value; it is not true, as Adam Smith says, that "value comes from labor" (p. 386). These two factors working jointly make production easier and the output greater, therefore a greater share to labor. He further believes that a natural law applies here, which makes it easier for labor to rise to the rank of capitalist and employer, in line with the general tendency of wages to rise. Bastiat was apparently more concerned with answering the socialists and the communists on wages issues, rent, and land monopoly, than in evolving a theory of wages. His discussion was unfinished but the general direction of his arguments indicates his beliefs in a rising rate of wages and easier conditions of employment. However, much remains unanswered.

Bastiat emphasizes the importance of the consumer over the producer. "Political Economy," he writes, "should be studied from the consumer's standpoint," also that "consumption is the great end of Political Economy" (p. 338). By this he means that public or general interest and welfare comes before private. He believes consumers have a responsibility for educating people to develop a "taste for good living" (p. 336). While he does not advocate a curtailment of wants in the cameralist sense, he does register objections to depraved desires which may lead

---

[26] His chap. xiii, "Rent," is only five pages long and contains nothing helpful in explaining rent. His translator, P. J. Sterling, remarks that "two or three short fragments are all the author left us on this important subject." The chapters on "Property-Community" (viii) and "Landed Property" (ix) contain his views, many of which are intended to refute the theories of the socialists and the communists, rather than to develop a theory.

to worthless production. He says, "A frivolous people requires frivolous manufacturers, just as a serious people requires industry of a more serious kind. If the human race is to be improved, it must be by the improved morality of the consumer, not the producer" (p. 338). This view is praiseworthy. Indeed, Gide and Rist state, "Bastiat's contribution to this subject is quite first-class, and may possibly be his best claim to a place among great economists." [27]

Bastiat disavows the teachings of Malthus on population but he does not state clearly to what he objects. Again, he lacks the argumentative approach, originality, and thoroughness of Carey. Such dire consequences as Malthus's theory predicted were unthinkable in the harmonies of nature, and therefore there was no problem. His thinking here was in line with his general beliefs on the basic goodness of the over-all plan of the Creator which would admit no disharmonies.

Enough has been presented to show the trend of his thoughts. He believed he had a mission to fulfill, namely, to acquaint mankind with the munificence of the world in which he found himself. His time proved almost too brief to fulfill the mission. Little is to be gained in weighing the arguments for or against the plagiarism charge of Carey. Without doubt Bastiat envisioned a better life for his France than she had had up until his time. He saw a better side to man and nature; this he wished to develop. The same may be said of Carey. Teilhac, who devotes many pages to the Carey-Bastiat plagiarism case holds that each had a common stimulus in the political regime of the two nations, the spirit of revolution, but mainly in a common *inspiration*: J. B. Say. He says, "The very coincidence of the intellectual milieu, an identical doctrinal atmosphere, makes it possible to sift out Bastiat's contribution." [28] Indeed this appears to be a fair evaluation. If some ideas were plagiarized, they were not an especially significant loss to Carey, for in thoroughness of analysis and in originality of argument, Bastiat is the one who suffers by comparison. Bastiat excels only in cleverness of style and succinct expression. It may be to the credit of Bastiat that his arch enemies whom he wished to discredit were the socialists and communists, especially the latter. Could it be that he was one of the first to point out that "Communism is slavery"? (*Harmonies*, p. 269.)

Bastiat's influence in the politico-economic world was not nearly so great as that of Carey. In large measure Bastiat's work was an unfinished symphony. He did not change the economic trends in France nor did he initiate any new ones. Carey's influence upon the protectionistic movement in America, although not identifiable quantitatively,

[27] *History of Economic Doctrines* (1915 ed.), p. 343.
[28] See E. Teilhac, *op. cit.*, p. 111.

was pronounced. Bastiat's attack on economic practices in France was germane, but it cannot be shown to have borne fruit in subsequent reforms. He says in the opening essay to *Harmonies of Political Economy*, which he addresses to the youth of France, "All I have aimed at is to put you on the right track, and make you acquainted with the truth, that *all legitimate interests are in harmony*." It is questionable whether his aims were accomplished and doubtful that the youth of France realized his purpose. His works may still be read with interest and profit as an antidote or even an anaesthetic for the gloomy outlook associated with certain classical teachings. An occasional injection of optimism such as Carey and Bastiat tried to give is probably beneficial for the individual and the world alike.

16

The Historical School of Economics

The student must be impressed by the extent to which criticism permeates economic thought. Disagreements among themselves, which border on criticism, appear in the writings of early mercantilists. Some elements of Smith's work were criticized almost before the ink was dry. In subsequent years it became the privilege of writers of every land, with every shade of learning, to criticize previous theory or development. As has been pointed out, there were criticisms of the methods used, of the underlying assumptions, of premature generalizations, of generalizations which were treated as "laws," of shortcomings in exposition; or it might be charged that the whole structure was completely wrong. If none of these objections could be used in whole or in part, it was then the habit of the critics to use a tactic resembling the peremptory challenge in selecting jurors—dismissing the whole thing by simply saying, "Other doctrines do not apply to us; we will have no part of them." Such was the contention of the group of German scholars known as the historical school, and to some extent of writers in other lands, in most of the last half of the nineteenth century (roughly 1843-1883). When one considers the criticism heaped upon orthodox economic doctrine by critics prior to the historical school, as well as by the historical school and by the socialists (who are discussed in the next chapter), the remarkable thing is that any of the original economics remains.

Not all criticism was made merely to be critical. Much was germane. A good deal of the criticism rested upon the historical fact that all conditions had changed. Marked advances had been made in all branches of learning, in production of goods, and in trade and commerce. Advances in transportation and communication changed the isolation and provincialism of areas and nations. Although nationalistic tendencies were probably greater, there arose an international awareness of common problems. Survival of classical doctrines depended upon the strength and truth of the doctrines, not necessarily upon any *Fidei Defensor*. None of the Germans, and indeed not all of the English, felt any responsibility to defend the citadel of orthodoxy against criticism.[1] Indeed, the historical progress of the peoples of most nations subsequent to the publication of the *Wealth of Nations* tended to challenge classical generalizations and raise the question of their universal applicability. In this respect, then, most of the so-called criticisms should be viewed as chronicles of social and scientific progress rather than as denials of earlier generalizations. The distinguishing characteristic which makes the German contribution differ from others is the attempt to identify and trace the trends of human development and then to develop them instead of relying on theoretical generalizations. The historical school is therefore characterized by a method known as the "historical method," in which the emphasis is placed upon the history of peoples as the only means of studying their economic progress.

Background to the German Historical School.—The historical method is characterized by an attempt to explain economic life and economic behavior by re-examining every phase of human life. The whole gamut of cultural development, including the art, literature, language, habits and customs, commerce and industry, religion and folkways—in fact, every element of civilization—was included in the extensive researches. In addition to the researches into the past, there stands out a strong conviction that the early practices were good, and that they furnish a unifying principle in the scheme of things. The origins of these basic conceptions are deep-seated in German scholarship and research. Many elements of them may be observed in the early cameralist writings.[2]

Hegel (1770-1831) took the position that the cultural level of a people was but an unfolding of the human spirit of the people. The state was first and foremost in the scheme of things; it preceded the family and civil society, which could exist only under the protective shelter of the state. For Hegel, the state was the ultimate in concrete freedom. This theory was in direct conflict with all doctrines of individualism and natural rights which characterized much of the eighteenth century economic and political thinking. The Hegelian concept of the state provided a logical basis for absolutism under German monarchs and, even more decidedly, for totalitarianism under the Nazis. The concept is a difficult one for people of democratic states to grasp.

Another influencing factor which contributed to the development of the historical method was drawn from the juristic field. This influence came mainly from the teachings of Friedrich Carl von Savigny (1779-1861), who taught law at the University of Berlin from 1810 to 1842

---

[1] J. E. Cairnes (1824-1875) and Henry Fawcett (1833-1884) may be regarded as the last defenders of the orthodox classicism. See Chapter 13.

[2] Cf. Chapter 7, especially the works of Von Justi and Sonnenfels.

and became the first rector of the University. His theory was that the laws of a people, like its language, customs and songs, were but a part of the Volksgeist (the spirit or soul of the people). He studied the development of Roman law from the sixth century A.D. with a view to establishing German law as a part of, or product of, national culture. His work had a pronounced success in Germany, and the method of research was emulated in historical economics. Comparative philology was also used in attempting to trace the origins of words and language and through them, ideas which might have economic significance.[3]

It was pointed out in the preceding chapter that Friedrich List held similar views. List viewed the state as the all-important entity to which the individual must subordinate all his interests. The state, being a unity of language, customs, manners, and the like, which he calls "nationality," is thereby given a reason for existence as a unity much more significant than "the geographical accident of a boundary." He not only extolled the German past but advocated many national reforms and changes in policies. List was more than a forerunner of the historical school. He deserves to rank with the best of the historical economists.[4]

Several years elapsed between List's work and the work of the writers of the historical school proper. In these years Germany made great national strides. The Zollverein, or customs union, established in 1834, gave impetus to the rising tide of nationalism. Industrial expansion brought many problems; labor was becoming vocal; socialist criticisms of the existing order could not be overlooked; the role, as well as the form, of government was taking on new dimensions; unification and expansion presented new and different problems for which no adequate solution was offered by any economic doctrines hitherto expounded.

The Earlier Historical School

The doctrines of the historical school were first developed by the triumvirate Wilhelm Roscher (1817-1894), Bruno Hildebrand (1812-1878), and Karl Knies (1821-1898). Chronologically they have been

[3] See M. Wolowski, Preliminary Essay on the Application of the Historical Method to the Study of Political Economy, translated by John J. Lalor in William Roscher, Principles of Political Economy (New York, 1878).

[4] Hermann Schumacher says (Encyclopaedia of the Social Sciences, V, 371) that List's "importance for theory was not recognized by his first biographer, Ludwig Häusser, in 1850, and was generally ignored for a long time. Since the discovery in 1925 in the Archives of the Institut de France of the manuscript of his Paris prize essay, Das natürliche System der politischen Oekonomie [1838; tr. from the French and ed. by E. Salin and A. Sommer as vol. iv of Schriften, Reden, Briefe . . . , Berlin 1927], there is no reason for not considering him a member of the historical school proper."

identified as the "older school," whereas the second group, of which Gustav Schmoller (1838-1917) was the leader, has been called the "younger school." This grouping has no significance other than for identifying the issues of the time in which the writers lived and for their attitude and stand on the issues.

Wilhelm Roscher's Formulation of the Historical Method.—Roscher was the founder and leader of the school. Not only was he the leading German economist, but through the school he exerted great influence in German-speaking countries for many years.[5] Our interest is in the so-called historical method and in the contributions of the group to economics.

The broad outlines of the historical method as set forth by Roscher are found in his *Grundriss*. He does not denounce theory but declares that history must be drawn upon to supplement what has already been done. The aim, as set forth in the preface, is "simply to describe what people have worked for and felt in economic matters, to describe the aims which they have followed and the successes they have achieved— as well as to give the reasons why such aims were chosen and such triumph won. Such research can only be accomplished if we keep in close touch with the other sciences of national life, with legal and political history, as well as with the history of civilization."[6] Again he states, "Our aim is simply to describe man's economic nature and economic wants, to investigate the laws and the character of the institutions which are adapted to the satisfaction of these wants, and the

[5] **Wilhelm Roscher** (1817-1894) studied jurisprudence and philology at the Universities of Göttingen and Berlin. He taught first in Göttingen (1844-1848) and then in Leipzig, where he served for nearly fifty years. He was the author of books and articles on the corn trade, colonial system, forest and agricultural economy. In 1843 he published his famous *Grundriss zu Vorlesungen über die Staatswirthschaft, nach geschichtlicher Methode* (Göttingen, 1843; *Outline of lectures on political economy according to the Historical Method*). He also wrote *Zur Geschichte der englischen Volkswirthschaftslehre [im sechzehn und siebzehnten Jahrhundert]* (Leipzig, 1851; *History of English political economy in the 16th and 17th centuries*). The *System der Volkswirthschaft (System of Political Economy)*, published in five volumes, appearing from 1854 to 1894, attests to the scope of his researches. They are: *Grundlagen der Nationalökonomie* (Stuttgart, 1854; *The Principles of Political Economy*, translated from the 13th ed. by J. J. Lalor, 2 vols., New York, 1878); *Nationalökonomik der Ackerbaues und der verwandten Urproductionen* (Stuttgart, 1859; *The Economics of Agriculture and Related Primary Production*); *Nationalökonomik der Handels- und Gewerbfleisses* (Stuttgart, 1881; *Economics of Commerce and Industry*); *System der Finanzwissenschaft* (Stuttgart, 1886; *System of Finance*); *System der Armenpflege und Armenpolitik* (Stuttgart, 1894; *System of Poor Relief and Policy toward the Poor*). His great work *Geschichte der Nationalökonomik in Deutschland* (Munich, 1874; *History of Political Economy in Germany*), is well known to students of economics.

[6] Quoted from C. Gide and C. Rist, *History of Economic Doctrines* (2d ed., New York, 1948), p. 382.

greater or less amount of success by which they have been attended." [7]
In his quest for truth he liked to think his approach was similar to that
used by "the investigator of nature"; in fact he referred to his method
as the "Historical or Physiological method." He believed the historical
approach was practical and susceptible to scientific method. The whole
history of mankind was believed to be a series of successive steps in the
evolution of humanity. In order to understand this development, every
phase of the evolution must be examined with a completely open mind.

Roscher was sincere in his belief in what he expected to accomplish.
He did not propose another method of attack on the citadel of classical
economics; he had the firm conviction that the broad sweep of history
would illustrate, supplement, and round out theory and at the same
time aid in shaping national policy. He believed that the manifold
elements which make up the complete cultural pattern of a nation
should be examined and understood in the light of their own setting.
German patterns were different in many respects from those of England
or France; therefore, the problems and their solutions must be interpreted by a complete analysis of all the cultural factors historically responsible.

To this end, therefore, Roscher devoted his talents and his life. His
historical monographs and finally his *System Der Volkswirtschaft* (5
vols., 1854-1894), about which Gide and Rist say, "every installment
was received with growing appreciation by the German world of letters" [8] constitute in a very real sense a completion of his work. Subject
matter is traced as far back as historical materials permit, and from the
researches are derived laws and explanation applicable to Germany's
national problems. There is no doubt that this is a great undertaking.
It carries historical research to high levels of thoroughness in both
breadth and penetration.

The Historical Method Applied.—A brief examination of his work,
Die Nationalökonomik des Handels- und Gewerbefleisses (*The Economics of Commerce and Industry*, 1881) will show how he used the
historical method. First he considers what he calls "The Theory of
Municipal Affairs in General" and brings to his aid the topography of
an area, as well as its history, as influencing factors in metropolitan
city development. Then in the first section of 13 chapters he develops
the subject "Commerce," by starting with the theory of commerce in
general; next he speaks of the main branches of commerce, wholesale
and retail trade and trade of the lower culture strata. In the chapter
on international trade he discusses the mercantilist theory of trade bal-

---

[7] *Principles of Political Economy*, Vol. I, p. 111.
[8] *Op. cit.*, p. 386.

ance, free trade, improvement in Smith's doctrine, international commercial treaties, and so on. Next he devotes several chapters to developing the history of coinage, paper money, exchange, and banking, followed by chapters dealing with problems in the development of transportation. In these chapters he again goes back to the Middle Ages for early historical materials and follows the developments through the years in France, Germany, and England. It is here that he assesses the part played by railroads, telegraph, ocean shipping, harbors, and the like, in national economic development. He ends the first section with a discussion on standards of measurement.

The second section of 12 chapters is entitled "Industry in the Narrower Sense." In this section he discusses the growth of industry in general, the creation of industry, large- and small-scale industry with a fine essay on the development of industry from the handicraft system to the factory. He devotes a chapter to machinery, in which he emphasizes the superiority of machine production. In the next few chapters he traces the development of trades from the early gilds, and shows how trade was influenced by premiums and taxes. He considers trade regulation by the state covering such matters as factory regulation, protection to child workers, and inspection of factories by the state. He devotes a chapter to state promotion of industry and discusses how trade instruction could be given, engineering and trade schools, museums and exhibitions of products, patents, copyrights, and trademarks. One section ends with a valuable treatment of what he calls "sales crisis" (*Absatzkrisen*), in which he discusses the causes of a crisis, the social effects, how the state may alleviate the crisis, and so on. His last chapter deals with the economics of mining. His treatment of the general subject is thorough. Viewed as a whole the problem appears to be: What use could a German industrialist make of this sweep of history in keeping with his own contemporary problems of domestic and foreign competition?

In his famous *Geschichte der Nationalökonomik in Deutschland* (*History of Political Economy in Germany*, 1874), which is indeed a great work, he grouped the writers chronologically and placed them in three periods: first, the years prior to 1648, which he calls the *Theological Humanistic period*; the years from 1648 to about 1750-1780, which he calls the *Cameralistic period*; and the years after the cameralistic period, which he calls the *Scientific period*. In this long volume he describes the work of over a thousand writers who wrote on every phase of economics; he also deals with "schools" of thought, with the background or setting and the economic history of the time, as well as with the theoretical views of the men or the school. He gave the same sort of treatment to the history of political economy in England in the sixteenth and seventeenth centuries. His works, both in quality and in quantity, rank him as one of the first, if not the foremost, of German economists.

Bruno Hildebrand.—Another German economist who employed the historical method was Bruno Hildebrand.[9] His attack on classical doctrines, both in subject matter and in method, was more sharp than Roscher's. He rejected the natural laws of classical doctrines and denied the applicability of universal generalizations drawn from the behavior of people at different periods. Like most German scholars, Hildebrand refused to make the individual the end of society; he wanted a science of culture (*Kulturwissenschaft*) embracing the complete economic development of all societies examined; from these historical (and statistical) researches he would arrive at a complete understanding of contemporary cultural standards and be in a better position to point the way to even higher cultural levels. He thought that the knowledge of history would not only revitalize economic science but would help recreate it along more realistic and scientific lines. In the preface to *Economics of the Present and Future* he says the object is to "open a way for an essentially historical standpoint in political economy and to transform the science of political economy into a body of doctrines dealing with the economic development of nations" (p. v).

Hildebrand was more certain of what the historical method could accomplish than was Roscher. The works of Roscher show more tolerance and willingness to compromise; he would supplement the existing doctrines with historical materials, even to the extent of giving them an eclectic treatment. Hildebrand was more absolute in his views, going so far as to criticize Roscher for partially recognizing the existence

---

[9] **Bruno Hildebrand** (1812-1878) studied history and economics at Breslau. He held teaching appointments in Breslau and Marburg. Because of political differences with a reactionary (Hessian) government he fled to Switzerland; while there he taught in the Universities of Zurich and Berne. In Berne he established the first statistical bureau in Switzerland. In 1861 he returned to Germany and became professor at Jena, where he remained until his death. His teaching career in the four universities totaled approximately forty years.

In 1863 he founded the *Jahrbücher für Nationaloekonomie und Statistik* (*Yearbook for Economics and Statistics*), of which he served as editor for ten years. The *Yearbook* still is a distinguished publication. He was always actively interested in social reforms and was one of the founders of the organization known as the *Verein für Socialpolitik* in 1872. His interests were very broad; he was concerned with politics, social affairs, business, as well as with the disciplines which he used in his teaching and writing. He wrote articles on many topics for the *Yearbook*, but the work which sets forth his attitude toward classical economics and his belief in the historical method was his *Die Nationalökonomik der Gegenwart und Zukunft* (*Economics of the Present and Future*, 1848). This was intended to be a comprehensive work of two or more volumes but only the first was completed.

of natural laws. He had no use for generalizations in the form of natural laws with eternal continuity and universal applicability.

Hildebrand exerted considerable influence on German (especially subsequent members of the school) and foreign scholars through his writings and in his seminars. His interest in and use of statistics as an aid in research constituted a distinct contribution. However, his criticisms of classical economics show an intolerance bordering on narrowmindedness.[10] It is doubtful that the "damage" done by Hildebrand to classical doctrines is significant. Some of his historical monographs which dealt with certain German industries (notably woolen and linen manufacturing) and his analysis of the economic growth and life of people under what he calls natural, money, and credit stages are good examples of the historical method.

Karl Knies.—The third member of the historical school was Karl Knies.[11] In general it may be said that Knies was the most persistent and thorough of the three in expounding historical method. In his work *Political Economy from the Standpoint of the Historical Method* (1853), he presents his explanation and his defense of the historical method as applied in economic science. He contends that the economic make-up of society at any time and the theoretical concepts applicable to that society are a result of definite historical development. All the elements which characterize that society attest to its progress and development at any one time. The level which that society has attained is but a phase or stage in its continuous development; ethical evaluations of the goodness or badness of the stage of current development are not significant; only the cultural level of that society in its continuous historical evolution is significant. Therefore, doctrinal economics cannot have universal applicability; its value can be only for a given time and place; it lacks continuity and fails to record social evolutionary change.

---

10 Hildebrand was also a severe critic of socialism, which was rapidly growing in most continental European states. He was especially critical of Proudhon and the earlier utopian socialists.

11 **Karl Gustav Adolf Knies** (1821-1898) taught in Marburg, Freiburg, and Heidelberg, where he spent thirty-one years (1865-1896). His seminars were attended by many American scholars. His views on method are found in his theoretical work, *Die politische Ökonomie vom Standpunkt der geschichtlichen Methode* (*Political Economy from the Standpoint of the Historical Method*, Brunswick, 1853). The second edition of 1883 bore the title, *Die politische Ökonomie vom Geschichtlichen Standpunkte* (*Political Economy from the Historical Standpoint*). It is generally stated that this work went unnoticed until Schmoller and his group called attention to it. His *Geld und Kredit* (2 vols.; Berlin, 1873-1879) is one of the best treatments of money, capital, credit, and interest found in the German language. *Die Eisenbahnen und ihre Wirkungen* (*The Railroads and Their Effects*, Brunswick, 1853) established his skill in the economics of transportation. He contributed generously to German periodicals and yearbooks.

Knies likewise contended that the concepts of economic and social institutions change; such institutions as private property, the productivity of certain types of labor and the self-interest concept of classical doctrines have changed with time, place, and peoples; hence, the methods used to arrive at final truth must necessarily change. By examining the historical background of other peoples at different periods, similar but not identical characteristics might be found. Since laws were developed from common characteristics which permitted generalization and since, according to Knies, the generalizations were not universally true or applicable, the deductions could not be scientific laws. The generalizations could only be analogous; they could not be causal.

It is not to be assumed that everything Knies wrote was according to the plan of the historical method, free from deduction and theoretical analysis. His works on money and credit, railroads and transportation, telegraphs and statistics (in the use of which he was very proficient) are theoretical and comprehensive. In them he is not concerned solely with method.

There was considerable disagreement among the three founders of the school. For instance, Roscher and Hildebrand were rather severely criticized by Knies. They were all agreed, however, in their critical attacks on the narrow abstractions of the classical economists which were given the weight of positive laws. Likewise, they were agreed that final truth depended upon a free and full investigation of the evolution of the subject at hand. But they disagreed as to details and points of emphasis. Knies criticized Roscher for the sense in which he used the historical method and for his tendency to admit that some laws exist which have universal applicability, such as have the laws in the physical world of exact science. He criticized Roscher for approving any element of the classical method. He criticized Hildebrand for making concessions to pure theory. It was noted that Knies changed the title of the second edition of his work to read, *Political Economy from the Historical Standpoint*. He did this in response to criticism and to indicate that he did not advocate a one-sided approach. He preferred that less emphasis be placed upon method per se, and that the historical point of view be used in economic works. In this aim he failed to accomplish his own objective. It was attained to a large extent by Schmoller and others to be discussed subsequently.

There can be no doubt that the three men identified with the older historical method held views on the scope and method of political economy which were quite different from those developed by the classical economists—Smith, Ricardo, Malthus, and even J. S. Mill. The scope of classical economics was much more narrow than the all-embracing sweep of *Historismus*.[12]   Classical economists had emphasized self-interest, wealth, value, price and its component parts, trade, free competition—the economics of an exchange economy.   The deductions of the classical economists were aimed at explaining economic phenomena as they were seen, and not for the purpose of showing a complete social integration.   The ultimate ends of the two were entirely different.   The fact remains that the classical economists did not recognize, or at least did not admit, the interdependence of the various social sciences.[13] This may be regarded as a criticism of classical economists but it does not impair the validity of their doctrines.   The German triumvirate resented, intellectually, the transplanted English doctrines; in self-defense they attempted to free themselves and at the same time develop an indigenous German product.   Their efforts resulted in both gains and losses.   They gave a fresh impetus to scholarly research which was rewarded by many fine studies.   They lost in pure theoretical refinements, a loss which German scholarship subsequently has never regained.   They carried their investigations into fields which yielded fruits of interdependence before unknown, yet the dragon which they slew in classical doctrines proved no formidable monster.   The more temperate views of the later historical economists sometimes called the "younger" historical school follow.

The Later Historical School

The framework of the historical method was developed by the three economists, Roscher, Hildebrand, and Knies.   The actual historical research was most effectively done after 1870 by a group of which Gustav Schmoller was the leader.[14]

[12] The term means a tendency to regard all the intellectual structures in history (such as law, morality, religion, etc.) as products of historical development; they are regarded and evaluated as historically conditioned; therefore the elements, postulates, and norms which are rooted in the very structure of society and civilization are recognized and developed.

[13] The exception is J. S. Mill, who was greatly impressed with the views of Auguste Comte, but he fell short of integrating the social sciences in his *Principles of Political Economy* (1848).   Comte's *Philosophie Positive* (6 vols., 1830-1842) was known to Mill.   Knies admits in the second edition of *Political Economy from the Historical Standpoint* (1883) that when he wrote the first edition in 1852 the work of Comte was entirely unknown to him and, he adds, probably to all German economists.   Mill at least knew the Frenchman's views and made some use of them, but they escaped German scholarly vigilance.

[14] Gustav von Schmoller (1838-1917) was one of Germany's greatest economists. He held professorships in Halle, Strasbourg, and Berlin.   Most of his academic years were spent in Berlin (1882-1917), where he became famous both as a teacher and writer.   Many American students attended his seminars in Berlin.   He was one of the founders of the *Verein für Socialpolitik* in 1872, an organization devoted to social reform.   He lived in the formative years as well as in the capital of the

Schmoller knew both classical theory and the works of the older historical school, especially those of Roscher. He was therefore a little more tolerant of classical doctrine than his predecessors. He was interested in the inductive method and preferred it, but he was not averse to using deduction. He wished to make economics a part of a larger concept of social science—an integration of history, political science, sociology, philosophy, ethics, and all elements of social life. It would be a science of society dealing with people first and with economic goods and wants last. Schmoller would not deny that there were laws of society, but he doubted that they could be discovered. Economic laws, he would admit, existed; but he was convinced they could not be discovered by the methods of the classical economists. Theory, he believed, should rest upon a historical foundation, which, in turn, rested upon empirical facts. He conceived the real task to be that of finding the laws, once the empirical facts were known. In searching for the facts he would use both induction and deduction, but he preferred greater use of the former. By not delimiting his method and by drawing upon a broad, all-inclusive sweep of all elements entering into a culture pattern, he hoped to place economic science on a higher plane and also produce a science that could contribute to the shaping of national policy.

Schmoller's Outline of General Economic History.—The program was indeed an ambitious one. After a series of monographs and books on numerous topics, he began what was intended to be his epitome of historical research. The first volume of his *Grundriss* appeared in 1900 and the second in 1904. There is no doubt that this is Schmoller's greatest work and the best exhibit of the historical school. A look at the plan of the work will show the materials which he regarded as falling within the scope of the science of political economy.

Volume I contains an Introduction of two major parts, one consisting of nine chapters and the other of five. In the first part he deals with socio-historical subjects and the psychical, ethical, and legal foundations of political economy and society in general, and with the literature and methods of the science. His chapters treat of such interesting subjects

---

new German Empire. This fact influenced his work and tended to shape his thinking in the general direction of problems confronting the new empire.

Schmoller's works were many, but his *Grundriss der allgemeinen Volkswirtschafts-lehre (Outline of General Economic History)*, the first volume of which appeared in 1900 and the second in 1904, was probably his greatest. He published articles in the *Jahrbuch für Gesetzgebung, Verwaltung und Volkswirtschaft im deutschen Reich (Yearbook for Legislation, Administration and Political Economy in Germany)*, which he founded and edited. He wrote *Geschichte der deutschen Kleingewerbe im 19. Jahrhundert (A History of German Small Industry in the 19th Century,* 1870) and many other articles and monographs.

as the purpose and means of social union; the psycho-physical means of human communication—language and writing; the individual and his requirements; human impulses; the moral or ethical organization of social life, custom, law, and morality; and, finally, the general connection between economic and moral life.

The second major part of the Introduction is entitled "The Historical Development of the Literature and Method of Political Economy." In this part he draws heavily upon history and traces first the beginnings of economic theory until the sixteenth century. Next he treats of the awakening of science and natural law in the seventeenth century, and follows with a chapter on the prevailing systems of the eighteenth and nineteenth centuries. To these he applies his analysis of the method of political economy. Last he shows how political economy developed into a science in the nineteenth century.

In Book I, which he calls "Land, Rent and Technique as Mass Phenomena and the Elements of Political Economy," he deals with the dependence of political economy on natural conditions: race and peoples; the population—its natural structure and movement. In the fourth and last chapter of this book he discusses the development of techniques and their economic significance.

Book II covers the social nature of political economy, its origins, and its present state. In this book he discusses the family; the manner of settlement and the way of living of social groups; the economic life of the state and the community; the social and economic division of labor; the nature of property and its distribution; the formation of social classes; and finally the development of forms of business and their management.

The second volume contains Book III, which is entitled "The Social Process of the Exchange of Goods." Here he comes to grips with problems of the market, commerce, and trade; competition; measures, weights, and coinage; value and price; wealth, capital, and credit, including capital rent and the rate of interest; credit organs and their modern development, including banking. He has a chapter dealing with labor relations, the right to work, labor contracts, and wages. This is followed by a chapter dealing with the more important modern social institutions: social security and insurance, the labor market, trade unions, and courts of arbitration. The last chapter of the book deals with income and its distribution, with subtitles on profits to enterprise and rent and income from property and from labor.

The fourth and last book is entitled "The Development of Economic Life as a Whole." In this he explains the fluctuations and crises of the economy. The second chapter sets forth his views on the class struggle and its control by means of the state, law, and reform. He then treats of the economic relations and struggles of the states among themselves and the policy of the state in regard to trade. The last chapter deals with the economic and general development of mankind and of individual peoples, including their rise, flowering, and decay.

The chapter content of Schmoller's two volumes is given in some detail to enable the student to appreciate better the tremendous sweep of *Historismus*. In these pages (approximately 1,330) is found a very comprehensive coverage of materials, as envisaged by the best of the historical scholars. It is probable that there is no rival of the work in either the German or the English language. Certainly it is ambitious and all-inclusive, omitting few, if any, elements of socio-economic life. Fault may be found with Schmoller's research but not with the sweep of materials in his *Grundriss*. He drew upon both historical and statistical materials and theories of both early and contemporary writers; while critical of classical economics, he avoided the metaphysical elements formerly associated with man and dealt with real people as revealed by the broad scope of history, biology, anthropology, and other sciences enlisted to portray every facet of man in his setting.

Schmoller was indeed the authoritative exponent of economic science as conceived by the historical school. The work of earlier members of the school, though valuable, hardly compares with the mature work of Schmoller which was done with finality. Despite the many articles and monographs which were critical of former economics and promised great things as an outcome of the new "historical diversion," the *Grundriss* was the first work seriously undertaken by any of the historical scholars, old or new.

It is to the credit of Schmoller and his work that he departed somewhat from the strict historical method blueprinted by the older school. He did not show the distrust of all economic theory exhibited by older members of the school. Instead, he chose to seek theoretical as well as historical bases by which all phenomena of economic life would be explained better than they had been by classical economists and which would also be more in harmony with his times. Economic life, he believed, was a part of an active culture pattern which was both dynamic in an evolutionary sense and self-revealing. He believed that it was the task of economic science to determine the means or laws of this cultural exfoliation in its economic aspects, thus providing a sequence of cultural changes of growth and decline. Since history shows a repetitive sequence of events, a comprehensive record of past cultural developments would therefore provide a historical cultural prospective for the future. Short-run, environmental elements would not do more than briefly interrupt the cultural trend; they would not alter the final outcome of the dynamic march of cultural progress or of the cultural process. This reasoning provided Schmoller with a logical method of making historical inquiry the most important means of determining the laws of economic and other cultural development.

There can be no doubt that Schmoller's work was of first magnitude. It represented, in a real sense, an epitome of German historical scholarship. Although it may be criticized on the ground that sometimes he departed from the plan, and that he failed to develop all the aspects of many of his topics, he did present a most comprehensive work. He was inclined, when discussing some issues, to resort to appeal and admonition, even moral suasion, thus departing from a scientific, objective method. At times "he harks back again to the dreary homiletical waste of the traditional Historismus." [15]　However, he is not so palpable in this as Roscher. In the broad sweep of Schmoller's generalizations he may be forgiven for a few digressions from the narrow path. He, like Roscher, reflected to a considerable extent the tradition of German cameral science which was devoted to state-management. It taught young men how to be servants of the state, and that what was taught was right. There can be no doubt that cameralism influenced all German economic thought for many years. To this tradition both Roscher and Schmoller were indebted. From the historic past they reasoned to both the present and the future. Schmoller, however, did the better work by any and all standards of evaluation.

G. F. Knapp and L. J. Brentano.—No other economist of the German historical school approached the stature of Schmoller, yet some were distinguished in special fields. Among the better-known followers was George Frederich Knapp (1842-1926), who did distinguished work in agriculture and money. He spent many years as professor at the Universities of Leipzig and Strasbourg. Knapp followed the general historical method but also depended heavily upon statistical method, the limitations of which he recognized. His study of agricultural development in Germany [16] is an excellent historical study of the development of agriculture and land ownership from the earliest times through their feudal relations, manorial estates, and finally to contemporary ownership and subsequent measures of rural reform. More controversial, however, was his last work, that on money. [17] He considered paper money to be more desirable than metal. The value of money should rest, not

---

[15] Thorstein Veblen, "Gustav Schmoller's Economics," *Quarterly Journal of Economics*, XVI (November, 1901), pp. 69-93. This is a critical review of the historical method and of Volume I of Schmoller's *Grundriss*.

[16] *Bauernbefreiung und der Ursprung der Landarbeiter* (*Liberation of Farmers and the Origin of the Farm Laborer*, 2 vols.; Leipzig, 1887).

[17] *Staatliche Theorie des Geldes* (Leipzig, 1905; 4th ed., Munich, 1923; trans. by H. M. Lucas and J. Bonar, as *State Theory of Money*, London, 1924).

on intrinsic worth as was true in metal money, but on the validity of the issuing agent—in this case the state. His "state theory of money" was a controversial issue at the time it was offered and in subsequent years it has been re-examined and even used in modified forms in some European states. The regulatory measures proposed by Knapp indicate that he was aware of the dangers as well as the advantages of his theory.

One other of the younger group, and a close adherent to the Schmoller pattern, was Lujo Brentano.[18] Like Schmoller, he spent many years as a teacher whose seminars were attended by students from many nations. His fame as a lecturer has been told and retold; in this sphere he had few equals. As a writer on economic subjects he ranks with the best ever produced in Germany. He used the broad sweep of materials as did Schmoller in developing his subjects and presented them in brilliant style. In some respects his *Anschauung*, or outlook was even more broad than Schmoller's. Brentano had a conception of the state different from that held by most German writers. He did not recognize the state as being omnipotent and above the individual. He did not trust the motives of the state or of its statesmen. Too often the state abused its power, and its servants misused their offices to further their own selfishness. The fact that he favored free trade may account for his general opposition to direct state legislation. He was apprehensive that special legislation, such as tariffs, rested upon sectional or special interests—not on national interests. Tariffs, if established, could and probably would be beneficial to the protected groups but this could not be for the national good. Throughout his writings and in his public service he showed his strong belief in the importance of the individual. He had faith that the individual, through his reason and intelligence, could bring about reforms far more useful than those which the state could instigate and which would necessarily carry with them an element of compulsion.

[18] **Ludwig Joseph Brentano**, more frequently called Lujo Brentano (1844-1931), spent his academic years in Breslau, Strasbourg, Vienna, Leipzig (he succeeded to Roscher's chair), and Munich. In addition to his work in economics he devoted much of his best efforts to the cause of peace. For this he received the Nobel Peace Prize in 1927. He was known for many years as the leading pacifist in Germany. His work at international peace conferences made him a world figure. Of his many writings in economics, the best known works are: *Die Arbeitergilden der Gegenwart* (*The Labor Gilds of the Present*, 2 vols., Leipzig, 1871-72; English translation by J. T. Smith as *English Gilds*, London, 1870); *Der wirtschafende Mensch in der Geschichte* (*The Economic Man in History*, Leipzig, 1923); *Geschichte der wirtschaftlichen Entwicklung Englands* (*History of the Economic Development of England*, 3 vols., Jena, 1927-29; *Ethik und Volkswirtschaft in der Geschichte* (*Ethics and Economics in History*, Munich, 1901); *Die Entwicklung der Wertlehre* (*The Development of Value Theory*), Munich, 1908.

Brentano's works in the field of labor and wages, gild history, law and labor, wages and productive efficiency were excellent early research studies, still very much worth reading. His *History and Development of Gilds and the Origin of Trade Unions* (1870) is still the best brief account of English gilds extant. In this work he was able to make use of his knowledge of the English language (he studied at the University of Dublin and spent many years in England) and of the wealth of neglected research materials of the Middle Ages. He portrayed the gilds as a part of the great social system of the Middle Ages, not as a local institution. He treated them as a part of the great advance of economic and social history.

His work on labor [19] discusses in Book I the early gilds and the development of the labor question, the origin of trade unions, the factory system, the early antilabor laws and regulations, the reform movements, the development of the English trade unions, and finally the development of the labor contract. In his discussion of the economic principles involved in the labor question (Book II), he develops—among other topics—labor as a commodity, wage rates and productivity of labor, ways of settling industrial disputes, and finally the legal equality of employers and laborers. In this discussion Brentano uses the historical development of the wage and factory systems, classical wage theories, utopian and reform measures, and so on for background material, yet he applies theoretical analysis in a measure beyond the usual historical treatment. He is a firm critic of the wages-fund theory and shows his confidence in trade unions serving as quasi-private units which could best provide their own relief measures, including insurance, rather than entrust that function to the state. To view this as a quasi-private responsibility was not to compromise with his faith in individualism. Brentano's work in labor economics was among the best as well as the earliest in the field. His monographs and articles are still very worth-while materials for historical as well as analytical treatment.[20]

It is true that Brentano's work in general is far removed from the pattern used by Roscher and the members of the older school. His economics shows a greater catholicity; he was less concerned with method than were other members of the school.[21] His researches, which were mainly historical, were not entirely devoid of theory. However, like other German scholars of the younger school, he virtually

---

[19] *Das Arbeitsverhältniss gemäss dem heutigen Recht* (1876; translated by Porter Sherman as *The Relation of Labor to the Law of Today*, New York, 1890).

[20] See also his *Hours and Wages in Relation to Production*, translated by Mrs. Wm. Arnold (New York, 1894). (Originally this was an article in Holtzendorff's *Jahrbuch*, Leipzig, 1876.)

[21] The famous controversy between Schmoller and Menger over method is discussed in Chapter 19.

abandoned classical theory, an act which cannot easily be condoned. It is apparent now that the historical scholars in abandoning theory in general, committed an error. The errors in classical theory came from excessive deduction, from uncertain facts, and shaky premises. Universal laws cannot be deduced if the empirical facts are faulty.

These common beliefs were generally held by Brentano but he went beyond them. He avoided the controversies which entrapped some, and, along with others of the school, proceeded to turn out monumental studies which we would now place in the fields of economic history and institutional economics and which would provoke no methodological controversy. It should be kept in mind that German economists —from the cameralists on—have been interested in state and social reforms. Wide differences, however, are apparent between the views held by von Justi, for example, and those of Schmoller or Brentano. The views range from a strong belief in state supremacy to mild opinions that the will of the state should be bent to provide greater welfare for the individual—not that the individual be lost in the larger state concept. This was in line with Brentano's liberal views and in accord with his faith in social change and reform. Rigid laissez faire was opposed, as was also political absolutism. Both the individual and the state would, he held, fare better if moderation in political and economic measures was practiced. Society had made its governing ordinances, which it alone could change; they were not products of any natural, immutable laws. The changes which they would make, being the result of a social evolution not a revolution, led critics to refer to the whole group as "socialists of the chair," which title they willingly accepted.[22]

Some evidence of the esteem in which Brentano was held by his fellow countrymen is shown in the two-volume work entitled *Die Wirtschaftswissenschaft nach dem Kriege* (*The Science of Economics after the War*, 1925). This was a memorial publication on his eightieth birthday. Contributions included those of well-known German and foreign economists such as E. R. A. Seligman, Bertil Ohlin, Charles Gide, Graziani, Palyi, and others. The introductory essay by M. J. Bonn has some significant passages which bear repeating. In spite of the long list of Brentano's publications, Bonn remarks, "He has not been a man of textbooks. No textbook or handbook bears his name" (p. 4). It was pointed out that Brentano had what might be regarded

---

[22] Prof. J. K. Ingram, A *History of Political Economy* (1923 ed., p. 123), calls them "socialists of the (professional) chair." *Katheder-Socialisten* was a nickname invented by H. B. Oppenheim. E. Heimann says the name was "bestowed on them by the members of the Manchester school" (*History of Economic Doctrines*, p. 179). Their views on trade were intermediate between complete free trade as proposed by the Manchester school of Cobden and Bright and a socialistic program as proposed by the leading socialists of the time in Germany and England.

as a system of his own; Bonn remarks that "he had a horror of bloodless abstractions. He could not think of a system separated from or not covered by the flesh of life" (p. 5). In referring to Brentano's skill as a lecturer and scholar he says, "Whoever sat at his feet and was allowed to listen how he, with word and gesture, recreated economic life that generations who are long since under the sod once lived, will never forget in gratitude that he taught them to regard history, and not in the least economic history, as a science which must be practiced with strict critical [scientific] methods but that beyond this, history is an art, and that only art makes it alive" (p. 5).

Brentano always championed the rights of the suppressed and social reform movements. His liberal views were attacked by many but he held steadfast to his convictions. His approach to economics was objective. The development of national economic policies he regarded as a fine art, far above mere politics which was a profession. Brentano stood for the best in scholarship and in social reform.

The influence of socialist writers and socialism was without doubt a conditioning factor in the thinking of most members of the historical school. The tenets of socialism, if not in direct conflict, were at least thorny problems to the absolute monarchy of the newly created German Empire after the Franco-Prussian War. The empire was expanding industrially at a rapid pace. Capitalism in the new German state was very dynamic, and the flames of class conflict were fanned by the teachings of such socialist leaders as Lassalle, Rodbertus, Marx, and Engels in Germany, and Saint-Simon, Fourier, and Proudhon in France. The *Deutsche Verein für Sozialpolitik*, to which many of the economists belonged, was active in encouraging the state to grant many of the demands made by the socialists. Thus the *Verein* group could be liberal-minded and aid in granting reforms within the framework of a nearly absolute state, the Empire. Very few of the many German economists were liberals in a contemporary sense. However, when viewed in their own setting, which had always been a conservative one, they advocated social reforms to an extent which would require them to be classed as liberal reformers. However, always there appears the motive, although not vigorously pursued, of combating the rising tide of Marxian socialism which was held to be incompatible with unifying and strengthening the Empire.

Other Representatives of the Later Historical School.—The task of giving each of the many German writers who fall within the historical group a full treatment is far beyond the scope of this volume. It is unfortunate that so few of the many publications have been translated and that the language barrier is so formidable to many. Perhaps in time someone will do a thorough study of the works of the lesser known authors. Viewed in retrospect this group of German scholars, beginning with Roscher (*Grundriss*, 1843) and perhaps ending with Sombart (*Der moderne Kapitalismus* (*Modern Capitalism*, 6 vols., 1919-1927) represents the very best of all German scholarship in economics. Though economic theory suffered at their hands, they offered monumental historical researches which are unrivaled in any language. They had an indeterminable influence on American scholarship and research culminating in the so-called institutional school. Scholars in some other lands tended to follow the general pattern of the historical school.

The authors presented are typical of the historical school and probably its best known exponents. However, many others have contributed heavily to the great list of monograph materials, books, and articles in German periodicals. Only a few of the best known are named here. Karl Bücher (1847-1930) is the author of the well-known *Entstehung der Volkswirtschaft* (*The Rise of National Economy*, Tübingen, 1893), a book which has been read by many students under the title of *Industrial Evolution* (tr. by S. Morley Wickett from the 3d German ed., New York, 1901). In the first two chapters he treats "pre-economic stages of industrial evolution" preceding the dawn of civilization, drawing heavily on existing materials in every language and from every clime. His knowledge of ethnology and anthropology is clearly shown in these two chapters. In the third chapter ("The Rise of National Economy") he traces the rise of national economy through the developmental stages of the household, town, and nation, and emphasizes the industrial relationships existing between producer and consumer. He explains the rise and use of capital, income, and wealth and relates them to industry and to the complexities which accompany an advanced economic society. The entire economy, having passed through simple stages of development, has advanced to the stage of complex interdependence in which even "a sack of wheat is knit by a strong cord to the great intricate web of national commerce" (*op. cit.*, p. 148). In Chapter Four ("An Historical Survey of Industrial Systems") he presents an excellent survey of industrial systems, tracing the stages of domestic work or housework, wage-work, handicraft, commission work (house industry), and finally factory work. He develops these subjects from the point of view of their historical evolution and he regards them as a phase of an evolving cultural pattern leading "mankind towards more and more perfect forms of existence" (*op. cit.*, p. 184). The remaining chapters (5-10) present analyses of the processes of industrial evolution, such as the decline of the handicrafts, the genesis of journalism or the press as a means of intellectual integration, the evolution of the union of labor, the division of labor and its economic effects, the growth of social classes over the centuries, and finally the movement of population and the growth of towns and cities. Each chapter is an essay in itself, rich in historical material and balanced in presentation and emphasis. The work remains to this day one of the best of its kind. Bücher contributed many other monographs and articles in yearbooks, all of which follow the general pattern of historical research.

Adolf Wagner (1835-1917) was a professor at the University of Berlin for forty-six years (1870-1916). He exerted wide influence both at home and abroad by his teaching and writings. His most important works from an imposing list of publications are his *Finanzwissenschaft* (*Science of Finance*, 4 vols., Leipzig, 1877-1901) and his *Grundlegung der Politischen Oekonomie* (*Foundations of Political Economy*, 1st ed., 1876; 3d ed., 1892-94). In the former work he treated public finance as a well-developed, scientific subject, free from the cameralistic brand of state finance doctrines. He regarded public finance not solely as a problem of income and expenditures but as a broad social and national problem. To him *Finanzwissenschaft*, or the science of finance, should be an agency for effecting a redistribution of wealth: it could provide the effective means by which the state would redistribute wealth and take the "unearned increment" which accrued especially to property owners in urban areas. He held that unearned appreciation belongs to society, not to private individuals. This was indeed advanced and liberal thought.

In the *Grundlegung* his kinship with Savigny and the juristic background appears. He leans heavily upon the evolutionary juristic elements of society and holds that all economic elements should be examined in their juristic or legal, as well as their economic, setting in order to arrive at the present stage of development. He held that the individual, having been the creator of his own society, could not fall back upon any natural rights: therefore he disputed the classical doctrines, in which he was well versed, of individual natural rights which underlie the tenets of classical economics. Man, he maintained, was conditioned in his society by elements, largely legal, which had to be reexamined in the light of their evolutionary development and present levels of attainment. Only this could fully explain society and the degree of freedom and progress of the members of the society under consideration. His method was partly historical and partly deductive. He accepted self-interest as the only constant motive and held that the classical economists had made false applications of sound economic principles. He did not approve of the repudiation of deductive and abstract reasoning, as many of the German historical economists did.

Wagner was a reformer but not a revolutionary. He believed that society, both economic and social, had to be thoroughly reorganized if it wished to survive. His belief that state or governmental ownership would have to displace private ownership of most elements of capitalistic production made him an advocate of reforms far ahead of most of his contemporaries. He saw a social good far greater in its importance than the retention of private capital. He has been called a "conservative socialist"; he was one of the organizers of the *Verein für Sozialpolitik*; in this and other organizations his efforts as a social reformer were influential in Germany and well known throughout the world.[23]

Wagner's real influence in shaping social changes is difficult to estimate. He was intimate with Bismarck, and one is inclined to associate his social policies with those of Bismarck in the 1880's. What the "Iron Chancellor" owed to Wagner and his group is certainly considerable. At this time Wagner was regarded as "the foremost scientific exponent of state socialism in Germany." He was a monarchist at heart yet some of his work would lead one to regard him as the foremost member of the "socialists of the chair." He was a member of the Prussian legislature (1882-1885) as a member of the Conservative party. In 1910 he was made a life member of the Prussian House of Lords. His political affiliations and his writings on social reform lead one to wonder if he was sincerely concerned with reform. His works at least provided an intellectual justification for many of the social reform measures of the Bismarck regime. Wagner may be regarded by some as a propagandist. He left no fundamental economic theories and no devoted followers to carry on his doctrines.

Sufficient material has been presented to show the method and scope of the historical school in Germany. As viewed in retrospect, historicism has a formidable list of gains and losses. In denying the universal validity of classical doctrines they were right, but in denying the validity of theory and analysis they suffered irreparable losses in scholarship. Theory and history are mutually interdependent: history alone is incomplete, and theory without history is inadequate. Thoroughness demands that each be used and weighted according to the issues under study. In denying theory the Germans lost heavily in theoretical refinements and fell far behind scholars of other nations. They turned deaf ears to the original work of Menger and the Austrian marginalist school, which was gaining wide acceptance. The violent polemics engaged in by Schmoller and Menger over method (the *Methodenstreit*) showed an unexpected

[23] See D. O. Wagner, ed., *Social Reformers* (New York, 1934), chap. xxii. In addition to the writers presented, German economic literature has been greatly enriched by a host of others whose names follow. A study of their work would require at least one volume in itself: Max Weber (1864-1920), A. Held (1844-1880), G. V. Schönberg (1839-1908), J. Helferich (1817-1892), Gustav Cohn (1840-1914), E. Nasse (1829-1890), L. von Stein (1815-1890), Schäffle (1831-1904), and many others.

narrowness on Schmoller's part which tended to alienate him and his followers from world scholarship. It appears that, even though the members of the historical school were committed to studies of their contemporary life and how it came about, they missed their objective by a wide margin. They were, generally speaking, reformers in a sense, and many reforms can be attributed to them directly or indirectly. The form of government, as well as their attitude toward the proper functions of the state, made reform difficult. The *Verein*, their main organized front, met with both success and failure; in any event, reforms were dearly bought. Socialism was only mildly attacked, at least not severely enough to halt its growth.

By monographic studies on many phases of economic life and development they greatly enriched the literature of economics. German thoroughness in both quality and quantity is apparent in the monographs, volumes, and many handbooks and encyclopedias. However, in theoretical economic analysis they are responsible for German scholarship's being both poor and inadequate. In fact it can be questioned whether the Germans ever made any significant contribution to economic theory.

English Followers of the Historical Method

The historical method and criticism of classical doctrines was not a German monopoly. Indeed, criticism was a prerogative of scholars everywhere. The use of the historical method was largely a German product both in origin and in refinements. It reached its highest levels of perfection in Germany, and was clearly a school with preceptors and followers. The case was different in English-speaking areas. There were writers who used the same technique used in Germany, but no school developed. There is no clear evidence that the English writers who were critical of earlier economic principles and who used the historical research technique were German-inspired. It is more accurate, therefore, to refer to them as users of the historical method than as a school related either to the German scholars or to a group of followers in their own land. A few of the English-speaking group are presented to show both the bases on which contemporary criticism rested and the use of the historical method.

Walter Bagehot and T. E. Cliffe Leslie.—On the basis of criticism and method of research Walter Bagehot (1826-1877) deserves attention. His criticism of classical doctrine appeared in his *Economic Studies*, ed. R. H. Hutton (London, 1880). He devoted several essays to examining and criticizing the assumptions of English classical doctrines. He contended that they rested upon assumptions which were not universally true but realizable only under narrow, specific conditions, and therefore lacking in universal validity. They were not true of conditions in England in his own time. He drew from the general field of the social sciences much as the Germans had done, but his use of these disciplines was broader. As a social scientist he was less inclined to any narrowness of emphasis.

Bagehot was both a practical banker and a writer on financial subjects. He was editor of the *Economist* for many years and in this capacity exerted considerable influence on contemporary finance. His work *Lombard Street* (London, 1873) remains as one of the best realistic descriptions of the English banking system and the functions of banking and of money. He also treats historically the developments of capital in the early stages of society and then views the economic and social aspects of money in advanced society. The scope of the treatment of the monetary aspect of society and the financial institutions which are found in an advanced society make the book a classic in the field.

Probably the leading English writer to use the historical method was T. E. Cliffe Leslie (1825-1882). He was educated in Trinity College, Dublin, in both law and political economy, and his works attracted wide attention. His *Essays Moral and Political* (London, 1879), originally published as articles in the *Fortnightly Review* and other magazines, offer a philosophic explanation for the historical method. The book was called by Professor Ingram, himself belonging to the same group, "the most important publication on the logical aspect of economic science which had appeared since Mill's essay in his *Unsettled Questions*." [24] Leslie studied law under Sir Henry Maine, who gave his thinking a juristic and historical bias much the same as Savigny had done for some scholars in Germany. He was also a student of Comte, although not quite a Comtian. These two sources gave him a background which was strongly reflected in his writings. The legal aspect of institutions and the Comtian insistence on the unity and interdependence of the social sciences show heavily in his writings.

Leslie is critical of classical economics in general and Ricardian economics in particular. He says that "political economy is not a body of natural laws in the true sense, or of universal and immutable truths, but an assemblage of speculation and doctrines which are the result of a particular history, colored even by the history and character of its chief writers; that, so far from being of no country, and unchangeable from age to age, it has varied much in different ages and countries and even

[24] Ingram, *op. cit.*, p. 222.

with different expositors in the same age and country." [25]   He believes
that Adam Smith had used historical research in making his generalizations and that to that extent his work was inductive.   He contends that
Smith did not make selfishness a fundamental principle in his theory
and that while Smith's method combined a "vein of unsound a priori
speculation" it was in large measure inductive.   Ricardo, he says, reasoned "entirely from hypothetical laws or principles of nature, and dis-
carding induction not only for the ascertainment of its premises, but
even for the verification of its deductive conclusions" (p. 151).   Leslie
holds that "no branch of philosophical doctrine can be fairly investigated or apprehended apart from its history" (p. 149).   His criticism of
classical doctrine is very sweeping; he writes, "The abstract and a priori
method yields no explanation of the laws determining either the nature,
the amount, or the distribution of wealth . . . the philosophical method
must be historical, and must trace the connection between the economical and other phases of national history" (p. 241).   The nature, the
amount, and the distribution of wealth all reflect profoundly the "entire
state of society" and "the whole history of a nation."   They are all evolutionary in character.   He ends his discussion on the philosophical
method of political economy (Chapter XIV) with the statement that
"the method of political economy must be one which expounds this
evolution" (p. 242).   These views may be challenged but it is difficult
to refute them.

Leslie was also critical of specific theories which bore classical ear-
marks.   He refuted the wages-fund theory as others had done (notably
Longe, Thornton, and Walker).   He denied the possibility of free competition as a regulator or equalizer of wages or profits; this would, then,
make classical cost of production theory untenable as an explanation of
value and price.   He tended to a supply-and-demand theory of value for
both domestic and foreign values, following somewhat J. S. Mill's idea.
However, he did not work out a theory of value per se.   He was apparently more interested in criticizing the unrealities of the Ricardian theory
than in developing his own.

In the field of taxation he was most critical of the taxes which caused
great inequalities.   He advocated abolition of all forms of indirect
taxes and only the use of direct taxes.   In his essays he showed an
acquaintance with statistics when applied to prices in certain European countries, value of precious metals, systems of land tenure, and
movements of labor groups.   His forte was his criticism and his essays
in methodology.   The manuscript which bore his own conception of
political economy was lost by accident in 1872 when he was traveling in

[25] Leslie, op. cit., chap. x, "The Political Economy of Adam Smith," p. 148.

France. He did not live to rewrite it or to complete any major historical or theoretical work. On the basis of his essays and general philosophy one can only speculate on what use he would have made of his fine talents and background in developing a work in political economy.[26]

John Kells Ingram, Arnold Toynbee, William Cunningham, and William James Ashley.—Most students of the history of economic thought are familiar with the *History of Political Economy* by John Kells Ingram (1823-1907). The student may be so immersed in the approach used by Ingram as to be unaware that this book, which has for years been regarded as one of the best in the field, follows the pattern of the historical school.[27]

Ingram, like Leslie, was educated at Trinity College, Dublin, and attained a great degree of proficiency in many subjects.[28] He was a friend and associate of Leslie at the University and held essentially the same economic views. Like Leslie he held strong Comtian views, especially that political economy should not be separated from the other social sciences. One of his criticisms of classical economics was that it devoted too much emphasis to a study of wealth, isolated from other social phenomena and that it was too deductive and unhistorical. Ingram was also a sociologist and held a strong conviction that economics belonged in a larger sociological concept and should devote itself to empirical studies of social (including economic) evolution.

These views were strongly enunciated in his address entitled "The Present Position and Prospects of Political Economy," before the Section of Economic Science and Statistics of the British Association for the Advancement of Science in a meeting in Dublin in 1878. He also criticized classical doctrine for unreality, for excessive abstraction and deduction, and for being out of touch with the advance of science and social change. His criticism of classical economics was warmly received in Germany, where his address was published in 1879 with an introduction by von Scheel. Likewise, his views on the proper method of political economy struck a responsive chord among German adherents of the historical method. However, Ingram did not support the Ger-

[26] In addition to his *Essays* he wrote *Land Systems and Industrial Economy of Ireland, England and the Continental Countries* (London, 1870). He had an article on "Financial Reform" in the *Cobden Club Essays* (London, 1871-72).

[27] The *History of Political Economy* (New York, 1888) was a republication from his article in the ninth edition of the *Encyclopaedia Britannica*, Vol. XIX, 1885, new ed., with a chapter by W. A. Scott and introduction by R. T. Ely (1915). In addition he wrote *Outlines of the History of Religion* (London, 1900), *Human Nature and Morals According to Auguste Comte* (London, 1901), and other books on the same general subjects.

[28] Ely says in his Introduction, p. xiv, "Several of his associates after his death said that he was probably the most learned man in the world."

man position that economic laws could not be formulated; he held that evolutionary development could be stated in terms of laws of social change.

Ingram was more of a Comtian than a follower of the Germans in his method. Moreover, he held, from his early years, a strong religious conviction and a genuine desire to promote human welfare. This desire seems to surmount all other considerations in his writings. He was able, however, to maintain balanced objectivity in his *History of Political Economy*. The student today may read the book, fascinated by the scope of its coverage and the elegance of its composition, without being aware that it is one of the classics in the English language written in the historical method.

Another critic of great promise was Arnold Toynbee (1852-1883) whose work was prematurely ended at an early age. He was first a reformer and second an economist; however, he was able to blend his reforms and his economics into an orderly whole. He had a wide grasp of historical facts which he used to good advantage in disproving most of the long-run tendencies in Ricardian economics. Interested as he was in human betterment, he argued that the human lot could be improved within the framework of the current economic and social order. He advocated an extension of government activity into public housing. He was friendly to the trade unions, cooperatives, church movements, and urban social reform. He was a capable lecturer and teacher. While at Balliol College, Oxford, he delivered lectures on industrial problems which presented the whole evolutionary development of capitalistic enterprise and its problems. The lectures were published posthumously under the title of *Lectures on the Industrial Revolution of the Eighteenth Century in England* (London, 1884; new ed., 1908). Not only did he coin the term, "Industrial Revolution," but he gave a new impetus to the study of economic and industrial history.

His method was to show first that writers were influenced materially by their own environment and that schools of thought reflected the setting in which the members found themselves. Next he made use of theory but bolstered it with statistical data to test and to support the theories. He depended upon historical facts, not deductive logic, to support his contentions. He visualized a close coordination between the subjects of history and political economy; history could provide factual bases for theory, and history could be more readily understood when principles of political economy were available for explanatory purposes. His views are indeed intelligible; literature in the two fields now uses the combination so readily that one may wonder why the interrelationship ever was an issue at all. Had Toynbee lived, it is likely that literature in economics would have been further enriched by his writings.

Two English economic historians belong in this group, William Cunningham (1849-1919) and William James Ashley (1860-1927). Cunningham began to teach economic history in Cambridge University in 1878. Because of the lack of an introductory type of book in the field he wrote *The Growth of English Industry and Commerce* (Cambridge, 1882), which was the pioneer work in the field. Cunningham was the first of the long and distinguished line of English economic historians. The edition of 1882 was subsequently expanded to three volumes (5th ed., 1910-12) and is still generally recognized as one of the leading works in the field. Throughout his writings he emphasized the interdependence of economic, industrial, and political history. In his essay on *Western Civilization in its Economic Aspects* (2 vols., Cambridge, 1898, 1900) he emphasized the evolutionary development of civilization instead of following the pattern commonly used in the first work, which regards political changes as the determining causes of economic events. Cunningham was not directly critical of classical doctrines. Rather, he was a historian, and the evolutionary sweep of historical economic research concerned him more than polemics against classical errors.

William J. Ashley has earned a more honored position than Cunningham in the field of economic history. Educated at Balliol College, Oxford, he, like some of the other English economists already mentioned, studied under Sir Henry Maine and Arnold Toynbee. He was very familiar with the writings of the German historical school as a result of study and travel in Germany. He came to the University of Toronto in 1888 and to Harvard in 1892, to hold the first chair of economic history established in any country. He held this chair until 1901. One of his best known works was *An Introduction to English Economic History and Theory* (2 vols., New York, 1888-1893). This book was soon translated into the German, Russian, French, and Japanese languages. He was knighted in 1917 for his work in academic circles and as a public servant.

Ashley escaped a narrowness which was shown by some writers and indicates no prejudice for or against issues, men, or methods. His work reflects eclecticism and balanced scholarship. In the Preface to his *Introduction to English Economic History and Theory* he writes,

. . . two causes, above all others, sometimes working separately, sometimes in conjunction, have gradually modified the character of economic science. These two causes are the growing importance of historical studies and the application to society of the idea of evolution. The first to make itself felt was history: in the hands of Savigny it became the foundation of a new method of jurisprudence, the value of which has been signally illustrated in our own time by Maine; and from the lawyers the historical method passed to the economists. Yet the lessons of Roscher, of Hildebrand, and of Knies, remained for over a quarter of a century unheeded; nor did they begin to carry their due weight until the practical needs of modern life had shown the deficiencies of older economic methods. But meanwhile, the idea of an orderly evolution of society had been slowly making itself felt— an idea which, whether conceived, as by Hegel, as the progressive revelation of spirit, or, as by Comte, as the growth of humanity, or, as by Spencer, as the adaptation of the social organism to its environment, had equally the effect of opening to the economist undreamt-of perspectives of the past and the future.

He further states what he regards as the true principles by which investigation is guided; they are:

(1) Political Economy is not a body of absolutely true doctrines, revealed to the world at the end of the last and the beginning of the present century, but a number of more or less valuable theories and generalizations.

(2) No age, since men began to speculate, has been without its economic ideas. Political Economy was not born fully armed from the brain of Adam Smith or any other thinker: its appearance as an independent science meant only the disentanglement of economic from philosophical and political speculation.

(3) Just as the history of society, in spite of apparent retrogressions, reveals an orderly development, so there has been an orderly development in the history of what men have thought, and therefore in what they have thought concerning the economic side of life.

(4) As modern economists have taken for their assumptions conditions which only in modern times have begun to exist, so earlier economic theories were based, consciously or unconsciously, on conditions then present. Hence the theories of the past must be judged in relation to the facts of the past, and not in relation to those of the present.

(5) History seems to be proving that no great institution has been without its use for a time, and its relative justification. Similarly, it is beginning to appear that no great conception, no great body of doctrines which really influenced society for a long period, was without a certain truth and value, having regard to contemporary circumstances.

(6) Modern economic theories, therefore, are not universally true; they are true neither for the past, when the conditions they postulate did not exist, nor for the future, when, unless society becomes stationary, the conditions will have changed (p. xxi).

He points out that the economists have tended to use the "method of deduction practiced by Ricardo and defended by J. S. Mill and Cairnes"; that "from certain assumptions, such as that man is governed by self-interest, that there is freedom of competition, that labor and capital are transferable . . . and from these they deduce certain hypothetical conclusions . . . and to arrive at an explanation of particular problems." The others proceed by "historical inquiry and observation of actual facts." The historical school objects to "general formulas as to the relations between individuals in a given society, like the 'old' laws of rent, wages and profits." He states that historical scholars want to "discover the laws of social development . . . generalizations as to the stages through which the economic life of society has actually moved. They believe that knowledge like this will not only give them an insight into the past, but will enable them the better to understand the difficulties of the present" (p. xiii).

In his book, he considers the period from the eleventh to the fourteenth century with chapters on the manor and village community, merchant and craft gilds, and finally economic theories and legislation. In the compass of the three chapters he presents many valuable historical materials. The last chapter deals with the influence of the church in economic affairs in the medieval period, Aquinas and the concept of just price, the concept of usury, regulation of weights and measures, regulation of trade, and other issues from the early period in the growth of capitalism. The manner of treatment leaves no doubt concerning Ashley's mastery of historic research.

Summary and Evaluation

The historical school of Germany has been treated at some length mainly because the writers of this school made greater contributions to economics than any other group of German writers. It is an indigenous German product just as classical economics is an English product. The school included a larger number of German writers than produced by any other German school. The situation was different elsewhere. The number of English followers of the historical method was few and never did the movement assume the proportions of a "school." Many critics produced great quantities of criticisms, but each tended to show his own individualism in choosing the vulnerable points for attack. Few writers anywhere have shown a disposition to glorify the past as did the German writers. Nor has the evolutionary development evoked much more than a historical interest in the past. The pragmatic point of view held that the past was of interest if it helped in solving contemporary problems. The Germans carried the same view further; they used the past to explain the whole of social and economic conduct: apparently they had less fear of "the skeleton in the closet" than most peoples. Despite their painstaking efforts, it is doubtful whether their attitude made German life any fuller or its institutions any more responsive and reliable. Probably the net total gains appear in the wealth of literature which covers such a broad sweep of human culture. In this country the

so-called institutional school, subsequently to be discussed, is traceable
directly or indirectly to the German historical school. Today the excitement caused by the institutionalists has subsided and scholars take the
historical method in their stride, using it when they feel a background
is needed, or passing it up. Scholars do not feel the need for historical
method more than for another method. All seek the truth, and any
method is useful only if it leads to the desired end. There are many
items in the scholar's tool kit; any one or all may be needed on different
occasions. Historical method is but a part of the modern scholar's productive machinery; it is not everything in itself; it is but a part of a
larger whole.

17

Socialist Criticism

The literature on socialists, socialism, and socialist criticism probably surpasses quantitatively all other economic materials. Every conceivable shade of emphasis has been developed; there are dozens of books on books dealing with this subject, representing all shades of conviction; there are equally keen critics and defenders of the faith. There are followers with all degrees of enthusiasm from mild indifference to militant revolutionary ardor. Socialism in some form may be found in the earliest records of mankind; throughout all the travail that has beset mankind it has lived and, at times, really flourished. In most nations and at one time or another the tide rose, then ebbed, until today socialism, in one form or another and in greater or lesser degree of emphasis, may be found in every nation of the world. In some nations the issues may not be identified as "socialistic" but as "liberal" or "progressive." Many of the reforms of the Social Democratic parties in European states were introduced within the framework of the established government and caused no especial disturbance. In our own country, many of the issues decried as "socialistic" when they were proposed have long since been made a part of our national political and social economy. The extremes in the nature of sweeping changes in the entire structure appear in the movement in the Scandinavian countries, in Great Britain, and the most extreme of all in the Soviet Union.

The purpose of this chapter is not to write a history of socialism—a task almost approaching the impossible, but to present materials written by men whose work had some part, although small, in shaping the trend of economic thought and doctrines.[1] This task alone appears formidable. At the outset we are confronted with the question of what socialism means. Literature in this general field is filled with definitions, each presented for a different purpose. Indeed there are no greater disagreements to be found than among the self-admitted so-

[1] For details on the men the student is referred to two excellent sources: H. W. Laidler, *Social-Economic Movements* (New York, 1945), and Alexander Gray, *The Socialist Tradition* (New York, 1946).

cialists over the definition of terms. Since the tendency is for each
definer to define for specific purposes, it seems advisable to dodge the
question entirely except to recognize in general terms that socialism demands the abolition of private ownership of much, or all, wealth; that
the wealth transferred from private ownership should in some way be
owned and operated by the community as a whole. Further refinements
beyond these basic fundamentals, while of exceedingly great interest, are
not germane to our purpose here.[2]

It is much easier to decide who, among the socialist writers, are important. Admittedly there can easily be disagreement here, for many
would contend that there is nothing worth while before Marx. Others
hold that the "revisionists," improving as they have on Marx, have the
last word. Still others abandon Marx and any revision of his doctrine
to pattern a national policy of "moderate socialism" from a mold of
their own dimensions. This is the pattern of the modern British state.
Few in its high places would admit intimate acquaintance, certainly not
blood kinship, with Marx or his doctrines.

Yet the vast span of history is replete with the works of men who fall
in the generic group of socialist writers. Just what impact they had in
shaping or directing economic thought is the subject of the following
pages. It may be that the influence of some was negligible at any given
time, but the influence, however small, is cumulative. The same was
found to be true of the critics of classicism, whose criticisms were directed against Smith *et al.* for entirely different reasons. In totality the
criticisms make formidable dents on the citadel, thereby causing new
methods of both defense and attack. It could also be argued that some
socialist criticism completely bypassed the fort and swept on to greater
victories. In any event, this survey briefly examines the generals and
their weapons of attack used on the established order.

Criticism of the established order by the socialists differed in both
aim and objective from that of the critics heretofore presented. Socialist criticism was leveled at the basic wrongs in the social order whatever their origin, not at particular doctrinaire refinements. In fact,
some criticism antedates economic doctrines. The wrongs of the prevailing order were pointed out as they affected the masses of the people.
In few, if any, instances could wrongs be traced to persons purporting
to be economists or to their doctrines, but to a social system which permitted economic practices that led to social and economic wrongs.
Socialist criticism in general, therefore, is much broader in scope than
any other criticism to be found in all economics. It had an aim of

---

[2] See R. H. Blodgett, *Comparative Economic Systems* (New York, 1949), pp. 24 ff.,
for definitions of socialism.

socio-economic reform far more sweeping than anything yet encountered. Criticism thus far called for change or corrections within the framework of existing institutions. Socialist criticism went far beyond this; it would change the structure of hitherto existing institutions and set up a new and purportedly better world. Since the world has been basically more or less a capitalistic world for many hundreds of years, the evils of capitalism would be supplanted by new institutions designed to make it a better place in which to live—at least, so say the socialist critics and reformers.

Early Utopian Writers.—One may find criticism of abuses in the then existing order in the utterances of the prophets of the Old Testament. Amos, Isaiah, and Jeremiah denounced existing conditions and threatened dire consequences for the rulers who were held to be responsible for the suffering. Jesus likewise denounced as evil many of the practices he encountered. He was revolutionary in his teachings, for he talked in terms of a Kingdom of God on earth against which no one could stand. He taught that the abuses of cruel rulers would end and a spirit of love, devotion, service, and self-sacrifice would prevail. There would no longer be rulers and ruled. While his teachings had an ethico-religious bent, they were, nevertheless, revolutionary.

Plato's *Republic* dealt with justice in his ideal state. In this state there would be neither poverty nor riches; civil society would be carefully developed, each person fitting into his proper niche; the rulers would mete out justice to all according to well-ordered plans, "for our object in the construction of the State is the greatest happiness of the whole, and not of any one class; and in a state which is ordered with a view to the good of the whole we think we are most likely to find justice. . . ." [3] Plato conceived of communal relations in family as well as property. His concept of communism was a dictatorship of the aristocratic philosophers, of the elite. His republic was a utopian concept, based on the hope that he might recapture some of the real or imagined glories once prevailing in a city-state undisturbed by world events. No one can find fault with his objectives; however, it was a dream state even in his day. It further appears that his scheme, however appealing it may have been, was not significant as a pattern for state experiments in subsequent years.

One of the first writers to visualize a better world was St. Augustine (354-430) who wrote the *Civitas Dei* (*City of God*, 413-426) after observing the misery caused by oppression and wars. In this work he drew

---

[3] *Republic* (Jowett translation), Bk. IV, p. 243. The entire book is devoted to a discussion of justice and happiness.

a picture of a spiritual realm which he believed to exist beyond the temporal sphere. This realm had contacts with the temporal sphere in the spirits of godly and good men. It was a kingdom of the spirit. Despite the lack of realism of St. Augustine, he was the dominant figure from his own time down to St. Thomas Aquinas and beyond. Aquinas refers to St. Augustine many times in his own writings.

In the Middle Ages many writers expressed views, usually ecclesiastic in their setting, designed to make living more tolerable.[4] St. Thomas Aquinas, whose writings provided standard rules for behavior from the thirteenth to the fifteenth centuries in many elements of economic dealings, sought for more just and fair dealings among men. While St. Thomas was not a socialist, he taught in the Christian tradition of fairness, equality, and brotherly love. Economic abuses and wrongs did prevail which he strove to correct. However, the grave wrongs which appeared concurrent with capitalism were not present in his time.

The first and one of the best of all the books in socialist literature was Sir Thomas More's (1478-1535) *Utopia*. Written originally in Latin in 1515-1516, it was translated into English in 1551 and into German, French, and Italian. It became the prototype for all subsequent writings falling in the generic group known as utopian. In the book Sir Thomas More dealt with the evil conditions prevailing in England and in other European states as well, at the time it was written. He attacked the institution of private property, idleness, waste, conditions of poor tenants, the enclosure system, and, in general, the economic structure of the time. He followed this with a description in Book II of his ideal city-state (somewhat resembling Plato's *Republic*): basically agricultural, everyone a worker (six hours for work, the remainder for rest and cultural betterment), with no idleness, everyone with a voice in government, with the ultimate aim of happiness for all. There would be no superfluous wealth or poverty; all would work for the good of society.

The book was written as a satire and meant as an indictment of contemporary society. The utopia he set up was fantastic, but he had in mind social and industrial reforms that might be adopted in time. It was an ideal state within the framework of pure reason. More took this indirect method of calling to everyone's attention many of the most grievous wrongs and their need for correction. His work touched off an avalanche of writing by writers in the fields of social reform and literature. While most would admit that utopia is unattainable, there are many who maintain that utopia can be reached but only after a long

---

[4] Notably St. Ambrose, St. Basil, St. Clement, and others. See Alexander Gray, *op. cit.*, chap. ii, for detailed treatment; see also H. W. Laidler, *op. cit.*, chap. ii.

journey through semi-utopia. The road maps for the journey are, happily, not a responsibility of this writer.[5]

French Utopian Writers—The Associationists.—The first utopian writers were English; however, forces were at work in France which produced a great harvest of writings. The years of wars and waste brought about by profligate rulers (Louis XIV, 1643-1715; Louis XV, 1715-1774) and the grinding burden of taxes for supporting a corrupt government brought bitter hatred for the whole political setup. In time that resentment erupted in the form of one of the greatest social upheavals of all time. France was, therefore, a fertile ground for almost any doctrine that promised to better the lot of the people. One of the first of the utopian writers was François Babeuf (1764-1797) who taught a doctrine of absolute equality. "The aim of society is the happiness of all, and happiness consists of equality." He opposed private ownership of property and advocated state ownership of all property. He edited *The Tribune of the People*, probably the first communist newspaper ever published, and through this medium he enlisted many thousands of followers. Naturally his ideas ran afoul of the state and his career was ended by the guillotine.

Etienne Cabet (1788-1856) was the author of *The Voyage to Icaria* (1840), a social romance with many fantastic ideas. He was an ardent follower of Robert Owen and spent some time in England in exile. He wrote *The Voyage to Icaria*, when in London, after reading More's *Utopia*. In an effort to prove that his ideas were practical he promoted a band of 1,500 "Icarians" which sailed to America in 1848, to settle a tract of land on the Red River in Texas. Because of internal strife and other difficulties the group never reached Texas but moved instead to Nauvoo, Illinois, the former Mormon settlement. Cabet was unable to hold the group together and it broke up. He died in St. Louis, Missouri. His was one of the early attempts to found a society based upon what he held to be fundamental: equality of all under a communal ownership of property.

Another French utopian was Comte Henri de Saint-Simon (1760-1825). He was an eccentric nobleman who could claim descent from Charlemagne. He served in the French and the American armies, in the latter taking part in the famous siege of Yorktown. Army life did not appeal to him and he devoted himself to political and social reform and revolutionary activity. To this cause he gave all his energies and

---

[5] Francis Bacon's *New Atlantis* (1627), Tommasso Campanella's *City of the Sun* (1623), and James Harrington's *Oceania* (1656) were early works patterned along the same lines as More's book.

forfeited what was then a large fortune. His last years were spent in poverty.

Saint-Simon was not a socialist but a collectivist. He stood for equality of opportunity and abolition of privilege, abolition of class distinctions, and the establishment of industrial equality. He did not advocate abolition of private property but held that the owners of wealth and property must be made to know that their possessions were to be used for the public good. He believed that knowledge and industry should unite to govern the world as, he asserted, had been done in the past by industry and warfare. Peace must be established and knowledge and industry must govern the world and thereby form a new social system based upon universal association. He became a leader of the so-called "associationists."

The curious doctrines attributed to Saint-Simon and his followers became almost a religion. Under the leadership of Enfantin and Bazard the movement reached its peak of development and absurdity. They sought to reduce the extremes of riches and poverty by proposing that industry be transferred from private to public ownership. Each person must work according to his capacity and his reward was to be based on services rendered. Private property would then be confined to consumption goods. Industrial production was to be teamed up with knowledge and administered by knowledge that was rather vaguely defined; there would be leaders, natural leaders, whose abilities would be clearly manifest, somewhat on the *Führerprinzip* of Hitler's Germany. Cooperation would rule. Inheritance would be abolished because it interfered with equality and life would be, in current slang, "a bowl of cherries." It is questionable how influential this sort of comic opera thing known as Saint-Simonism was either in its own time or later. Auguste Comte was purportedly a follower and John Stuart Mill was interested in both Comte and Saint-Simon. Rodbertus and other socialists were at least interested. The gyrations of the Count and his followers, especially Enfantin, make interesting and even exciting reading; but it appears that this "act," though rather original, furnished little either to direct or to divert the trend of socio-economic thought.[6]

Charles Fourier (1772-1837) was a utopian writer who outshone Sir Thomas More in imagination. Fourier who, if not a lunatic, would surely be put in the "lunatic fringe," dreamed the most preposterous of

[6] Saint-Simon wrote the following books with collaboration by his followers. *L'Industrie* (1817-1818), *Le Système Industriel* (1821-1822), *Catéchisme des Industriels* (1823-1824), and *Le Nouveau Christianisme* (1825). It could be argued, but would be hard to prove, that his influence was felt in liberal movements in most European states and in Latin America, especially in a group of intellectuals. Any tie between Saint-Simonism and economic planning under capitalism appears to the writer as extremely remote.

schemes which were so fantastic as to cast some suspicion on those who saw anything of economic value in them. Fourier was not a nobleman like Saint-Simon but one of the common people. Early in life he learned to distrust the accepted business techniques with which he was acquainted and thereafter devoted himself to reform.[7] His success as a practitioner of his own nostrums was nil. The underlying tenet of his social philosophy was an ever-present power in the world to draw men together for united action. This power of attraction assumed social harmony which could be best expressed in a social unit known as a phalanx. The phalanx should consist of 400 to 2,000 citizens who would live on a communal basis, each doing what he was best fitted to do under a division-of-labor arrangement. Productivity per person would increase greatly—in fact, so greatly that a man would produce enough between his eighteenth and twenty-eighth birthdays to permit him to live in comfort and leisure the remainder of his life. Fourier really believed that a sizable surplus would accrue to the unit which could be divided among labor which would get five twelfths; capital, four twelfths; and what he called talent, the remaining three twelfths. There would be no need for an expensive government with all its costly outlays but there would be a capital of the world phalanxes at Constantinople. Eventually the family and marriage would disappear.

The millennium of Fourier had much to offer to the believer. Politically, all that his fantastic ravings accomplished was to point up the waste of capitalistic competition, the hardships of labor, and the possibilities of cooperation. He advocated a "back to the land" type of movement on the strength of an assumption that agriculture was of first importance in production, and that industrial production could then follow.[8] Some of his experiments were tried in France but failed. About 1840, the phalanx idea was brought to the United States; thirty-four experiments were tried, all of which failed.[9] The Brook Farm in Massachusetts was a notable example whose personnel were notably intelligentsia: Margaret Fuller, Nathaniel Hawthorne, and others of the Transcendentalist group. These and other writers made greater contributions to social reform than the experience gained by all the units put together. It is little wonder that the more realistically minded socialists had little use for Fourierism. It appears, however, that there are some who will follow any cause, however fantastic it is.

[7] He wrote *Theory of the Four Movements and the General Destinies* (1808); *The Theory of Universal Unity* (1822); and *The New Industrial and Social World* (1829).

[8] In fact, he believed that poultry raising alone could become so significant that six months of production and sale of hens' eggs would be enough to pay off the entire British national debt. He wrote this in 1829. How unfortunately untrue!

[9] See J. H. Noyes, *History of American Socialism* (Philadelphia, 1870), chap. xi.

Louis Blanc (1813-1882) was the first of the socialist group to attempt reforms by means of political institutions of his own time. Blanc was a member of the Provisional Government of 1848; and in that capacity he demanded that the state set up a Ministry of Labor and Progress. This agency would provide work for everyone unable to find employment elsewhere. That everyone should have the opportunity to work was but a part of his desire to have all given the opportunity for a well-rounded mental, moral, and physical growth. He found that this goal was unattainable under laissez faire, for it leads to murderous competition with resulting want and misery.

To overcome this obstacle, he advocated that work be guaranteed through what he called social workshops, which would be operated to provide employment and to produce what people most needed.[10] Private capital and private producers could come into this arrangement; they were, in fact, encouraged to enter, for in time they would disappear since they could not compete, and a socialistic state would follow. He did not expect all entrants to be equally productive, but unlike his predecessors (Saint-Simon and Babeuf) he believed production would be "from each according to his ability, to each according to his needs." Blanc was an associationist, not a utopian in the strictest sense. He believed people could live and work together under the state, which was to serve as the banker and at first as manager of the cooperative workshop. The idea never had a fair trial, even though an abortive attempt was made by the government. He viewed the state as the regulator of industry, not as an entrepreneur; he had a firm belief that his idea would work, but in practice the problem was more complex than he had thought.

Blanc was more realistic in his thought than most of his predecessors. Although utopian in a very limited sense, he nevertheless believed that reform was near at hand and possible under state guidance. He was certain that, under state guidance, people could find employment and thus be afforded their natural right to work (droit au travail). The fact that he was given a state funeral seems to indicate that his ideas and his efforts were held in rather high esteem. His direct influence on socialist thought, however, seems negligible.

The last, and in some respects the greatest, of the French utopians was Pierre-Joseph Proudhon (1809-1865), who almost defies classification. He was a severe critic of everything: he was an anarchist, at least in his views, a syndicalist, and a revolutionary in general. Nothing of temporal or spiritual institutions escaped his withering criticism; he de-

---

[10] His ideas are found in his *Organisation du travail* (*Organization of Labor*, 1841; 5th ed., 1850).

spised authority regardless of its source or its purpose. What he said and what he wrote were frequently little more than ambiguous phrases defying explanation. Yet, despite all the errors and inconsistencies which may be attributed to him, he did exert a tremendous influence on socialist development.

Proudhon's ultimate aim in life was to bring about justice, a term which had a meaning all its own to him. He bitterly opposed property because it was the root of the evil—injustice. Perhaps inequality would be a more fitting term. He held that all inequalities arose because of the ownership of private property, which made government and authority necessary; since government required a giving up of freedom by the individual, the entire blame for all inequality and injustice rested on private property. This provided the justification for his work, Qu'est-ce la propriété? (What is Property?, 1840). In this he showed the evils of private property and developed the idea of labor time as a measure of value. In discussing private property, the possession of which depends largely upon inheritance, he would not permit it in his ideal scheme of things, for "property is theft." (La propriété, c'est le vol.) What he apparently means is that the use of property brings abuses; the ownership of property means that the owner may exact revenue from others, and this privilege constitutes an abuse. In his ideal scheme the use or productivity of property (mainly land) would be a social return and no longer a monopoly which makes theft possible.

His labor theory of value was arrived at by maintaining that the value of goods was measured by the amount of time and labor required for their production. The capitalist employer, like the landlord, took more than he was entitled to take over bare costs, and even added a percentage to the cost of the goods, thereby robbing society. Proudhon believed he could make the labor theory work by establishing an exchange bank, which would make it possible for workers to get what they desired by exchange of labor time without price. The bank would issue paper notes which could be exchanged for commodities deposited in the bank; it would serve as the exchanging agent only. The notes would then purchase an equivalent amount (in labor) of a desired commodity. He planned to put a progressive tax on salaries of government officials and a tax on property to raise capital for the bank. There would be a central bank and branches would be established throughout France. The rate of interest on loans at the bank was to be low and would ultimately reach zero. The patron of the bank—the laborer— would always get an amount of goods equivalent to what he himself had created by the expenditure of his own labor time; this would constitute complete justice. Needless to say, the scheme, which was tried in 1849, failed.

Proudhon apparently had faith in free association. In his blissful order there would be no state, no master. Yet he was an associationist mainly because he distrusted any utopian plan. He preached "liberty, equality, fraternity," yet he showed distrust of fraternity. He stated, "The highest perfection is found in the union of order and anarchy," [11] yet he was at best (or worst) only a philosophical (nonbomb-throwing) anarchist. He would have no part in the revolution of February, 1848, because he believed that any form of government was bad and wrong no matter who won. Little wonder that he is eligible for enlistment in so many camps.

In 1846 Proudhon wrote *Système des contradictions économiques ou philosophie de la misère (System of Economic Contradictions or the Philosophy of Poverty)*, which was a bitter criticism of socialist and communistic theories. Even though he tore both theories to shreds he presented no constructive plan of his own. Marx attacked Proudhon and at the same time gave expression to his own doctrines in his *Poverty of Philosophy.* This work provided an opportunity for Marx to effect a doctrinal break with Hegelian philosophy. Proudhon's work is entirely negative. He blasted every known institution yet never built anything to take its place. He was really "a bull in the china shop" of established social institutions. As such, he is well remembered.

English Socialists—Robert Owen.—English socialists are treated en bloc largely because they are English. Their thought and their work are not to be regarded as separate and distinct from those of the French, for indeed the tie of utopianism and association bound both French and English reformers. Saint-Simon influenced all shades of economic and political leanings from Robert Owen to J. S. Mill. Indeed, where would one look to find excesses as great as those which came with the Industrial Revolution in England? There the industrial abuses matched or surpassed the political excesses and abuses in France. The pot of criticism which started boiling early in England was stirred vigorously by Robert Owen and others whose influence must be regarded as important as that of the French socialists.

The leading English utopian and associationist was Robert Owen (1771-1858), an industrialist of Welsh birth, who enjoyed a successful business career in both England and Scotland, and who is sometimes known as "the father of English socialism." The strength of his views was so great that he sacrificed many hundreds of thousands of dollars of his own money and a potentially outstanding record as either a businessman or a social reformer, or both. He started out as a successful textile mill operator and an employer who put his reforms into practice;

[11] *Oeuvres complètes* (Paris, 1865-76), Vol. I, p. 214.

yet in the end disappointment tended to make him lose his perspective and consequently the respect of his fellow men. Only in recent years has Owen's heresy been forgiven. Students now recognize that his good works more than offset his errors.

Owen successfully operated a textile mill at New Lanark, Scotland. In this enterprise he introduced advanced reforms affecting employees both within the mill and in their homes and social life. Disappointed that others had not followed his leadership, he came to America in 1824 and bought out a Rappite community of 30,000 acres in Harmony, Indiana, which he renamed New Harmony. The communal experiment failed in three years, as did Owen's money.[12]

The philosophy underlying his efforts was simple: he worked for the happiness of his fellow man.[13] He believed that man is inherently good and that social and economic evils are largely traceable to the capitalistic system. He believed people could be educated to a level which would permit cooperative associations in which all should share in the productivity of others. Competition was not to the best interests of any society and profits should not exist; cost of production should provide the just selling price for goods. Money should be used only to facilitate exchange; it should not be speculated in nor should gold and silver be used as money. He advocated labor notes based upon labor time required for production of goods.

After 1821 Owen's views were completely communistic. He denounced private property and the accumulation of riches as basic causes of unhappiness. Equality alone could eliminate the inequalities arising under capitalism, and he believed association of equals would solve the problem. In the last years of his life he was less inclined to communistic beliefs. Owen's place in the parade of social reformers and critics is difficult to ascertain. His communal associations were failures both in America and in his native land. His criticisms of capitalistic waste and the terrible conditions of employment in English industry and his plea for cooperation in production and distribution of wealth did not fall on deaf ears. He was deeply involved in the legislation which ultimately gave Britain her first effective factory laws, the Factory Act of 1844. His emphasis on land and industry as cooperative agents in production tended to encourage a balanced economy. However, Owen was a prophet of better times which he never lived to see. In time his ideas did have a profound influence in social reform; there is now a tendency

---

[12] See A. E. Bestor, *Backwoods Utopias* (Philadelphia, 1950), for the best account of the New Harmony experiment.

[13] Owen's best known writings were *A New View of Society* (London, 1813-1814); *The Book of the New Moral World* (London, 1820); *Social System* (London, 1821); and *What is Socialism?* (London, 1841).

to credit him with progressive reform measures he tried to accomplish rather than with the ones he did achieve.

Ricardian Socialists.—The English writers to be considered were neither utopians nor Owenites. They were so different from other socialists in England and France that they are frequently treated as simply pre-Marxian; some refer to them as Ricardian socialists. The group had at least one common characteristic—their belief that labor is the standard of value; thus they anticipated the Marxian surplus value theory. They are identified as Ricardian because they held a value theory resting upon Ricardo's concept, namely that the exchange value of a commodity is a result of labor and is measured by the amount of labor necessary to produce the commodity under most favorable methods of production. Likewise, the wage concept of Ricardo was accepted by them as a fact, not as a tendency. They believed wages would not reflect the productivity of the worker, which would, or at least might, increase with every advance in productivity, but that earnings would be ground down to the level of subsistence which would permit "neither increase nor diminution" in the number of workers (cf. Chapter 12, p. 232). These two issues, spoken of by Ricardo as tendencies, were keynotes in the ideology of socialist theory. The extent to which they have been used and also modified by later theory will appear in the following pages.

Charles Hall (c. 1745-c. 1825) held views that made him a defender of the poor against the privileged minority. He saw a gradually widening gap between the rich and the poor and blamed inequalities in the possession of wealth for all injustice, war, misery, and suffering. His views, set forth in his one book *The Effects of Civilization* (London, 1805), pointed up what he saw as a practicing physician. His solution for the struggles that arise because of the extremes in the distribution of wealth was the nationalization of land. By making agriculture a basic industry, all the evils resulting from the factory system, which made the poor poorer and more dependent on the owners of capital, would be removed. Man could then claim the products of his own labor. Hall would permit only limited manufacturing and that only if it contributed to a vaguely defined "human happiness." He saw in his professional capacity the extremes of poverty; and the causes, obviously partially true, were explained with the same deep sincerity as were the cures he proposed.

William Thompson (1785-1833) was a far more significant figure in early socialist literature than Hall. He wrote *An Inquiry into the Principles of the Distribution of Wealth Most Conducive to Human Happiness* (London, 1824), and *Labour Rewarded* (London, 1827), the latter being a reply to the English socialist Thomas Hodgskin's work, *Labour Defended.* In the first book Thompson showed strong utilitarian leanings in his interpretation of Ricardo's economics. The concept of "greatest happiness to the greatest number" as the aim of human endeavor was the starting point in his economics. He held that labor is "the sole parent of wealth." [14] With labor as the only source of value, Thompson held that the worker should receive the whole of his product, which he could not get in a capitalist society because the owner of the capital took a share. He admitted that capital used in production enhanced the value of the goods produced but he objected to the capitalist's taking the surplus value; he was really toying with a surplus value theory later to be refined by Marx. He also implied "capitalist accumulation," or an accumulation of wealth in the hands of the owners of capital who could keep the surplus at the expense of the less fortunate working class which produced it. Although his criticism of capitalism was cogent, his ideas of social reform were not clearly developed. He agreed with Owen's belief that cooperation would solve the problems. This was his thesis in *Labour Rewarded,* which was somewhat of a criticism of Hodgskin who would not permit interest or profit to accrue to anyone. Thompson defended capital as an agent in production and its owner, the capitalist, and admitted each was necessary. The solution rested upon cooperative arrangements, with the capitalist doing most of the cooperating.

Thomas Hodgskin (1787-1869) was a pre-eminent forerunner of Marx. In 1825 he wrote *Labour Defended against the Claims of Capital.* He really was defending the organization of workers provided they had as their aim the recapture of what had been taken from them by the capitalists. He held that capital is unproductive; fixed capital is but a form of stored-up labor whereas circulating capital is "coexisting labor." The capitalist, as the person between the laborer and his product, takes something to which he is not entitled. He adhered to the Ricardian wage theory, which held no hope for wage advances under capitalism. Hodgskin saw the capitalist in a position where he could exact from labor a heavy toll of all that it produced. It seems that he did exert considerable influence; however, his arguments never quite prevailed. It remained for a keener analyst to weld them into basic socialist doctrine.

John Gray (c. 1799-c. 1850) wrote in 1825 his one work, *A Lecture on Human Happiness,* in which he quoted Adam Smith's famous phrase, "man's propensity to truck and barter." Gray held that the propensity is to exchange labor for labor. He regarded labor as the sole producer of wealth and then contended that, under the then existing system,

[14] *Inquiry into the Principles of the Distribution of Wealth,* pp. 6-7.

the laborer got but a small part of what he produced. He denounced as parasitic all those who do not labor but collect incomes in the form of rent, interest, and profits. He believed that the laborer could never improve his position so long as the contemporary exploitive system prevailed.

Another English socialist who closely approached Marxian premises was John Francis Bray (c. 1809-1895). Little is known of this man, but his one book, *Labour's Wrongs and Labour's Remedy* (London, 1839), gives the impression that he embraced ideas similar to those of many socialist writers, as well as those of Marx. He showed utilitarian leanings, as did most of the English writers, but in addition he was akin to Owen—and even Godwin—in attributing man's behavior mainly to the influence of his environment. He held a doctrine of equality which would not permit the accumulation of private property and believed that all who labor should receive a reward equal to the labor time they expended. Unjust exchange was the cause of social evils. He would make all economic dealings rest upon a universal exchange arrangement which could be expedited through paper money issued by labor groups or trade unions. In the end, he saw a society of many exchange units, all producing, exchanging, and laboring for one another. Bray's work had more unreal than real elements in it, yet it, like the others, added grist to the socialist mill.

These brief sketches of the ideas of the early English socialists indicate common points of criticism and, to some extent, common measures of reform. They drew upon Ricardo's value theory to prove labor was the sole producer of wealth and the cause of value, and also upon his "iron law of wages" to prove that wages could never rise above subsistence level. Their emphasis upon happiness was not Ricardian but the best of Benthamism. They lived and wrote at the time when the factory system was getting started, when laws of a regulatory nature were nonexistent, and when working conditions were at their worst. Many, in addition to the persons mentioned, saw the excesses and protested against them; each critic represented different degrees of criticism and likewise different extremes in the reform measures he advocated. None of the English could be regarded as revolutionaries in the Proudhon sense, nor were they "associationists" à la Fourier. They worked toward a Benthamite ideal of "greatest happiness for the greatest number" but within the existing framework of government, in which significant laws could be changed and new ones enacted. Their attack tended to be focused on the distribution of property with its concurrent evils, rather than upon property per se, which was of course essential to production. While many ideas were held in common by this group, their attack on the basic causes of social inequality was neither sweeping nor forceful. It remained for Marx to give it force and direction.

State Socialism.—Two socialist writers deserve attention before the spotlight is turned on Marx. In Germany, Johann Karl Rodbertus (1805-1875) developed ideas which were asserted (mainly by his German admirers) to have been more penetrating than those of Marx. In contrast to many other socialists, he lived a quiet, inactive life, far away from the battlefront of dynamic socialism. He was a Prussian lawyer turned landlord and master of an estate at Jagetzow (formerly in East Prussia), hence the name Rodbertus von Jagetzow. He spent his life managing his estate and speculating on how he would improve the world in five hundred years; he also served briefly in the Prussian National Assembly in 1848.

Rodbertus' ideas are found in three works, none of which attracted much attention.[15] He followed the Ricardian wage theory and held that wages are never for very long above subsistence levels. Coupled with his wage theory was a belief that national wealth was increasing; therefore, wages being more or less rigidly fixed at a subsistence level, the share of national income devoted to wages would decrease; from this he derived his law of a diminishing wage share. He observed that the number of workers increased as population increased but that, even though the total amount paid in wages would increase, the proportion of the total national income for labor would decrease. Workers' wages would tend to become less and less.

Rodbertus held that production was solely for profit and that all production was a result, directly or indirectly, of labor efforts. This standard socialist doctrine, when joined with his beliefs on diminishing wage share, led him to a theory of crises. All wealth being a product of labor, the laborer with his declining wage share was unable to buy back the products he produced. Markets would be flooded with goods which would bring falling prices and unemployment and, finally, precipitate an economic crisis. To relieve the situation Rodbertus proposed that the state take over; thus he is sometimes regarded as a state socialist. He felt that the root of the evil lay in private ownership of land and capital. Ownership of the means of production (land and capital) would be taken over by the masses who supply the labor, and

---

[15] *Zur Erkenntniss unsrer staatswissenschaftlichen Zustände* (*To a Knowledge of Our Economic Condition*, Neubrandenburg, 1842); *Zur Beleuchtung der Sozial-Frage*, 2 vols. (*To the Illumination of the Social Question*, Berlin, 1875); and *Der Normale Arbeitstag* (*The Normal Work Day*, Berliner Revue, 1871). See also *Schriften von Dr. Karl Rodbertus*, 4 vols. (*Writings of Dr. Karl Rodbertus*, new ed., Berlin, 1899); *Soziale Briefe an von Kirchmann* (Berlin, 1850-51; translated by Julia Franklin as *Overproduction and Crises*, 2d ed., London, 1908).

the entire product would then belong to all. He believed this would come about by a slow evolutionary process which might require five or six centuries.

This theory represented his long-run evolutionary views. In the meantime, however, he believed conditions could be improved by reforms instituted by the state. The state should prescribe the amount of work to be accomplished and the length of the workday. This would tend to equalize labor and at the same time to assure greater exchange in goods, for money would be dispensed with and labor would be paid in certificates indicating the exact amount of work put in and product turned out. These, in turn, would exchange for commodities representing equivalent productivity and time. The scheme would have the effect of fixing prices. He held that this arrangement would preserve the existing equities of landlord and capitalist and bring a much larger return to the laboring masses.

Rodbertus was better educated and more widely read than most of the socialists thus far considered. He knew Smith's *Wealth of Nations* and criticized him for his belief in competition and laissez faire. He used the historical method to disprove Smith's ideas of natural harmony in a primitive state and contended that history shows disharmony and perpetual inequality. He hoped that mankind would bring about improvements in the social system peacefully, for he had a horror of revolution.

Rodbertus' place in the development of socialism is hard to evaluate. He was the high priest of socialism to a group of German followers and his influence on Lassalle was considerable. Rodbertus had a loyal follower in Adolf Wagner, who, nevertheless, disagreed with him on many points. A landlord himself, his theories and practices were quite at variance. He opposed the absolutism of the monarchy and Bismarck, but toward the end of his life he fell in line with the Bismarckian policies, nor would he have anything to do with the "socialists of the chair."

It is apparent that anyone who desired social reforms of some import in his lifetime would not regard Rodbertus' works and ideas very highly. Certainly the dynamic Marx had no patience with doing patchwork on the old regime. Rodbertus really belongs to the advocates of state socialism, and to that cause he made his greatest contribution.[16]

One other remains to be considered under state socialism, yet the classification is not strictly accurate. The greatest enigma, firebrand, orator (or rabble-rouser), and propagandist of all socialists was Fer-

[16] C. Gide and C. Rist have a good discussion of Rodbertus in *History of Economic Doctrines* (2d Eng. ed., New York, 1948), pp. 417-33.

dinand Lassalle (1825-1864). As a socialist, the sincerity of his motives was probably always subject to question. Of Jewish extraction, with a strong flair for the center of attraction, his life was one of revolutionary activity (he was a Marxian revolutionary at the age of 23) and active political agitation, which was ended in a duel.

Lassalle (originally spelled Lassal) was educated in law at Breslau and Berlin. He was, without doubt, a very brilliant person yet his general behavior at times showed a marked lack of balance. His writings, notably *Das System der erworbenen Rechte (The System of Acquired Rights*, Leipzig, 1861), showed very promising scholarship.[17] His scholarly interests soon took a turn in the general direction of socialism and politics. His early acquaintance with Marx and with the *Communist Manifesto* of 1848 started him on an active career as a Marxian, yet he broke with Marx on a few important issues. He carried both Marxian dogma and his own revolutionary ideas directly to the people. His speeches to labor groups were published and usually reflected the Marxian ideology. Since his death in 1864 preceded the publication of *Das Kapital* (1867), he had to learn his Marxism directly from the master; generally he was an apt pupil.

At this time there were many German Workingmen's Associations. It was to these groups that Lassalle made his direct appeals in behalf of social reform. One of these was led by a person named Schulze-Delitzsch, a prominent member of the liberal party, a quasi-philanthropist, economist, and do-gooder. This party and this person are significant because they were stepping-stones for Lassalle. First he spoke to the Association at Leipzig (March 31, 1863) and thus began the organization, *Allgemeiner deutscher Arbeiterverein* (General Association of German Workers), of what was later the great Marxian party known as the German Social Democratic party. Next he used his bitter dislike for Schulze-Delitzsch as an excuse for his book, *Herr Bastiat-Schulze von Delitzsch* in which he vented his hatred for the man and at the same time expressed some of his own economic views, which have become catch phrases in economic literature.

Lassalle accepted Ricardo's wage theory and held that while the worker gets a bare subsistence, the capitalist-employer takes the remainder. In Lassalle's hands this tendency had tremendous propaganda appeal in what he called *das eherne löhngesetz* (the iron, or the brazen, law of wages). It was a combination of Malthusian population pressure which was used by Ricardo as a statement of a tendency; as a theory it held that the supply of and the demand for labor would automatically bring about a subsistence wage by making the supply of labor

[17] *The System of Acquired Rights* was pronounced by the jurist Savigny the ablest legal treatise written since the sixteenth century. (See Laidler, *op. cit.*, p. 225.)

dependent on the products or commodities on which it subsists. Wages would, therefore, never be more than just enough to perpetuate the supply of labor (the race) "without increase or diminution." [18] This had terrific meaning when hurled at workers' groups with the oratorical force which Lassalle could command.[19]

In the same diatribe against Schulze he gave his famous philippic against Senior's abstinence theory. Senior had used the term "abstinence" as a factor in production in place of the term "capital." (Cf. Chapter 13, page 251.) Lassalle found this explanation ridiculous and quite to his liking as proof of the perversity of the capitalists. He says with perfect invective, "The profit of capital is the 'wage of abstinence.' Happy, even priceless expression! Like Indian penitents or pillar saints they stand; on one leg, each on his column, with straining arm and pendulous body and pallid looks, holding a plate towards the people to collect their wages of abstinence. In their midst, towering up above all his fellows, as head penitent and ascetic, the Baron Rothschild! This is the condition of society; how could I ever so much misunderstand it?" [20]

Lassalle and Marx were agreed on the value and wage theories of socialism but they broke on their belief in state activity. Lassalle had opposed the credit unions and cooperative societies proposed to the Workers' Association by Schulze-Delitzsch as being ineffective palliatives. He advocated a working-class organization which would guarantee to the workers their total productivity. In this he would enlist the state as the one agency best fitted for the purpose. He preached to the workers that they were the State and that as such they could and should function. He ridiculed the function of the state as generally held, viz., as a protector of the people, a watch-dog (Nachtwachteridee) as he called it. On this point Marx violently disagreed. Likewise on this point rest the most valid reasons for putting Lassalle in the state socialist group. He did not advocate the overthrow of the Prussian state nor did he ever expect the state "to wither away," as Marx prophesied, once the dictatorship of the proletariat was established. His deviation from the Marxian blueprint may have been due to the fact that he never had a chance to read Das Kapital; therefore how could he know the lines?

Lassalle's contribution was in socialist action, not in socialist theory. He helped make the workingmen's associations vocal. He was the

---

[18] Cf. D. Ricardo, *Principles of Political Economy and Taxation*, chap. v. Also Chapter 12, p. 232.

[19] He is reported usually to have called it *das eherne und grausame Gesetz*—the iron and cruel law. Cf. A. Gray, *op. cit.*, p. 336.

[20] *Herr Bastiat-Schulze von Delitzsch*, p. 121. See also E. Böhm-Bawerk, *Capital and Interest* (London, 1890), p. 276.

founder of the General Association of German Workers, which was represented by units in all the large German cities. From this movement there ultimately developed the Social Democratic party. Lassalle, although credited with founding the party, somehow failed in its leadership. His unorthodox gyrations were not becoming to a real leader in the movement, and his influence was soon eclipsed by the so-called "scientific socialism" of Marx. However, as a coiner of economic phrases, and as a dynamic and gifted propagandist, he had no equal. It appears that he will be remembered more for his utterances than for the larger political impetus he gave to workingmen's groups, or more specifically the German workers' movement.[21]

Scientific Socialism—Karl Marx and Friedrich Engels.[22]—Karl Marx is sometimes given credit for purging the socialist thought and materials of the nonworth-while elements (which previously characterized it) and setting socialist dogma once and for all on a scientific plane second to no other science. Whether he did this or not depends upon the *raconteur* of the story, for indeed Marx means all things to some people and utterly nothing to others. Probably no man in the history of economic thought has had as much written about him, both praiseworthy and critical. There are volumes on "what Marx means" and volumes on what he "did not mean." Then we have criticism of Marx followed by criticism of the critics. His views, in accordance with his own or some others' interpretation, have been used to prove him a devil incarnate or a savior of mankind who founded a religion even more potent than that of Christ or Mohammed. Certainly, many dynamic social forces throughout the world today were conceived in the name of Marx. The brew concocted by Marx has influenced more people (even if it hasn't won more friends) than the combined ideas of all the economists up to his time. Yet the strange fact remains that every idea (a bold statement, yet true) he used in all his writings may be found lurking somewhere along the tortuous paths of economic, political, or social thought.

In this chapter, Marxian theories will be treated as influences in shaping or directing the trend of economic thought. The merits or demerits of Marxian ideological controversies are not a part of this work. Being

[21] The best collection of Lassalle's works is *Gesammelte Reden und Schriften* (*Collected Speeches and Writings,* ed. by Eduard Bernstein, 12 vols., Berlin, 1919-1920). George Meredith used the story of Lassalle's life in his novel, *The Tragic Comedians.* See also Georges Brandes, *Ferdinand Lassalle* (New York, 1911).

[22] Friedrich Engels (1820-1895), the lifelong friend and benefactor of Karl Marx, is treated along with Marx. Their ideas were in complete accord with one another after the two men met in Paris in 1844. After Marx's death in 1883, Engels began the work of editing the second and third volumes of *Capital,* which appeared in 1885 and in 1894.

fully aware that, no matter what one says, it is either too much or too little, let us proceed with our examination of the materials.

Karl Marx [23] lived in an extremely turbulent period in European and especially German history. The Industrial Revolution had more or less run its course in Europe and had left in its wake a vast amount of wealth and poverty. Marx saw two classes as the outcome from the haphazard growth of capitalism—the bourgeoisie and the proletariat. They represented the logical results of unrestrained laissez faire, which caused all the misery heaped upon man by his fellow man. Regardless of the accuracy of his observation, the spread between the classes and

[23] Karl Marx was born in Trèves, near Coblenz in the Rhineland, May 5, 1818. His parents were Jewish but when he was six years old they renounced the Jewish faith and embraced Christianity, probably for two reasons: to escape antisemitism and to be better aligned with a German romantic nationalistic movement. Harold J. Laski remarks that "to the end of his life he remained somewhat of an anti-Semite." He was educated in the local schools where he showed an unusual brilliance. He attended first the University at Bonn for one year, 1835, studying jurisprudence. In 1836 he went to the University of Berlin, where he began his first serious studies and work. Berlin was the great stronghold of Hegelian philosophy, which for a time he embraced in totality. Because of changes in the fundamental views of members of the Berlin faculty, Marx did not get a doctor's degree from Berlin but from the University of Jena in June, 1841. Marx hoped to get a teaching appointment at Bonn with his friend Bauer but it happened that neither received one. Marx then went to Cologne where he became editor of the *Rheinische Zeitung*, a Cologne newspaper of moderately liberal leanings, which was started January 1, 1842, and suppressed by a conservative government in March, 1843. Marx had married a Quakeress, Jenny von Westphalen, the daughter of a privy councillor, and was faced with the problem of making a living—a problem he never solved by his own efforts.

Next Marx went to Paris in October, 1843, to become editor of the Franco-German Yearbooks, but that venture ended after publication of the first issue. One article contributed to the Yearbook led to his meeting and life-long friendship with Friedrich Engels. The Yearbook also furnished Marx the opportunity to throw off the mantle of Hegelian philosophy which had enmeshed him mentally. He criticized Hegel's basic philosophy of the individual and proceeded to make history the center of his own philosophy. Marx also broke with the established concepts of religion, which he held enslaved mankind. For the Yearbook he wrote an article, "Zur Kritik der Hegelschen Rechtsphilosophie" ("Introduction to a Critique of the Hegelian Philosophy of Right"), in which he wrote, "Religion is the sigh of the oppressed creature, the feelings of a heartless world, just as it is the spirit of unspiritual conditions. It is the opium of the people." He not only broke with Hegelian philosophy but he set up a revolutionary doctrine which called for a complete break with the past and an emancipation of the proletariat from reactionary fetters. In Paris he met Proudhon, Cabet, and other leaders of the socialistic movement. His stay in Paris was profitable in that he was seeing and learning socialism firsthand. But the long arm of the Prussian police forced him to leave Paris as an exile. He went to Brussels, where he remained, except for short intervals, until the outbreak of the Revolution of 1848.

In 1847 Marx, who had been friendly for a time at least, with Proudhon, wrote the *Misère de la Philosophie* (*The Poverty of Philosophy*), which was his reply to Proudhon's *Philosophy of Poverty*. In this work Marx severely criticized the ideas of Proudhon, which were semi-utopian and which lacked a full grasp of the evolution-the misery of the workers became powerful weapons for an attack on the existing order. Marx searched the pages of history to find proof of the class struggle and also proof that socialism was the logical end-product. On this latter point he used his Hegelian training to prove one of his first cardinal points. Hegel had taught that everything developed by conflict or by a "clash of opposites." Every condition develops its negation, and the interaction of the two begets a new situation. The new or resulting condition soon has its negation and the struggle continues. Or, every thesis has its antithesis and the clash between them then provides a new synthesis. This, in turn, becomes the new thesis and opposed to it is a new antithesis from which clash again

ary impact of history and of the certainty of the class struggle. This book established Marx's thesis that social evolution and economic revolution were inevitable.

One of the German workers' associations, with numerous branches in the chief European towns, was the League of the Just, organized in 1836. The League held its first congress in London in the summer of 1847. Under the leadership of Engels the League became known as the Communist League, and its second congress was held in London in December, 1847. Marx and Engels were commissioned to prepare a statement of principles and a program for action which were completed and published as the *Communist Manifesto* in January, 1848, just before the outbreak of the revolution in Paris.

Marx was banished from Brussels and went to Paris, where he remained but a short time before going to Cologne in the Rhineland, which was then seething with revolt, and starting a revolutionary paper, the *Neue rheinische Zeitung*. The paper lived less than a year before he was again obliged to leave ahead of the police. He went to Paris in June, 1849, and in July the French again banished him to rural Brittany—a beautiful place to live but no place for a revolutionary. He left there for London where he lived, except for brief intervals, until his death in 1883.

His thirty-four years in London were the most creative years of his life. Much of his working time was spent in research in the British Museum library; as a result he had little contact with labor and liberal leaders in London. He had no regular income and depended upon the regular annual bounties of Engels to keep him and his family from starvation; indeed, they appear to have been at the mere subsistence level most of the time. Marx contributed articles to the *New York Tribune* but income from this source was small and irregular. He sacrificed everything for his work. The painstaking research given to *Das Kapital* (1867) established his scholarship and mastery of materials. He is reported to have had few friends, except Engels, outside his family. He did not trust the revolutionaries then in London, much less the Russians there and especially Bakunin.

His health, which was never very good, broke despite trips to Karlsbad and Algiers. He died March 14, 1883, and was buried in a cemetery at Highgate. The funeral oration was delivered by Engels and attended by eight persons.

For details see Otto Rühle, *Karl Marx, His Life and His Work*, trans. by Eden and Cedar Paul (New York, 1928); H. W. Laidler, *Social Economic Movements* (New York, 1944), chaps. xiii-xvii; Sidney Hook, *Towards the Understanding of Karl Marx* (New York, 1933); Max Beer, *The Life and Teaching of Karl Marx* (London, 1893). The most important writings of Marx were: *Die Heilige Familie* (1844); *Die deutsche Ideologie* (1845); *Misère de la Philosophie* (1847); *Communist Manifesto* (1848); *Der Achtzehnte Brumière* (1852); *Zur Kritik der Politischen Ökonomie* (1859); *Das Kapital* (vol. i, 1867; vols. ii and iii were finished by Engels and published in 1885 and 1894, respectively). In 1904 Karl Kautsky edited a collection of materials known as *Theorien über den Mehrwert*.

comes a further synthesis. For example, in the clash of opposites let us say the conservative element (thesis) has as its antithesis, the radical, —their synthesis being a liberal fusion. Or, the clash of the proletariat with· the bourgeoisie brings a new economic society. Marx held that change was inevitable; capitalism was but a phase of the change. Since change was inevitable neither economic institutions such as private property and capital nor social institutions were permanent. In fact, Marx reputedly had a motto, "de omnibus dubitandum"—"doubt everything."

Marx used the Hegelian dialectic to develop the first of his cardinal principles, the theory of the class struggle. The *Communist Manifesto* (1848) begins with the statement, "The history of all hitherto existing society is the history of class struggles. Freeman and slave, patrician and plebeian, lord and serf, . . . in a word, oppressor and oppressed . . . carried on a fight that each time ended, either in a revolutionary re-constitution of society at large, or in a common ruin of the contending classes." The concept of the "class struggle" is inseparable from his materialistic concept of history. Marx held that all history is but a cruel record of man's efforts to gain material ascendancy. He believed that every conflict rested upon economic issues, which were struggles between those who have and those who do not. These struggles, he believed, were basic in the capitalistic society and the inevitable and absolute reason for international conflicts.[24]

Marx held that capitalism has produced two classes, the bourgeoisie and the proletariat. The former are the owners of capital, who live by exploiting the masses of workers. The latter are the masses of wage earners, who have no property, productive capital, or surplus money funds, but must depend upon selling their productive power to the owners of capital for a wage which is only sufficient to maintain a minimum subsistence level. The petty bourgeoisie, shopkeepers, small manufacturers, peasants, and artisans, constituted a middle class. This group would gradually disappear into the proletariat group in the progress of capitalism. The groups would, therefore, in their struggle for economic power, overthrow the capitalistic system and establish a classless society.

It should be remembered that Marx was arbitrarily setting up two classes which he thought he saw in early times and clothing them with living reality. It was ridiculous then, as it is now, to attempt to prove that society is made up of two groups with antithetical economic interests. That groups should be continually at one another's throats has proved to be historically untrue. Cooperation in its many forms has

24 See M. M. Bober, *Karl Marx's Interpretation of History* (Cambridge, Mass., 1950).

proved much more of a social force than Marx ever imagined. Only those possessed with the zeal of a religious fanatic could believe implicitly in such unreal doctrines, which, however, have been extremely effective for propaganda purposes.

Value Theory.—The second major point in Marxian economics is the value theory. The theory as developed by Marx is Ricardian in origin, which, in turn, was partly borrowed from Smith. McCulloch, Petty, Cantillon, and others also attempted to explain value or price. However, on careful examination, their explanation proved not to be applicable to existing market prices today or even to prices when they wrote, but to the prices which would prevail under assumed conditions. If the assumptions were unreal, then the explanation and conclusions would be worthless. There is nothing wrong in using supply as one factor to explain value or price, but the demand side must not be neglected. The early explanations emphasized the relative abundance or scarcity of the supply of goods which, in most instances, did reflect the high or low cost of their production or procurement. While there were many early writers who gave some attention to the demand for goods, the problems of production far overshadowed those of demand; most goods were in short supply while demand was generally inordinately great. Hence, the most pressing problems were centered around production costs. How to keep them down was always a problem to the early writers, for seemingly each feared that lower production costs in other nations would bring disastrous competition in foreign markets.

When Marx wrote in 1867, the old supply or cost-of-production doctrines of Smith, Ricardo, and J. S. Mill still prevailed. In a few years, however, value as explained by the Austrian economists took the other extreme, with emphasis on demand. Marx followed a traditional, classical pattern by approaching value from the supply or cost-of-production side, but with his own qualifying conditions. All value theory before and after Marx had but one objective, namely, the explanation of price. But Marx's theory of value is not a theory of price; in fact, it is probably anything but a theory which purports to explain the price at which any commodity is sold. It does not explain either the level of prices or why they fluctuate. Since economists and writers on economic subjects have for years been concerned with explanations of price (which is defined as value in terms of money), one may ask what Marx means by his theory of value. If it is not a theory of value, what is it? In reality it is an attempt to explain how labor is exploited under a capitalistic economy of profits. "It is not a theory of value but a theory of capitalistic exploitation." [25]   Little wonder, then, that the theory is so vulnerable and can so easily be proved totally inadequate in explaining market price as it is known in a capitalistic society.

Marx considers value, the consequence of labor, as something apart from price. The orthodox treatment of value and price considers the sum total of the costs of each of the factors of production as the price which the commodity must bring in the long run, otherwise it will not be produced. To Marx "value" means what a commodity is really worth as the result of certain amounts of labor which are directly or indirectly embodied in it. Its value has no direct relation to what price it will bring in a market. The sole basis for value of any commodity is the human labor expended in its production. Value then consists of what man by his labor is able to add to basic materials already supplied in some form by nature.

With this in mind, let us examine first Marx's labor theory of value, then the surplus-value doctrine which is developed from it. He begins his discussion with "the two factors of a commodity," its "use value" and "exchange value," the time-worn concepts used by Aristotle, Smith, and others. The older writers who used the concepts were concerned primarily with exchange value, but use value was regarded as necessary. In other words, value in use was implied or the commodity would not be an object in exchange. Classical economists regarded "value in use" as a qualitative characteristic of the commodity which contributed to the satisfaction of human need or desire. "Exchange value" was regarded as a quantitative relationship of commodities. The concept of the price of goods was built around the "exchange value," whereas "use value" had nothing to do with prices directly. Modern usage makes no significant distinction between them—any qualitative difference being disposed of in the price-quantity relationship. But Marx did not give them the same meaning; his usage should not be confused with the classical meaning of the terms. To him "use value" is very similar to utility as it is commonly thought of. It is the useful aspect or character of anything or the useful material qualities of the commodity. Thus, "Use values become a reality only by use or consumption; they also constitute the substance of all wealth, whatever may be the social form of that wealth." [26]

For Marx, exchange value or value in exchange, which in the orthodox sense was always used to mean what a thing would bring in the market, had no objective price relationship or price-quantity equivalent. Thus

[25] G. D. H. Cole, *What Marx Really Meant* (London, 1934), p. 206.
[26] *Capital*, trans. by E. Untermann (3 vols., Chicago, 1908), Vol. I, pp. 42, 43. All references are to this edition.

he writes, "Exchange value, at first sight, presents itself as a quantitative relation, as the proportion in which values in use of one sort are exchanged for those of another sort, a relation constantly changing with time and place. Hence exchange value appears to be something accidental and purely relative, and consequently an intrinsic value, i.e., an exchange value that is inseparably connected with and inherent in commodities seems a contradiction in terms." [27] When comparing the exchange of a quarter of wheat for Y silk or Z gold, which are all equal to each other, their exchange values are also replaceable by each other; ". . . the valid exchange values of a given commodity express something equal; secondly, exchange value, generally, is only the mode of expression, the phenomenal form, of something contained in it, yet distinguishable from it." When Marx says one unit of X equals one unit of Y, he means that "there exists in equal quantities something common to both" (I, 43). On the next page he states, ". . . exchange values of commodities must be capable of being expressed in terms of something common to them all, of which thing they represent a greater or less quantity." This "common something," it would appear, might be use value, but he eliminates that in the following extract, "As use-values, commodities are, above all, of different qualities, but as exchange values they are merely different quantities, and consequently do not contain an atom of use-value. If then we leave out of consideration the use-values of commodities, they have only one common property left, that of being products of labor." By eliminating qualities of the workers who produced the commodities "there is nothing left but what is common to them all; all are reduced to one and the same sort of labor, human labor in the abstract" (I, 44, 45). He makes this common element—labor power—the value of a good which, as previously stated, is far from a price concept. He asks, "How is the magnitude of the value to be measured?" The answer is "plainly by the quantity of the value-creating substance, the labor contained in the article. . . . The magnitude of the value of any article is the amount of labor socially necessary for its production" (I, 45, 46). "Socially necessary" labor, which is that average amount of labor necessary to create a thing for which there is a demand, does not mean all labor. The mere spending of labor time to produce a commodity does not necessarily give it exchange value, since there must be use value as well. If there is a superfluous amount of labor time spent in producing goods (say linen) which cannot be exchanged in the market, "the effect is the same as if each individual weaver had expended more labor-time upon his particular product than is socially necessary" (I, 120). In other words, either more labor

[27] *Capital*, Vol. I, p. 43.

time has been spent inefficiently than was needed to make the goods, or producers have failed to estimate accurately the effective demand. Finally, if more goods are produced by labor than are needed or demanded, no value will be created. The emphasis is on the demand *for the products* which labor creates, which is not the same demand used in explaining value or price of goods. In fact, one of the cogent criticisms of Marx is his neglect of the influence of demand in value and price analysis and his emphasis upon supply behind which lies the labor-cost emphasis.

Marx would not deny that goods could exchange on the basis of their intrinsic value, but it would always be constant and unrelated to price. This exchange could take place only in an ideal society, such as he would establish, in which social needs played the leading role. His value explanation, then, hinges on a social concept. He expresses it as follows, "In saying that the value of a commodity is determined by the quantity of labor worked up or crystallized in it, we mean the quantity of labor necessary for its production in a given state of society, under certain social average conditions of production, with a given social average intensity, and average skill of the labor employed." [28] In other words, he means the average amount of labor which is necessary to produce a certain commodity. In Volume III of *Capital* the idea is more fully stated: "In the determination of value the question turns around social labor time in general, about the quantity of labor which society in general has at its disposal, and the relative absorption of which by the various products determines, as it were, their respective social weights" (III, 1028).

Furthermore, he makes no issue of quality of labor and holds generally to the quantity or amount of labor needed in production. Consequently, "It is the expenditure of simple labor power, i.e., of the labor power which, on the average, apart from any special development, exists in the organism of every ordinary individual. . . . Skilled labor counts only as simple labor intensified, or rather, as multiplied simple labor, a given quantity of skilled being considered equal to a greater quantity of simple labor" (I, 51). The quality differences thus being ignored, there appears to be only one common element in all labor, namely, the bare fact of being human labor.

It is labor, then, that gives value to commodities; not labor of a special sort but a quantity of labor, resting on or depending upon its duration, determines the value of the commodities produced. Marx says:

. . . that which determines the magnitude of the value of any article is the amount of labor (as already defined) socially necessary, or the labor-time

[28] Karl Marx, *Value, Price and Profit* (Chicago, 1913), p. 62.

socially necessary for its production. . . . Commodities, therefore, in which equal quantities of labor are embodied, or which can be produced in the same time, have the same value. The value of one commodity is to the value of another, as the labor-time necessary for the production of one is to that necessary for the production of the other. As values, all commodities are only definite masses of congealed labor-time (I, 46).

Again he says, "As values, commodities are mere congelations of human labor" (I, 58). In other words, value is homogeneous labor-time; labor can have value only as its efforts, "congealed in a commodity," have value.

In an exchange of goods, then, the homogeneous labor element makes it possible to equate them. Exchange could then take place without money. If money is used in exchange, it serves as a commodity in which the values intrinsic in other commodities may be expressed. He recognizes no intrinsic value in money; it gets its value from the labor power which it embodies. For example, a given amount of gold has a certain value because the producers of that gold have spent a certain amount of labor in a given time period and have consumed (with their families) a certain amount of commodities. Or, the value of the commodities is reflected in the value which is ascribed to the gold. Gold was not regarded as a commodity having both monetary and intrinsic value as is currently held.

It is clear that Marx in the first volume of *Capital* is trying to state a law of value, not a law of price. Labor power, being the embodied element in goods, exchanges for labor power embodied in other goods. The ratio of exchange should be equal, but under capitalistic exploitation Marx finds the ratio is not equal. The value at which goods exchange under capitalism is a long-run "natural" exchange value, which means a sort of long-run average level of value of the commodity around which market (short-run) values would fluctuate. (This corresponds to "normal" and "market value" as currently used.) Thus, the law of value equates embodied labor power. It was not until the third volume of *Capital* came out, twenty-seven years later in 1894, that a distinction was made between value and price. In this he stated that commodities seldom or rarely exchange at their "value," but at a price which may be above or below their value. This injection of price into the picture makes the meaning of value as used by Marx even more confusing. He does not present either a theory of value or a theory of price; in fact, he never says what he means by either value or price. Even Cole, who professed some confidence in knowing what Marx really meant, says that the Marxian theory of value is somewhat unique in not being a theory of prices and adds that "it is doubtful whether in the end it has any point of contact at all with price." [29] Certainly the value theory of Marx, if it may be so called, has little if anything to offer.[30]

The surplus-labor theory rests fundamentally upon the labor-cost or labor-power theory just described. The theory assumes a wage system and an absentee ownership of the capital used in production. The worker presumably does not own the means of production; this fact makes it impossible for him to produce any goods either for his own use or for exchange. The capitalist, who owns the tools of production, offers the worker no more than subsistence wages for his services in production over a given time-period. However, capital and labor produce, over and above the bare subsistence wage paid to the worker, an excess which is the surplus value taken by the capitalist. The worker, producing more value than he receives, is thus exploited by the employer. The amount taken by the employer is his income, which is really the uncompensated labor of the worker. For example, a worker in one day might produce ten units of a commodity; however, his subsistence wage in units might be, let us say, six. Hence the worker is deprived of his full productivity, the difference (four units) being pocketed by the capitalist employer. This is the fundamental injustice in capitalism, according to Marx. Furthermore, it is a characteristic of capitalism. It does not mean that the employer is basically dishonest, but it is the way in which capitalism operates. The employer is just as much a tool of capitalism as is the exploited worker. If the workers' and employers' positions were reversed the results would be the same.

Marx holds that goods exchange in the market at something other than their labor-cost values. From the exchange of goods the capitalist-producer gets a total income made up of two parts: one, the amount necessary to reimburse him for wages paid to the productive worker; and the other, the surplus value. This does not mean that the producer sells the goods for more than they are worth or that the producer pays the worker less than his labor power is worth. He is simply doing what is expected of him under capitalistic production. Marx recognizes that economic forces may cause both wages and prices to fluctuate around a long-run natural return, which would temporarily increase or decrease the surplus value. In this long run the employer makes a surplus-value even though he pays a natural price for wages and receives a natural price for the product. On this point Marx adds,

[29] G. D. H. Cole, op. cit., p. 206.

[30] Böhm-Bawerk says, "No one, with so powerful a mind as Marx, has ever exhibited a logic so continuously and so palpably wrong as he exhibits in the systematic proof of his fundamental doctrine." *Karl Marx and the Close of his System* (London, 1898), p. 152. See also a reply by Rudolph Hilferding, *Böhm-Bawerk's Criticism of Marx* (Glasgow, 192—?).

The value of a commodity is determined by the total quantity of labor contained in it. But part of that quantity of labor is realized in a value, for which an equivalent has been paid in the form of wages, part of it is realized in a value for which no equivalent has been paid. Part of the labor contained in the commodity is paid labor; part is unpaid labor. By selling, therefore, the commodity at its value, that is, as the crystallization of the total quantity of labor bestowed upon it, the capitalist must necessarily sell it at a profit. He sells not only what has cost him an equivalent, but he sells also what has cost him nothing, though it has cost him workman labor. The cost of the commodity to the capitalist and its real cost are different things; I repeat, therefore, that normal and average profits are made by selling commodities not above, but at their real values.[31]

The surplus value thus becomes an exploitive return to the capitalist because the whole system itself is exploitive.

The Future of Capitalistic Society.—On the basis of his analysis of the factors, Marx made certain predictions on the future of capitalistic society. He prophesied a succession of crises in capitalism which would become progressively worse with each recurrence. As a result of the damage done by the trade or business cycle, the small capitalists would lose everything to the large capitalists, thus bringing about greater and greater capitalistic accumulations. With each recurring cycle, producers would cut prices on their products in order to dispose of their inordinately great supply. The corollary of falling prices would be falling wages. Thus the workers, who are also consumers, would be unable to buy the goods they had produced.[32] This would further accentuate the misery of the working class, which by now would include most of the petty bourgeoisie, and they would finally rise up and forcibly overthrow the entire exploitive system and set up a dictatorship of the proletariat. This is the end of capitalistic society as forecast by Marx. The Hegelian dialectic will therefore have run a part of its course and the new synthesis will be a better society, or so Marx would have one believe!

Marx arrives at this final stage in his reasoning only by setting up his own assumptions. He makes labor (as he defines it) the sole creator of value by excluding capital, which to him is but congealed labor and not a separate production factor. In his scheme of things the capitalist exploiter is not entitled to what he takes from labor and is, in reality, an enemy of the working class. There is no place for the landlord or any rentier. No provision is made for entrepreneurial rewards nor is there any governmental aid or interference with which to be concerned.

---

[31] *Value, Price and Profit*, pp. 87-88.

[32] Both the theory of the recurring cycle and the theory of a declining wage share are found in the writings of Rodbertus.

Marx held to the Ricardian "iron law of wages," which sets up the hypothesis that under capitalism the tendency is for wages to sink to a bare subsistence level. Interest, being explained as a surplus taken by the capitalist in the exploitive process, is regarded neither as a reward for saving nor as a legitimate return for risk. The explanation of the function of the productive agents is probably the most unsatisfactory part of Marx's work. His conclusions rest upon an arbitrary meaning and use of the production factors. It is an ascribed meaning that was intended to serve the foregone conclusion, namely, the basic contradictions of capitalism and its final and complete demise.

Marx was notoriously careless in defining his terms. The reader is left in a quandary as to whether Marx had in mind a primitive society or a future society; certainly it was not his own contemporary world that he was describing, although his work purported to be a critique of capitalism in his day. The meanings of such ordinary terms as value, price, labor, exchange, and capital are but a few of those which are enshrouded in mystery. Even the admirers and adherents have been unable to agree on what Marx said and what he meant. The lack of agreement on what he meant could only rest on misunderstanding of and disagreement with what he said. Despite the many statements of Marxians that *Capital* is a perfectly lucid book, there is no way of telling for whom or about whom it was written. Authorities seem to agree that he dealt with an abstract world that never did or never could exist. It was a study of a "hypothetical capitalism," to use Dr. Lindsay's term.[33] Then, too, much of the body of Marxian socialism rests upon the teachings in Volume I of 1867; yet the tenets of this volume were not fully explained until after the publication of Volume III in 1894, which in turn cast a different meaning upon much of Volume I. Despite all doctrinal contradictions the work had a terrific impact on economic thought, regardless of whether it was understood or misunderstood.

Marx's value theory rests on assumptions as unreal as any ever propounded. Adam Smith, in a sense, avoided or at least qualified his labor cost theory by making it applicable in "that original state of things" when the whole produce belonged to the producer for he had "neither landlord nor master to share with him." [34] Smith shifted uneasily from a "labor cost" to a "labor command" explanation which Ricardo criticized and then tried to restate. But Ricardo ended up so completely dissatisfied that he hoped "a more able pen" would finally

[33] A. D. Lindsay, *Karl Marx's Capital* (London, 1925), p. 25.
[34] *Wealth of Nations*, ed. E. A. Cannan (2 vols., London, 1904), Bk. I, chap. viii, I, 64. See also David Ricardo, *Principles of Political Economy and Taxation*, chap. i, sec. 1.

work out the correct explanation.[35] Marx believed he had avoided the
errors of the classical writers by giving value a meaning apart from
price. Thus the concepts as well as the problems of "normal price"
and "market price" were avoided. Some emphasis has been placed upon
the Marxian "theory of value" for the reason that it plays such an
important role in so-called Marxian economics. The student is reminded that Marx's purpose was in reality to explain capitalistic exploitation, not pricing under capitalism. The motive and the method
are therefore suspect.

The Accuracy of the Marxian Predictions.—History, upon which Marx
drew so heavily to prove his theses, records the incorrectness of his
prophecies. The history of the development of capitalistic nations has
not been according to the Marxian predictions. It is true that those nations have not had smooth sailing, but few, if any, have cracked up on
Marxian rocks. Wars have proved the great disturbing elements in the
economies of nations since Marx wrote, but he would say they came
as a result of capitalistic imperialism and were explained by the materialistic conception of history. The wars of the twentieth century
have infinitely more complex causes than the development of financial
capitalism and imperialism.

The Russian revolution, which established the present regime in
that country, did not follow the Marxian blueprint very closely. Conditions in Russia, resulting from defeat on the battlefield, provided the
opportunity for a small but desperate minority to seize control. The
conditions for revolution were not as Marx prescribed; there had been
a breakdown of the woefully inadequate forces of production but there
was no lack of homogeneity in the ruling class as Marx had foretold.
Strikes, riots, and mass demonstrations led by dynamic revolutionaries
did prevail.[36] The lack of national leadership after the complete surrender meant a breakdown of authority which led to anarchy and
revolution. Marx never thought that Russia would be the state in
which the socialist revolution would take place. He believed it would
come in the most advanced capitalistic countries and of these, England
or Germany would be the first. Little did he suspect that the least
advanced of the capitalistic nations of the world would be the ones in
which his predictions came nearest being true. His prediction that the
state would "wither away," after the revolution and subsequent temporary dictatorship of the proletariat, is proving altogether untrue in
Russia, where a deeply entrenched bureaucracy of quasi-state socialism

[35] See Chapter 12, pp. 225-26.
[36] See Sidney Hook, *Toward the Understanding of Marx* (New York, 1933), p.
276.

shows no sign of impermanence. It is doubtful that any of the Marxian predictions have been fulfilled. Capitalism, despite its uncertainty of action at times, shows little disposition to "dig its own grave."

The Influence on Subsequent Economic Thought.—It is not possible to cover the entire sweep of Marx's influence on all issues and movements purporting to be Marxian in origin. Socialism, especially the so-called scientific socialism, is the trunk from which many branches have sprung. Communism, also, is Marxian in derivation. Social, economic, and political reforms of many shades may trace some element to the Marxian font. That does not imply that all reforms are inspired by Marx, but there is a tendency for so-called reforms or changes to beget others; in this manner many reforms may be indirectly associated with basic doctrines which are rightly or wrongly associated with Marx. In a real sense, Marx pointed up, in sharp relief, some of the economic extremes which prevailed in all countries. Even if it could be argued that reforms would have come without Marx, the fact remains that he did hasten the changes and create an awareness of prevailing inequalities.

Marx was not an original thinker, although his synthesis was original. It is relatively easy to trace the origins of his fundamental ideas. The influence of Hegel was mentioned earlier. The labor theory of value rests upon a narrow interpretation of some loose sentences from Ricardo which he himself admitted were not right. Ricardo's explanation set up certain qualifications in stating that the value of any commodity is measured by the quantity of labor required in its production. Marx ignored the qualifications and offered an explanation very different from Ricardo's. The surplus value theory may be found in Rodbertus and it was more or less clearly stated by English socialists, such as Bray and especially William Thompson, since the beginning of the nineteenth century. Neither theory has stood the test of criticism; both are out of harmony with the facts and completely inconsistent. Nor does it avail much to point out the inconsistencies and incompleteness in his theories of distribution. These facts make little, if any, difference to the confirmed Marxian. Nor can anything be gained in attempting to refute any of the other dogmas. The materialistic interpretation of history, the theory of capitalistic accumulation, the increasing misery of the masses, and the theory of capitalistic crisis are held to be true by the ardent Marxists not because of historical facts or irrefutable logic but because these doctrines were held by Marx. Socrates was put to death not so much for what he said as for what some people thought he said. Marx has achieved a high degree of immortality not from the irrefutable logic of his utterances but solely from the fact that he uttered them. In the face of this type of entrenched belief any attempt at refutation is conducted at cross purposes.

Despite all the basis errors in what he wrote and espoused, he was in his time, and still remains, the leader of socialist thought and one of the outstanding figures of the nineteenth century. Upon the publication of *Capital* his name, although already well known to liberals, became that of a messiah among the masses of Europe and Russia. The book, written in German, was translated into all languages and never lost its predominant position in the socialist canon. It became the "fire and sword" for both agitating the working classes and uniting them into revolutionary groups, the importance of which could not be overlooked by any state.

Marx was in a real sense more of a historian than an economist, and more a socialist than either historian or economist, yet he drew heavily on all economic, political, and social writers and movements. In the pages of his many works may be found slogans and battlecries which afforded to some both a rallying cause and a propaganda appeal. It mattered little whether his writings were read or understood, the fact remained that he had used the whole sweep of history to prove that the masses were downtrodden and that revolutionary change must follow. With almost dramatic suddenness the "toiling masses" throughout the world were supplied with a complete blueprint of things present and things to come. Their part was to carry out the historic mission. The extent to which it has been carried out in various states of the world is a story of many volumes in itself. Nor is the end in sight. The socialization program in Great Britain and the communization of great land areas in Europe and Asia and elsewhere are but a part of the harvest of the dragon's teeth.

The academic economists of all nations were severely challenged in their beliefs by the rising tide of Marxism. There were some who, like Böhm-Bawerk, risked direct conflict and came out with only a moral victory. Others by-passed the Marxian roadblock completely, or at most gave it only a passing glance and proceeded to their work of explaining the elements of a going capitalistic economy.

In Germany, the so-called historical school re-examined history as did Marx, but they came out with a different answer. Their *Verein für Socialpolitik*, founded in 1872, was formed as the result of a minor intellectual revolution in recognizing pressing social, economic, and political problems which demanded reform. The *Verein*, made up as it was of German academic leaders, was organized not so much because of direct socialist agitation as of the indirect realization that reforms were needed in those areas on which socialism, and ultimately revolution, feeds. These "socialists of the chair" (*Katheder-Socialisten*) stood for gradual reform in nearly every element of the state's functions such as education, taxation, regulation of trade unions, factory working conditions, agrarian laws in the broadest sense, and so on. Just how many reforms in German laws subsequent to 1867 are directly traceable to Marxian doctrines is unascertainable, but certainly their influence was pervasive. The Austrian economists (treated in Chapter 19), while primarily and directly concerned with the development of utility analysis of value and price, were indirectly disproving the labor-cost concept.

In England many elements of socialism were discernible long before Marx; this was likewise true in France and other countries. The groups have been called utopians or pre-Marxians—depending largely upon the writer's choice. The German historical school, as was shown in Chapter 16, had no powerful counterpart in England, nor did Marx have the revolutionary appeal to the English masses that he had in Germany. John Stuart Mill had socialist leanings, and his *Principles of Political Economy* showed some influence of Saint-Simon and Sismondi. In fact, he had planned to write a book on socialism (of which only the first four chapters were completed) neither because of Marx nor in spite of him, for their paths never really crossed. The Chartist movement, which was most active between 1838 and 1850, lost its popular appeal as its members gained more economic concessions and fell far short of a revolutionary movement. The Owenites participated to a greater or less degree in the spread of liberal doctrines and in pressing for social reform laws. Writers such as Cairnes (who followed Mill), Bagehot, Leslie, and others injected social reform ideas into their writings but they did not adopt the Marxian line. These groups, and especially the Fabians (founded in 1884), believed in reform of a gradual or evolutionary type, with no interest in the revolutionary, direct-action type of approach as advocated by Marx. While Owenism passed out of the socialist picture long ago, Fabianism has grown; over the years it has included such well-known persons as Beatrice and Sidney Webb, Graham Wallas, Ramsay MacDonald, G. D. H. Cole, G. B. Shaw, and many others. Just what blood relationship, if any, they would claim to Marx is indeterminable.

Some of the first socialists were Frenchmen. Saint-Simon, Blanc, Proudhon, Fourier, and others gave to that country the advantage of an early start. The world-shattering force of the French Revolution of 1789-1797 had lasting effects. The criticisms of the excesses of private property and the abuses of privilege which brought on the first revolution produced the second revolution of 1848, but that failed to overthrow the state as Marx had hoped and expected. The atmosphere was not friendly to socialism and it is entirely possible to view subsequent French liberalism as a reaction against socialism. Bastiat showed this tendency in his writings; he would out-liberalize the liberals and the socialists, but within the framework of the French capitalistic state. Over the years France, like many other states, has witnessed more or less activity by groups variously known as Socialists (of many shades), Syndicalists, Anarchists, Collectivists, Neo-Marxians, and what not.

The American soil was never as fertile as the European soil for Marxian ideology. Although there were numerous disciples, this country never produced any high priests. Academic writers were generally optimistic in tone and none could clearly visualize a coming revolution. The open frontier tended to keep wages high in the cities, an attraction which encouraged thousands of persons to emigrate to America. Early writers such as Arthur L. Perry [37] and Francis A. Walker showed an acquaintance with Marxian dogma, but only that. Perry shows no evidence of socialistic leanings; Walker urges higher wages lest labor be degraded and brutalized as it was in Europe. Socialist leaders and socialist movements appeared temporarily in the limelight, largely as a result of labor outbreaks which occasionally occurred in major depressions, but upon the return to better times the leaders and the movements tended to lose force. This nation never had the identifiable "classes" of Europe and the American "masses," who never classified themselves as a "proletariat," have aspired to become "bourgeois," wherein they have been pre-eminently successful. Liberal social reforms have been instituted in America to a greater extent and at a lower cost in lives and blood (but not in money) than in any other nation.

The Influence of Socialistic Teachings.—Socialism has had significant beneficial effects on the development of economic thought, directly and indirectly. Liberal movements (usually progressive) have been prevalent in most capitalistic nations during the past hundred years; however, for many reasons there has been an unevenness in their development and it would be a difficult task to attempt to trace the origins of the movements. The fact remains that the governments of most states have secured and then retained power by making or promising liberal reforms. Economic doctrines likewise have been refurbished since Smith wrote, both in spite of and because of Marx. In the course of time the association of much of economic doctrine with certain authors is lost and ideas, once possibly radical, lose their identity. Economists have used what they felt was worth while in Marx and discarded the rest. The same applies to classical doctrines. The great body of economic doctrine has proved to be larger than any one man or group. It has a flexibility which permits change within an existing structure, something

[37] *Elements of Political Economy* (New York, 1873).

which Marxian dogma does not do. Events have to follow the Marxist formula; otherwise, the end cannot be achieved. "Vulgar economics"— as Marx would call it—is really a study of change; the only constant characteristic it has is that it is not fixed and rigid. Some of the changes which have come in the materials of economic thought and in emphasis on these materials are now set forth; they are presented without any assertion of direct relationship to Marx specifically or to socialism generally.

First, the emphasis upon historical growth and interdependence of social institutions removed the metaphysical element from economics. No longer could a "natural law" or "natural order" be made the basis for economic activity. The complexities of social or group action motivated by basic human wants gained ascendancy. This group action, reflected in supply and demand relationships, is used in explaining value and price analysis, personal and social income distribution, as well as the more recent national income analysis. The concept of the "economic man" has yielded to the larger social concept.

A corollary of this is the emphasis upon distributive justice, which has become a problem of both academicians and statesmen. With this are tied the problems created by "capitalistic concentration"—perhaps the truest of the Marxian predictions. Great concentrations of capital have shown tendencies toward monopoly practices which are presumably antisocial; yet in England, where socialization is now running its course, capital concentration has made the problem of socialization easier.

While there have been unmistakable tendencies toward great capital accumulations in the form of large concerns, especially in America, such organizations have been instrumental in producing goods in unprecedented amounts. These concerns have made profits and taken losses as well. It is likewise true that on certain occasions the large concerns have followed practices antithetical to the public interest, but it would be difficult to prove that the entire record of capitalists has been antisocial. The present tendency of government is to expand the control of laws over most business practices. The limits to which government or social control of business may go are unpredictable. In any event, the forces at work tend more toward leveling, rather than creating, extremes of capitalism. The corollary of this is that the Marxian concept of the capitalistic crisis is bound to be inaccurate. So long as policies of national interdependence prevail, the cooperative element, unrecognized by Marx, will tend to mitigate or at least minimize the crisis in any nation. Nations must, to paraphrase Benjamin Franklin, hang together or they shall all hang separately. The weight of the evidence points to international cooperation. In a sense this is socialistic, not Marxian. Cooperation is an extremely dynamic force in domestic as well as in international relations; it rests upon a free choice of free peoples, not a decision of a dictatorship of the proletariat or of a bureaucracy.

Academic economists generally have maintained objectivity in both teaching and writing on subjects involving socialism and the socialistic approach. Courses dealing with the various "isms" are offered in most colleges with few, if any, "bad" results. Academicians and laymen will doubtless continue to criticize or accept Marx in whole or in part as they choose. In any event, Marx as the leading critic of capitalism has forced a re-evaluation both of economic doctrines and of methods of analysis. His rigid adherence to the labor-cost theory of value helped in its demise and probably hastened the refinements of later writers, from Marshall with his equilibrium analysis, to the more recent theory of imperfect competition, and finally to the economics of oligopoly. Joan Robinson[38] has attempted to compare the economic analysis of *Capital* and current academic teaching, with interesting results. She credits Marx with "the elements of a theory of effective demand" which "orthodox economics used to eliminate . . . and to justify the assumption of full employment by appealing to Say's law" (p. 50). She also shows that the "main outline" of the general theory of employment "is clearly to be seen in Marx's analysis of investment" (p. 79). Other comparisons presented by Mrs. Robinson make her brief essay very useful to the student. Most scholars will continue to be eclectic and retain their independence in developing their views. A few will adhere rigidly to the Marxian dialectic and apply its methods to contemporary learning.[39] Others, like Eugene Varga, will continue to outdo Marx and explain the whole of political, economic, and social change as Marxian. Only Varga would attempt to compute the surplus value on American industry from 1899 to 1932.[40]

The influence Marx had on men like R. T. Ely, J. B. Clark, Henry George, Alfred Marshall, and even Thorstein Veblen is not clearly discernible. The productivity theory as used in distribution might owe some refinements to the Marxian emphasis on labor cost; possibly the functions of capital and the rate of interest return may have had theoretical sharpening by Marx's dogma. The theory of crises, which Marx held to be a "disease of the capitalistic system" and a thing which would hasten the end of capitalism, has prompted most penetrating work in the area and pointed up the importance of national income, full em-

[38] *An Essay on Marxian Economics* (London, 1942).

[39] See J. B. S. Haldane's *The Marxist Philosophy and the Sciences* (London, 1939). He applies Marxist principles to mathematics, chemistry, biology, psychology and sociology.

[40] Eugene Varga, *The Great Crisis and its Political Consequences* (London, 1934), pp. 174-75.

ployment, fiscal policy, and so on—measures designed to perpetuate capitalism, not to destroy it. Even if credit should be given to Marx for remotely stimulating economists to write better theories, the stimuli, even as a leavening influence, are long forgotten. It seems that Böhm-Bawerk's last paragraph in his *Karl Marx and the Close of His System* is a fitting one with which to end this section on Marx.

Marx, however, will maintain a permanent place in the history of the social sciences for the same reasons and with the same mixture of positive and negative merits as his prototype Hegel. Both of them were philosophical geniuses. Both of them, each in his own domain, had an enormous influence upon the thought and feeling of whole generations, one might almost say even upon the spirit of the age. The specific theoretical work of each was a most ingeniously conceived structure, built up by a magical power of combination, of numerous storeys of thought, held together by a marvelous mental grasp, but—a house of cards.[41]

[41] P. 221. It is not within the scope of this work to present either the tedious details of the whole of Marxian economics or a refutation of the main arguments. The author's purpose has been to present a brief treatment of the recognized high points and proceed to a discussion of the influence of Marx on the development of economic thought after 1867. Everyone is entitled to the "thrills" of being a "thorough Marxian" or to a "savage delight" in showing the inaccuracies and inconsistencies in Marxian economics. For a thorough and patently fair presentation of the theories and criticisms in great detail see R. H. Blodgett, *Comparative Economic Systems* (1949 ed.), Part II, chaps. xxvi-xxx. Also H. W. B. Joseph, *The Labour Theory of Value in Karl Marx* (London, 1923); G. D. H. Cole, *The Meaning of Marxism* (London, 1948); and Alexander Gray, *The Socialist Tradition* (New York, 1946).

PART V

The Development of Marginal
Utility Economics

18

Early Developments of the Marginal Concept

Utility Theory to Smith and Say.—In the preceding chapters it was shown that value theory or price was generally made to depend on what it cost to produce the commodity in question. Cost was reduced to a labor-time outlay and related to the subsistence level of the laborer. This provided the reasons for thinking that value was inherent in the commodity or that a good had value (use value) simply because it "cost" so much labor to produce it. Plato held such views. Aristotle considered that goods had both use and exchange value. (Cf. Chapter 3.) Both held that exchange should be *fair or just*: a concept of what exchange *ought* to be. The teachings of the ancient philosophers provided a foundation for the "just price" doctrines of the Middle Ages. That goods were to exchange at their "just" price was a cardinal doctrine of Thomas Aquinas; in such an exchange neither party would be injured and equivalent values would be gotten by the exchange. Toward the close of the Middle Ages the doctrine gave way to different methods of pricing in which not only were the costs covered but a profit was made. With the growth of trade and commerce the ethical ideas of long standing were abandoned and prices were set at levels which covered the cost factors.

Although, as has been noted, many early writers gave at least lip service to the fact that the "use" of a good had a significant influence on its value and price, the idea was never fully investigated—possibly because it was believed unimportant—hence, it was never fully understood. The tendency in production was that unwanted goods would not be produced; goods were generally in short supply and the problem was seldom or never one of creating a demand. Instead, the main problem was how to increase the supply. The functions of capital were not clearly understood in the time of the early writers on economic subjects; about the only factor which really demanded a payment was the laborer, who was paid a wage which approximated his subsistence; returns to other factors, including profits, were uncertain. With the growth of capital and capitalistic or machine production, theories and practices changed ma-

399

The Development of Marginal Utility Economics

1630 40 50 60 70 80 90 1700 10 20 30 40 50 60 70 80 90 1800 10 20 30 40 50 60 70 80 90 1900 10 20 30 40

Expressed but undeveloped ideas on utility

x 1632

x 1640 N. Barbon x 1698 x
A Discourse on Trade, 1690

John Locke x 1704 x
Some Considerations, etc., 1691

x 1680 R. Cantillon 1734 x.........x
Essay on the Nature of Commerce in General, 1755

Smith, Malthus, Ricardo, Senior, J. S. Mill and others recognized utility as a characteristic of a good. Total utility concept only.

x 1767 J. B. Say x 1832 x
A Treatise on Political Economy, 1803

x 1802 Mountifort x Longfield 1884 x
Lectures on Political Economy, 1834

x 1795 W. F. Lloyd x 1852 x
Lectures on the Notion of Value, 1837

x 1833 F. Jenkin x 1885 x
Graphic Representation of the Laws of Supply and Demand, 1870

Fully developed marginal utility concept and analysis

"Worth of the Last Atom" x 1810 H. H. Gossen x 1858 x
The Development of the Laws of Exchange, 1854

"Final Degree of Utility" x 1835 W. S. Jevons x 1882 x
Theory of Political Economy, 1871

The Austrian School
"Grenznutzen" x 1840 Carl x Menger 1921 x
"Marginal Utility" *Grundsätze, Principles of Political Economy, 1871*

x 1851 F. von x Wieser 1926 x
The Origin and Leading Principles of Economic Value, 1884
Natural Value, 1889

x 1851 E. von Böhm- xx Bawerk 1914 x
Capital and Interest Theories, trans. as Capital and Interest, 1890
Positive Theory of Capital, 1891

The Lausanne Economists
"Rareté" x 1834 Léon x Walras 1910 x
Elements of Pure Economics, 1874

"Ophélimité" x 1848 Vilfredo Pareto x 1923 x
Course of Political Economy, 1896

"Specific Productivity" x 1847 J. B. Clark x 1938 x
Distribution of Wealth, 1899

terially. Since the cost-of-production explanation has had a long, even though undistinguished, existence in doctrinal development, attention is next directed to the early ideas on use value which preceded the fully developed marginal analysis. (See p. 400.) That is to say, the purpose here is to observe the decline of the labor-cost theory and the development of what was believed to be a more adequate value theory.[1]

It was shown that Aristotle referred to the use and the exchange value of shoes. Aquinas recognized that the usefulness of an article might be greater to one or the other party in an exchange.[2] The old mercantilist Nicholas Barbon (c. 1640-1698) was one of the earliest writers to recognize use or utility of a good. In his book, A *Discourse of Trade* (1690), he wrote:

> The Value of all Wares arise from their Use; Things of no Use, have no Value, as the *English* phrase is, *They are good for nothing*. . . . The Use of Things, are to supply the Wants and Necessities of Man: There are two General Wants that Mankind is born with; the Wants of the Body, and the Wants of the Mind; To supply these two Necessities, all things under the Sun become useful, and therefore have a Value (pp. 13-14).

He recognized both scarcity and use as the main factors in the value of commodities. John Locke (1632-1704), in his work *Some Considerations of the Lowering of the Interest and Raising the Value of Money* (London, 1691), showed that "the vent [sale] of anything depends upon its necessity or usefulness."[3] He recognized the differences between goods which were absolutely essential to life and those less essential, the importance of which, in some cases, would change in time and under different circumstances. The idea of the use or utility of a commodity is clear, however.

Richard Cantillon (1680-1734) had advanced ideas on utility as a factor in value and price. His theory was one of the earliest, if not the earliest, supply-and-demand explanation. He accepted the earlier cost explanation as the factor behind supply, but demand was given an equivalent importance. He made prices rest on "altercations" between the buyers, on the one hand, and the suppliers, on the other. He was very clear in his views on price, making it depend on both demand and supply. However, his concept lacks the necessary analysis of a fully developed equilibrium theory.[4] Adam Smith, as was shown in Chapter

---

[1] Eric Roll, in his *History of Economic Thought* (New York, 1942), very aptly calls it the "Break-up of the Labor Theory."

[2] *Summa Theologica*, Question 77, First article in A. E. Monroe, *Early Economic Thought* (Cambridge, Mass., 1924), p. 53.

[3] *The Works of John Locke* (London, 1823), Vol. V, pp. 30-31.

[4] Both John Law and Turgot held fragmentary ideas that value depended upon utility. Law used the analogy of water and diamonds in a manner similar to that

10, recognized that "the word value . . . has two different meanings, and sometimes expresses the utility of some particular object, and sometimes the power of purchasing other goods which the possession of that object conveys. The one may be called 'value in use,' the other 'value in exchange.'" (*Wealth of Nations*, chap. iv.) He then proceeded with the familiar illustration of the use and the exchange values of diamonds and water. Even though he understood that use is an indispensable quality of a good, he did not make it a factor in determining price but continued with a labor-cost doctrine. Ricardo, building on Smith's fundamentals, did not add to the utility concept. He said, "Possessing utility, commodities derive their exchangeable value from two sources: from their scarcity, and from the quantity of labour required to obtain them." [5] He ends his theory with an admittedly unsatisfactory explanation of labor cost, giving no emphasis to the demand or utility side of the equation. (Cf. Chapter 12.) It was shown in the chapter on socialist criticism that the labor-cost theory of value of Marx and others continued to prevail. We must look to other, sometimes less well-known, names for significant developments. Certainly the so-called classical economists held to the "straight and narrow" cost-of-production-and-supply explanation. Even the few writers already mentioned made so little use of the concept that it was of small consequence as a tool in price analysis. In each case, utility was at best a total-utility concept, with little comprehension of diminishing utility and none of the marginal concept.

A very early writer who used the utility explanation was the Frenchman Abbé Condillac, writing in 1776, who held that value depended upon wants. He said, "A thing does not have value because of its cost, as some suppose; but it costs because it has value." [6] Value is the most important thing in political economy, whereas utility, he believed, expresses the relation of a felt want for a good to the scarcity or abundance of it. He believed that land and capital, as well as labor, are jointly responsible for production of goods and that the value of the goods they produce reflects more than the labor cost alone. The prices of the goods thus produced also result from the joint action of supply and demand. He was unquestionably an early exponent of equilibrium analysis and of subjective economics. He recognized scarcity or abundance of goods as exercising important influence in determining their value or price. He abandoned any concept of intrinsic value and made

---

of Smith. See John Law, *Money and Trade Consider'd; with a Proposal for Supplying the Nation with Money* (Glasgow, 1705; 2d ed., London, 1720).

[5] *Principles of Political Economy and Taxation*, chap. i, p. 6.

[6] E. B. de Condillac, *Le Commerce et le gouvernement considérés relativement l'un à l'autre* (1776), Part I, chap. i.

value rest on the use or utility of the commodity as related to a felt need for it. This idea was far advanced and certainly akin to the refinements which were developed almost 100 years later. Although Condillac lived and wrote in the late physiocratic period and held some of the views of that group, his ideas were generally in advance of most of the physiocratic doctrines.[7]

It is probably true that Jean Baptiste Say (1767-1832) was indebted to Condillac for some of the ideas which he used to supplement Smith's doctrines. He disagreed with Smith in making labor the cause of value. Say contends that Smith "drew a false conclusion that all values represent pre-exerted human labour or industry, either recent or remote." [8] It was pointed out (Chapter 14) that Say made progress toward an equilibrium, supply-and-demand analysis. He criticized the labor-cost theory, and declared "the desire of an object, and consequently its value, originates in utility" (p. 287). His well-known "Say's Law" made demand and supply mutually determining. He clearly emphasized utility as a determinant of value. While Say did not contribute significantly to utility analysis as such, he broke with his preceptors on the labor theory and moved toward establishing an equilibrium analysis.

Marginal Analysis in England Before Jevons.—An English writer, Lord Lauderdale (see Chapter 15), not only severely criticized Smith's work but made some very cogent observations on a value theory in which utility and scarcity were coordinate factors. He criticized Smith's theory which made labor an accurate measure of value, and he contended that value rests on a supply-and-demand relationship—"the value of everything is so completely dependent upon the proportion betwixt the demand for it and the quantity of it." [9] He listed eight causes of changes in value of which the four main ones are: a diminution in its quantity, an increase in its quantity, an increase in demand, and a diminution of demand (p. 58). He made considerable progress in showing the influence of demand on price, even presenting ideas on elasticity of demand, but he failed to give a clear explanation of the utility concept. Lauderdale came nearer to presenting a supply-and-demand equilibrium analysis than to an explanation of utility as the factor determining demand.

In Chapter 13 it was pointed out that N. W. Senior, the first occupant of the Drummond Chair of Political Economy at Oxford, lectured on

[7] Gide and Rist write, "It is possible that Turgot inspired Condillac and that he himself owed his inspiration to Galiani." A History of Economic Doctrines (2d Eng. ed., New York, 1948), pp. 64-68.

[8] Treatise on Political Economy, Prinsep translation, chap. iv, p. 76.

[9] An Inquiry into the Nature and Origin of Public Wealth (Edinburgh, 1804), p. 15.

many economic subjects, including value. He held the view that utility
is a necessary attribute of value but that limitation of supply, or relative
scarcity, is of greater importance than utility. While Senior recognized that utility is important in explaining value, he did not develop
it into a theory. It may be said with considerable accuracy that his
explanation of value was an equilibrium theory, but the emphasis was
overbalanced on the supply side. The same may be said about the
theory developed by Malthus and, in a limited sense, of all the classical
group. None of this group did more than recognize utility as an attribute which gave value to a commodity.

The successor to Senior at Oxford was Richard Whately (1787-1863),
who held the chair from 1830 to 1831, after which he became Anglican
Archbishop of Dublin. Most of his writings dealt with religion; however, his only work in political economy, *Introductory Lectures on Political Economy*, has some worth-while ideas on utility. In Lecture II
he presented his objections to the current practice of making wealth
the subject of political economy, and proposed that the term "catallac-
tics" or the "science of exchanges" more nearly describes the subject
matter than does political economy. While his lectures have a strong
ecclesiastical and moral bias, he did manage to incorporate much economics in them, although he failed to establish any principles of economics. He did not present a theory of value, and though it is reasonably certain that he understood utility, he treated it, like wealth, as
subjective and entirely relative. These points he illustrated by examples
selected from the practices of various tribal groups, as well as by current
examples. He did not hold to a labor-cost theory but he did emphasize
the subjective side of value enough to prove that he understood utility;
his explanation—such as it was—fell short of any clearly definable
theory. His interest in political economy, as is evidenced by the lectures, was not in developing a body of doctrines, but in a semireligious
presentation of materials associated with political economy. His
familiarity with the importance of utility may be seen from the famous
quotation: "It is not that pearls fetch a high price because men dived
for them; but on the contrary, men dive for them because they fetch
a high price." [10]

Whately, after becoming Archbishop of Dublin, founded and endowed a Chair of Political Economy in Trinity College, Dublin, similar
in requirements to the Drummond Chair at Oxford. The first occupant,
Mountifort Longfield (1802-1884), was appointed in 1832 and subsequently published the lectures given in 1833. These lectures are vastly
superior in their content to those delivered by Whately. In Lecture II

[10] *Introductory Lectures on Political Economy* (London, 1831), p. 253.

Longfield defined political economy as "the science which teaches the laws that regulate the production, accumulation, consumption and distribution of wealth." He then discussed the implications of the meaning of the term "wealth" and the impossibility of defining the term. In this lecture he dealt with value. He referred to Smith's "value in use and value in exchange" and identified "use" with "utility," defining the latter as "the power which an article has in satisfying one or more of the various wants or desires of mankind."[11] Value he defined as "the power of [a good] being exchanged for other goods." Like many of his predecessors, he declared, "It is plain that without some utility a thing can have no value, since nobody would give any thing or bestow any labour for that which would not satisfy any want or wish" (p. 26). He insisted, however, that "all the materials of wealth must be both useful and valuable; but it is with their value, not their utility, that the elements of Political Economy are principally conversant, in so much that it has been called the science of values, or the science of exchanges" (p. 26). Further on he stated that the "science may be divided into two branches of theoretical and practical Political Economy. The former is conversant about value, the latter about utility" (p. 27). All exchange has "some utility"; and if not, exchange will not take place. "When an exchange is made therefore it may be fairly presumed that each party to it has gained something, by receiving for the article he disposed of something . . . which is, *relative to him*, of more utility . . ." (p. 28).

In discussing what constitutes an adequate measure of value he writes, "The most unsatisfactory reasons have been given to shew not only that labour is (as it undoubtedly is) the best, but also that it is the only real measure of value, which undoubtedly it is not" (p. 29). After pointing out the limitations of labor as a measure of value, he finally came to the conclusion that "labour is the best measure of value, because it admits of being directly applied to or compared with every other important commodity whose value we desire to learn" (p. 32). He admitted that there are exceptions but considered them of little importance. In actual exchange of goods he identified both market price and natural value, or "the production price," as he calls it (p. 36). Likewise, price is said to depend "upon the proportion between supply and effective demand" (p. 37). The long-run influence of demand and supply is seen in the following quotation: "Besides the adjustment between supply and demand, the cost of production or natural value of any commodity always exercises a very considerable influence upon its price. The cost of production regulates the supply, and keeps it pretty nearly

[11] *Lectures on Political Economy* (Dublin, 1834), p. 25.

in that proportion to the demand which may produce a conformity between the exchangeable and the natural value" (p. 47).

Longfield came near to developing a marginal concept in Lecture VI. He restates his former thesis that "price is regulated by the demand and the supply, and will be such a sum as is sufficient to produce an equality between the supply and the effectual demand" (p. 111). Behind supply is cost of production, and behind demand is utility. Thus, "The measure of the intensity of any person's demand for any commodity is the amount which he would be willing and able to give for it, rather than remain without it . . ." (p. 111). "Market price," he states, "is measured by that demand, which being of the least intensity, yet leads to actual purchases" (p. 113). He argued that "each individual contains as it were within himself, a series of demands of successively increasing degrees of intensity; that the lowest degree of that series which at any time leads to a purchase . . . is that which regulates the market price . . ." (p. 115). He came close to stating a marginal price when he said that if prices are moved "one degree" above the market price, "the demanders, who by the change will cease to be purchasers, must be those the intensity of whose demand was precisely measured by the former price" (p. 113). While no precise marginal analysis is claimed for Longfield, his views were both accurate and to the point.

The marginal productivity of labor is inherent in his wage analysis and also in his interest theory. Lecture IX, which dealt with capital and interest, contains some pointed statements which carry strong marginal productivity connotations. Thus, in speaking of labor and capital when used in production, he writes, "The sum which can be paid for the use of any machine has its greatest limit determined by its efficiency in assisting the operations of the labourer, while its lesser limit is determined by the efficiency of that capital which without imprudence is employed in the least efficient manner" (p. 188). Should the supply of capital instruments be increased, additional laborers must be employed to use the capital and the "rate of profits must be determined by those cases in which the efficiency of capital is the least" (p. 192). In Lecture X he made wages depend upon supply and demand; the former is the "existing race of labourers" (p. 209); the latter depends upon "the utility or value of the work which they [the labourers] are capable of performing" (p. 210). He contended that the "labourer must earn certain wages according to his real or imaginary wants" (p. 204) but that the "wages of the labourer depend upon the value of his labour, and not upon his wants, whether natural or acquired" (p. 206).

Enough has been presented to show that Longfield was an extremely keen analyst and an early expositor of utility and marginal productivity doctrine. While the general overtones are those of Smith and classical doctrines, his value analysis and his ideas on distribution are much more penetrating. The eleven lectures were not intended to encompass the whole of economic science, but within the limits which he prescribed for the lectures they are extremely well developed and deserve careful reading. Certainly his thoughts on utility and value show advanced and original contributions.[12]

William Forster Lloyd (1795-1852) was Whately's successor to the Drummond Chair of Political Economy at Oxford from 1832-1837. His best-known lecture and the one which shows his originality in utility and value analysis is entitled, *Lecture on the Notion of Value, as Distinguishable not only from Utility but Also from Value in Exchange*, 1833.[13]

Lloyd had clear views on both value and diminishing utility. He showed that the wants of primitive peoples were quickly satisfied but that advanced civilizations have insatiable wants which make it possible for wealth to accumulate and ultimately become the sole objective of society. Even though there is no assignable limit to human wants, yet an increase in the supply of one specific object, will bring satisfaction to a point where the value of the object will vanish. He explains what happens to utility and value as the supply is increased as follows: "We have come to the conclusion that an increase of quantity will at length exhaust, or satisfy to the utmost, the demand for any specific object of desire. Having reached this point, let us now inquire, what happens with respect to value, at the time when the demand or want is thus fully satisfied? It will be found that, in the case of every commodity, its value vanishes at the very instant of satisfaction." [14]

Lloyd was certainly one of the first persons, if not the first, to use marginal analysis in explaining the relation between utility and value in exchange. Likewise, he was one of the first to use the principle commonly known as diminishing utility. He used a familiar example of a hungry man and bread and showed that with only one ounce its importance to the consumer is extremely great; but if a second and a third ounce are available, the importance of each successive ounce becomes less than that of the preceding one. "Thus while he is scantily supplied with food, he holds a given portion of it in great esteem—in other words, he sets great value on it; when his supply is increased, his esteem for a given quantity is lessened, or, in other words, he sets a

---

[12] See E. R. A. Seligman, "On Some Neglected British Economists," *Economic Journal*, XIII (1903), pp. 46-54.

[13] Published in 1837; reprinted in *Economic History*, Vol. I (London, 1926-1929), pp. 168-83.

[14] *Economic History*, Vol. I, pp. 171-72.

less value on it." [15]　Although he did not use the terms "marginal" and "total" utility, he clearly distinguished between them and showed that value is in proportion to the intensity of desire for the last unit of a commodity.

Lloyd, like Lauderdale, recognized that elasticity of demand for goods varies.　He illustrates this by the analogy of a coiled spring: the tighter the coil, the greater the utility.　For example, the smaller the harvest, the greater the spring tension; the larger the harvest, the weaker the spring.　His value theory, so abundantly and ably illustrated by both examples and analogies, was very far advanced.　The extent to which his ideas were original has been questioned by Miss Bowley, who holds that some of his views were taken from Senior.[16]　It is entirely possible that Lloyd did make some use of Senior's ideas on utility without repeating the statements.　The ideas on utility in connection with value explanations were fairly prevalent and not the monopoly of any one person. It is perfectly safe to regard Lloyd's ideas as being in the marginal pattern which was then developing.[17]

The persons discussed thus far made significant contributions to the development of marginal analysis, but their contributions, like their names, are less well known than those of some others whose views have gained wider acceptance.　Even though "discovered" in relatively recent years, their ideas were original and generally similar to later developments.　Of the better known writers, Senior used utility to good advantage in his value theory, but he failed to develop the concept as such. John Stuart Mill gave some attention to utility "as the estimation of the purchaser," [18] but he made no significant use of the concept as an influencing factor behind demand.　The same is true of J. B. Say, who broke with the labor theory of value and placed greater emphasis on utility than did his contemporaries or predecessors.　He came close to developing an equilibrium theory of value, but fell short of his objective. Cantillon, Law, Locke, Condillac, and others more or less toyed with the concept but all failed to see in it anything other than an attribute of a good which was essential to its value.

Before considering the "big three" (Jevons, Menger and Walras) of early marginal utility development, attention should be given to a Scottish professor of engineering at the University of Edinburgh, named

[15] *Ibid.*, p. 172.

[16] Marian Bowley, *Nassau Senior and Classical Economics* (London, 1937), p. 108.

[17] Professor Seligman states, "It will come as a surprise to many to be informed that the theory of marginal utility is, after all, an English discovery, and that what is a virtually identical doctrine was advanced by Professor Lloyd in 1834, a decade before Dupuit, two decades before Gossen, and considerably more than a generation before its rediscovery by Jevons, Menger and Walras." *Op. cit.*, p. 25.

[18] *Principles of Political Economy*, Bk. III, chap. ii.

Fleeming Jenkin (1833-1885). His interest was in demand and supply as they exist in the market, not in any psychological attributes of consumption or in problems of production. His book *The Graphic Representation of the Laws of Supply and Demand, and their Application to Labor* (Edinburgh, 1870), was a clear attempt to show the relationships existing among supply, demand, and price, and how the relationships change with either an increase or a decrease in any of them. He used graphic means to show the relationships; the only difference between his method and the method currently in use is that he used the vertical scale to show quantities and the horizontal scale to show prices. He held that the market price of a commodity at a given time would be at the point of intersection of the supply and demand curves.[19] Jenkin followed Cournot more closely than he did Jevons in that he was not interested in the psychological aspects, or for that matter in the cost aspects, of value analysis. He believed, however, that the long-run tendency would make the price of an article tend to be its cost of production and the quantity demanded would be determined mainly by the demand at that price (*op. cit.*, p. 89). His long-run cost of production would include a necessary or normal profit for the producer. Jenkin's work, especially his graphic presentation, was suggestive, but nothing came of it. He was one of several whose ideas bore little fruit.[20]

The Contribution of Gossen.—A writer whose early work in theory anticipated fully developed marginalism was Hermann Heinrich Gossen (1810-1858). This German worked out his ideas independently and published them in a work entitled, *Entwicklung der Gesetze des menschlichen Verkehrs und der daraus fliessenden Regeln für menschliches Handeln* (*The Development of the Laws of Exchange among Men and of the Consequent Rules of Human Action,* 1854). The book received little attention when published. After four years the disappointed author had it withdrawn and ordered it to be destroyed. However, a copy was found in 1878 in a German bookseller's catalog by Professor Adamson of Manchester who succeeded in purchasing it. Jevons called the book to the attention of students of economics in the preface to the second edition of his *Theory of Political Economy* (1879), in which he said Gossen had "completely anticipated him as regards the general principles and methods of economics." Gossen's work was reprinted in German in 1889 but it has not been translated.

[19] See Fleeming Jenkin, *The Graphic Representation of the Laws of Supply and Demand, and their Application to Labor* (1868-1884), London School of Economics, Reprints of Scarce Tracts, No. 9 (London, 1931), pp. 76-93.

[20] Jevons mentions Jenkin in *The Theory of Political Economy* (4th ed.; London, 1911), p. 333; but that is about all. Marshall refers to him only in a footnote. *Principles of Economics* (London, 1890), p. 455.

The hopeful Gossen believed that he had made a discovery, which would have results in the social sciences comparable to the work of Copernicus in developing the physical laws of the universe. He believed that the confusion which existed in economic doctrines was due to the absence of precise, mathematical measurements. He set out with the purpose of reducing the consequences of economic forces to mathematical exactness. Although exact measurements were not then possible, he believed that it would be feasible, by use of geometry and mathematics, to measure unknown quantities in economics just as science is able to measure distances in astronomy. Thus he was one of the first to try to adapt economics to mathematical computations.[21]

Gossen was influenced by Bentham, but the final ideas which he developed were distinctly his own. His main contribution to economics was an explanation of what later became known as the principle of marginal utility and of its application to value and price. He started with the assumption that the aim of human conduct is to maximize pleasure and minimize pain (used in the sense of sacrifice or disutility). Simple, two-dimensional diagrams and algebraic formulas are used to show the relations between utility and disutility. On the basis of his fundamental assumption, he arrived at generalizations or principles which have become known as the "Three Laws of Gossen." The first law, which is a clear statement of the principle of diminishing utility, is that the amount of satisfaction derived from the consumption of a good decreases with each additional unit of the same commodity until the point of satiety is reached. The second law, briefly stated, is that the individual must endeavor to keep the marginal utility of goods equal if he is to attain maximum satisfaction. If it is not possible for the individual to satisfy all wants to the point of zero satiety, then it is necessary for him to discontinue consumption (and by implication, satisfaction) at the point where the intensity of the desires for, and the enjoyment from consumption of, different goods is equal. Or, since it is impossible to satisfy all wants fully, the individual will maximize utility at the point where the satisfactions derived from the use of the last unit of each good are equal. If money is used, then the individual is to spend it in such a way that the amounts paid for different goods bring to the spender equal satisfactions. The third law, which is derived from

[21] A French engineer, A. J. E. Dupuit (1804-1866), was the first person to draw supply and demand curves similar to those at present used in economics. He was also the first to conclude that, as prices fall with a decrease in demand, those who would have paid more than the price they are finally obliged to pay, gain in the exchange. This is the "consumers' surplus" of Alfred Marshall. See W. S. Jevons, *The Theory of Political Economy* (2d ed., 1879), p. xxxviii.

the first and second, states that subjective (use) value attaches to a good only when the supply of the good is smaller than the quantity demanded. As more units are supplied, the subjective value of the additional units approaches zero. The entire analysis rests on a hedonistic, utility-disutility or pain-pleasure, calculus on the part of the individual. Cost, in the classical meaning, does not enter into the calculations.

Gossen understood utility and the marginal concept, although he did not use the latter term. He used "Werth der letzten Atome" (value of the last atom) as the equivalent of marginal utility. His entire work was given to developing the principle of diminishing want satisfaction and the laws derived therefrom. The theory was subjective throughout and rested upon a relationship between the object and the subject. He then classified objects into three classes: consumers' goods, complementary goods, and goods used in production. The practice of identifying goods still prevails, but the grouping carries no significant emphasis in economic analysis. Gossen did not dismiss cost of production as unimportant but, like most of his successors in marginal analysis, he emphasized utility or the demand for a good as of greater importance. Cost, or disutility, reflected different degrees of sacrifice or exertion which would show in the value of the goods. The value of the good to the consumer would be equal to the disutility or cost of the good. Since many goods enter into one's consumption, Gossen would say that the utility of any good is equal to the disutility of producing it at the margin of production-cost or disutility. This explanation is obviously not satisfactory; the disutility incurred as a cost is even less incisive than the labor-cost of earlier writers.

No credit should be claimed for Gossen as a developer of a value theory. He was concerned with the basic reasons underlying human wants and the manner in which the individual responded to these wants. On this score, then, he was attempting to develop the subjective approach to value; his ideas of marginal utility were very precise, but when he attempted to coordinate them with marginal disutility he met with less success. The incompleteness of his analysis, together with his heavy, complex style, no doubt contributed to the unpopularity of the work. Despite its shortcomings, this work contains the fundamentals of the theory later developed by Jevons and the Austrian economists.

William Stanley Jevons.—The English economist Jevons rates a front-rank position not only in the development of marginal analysis, but also for his many other contributions in value and capital analysis, in distribution theory, and in statistical research in economics. On the time scale his works fit between those of John Stuart Mill and Alfred Marshall, two of England's great economists, and measure very well with them.[22]

Jevons is of interest here primarily because of his pioneering work in value and distribution theory. The theories of the classical writers, as put in final form by J. S. Mill, generally prevailed at this time and placed especial emphasis upon the supply side. Jevons changed the emphasis to demand and depended upon utility to explain value.[23] He accepts the Benthamite idea that pleasure is conditioned by intensity and duration, certainty and remoteness. Both pleasure and pain were regarded as having two dimensions—intensity and duration. These two premises are important when the measurement of utility is considered. For example, the effect of a stimulus is likely to be less intense as time goes on, even to a point where the stimulus brings no response. This fact, Jevons held, can be reduced to measurement, which he did diagrammatically by placing intensity on the vertical (OY) axis and time on the horizontal (OX) axis. Pain and pleasure may be shown in the same

[22] William Stanley Jevons (1835-1882) attended University College, London, from 1851 to 1854; there his main interest was in the exact sciences, especially chemistry. Toward the end of 1854, when he was but eighteen years of age, he went to Sydney, Australia, as assayer of the mint, a position which he held until 1859 when he returned to England. On his return voyage he stopped in cities of the eastern United States and even made a trip to Minnesota, where a brother lived. Upon his return to England he resumed his academic studies, and graduated with an A.B. from University College, and received the M.A. in 1863. He next went to Owens College, Manchester, as a tutor, becoming the Cobden Professor of Political Economy in 1866. In 1876 he became a professor at University College, London.

His writings cover a wide range of subjects. The first publication to gain him recognition was The Coal Question (1865). He appeared before English learned societies, where he presented papers on contemporary questions. His Principles of Science and Elementary Lessons in Logic appeared in 1874 and 1870, respectively. His main work in political economy, Theory of Political Economy, appeared in October, 1871 (subsequent editions in 1879, 1888, and 1911). He was strenuously engaged in many activities besides teaching. The result was a break in health which impaired his work during his last ten years. While at a health resort he drowned in August, 1882.

Jevons was interested in philosophy, logic, and natural science, as well as in political economy. He was a pioneer in mathematical statistics and business forecasting. He even devised economic and statistical correlations to sell to businessmen for use in business forecasting, a pioneer idea at least fifty years ahead of his time. He learned of Gossen's work in August, 1878, and readily admitted its original elements. For a man whose life was cut short at forty-seven years, he accomplished much and earned for himself an enviable position among English economists. The best biographical sketch is by H. S. Jevons, Letters and Journal of W. S. Jevons (London, 1886).

[23] "Repeated reflection and inquiry have led me to the somewhat novel opinion, that value depends entirely upon utility. Prevailing opinions make labor rather than utility the origin of value; and there are even those who distinctly assert that labor is the cause of value. . . . Labor is found often to determine value, but only in an indirect manner, by varying the degree of utility of the commodity through an increase or limitation of the supply." W. S. Jevons, Theory of Political Economy (4th ed., 1911). All references are to the fourth edition unless otherwise stated.

illustration, for he regarded pain as negative pleasure; or more accurately, pain and pleasure are negative and positive quantities of the same thing. Anticipation, uncertainty of future events, man's social and mental outlook, all influence the calculus. He made this the central core of his economics: "Pleasure and pain are undoubtedly the ultimate objects of the Calculus of Economy. To satisfy our wants to the utmost with the least effort—to procure the greatest amount of what is desirable at the expense of the least that is undesirable—in other words, to maximize comfort and pleasure, is the problem of Economy." [24]

Next, he defined "some terms which will facilitate the expression of the Principle of Economy." A commodity is defined as "any object, or, it may be, any action or service, which can afford pleasure or ward off pain." Utility is used to "denote the abstract quality whereby an object serves our purposes, and becomes entitled to rank as a commodity" (p. 45). He made the laws of human wants the basis of political economy, or as he said, the "whole theory of Economy depends upon a correct theory of consumption" (p. 47). He gave this point added emphasis, "Thus the demand for, and the consumption of, objects of refined enjoyment has its lever in the facility with which the primary wants are satisfied. This is the key to the true theory of value" (p. 51).

It will be recalled that the problem of intrinsic value caused difficulty for some writers. Jevons emphatically stated, "Utility, though a quality of things, is no *inherent quality*." He thought it might be more accurately described as "*a circumstance of things* arising out of man's requirements" (p. 52). He made the decision of whether a good has or does not have utility rest upon the individual who feels the want and the relative availability of the good. He had an advantage over his predecessors in that he clearly distinguished between total utility of a good and the utility of a portion of it. Again, he used a diagram to show how the utility of an additional portion of a good diminishes as the supply is increased. The concept of total utility is the sum of the utilities attached to each unit of a given supply. But this is not the important point at issue; "we seldom need to consider the degree of utility except as regards the last increment which is consumed, and I shall therefore commonly use the expression *final degree of utility* meaning the degree of the last addition . . . of a small, or infinitely small, quantity of the existing stock." [25] He pointed out that economists, generally speaking, failed to distinguish between total utility and final de-

[24] W. S. Jevons, *The Theory of Political Economy* (1871 ed.), p. 44.
[25] P. 61. In a paper delivered before Section F of the British Association in 1862, he called it the "coefficient of utility." Reprinted in the 4th ed. of the *Theory*, pp. 303-14.

gree of utility—and that their failure to do so caused confusion and perplexity.

Next, Jevons stated as a general law that "the final degree of utility *varies with the quantity of a commodity and ultimately decreases as that quantity increases*" (p. 62). The law of diminishing utility is graphically illustrated by means of a curve, convex to the point of origin and similar to the demand curve as commonly used. The quantity of the commodity is shown on the OX axis; the degree of utility, or intensity of the desire (and effect) on the consumer, is shown on the OY axis. The curve shows how the utility of successive units consumed declines, and illustrates the principle known as diminishing utility. Jevons was the first English-speaking person to explain this principle. He likewise pointed out clearly the difference between *final degree of utility* and *total utility*. For example, the supply of water is so great that the utility of any unit is zero or negative. Diamonds, on the contrary, are so scarce that the utility of the last one available would be extremely high. The utility of water would be infinite, but the utility of any given unit would be negligible. For commodities whose supply is limited, the utility of one unit, especially the last unit, would be very great; it is to this unit, therefore, that a value or price is attached, which in turn influences all the units of the group. "The fact is, that labour once spent has *no influence on the future value of any article*; it is gone and lost forever. In commerce bygones are forever bygones; and we are always starting clear at each moment, judging the values of things with a view to their future utility" (4th ed., p. 164). He admitted that, although labor is "never the cause of value, it is in a large proportion of cases the determining circumstance." Labor affects supply and the supply affects the degree of utility, which, in turn, governs the ratio of exchange or value. He gave typographical prominence in the restatement of his theory as follows:

> Cost of production determines supply;
> Supply determines final degree of utility;
> Final degree of utility determines value (p. 165).

The fault he found with Ricardo's theory was in assuming quantities of labor as uniform. But Ricardo, he observed, was aware that labor differed greatly in both quality and efficiency so that each kind is more or less scarce and makes for a higher or lower rate of wages. While these were disturbances affecting the rate of wages for which allowances had to be made, the theory still rested upon an assumed equality of labor. But Jevons held that labor was a variable, the value of which "must be determined by the value of the produce, not the value of the produce by that of labour" (p. 166). Jevons opposed the Ricardian view that labor cost was the determinant of value on the supply side. However, he admitted that labor was a factor. Nor did he subscribe to the wage-fund theory, which he regarded as a truism. The wage-fund idea which would make the general rate of wages depend upon amount of capital set aside for the payment of wages, divided by the number of laborers, was, like the Ricardian cost-of-production doctrine of value, untrue. In the preface to the fourth edition he remarked that "the only hope of attaining a true system of Economics is to fling aside, once and forever, the mazy and preposterous assumptions of the Ricardian school. Our English Economists have been living in a fool's paradise" (p. xliv).

The purpose of this excursion into distribution theory was to examine briefly the part played by labor in value theory. Jevons held that labor, though never a cause of value in the classical sense, was in many cases the determining factor in an indirect way. He did *not* deny that wages paid to labor have no part in value theory, but he saw that all factors of production bear about the same relationship—that of scarcity—to value. "We must regard labour, land, knowledge, and capital as conjoint conditions of the whole produce, not as causes each of a certain portion of the produce" (4th ed., p. xlvi). Since he proposed no specific or exact causes for rent or wages, while interest was determined by the marginal productivity of a quantity of capital, the precise part each of the factors played in distribution was indeterminate.[26]

The central core of Jevons' theory of value lies in the principle of diminishing utility. As successive units of a commodity are used, the utility realized from each unit declines. If a commodity is scarce, the utility of the last unit to be consumed, *the final degree of utility*, will be high and hence its value will be high; on the contrary, if the commodity is plentiful, the utility of the last unit will be low and its value low. Value, therefore, is determined by the conditions of demand in relation to a given supply.

Even though Jevons did not succeed in putting his concepts into a form acceptable in later analysis, his principle of diminishing and marginal utility was both a notable and an original contribution to economic thought. His work gave a new impetus to theory and, though his influence is somewhat lost from being overshadowed by the great work of the Austrian school, he will always be regarded as a codiscoverer of the

[26] See George J. Stigler, *Production and Distribution Theories* (New York, 1941), chap. ii, for a criticism.

theory. His independent work assures to the English an equity, along with the German, Gossen, the Frenchman, Walras, and the Austrian, Menger, in the development of utility analysis.

Jevons should be recognized and remembered as a logician, philosopher, and reformer. He neither founded a school nor created a system of economics. Yet as Alfred Marshall said, "He was a Classic." [27] It was the breadth of his interests and the fertility of his imagination, rather than a finally perfect theory, that assures him a place among the great English economists of the nineteenth century. As Keynes put it, Jevons' Theory of Political Economy, "lives merely in the tenuous world of bright ideas when we compare it with the great working machine evolved by the patient, persistent toil and scientific genius of Marshall. Jevons saw the kettle boil and cried out with the delighted voice of a child; Marshall too had seen the kettle boil and sat down silently to build an engine." [28] Jevons' theory was both a challenge and a portent of things to come. He was not a critical destroyer as some of his predecessors had been; rather he was a creator of patterns which showed the way to more thorough analysis and refinements leading to a unification of the whole subject matter of economics.[29]

Summary and Evaluation.—Many writers, beginning with Aristotle, recognized that the "use" of a good was important in determining its worth, but "cost" explanations had the greater appeal. Lauderdale, Lloyd, Senior, Whately, Longfield, and others all scored "near misses" on the target of a marginal utility concept. Gossen in 1854, Jevons and Menger in 1871, and Walras in 1874 are the ones generally honored with the "discovery." While their contributions are indeed considerable, it is the Austrian economists, discussed in the following chapter, who are credited with the full development of marginalism. Gossen's idea fell upon deaf ears, whereas the original ideas of both Jevons and Walras (discussed in Chapter 20) provided permanent footholds in the tortuous, upward climb of the currently accepted value theory. Of the two men, it appears that Walras has a larger share in the development of the theory than Jevons does. Walras' analysis, though not entirely complete, does lead to a more rational use of supply (or cost) than that offered by Jevons, which rests upon circular reasoning. The fact that Jevons had a wider reading public and that his theories became better known tended to enhance his academic stature, but from the standpoint of analytical finesse, which would permit the application of empirical

[27] A. C. Pigou, ed., Memorials of Alfred Marshall (London, 1925), p. 374.
[28] J. M. Keynes, Essays in Biography (London, 1951), pp. 155-56.
[29] See Lionel Robbins, "The Place of Jevons in the History of Economic Thought," The Manchester School, VII, No. 1 (1936).

data, the Walrasian analysis was superior. In total contributions to economics, Jevons, with his work in statistics, money, trade cycles, and current economic problems, surpasses Walras. However, in purely theoretical refinements of value analysis Walras is clearly the greater of the two.

One of the interesting points in the development of economic thought is the persistence of the cost-of-production doctrine of value or price, with its emphasis upon supply. Practically every writer since Adam Smith, and even a few before him, held that an article must have a value in use. It might be argued with reasonable accuracy that consumption, or the demand for goods, was not a problem, for goods were generally in short supply; the real problem was production. Market gluts were virtually unknown and the problem of why people do or do not want goods is not as insistent as the problem of how to get them. Many economists, notably Lauderdale, Lloyd, and Senior, came close to developing a value theory with utility as the chief motivating factor, but the real significance of their ideas was never appreciated. After J. S. Mill restated the classical doctrines in 1848, theoretical economics, especially in England, stagnated. The long-winded criticisms of classical doctrines made by many were rather effective in questioning the classical formulation, but none of the critics had anything better to offer in its place. Socialist labor-cost theory was no improvement over classical theory, from which it actually derived. Historicism in Germany completely by-passed theoretical analysis. It seemed to be "about time," therefore, that the whole of value theory be re-examined.

It should not be inferred that marginal utility analysis was "discovered" by economic explorers who set out to find the promised land of a new value theory. Gossen's analysis was stillborn. As an economic explorer, he was rescued by Jevons, who himself had considerable difficulty in establishing his own discovery. Even then he was not entirely certain of his new theory. However, the year 1871 proved to be significant because of the publications of Jevons and Menger, whose pioneering works established marginal utility theory and gave a new impetus to economic thinking. Walras' claim, which came three years later in 1874, has also become permanent, not because of the time of the discovery, but because of the finesse of his development.

Refinements in marginal utility theory were made by others, both in analysis and in exposition. Mathematical symbols and diagrammatic methods have materially aided in exactness and clarity of exposition. The utility-disutility, pain-pleasure calculus, or hedonistic psychology, loses some of its mysticism and metaphysics when clothed in the refinements of recent analysis. The fact remains, however, that total utility or marginal utility can never be reduced to a mathematical exactness similar to that of marginal cost analysis, mainly because utility rests basically upon one's own subjective estimate of the want-satisfying power of the article. Nevertheless, marginal utility remains a significant part of theoretical economics.

19

The Austrian School of Economics:
Fully Developed Marginal Utility Analysis

Three men, at one time or another professors at the University of Vienna, compose the triumvirate who are generally credited with the development of marginal utility economics. Around them the tradition known as the "Austrian school" has developed. The contributions of the men and the influence of their theories rank them above all others after the classical school. Indeed, a comparison of the height of the "pinnacles of fame" for the two schools would probably give the Austrians the advantage. Certainly no other group added so much to the body of pure economic theory as did the Austrians. The intellectual debt of all economists to the body of doctrines developed in the years from 1871 to 1889 by the Austrian economists is indeed great. Their contributions provide some of the strongest warp threads in the garment of economic theory.

Carl Menger

The leader of the "school" was Carl Menger, a leader in the broadest sense of the term, for his basic theories were used as the foundation on which the whole edifice of Austrian economics, except for minor modifications, was built.[1] The fundamentals were in the *Grundsätze*, a

---

[1] Carl Menger (1840-1921) was born and reared in the once-Polish area of Galicia. After obtaining a doctor's degree at the University of Cracow, he spent some time in journalistic endeavors before accepting a civil service position in the Austrian prime minister's office. In 1873, two years after the publication of the *Grundsätze*, he was made professor extraordinary in the University of Vienna and resigned from his government position. During the years 1876-78 he became private tutor in political economy and statistics and traveling companion of Crown Prince Rudolph. Their travels took them through most of the European states. Upon his return, he was appointed in 1879 to the chair of political economy at Vienna and settled down to the quiet and secluded existence of the scholar, which characterized the last half of his long life. He held the professorship until 1903, when he resigned (at the age of 63) to devote all his time to research and writing. In 1900 he was made a life member in the upper chamber of the Austrian parliament, but he did not care for the appointment sufficiently to take any very active part in

slender volume of 285 pages, which appeared in 1871; few books have
had a comparable influence, not because it was widely read or well received, but mainly because of the author's able students and followers
who put across his theories. The book was a carefully planned, introductory part of a larger, more comprehensive treatise, which never appeared. It will be recalled that Jevons' *Theory of Political Economy*
appeared in the same year, and Walras' *Eléments d'économie politique
pure* in 1874. Each developed substantially the same theories independently. In a sense, Jevons had the prior claim, since he delivered
in 1862 and published in 1866 a public lecture which dealt with marginal
analysis, but it received little attention. Menger, too, had difficulty in
launching his new theories. In England, J. S. Mill's restatement of
classical doctrines was quite satisfactory, and in Germany the historical
school reigned supreme. However, the last quarter of the century saw
a rapid decline in classical economics, which suffered mortal injury from
the blows of the numerous critics, especially from the historical school
in Germany. It has been shown in Chapter 14 that, for numerous reasons, classical doctrines never did gain permanent acceptance in Germany. By the time Menger and other Austrian writers appeared, theoretical speculations had been so nearly discredited that the problems
of presenting logically consistent theoretical analyses were extremely
great. It was in defense of the logical, theoretical method that Menger
allowed himself to be diverted from his larger objective, and to become
involved in the controversial squabble with Schmoller over method.

deliberations or show any interest in politics. No indications of either liberal or
conservative political views appear in his writings. He is, therefore, best known as
a teacher and author. He was extremely well-read in the literature of all the social
sciences. His economics library was one of the three or four greatest private collections of economic works. All his books on economics and ethnography are now
in the Tokyo *Shoka Daigaku* (Tokyo University of Commerce). The part of the
Menger collection dealing with economics alone has more than 20,000 entries.

Menger's best-known writings are: *Grundsätze der Volkswirthschaftslehre* (*Foun-
dations of Political Economy*, Vienna, 1871; 2d ed. by Karl Menger, Jr., 1923);
*Untersuchungen über die Methode der Sozialwissenschaften, und der politischen
Oekonomie insbesondere* (*Inquiries into the Method of Social Sciences and par-
ticularly Political Economy*, 1883); *Die Irrthümer des Historismus in der deutschen
Nationalökonomie* (*The Errors of Historismus in German Political Economy*, 1884);
Zur Theorie des Kapital (*On the Theory of Capital*, 1888). He contributed several
articles in the *Jahrbücher für Nationalökonomie und Statistik zur Theorie des Kapital*
(*Yearbook for Political Economy and Statistics for the Theory of Capital*). His successor to the chair of political economy was Wieser, his son-in-law. Böhm-Bawerk
subsequently taught in the University of Vienna.

See F. A. von Hayek's introduction to the reprint of the *Grundsätze*, No. 17 in
the London School of Economics series of Reprints of Scarce Tracts in Economic
and Political Science (1934), for intimate glimpses of Menger's life and a general
outline of his work. See also J. Schumpeter, "Carl Menger," *Zeitschrift für Volkswirtschaft und Politik* (*Writings on Political Economy and Politics*), N.S., I (1921),
197-206. *The Economic Journal*, XXXI (1921), 271-72, carries an obituary.

The *Grundsätze* survived the buffeting of troubled academic seas, and even though Menger would not permit a translation or reprint in his lifetime, the book has gained a rank equal to the greatest tracts in economic literature.[2]

The *Grundsätze*, dedicated to Wilhelm Roscher, is scarcely more than a syllabus. Its eight chapters ("The General Part") deal with the general theory of the good, the economy and economic goods, the theory of value, exchange, price, value for use and value for exchange, the theory of commodities, and the theory of money. His son, who edited the second edition in 1923, stated in the preface that manuscript notes indicated the second part was to have dealt with "interest, wages, rent, income, credit and paper money, and the third part with the theory of production and commerce, and the fourth part was to present criticism of the present economic order and proposals for its reform." Of this elaborate plan only the first part was completed.

In Chapter I Menger states that "all things are subject to the law of cause and effect." Our own personalities and their many aspects are parts of what he calls "this great cosmic interrelation." The things which can be placed in this interrelation in the satisfaction of human wants (*Bedürfnisse*), we call utilities (*Nützlichkeiten*). In order, therefore, that a thing may be a good (*Gut*), or in order that it may acquire a goods-quality (*Güterqualität*), four conditions must be fulfilled:

1. There must be a human need.
2. The qualities or properties of the thing must be such as will satisfy the want.
3. There must be a recognition of this want-satisfying power by man.
4. There must be enough control over the thing to make it subserve the given need.

Goods (*Güter*) have the capacity of satisfying all four conditions: the loss of any one affects the *Güterqualität*, or the quality which makes it a good. Producers' goods which are not consumed directly also have *Güterqualität* because they can be transformed into goods which are want-satisfying. Here he introduces his concept of goods of different orders: consumers' goods are "goods of the first order" (*Güter der ersten Ordnung*), for example, bread; flour and the ingredients together with the bakers' skill would be of the second order; wheat would be of the

---

[2] James Dingwall and Bert F. Hoselitz have translated the *Grundsätze* as *Principles of Economics* (Glencoe, Ill., 1950), to which Professor Frank H. Knight has added an interesting introduction. The nearest thing to a translation, prior to the recent publication of the entire work, was by A. W. Small and appeared in the *American Journal of Sociology*, XXIX (January, 1924), pp. 455-88.

third order; wheat land, etc., of the fourth order, and so on. The main purpose of setting up the idea of orders or ranks is to differentiate between producers' and consumers' goods. Menger was emphasizing the importance of consumers' goods and he used the device of "orders" to show cause and effect relationships as well as their complementary aspects. In other words he made the value of goods rest upon a demand which was derived from a complementary use of the good. Demand for a good (Bedarf) included both a quantitative and qualitative satisfaction of man's wants in a given period of time. The chain of complementary relations runs as follows. For example, the demand for bread creates a demand for flour, which in turn creates a demand for wheat and all that the production of the commodity implies, such as agricultural land, machinery, fertilizer, and so on.

This leads to the theory of "imputation" (Zurechnung), a term used by von Wieser, which makes the value of the productive agents rest upon the value of their products. Here again the complementary nature of goods is emphasized as well as the fact that behind the whole series of dependencies lie unsatisfied human wants. He makes the whole of economic activity rest upon the Wirtschaftende Menschen (men engaged in economic activity). No ethical or social rules are made to apply to man's economic activity. The origin of all economic value is the relation between a human want and the available economic goods capable of satisfying the want. Here, and for the first time, he makes the distinction between free goods and economic goods rest solely upon scarcity, or what he calls "insufficient quantity."

Throughout his analysis Menger emphasized the importance of the time element. Credit for developing the time element is frequently given to Alfred Marshall; however, Marshall was antedated by Menger, who recognized that problems of uncertainty arise when goods used in immediate consumption are compared with goods for future use. One cannot determine in advance either the total number of wants or their intensity; nor can their supply be known. Likewise, the amount of goods available for present consumption may be changed, destroyed, or deteriorate before final consumption. The whole scheme of order or rank of goods rests upon the *time* element, for goods of the second order are dependent upon the use made of the first; the third in turn depends upon the second; and so on. The productive process would then depend upon a time lead-lag relationship, beginning with the individual, where the original demand arises. The relationship of the order of goods is somewhat analogous to the waves set up when a pebble is dropped on the smooth surface of a pool. The highest wave around the point of impact may be likened to the demand for the good of the first order; succeeding waves reflect the intensity (height) of the preceding wave. In consumption it is the intensity of the felt demand that activates the demand for all contributing factors. Obviously, in real life the relations are neither so simple nor so direct, and indeed the idea of goods of different orders is of questionable value. However, in Menger's analysis it is effective in showing how the value of goods is derived from the very center of value, which lies within the individual.

Menger's Value Theory.—Menger's theory of value was entirely subjective. In Chapter III, "Die Lehre vom Werthe" (The Theory of Value), he points out that value arises as a result of the relation between a human want and the available economic goods capable of satisfying the want. The available supply of such goods may be large or small at any given time; thus satisfactions will increase or decrease as the supply is increased or decreased. Therefore, Menger's theory then provides that the individual attach an importance to the good in proportion to its supply. It is not an inherent quality or property of the good that gives it value; it is a relationship between the well-being of the individual and the available supply of the good which contributes to his well-being that gives the good its value. Value, then, is the indispensable condition on which the satisfaction of the want actually depends. For example, bread and water are useful to man; but if both were abundant they would have no value for him—not even value in use—unless the satisfaction of hunger and thirst depended upon a particular loaf of bread or cup of water; then it would have value. If a good should satisfy no want, it would have no importance in the welfare of the individual and would therefore have no value to him.

But not all goods have the same importance in want-satisfying power, mainly because of the intensity of the want in relation to the supply of the good. Again, some goods satisfy wants directly and others indirectly. In any event, the central point of the theory makes the value one attaches to an article depend upon the *least important* use to which it is put. If one prefers to use an antique chair for kindling wood, then it has only kindling-wood value; the *least important* use is determined from the fact that as the supply of antique chairs is decreased, they cease to be used for kindling wood.

This leads next to the marginal concept. Jevons used "final degree of utility" and Walras used "rarity" to express the concept of the marginal use. Menger did not use the term marginal utility in his explanation of value. However a term was coined by von Wieser—*Grenznutzen* —which has since been identified with marginal utility. He emphasized the dependence one must feel on a good as necessary to satisfy our wants. The value of an article is therefore the importance one attaches to it as a satisfier of the least important want; the article is an indispensable condition to the satisfaction of that want and not to any other. This value, being subjective, does not depend upon total utility but on the *Grenznutzen* or "marginal utility," which is the least, or lowest, actual utility that one gets from the article. The consumer would therefore be able to impute or attribute a value to the last article by judging his own well-being if he had more or less of the article. If he used positive imputation, he would add more articles and see how much his well-being would be enhanced; or, if negative imputation was used, he would ascertain how much his well-being had suffered from the loss of an article.

The theory of imputation (*Zurechnung*) is the first attempt at a scientific explanation of distribution. The classical economists never considered distribution as a problem of value by discussing the pricing of productive factors in combination; they treated the returns to each factor as income to social classes—the landlord receiving rent; the capitalist, interest; and the laborer, wages. Menger made the value of productive factors depend upon their contribution to the value of the product they created. Producers' goods (goods of a higher order) which satisfy wants indirectly get their value from consumers' goods, which directly satisfy human wants. Assuming that the factors of production are jointly responsible as producers' goods in the production of consumers' goods, the withdrawal of a factor for any reason whatever, such as more profitable employment elsewhere, would cause a computable loss to the consumer. Conversely, the addition of a productive factor would make a computable addition. The computable gain or loss would then be the measure of the value of the factor as reflected in the value of the product.

The theory of imputation, although the best thus far proposed, is not complete. Menger neglected to apply diminishing returns to the factors and he also avoided the problems of production under so-called increasing, constant, and decreasing "cost conditions." Menger never treated land, labor, and capital as separate factors but always as complementary factors of production. Whether the units which were added or subtracted were large or small was never clearly shown. The complex problem of actually measuring the amount contributed by each factor is virtually impossible, even now with modern accounting methods. For purposes of final pricing, however, figures are arrived at which purport to be the costs of the various factors which are included in final price. Menger made the price of the factors depend upon a combination of two sets of laws: those which govern the value of the materials which the factors produce, and, next, the laws of complementary goods, which are in reality consumers' goods. Durable goods and goods of the different orders and their services are not differentiated. This is a weakness in his consideration of both land and capital as factors of production. More emphasis was placed upon the complementary relations than upon the analysis of the factors involved in developing his distribution theory.

Menger's theory of subjective value, and its elaboration by the Austrians, with its emphasis upon demand and utility analysis, might be likened to a pendulum which has moved to the opposite extreme from classical supply-and-cost analysis. The pendulum swings back again and comes to rest, in a sense, with the partial equilibrium analysis of supply and demand as developed by Alfred Marshall and neo-classical economics. Menger left a serious gap in value analysis by failing to explain the role of cost of production in the valuation process. He never developed a cost analysis, although he recognized that costs had to be considered. Likewise, he did not develop a theory of price. It has been maintained that Menger and the Austrian school were chiefly concerned with an exposition of the principles governing value as arising within the individual, and that they neglected the laws of price. Böhm-Bawerk remarked on this point, "Price, or 'objective value' of goods is a result of different subjective estimates of the goods which the buyers and sellers made in accordance with the law of final utility." [3] But this is not very satisfactory. Though Menger did suggest alternative or opportunity cost, it was Wieser who developed what is now known as "opportunity cost" or, as it is sometimes called, "Wieser's law." Simply stated, the value of the factors of production is measured by the best alternative use to which they might have been put had this particular commodity not been produced. The value of the product thus produced will not be less than the value of the product produced by an alternative use of the factor or factors under consideration.

It will be recalled that classical theory made price the sum total of the costs of production, or better—the expenses of production. This theory made the value (price) of a good come from its *past* cost. The good had to sell (at least in the long run) for an amount that would cover the costs of production or it would not be produced. The Austrian analysis based on Menger's fundamental theory made the causal connection run the other way—from the final product *back* to its cost. They would say that the value of a good comes from its future use, not from its past; in other words its value arises from its use in consumption, not because it cost so and so much to produce. Goods therefore stand midway between production and consumption. Menger had no place in his theory for historical cost as influencing value; he would say that "value

[3] Eugen von Böhm-Bawerk, "The Austrian Economists," *Annals of the American Academy of Political and Social Science*, I (January, 1891), 361-84.

sanctions costs" but is not determined by them. In his analysis, cost of production is itself first determined by the marginal product, and the value of the marginal product depends on the extent to which it is an *indispensable condition* of the well-being of the individual. His interest was in developing a theory of subjective value, not a price-theory. Böhm-Bawerk alone developed the marginal utility theory of value into a detailed theory of price.[4]

The Menger-Schmoller Controversy over Method.—Enough of Menger's theory has been presented to show the genesis and development of the Austrian marginal utility analysis. One should not leave Menger without noting in some detail the controversy between him as leader of the Austrian school and Schmoller, the leader of the "younger" German historical school. The controversy has little or nothing to do with marginal analysis as presented. It does represent, however, one of the keenest controversies ever engaged in by economists over methodology. Even though it ended precipitately in 1894 between the two "giants," the polemic was carried on by their respective followers for many years.

The German historical school (see Chapter 16) was at the zenith of its influence in the seventies and eighties. Schmoller was at that time the recognized leader of the school which had not only succeeded in "demolishing" classical doctrines but had made marked progress in establishing its method of analytical research. Its break with deductive method in particular and theory in general was complete. Most German economists adhered to the historical method and believed that history alone could illustrate and explain economic phenomena. Menger's *Grundsätze*, which was pure theory, was not read in Germany, where theory was virtually excluded from the universities. Menger's theory was held to be simply a useless theoretical analysis scarcely worth their attention.

Though Menger failed to arouse their interest with his pioneering theory, he did arouse their anger with his *Untersuchungen über die Methode der Sozialwissenschaften und der politischen Oekonomie insbesondere* (*Inquiries into the Method of the Social Sciences and particularly Political Economy*, 1883). This was his second great work and in its particular field it was as significant as the *Grundsätze*. While he was not acrid in this book, there can be no mistaking the focal point of his attack. In the preface he contended that the Germans had

---

[4] For development and for criticism of the Austrians see George J. Stigler's *Production and Distribution Theories* (New York, 1948), chaps. vi-viii; and Wm. A. Scott, *The Development of Economics* (New York, 1933), chaps. xx-xxii, and especially "Criticism of the Austrian Doctrines."

ignored the differences between the formal nature of political economy and other sciences and that misunderstandings had played a decisive role in the recasting of political economy. One passage from the preface sets forth his criticism:

. . . curious misunderstandings have played a decisive role in the reform of political economy, especially by its German reformers. The new types of investigation were in no slight degree the outcome of misunderstood analogies and of disregard of the real tasks of political economy.

Meanwhile, even in quarters where a type of research which was in itself legitimate made itself effective, it was not the product of a comprehensive insight into the system of tasks which science must perform within the field of public economy. The phenomenon was everywhere repeated of types of research of more or less subsidiary significance assuming that reform of political economy depends exclusively upon their results, while they denied the legitimacy of every other type of investigation. The endeavor to remove the unsatisfactory condition of political economy by inaugurating new schemes of investigation led, in Germany, to a series of partly mistaken, partly one-sided conceptions of the nature of our science, to conceptions which segregated German national economy from the literary movement of all the other peoples. Indeed the one-sidedness of those German innovators in particular cases made them unintelligible to foreign economists. This being the situation, it scarcely need be said that a reform of political economy upon the above suggested universal bases did not come within the range of the German reformers' ideas.[5]

Menger admitted that the monograph was a polemic. He said that "not in a single passage did it spring from ill will toward meritorious representatives of our science. . . . It was a necessary consequence of my conception of the present condition of political economy in Germany. Agitation against the tendency at present chiefly controlling political economy in Germany was not for me an end in itself, nor was it a mere external gratuity. It was an essential part of my task. It needed to be penetrating and thorough, even at the peril of wounding certain sensibilities" (ibid.). He further lamented the trend of political economy in Germany which, he said, "is little enough noticed at best in other countries" and has suffered isolation. He stated his objective to be "reawakening consciousness in Germany of the essential tasks of political economy, to rescue it from fatal one-sidedness, to free it from isolation from the great literary movement, and thus promote the reform that is so much needed." He sought to "bring the German mind back to its proper attitude towards economic problems" and not to belittle his German colleagues.

[5] A. W. Small, op. cit., pp. 473-74.

Despite his clear statement of objective principles, he started the intellectual "battle of the century," commonly referred to as the *Methodenstreit* (controversy on methods). Schmoller, the leader of the historical school, replied in an extremely bitter article [6] which in turn aroused the dignified Menger. He replied forthwith in an 87-page pamphlet, "Die Irrthümer des Historismus in der deutschen National-oekonomie" ("Errors of Historismus in the German Political Economy," 1883), written in the form of letters to a friend, in which he outshone the pompous Prussian in style, brilliance, and forceful argument. Schmoller did not reply to the "Irrthümer"; in his yearbook he announced that although Menger had sent him a copy he was unable to review it because he had immediately returned it to the author. He reprinted the insulting letter which he sent with the returned pamphlet.[7] The pamphlet adds little to the *Untersuchungen*.

The controversy between these two men brought some significant contributions. The historical school denied the existence of all economic laws and believed only in what it called "regularities" which could be discovered by historical research alone. Its members even held the word "theory" in contempt and substituted "doctrine" in its place. They held that economic theory had nothing to do with scientific research; only history and, to some extent, statistics were useful. Menger defended theoretical analysis and deductive methods. He recognized the value of historical research but he insisted that theoretical analysis and deductive method were also necessary. Schmoller held out for the inductive method but would allow deduction only in developing a perfect, exact science. Menger, being primarily a deductive theorist, would also defend induction and historical investigation. Schmoller misrepresented Menger in the controversy but possibly both exaggerated the differences in each other's views.[8]

The net gains fall in the general field of social science rather than in economic theory. According to von Hayek, "Probably it [*Untersuchungen*] did more than any other single book to make clear the peculiar character of the scientific method in the social sciences." He further remarks, "Its main interest to the economist in our days seems to lie

[6] Cf. G. Schmoller, "Zur Methodologie der Staats- und Sozialwissenschaften" ("On Methodology of Political and Social Science"), *Jahrbuch für Gesetzgebung, Verwaltung und Volkswirtschaft im deutschen Reich* (*Yearbook for Legislation, Administration and Political Economy in Germany*, 1883), pp. 974-94.

[7] See G. Schmoller, *Jahrbuch* (1884), p. 677. The last line of the article reads, "Viel Feind, viel Ehr" (Many enemies, much honor).

[8] See Joseph Schumpeter, "Epochen der Dogmen- und Methodengeschichte" ("Epochs of the History of Dogmas and Methods") in *Grundriss der Sozialökonomik* (1924), Vol. I, chap. ii, p. 108. Professor Schumpeter says that Schmoller was especially guilty of exaggerating the differences of their opinions.

in the extraordinary insight into the nature of social phenomena which is revealed incidentally in the discussion of problems mentioned to exemplify different methods of approach, and in the light shed by his discussion of the development of the concepts with which the social sciences have to work." [9]

The controversy was continued by the followers of the two masters for many years. It enhanced the stature of Menger and seriously detracted from Schmoller and German economics in general. The Austrians as a group went on to greater fame, whereas in Germany economics retrogressed. Many splendid historical researches came from Germany but in theory they never caught up with the Austrians. The Germans lost prestige as they resisted the doctrines from Vienna, and in all probability the whole of economic science lost when Menger allowed himself to be sidetracked by methodological controversy instead of developing further theoretical analysis as he had promised in the *Grundsätze*.

Menger's fame as a teacher spread. His lectures attracted students from both Europe and America. The influence of Menger and the other members of the Austrian school has penetrated every phase of economic science. The seeds of marginal utility analysis were sown by many former writers including Lauderdale, Lloyd, Senior, Mill, and others. Only under the Austrians did it become one of the richest of economic developments.

Friedrich von Wieser

The second member of the Austrian trio was Friedrich von Wieser.[10] As a member of the school, he generally followed the subjective analysis of Menger, but in this he went much farther. He not only elaborated

---

[9] von Hayek, ed., *op. cit.*, pp. xx, xxi.

[10] Friedrich Freiherr von Wieser (1851-1926) was born in Vienna and spent most of his life there. Although his interests, as a young student, were in history and social phenomena, he studied jurisprudence, which was the traditional course for his social class at that time. He graduated from the University of Vienna in 1874, and spent the next two years (1875-77), together with Böhm-Bawerk, in Germany studying under the leaders of the historical school, Knies, Roscher, and Hildebrand. In spite of his own interest in historical research, he did not become a follower of the historical school. In 1884 he went to the University of Prague and in 1889 became professor of political economy. When Menger resigned at Vienna, Wieser was offered that chair, which position he held from 1903 until 1922. He was made an honorary professor and continued to lecture until 1925, mainly on sociological subjects in which he was always interested.

He was appointed to the Upper House in 1917, and served with distinction as Minister of Commerce in the last two cabinets of the Austro-Hungarian Empire. Although a born aristocrat, which might imply militaristic tendencies, he was politically a pacifist. Wieser was an original thinker whose outlook was broader than that of Menger, his father-in-law, or Böhm-Bawerk, his brother-in-law. While he

Menger's analysis but independently developed his own theories. There is evidence of both agreement and disagreement in the family. Wieser and Böhm-Bawerk were not always in complete accord, especially as to distribution theories, but the three were in substantial agreement on the importance of the subjective approach. In some respects, especially in his analysis of the productive contribution of a factor of production, Wieser's theories resembled those of Walras. He also held a much broader view of the scope of economics than Menger, and because of this he came closer to presenting a complete work on social economics.[11] Indeed, Wieser's *Theory of Social Economics* ranks as one of the greatest, and by far the most comprehensive, work of the triumvirate.

Wieser's first significant work was the *Ursprung und Hauptgesetze des wirtschaftlichen Werthes (The Origin and Principal Laws of Economic Value)* in which he reaffirmed the general views of Menger; however, he carried the latter's ideas further and drew independent conclusions from them. In place of Menger's "least important" use idea there appears for the first time (*Ursprung*, p. 128) the word *Grenznutzen*, which is known to English-speaking students as marginal utility —a name which sometimes characterizes the school.

Wieser used Menger's fundamental proposition that value exists in an article which directly satisfies a want and is thus a consumers' good; producers' goods derive their value from the value of their products which in turn are used to make consumers' goods. In other words, the value of a producers' good was imputed to it only because of the part it played in making a consumers' good. Wieser's explanation was more comprehensive than that of Menger in that he applied the imputation theory to factors of production under differing conditions of supply and demand.

Natural Value.—Additional points of agreement and disagreement appear in his best work on theory, *Der natürliche Werth (Natural Value, 1889).*[12] Wieser begins with the question: Whence do things get their value? He answers his question: from their utility. But he points out

accepted Menger's basic fundamentals he went much further in developing them into a system. His seminars attracted many students. His best known writings were *Ursprung und Hauptgesetze des wirtschaftlichen Werthes (The Origin and Principal Laws of Economic Value*, 1884); *Der natürliche Werth (Natural Value*, 1889; English translation edited by William Smart, 1893); *Theorie der gesellschaftlichen Wirthschaft (Theory of Social Economics*, 1914; translated by A. F. Hinrichs, New York, 1927).

11 For critical evaluation see George J. Stigler, *Production and Distribution Theories*, chap. vii, and Wm. A. Scott, *The Development of Economics*, chap. xxi. See also Oscar Morgenstern, "Friedrich von Wieser," *American Economic Review*, XVII (December, 1927), 669-75.

12 This work was translated by Mrs. Christian A. Malloch and edited, with a preface, by William Smart (London, 1893).

that the utility of goods varies under changed circumstances and that the value of the good will therefore also change. After observing how earlier writers had explained value, he remarks that "the economist who undertakes to explain value has to explain the procedure of those who value" (p. 5). Thus he contended that the value of a good rests upon, or is derived from, the intensity of the wants and the want-satisfying power of the good. He then used the principle of diminishing satiation of wants (similar to Gossen's law) to show that successive quantities of a good available to one consumer change that consumer's demand from satisfaction to surfeit even to disgust. However, economic goods, which imply limitation in supply, do not exist in quantities which permit such usage; hence, with supply limited it is important that consumption proceed only to the point of "marginal utility." It has been pointed out that he used the term *Grenznutzen* to express the last or marginal use to which a good is put. Thus his approach is purely subjective or psychological and patterned on Menger's doctrine.

In Book II ("Exchange Value and Natural Value") of *Natural Value* he developed a price theory and finally explained what he meant by natural value, which he defined as "value as we should find it in a community at a high stage of development carrying on its economic life without price or exchange." He reasoned that "exchange gives rise to a phenomenon which, originating from value, reacts upon it in the most powerful manner; this phenomenon is price" (p. 39). His concern with price is to show that it is but the money equivalent of the marginal utility of the marginal buyer or consumer. Wieser develops subjective value as subjective-use value and subjective-exchange value. The idea, simply stated, is that a good may be used either in consumption or in exchange. For example, wheat may be used for seed or for bread. The marginal utility calculations of the individual will decide which use will prevail, since wheat has two possible uses. All goods brought on the market will exchange at their marginal value; under what he called the "general economy" they must use the market structure, however imperfect it may be, to facilitate exchange. There always remains, however, the value-in-use, which measures utility and the value-in-exchange, which "measures a combination of utility and purchasing power" (p. 57).

The foregoing characterizes the "general economy" which prevails. Next he develops natural value as it would exist in a communistic state which is assumed to be a perfect state with everything well-ordered, with no misuse or abuse of power, and in which "no error or any kind of friction will ever occur" (p. 61). Under this idealized concept goods would exchange according to their utility. However, human imperfections, fraud, error, inequalities in wealth, and the like all affect purchasing power or exchange value. Wieser then points out the unreality of the former and the reality of the latter characterization and sets about to discover the economic laws which prevail in the "general economy."

Wieser's greatest contribution to value theory was his doctrine of Zurechnung, or the imputation theory. One of the leading principles developed by Menger and subscribed to by the "school" was that value exists in goods of the first order, or those entering into direct consumption. The value of all factors which had a part in producing goods of the first order is reflected in both factors and goods of lower orders. Wieser said, "Every means of production, every tool, every piece of land or raw material, every service of labor, represents a share in an undertaking. This share contributes to the result of the undertaking, and consequently gets ascribed to it a quota of the result, and upon the amount of this result its value must depend" (p. 71).

The emphasis in Book III is on imputation. The first point stressed is that imputation follows the marginal law which accounts for the value of the good produced by complementary factors. Next, he disagreed with Menger's explanation of imputation, which was that value would be determined by the loss that would result if a good were withdrawn, or by negative imputation. Wieser argues (Chapters III-IV) that "if in a stock of goods of the same kind . . . I take away one good from the others, it is this one good alone and nothing else that is taken away." But in the case of "heterogeneous and cooperating production goods, if I remove one, I deprive the others also of a portion of their effect" (p. 84). In other words, the withdrawal of an agent of production reduces the productivity of the remaining agents.

Wieser believed that Menger's analysis needed "only a very slight turn" to correct it. Thus, "The deciding element is not that portion of the return which is lost through the loss of a good, but that which is secured by its possession" (p. 85). Wieser's solution, then, was to determine what he called the "productive contribution" of each factor; this, he thought, could be computed by a series of equations showing the results of varying combinations of the factors of production. The thoroughness of the discussion implies that Wieser believed he had developed an explanation applicable to all possible conditions. However, the amounts attributable or imputable to any one factor of production in combination with others remain subjective; they are not mathematically accurate.

Wieser considered costs of production in Book V. He contended that the cost of production as used in classical theory was only a utility concept. He argued that the value of production goods was determined from the value of their products; production goods (barring monopoly) receive their value from the least valuable one produced, or from the marginal product. Since it is the value of the marginal product which really determines the value of the articles (or their costs), the classical cost of production would be only a special case of the general marginal utility law of value. Wieser found no opposition between costs and utility. He viewed cost of goods in terms of their marginal utility. "Whoever thinks of 'utility' without thinking of 'costs' simply neglects, in the utility of one production, the utility of the others." Again he states, "Where the law of costs obtains, utility remains the source of value. More than this, marginal utility remains the measure of value" (p. 183).

Throughout the discussion he holds with grim determination to his utility explanation of cost. Wieser was extremely critical of labor-cost theories of value, regardless of their origin. He viewed any theory which spoke of the costs of production of human labor as a "monstrous idea." He consistently held that labor, like all other factors, gets its value from its products. Wieser used cost as social cost, not as a capital outlay. The "opportunity cost" element is present, but it is a social rather than an individual concept. The whole community (or society) gains or loses as total production enhances or diminishes the community wealth. He remarks, "Production not only creates value, it also destroys value. The whole of human wants and the whole of economic goods necessary to supply them must be considered, not the costs of any single factor of production" (p. 173). He proudly states that "possibly it is the greatest triumph of the theory of marginal utility that it fully explains the obscure conception of costs, with which every other theory had to reckon, with which no theory could come to any reckoning" (p. 185). Costs to Wieser were only a symptom; marginal utility sanctions cost and is basically the source of value.

Wieser's analysis of cost is both subtle and involved and always leads, by tortuous paths, to utility as the real cause of value. There is no place for "sacrifice" or disutility in his cost concept; utility alone explains all. Wieser recognized that Menger had neglected cost analysis; therefore his treatment was designed to fill in the missing analysis. His work in cost analysis was completely original. He did more than any other member of the school to establish the individual marginal utility approach and effect a complete break with objective cost doctrines of the classical school. Wieser conceived of economics as a social science which should explain the social economy. The shortcomings of his analysis, though real, do not prevent *Natural Value* from remaining the fullest statement of the entire body of marginal analysis made by any member of the school.

Wieser's Panoramic View of Economics.—In some respects Wieser's *Theorie der gesellschaftlichen Wirthschaft* [13] was his best work. Mitchell remarked in his preface that "Wieser's *Social Economics* holds a place in the literature of the Austrian school such as John Stuart Mill's *Political Economy* holds in the literature of classical theory. It sums up, systematizes, and extends the doctrines developed by the founder of the school, the author, and his fellow workers" (p. ix). *Social Economics* was the first systematic treatise on economic theory produced by the Austrian school. Unlike Mill's *Principles*, which was a restatement of classical doctrine, Wieser's treatise was an original work and displays typical German thoroughness. Unfortunately, *Social Economics* came out in 1914 and was virtually lost to world scholarship during the turbulent years of the war and subsequently, until a second edition appeared in 1924. The translation in 1927 made the volume available to English scholarship, which has belatedly recognized the value of his work.

The work is divided into four books and a brief look at the contents is in order. In Book I, "Theory of Simple Economy," he examined the subjective elements in economic analysis, such as human needs, satisfactions, and the appraisal of future needs. Then he examined goods as means of satisfying wants; the process of production; and land, labor, and capital as factors of production. In subsequent topics of the book he restated the fundamental doctrines of the school, including "marginal utility," and showed that costs are but a part of the law of utility. In the "simple economy" he considered the problem of wants and their satisfaction without complexities, such as monopoly. The last section of Book I deals with economic value. Here he restated his concept that "the economy arises whenever the means for the satisfaction of needs exist in economic proportions." The object of the economy is to secure the highest utility that is possible. He held that the laws which prevail and the ones to which we submit are "none other than the laws of computation of utility." In acquainting ourselves with these laws "we have fulfilled the mission of the theory of value as regards the simple economy." Thus he defines "economic value" as the "value which is assigned to units or groups of commodities and of labors employed in economic transactions" (p. 143). This is a wider definition than was used by Menger, since both labor and commodities are included. Wieser makes men conscious of their economic activity; he

[13] Translated as *Theory of Social Economics* (New York, 1927) by A. F. Hinrichs with a preface by Wesley C. Mitchell. It was written in 1914 as the theoretical volume in a series, *Grundriss der Sozialökonomik* (*Outline of Social Economy*), edited by Max Weber. See also Wesley C. Mitchell's "Wieser's Theory of Social Economics," *Political Science Quarterly*, XXXII, 95-118; reprinted in *The Backward Art of Spending Money* (New York, 1937), pp. 225-58.

is concerned not only with satisfying wants but with providing means of satisfying wants.

Book I is, in a sense, a complete volume because it has the foundations upon which the subsequent books are built. The treatment of the behavior of a single individual in a "simple economy," where there are no laws of price, no monopoly or pressures, and where the individual is rational and not influenced by any external or internal pressures, was intended to establish a universal pattern of individual behavior. He then admits other influencing factors to the static relationship in order to "exhaust the entire sphere of the phenomena of value without exception."

In Book II, "Theory of the Social Economy," he considers how an entire population acts in a complex economy where each person follows his own interest, where many social classes exist, and where prices prevail in both competitive and monopolistic market conditions. All the institutions of capitalistic exchange exist, such as money and credit and a complex price system. Private enterprise, the profits motive, wage-systems, rentiers, capitalists, and the whole list of capitalistic institutions in a complex economy are examined in their interrelationships with one another. In this book he assumes that the state does not interfere with the individual in pursuing his self-interest. This book is the longest (259 pages) and most thoroughly developed of the four. It is his fullest statement of the workings of the complex economy and establishes his knowledge of economic institutions and their interrelationships.

In the 14 pages of Book III, "Theory of the State Economy," he introduces state interference and makes the individual a subordinate of the state, which performs many economic functions for the common good. The state is to aid in making production possible but not to engage in production. To accomplish the aims of the state, taxes are necessary to produce revenues which are expended for the public good, even for operation of some agencies at a loss. The utility principle applies here just as it did in the simple economy. The principle of greatest utility then decides what function the state should undertake and how the costs should be allocated. However, the state should not use its taxing power to equalize income and wealth.

The brief fourth book of 25 pages, "Theory of World Economy," considers how the single state, as described in Book III, would operate when surrounded by similar states. The interstate problems of prices of goods, flow of gold, balance of payments, and tariffs are taken up. He believed that price equilibrium could never be attained as in a domestic economy. He would permit tariffs to protect infant industries; however, classical economists were right in advocating free trade.

But, because of the lack of natural resources, some nations can never diversify their industries. Therefore they must adjust themselves to their best advantage and make the most of their resources.

Social Economics is a comprehensive work dealing with man's economic activity in satisfying his wants. Man's aim is to obtain the greatest utility, which will therefore afford maximum satisfactions. Wieser developed this idea from his "simple economy" concept to the complex world economy. His explanations throughout the four books do not support the statement made in the opening line, "This investigation uses the method recently designated as the 'psychological.'" The analysis should be designated as "logical" rather than "psychological" in the generally accepted meaning of the latter term.

This work shows Wieser's ability to build a comprehensive economic treatise on Menger's fundamentals. Numerous references to classical economics and copious footnotes show his wide acquaintance with economic literature. A modified "historical method" is employed in developing his thesis, especially in Books I and II. No similar work was attempted by Böhm-Bawerk, whose main efforts were devoted to capital and interest theories. Social Economics, therefore, is the final and complete statement of Austrian marginal utility analysis.

Eugen von Böhm-Bawerk

Böhm-Bawerk, the third member of the Austrian school, was, in some respects, the greatest.[14] He is probably better known to English-speak-

[14] **Eugen von Böhm-Bawerk** (1851-1914) entered government service after graduating in law at the University of Vienna. He had also studied political economy at Heidelberg, Leipzig, and Jena. He became a professor at the University of Innsbruck in 1881 and served there until 1889, when he re-entered the finance ministry. His progressive measures were responsible for his appointment as Minister of Finance in 1895, again in 1897, and a third time in 1900, and his work as Minister of Finance was outstanding. He left the government service in 1904 and became a professor at the University of Vienna. His best known writings include *Kapital und Kapitalzins* (*Capital and Interest Theories*, 2 vols.). The first is *Geschichte und Kritik der Kapitalzins Theorien* (*History and Criticism of Interest Theories*, 1884; 2d ed., 1900; 3d ed., 1914); and the second, *Positive Theorie des Kapitales* (*Positive Theory of Capital*, 1888; 3d ed., 1909). Both volumes were translated by Professor William Smart of the University of Glasgow as *Capital and Interest* (1890) and *Positive Theory of Capital* (1891). Böhm-Bawerk's monograph *Grundzüge der Theorie des wirtschaftlichen Werthes* (*Outlines of the Theory of Commodity Value*) appeared in 1886. His additions to the second edition of Volume I of *Kapital und Kapitalzins* were translated by W. A. Scott and S. Feilbogen as *Recent Literature on Interest, 1884-1889* (New York, 1903). His minor works were collected by F. X. Weiss in *Gesammelte Schriften* (*Collected Writings*, 2 vols., Vienna, 1924-26). His criticism of Marx appears in *Karl Marx and the Close of His System*, trans. Alice Macdonald (London, 1898). He contributed many articles to the economic journals of Europe and America.

ing scholars than either Menger or Wieser. He proceeded from the same starting point as did Wieser—Menger's *Grundsätze*—but carried his analysis much further. The books, *Capital and Interest* and *The Positive Theory of Capital*, form a core around which his theoretical analysis is built. They are not treatises on capital and interest solely, but they deal with price, production, and distribution theory, and a theory of the whole economic process. His production theory, under which he treats distribution, was borrowed from Wieser's *Natural Value*, in which the opportunity cost principle was developed. His theories of capital and human motivation rest upon his own concept of the significance of time as a factor in production. Böhm-Bawerk was outstanding as a theorist. He avoided the polemics over method which proved so unfruitful, but entered freely into doctrinal controversies and argued with confidence and finality. He did more than either of his coworkers to raise Austrian theory to a high plane of general acceptability. In his chosen field of capital and interest, his works were pioneers; he probably did more to stimulate interest in that general field of economics than any other person.

Critiques of Interest Theories.—The first of Böhm-Bawerk's writings to be considered is *Capital and Interest*, a volume of considerable interest to the student of economic thought. In the Introduction, which he called "The Problem of Interest," he attempted to prove that anyone who owns capital is able "to obtain from it a permanent net income, called Interest." He remarked that this income had "notable characteristics" and flowed to the capitalist "even where he has not moved a finger in its making." "The phenomena of interest," as he called it, "presents a remarkable picture of a lifeless thing producing an everlasting and inexhaustible supply of goods" (p. 1). He identified two problems: first, the theoretical problem of interest, which deals with the relations of capital and interest and leads to the question of why there *is* interest on capital. The second problem he identified as the "social and political problem," which asks whether interest *should* be paid on capital—whether it is just and fair or whether it should be modified or abolished. His concern was chiefly with the first problem. To this end he says, "We shall have to explain the fact that, when capital is productively employed, there remains over in the hands of the undertaker a surplus proportional to the amount of this capital. This surplus owes its existence to the circumstances that the value of the goods produced by the assistance of capital is regularly greater than the value of the goods consumed in their production. The question accordingly is, Why is there this constant surplus value?" (Pp. 77-78.) Simply stated, why does a principal of $100 bring an interest return of two, three, or four or more dollars in addition to the repaid principal at the end of the year?

The question he poses is really answered not in this volume but in his later volume, *The Positive Theory of Capital*. In Book I of *Capital and Interest*, "The Development of the Problem," he begins with a discussion of the opposition to interest in the earliest literature and follows the issue through the Middle Ages and the church teachings. Practically every writer who expressed an opinion on interest is treated; included are Grotius, Justi, and Sonnenfels of Kameralism fame; the mercantilists Child, Locke, Stuart, Hume; Bentham, Galiani, Turgot and Adam Smith also receive attention. The "Colourless theories" in Germany, the theories of Rau, Ricardo, Torrens, and McCulloch in England are brought under examination.

In Book II, "The Productivity Theories" of Say, Lauderdale, Carey, Thünen, and others are considered. His grouping and criticism of the productivity theories may be briefly summarized as follows. Two groups of theories are identified; the first group claims for capital a direct value-producing power. They state that capital is productive and any surplus value created by capital results from its productive power. He called these the "Naïve Productivity" theories. The theories which held that the productive powers of capital created a surplus which went to the capitalist, he called "Indirect Productivity" theories. Böhm-Bawerk criticized these theories on the basis that they confused quantity of the product with value of the product; the theories failed to distinguish between quantity and value and likewise failed to show any necessary connection between them. He showed that the problem of capital is a problem of surplus value and argued that capital cannot produce value directly; his subjective analysis is the basis for his argument that the value of capital comes from consumption, not from production. He does not deny that capital is productive, but he insists that interest is not its product. He asserts that "to ascribe to capital a power of producing value is thoroughly to misunderstand the essential nature of value, and thoroughly to misunderstand the essential nature of production. Value is not produced, and cannot be produced. What is produced is never anything but forms, shapes of material, combinations of materials; therefore things, goods."[15] Thus capital creates or produces goods, not interest.

Book III, "The Use Theories," critically examines the ideas of Say, Hermann, Menger, Knies, and others. The use theory, which is primarily a German one, is somewhat related to the productivity theory.

---

[15] *Capital and Interest*, p. 134. See W. A. Scott, *The Development of Economics*, chap. xxii, for more detailed criticisms of the theories.

(Say first suggested the theory, Hermann worked it out, and Menger gave it the most complete form; Böhm-Bawerk says that in Say's writings the "Productivity and the Use theory grow up side by side" p. 189.) In fact, he calls it an "offshoot of the Productivity theories, but an offshoot which quickly grew into an independent life of its own" (p. 185). The fundamental idea of the use theory is that besides the substance of capital, the *use* (*Gebrauch* or *Nutzung*) of capital is an object of independent value. Or, in familiar terms, "Interest is the price paid for the use of capital." His criticism of the theory centers around a mistaken belief that a distinction exists between the value which goods have in themselves, and a value which the use of the good has (see Book III, chap. xi). He argued that the theory was untenable in making the *use* of capital something different from the *using-up* of capital. The fault, he believed, is attributable to a wrong interpretation which tended to make all capital the same as durable goods. He believed that use theories raised all the problems of the productivity theories and solved none of them.

In Book IV, "The Abstinence Theory" of Senior and Bastiat is severely criticized; although he admitted that it has a "core of truth in it" (p. 276), he said that it does not explain interest. It confuses the origin of capital with the cause of interest. The theory would possibly explain why the owner of capital has a sum which he would loan, but it would not account for an increase in the sum at the end of a year as a result of interest accumulation. Its popularity as a theory was due "not to its superiority as a theory" but to the fact that it appeared at a time when its argument could be used "to support interest against the severe attacks that had been made on it" (p. 286).

Book V, "Labour Theories," which considered interest as a "wage for labour rendered by the capitalist" was held by James Mill of the English group. The French group (notably Courcelle-Seneuil) called it labor involved in saving of capital; the German group, represented by Schäffle, held capital to be a result of the labor of the entrepreneur. Böhm-Bawerk regarded these generally as inadequate explanations. The "Exploitation Theory," developed in Book VI, which is perhaps the best of the seven books, contains destructive evaluations and criticisms of the socialist theories of Rodbertus and Marx. He vigorously opposed the proposition of Rodbertus "that all goods, economically considered, are products of labour and of labour only." Marx, who adopted this view, was criticized not only for accepting the view but for failing to see that time is also an influence of large proportion in the analysis. This criticism of labor as a sole determinant in value theory is in line with his general criticism of socialist doctrine. In Book VII, "Minor Systems," he dealt critically with the eclectics, a group which includes Jevons, J. S. Mill, Schäffle, and Henry George.

In conclusion he remarked that after examining the "motley array of interest theories," he found that none of them "contains the whole truth . . . taken together they form nothing but a chaos of contradiction and error." He held that the problem of interest is to "discover and state the causes which guide into the hands of the capitalists a portion of the stream of goods annually flowing out of the national production." To this he added that there "can be no question then that the interest problem is a problem of *distribution*" (p. 421). However, he later added that if one should treat interest only as a distribution problem, he falls short of complete comprehension of the problem; one must go back to the basic causes of wealth—economic goods and their supply in relation to human wants. Thus he concluded that "the interest problem in its last resort is a problem of *value*" (p. 425).

The two theories which "constitute the lowest step in the development" were the naïve productivity and the socialist exploitation theory. Neither of them touched the distinctive problem. In fact, Böhm-Bawerk systematically disposes of each theory as being inadequate either in its underlying premises, analysis, reality, or in its final scientific objectivity. He ends the book with only one hint as to his own theory by the remark that "I may just mention the element which seems to me to involve the whole truth. It is the influence of Time on the valuation of human goods" (p. 428). He promises to expand this in the "second and positive" part of his work which followed, namely, the *Positive Theory of Capital*. Thus, in his own estimation, he succeeded in sweeping the board clean for his own theories, which are developed in the following pages.

Capital and Its Function.—The *Positive Theory of Capital*, published in 1888 while Böhm-Bawerk was a professor at the University of Innsbruck, is his best work. It is more than a treatise on capital and interest; a glance at the subjects of the seven Books indicates that it contains his conception of value and price, as well as an explanation of capital and interest. Book I treats of the "Nature and Conception of Capital"; Book II, "Capital as Instrument of Production"; Book III, "Value"; Book IV, "Price"; Book V, "Present and Future"; Book VI, "The Sources of Interest"; and Book VII, "The Rate of Interest."

Böhm-Bawerk generally regarded capital as a "group of products which serve as a means to the acquisition of goods," a concept generally held by Adam Smith and others of the classical group. Next, he considered the end and aim of production to be the making of things which satisfy our wants—or consumption goods. In production we may produce the goods directly, or indirectly by a roundabout method or process. Or, as he says, "we may put forth our labour in such a way that it at once completes the circle of conditions necessary for the emergence of the desired good . . . or, we may associate our labour first with the more remote causes of the good, with the object of obtaining, not the desired good itself, but a proximate cause of the good" (*Positive Theory of Capital*, p. 17). The latter explanation is his "roundabout" process or method of production; a process which calls for the production of producers' goods before final consumption. He illustrates the process by an example of a peasant who may satisfy his thirst by going directly to the spring each time he is thirsty, or he may carry water by means of a pail, or, better still, he can bring the water to his hut by means of hollowed logs joined together.

The primitive example illustrates the superior advantages of the "roundabout" process over the "direct" method of satisfying wants, and finally of producing goods. Naturally this implies, as a necessary part of the roundaboutness, the energy or sacrifice in first procuring tools or implements for making the particular capital (in this case the hollowed logs) and the natural resources from which both the tools and the final capital were made. Böhm-Bawerk maintained that the roundabout process has at least two advantages. First, roundabout methods lead to greater results than direct methods; in other words, they are more highly productive. Second, beyond both the greater productivity and time elements, in most instances, there is no other way in which certain goods can be obtained (p. 19). This method "which has long waited for expression . . . is nothing else than what economists call Capitalistic Production" (p. 22) as opposed to direct production. He then defines capital as "nothing but the complex of intermediate products which appear on several stages of the roundabout journey" (p. 22). Subsequently he defines capital "as a group of Products which serve as a means to the Acquisition of Goods . . . or a group of Intermediate Products" (p. 38). He preferred the term "Acquisitive Capital" to the term "Private Capital," and "Social Capital" was treated as "Productive Capital." He treated capital as a factor in production and capital as the source of interest as "having enough in common to allow their being formally coupled under one definition, and then distinguished as narrower and wider conceptions" (p. 40). His view was that society as a whole "cannot acquire except through producing, [and] the goods which constitute the produced means of acquisition (capital in the wider sense) coincide with the goods which constitute the produced means of production, or capital in a narrower sense or social capital" (p. 40). In other words, he finally arrived at a view which treats "capital as an instrument or tools or means of production" (Bk. II, chap. i).

Next he considered the function of capital in production. Here he treated capital as a "symptom" of a profitable roundabout production. The term "symptom" is used rather than "cause" of profitable methods of production, for the very presence of capital "is rather the result than the cause" (p. 93). He raised the question of "whether capital is a third and independent factor of production alongside labour and nature" (p. 95). To this question he said, "The answer must be a most distinct negative." It is, so far as his treatment is concerned, "an intermediate product of nature and labor, nothing more." Its own origin, its existence, its subsequent action, are "nothing but stages in the continuous working of the true elements, nature and labour" (p. 96). He did not regard capital as having any independent productive powers, but as a "medium through which the *two* original productive powers (nature and labor) exert their instrumentality" (p. 99). Then he asks, "Is capital not productive at all?" To this he replies, "Certainly it is . . . first because it finds its destination in the production of goods; further because it is an effectual tool in completing the roundabout and profitable methods of production once they are entered upon; finally because it makes the adoption of new and profitable methods possible" (p. 99).

Value and Price.—Value theory, the subject of Book III, is a treatment of a special phase of value along marginal utility lines of reasoning. He used the terms subjective (use) and objective (exchange) value and ascribed to value theory the double task of explaining each of them. Value he formally defined "as the importance which a good or complex of goods possesses with respect to the wellbeing of a subject" (p. 135). Scarcity and usefulness are the necessary attributes of a good conducive to its having value. In the final analysis, however, its value is determined by the amount of its marginal utility which is "the keystone of our theory of value" (p. 149). Here he introduced the famous illustration of the five sacks of corn to which their owner attaches a different value designed to represent his scale of wants all the way from the most urgent to the least urgent. The utility of any one sack, since the sacks are all by assumption interchangeable and exchangeable, is no greater than of any other one. Should the owner's wants change because of faulty judgment or otherwise, the utility of the marginal bag might be changed. The value of this, or of any commodity, would therefore depend on the utility of the last or marginal unit of the stock. Again, marginal utility is determined by the usefulness and scarcity of the goods.

His treatment of the value of complementary goods was held to be "the key which will solve one of the most important and difficult problems in political economy—the problem of distribution goods as made in the present state of society. . . . All products come into existence through cooperation of the three complementary factors of production, labour, land and capital" (p. 176). He held that "the joint product may economically be considered as due to each of these, and what share may accordingly be assigned to each of them"; the theory of the value of complementary goods also shows at the same time "the most decisive basis for determining the amount of remuneration which each of these factors obtains" (p. 177). The theory, he argued, explained labor and land as factors and wages and rent as the quota which each of the owners receives. "But the quota which falls to the cooperation of capital is not interest. . . . It is first a gross remuneration for the cooperation of capital and out of this interest is got, like a kernel out of a shell, because . . . something remains over after deducting from the gross remuneration of the value of the worn-out capital" (p. 177). This is interest as he uses the term.

Böhm-Bawerk's theory of value is not concisely described in one chapter, but elements bearing on this subject are interspersed through several chapters in Books III and IV. After restating Menger's division of goods into ranks, he concludes that the only difference between consumers' and producers' goods is that in the case of goods for immediate consumption, "the good and the satisfaction stand beside each other in a direct causal relation; while in productive goods, there is interposed between them and the satisfaction finally dependent on them, a more or less lengthy series of intermediate members, their successive products" (p. 181). Costs are "the complex of those productive goods . . . which must be expended in making a product" (p. 183). Despite issues which may be involved in the analysis of value, the marginal utility of the marginal product is about all that counts. "The whole truth about the celebrated Law of Costs" is that it is only a "particular law" applicable where goods can be "freely reproduced," and even in cases where the law holds (and he admitted there were a few) "costs are not the final but only intermediate cause of value." "In the last resort they do not *give* it to their products, but receive it from them" (p. 189). The value of goods in his analysis falls under the "all-embracing law of Marginal Utility." He did not add anything to the Mengerian analysis except in exposition. The analysis was necessary, however, as a background for Book IV, which deals with price.

The basic assumption underlying the exchange of goods was that the "economical condition" of the parties to the exchange was bettered. He moved in his analysis from isolated exchange first, to one-sided, then to two-sided competition, which "is the most common in economic life." Here he developed the idea of the "marginal pairs." In competition in a horse market, which he used for his example, the market price is determined within a latitude whose limit is established by the valuation of the last two buyers and of the last two most capable sellers who actually exchange. Finally, market price will be determined by the subjective valuations of the last two buyers and the last two sellers, which he called the "Marginal Pairs" (p. 209). This now familiar device serves to bring into focus the area within which final market price is established under competition.

Böhm-Bawerk found great ambiguity in the expressions "Supply and Demand" which "bring innumerable errors and misconceptions in their train" (p. 215). He preferred to develop price by an analysis of "determinants" which included both the extent and the intensity of demand as well as of supply, but in the final analysis the last four valuations are made by the "marginal pairs."

This led him next to his "Law of Costs" (chap. vii), in which he sought to "describe the concatenation between Value, Price and Costs." He promised that "to understand clearly this connection, is to understand clearly the better part of Political Economy" (p. 224). Again he reminds his readers that "value and price takes its start from the subjective valuations put upon finished products by their consumers" (p. 224). The demand for the products by consumers stands opposed to the supply of products, with final price depending upon the estimates of the marginal pairs. He illustrated his case with commodities selected from the market and concluded that the "causal relation which has ended in price . . . runs in the clearest possible way, in an unbroken chain from value and price of products to value and price of *costs*—from iron ware to raw iron, and not conversely" (p. 226). The "links in the causal chain" run first from subjective valuation of the finished product, then to demand and money-price, then to iron, then to exchange value of producers and sellers, and finally to the market price of iron, or of any other commodity. This is "simply the great law of marginal utility fulfilling itself. . . . In any individual economy . . . the value which emerges . . . is purely a personal subjective value. In the more extended sphere of the market . . . money being the neutral common denomination for wants . . . here emerge the employments . . . represented by the highest money valuation . . . and the value which results is objective exchange value" (pp. 226-27).

Böhm-Bawerk admitted the smooth working of his principles were affected by "disturbing causes" or "frictions" which were innumerable. Among them were changes in human wants, the changes in production which resulted from profits or losses, the "Lapse of Time," as he called it, which occurs between the inception of the idea and the original production, to the finished product. It is this last "disturbing cause that gives rise to Interest" (p. 234). The development of the interest theory follows in Book V, "Present and Future."

Böhm-Bawerk's Own Theory of Interest.—Böhm-Bawerk developed the theory that capital or capital goods are the final result of roundabout methods of production, which necessarily cause consumption to be postponed to a future time. Direct methods of production presumably satisfy wants directly and immediately. Capital goods, so far as immediate satisfaction of wants is concerned, are in reality future goods and are therefore discounted in value. Because of this, "Present goods are, as a rule, worth more than future goods of like kind and number. This proposition is the kernel and center of the interest theory which I have to present" (p. 237). Three reasons (*drei Gründe*) account for the proposition: first, differences in wants and provision for them in the present and future; next, the tendency to underestimate the future; and last, the technical superiority of present goods.

These three points are developed with considerable thoroughness in chapters ii, iii, and iv of Book V. The first point rests upon differences in the wealth and welfare of persons as affecting their present wants and future expectations. Next, "less importance is attached to future pleasures and pains simply because they are future." He argued that "we systematically underestimate future wants and the goods which are to satisfy them" (p. 253). The causes for this are "incompleteness of the imaginations," "a defect" in the will which tends to make a "decision for present pleasure" rather than a future one, and last the "shortness and uncertainty of life." These characteristics, although they manifest themselves differently in various individuals, are nevertheless most important factors in the theory of capital and interest. The "technical superiority" arises because "present goods" make possible roundabout production, which is more productive and also more remunerative than direct production. In conclusion, he held that all these characteristics have a cumulative effect and that

. . . to the overwhelming majority of men the subjective use value of present goods is higher than that of similar future goods. From this relation of subjective valuations there follows in the market generally, a higher objective exchange value and market price for present goods; and this, reflecting back on present goods, gives them a higher subjective (exchange) value even among those whose personal circumstances happen to be such that the goods would not naturally have any preference in subjective use value (p. 281).

Finally, there are leveling forces in the market which tend to bring reduced value of future goods into regular proportion to their remoteness in time. Future goods have less value, both subjective and objective, depending upon their remoteness in time.

Book VI, "The Source of Interest," treats both the cause and the rate of interest. Subjective valuations tend to influence the market price in favor of present goods. Therefore, a borrower of money will be obliged to make a payment to reward the lender for abstaining from present consumption. He must thus pay an "agio" or premium (Aufgeld) for the use of the funds and this premium is interest. "Interest comes in the most direct way, from the difference in value between present and future goods" (p. 286). This theory is often called the exchange theory of interest.

The rate of interest (Book VII) is explained by an analysis which called for a quasi-general equilibrium relationship between supply of and demand for the factors of production. He arrived at his answer by a circuitous method. He considered the rate first in an isolated exchange, and later under market conditions. It was demonstrated in Book VI that interest originates as a result of the desirability of present goods over future goods for which an agio or premium must be paid. However, this is only a special case of the exchange of goods in general; all such exchanges conform to the same general pattern and are subject to the same general laws as govern all exchange. Since the value placed on future goods varies widely for different persons even at the same time, the agio will vary from nothing (zero) to a high percentage, depending upon the "skill and staying power" displayed by the persons conducting the negotiations. In a complex market situation, however, the problem becomes much more difficult. Assuming that, on the basis of former analysis, an agio has to be paid to induce the owner of present goods to forego consumption, the question of what determines the amount of the agio remains to be answered.

In explaining this point Böhm-Bawerk used an equilibrium analysis of labor as a commodity having peculiarities which make it comparable to a productive loan. He held that "a capitalist will count the value of labour equal to just as many present shillings as it will bring him in the future" (pp. 382-83). But "labor" has certain peculiarities not found in other commodities. "Every other commodity . . . has a predetermined subjective value to the one who wishes to buy it. Labour has not, and for this reason. It is valued according to its prospective product" while the prospective product varies according as that labour is invested in a short or in a long production process" (p. 382). Under market conditions the fund of capital and the fund of labor (used in the sense of total supply in each case) are constantly bidding against one another for greater shares in total productivity. This, he believed, is desirable, for it insures greater productivity of each factor. But the productivity depends upon the "length of the production period," which in turn affects the amount of the product which the capitalist (in the en-trepreneurial sense) obtains from the amount of labor he buys, or the wage he pays for the labor. He made the assumption that "the whole supply of labour and the whole supply of present goods, come to mutual exchange" (p. 386), or that the whole disposable fund of subsistence is sufficient to pay for the entire quantity of labor; thus in a long period equilibrium prevails. But in a shorter period no balance would exist, and some capital would remain unemployed; if the period were longer, not all the laborers could be provided for and "unemployed economic elements" would result.

Not only are the length and the productiveness of employment treated, but the wage rates are important considerations. He attempted to show these relationships by a series of tables which show changes in the total annual product as related to the number of employed at different wage rates (pp. 381-402). The point he was attempting to illustrate is that the capitalist may employ a small number of laborers over a longer period, or vice versa, and that he will select the period and combination which bring him the largest returns. He also held that competition will equalize any unbalance that may exist within a produc-tion factor. If one wage prevails and not all labor is employed, com-petition among the unemployed labor will force wages down to a point where all may be employed at a wage and for a time period most profitable to the employer. The converse would work just the same. If, at a given wage, all labor is employed but some capital remains un-employed, competition between capitalists will force wages up to the point where all capital will be employed in the most productive opera-tions at the new equilibrium wage.

The analysis therefore has "three elements or factors" as he calls them, which are "decisive determinants of the rate of interest; the amount of the national subsistence fund; the number of labourers pro-vided by it; and the degree of productivity in extending production" (p. 401). The three factors affect the rate of interest as follows: "In a

community, interest will be high in proportion as the national subsistence fund is low, as the number of labourers employed by the same is
great, and as the surplus returns connected with any further extension
of the production period continue high. Conversely, interest will be
low the greater the subsistence fund, the fewer the labourers, and the
quicker the fall of the surplus returns" (p. 401).

Böhm-Bawerk confidently declared that in actual life the formula
has the most "complete verification." He stated that

. . . it is one of the best accredited and most recognized facts of economic history that an increase of the subsistence fund . . . or the increase
of the community's capital, has a tendency to depress the rate of interest.
Second . . . the relation between that capital and numbers of the population . . . an increase of population without a simultaneous increase of
capital, has a tendency to raise the interest rate. And, thirdly, it is also an
acknowledged empirical fact that the discovery of new and more productive
methods of production, outlets, business opportunities, etc., which conduce
to check the fall of surplus returns, tend to raise the rate of interest, while
the closing of former opportunities of production or sale, or other occur-
rences which end in a reduction of the previous degree of productiveness,
tend to lower the interest rate. We find, therefore, that all those factors
to which, on the lines of our former inquiry, we were forced to ascribe a
decisive influence on the interest rate, do, as a fact, possess and exert that
influence (p. 402).

Thus far, Böhm-Bawerk's assumptions made the annual product of
the worker and his annual wage the same in all employment. He admitted this was not true in actual life but believed that it did not affect
the normal relationship; the general principle held. Also, he admitted
it was not true in actual life that the demand for present goods came
solely from the wage-earner. There are additional competitors in the
capital market—"suitors," as he called them—for consumption credit,
including landowners, and capitalists themselves. The additional competitors do not affect the fundamental principles of the theory; they
only decrease the national subsistence fund available for the support of
productive labor and, to that extent, decrease the rate of wages and
raise the rate of interest.

The long and somewhat tedious discussion of Book VII may be
summed up briefly as follows: the famous drei Gründe, which include
both subjective and objective (or technical) factors, as well as the time
element in both production and consumption, are the most significant
points. The subjective element makes the individual place a higher
valuation on present than on future goods and therefore a higher value
on present income than on future income; that is, the marginal utility

of present goods is greater than their marginal utility in the future. Thus, in order to induce the individual to forego present consumption, an agio or premium must be paid on present goods. The third factor or element, and the one which directly affects production, emphasizes the technical superiority of roundabout, or indirect, production. This method of production requires great arrays of tools and machines, which in turn create a demand for capital. Because they are highly productive when so employed, the owner of the capital could demand and get an agio which would serve to compensate for postponement of present consumption of those goods which made future production possible. This was Böhm-Bawerk's explanation of why interest could be paid and also why it had to be paid. The rate of interest that was finally paid was determined by the amount of the national subsistence fund, the number of laborers, and the surplus returns from production under his prescribed methods. Despite pages of analytical discussion of the theory, no specific rule for determining the amount of interest is given. The number (actually seven; see p. 447 for the three most important) of "determinants" which influence the rate of interest, consists of economic, psychological (subjective), and social elements or causes, which represent the forces at work that finally resolve themselves, under the "principle of harmonious satisfaction," to a level where the principle of marginal utility equates everything (p. 410). Despite his patience with detail and thoroughness of analysis, the theory remains both inadequate and unreal.

Böhm-Bawerk was apprehensive lest the reader might interpret his subsistence fund as similar to "the notorious Wage Fund theory of the older English school" (p. 419). While very reluctant to admit it, he did, in fact, revive and refine the wages-fund theory for his own purposes. The wage fund, he believed, could be spent over different periods of investment; yet the rate was not determined by simply dividing the fund by the number of workers currently employed. The fund, as money, was to be actually used for the purchase of the means of subsistence for those engaged in current production. The fund therefore was a "variable proportion of the community's wealth" or a "stock of wealth accumulated in a community" (p. 420), not a certain predetermined amount. This subsistence fund is as unreal as the wages-fund doctrine of classical economics; however, the purpose of the fund as developed by Böhm-Bawerk was entirely different from that of its classical proponents. Likewise, despite his extended criticisms of the productivity theory of interest, he actually uses it throughout the analysis.

A Brief Criticism of Austrian Theory

The theories of the Austrian trio have been subjected to long and vigorous criticisms.[16] The premises as well as the realities of the analysis of the theories have been challenged. Since the theories stem from subjective evaluations, the first general criticism is directed at the hedonistic, pain versus pleasure, calculations. The theory makes value not an attribute of the goods but an attribute dependent upon a psychological determination of utility as conceived by each individual who responds to a host of environmental factors. As Gray put it, "Value, then, is a judgement of the mind; not a property of the thing or an independent entity." [17] The imputation theory, either positive or negative, as a means of ascertaining what one factor contributes to the total, lacks scientific accuracy. The productivity of all factors would be affected by the addition or withdrawal of any one factor, since they are jointly responsible in total production; thus the product of any one could not be independently computed. The concept of different orders of goods, which makes the value of a good reflect throughout all goods which in any way contributed (directly or indirectly) to its production, is not an untrue concept. It is the same as "derived demand," as developed by Alfred Marshall. In strict analysis, all demand is derived

[16] Among the many criticisms the following will be found extremely useful.

James Bonar, "The Austrian Economists and Their View of Value," *Quarterly Journal of Economics*, III (Oct. 1888), 1-31.

Francis A. Walker, "Dr. Boehm-Bawerk's Theory of Interest," *Quarterly Journal of Economics*, VI (July 1892), 399-416.

Eugen von Böhm-Bawerk, "The Positive Theory of Capital and Its Critics," *Quarterly Journal of Economics*, IX (Jan. 1895), 114-31.

J. B. Clark, "The Origin of Interest," *Quarterly Journal of Economics*, IX (Apr. 1895), 235-36, 257-78.

J. B. Clark, "Concerning the Nature of Capital, A Reply (to Dr. Eugen von Böhm-Bawerk)," *Quarterly Journal of Economics*, XXI (May 1907), 351-70.

Eugen von Böhm-Bawerk, "Capital and Interest Theory Once More," *Quarterly Journal of Economics*, XXI (Nov. 1906), 1-21, 247-82.

Z. C. Dickinson, "The Relations of Recent Psychological Developments to Economic Thought," *Quarterly Journal of Economics*, XXXIII (May 1919), 377-421.

E. H. Downey, "The Futility of Marginal Utility," *Journal of Political Economy*, XVIII (Apr. 1910), 253-68.

Jacob Viner, "The Utility Concept in Value Theory and Its Critics," *Journal of Political Economy*, XXXIII (Aug. 1925), 369-87, 638-59.

George J. Stigler, *op. cit.*, chaps. vi, vii, viii.

Wm. A. Scott, *op. cit.*, chap. xxiv.

Frank H. Knight, *Ethics of Competition*, especially chap. v, "Marginal Utility Economics."

See also Eugen von Böhm-Bawerk, *Recent Literature on Interest, 1884-1889* (New York, 1903), especially pp. 10-13.

[17] Alexander Gray, *Development of Economic Doctrine* (New York, 1933), p. 349.

demand. However, if one is interested in price theory, the analysis must be more specific and less all-inclusive, with some recognition being given to circumstances of time and place and prices of other factors and products. The marginal concept and its use, although necessary for a subjective analysis of demand, place a heavy responsibility on the individual. Final choice is dependent upon many other factors besides the expected pleasure or satisfaction as balanced against the dissatisfaction of doing without. There are many socially prescribed elements that enter into the valuation of goods and consciously or unconsciously influence one's choice. The Austrian analysis would make the individual a calculating machine which would always come up with the right answer on the value of products, hence the amount that would be supplied, and so on. The pricing process in the market is not as simple as that.

Finally, the value theory is completely monistic. When considered by itself, it is indefensible. The Austrians excluded supply or cost of production as being of significance and the concept of mutual dependence of supply, demand, and price as well. They were obliged however to make some use of supply but only in an indirect manner; they reasoned that cost of production determines supply; supply determines marginal utility and marginal utility determines value. The reverse is just as inadequate; as Marshall pointed out, "If this series of causations really existed, there could be no great harm in omitting the intermediate stages and saying that the cost of production determines value. For if A is the cause of B, which is the cause of C, which is the cause of D; then A is the cause of D. But in fact there is no such series." [18] Neoclassical economics holds the Austrian analysis to be inadequate because of the failure to consider supply as a factor correlative with demand in determining value and price, and the failure to recognize the mutual interdependence of supply, demand, and price.

As one surveys the marginal utility development, so carefully developed by the Austrians, the impression is gained that little or no progress was made. Their price theory and their distribution theory as well were not left in final form. The high esteem in which the men and their theories have been held, cannot camouflage their rather barren contribution to economic thought. Many of their errors have been corrected by subsequent writers, yet it is safe to say that neoclassical developments have eclipsed the Austrian doctrines. It appears doubtful if any of the modern economic theories owe their origin directly to the Austrian school.

[18] Alfred Marshall, *Principles of Economics* (8th ed.), p. 818.

Probably the most acute criticisms have been directed against Böhm-Bawerk's theory of interest. The pioneering work in this general field served to stimulate much research and writing on the subjects of capital and interest, as well as to stir up the liveliest of academic controversies in which Böhm-Bawerk himself was a frequent participant. His theory of interest was attacked on at least three grounds: first, that he had either misunderstood or misinterpreted (or both) former writers on the same subject; next, that his own theory was but a restatement of earlier ones; and finally, that his own assumptions and reasoning were inadequate. After disposing of all former interest theories (at least to his own satisfaction) he enlisted the general marginal utility analysis to explain interest.

The theory developed by Böhm-Bawerk, while purporting to rest on marginal utility analysis, turns out to be a theory resting on marginal productivity. Thus, all a marginal productivity theory can do is explain *how* returns *can* be made to agents of production (the basis of a demand curve), not *why* they *must* be paid to offset disutility (the basis of the cost or supply curve). It is apparent that Böhm-Bawerk's theory of distribution, like his value theory, is monistic. Despite this criticism, his general contribution to demand analysis as a part of value analysis must not be underestimated. Specific criticisms may be directed against the importance Böhm-Bawerk attributes to the roundabout process of production and the importance of capital in this process. He tends to minimize the importance of labor, land, and management in the process, yet he recognizes them as cooperating factors in production. Irving Fisher and others challenged the assumption of the "technical superiority" of present goods.[19] Böhm-Bawerk held that present goods possess a technical superiority over future goods in that they permit a producer to undertake roundabout production now, which is admittedly more productive than direct production. This fact, though true, needs additional supporting evidence. The agio or premium whose payment for the use of capital makes this method of production possible would appear to be a payment made in advance of production; yet interest is a return which is paid to only one factor of production, and paid out of final productivity. As Professor Knight remarked, "after almost a thousand pages of prolix argumentation, he gave a few pages of none too clear but reasonably correct statement of the productivity theory, somewhat vitiated by the admixture of the wages fund view of the relation between capital and wages."[20]

[19] See F. A. Fetter, "The Roundabout Process in the Interest Theory," *Quarterly Journal of Economics*, XVII, 13. Irving Fisher, *The Rate of Interest* (New York, 1907), pp. 55 *et sqq.*

[20] Frank H. Knight, *Ethics of Competition* (New York, 1935), pp. 157-58.

In the light of neoclassical economic theory and analysis, one must agree with Professor Knight that "the utility theorists were no nearer the truth than the classical economists" (*ibid.*, p. 154). The explanation of price by means of the Walrasian general or Marshallian partial equilibrium analysis with emphasis of interdependence of supply, demand, and price marked, we believe, a forward step. Many refinements have been made in both supply and demand analysis to effect the presently generally accepted value and price explanation. No one would maintain, as did John Stuart Mill over a hundred years ago, that value analysis is in its final form; yet so long as value and price analysis remains a part of the total picture of economics, the brush marks of the three Austrian economists will always be discernible.

20

The Lausanne Economists:
Léon Walras and Vilfredo Pareto *

The two previous chapters traced the development of the concept of marginal utility and also emphasized the other contributions of the writers concerned with the task. This chapter deals with the work of Léon Walras and Vilfredo Pareto, who also were pioneers in their chosen fields of economics. Walras has a legitimate claim to originality in developing the marginal utility concept, which he did without the knowledge of the theories of Jevons or Menger. His work was published in 1874. The dates of the publications of Pareto are not significant in the development of marginal utility theory. This chapter will attempt to develop the main parts of the work of the Lausanne economists, of which marginal utility is but one aspect.

Léon Walras,[1] the first of the Lausanne economists, is recognized as a codiscoverer of marginal utility analysis, or the marginal utility theory

* The author gratefully acknowledges the assistance of Professor A. Stuart Hall of the Economics Department at the University of Illinois for his aid in the preparation of this chapter. Dr. Hall has done extensive research in preparing a Ph.D. thesis entitled "Historical and Philosophical Aspects of the Economics of the Lausanne School," submitted to the Graduate College in 1951.

[1] Marie Esprit Léon Walras was born in Evreux, France, December 16, 1834. His father, Antoine-Auguste Walras (1801-1866), was at one time a professor of philosophy in the Royal College of Caen and later an economist of some note. In 1831 the father wrote *De la nature de la richesse et de l'origine de la valeur* (*On the Nature of Wealth and the Origin of Value*); this book provided the son, Léon, with many of the terms and concepts later used in his own works. The pioneering work of Augustin Cournot, *Recherches sur les principes mathématiques de la théorie des richesses* (*The Mathematical Principles of the Theory of Wealth*, 1838), was also held in high esteem and served as Walras' first introduction to mathematical economics.

Léon Walras graduated in 1852 from the *Lycée* at Douai with the degree of Bachelor of Letters. He then decided to enter the *École polytechnique* in Paris but felt incompetent in mathematics which he hoped to correct by still another year at the *Lycée*. This earned him the degree of Bachelor of Science (1853). He failed the entrance examinations to the *École polytechnique* on two occasions. He entered the *École des Mines* in 1854 but withdrew in less than a year. His tastes

of value. Whatever distinction this may have brought to Walras is now eclipsed by the greater glory of being the founder of the so-called "Lausanne school," the founder of the "mathematical school," and the originator of "general equilibrium economics." It is the purpose of this chapter to examine the work of Walras and his successor, Pareto, in an effort to appraise their contributions to economics.

were leading him toward philosophy and literature. His interest in literature finally led to the publication of his only novel, *Frances Sauveur* (1858), which proved to be a literary failure. Then followed his decision to enter the field of political economy with the view to "reconstruct the social sciences."

Walras secured a place on the staff of the *Journal des économistes* and later with *La Presse*, neither of which positions were of long duration. He subsequently attempted without success to establish a journal of his own. Following this, he became interested in the cooperative movement, a life-long interest. In connection with the movement, he and Léon Say were the prime movers in founding a bank for producers' cooperatives in 1865. The bank failed in 1868. Up to that time Walras had met with more disappointment than success. The journals would not accept his articles, he had been unable to obtain an academic post in France, and the disastrous bank failure ended a business career.

One episode in Walras' early attempt to enter the field of political economy should be noted. It served to introduce him to Lausanne as well as to political economy. In 1860 an International Tax Congress met at Lausanne which was attended by public officials and laymen. The Council of State of the Canton of Vaud resolved to offer a prize for the best paper dealing with the fiscal problems of the canton. Walras submitted a paper entitled *Théorie critique de l'impôt* (Paris, 1861), in which he advocated nationalizing the lands of Vaud. The first award went to Pierre-Joseph Proudhon for his *Théorie de l'impôt* (Brussels, 1861). This is an interesting occurrence, especially in light of Proudhon's views on property and income and his socialism in general. Even more curious is the fact that Walras' first economic work, *L'économie et la justice* (1860), which was an attack on Proudhon's monetary theories, was then in the process of being printed. Even though the judges recognized Walras' paper as "well and closely reasoned," he was awarded fourth place.

In 1869 the Canton of Vaud enacted legislation for reorganization of the *Académie* at Lausanne, one part of which provided for a chair of political economy in the faculty of law. After some delay, Walras was appointed to this post and began his academic career in December, 1870, at the age of thirty-six. It had taken him ten years to attain even a modest beginning in the profession to which he consecrated himself. He held the position until he resigned for reasons of health in 1892.

Walras was the author of many books and articles. The best known books are *Eléments d'économie politique pure (Elements of Pure Economics), which falls into two parts: Theory of Exchange, 1874; Theory of Production, 1877; 2d ed., 1889; 3d ed., 1896; 4th ed., 1900; and the last, definitive edition, 1926. His other major works in economics were *Théorie mathématique de la richesse sociale* (*Mathematical Theory of Social Wealth*, 1883) and *Etudes d'économie sociale* (*Studies in Social Economics*, 1896); the latter was concerned with problems of social ethics, such as communism, individualism, private property, nationalization of land, and public finance. His *Etudes d'économie politique appliquée* (*Studies in Applied Economics*, 1898) dealt with practical problems of bimetallism versus monometallism, monopoly versus free competition, free trade, the role of banking and credit, uses and abuses of stock market speculation, and so on. He prepared a sketchy autobiography, published in 1908. He died January 6, 1910.

Walras at Lausanne, 1870-1892

Walras began his career as a teacher at Lausanne in December, 1870, without prior instructional experience. He had studied and written in the general field of political economy, but he had not yet definitely tested his own ability or clearly shaped the direction of his thought. Not much can be said with certainty about the manner of his teaching, or his lectures, or even the general tenor of his course in political economy, although the lectures were reputedly popular. The tendency has been for writers to identify Walras primarily with mathematical economics, but he himself was convinced that the study of political economy fell naturally into three parts, each indispensable and each of equal importance with the other two. The parts were (a) pure theory, (b) the application thereof, and (c) the social aspects and implications of economics. In general, his writings, as their titles indicate, deal with the three aspects of economics.

After retirement in 1892 he lived in Clarens, a small town near Montreux on Lake Geneva. After a year of rest he again devoted himself to writing and published his *Etudes d'économie sociale* (1896) and the *Etudes d'économie politique appliquée* (1898). These two works were not what he would have wished, for he was plagued by ill health. Their titles do not accurately describe the contents: a group of more or less related articles which had been previously published elsewhere, together with a few unpublished ones. In 1903 he wrote a condensed and simplified version of his famous *Eléments d'économie politique pure*, which was not published until many years later.[2] In 1906 he competed for the Nobel Peace Award, submitting an essay on his favorite theme of land nationalization. He failed in the competition; the award for that year went to Theodore Roosevelt.

Throughout his lifetime he kept up a steady correspondence with economists from practically everywhere.[3] Much of the correspondence deals with controversial points in his work and answers to questions about it.

[2] The work was published in 1936, edited by Gaston Leduc, with the title, *Abrégé des éléments d'économie politique pure.*

[3] The Library of the University of Lausanne contains hundreds of letters received from eminent people in many walks of life and also copies of the letters sent by Walras to his correspondents. The letters were meticulously written in longhand and then carefully corrected before being finally rewritten. They are well preserved and catalogued under the title of *Fonds Walras.* He corresponded with Jevons, Böhm-Bawerk, H. L. Moore, John Bates Clark, Irving Fisher, Marshall, Seligman, Schumpeter, Wicksell and many other eminent economists. Edgeworth called him the "Helvetian Jevons" and at times was even scornful in his criticisms.

Of all the economists whose original contributions put them in the first rank, there is no one whose fundamental ideas have been so obscured, whose personality has been so hastily—and incorrectly—appraised as the "founder" of the "Lausanne School." He has been called a "mathematical economist," a "Saint-Simonian," a "socialist of the chair," and a "reformer." None of these terms appropriately characterizes the man, and to apply any particular one necessarily obscures other aspects of perhaps equal importance. He used mathematical techniques, but there is far more to the Walrasian system than the symbolic logic which he chose to expound a part of it. He did refer to himself now and then as a socialist but for him the term had a specialized meaning. He says, "My socialism predisposes me to favor the authority of the state against that of the individual, and not always simply in matters of politics but sometimes from the viewpoint of economics as well . . ." [4] Walras was sympathetic with some of the aspirations of socialism, but he regarded many or even most of their ideals as ill-conceived and impractical. In his opinion, "The day when a true social science is born, there will be no more socialism." [5] He was much more interested in developing a true social science than in becoming a practitioner of socialism.

Although his interest in reform was great, he was not a "reformer" in the generally accepted sense. He deeply desired to see society reorganized on a more "rational" basis but not by jettisoning its institutions. The whole, embracing purpose of his work was social betterment; the theoretical economics on which his claim to fame now rests was to him merely the first step toward this final objective. He had great faith that a "scientific" society could be created and great hope that his work would be "scientific"; therefore he used mathematics as the true language of the scientist. He ridiculed the economic policy of laissez faire and held that "orthodox" economists were unable to create a genuine social science.

It is incorrect to identify Walras solely as a mathematical methodologist although he made great use of mathematics. He had faith in the ability of science to make a better society and in that sense he was a reformer; he may have had socialistic tendencies, for he did advocate the nationalization of land and believed that conditions could be improved by state intervention. No one of these classifications is especially significant now or redounds to his credit or discredit in view of the importance of his contributions to economic science.

[4] *Etudes d'économie sociale*, pp. 165-66.
[5] *Ibid.*, p. 72.

Marginal Utility Analysis.—Walras' *Elements of Pure Economics* contains the theories which established the author's originality and indicated the direction which he believed that scientific economics should take. It has already been indicated that he was a codiscoverer of the marginal utility principle, along with Jevons and Menger. However, he alone has the credit for the original development of general economic equilibrium analysis.

Although his *Eléments* appeared in 1874, three years after Jevons and Menger had "staked their claims," their works were unknown to him.[6] Walras used the same basic concepts as Jevons in developing his subjective value theory—utility and limitation of the supply of the commodity. He employed the term *rareté* (a term developed and used by his father) as "l'intensité du dernier besoin satisfait par une quantité consommée de marchandise." (The intensity of the last want satisfied by consuming one unit of goods.)[7] *Rareté* was defined as "la dérivée de l'utilité effective par rapport à la quantité possédée." (The derivative of effective utility in relation to the quantity possessed.)[8] *Rareté*, in short, is marginal utility. The term has the same meaning as Jevons' "final degree of utility" and Gossen's "value of the last atom."

Walras held that the individual's own choice was basic. The individual, always wishing to maximize his own satisfactions, will resort to an exchange of goods to accomplish this end. This desire, when coupled with the amount or supply of goods available to each individual, makes it theoretically possible to arrive at a determinable supply and demand for the individual. The relationship can then be shown either symbolically or graphically. Under competitive market conditions, an equilibrium will be achieved when the price which prevails equates supply and demand. Walras' own account of the nature of equilibrium is something like this: Persons come to the market with certain amounts of commodities and with certain desires to dispose of them (*dispositions à l'enchère*) at various prices. If all commodities are disposed of at these prices, then supply and demand are equal and an equilibrium exists in that market. But if supply and demand are not equal, prices will be changed until an equilibrium is reached. This is the general equilibrium theory of exchange and the theory for which Walras is best known, his concept of marginal utility and other contributions notwithstanding.

---

[6] A student at the University of Leyden (Holland), one M. Bourouill, wrote Walras in May, 1874, pointing out the similarity of his work to Jevons' *Theory of Political Economy*. Walras promptly wrote Jevons, admitting the priority of the latter's theory. These letters are in the *Fonds Walras*.

[7] *Eléments* (5th ed., 1926), p. 76.

[8] *Ibid.*, p. 103.

The novel element in Walras' analysis was not that he emphasized demand and supply, for others had done that, but that he stressed the functional interdependence of demand, supply, and price. He did not anticipate all the possible market situations that could exist, but for most situations he believed that the subjective marginal estimates of the individuals would ultimately establish a balanced, stable equilibrium of demand, supply, and price which fully expressed the *rareté* of the good. Thus, once an individual equilibrium is established, the general exchange equilibrium follows, which rests on a general system of interdependence among demand, supply, and price. While there remains an unreal element in his marginal utility emphasis, as well as a tendency to overlook the nature of costs, his equilibrium analysis is very significant. It might be contended that he was so concerned with equilibrium that he overlooked problems other than those directly bearing upon equilibrium. Likewise he held a naïve faith that competition would maximize utility, as did Jevons, although that is not necessarily true. Nevertheless, the Walrasian equilibrium theory has wide implications.

General Equilibrium Analysis.—A marginal utility concept was only his first step in developing what is familiarly known as the Walrasian system of general equilibrium. Indeed, if this had been all there was to his system, one would have to agree with Professor Jaffé that Walras would be remembered only as a codiscoverer of marginal utility.[9] But the system encompasses the whole field of value and price in a much more comprehensive manner than had been presented by any previous economist.

Walras assumed perfect competition and uniformity of price throughout the given market. Then he demonstrated mathematically that general equilibrium in this market requires the following conditions to be satisfied. First, each individual will have a utility curve for each good and service offered in the market. Next, he will maximize his utility by exchange. And last, he will then obtain the greatest possible satisfaction when the prices paid in the exchange are proportional to the marginal utility of the good purchased. Further, a necessary corollary is that the supply of each good and service must equal the demand for it. It follows then that the price of each good or service must in the long run equal its cost of production. Walras could thus arrive at a static equilibrium analysis under perfect competition, one of the most useful concepts in economic theory. Hicks remarks, "Although static equilibrium is far from being the whole of economics, it is an in-

---

[9] William Jaffé, "Unpublished Papers and Letters of Léon Walras," *Journal of Political Economy*, XLIII (April 1935), 187-207.

dispensable foundation, and the greater part was laid by Cournot and Walras. There are very few economists who have contributed so much to the permanent body of established truth as Walras did." [10]

Walras, as has been indicated, was not especially concerned with cost theory as such. General equilibrium emphasis, in which he was mainly interested, was superior to any labor-cost analysis in the Ricardian sense —a classical tradition. However, since in his equilibrium analysis he held that the price of the product was equal in the long run to the cost of production, one may well ask what cost he had in mind. The implications are that he held to an "alternative" or "opportunity" cost doctrine. He arrived at this by use of equilibrium, reasoning that if prices exceed cost of production, a profit results which leads to an expansion in production and an increase in supply of goods; supply then exceeds demand, and a fall in price is inevitable. The reverse is just as true: a loss on the sale of goods leads to a diminution of supply and a subsequent rise in price in response to demand. His reasoning requires that all exchange depends upon the maximization of satisfactions. Therefore resources will be utilized by the producer in such a manner that his maximum satisfaction as a producer is obtained in the same manner as is the satisfaction of a consumer, for the producer is likewise a consumer of his own products or those of others. It is just as important for the producer to maximize his satisfactions as it is for the consumer, since this leads to equilibrium when each has attained the maximum.

Profits occupy an important place in his analysis. He used profits in the sense of "normal" profits which are a part of production costs (i.e., profits which could be earned by an entrepreneur in alternative activities). Edgeworth, the English mathematical economist, was severely critical of Walras for making price (including normal profits) equal cost of production; however, the issue between them is now of only academic interest.

Even though it may be argued with considerable accuracy that Walras' treatment of cost and supply seems inadequate in the light of recent theory, his analysis gave an exact version of the "opportunity" cost element in value. In the end, all costs become the same, and whether they are identified as "alternative" or "real" costs (in Marshall's sense) is a distinction without a difference. Walras held fast to his belief in subjectivism and used it effectively for both demand and supply analysis. He broke with labor-cost value theory as sharply as did the Austrians and more sharply than did Marshall.

[10] J. R. Hicks, "Léon Walras," *Econometrica*, II (1934), 347.

The really significant contribution of Walras was his general equilibrium analysis. He succeeded in linking together two markets: the
first one was the market for goods; and the second, the market for the
services of the factors of production. This did not imply a market for
only a single commodity but for all commodities and for all productive
factors. He visualized the whole economy as a series of interdependent
markets, with demand, supply, and price influencing one another and
also what he called "the productive services" of the factors. For example, an individual purchases a commodity in a competitive market at
a price which is a result of demand and supply under a given set of
market conditions. The commodity may be manufactured by a concern which draws some raw materials from mines, some from agriculture,
and so on. Walras would then contend that the producer of the commodity in turn would be buying the "productive services" of the workers
in the mines, the fertility of the lands, and the productivity of capital.
The laws of exchange under competition would establish the wages paid
to labor, the rent to land, and the interest to capital, which are the
productive factors. The price paid for the commodity, just as in the case
of the price of the productive factors, would be determined by the laws
of supply and demand. Those laws would also equate the amount of
"productive service" demanded and the amount offered. Thus the
price of goods and the price of "productive services" are linked together
in an equilibrium which runs throughout the entire economic structure.

The basic laws which are at work to bring about the equilibria are:

1. There can be only one price for one class of goods in the same
market.
2. The price of the commodity will make the amount offered and
the amount taken equal.
3. The price will thus give maximum satisfaction to both buyers
and sellers.

The operation of these laws would assure equilibrium. They would
be applicable to a commodity or service not only at the consumers'
level, but also at the producers' level. Assuming that factors of production flow freely in response to various uses, an equilibrium would be
established as a result of the supply of and the demand for the factors
for all possible uses. But the entrepreneurs in a competitive economy
are really buyers of services from the owners of the capital goods and
from labor and land. Here again the price of the service would be
equated by supply and demand. Likewise, in the market for finished
goods equilibrium prices would equate supply and demand.

Walras' treatment of equilibrium is both exhaustive and complex. He was the first to bridge the gap in the analysis of the value of resources and their services. In his analysis the prices of *all* goods and services were considered. Most students, familiar with the partial-equilibrium analysis of Alfred Marshall and neoclassical economists, think in terms of "other things being equal." That is, both demand and supply of a commodity would vary with a change in price, on the assumption that all other prices remain unchanged. Walras' formula brought in all other prices, and thus presented a most comprehensive analysis of general equilibrium.

Walras made significant contributions to capital theory in distinguishing between capital goods and their services. Stocks of goods and cash balances enter into his equilibrium analysis and are considered on a high and theoretical plane. He also laid the foundation for the integration of value theory and monetary theory.[11]

Many writers on economic subjects had attempted an equilibrium analysis, starting with Cantillon in 1755. No one was as successful as Walras, yet his general equilibrium theory and other contributions tend to be overlooked because he is so frequently remembered for his *rareté* and nothing else. His use of this term has been largely responsible for linking him with Jevons and Menger, when actually he should be linked more closely to Alfred Marshall and neoclassical equilibrium analysis. What separated them seems to have been matters of interest and emphasis, not technique in analysis. In some respects Walras was a keener, sharper analyst than Marshall. Walras sought for the general principles underlying economic behavior which led to general equilibrium; Marshall sought for analytical economic instruments or "tools" of universal application. Marshall was forging research tools; Walras was drawing an analytical picture of the whole economy in operation. The two systems have tended to become one over the years, and the major share of the credit for developing equilibrium analysis has gone to Alfred Marshall.[12]

Walras wished to make economics an abstract science in which pure economics would be separated from applied economics. He had no intention of making it a complete social science; indeed, he did not regard theoretical economics as a social science but as a pure science. In this respect he resembled Jevons and Gossen. Walras placed great

[11] See Arthur W. Marget, "Léon Walras and the 'Cash-Balance Approach' to the problem of the Value of Money," *Journal of Political Economy*, XXXIV (1931), 569-600.

[12] In December 1934, the American Economic Association, the American Statistical Association, and the Econometric Society held a joint Walras Centennial Program. Some of the papers presented at this meeting are extremely valuable. They are reprinted in the *Journal of Political Economy*, XLIII.

faith in *rareté* as a concept which would lead to the maximization of want satisfaction; both demand and supply depended on *rareté* and they in turn depended upon the maximization of satisfaction; in market exchange a single price would result which would be an expression of equilibrium maximizing the satisfaction of both parties, i.e., the buyers and sellers. This analysis is applicable to any number of commodities, not only to two as in Jevons' analysis. The novel element in the Walrasian analysis is the functional interdependence of demand, supply, and price, all of which are ultimately determined by *rareté*.

Despite the equilibrium and interdependence of the three determinants, the concept of *rareté* still remains subjective. More recent theories hold this explanation to be unsatisfactory in value analysis. Yet the fact remains, as the Austrians have contended, that the center of value is within the individual, who is the final arbiter. If goods are not wanted, they will not be produced, at least not for long. Goods stand midway between production and consumption; the pre-Walrasian theories made the value of goods rest on the former; the theories of Gossen, Jevons, and Walras made it rest on the latter. A great deal of modern economic analysis is very little concerned with the value or price theory but rather with whether or not people have income with which to buy the good. Could it not be that if they possess income, their decisions to buy are largely or even purely subjective? Walrasian economics will be discussed further in conjunction with the economics of Vilfredo Pareto.

Vilfredo Pareto, The Second Lausanne Economist

Vilfredo Pareto succeeded Walras in the chair of political economy at Lausanne, and his contributions to economic science are also outstanding. Pareto entered the field of political economy at the age of forty-five after abandoning a career as engineer.[13] His interest in theo-

[13] Vilfredo Pareto was born in Paris July 15, 1848; his mother was a Parisienne and his father an Italian *marchese* from Genoa. For political reasons the elder Pareto spent much time in exile. In 1858, when the Italian government proclaimed a general political amnesty, the Pareto family returned to Italy where Vilfredo Pareto remained until he left for Switzerland in 1893. Pareto was educated in the Institute of Technology and later the Polytechnical School of the University of Turin, specializing in mathematics and physics. Apparently he had no interest in the social sciences at this time.

In his early years he was employed by the Italian railways and next by a large iron works for sixteen years; the latter position afforded the opportunity for extensive travel in England and on the Continent; since his connection with the concern was that of manager-director, he was in touch with many problems in applied economics. On various occasions he came in contact with the contemporary literati who stimulated his interests in several fields. As a result of this and of his own intellectual bent he read widely in ancient and contemporary philosophy, especially

retical economics was probably aroused by Maffeo Pantaleoni, a professor of political economy in the University of Rome, who was not
himself a mathematical economist but a great admirer of Walras and
his work; he was instrumental in awakening in Pareto an appreciation
of Walras' contributions to economics. G. H. Bousquet quotes Pareto
as saying, "I had read Walras, and . . . had failed to see anything in
his work but barren ore of metaphysical argument. I therefore put the
book away in disgust. . . . But after reading Pantaleoni's 'Principles' I
modified my previous opinion, I reread Walras, and this time I found
in his work the vein of gold, that is to say, the concept of an economic
equilibrium." [14] Thus, Pareto's appointment to the University of Lausanne gave him an opportunity to pursue his own intellectual interests
in much more friendly surroundings than were afforded him in Florence,
Italy, where he then lived. In view of Pareto's alleged connections with
Fascism, discussed subsequently, it is well to note that Pareto was not
friendly toward the preceding Italian government. He attacked it for

Comte, Spencer, and Darwin, ancient languages and institutions, religious dogma,
and so on.

His early writings, most of which appeared in journals, bore the tone of a "liberal"
on current issues of wages, government ownership, and other problems arising in a
government which was becoming more democratic.

In 1890 he inherited a comfortable fortune and retired from business to devote
himself to his studies. He seems to have had hopes of securing a chair of political
economy in Italy. In the meantime, Walras' health had failed and forced his retirement at Lausanne. Walras was privileged to nominate his own successor to the
chair of political economy. It is probable that the acquaintance between Walras
and Pareto was confined to their correspondence, but in any event Walras recommended that Pareto become his successor. This was welcome to Pareto for he
wished to leave Italy and also to advance the cause of pure economics.

Pareto went to Lausanne in April 1893 with the rank of professor-extraordinary
and entered the second phase of his career (first an engineer; then, an economist;
and last, a sociologist). His work was successful and he was promoted to a professorship the following year. He lectured on "pure" economics for one semester and on
"applied" economics the next. From 1897 to 1898 he taught sociology as well
as political economy. In 1900 Pareto suffered a long illness and Boninsegni, his
assistant, took over his duties and continued to do so intermittently for about four
years. In 1906 Pareto again became ill and in 1909 he resigned his chair at Lausanne. He retired to his villa "Angora" near Céligny on Lake Geneva, where he
lived and worked until he died in August 1923.

Despite ill health he produced a prodigious amount of work after retirement. His
best known works are *Cours d'économie politique* (Lausanne, Vol. I, 1896, Vol. II,
1897); *Les Systèmes Socialistes* (Paris, 1903); *Manuale d'economia politica* (Milan,
1906); *Trattato di sociologia generale* (Paris and Lausanne, 1919; translated as *Mind
and Society*, 4 vols., New York, 1935). For intimate biographical sketches see M. M.
Einaudi, "Pareto as I knew him," *Atlantic Monthly*, CLVI (1935). Arthur Liv-
ingston, "Vilfredo Pareto, a Biographical Portrait," *Saturday Review of Literature*,
XII, No. 4 (1935); Georges-Henri Bousquet, *Vilfredo Pareto: sa vie et son oeuvre*
(Paris, 1928). Joseph Schumpeter, "Vilfredo Pareto," *Quarterly Journal of Eco-
nomics*, LXIII, No. 2 (May 1949); reprinted in his *Ten Great Economists* (New
York, 1951).

[14] *Vilfredo Pareto: sa vie et son oeuvre* (Paris, 1928), p. 18.

its corruption and favoritism, its protectionist policy, militarism, crushing taxes, and lack of leadership and his criticisms were sharp and telling. His change of residence to Switzerland was welcome to both parties.

Pareto's lectures at Lausanne followed the plan used by Walras of "pure" economics for one term, after which came "applied" economics. His work, *Cours d'économie politique* (1896-97), was not a required text for his course, and he may have conducted his lectures without the aid of mathematics.[15] The chair of political economy at Lausanne was under the jurisdiction of the faculty of law; this fact may have had some influence on the manner in which the materials were presented. He lectured in both political economy and sociology from 1897 to 1900; but upon his return to the University after a four-year illness he lectured in sociology only. He explains this change in his major interest as follows:

Having arrived at a certain point in my researches in political economy, I seemed unable to continue ahead. Many obstacles confronted me . . . and among these was the truly interdependent relationship which exists among the social phenomena of all sorts. Just as in our times it has come to be realized that the theory of chemistry is linked with that of electricity, and vice versa, so also it is evident that no single social study can progress far without the aid of all the others.[16]

His *Cours* was out of print and he decided not to prepare another edition; instead he began work on his *Manuel*,[17] which was intended to be a transition from pure economics to sociology. His career at Lausanne was cut short in 1909 by a severe heart condition which made him unable to continue on the faculty and to attend the Walrus Jubilee held that summer. Despite his enforced retirement, he produced some of his best work in the last years of his life.

Pareto's name has been associated with the fascist movement in Italy. He was even called the "Prophet of Fascism" and the "Karl Marx of the Bourgeoisie." He had witnessed the disturbing events in Italy after 1914 and expressed opinions antithetical to democracy. His sociological views, in which he held a theory of the superiority of the elite, might be construed as supporting a strong dictatorial government. Despite this, Pareto disclaimed any active support of the leader or of the movement. It is both illogical and unfair to impute to Pareto the role of either founder or supporter of Fascism.

[15] Guido Sensini, *Corrispondenza di Vilfredo Pareto* (1948) indicates (p. 5) that such was the case.
[16] *Jubilé du professeur Vilfredo Pareto* (Lausanne, 1917), p. 54.
[17] *Manuel d'économie politique* (Paris, 1909) is the French edition of the *Manuale d'economia politica* (Milan, 1906).

Pareto's Economics: The Meaning of Pure Economics.—Both Walras and Pareto used the term "pure" economics, a term which carried the connotation that economics could become as "pure" or as exact as any physical science. The Lausanne economists conceived the abstract science of pure economics to be related to practical problems in economic life in accordance with the then prevailing philosophy, and expressible in terms of the latest scientific accuracy.[18]

Both Walras and Pareto referred to their work as "pure economics" and believed it to be sharply differentiated from the work of other economists. Their nomenclature was both a hallmark and an expression of a conviction that, comparatively speaking, their work was scientific. At least three features characterize their use of "pure" economics: (1) a strenuous insistence on the truly scientific value of the system; (2) the importance assigned to mathematics; and (3) the complete rejection by them of all causal theories which purport to explain economic phenomena and the supplanting of such cause-and-effect relationships by a generalized theory of *mutual* dependence among economic quanta.

Since Walras was the originator of the term, one would expect to find it clearly identified in his writings. But this is not done with incisiveness. He says, "Pure economics is . . . essentially the theory of price-determination under a hypothetical regime of absolute competition." [19] In another work he defines it as "the science which proves that free competition combines services and natural resources in such a way that maximum satisfaction is the result." [20] Later in the same book he says that pure economics is "not alone the rational science of physiologico-economic men and their division of labor, but also the mathematical determination of the prices of exchangeable goods through the mechanism of free competition." [21] The first definition is the one most frequently cited; it appears early in his major work which deals exhaustively with pure economics. The next definition indicates the end product of the science; the last characterizes some of his basic assumptions, especially free competition. None are very illuminating; it is clear, however, that he regarded scientific economics as a means of providing a basis for reform of economic society. Or, as he stated in

---

[18] It may be argued with logical consistency that the work of Walras and Pareto in "pure" economics was motivated by the positivism of Auguste Comte which had gained widespread popularity at this time. The Comtian theories were a conspicuous part of the intellectual life of the nineteenth century. Likewise, the advances made by French and Italian scholars in mathematical science, together with the early training of both men in mathematics and engineering, presented an amalgam which greatly influenced both the nature and the quality of the work of the Lausanne economists.

[19] *Eléments d'économie politique pure* (5th ed., Lausanne, 1926), p. xi.

[20] *Etudes d'économie politique appliquée* (Lausanne, 1898), p. 265.

[21] *Ibid.*, p. 451.

still another place, ". . . first, work out a science of pure economics upon which to establish an applied economics; then, perfect this latter with a view to social reform." [22] Pure economics is that division of economics which pertains to science; applied economics relates to industry; social economics relates to morals—social morals, the ultimate perfection of which was always foremost in his mind.

Pareto was admittedly a follower of Walras—at least in his desire to give "pure" economics the stature of a science. To a considerable degree, he was content to allow the Walrasian concept of "pure" to stand. Pure economics, according to Pareto, was simply "a first approximation of the phenomena which enter into, and of the general conditions prerequisite for, an economic equilibrium." [23] While he treated pure economics as a first approximation, he regarded applied economics as making the many successive approximations necessary to explain the working of economic forces, but not to ascertain the economic behavior of an individual. Although this statement reveals something of the nature of pure economics, it is really not "defined" in a sense which would differentiate it from other economics. It was, however, treated by the Lausanne economists as a "rational" science, abstract and mathematical, which are attributes by no means applicable only to pure economics. In any event the Lausanne economists, reflecting the philosophy of Positivism, were confident that economics could become a science and that it could be best expressed in mathematical symbols. Both held a strong belief in the functional rather than the causal approach to economic phenomena.[24]

The Role of Mathematics in Pure Economics.—Both Walras and Pareto used mathematics extensively in developing their pure economics. In fact, Walras has been credited with founding the mathematical school. Economists deal with quantitative problems of more or less, maximum or minimum, and so on. Since mathematics is the science of quantities, economic data, which were quantitative, clearly fell within its scope. That economic data were subjected to mathematical treatment has been seen in economic literature at least since Petty's *Political Arithmetic*. (See Chapter 6.) The use of mathematics by the Lau-

[22] *Ibid.*, p. 69.

[23] *Cours d'économie politique*, I, 3, 16-17. See also Pareto's *Manuel d'économie politique* (1909), p. 29.

[24] Pareto developed in the *Cours* a theory which has since been known as "Pareto's Law." Briefly stated, it held that definite proportions of the factors of production were required in order to insure maximum efficiency in production. In the *Manuel* he developed the "law" of income distribution statistically (in the chapter on population), stating that the greater the fortune the smaller the number of persons who possess it. Subsequent criticisms and changes have left very little of the original doctrines.

sanne economists was by no means a novelty. Both Walras and Pareto, having been trained in engineering, were inclined to use quantitative methods; therefore they developed pure economics as a mathematical discipline. Walras remarks, "Pure economics . . . that is, the theory of social wealth considered by itself, is a physico-mathematical science like mechanics and hydraulics, and its practitioners should not fear to employ the methods and language of mathematics." [25]   He believed that only mathematics provided the exactness which was badly needed in the science of economics and which would enable political economy to free itself of "alleged demonstrations which are nothing more than gratuitous assertions."   Likewise we can never have a "true science until demonstrations have taken the place of argumentation." [26] Thus Walras held to the mathematical presentation which, in his opinion, was the only way of establishing final proof.

Pareto, who was by far the better mathematician of the two, was less inclined to use mathematics to establish final truth. He regarded mathematics as a procedural convenience, not as a machine for authenticating previous conclusions. It was a necessary but an insufficient instrument for effective analysis of economic problems. He was critical of earlier economists who had attempted to establish in words propositions which, in reality, demanded the use of simultaneous equations. Ordinary discussions and verbal logic were satisfactory in setting forth cause-and-effect relationships, but helpless in dealing with interdependence of phenomena.

Even though Pareto spoke of the absolute necessity to use mathematics in pure economics, he has given his readers, in both the *Cours* and the *Manuel*, lucid expositions of economic phenomena in forceful language free from mathematical symbols. However, in developing the concept of mutual interdependence, upon which the Lausanne system of general equilibrium is founded, there is ample justification for the use of mathematics in treating the related variables.

The mathematical approach was vigorously defended by both Walras and Pareto as necessary to pure economics. The reasons for their defense rest upon their sincere desire to make use of the language of science—mathematics—and to produce a science which would be recognized and acknowledged as such. There seemed no other way to raise political economy to this objective level than by the generally accepted media of science. The fact that the authors of pure economics chose to use this medium for expression neither proves nor disproves the scientific accuracy of the theory. They chose this method of exposition; final

[25] *Eléments*, pp. 29-30.
[26] *Ibid.*, p. 427.

evaluation of pure economics must rest upon its achievements, not on the form of its expression.

The Theories of Walras and Pareto Compared.—Earlier in this chapter, Walras' concept of marginal utility, or *rareté,* and his general equilibrium analysis were discussed. Even though Pareto was admittedly the follower of Walras, the models of general equilibrium analysis developed by the two were not identical. They differed in methods of analysis and presentation. The technical superiority of the work of Pareto reflects his superior training as a mathematician. Likewise it is apparent that Pareto was extremely able and original, and he would not be likely to follow Walras in every detail. Some of the Paretian variations follow.

Walras introduced the term *rareté,* or "the intensity of the last need satisfied." Pareto introduced the term *ophélimité,* which he thought would be more expressive and would preclude disputes over the meaning of such terms as "utility" and "*rareté.*" The expressions "final degree of utility," used by Jevons, and *Grenznutzen,* as developed by the Austrians, were interchangeable with "marginal utility." Pareto hoped his "neutral" word, *ophélimité* (the power to give satisfaction), would take the place of all predecessors and avoid the use of "utility" with its shades of meaning. His hopes were not fulfilled, and the term has only curiosity value now.

Both Walras and Pareto made extensive use of mathematics, as has been indicated. In general, Walras used only algebra and plane geometry in developing his pure economics. Pareto employed the calculus in his exposition of equilibrium, particularly in the Appendix of his *Manuel.* The extensive use of mathematics by Pareto was not designed to display his peculiar skill and talent, but was a necessary technique for developing his concept of *ophélimité.* His three-dimensional graphs showed a high order of complexity, whereas Walras used the ordinary plane or two-dimensional graphs. In the *Manuel,* to explain his "theory of choice," Pareto made use of the "indifference curves" [27] which could be used in place of the usual demand curve. Pareto used the "indifference curves" without any connotation of utility. The new indifference curves were to replace utility postulates by postulates based upon observable behavior and thereby put pure economic theory on a more secure basis. Despite heroic attempts by Pareto and other subsequent writers, it may be observed that no one has succeeded in devel-

[27] Pareto fully acknowledged his indebtedness to the English economist F. Y. Edgeworth, who first developed the indifference curves in his *Mathematical Psychics* (London, 1881). See Pareto's *Cours,* Vol. I, p. 66 n.

oping an indifference map from a whole series of indifference curves
by means of empirical data.

The differences between Walrasian and Paretian theory were not
really acute. They indicated differences in point of view or procedure
rather than a fundamental disagreement over substance. However, the
two Lausanne economists did have sharply different ideas concerning
economic motivation. Both men agreed to the proposition that the
individual as well as the economic system, as an aggregate, has an
economic "center of gravity" and is subject to the usual "laws" of economic equilibrium. Each delineated a system of economic equilibrium
as he saw it, and each arrived at essentially the same conclusion, namely,
that in the individual and in the economic system as well, there is an
"equilibrium-seeking" tendency omnipresent in all economic activities.

The Lausanne economists agreed that such tendencies existed, but
disagreed on why they should exist. For example, the theories of value
held by the two may be used to explain the case at point. In his
Eléments Walras digressed from the "straight and narrow" of scientific
method and followed tradition by including discussions of the "causes"
of value in the theory of general equilibrium, although general equilibrium theory, inter alia, tacitly denies the validity of simple theories of
causation. Walras, it should be noted, strongly defended the concept
of rareté, originally developed by his father, Antoine-Auguste Walras,
in 1831 long before Léon developed his own theory of general equilibrium. When he wrote the Eléments, in which he introduced the
general equilibrium theory, he used and defended the rareté concept,
perhaps because of filial pride, or perhaps because of the persistence of
deep-seated convictions. In any event, this stand resulted in an inconsistency in the Eléments. In one place he writes, "It is certain that
rareté is the cause of exchange value." [28] Whereas, elsewhere he admits,
"Theoretically, all of the unknowns in the economic system are dependent upon all the equations of economic equilibrium" (p. 289). The
first of these two assertions cannot be reconciled with the definition of
pure economics (the theory of price determination under hypothetical
conditions of absolute competition, cf. p. 466) as the Lausanne economists defined it; it is merely an undemonstrated assertion, even if made
by the great Walras himself. Walras' rareté is treated here as a "cause"
of value side by side with his theory of general equilibrium which denies
simple theories of causation.

It appears at first glance that Pareto, too, violated the canons of consistency; he used ophélimité in place of rareté to mean precisely the
same thing, the "cause" of value. The "causal" discussion is followed

[28] Eléments, p. 102.

by the general equilibrium treatment so that Pareto, like Walras, seems to have presented two mutually exclusive theories. A closer reading indicates that the apparent parallel between Walras and Pareto on "cause" of value really does not exist. They agree that their favorite terms, *rareté* and *ophélimité*, are the mainsprings governing economic activity, but they disagree with one another on the motivating causes underlying each term.

Walras' concept makes *rareté* a function of the quantity of the good in which the consumer is interested at a given moment. Pareto makes his *ophélimité* conditional not only upon the number of units he already has, but also upon the number of units of other goods he can command. The latter is not inconsistent with general equilibrium theory, since in its origin *ophélimité* is but another manifestation of the mutual interdependence of phenomena, the controlling principle that underlies a general equilibrium of objective economic phenomena. Pareto was careful not to say that *ophélimité* was the cause of exchange value. On this point he allowed himself to depart from the purely scientific and accept "metaphysical" or undemonstrated propositions. However, he did not commit the error of maintaining that the cause of value (subjective) was also the cause of exchange value (objective) or price. Pareto's attempt to be completely scientific and free from metaphysical speculations is more nearly accomplished in his *Manuel* than in the *Cours*. Marginal utility theory, under whatever name, is absent from the *Manuel* and in its place appears "indifference analysis," or the theory of choice. He seemed to believe that the use of indifference analysis rendered unnecessary any discussion of reasons underlying economic behavior.

Pareto, in his efforts to be "scientific," discarded his concept of *ophélimité* and accepted indifference analysis. The choice netted very little scientifically. Despite refinements made by many economists in recent years,[29] the "theory of choice" seems no more realistic than the theory of marginal utility, since each of the theories simply offers a more or less plausible explanation of observed phenomena; the one is just as speculative or metaphysical as the other. It is difficult to see that indifference analysis has any more scientific objectivity than the subjective tenor of the marginal utility approach.

Both Walras and Pareto held theories of general economic equilibrium. That economic forces tended to work toward equilibrium was held by each to be a certainty, not a hypothesis. The dynamics of the tendency was attributable to competition. However, the two men differed as

[29] See J. R. Hicks, *Value and Capital* (London, 1939); Geo. Stigler, *The Theory of Price* (New York, 1946); A. L. Meyers, *Elements of Modern Economics* (New York, 1948); K. Boulding, *Economic Analysis* (New York, 1948); and others.

to the way in which competition worked, Walras holding a concept very similar to the "invisible hand" idea of Adam Smith in which competition could be relied upon to lead people to the most suitable occupations, to make the most advantageous exchanges, and so on—a benevolent point of view. However, Walras saw certain institutional obstacles to the free play of competition, such as private ownership of land, protective tariffs, monopolies, and the laws of inheritance. If and when monopolies had to be tolerated, the revenues therefrom should accumulate to the state. Barring this necessity, competition should prevail, leading to the fullest rewards to the factors of production and to society. Competition was not a struggle for economic power and wealth unless institutional limitations had restricted it and brought a corruption of the objectives. It was, on the other hand, basically natural and desirable in bringing about equilibrium.

Pareto, like Walras, also had a strong aversion to monopolies, but he did not share the same sanguine views on competition. His philosophy was that the strong invariably oppress the weak; when they cease to do this, they themselves fall prey to other oppressors. This philosophy, he thought, explained the persistence of special privilege, monopolies, corrupt government, and many other evils in society. His views on equilibrium, whether personal or general, were then merely a result of the balance of forces: equilibrium occurs when the diametrically opposed forces of *desires* and *obstacles* are in balance. Desires are human wants; obstacles arise because the supply of goods to satisfy these wants is limited, and because the goods must be transformed or changed in some or in many ways before they can satisfy the desires of individuals. In addition, similar desires on the part of other persons create obstacles which interfere with the satisfaction of wants of one another, and so on. As it is with individuals, so it is with the entire economic system. Equilibrium consists of balancing the whole myriad of conflicting forces and objectives, with a resulting compromise of the forces rather than a completely optimum state of affairs. Pareto also saw that, because of scarcity of materials, complete gratification of the desires of some would have to be, in part at least, at the expense of others. Since he was completely aware of the multitude of forces, and the differences in the strength thereof, he had less confidence in competition as a regulator. The tendencies of the economic system toward equilibrium were, in Walras' opinion, not only real but highly desirable. Pareto also recognized the tendency toward equilibrium but denied any ethical connotations; he also recognized that equilibrium would, at best, terminate in a relative, not absolute, position of rest.

Points of difference between the two great Lausanne economists, although significant, hardly place them poles apart. They were in complete agreement on such important fundamentals as the use of the language of mathematics to express abstract ideas, the desire to elevate pure economics to the status of a science, the dislike for the metaphysical or causal theories, the substitution of the concepts of mutual dependency and of a tendency toward general economic equilibrium in the place of these same causal theories. These are the basic attributes which permit the term "Lausanne school" to be applied to the work of these two men.

The "Lausanne School"–Fact or Fiction?–The term, "Lausanne School," has been studiously avoided thus far in this chapter for reasons which will appear hereafter. The works of each of the two famous Lausanne economists have been considered in areas of similarity and in points of disagreement. Generally speaking, the two men have been referred to collectively as the "Lausanne School." [30] Much has been written, especially by European scholars, on one or both of the two constituent parts of the so-called "Lausanne theory," viz., general economic equilibrium and the mathematics of this theory. The tendency has been to amplify the general economic equilibrium out of all proportion to the place which it actually occupied in the thinking of either Walras or Pareto. Likewise, the mathematics used by them has become a prolific source of polemics, although it was intended only for logical expression. The goal of pure economics was to develop a science that would actually work for the improved welfare of the whole society.

Was there a Lausanne school? There is no unanimity of agreement among writers on economic thought as to the contributions, if any, made by the Lausanne economists.[31] Some refer to the achievement of the Lausanne economists in general equilibrium theory,[32] while others refer to the mathematics of the economics. None treat the Lausanne school in totality or elucidate the doctrines of this supposed school —for good reason. The term, "school," should not be used unless there is evidence that the persons to whom membership is imputed were in substantial agreement with its leaders on some major principles or poli-

[30] It is believed that the first time the term "Lausanne school" was used was by Herman Laurent, professor of mathematics at the Ecole Polytechnique in Paris. The term appears in the title of his small book, Petit traité d'économie politique mathématique, rédige conformément aux préceptes de l'école de Lausanne, Paris, 1902. Common and popular usage of the works of Walras and Pareto brought a wide acceptance of the term. The University of Lausanne sanctioned the term and preserved it in a plaque honoring Walras. There is no evidence that either Walras or Pareto used the term.

[31] L. F. Haney remarks, "Nevertheless one puts down the 'pure political economy' with the feeling that little if anything has been added to real knowledge," History of Economic Thought (1949 ed.), p. 601.

[32] E. Whittaker, History of Economics Ideas (New York, 1940), p. 459 ff. or Suranyi-Unger, Economics in the Twentieth Century (New York, 1931).

cies. At this juncture the physiocrats come to mind as perhaps the truest example of a "school" that has existed (at least by definition) in all economic literature. It is unfortunate that the term, "school," which is frequently used in the social sciences, carries with it such a large residue of uncertainty as to both fundamental principles and objectives.

So it is with the "Lausanne School." Léon Walras and Vilfredo Pareto had almost nothing in common except a firm conviction that mathematics was the best way to express their theories, and a common belief that the economic system tends toward a position of general economic equilibrium. In many other respects the two men were in fundamental, even violent, disagreement.

It is certain that Walras hoped a "Lausanne School" would develop from his concepts of scientific economics. On the occasion of his Jubilee at the University of Lausanne he remarked, "I make so bold as to say that, to the utmost extent of my ability, I have endeavored earnestly—with what success only the future will know—to give to this place the glory of having established a 'school' from which, it may be, there will come forth a proliferation of solutions for the problems now obstructing the way to peace and the welfare of society." [33] Here he makes it clear that welfare is the ultimate objective of his life's work, not mathematical virtuosity or "model building." Boninsegni, who carried on when Pareto was ill and who later was his successor for a time, remarks that Walras left a legacy of work that was "incomplete and imperfect" and that Pareto had "continued Walras' work, perfecting it and giving it a new aspect, more complete and rigorous." [34] His remarks are applicable only to Walras' theory of general economic equilibrium, not to the full objective of Walrasian economics. Neither Pareto nor Boninsegni subscribed to Walras' conception of the perfectibility of man or agreed with Walras' view that the real reason for abstract economic theory is its potential usefulness in improving human welfare. Thus it appears that, even at Lausanne, from the beginning there was no real "school" but merely a tenuous nexus of interest in mathematical economics and a common desire to be scientific in an analysis of economic problems. Walras was bitterly disappointed that Pareto, the person he himself recommended to be his successor, should reject his cherished views of social reform through the advance of economic science.

In time the two Lausanne economists drew farther and farther apart. Pareto seemed to feel a somewhat patronizing contempt for Walras combined with some reluctant admiration. Walras held for Pareto an

[33] *Op. cit.*, p. 128.
[34] *Jubilé du professeur Vilfredo Pareto*, p. 11.

inveterate dislike and a conviction that his successor had betrayed him. Walras showed no disposition to maintain a professional aloofness; on the contrary, he tried to embarrass Pareto and disparage his work.[35]

Thus it appears that to impute the term "Lausanne School" to the two economists Walras and Pareto would denote a meaning far narrower than usually indicated by "school." The name "Lausanne School" is still in common parlance, however. No substantial agreement between Walras and Pareto appears on ultimate objectives, only on methodology. The two supposed members and founders of the so-called school were hardly kindred spirits and to regard them as a "school" does not rest on a knowledge of the facts. Therefore, to appraise the impact of Walras and Pareto one must differentiate between their contributions.

The Role of the Lausanne Economists in the Development of Economic Thought.—From the foregoing it is preferable to consider the contributions of Walras and Pareto as separate from one another. First, one usually looks at the impact the pioneering works had upon contemporaries. Next one looks for the survival-value of the doctrines and their influence on subsequent theory.

The immediate effect of the new theories of Walras was to arouse much adverse criticism. Doubtless many of the criticisms stemmed from personal antagonisms, especially on the part of French critics. Both Walras and Pareto had the ability to present their views with firmness and confidence, which brought challenges of validity and embroiled both men in controversies that raged for many years. Not all of the criticism stemmed from prejudice. In general, it was directed first against the intrusion of mathematics into economics. Next, the contemporary critics felt that human differences and activities were so many and so varied that it was impossible to create, mathematically or otherwise, a genuine social science. Many of the criticisms showed a failure to comprehend the purpose of the theories of the Lausanne economists. The French critics, most of whom were members of the Académie, were extremely hostile (except for a few, notably Antonelli and Aupetit), and in fact the Walrasian "pure economics" never did gain a significant foothold in France. The Italians of that period were no more friendly to Walrasian doctrines and dismissed mathematical economics as an abstraction that obscured rather than clarified the issues.

[35] Even though Pareto did not attend the Walras Jubilee (claiming ill health) he did write a letter praising him highly. Walras was never convinced of the sincerity of Pareto's remarks. The necrologies prepared by Pareto after Walras' death were always laudatory, although their relations were deep-seatedly unfriendly, to say the least.

Pareto fared only little better than Walras in France, but in Italy there soon appeared a small but influential group of "Paretians." The late Joseph Schumpeter has been quoted to the effect that Walras' work, together with that of Cournot, encompasses eighty per cent of modern economic theory.[36] On the whole, the Lausanne theories were attacked from all sides, with Pareto faring slightly better than Walras in the criticisms. Much of Walras' time was spent in replying to his critics and in explaining points at issue. Walras was ignored in France, and in Switzerland his influence was negligible.

The long-run or enduring elements can be objectively evaluated because nearly three-quarters of a century has elapsed since the publication of Walras' *Eléments* and nearly a half-century since Pareto's *Manuel* appeared. Although neither enjoyed widespread recognition and acceptance in his lifetime, neither died obscure, as did Gossen. In considering the extent to which Walras and Pareto influenced economic analysis one should look first at the methodological and then at the conceptual aspects of their work.

There is no doubt that the use of mathematics in economic analysis has been very general. Full credit for its first use in economics does not go to the Lausanne economists, since Cournot, Ceva and others preceded them. However, the lion's share of the credit should go to the pioneering work done at Lausanne. The perfections and refinements subsequently made have left the originals far behind, yet students are generous in recognizing the original applications of Walras and Pareto. Boulding refers to Walras as the Laplace of economics.[37] Pareto has been called the liberator who freed economics from its confines and perfected the methods of general equilibrium analysis. Indifference analysis has found a place in some economics texts even at the beginner's level. Much of the methodology of the Lausanne economists has been integrated into economics, a fact which entitles the codevelopers to an important place in the progress of economic science.

So much attention has been given to the mathematical techniques that other contributions tend to be obscured. Each of the two men had a much broader purpose in mind than is indicated in the mathematical virtuosity of their work. Pure economics was to them a theory of economic relationships based upon mutual economic dependence. This was always the objective of Walras. Pareto held the same views for quite a long time—at least long enough to feel that they had been

[36] Bousquet, *Vilfredo Pareto: sa vie et son oeuvre*, p. 77. Schumpeter also remarks, "Critics as competent as the late A. A. Young have been of the opinion that Pareto achieved nothing but 'arid generalizations.' But only the future can tell whether this is so." *Ten Great Economists*, p. 124.

[37] Kenneth Boulding, *Economic Analysis* (1948), p. 868.

established—and then he turned to broader questions of social inter-dependence and became a sociologist.[38] The broader views of these two men have been overlooked or neglected and are generally omitted from works on economic thought. Hence the methodological aspects of their work have outlived their conceptual contributions.

The New Lausanne School.—Attempts are currently being made to rehabilitate and bring into prominence the broader concepts of Léon Walras. The leadership of the movement is assumed by Firmin Oulès, who presently holds the chair originally founded for Léon Walras. The present task, as announced by Oulès, is to derive the great principles underlying economic activity with the expressed purpose of using them as guides to governmental policy. The objective of the "new" Lausanne school is to determine the conditions conducive to progress in a free society. This then calls for a repudiation of laissez faire and involves the setting forth of spheres of state authority which are needed to guarantee true economic liberty to the individual. The new Lausanne school seeks to find the place, or optimum point, where an equilibrium between government regulation and freedom of economic action by the individual can exist.[39] The slogan, "Enlightened Justice," is the battle cry and the area of inquiry is "Social Equilibrium." [40] The emphasis is on the Walrasian concepts. Only time will tell what success the new Lausanne school may have in attempting to establish that purpose in place of the method as originally conceived by Léon Walras.

Summary.—Enough has been said of the detailed work of the Lausanne economists to permit a short summary. Walras had great confidence in his economic discoveries and adaptations. That they were not more widely accepted was a great disappointment to him. Pareto moved beyond the framework of Walras and became a sociologist. Yet his sociology was not very far removed from his economic logic, for he made his sociology largely a study of political and economic processes.

[38] A treatment of Pareto as a sociologist does not fall within the scope of this work. In his greatest sociological work, Mind and Society, he develops his theories of residues, derivations, and the elite and its circulation. For a brief survey see Franz Borkenau, Pareto (Modern Sociologists Series, New York, 1936). See also, Joseph Schumpeter's article, "Vilfredo Pareto," in the Quarterly Journal of Economics, LXIII, No. 2 (May 1949). Reprinted in Ten Great Economists (1951), pp. 134-42.

[39] See Firmin Oulès, L'économie harmonisée (Collection de la Nouvelle Ecole de Lausanne, 1948). See also Marcel Boson, Léon Walras fondateur de la politique économique scientifique (a doctoral thesis, Lausanne, 1948), esp. "M. Firmin Oulès et la nouvelle école de Lausanne" and "L'idée fondamentale de l'économie harmonisée: la liberté en société," pp. 339-48.

[40] Recent publications of the new Lausanne school have a cut of the goddess, Justice, holding the scales of justice. a familiar monument in one of the city squares of Lausanne.

All things considered, Pareto's contribution to economics remains greater than his contribution to sociology.[41] Walras deserves to be remembered not only for his independent work in the early development of marginal utility theory, but also for his use of mathematics to present the larger contribution of general equilibrium theory. These remain the pinnacles of his theory but the social welfare aspect has been, lamentably, overlooked. Pareto's *ophélimité* has been placed with the economic curios, and for good reason. The refinements in mathematical techniques of analysis, of which indifference curve analysis is but one, together with further developments in general equilibrium analysis, have clearly earned Pareto a place in the "economic sun." From the foregoing it is apparent that the term, "Lausanne School," cannot be applied accurately to the theories developed by its two most famous men. Whether success rewards the efforts toward establishing a "new" Lausanne School remains an unknown in the equation of economic doctrines.

The Mathematical School

Several of the persons previously discussed, especially Gossen, Jevons, and Walras, are sometimes identified as mathematical economists and treated as members of a so-called mathematical school. Certainly these writers were not developing economics as pure mathematics, nor were they aware of membership in any school. The present treatment considers them as codevelopers of marginal utility analysis and also considers their other contributions. Their mathematical, or graphic, techniques of presentation were used for scientific expression. Many writers on economic subjects, even before the above-named trio, used mathematical symbols to express economic relationships. Indeed, mathematical economics consists of economic propositions and assumptions presented with the aid of mathematical symbols. However, no one would argue, except in a very limited sense, that by employing such symbols the user becomes a mathematical economist. Nevertheless, mathematical economics presently occupies an extremely important place in economic analysis. The knowledge of infinitesimal calculus has become almost an "indispensable condition" to both reading and understanding an introductory text on principles. If and when economics parts company with the great field of social science and becomes a series of hypotheses and complicated formulas, it bids fair to attain

---

[41] Borkenau remarks, "There would be hardly any reason, from the merits enumerated in this survey, to number Pareto among the important sociologists." *Op. cit.*, p. 168.

the unenviable position in which theory was held during the period of the historical school in Germany.

The best reason for the use of mathematics in economic theory is that mathematics is a useful method of reasoning which must lend itself to being translated into understandable, nonmathematical language. As a branch of logic it is orderly and sequential. It provides necessary techniques for expressing economic relationships in simple manner. Yet it is not indispensable, although extremely useful, as a means of expressing relationships. Economics deals with quantities which are finite, but not all the relationships involving human beings are finite. For purposes of orderly exposition the use of graphs and symbols is a part of the kit of tools of every economist. It is only when economics is taken from the category of social science and refined into higher mathematics that it ceases to be economics.

One of the early mercantilists, Sir William Petty, in his *Discourses on Political Arithmetic* (1691), made use of crude statistics in his attempt to provide more exactness in political economics. The first person to apply mathematics to economics was an Italian, Giovanni Ceva, who in 1711 wrote a tract in which mathematical formulas were generously used. Von Thünen's *Der Isolierte Staat* (1862-63) used mathematical formulas; one of these was $\sqrt{ap}$, which represented a natural wage, a being the subsistence minimum and p the full product of labor. The formula hardly revolutionized the science, but von Thünen's general work was on a high level.

The person generally regarded as the father of mathematical economics was Antoine Augustin Cournot (1801-1877), whose *Recherches sur les principes mathématiques de la théorie des richesses* (1838) was the first great pioneering work. It went unnoticed until Walras called attention to it in 1872. It is extremely important as the publication which stimulated others not only in theory but in method. Cournot was the first to use calculus in economic analysis, especially in the treatment of monopoly and cost analysis. He held that supply and demand determine price and, in turn, price influences both supply and demand. He used simple two-dimensional diagrams to express these relationships and showed that both supply and demand are functions of price. The pioneering work of Cournot was of great significance as a stimulus to such scholars as Alfred Marshall and Walras. (See Alfred Marshall, *Principles of Economics,* 1890, p. x.)

Gossen also used algebraic formulas and two-dimensional diagrams. The French engineer, A. J. E. Dupuit, used mathematical formulas for expressing his concepts of supply and demand relationships. Jevons excelled in the use of mathematical expression. The work of Léon Walras (1874) at Lausanne was the best in mathematical analysis up to that time. He is generally regarded as the founder of the mathematical school of economists. The University of Lausanne, with which he was connected, has enjoyed prestige in the field of mathematical economics, no small part of which is traceable to Walras and his successor, Vilfredo Pareto. In his work *Cours d'économie politique* (1896-97), Pareto systematized the laws of production and distribution so that they are known as "Pareto's Laws." (See note, p. 467.) He was one of the first (after Edgeworth) to make use of indifference curves, which purport to explain demand and obviate the frequent criticism that marginal utility, when compared with marginal cost, can not be measured.

The English economist Alfred Marshall used mathematics extensively in *Principles of Economics* (1890) but chose to relegate most of its use to mathematical appendixes rather than present it in the main body of his chapters. F. Y. Edgeworth, in his *Mathematical Psychics* (1881), made extensive use of mathematical techniques, which made him distinctly outstanding in the field. Knut Wicksell and Gustav Cassel, both of Sweden, were mathematical economists of the highest order. The Americans, Irving Fisher, H. L. Moore, and Henry Schultz, are only a few of the many who have done significant work in mathematical economics.

It should be noted that the so-called mathematical school, in contrast with all other schools thus far considered, is the only one which has carried through to the present time. The name may not be universal, but the mathematical technique of economic analysis is a thriving development. A full treatment of the development of the techniques and accomplishments of the generic group of mathematical economists in the past two or three decades does not fall within the scope of this work. It is one of the crowning achievements in economic analysis and a step in the general direction of making economics an exact science. The fact remains, however, that economics is one of the social sciences and will always be concerned with the problems of how man utilizes scarce resources in satisfying his wants. Mathematics is indispensable as an expository device and a means of expressing hypotheses for the analysis of relationships. Quantification is one of the bases for description, and the economist must think in terms of quantities. It is here that mathematics becomes an indispensable tool for the economist. The Lausanne economists used simultaneous equations in developing their general equilibrium analysis. Since then, mathematics has gained a firm foothold in economics at every level of analysis.

PART VI

The Development of Economics
in the United States

21

The Early American Economists

A treatment of American writers on economic subjects presents several problems. In the first place there was no clearly defined American economics as such. We had no definitive body of doctrines such as may be attributed to England and Germany, and possibly no "school" of economic thought—at least, none in the early period. This does not imply that there was no economic literature in that period, which for convenience is here treated as the first half of the nineteenth century until the Civil War. On the contrary, there were voluminous writings which dealt with the many applied problems and pressing issues of the day. The topics, argued pro or con, included money, banks, agriculture, Western expansion, exploration, slavery, transportation, tariff, free silver, and trusts and monopolies.[1] However, out of all these writings there came little in the form of theoretical economics of which to be proud.

The reasons for the paucity of theoretical economic tracts are possibly to be found in the general circumstances of the period. The nation was new and expanding rapidly in every endeavor. Many issues of economic and political nature arose which were pressing but with which few administrators had had any experience. This was true of such major issues as types of banks and kinds of money, tariff for protection, slavery, states' rights, and so on. Many writers expressed their views on issues as they arose but few indulged in the luxury of finespun theoretical writing as did certain English, French, and German writers. It has been asserted that the Americans were more engrossed in the dynamic growth and expansion of the new nation than they were in writing tomes. While this is probably true, the fact remains that the American state is a product of statesmanship as well as of acumen. No discernible metamorphosis took place the instant a "foreigner" set foot on American shores which transformed him into an American. Likewise, no discernible hiatus existed between "imported economics" and

[1] See the extensive bibliography in James A. Barnes, *The Wealth of the American People* (New York, 1949), pp. 866-90, for a well-selected list of materials dealing with every phase of American economic development.

most of the "academic economics"—at least with that which was taught in this country. Clearly, much of the European economics was not strictly applicable here and, lacking any incentive to make it applicable, only that part was retained which was wanted and the remainder was discarded.

It is true that early American writers did not develop a body of economic doctrines as such. The bulk of early writings centered around the tariff issue as an applied economic problem. Turner remarks, "Indeed, prior to 1880, American economics was little more than a byproduct of consideration on the tariff." [2] Later, other economic problems held the spotlight. Criticism of prevailing doctrines, especially of English doctrines, ranked after the applied economic problems. However, the early academic economics remained predominantly European despite sporadic efforts to introduce an indigenous American variety. Charles F. Dunbar, writing in 1876 on the economics of early America, attributes the "general sterility" of thought to deep-seated causes related to the development of the nation. He remarked, "Our position as a nation charged with the business of subduing a new world, and the rapid material development which has attended our success in this work have given to our life for the greater part of the [nineteenth] century an intensely practical aspect." [3] Indeed Americans, for the majority of the years in our history, were engaged in practical economic pursuits to the exclusion of theorizing. The same view was held by Richard T. Ely who stated, "Throughout the first half of the nineteenth century, our forebears were, generally speaking, too much engaged in the stupendous task of subduing a continent to reflect deeply on their activities." [4]

Many additional reasons might be advanced to explain the paucity of works in the general field of theoretical economics, but no such explanations seem necessary. The fact remains that in the early years no general tract of significance appeared. Some of the writers and their contributions follow.

First Writings on Economics.—Benjamin Franklin is frequently referred to as an economist along with his many other achievements. Some of his brief writings are rich in economic materials, notably his essay on population published in 1751. The most influential of all his economic writings was a little pamphlet, *The Way to Wealth* (c. 1757), which combined his ideas on individual enterprise, frugality, and the

---

[2] John R. Turner, *The Ricardian Rent Theory* (New York, 1921), p. 19.
[3] "Economic Science in America, 1776-1876," in *North American Review* (January, 1876). Reprinted in *Economic Essays* (May, 1904), pp. 22 ff.
[4] *Ground Under our Feet* (New York, 1938), p. 121.

dominant philosophy then of self-reliance. This pamphlet was probably "printed and translated oftener than anything else ever penned by any American. It appeared in more than 150 editions and was translated into every European language." [5] Franklin's views on population were less dramatically stated than those which Malthus stated nearly 50 years later in 1798, but they were far more balanced and rational. Since Franklin knew Adam Smith, whom he had met in London, it is possible that his views on population influenced Smith. [6] Both Franklin and Jefferson in their missions to France became acquainted with the leading physiocrats and were extremely sympathetic, if not converts, to many physiocratic doctrines (see Chapter 8).

In the Colonial period most of the discussion and writing centered around political relations with England, yet the economic aspects were extremely important. The goal of freedom from England naturally affected all trade, industry, and commerce. When independence was achieved and a Constitution was adopted in 1789, economic problems became of greatest concern. The most significant writing before 1800 was Alexander Hamilton's famous *Report on Manufactures*, presented to the Congress in December, 1791. This report is interesting in that it supplied "the ammunition" for much of the argument in defense of a protective tariff which is found in subsequent literature. [7]

The first quarter of the nineteenth century saw the virtually uninterrupted economic growth of the young American nation. The War of 1812-1814 served as a test of the strength and cohesion of the nation. In those years and subsequently, many colleges and universities were established throughout the land. These institutions served as proving grounds for old theories of European origin; they also created a demand for materials adaptable to college courses in general economics. The classics of Smith, Malthus, Say, and Ricardo were available and were probably widely read as they had been in England. The *Wealth of Nations* was still criticized as "too abstruse to be easily comprehended by the unphilosophic mind, besides, subsequent experience has elucidated much that was problematical or intricate, in his day." [8] The economic writings of several early scholars show strong criticism of English doctrines. The teachers in the early colleges, many of whom were clerics, found much to their dislike in the teachings of the English trio.

[5] Frank A. Fetter, "The Early History of Political Economy in the United States," American Philosophical Society, *Proceedings*, LXXXVII, No. 1 (1943), p. 52.

[6] Smith discussed the "Prosperity of New Colonies" in the *Wealth of Nations*, Bk. IV, chap. vii. Reference is made there to the American colonies.

[7] Recent researches indicate that Tench Coxe, not Alexander Hamilton, was the true author of the *Report*. The ideas, however, were those of Hamilton.

[8] *American Monthly Magazine*, July, 1817, cited in Joseph Dorfman, *The Economic Mind in American Civilization, 1806-1865*, Vol. II, p. 234.

It was shown in Chapter 15 that the criticisms of Lord Lauderdale, published in 1804, had pronounced influence on Daniel Raymond, an early writer in this country.

It is probable that the work of J. B. Say (1803) had a wider acceptance than the English works. It was first translated into English in 1821. In 1832 a well known Philadelphian, Clement C. Biddle, brought out a new American edition based on the last edition (5th) prepared by the author in 1826. Biddle remarked that Say's *Treatise on Political Economy* was "unquestionably the most methodical, comprehensive and best digested treatise on the elements of political economy that has yet been presented to the world." [9] Several reasons contributed to the popularity of Say's work. In the first place it was by a French author; next, the critics found less to their dislike in it. No distinction was made between "productive" and "unproductive" labor (Smith made the labor of clerics unproductive); the entrepreneur was placed in a quasi-heroic role as a builder of industry and, by implication, of wealth; above all, it was a well-organized, readable book. Nor was it entirely antithetical to preconceived views on the tariff and the rising tide of nationalism.[10] Despite the similarities in many doctrines between Smith and Say, the latter proved more to the liking of those interested in the general subject of economics. Say's book served as a standard text until others were prepared by American authors.

The first comprehensive book bearing the title "Political Economy" was Daniel Raymond's *Thoughts on Political Economy* (1820).[11] The book was fairly comprehensive for its day and sufficiently orthodox to gain for its author an offer to teach economics in a college. Raymond admitted that he had read foreign texts on political economy, as well as Hamilton's *Report*. It was largely for the purpose of breaking "loose from the fetters of foreign authority—from foreign theories and systems of political economy" (*op. cit.*, p. v) and for espousing the cause of protectionism that he wrote the book. He talked of the nation as being "a unity and possessing all the properties of a unity" and used this concept to declare that everyone benefited from protection. He set forth a paradoxical theory that high tariffs benefit the entire nation even though the burden of the tariff is borne by the entire nation. He believed that without high protective tariffs there would be wide unemployment; a high tariff was his prescription for full employment in all

[9] *Op. cit.*, p. vi.

[10] It is not within the scope of this work to develop the teaching of economics in early schools and colleges. A discussion of this phase will be found in Joseph Dorfman, *op. cit.*, Vol. II, chaps. xix-xxii, xxv.

[11] See Chapter 15, pp. 313 ff. for a more detailed treatment of Raymond's book.

circumstances. He based his generalizations on the economic experience following the War of 1812 and failed to comprehend the real causes of the depression of 1815 as well as the implications of a tariff policy. The errors in Raymond's work so far outweigh the merits that it is just as well that it was consigned to academic oblivion almost as soon as it was born.

Henry C. Carey.—Next in line both in date of publication and in emphasis were the works of father and son, Mathew and Henry C. Carey. Mathew Carey was an ardent follower of Hamilton and a supporter of the tariff movement. The son spread his interests and talents more widely than his father, but in the same general framework. His *Principles of Political Economy* (1837-40) and his *Principles of Social Science* (1858-59) represent high-water marks in the writings on economics before the Civil War.[12] Carey expressed great admiration for the work of Adam Smith, but for Ricardo he had nothing but criticism. His attempted refutation of the Ricardian rent doctrine and the Malthusian principle has proved disturbing in assigning much worth to his other writings. Next in importance to his refutation of the two English authors, was his espousal of the tariff issue. His general economic outlook was optimistic and dynamic; he would have none of the pessimism of the "dismal science" of the Malthus-Ricardo variety. In retrospect, what he retained from English theory was the worst and what he rejected, the best. He supported a wages-fund doctrine and a labor-cost theory of value. Too often his Anglophobe views outweighed what surely must have been his better judgment.

Despite doctrinal errors and a doggedly unorthodox position, his writings did attract wide attention both at home and abroad. His literary style was vigorous; he showed original, even bold, ideas which were expressed with a confidence matched only by J. S. Mill. No early writer equaled Carey in the variety and scope of interests and works. He was not wrong on all points; his vision of the great economic potential of the new nation and its future greatness was prophetic. Nor can one say that, in the long run, all the tariff measures for which he and others stood were bad. Friedrich List had urged that tariffs be imposed to develop industry so that this nation would not be solely a supplier of raw material for British industry. Our great diversification of industry has served this and other nations well on at least two occasions. The diversification is attributable to national policy and to the great national resources. The part played by the early advocates of protectionism in

[12] See Chapter 15 for details on Carey's writings.

bringing about our diversification was unquestionably great. The praise or blame assignable to any one will always remain unidentifiable.[13]

Free Traders: John McVickar, Thomas Cooper.—It must not be inferred that no one arose to support the free-trade doctrines of the classical writers. On the contrary, there were many writers who favored free-trade policy or at least a low-tariff policy. The following persons not only held strong views on the tariff issue but a few, subsequently treated, developed texts on general principles.

One of the earliest writers belonging in the free-trade camp was John McVickar (1787-1868), a minister and the first professor of political economy at Columbia College in New York from 1818 to 1857. He was a follower of Hamilton on all issues but the tariff. His *Outlines of Political Economy* (1825) was really an American edition of McCulloch's work which followed strict Ricardian lines. McVickar's numerous interpretive additions and contemporary illustrations gave it an American slant, but it was basically Ricardian. The scope of the work was extended beyond the Ricardian pattern to include discussions on money and banks, canals, education, and so on. He enthusiastically praised free trade as the ideal "liberal system" as opposed to tariffs, bounties, and monopolies.

Another early writer, Thomas Cooper, M.D. (1759-1839), was an English-born, Oxford-trained law student, who later, after becoming acquainted with Priestley, switched from law to medicine and chemistry. He came to America in 1795, at the age of 36, and actively participated in nearly every current issue. He wrote on the slave trade and other problems as well as occasional semiscientific articles. He had a tempestuous career and at times ran afoul of the law. His criticism of President John Adams and the Administration was so severe that he was fined and sentenced to prison for six months under the Sedition Act.[14] Upon his release from prison he became a land commissioner and a judge of the common pleas court. Soon he was impeached and removed from office. He spent several years in Philadelphia, where he

---

[13] Carey had a wide following among businessmen, journalists, and academicians. Among the many followers who may be mentioned was E. Peshine Smith (1814-1882), who decided to write a proper textbook. In 1853 he wrote a *Manual of Political Economy* which he intended to be the "American System of Political Economy." It was based largely on Carey's *The Past, the Present and the Future*. David A. Wells, an editor of popular scientific articles and writer on various subjects, became a firm supporter of Carey's doctrines. There were, in addition, many less well-known names. Carey was embittered in his last years because his views, especially on the tariff, were in general rejected in academic circles. Only Simon N. Patten, to be discussed subsequently, held protectionist views of the Carey variety.

[14] He believed the Alien and Sedition Acts were unconstitutional. He won his point and his fine of $400 was returned with interest.

advocated a tariff on the theory of protection for infant industries and for defense.

He was next a professor of chemistry at Dickinson College; and later held a similar position at the University of Pennsylvania. In 1817 he went to the University of Virginia to teach chemistry and law but he was obliged to resign as a teacher of law at the end of three years. In 1821 he became President of South Carolina College and also a teacher of political economy. He was obliged to resign in 1834. In South Carolina he became an ardent free-trade advocate and a champion of state sovereignty. In England he had been a bitter critic of slavery, but in South Carolina he not only defended slavery but became a leader in forming and defending a pro-slavery philosophy. At one time he was a staunch defender of the American constitutional democracy but later he assailed it and criticized the assumptions of the underlying philosophy of the Declaration of Independence. Once a critic of the Bank of the United States, he later became its defender. He had a remarkable capacity for switching affiliations; so much so that one is likely to regard with suspicion his *Lectures on the Elements of Political Economy*, written in 1826 while he was President of South Carolina College.

Cooper was not an economist by training or by profession. However, he had great cleverness which, when matched with his vast experience in business ventures and a moderate acquaintance with economic literature, permitted him to generalize on economic subjects. He could be a pro or con on most issues, according to what he observed the prevailing thought to be. He tended to be a follower of Ricardo although he dismissed the rent doctrines as "metaphysical," especially as affecting cost. When he saw many of the Ricardian doctrines popularly accepted, he changed to the popular side. He denounced the "protectionists" and the protectionist tariff in very scathing terms. No doubt his attitude toward a protective tariff supported the objections of the South to the tariff, which led to the nullification measures sponsored by John C. Calhoun in 1832.

Cooper's economic views were on applied economics. No theoretical refinements or skillful organization of materials grace his pages. He was laissez faire in doctrine mainly because he found it expedient to be so. His outspoken views must be acknowledged, but his contributions to economic literature do not warrant any recognition. His attitude on education, however, does demand some attention. Cooper opposed mass education except at an elementary level, but he believed that colleges should be state-supported; he held that schools of higher education were of national benefit. In South Carolina he popularized the subject of political economy and established there a department of political economy, the second in America.

Francis Wayland's Textbook.—The first well-balanced textbook in economics was written by Francis Wayland (1796-1865).[15] Wayland was a philosopher and theologian and served as President of Brown University from 1827 to 1855. Like the others thus far considered, he was not primarily an economist. However, his *Elements of Political Economy* (1837) was by far the best and most adaptable text written by any American prior to 1867.

Wayland defined political economy as "The Science of Wealth . . . By Science, as the word is here used, we mean a systematic arrangement of the laws which God has established, so far as they have been discovered, of any department of human knowledge."[16] He remarked that he was "struck with the simplicity of the principle [of the science of political economy] and the extent of its generalizations." In the light of this belief, he stated that his "object has been to write a book which anyone who chooses may understand." Wayland developed an eclectic text. He quoted from Smith and McCulloch and "Mr. Carey" and drew from classical Ricardian theory. With this were intermingled certain distinctly American views. He emphasized the law of supply and demand in price determination but the labor-cost theory still lurks behind his value theory. The author regarded land as capital and identified rent with interest. He was also inclined to treat rent as price-determining. He supported loan interest and held that usury laws were not needed since the laws of supply and demand would care for any excesses. He held no fears that the Malthusian forebodings would ever apply here, since subsistence far outstripped population growth. His wage theory, if any, was explained as resulting from the competition of the forces of demand and supply which tended to attain a level that would remain about the same over a period of time. Population and the level of wages, he held, were more or less self-regulating, yet each was dependent upon a sort of capital fund which was available to pay wages. His explanation of wages was closer to the wages-fund doctrine than to a productivity theory.

He held a productivity theory of rent in which both fertility and site were factors. For agricultural lands he used the differential surplus

---

[15] Among the many who wrote on or in the field of economics were Jacob Newton Cardoza (1786-1873), editor of the free-trade organ *Southern Patriot*, author of *Notes on Political Economy* (1826); George Tucker (1775-1861), author of *Wages, Rent and Profit* (1837); Henry Vethake (1792-1866), who wrote *Principles of Political Economy* (1835); Samuel Phillips Newman (1796-1842), whose *Elements of Political Economy* (1835) was but a simplification of Smith's *Wealth of Nations*. Tucker was probably the most original economist of this group. See J. R. Turner, *The Ricardian Rent Theory* (1927), for details on each of the above named.

[16] Francis Wayland, *Principles of Political Economy* (2d ed., New York, 1840), p. 15.

theory of Ricardo but, strangely enough, maintained that rent enters into prices. He recognized the cost of production on marginal land as being important but reasoned that the marginal cost is the effect rather than the cause of price.

He had chapters on banking and paper money, and in his book he supported the Bank of the United States. Borrowing from the English writers, he attacked the poor laws. He opposed speculation in stocks and commodities. The slavery issue was avoided in his text on economics. However, he was not opposed to slavery in the Southern states but he opposed such an extension of slavery as the Kansas-Nebraska Bill of 1854 would have provided. This attitude caused his economic text to be excluded from Southern institutions.[17]

Wayland's book gained wide acceptance. Its moral tone was high, and the simplicity of the presentation made it extremely popular for use in beginning classes in economics. It had a broad selection of topics, was laissez faire in general philosophy, strongly free trade on tariff issues, fairly liberal but withal cast in the mold of orthodox English economics.

The book supplanted all other texts, even J. B. Say's *Treatise*. It was translated into most languages, including Armenian. The book was made the basis for both teaching and writing of the earliest Japanese economics. The great Japanese scholar, Fukuzawa, translated parts of Wayland's book and incorporated them into his *Things Western*, Part II (1870). Through this work the fundamentals of Wayland became one of the basic sources of Western economic principles to which the Japanese had access.

Wayland's book was the only one which survived for any considerable length of time. It was supplanted by better books in general economics that were written after the Civil War. C. F. Dunbar, writing in 1876, remarked that "President Wayland's book (1837) is the only general treatise of the period which can fairly be said to have survived to our day." He further added that "it owes whatever value it has to its manner of presenting for easy comprehension some of the leading English doctrines."[18] In the two decades prior to the Civil War the tariff issue was no longer the furious struggle of the earlier years, the second United States Bank was but a memory, and "the great sectional controversy began to fill all minds, to the exclusion of every other public question."

Francis Bowen.—Of the few pre-Civil War textbooks on economics that appeared, the work of Francis Bowen (1811-1890) which bore the

[17] James O. Murray, *Francis Wayland* (New York, 1891), p. 140.
[18] *Op. cit.*, p. 12.

title *The Principles of Political Economy* (1856) was one of the best.[19] This book brought together ideas which the author had developed and presented in lectures and articles over several years of successful teaching at Harvard and writing in the *North American Review*. Although he made generalizations which characterize a "universal science of Political Economy" and are applicable to "all nations under the sun," his emphasis lay in making them apply to America.[20]

In developing his book he stated that he "subjected to a vigorous examination the leading doctrines of the science as taught by English writers, in order not only to test their general soundness and applicability to the condition and institutions of the American people, but to trace out and analyze the peculiar circumstances which first suggested them" (p. vi). Thus the classical writers were examined and "modified or rejected." He made no claim to originality, nor did he wish his book to be controversial; he really wanted to write a "convenient textbook of instruction in American colleges" (p. vii). He explained that "most of what is valuable . . . has come to us by inheritance from our English ancestors." However, much of that which characterizes our people

> . . . has been the subject of frequent and sharp criticism, not only by British travelers, but by British economists and statesmen. Thus, Mr. J. S. Mill, unquestionably the ablest living writer upon Political Economy and the Logic of the Inductive Sciences, and the one who . . . might be disposed to view with some favor the workings of the republican institutions, cannot speak in any more flattering terms than these of the inhabitants of the Northern and Middle States of America: "They have the six points of Chartism, and they have no poverty; and all that these advantages do for them is, that the life of the whole of one sex is devoted to dollar-hunting, and of the other to breeding dollar-hunters." (p. viii).

Bowen begins his book with a discussion of wealth and the various forms which it takes. He believes that there are general laws affecting its production and distribution. But he hastens to remark, "Political Economy is not, as many suppose, the art of money-making, any more than meteorology is the art of predicting the weather" (p. 13). He talks in terms of value and utility; the former means exchangeable value; the latter is an element of wealth, which consists in "fitness to satisfy any want or desire, however irrational, that is felt by any number of men" (p. 33). He was unable to throw off the English theory, as seen from the statement that "the essence of value consists in difficulty of attain-

---

[19] The full title of this edition was *The Principles of Political Economy Applied to the Condition, the Resources, and the Institutions of the American People*. The edition of 1870 was entitled *American Political Economy*. Bowen also wrote in the fields of history, politics, education, philosophy, religion, and literature.

[20] Francis Bowen, *Principles of Political Economy* (1856 ed.), p. vi.

ment, so the labor which overcomes that great difficulty is the great means of producing value, or creating wealth" (p. 34). Again he remarks that "value depends on difficulty of attainment" (*ibid.*), and that "how vain it is to expect that wealth can ever be created without labor, which is its natural and necessary price" (p. 35). He has chapters on the division of labor, laissez faire, the nature of capital, Malthusian theory of population, theory of rent, wages, profits, money, banks and bank currency, the protective system, and so on. The 546 tedious pages read in places more like classical than like American economics. He disclaims the Malthusian theory, and also the Ricardian rent analysis, but shows great admiration for Smith's theories. In fact, when he began to teach economics at Harvard in 1853, he "substituted for Wayland's textbook McCulloch's edition of Adam Smith, then he used McCulloch's own simplified treatise," [21] and finally his own book in 1856.

Bowen's views were extremely conservative. He saw man as engaged in a constant attempt to accumulate wealth beyond immediate needs. In addition, man is "sagacious enough to see what branches of industry are most profitable, and eager enough to engage in them, so that competition regularly tends to force wages, profits and prices to a level" (p. 3). He held the view that political economy was not an "art of money-making"; in fact, it was "not an art at all, but a science" (p. 13). Also general principles run throughout the science which may be applied to specific countries. Thus many of the tenets of classical economics were applicable elsewhere as well as in the English economy. Free-trade doctrines would be sufficiently flexible to permit some protection to special interests.

The laissez-faire principle was given a peculiar interpretation. To him it meant "that God regulates [things] by his general laws, which always, in the long run, work to good" (p. 23). Society instinctively chooses the things best for itself, if the "casual and unnatural impediments are removed from its path." All things which obstruct the working of natural laws, "the ordinances of Divine Providence, by which society is held together, are stumbling blocks. To remove such stumbling blocks is not to create, but to prevent, interference with the natural order of things. Legislation directed to this end is only a legitimate carrying out of the laissez-faire principle" (pp. 23-24). Therefore, he would say that in passing tariff laws the legislature aids in making the natural laws function in accordance with the plans of laissez faire. Such laws would make for greater liberty in permitting expansion of industry at home and "remove the impediment created by a foreign

[21] Dorfman, *op. cit.*, Vol. II, p. 843.

state far more serious and extensive than the obstruction which it pro-poses" (p. 25). This action would also make it possible to use capital in other ways than those to which it was formerly limited. His theory then permitted the removal of "external dangers" and allowed for re-taliatory measures, which, in a sense, his protectionist policies would be. In fact, his explanation made a protective tariff a complete necessity.

A few additional points of emphasis in his book are significant. His theory of value is a reproduction-cost or labor-saved theory. For ex-ample, if a machine is introduced which reduces the number of men employed from four to two, the value of the product thus produced will represent the labor of those persons who actually make the product. The labor actually required in production is a measure of the value produced (chap. iv). Competition would tend to equalize all returns to labor and profits to an entrepreneur; however, if differences remained they would be attributable to more skilful management.

Bowen held no brief for the Malthusian doctrine, which he said was "a mere hypothetical speculation, having no relation to the times in which we live or to any which are near at hand" (p. 141). After many pages of argument he found that whereas an increase of population in England meant lowering of wages because the workers had only their wages for subsistence, such would not be the case in America. Most workers in America were much more independent, more mobile, and could always take up land. However, the land policy, he thought, was too easy; it tended to make for an unnatural poverty in the West since it emphasized agricultural pursuits and dispersion of the population. No towns or cities would be built, since land was accessible and com-manded a low price. This problem was accentuated by a great influx of Irish laborers. He used this fact to defend a "protective tariff" on labor and to encourage greater employment in home industry, which would also be protected.

Bowen presented chapters on the money and banking controversy which was discussed at great length. From the entire discussion of nearly two hundred pages, a large part of which is historical, little, if anything, of significance is found which is of current interest. The banks were basically good; they did not bring on commercial crises every few years; money should probably be specie, and paper money of small denominations should be discontinued. He opposed any change in the gold content of the dollar after gold discoveries, and defended the dol-lar against any legislation which would depreciate its value. This was indeed a pressing political as well as economic issue when he wrote.

The last chapters deal with the protective system. Here he reiterates his former statement that the "general doctrine of free trade is per-fectly reconcilable with the policy of granting protection under special circumstances," and that "in order to foster the manufacturing interests here in America, which cannot flourish, or even subsist to any extent, without such favor" (p. 457). He attempts to refute the standard free-trade arguments, and in so doing denies that a protective duty raises the price of the commodity to the consumer in the home country. He also argues that if wages are kept up at home, everyone gains. Bowen would not deny that certain nations have peculiar advantages of "soil and climate which time and practice can never remove or essentially diminish" but he adds that "Americans can profitably raise and manufacture iron, steel, wool, flax and silk, for the production and fashioning of which we have as great advantages as the English." He adds that "We can profitably submit, for a certain number of years, to an additional tax for this purpose, appearing in the additional price which we must for a while pay for the domestic products" (p. 483). He would defend the "American system" at any cost.

Enough has been presented to show the type of Bowen's work. He had a marked ability to twist liberal doctrines into extreme conservatism. His views were more extreme than those of other protectionists; he might be excused to some extent for accepting the general philosophy which prevailed, especially in the Northern states, but the manner in which he attributed everything to Divine ordination and twisted liberal doctrines into reactionary arguments cannot be excused. There seems little reason to lament that the Bowen book failed to gain universal acceptance.

Amasa Walker's *Science of Wealth*.—As has been noted, the most popular treatise on general economics before the Civil War was Wayland's *The Elements of Political Economy*. During the war and shortly thereafter several works appeared. Amasa Walker (1799-1875) wrote the *Science of Wealth* (1866), which bore the subtitle, "A Manual of Political Economy embracing the Laws of Trade, Currency and Finance." The book went through several editions and was widely used in its day. Walker was a successful businessman, a teacher of political economy at Oberlin College (which he helped to found) from 1842 to 1848 and later at Amherst College, a promoter of railroads, and finally a political figure, serving as Secretary of State of Massachusetts. His political career was climaxed by his election to the United States Congress in 1862. He was a strong antislavery advocate and took an active part in the founding of the Free Soil Party in 1848. He held very strong views on the prohibition movement, as well as on the currency and banking issues.

Walker's *Science of Wealth* was a collaboration with his son, General Francis A. Walker, to be subsequently discussed. The work was popular both at home and abroad. While purportedly a work on general economics it had a strong money and general business bias which reflected, in large measure, his business experience and his fundamental interests. He remarked that he had "the desire to produce a work especially accessible and useful to businessmen, merchants, manufacturers, etc. They have a deep and immediate personal interest in all economical questions, and need particularly to be fully informed of the character of that instrumentality by which exchanges are made, and obligations discharged." [22] After devoting the first book to definitions, he treats in the succeeding books the subjects of production, exchange, distribution, and consumption. He drew upon the English classical economists, Bastiat, and John Stuart Mill whom he called "undoubtedly the ablest of living writers" (p. xiv). However, the book contains certain distinct elements which reflect the thinking of American writers of the period.

Political economy is the science of wealth according to Walker; it treats of the laws by which the production and consumption of wealth are governed. However, he regarded the term, Political economy, as an unfortunate one since it tended to associate what the science actually teaches with politics and government, from which it is distinct. To Walker, that government was best which governed the least. The fundamental purpose for which the science of political economy exists is to explain how human wants are satisfied. Value he explains as power in exchange. Or, "the value of a thing is the services or labor which it will command in exchange." Nevertheless, he remarks that "labor alone does not create value, but value never exists in an article, unless someone is willing to give labor . . . in exchange for it" (p. 13). He understood the difference between value and utility, the latter being an attribute of a good; however, its exchange value is the really significant item.

Walker denied every point of the Malthusian doctrines as applied to America, for to him a larger population meant abundance rather than scarcity. The subject of wages occupied his attention as it did his son's at a later date. He associated wages with capital and made profitable investment of capital the determining factor in making wage payments possible. High wages were not in "proportion to the wealth of a community, but rather to the disposition that exists amongst those possessing wealth to pay it out for labor." The "disposition" of the investor depended upon both the security and the profitableness of the investment. Walker did not oppose labor organizations, if voluntary, although he felt that they could not accomplish much except with the

[22] *Science of Wealth* (New York, 1866), p. xii.

ballot. Unions could not effect a permanent increase in wages; on the other hand, he had little hope that laws would aid materially the position of labor. He opposed the establishment of an eight-hour day mainly because it would reduce production, hence profits, and thus affect the funds for investment which, in turn, would decrease wages and employment.

The immigration issue was fast becoming one of great importance. Walker opposed restriction of immigration, holding that it was needed to increase the labor supply. Since native Americans held the positions of importance, the immigrant workers were needed to develop the resources and thereby help to improve the rewards of the native entrepreneurs.

Walker accepted the Ricardian rent doctrine. However, unlike Ricardo, he classified land as fixed capital. He remarked, "All capital is wealth, but all wealth is not capital. . . . Wealth is as it is *had*; capital as it is *used*" (p. 55). Since land is used wealth, it is therefore capital. Fixed capital yields rent; circulating capital yields interest. Walker made labor and capital the "two great agents by which all wealth is created" (p. 60). He believed the two factors must cooperate in production; in doing so they not only increase production but each will be sure to receive its just reward. Even though Walker accepted Ricardo's rent doctrine, the qualifications and interpretations he placed on the doctrine altered it considerably. Walker regarded rent as a return to fixed capital and not as a payment for the use of land. The principle of diminishing returns which was basic in Ricardian theory is omitted by Walker. Nor was he interested in intensive or extensive margins. Walker, unlike Ricardo, was more concerned about rents in cities than agricultural rents. He viewed the problem as it appeared in America. The backgrounds of their thinking explain their views; Ricardo saw population pressing on the available supply of land, whereas Walker was concerned with population pressure on urban rents. The Malthusian tendency was much more real in the Ricardian doctrine, but in America the vast land areas tended to keep the population pressure down.

Walker was a free trader—even opposed to a tariff for revenue—optimistic in national outlook and conservative in his general philosophy. His acquaintance with and interest in the currency and banking issues tended to give his book a financial bias. He opposed a large public debt mainly because the taxes needed to support it had a depressing effect on industry. He favored a 100 percent specie reserve for bank notes and was therefore regarded as a follower of the "currency school." He showed original thinking in his treatment of deposits as an important part of the currency. Deposits were created by loans and entered into circulation the same as bank notes. He made some cogent observations on the causes of panics and crises as they were affected by the monetary and banking structure.

Walker's book was well received and extremely influential. His inconsistencies are less annoying than those of Bowen and nowhere are issues presented as propaganda. Voluminous use of data and charts adds to the scientific presentation of materials. The book also reflects the high sense of moral values held by its author. The causes and cure of wars occupied his attention; he saw the dangers of an unlimited armament race which tended to induce war, and the disturbances subsequent to wars. He thought a Congress of Nations might by "acting in concert" achieve any object that "commends itself to the common sense of mankind." [23] Walker's economic views showed liberal economic convictions. His catholicity of interests and work in both domestic and world issues attests to the breadth of his vision. In general, he ranks as the leading economist of the early period.

A. L. Perry.—Probably the best known teacher and textbook writer of the early period was Arthur Latham Perry (1830-1905). He was educated at Williams College, where he afterwards taught for many years (1853-1905). He wrote a classroom text entitled *Elements of Political Economy* (1866), later called *Political Economy*, which went through twenty-two editions. In 1876 a list of ten "most salable books on political economy" was prepared. Perry's book ranked third, below Mill's *Principles of Political Economy* and Smith's *Wealth of Nations*.[24] The work was translated into many languages; the Japanese translation of 1876 became one of the main sources for the teaching of economics in the early years when Western ideas were being adopted in Japan.

Perry was a close friend of Amasa Walker; the theories and general beliefs of Walker were held and popularized by Perry. Professionally a college teacher, he wrote articles in newspapers and engaged Horace Greeley in debate on the issues of free trade, although as a polemicist, he did not have the acumen of his friend Walker. His views were unprejudiced, scholarly, sincere, and often reflected a strong and deep religious conviction. Sincerity and simplicity of exposition made his text on principles outstanding. Dorfman remarks that "few teachers of the day held as important a position in the classroom and in the outside world." [25]

Perry admitted that in his early teaching he had used Smith, Senior, Ricardo, and John Stuart Mill. Smith, he said, "has frequently been

23 Bk. V, chap. viii, p. 440.
24 Joseph Dorfman, *op. cit.*, Vol. III, p. 81.
25 *Ibid.*, p. 56.

called the father of Political Economy . . . [but] it is hardly just that that title should be given to any man." [26]   Despite the treatment by Smith of the division of labor, the freedom of enterprise, the benefits of commerce, and so on, the defects of the *Wealth of Nations* were: the "want of clear definitions, illogical arrangements, an inconsistency sometimes with its own principles . . . a preference in its theory of value, for material commodities; a want of clear perception of the difference between utility and value, and a consequent partial confusion in the whole doctrine of values; and lastly a prolixity which is at times tedious" (pp. 18-19).   As might be expected, Perry would have none of the Malthusian gloomy forebodings, or of Ricardo's "ingenious and complicated [rent theory] which is too mechanical and rigid to be applied to any existing state of facts" (p. 159).   He did not fear any monopoly in land ownership and denied that land rent is a payment to a nonproductive group.   He credited Frederic Bastiat with carrying political economy "to its most advanced position."   It was Bastiat who made "a vigorous demonstration of the harmonious mechanism of society, by which, through the agency of liberty and property, God has designed the progressive amelioration of mankind" (p. 20).   Perry's broader view of political economy caused him to drop the narrower concept that made wealth the center of man's economic activity; he preferred to make political economy a social science and treat man "in a state of society" not in "a state of isolation." [27]

Perry's concept of political economy was one which made the entire science revolve around value.   Production, as used in economics, meant the creation of value, not matter or objects.   "He who creates value is a producer.   But value is not an attribute of matter, but of services exchanged" (p. 91).   "Value," he stated, "is nothing but the relation between two services exchanged" (p. 94).   He did not regard value as an inherent attribute of a commodity "but it is the relative power which one thing has of purchasing other things" (p. 34).   He insisted, "Value must be carefully distinguished from price.   The price of anything is its purchasing power expressed in money; the value of anything is its purchasing power expressed in any other purchasing power whatever" (p. 59).   It is possible to express price in terms of money but value rests upon the capacity of a good or service to command other goods or services, which can never be accurately expressed.   His theory of value, resting as it does on one fundamental concept—a mutual exchange of

[26] *Elements of Political Economy* (1866 ed.), p. 18.

[27] P. 25.   In the preface to *Political Economy* he wrote, "The most of what is original in my book is an immediate or else an indirect result of absolutely dropping from the start the use of the word "wealth" as a technical term.   So far as I know, I was the very first economist to do this" (p. x).

service for service—is inadequate. He succeeded in rejecting wealth as the source of economic motivation but he failed to offer anything to take its place. Nothing but difficulty would be encountered in attempting to apply his theory.

Some other points of emphasis in Perry's work include his belief that the three factors of production are labor, power-agents, and capital. Labor he regarded in the generally accepted sense as an expenditure of human effort, mental or physical; power-agents referred to services of beasts of burden, domestic animals, wind and water power, the powers of nature, and the like; and capital he defined as "any product reserved to be employed in further production" (p. 133). He included all raw materials, machinery, "all funds destined to purchase these" (p. 134). Land also was capital. He pointed out that "lands are absolutely valueless until some portion of human efforts has been expended on them" (p. 153). Likewise, most of the attributes of land are God-given and inseparable from land itself, but it takes labor to adapt many of them to man's use. Hence it is not different from capital.

Wages he considered as being influenced by agreeableness of employment, ease or difficulty of learning a skill, constancy of employment, probability of success, custom and fashion, legal restrictions, and so on. However, the amount of wages depends upon the amount of capital available for the payment of wages to labor—or a wages-fund. "The presence of capital anywhere constitutes a demand for labor. The more capital there is anywhere, the stronger the demand for labor; and capital therefore is the poor man's best friend" (pp. 119-20). He further remarks that "the average rate of the wages of common labor will depend on the number of laborers compared with the amount of capital there present" (p. 120). He admitted however, that "the portion set aside for the payment of wages" may increase or decrease as a result of the aggregate amount of capital, but "the wages-fund (the portion set aside for wages) may remain stationary, or even diminish," depending on the increase in laborers and the amount going to each (p. 121). His theory made the rate of wages depend upon the wages-fund divided by the number of workers. The more laborers there are competing for employment, the further down wages will go, and conversely. He actually outstripped John Stuart Mill in developing the wages-fund theory.

Perry included two elements in cost of production—the costs of labor and of capital. These two "onerous elements" are assisted by the natural powers (power-agents) which, since they are always gratuitous, "they form no element in cost" (p. 170). Labor is paid its wages whereas capital must get "its profits and also have a sinking-fund to replace original capital when worn out and expended." So certain was Perry that these elements composed cost of production that he remarked, "It will be in vain to search for any other ingredient of cost than these two" (p. 170). It was Perry's idea that labor cost is purely a cost to the employer, not a cost associated with bringing labor to a productive stage. The money wage paid to labor, however, is but one element of the cost of labor; efficiency of labor and the value of money are factors which also affect the real cost of labor—or the wages paid to labor.

A sort of residual claimant theory for profits is expressed. The gross product is a result of the combined action of labor and capital; therefore the product belongs in common to the laborers and the capitalists. "The cost of labor being deducted, the rest goes to capital as a matter of course and the proportion of this part to the whole capital determines the rate per cent of profit" (p. 175). He regarded both the productivity of labor and the productivity of capital as mutually beneficial to each. "Both are alike interested in the combined efficiency of capital and labor . . . in the amount of gross product created" (p. 175). It is to the harmonious interest of each that the gross product is high. The costs of labor must be defrayed first; what is left is gross profits, and the relation between this amount and the amount of capital invested decides the percent of net profits.

The ever-present money issues found Perry supporting his friend, Amasa Walker, who was strongly opposed to the issue of any form of bank currency. Gold and silver were the best money because these metals were limited by natural supply, whereas paper money knew no limits. Perry even questioned the issue of paper money with a 100 percent reserve. Banks should confine their activities to lending coined money and accepting deposits; they should be prohibited from issuing paper money. His distrust of banks in general and his fear of an unrestricted issue of paper money by either the government or by banks reflected a long and deep-seated apprehension. The Civil War greenbacks were depreciating in value; the experience of both state and private banks in money matters had not been good; the newly established national banking system faced many difficult problems. Perry's bank and money fears, resting largely upon past national experience and coupled with his general conservatism, shaped his views, which could scarcely be regarded as constructive.

Perry was almost a fanatic in his belief in free trade, which occupied much of his attention in his writing and in his public addresses. He used every economic argument he could command; he appealed to common sense, and finally enlisted the Creator, Scriptures, and the Ten Commandments to prove that trade should be free. Trade, he held, was mutually profitable or it would never have been engaged in; to prohibit it was not man's prerogative. A high tariff meant high prices for everyone, which in turn diminished consumption and added to human misery. He answered all of Carey's arguments for protection by very effective illustrations drawn from actual trade figures, as well as by logical refutation. Probably no American economist of the nineteenth century took such an active part in the free trade versus protection controversy. Perry opposed it with a missionary zeal; to him it was the greatest national economic issue.

Perry's books on principles of economics were more widely used than any others for many years. Their forte was a simplicity of presentation and sincerity of motive. But Perry was such an ardent democrat and defender of the rights of the many against the privileged few that he failed to keep abreast of the changing times. The fact that he lacked flexibility of view was both a strength and a weakness—a strength in his courageous defense of what he thought, but a weakness when he failed to see that the same things which outmoded Smith's economics also outmoded most of his own.

Summary and Evaluation.—The foregoing writers set forth a very heterogeneous blend of economics. They present mixtures of criticisms of earlier economics with interpretations and applications of the doctrines to the American setting. The basic roots of their economics, like their entire cultural heritage, were English. It is not surprising, therefore, that strong English influences are found in their economics. Problems of economic growth and expansion of the new country were indeed different from those of the older economics of Europe. Tariffs, for either protection or revenue, slavery, states' rights, private banks, and internal improvements presented problems of national scale which could only be solved in their own national setting. English classical theory had little to offer on these issues.

From the materials presented it is apparent that the level of theorizing, as presently viewed, was neither very high nor original. Sectional interests tended to influence, even color, the thinking of some of the writers; however few, if any, defended special interests. Some espoused with a missionary zeal causes and issues which they believed in. Others were more moderate and sought common principles. Throughout all the writings is to be found a high ethical, moral, and at times even religious tone. A patriotic sincerity is likewise apparent; however, ardent nationalism is not outstanding.

Generally speaking the group opposed the Malthusian population doctrine, the Ricardian rent theory, and the classical distinction between physical capital and land, preferring to include land in the capital concept in both the physical and value sense. Likewise, they tended to regard rent and interest as simply two names for essentially the same thing. This was not the orthodox treatment. The American writers observed the fact that land here was as freely bought and sold as other commodities; it was an item which lent itself to both investment and speculation. The entire group tended to treat land as a form of capital and the investment value of land as a form of capital investment in business. Hence rent paid for the use of land (contract rent) would have to be an item in cost of production just as were wages or interest. In these respects they departed from classical theory.

The early writers, except for Perry, would have none of the wages-fund doctrines. They all opposed the "iron law of wages," or any doctrine which would tend to uphold a subsistence wage for the working population. The "escape valve" of free or inexpensive land tended to make any permanently low wage level impossible; besides, the general optimism which prevailed would have no such thing. Those who believed in the "American System" of protective tariff were both sincere and optimistic; they regarded it as the only way to guarantee the growth and independence of the nation, and they were equally certain of its beneficial results.

The early writers probably departed least from the English doctrines in value theory. A strong belief in a labor-cost theory of value as determining prices prevailed. There was some tendency by a few to consider the supply-and-demand aspects but the idea remained generally undeveloped. Carey's "cost of reproduction" doctrine enlisted no support. On that important subject the early writers made no contribution.

Many reasons might be given for the failure of early writers to make significant contributions to political economy. They did not completely fail to make original contributions, but the ones they did make can scarcely be regarded as significant. It would appear that the problems arising in a new environment might have led to new analyses and even a distinct brand of theory. But the writers tended to try to adapt English doctrines to sets of conditions far different from those which were found in England. Then, too, there was probably a significant obstacle of partisanship in the path of new theorizing. Prejudices in many forms, and pecuniary as well as regional or sectional interests, stood in the path of completely objective, scientific writing. Nationalistic convictions, however laudable, did serve, either consciously or subconsciously, to mold the thinking of the best of the writers.

Finally, it may be contended that few of the writers were trained in political economy. Professor Fetter remarked,"In political economy they were all self-trained amateurs, who, as it were, happened to wander into this field." [28] Some of them were ministers and journalists; others were trained in law, literature, medicine, and general business. The subject lent itself then, as now, to treatment even by the uninitiated. Nevertheless, despite the doctrinal inaccuracies and the faulty perspective of some, there still remains in the works of the early American writers much worth reading.

[28] *Op. cit.*, p. 60.

22

Later American Economists: Francis A. Walker, Henry George, Simon N. Patten, and John Bates Clark

Francis A. Walker's "Residual Claimant Theory"

Outstanding among the American economists in the last quarter of the nineteenth century was Francis Amasa Walker, son of Amasa Walker. Francis A. Walker (1840-1897) was a man whose interests and activities, together with his writings in several fields, attest a full life. Had his talents been centered on fewer activities his contributions might have been greater in those areas. However, he chose an active career which encompassed many interests.[1]

General Walker had both a theoretical and an applied interest in the general field of economics. While his early training in the theory and history of economics was received mainly from his father in their

[1] General Francis A. Walker (1840-1897) graduated from Amherst in 1860. His study of law was interrupted by the Civil War when he enlisted as sergeant major in 1861; he was discharged with the rank of brevet brigadier general. He was wounded in battle and also confined in Libby Prison at Richmond, Virginia. After the war he taught for a while and helped his father write *The Science of Wealth* (Boston, 1866). Walker served for a time on the staff of the *Springfield Republican*. In 1869 he went to Washington and became associated with the Bureau of Internal Revenue. He was superintendent of the ninth census in 1870 and also of the tenth census in 1880. In 1871 he became Commissioner of Indian Affairs. From 1872 to 1881 he served as professor of political economy at the Sheffield Scientific School of Yale University, without any previous academic training for such an appointment. He became President of Massachusetts Institute of Technology in 1881, a position he held until his death in 1897. He was one of the founders of the American Economic Association (founded in 1885) and served as its first President for seven years; he held the presidency of the American Statistical Association for fifteen years.

Walker's publications are *The Wages Question* (1876); *Money* (1878); *Political Economy* (1883; other editions, 1887, 1888); *Land and Its Rent* (1883); *International Bimetallism* (1896). These publications rightfully earned for him a worldwide reputation as a leading economist. See J. P. Munroe, *A Life of Francis Amasa Walker* (New York, 1923).

collaboration on the *Science of Wealth*, it proved adequate. His expositions of economics always contained realistic illustrations drawn from his many contacts with public life. The current controversies always enlisted his fighting support on one side or the other. Throughout his writings one finds an "American flavor" which revealed his desire for concrete applications to the local scene. He, like his predecessors, reflected an optimism and a vision of a great future for America. His writings were standard texts for many colleges both in this country and in England.

The first of Walker's writings was on the still unsettled wage issue. In his *The Wages Question* he decisively refuted the wages-fund theory of long, even if undistinguished, standing.[2] Walker was not the first critic of the theory, but his criticism was most devastating. His contention was that wages are paid out of the product of labor, not from capital. Even when advanced out of capital prior to final productivity, wages were finally paid from what labor produced. It is the promise of profit to result from production that induces the employment of labor. The prospects of profits decide whether there shall be any employment, and the wages that are finally paid depend upon the success of the forecast.

Having disposed of the wages-fund theory, he propounded his own, which is commonly known as the "residual claimant theory." He recognized four shares in distribution: wages, rent, interest, and profits. Thus the annual income is distributed in accordance with a rule which makes certain deductions natural, definite, and certain. Rent is the first deduction and must come out of income before wages are paid to labor. The amount payable as rent is a fixed sum determined by natural law. No rent appears on the lowest grades of land, only on the better grades. Interest is the next deduction, for capitalists must be paid a remuneration high enough to induce them to risk their capital in production. If they refused this risk, there would obviously be no production. The third and last deduction is known as profits, "the remuneration to the entrepreneur, who sets in motion the complicated machinery of modern production."[3] Hence, "wages equal the product of industry *minus the* three parts already determined in their nature and amount. In this view, the laboring class receive all they help to produce, subject to the deduction on the three several accounts mentioned."[4]

Walker's distribution theory differed widely from those held by English classical writers. He accepted the Ricardian view that rent be-

---

[2] See Chapter 13 for the theory as propounded by J. S. Mill and his subsequent recantation following Thornton's criticism.

[3] *Political Economy* (1883), p. 264.

[4] *Ibid.*, pp. 262-63.

longed to the landlord. Next he pointed out that the English doctrine allowed labor a share in accordance with the wages-fund doctrine and that which remained belonged to the capitalist-employer as his own profits. Profits consisted of two parts, one a return for the abstinence of the owner of the capital, the other due to the personal exertions of the employer of capital as such.[5] As opposed to the English view, Walker held that the entrepreneurial class were the owners of the whole product of industry, subject to definite charges against the product for the payment of rent, interest, and profits. In a recapitulation of the wage discussion he stated that he was "Rejecting decisively the doctrine of the wages fund, the doctrine . . . of a predetermined dividend which is irrespective of the number or industrial quality of the wages class, I hold with Professor Stanley Jevons, that wages equal the whole product *minus* rent, interest, and profits" (p. 284). The amount going for wages would be governed by conditions of competition, each man finding his best market, unhindered in any manner under full and free competition.

In an attempt to assure a free, competitive market, Walker supported limited state interference in behalf of labor. Only under state interference could imperfect markets be avoided which were injurious to the best interests of labor; such markets resulted from labor immobility, ignorance, poverty, and the like, and afforded opportunities for exploitation. Strikes would result from the market imperfections. Labor unions were generally approved by Walker and laws against unions were severely opposed. He recognized a need for organizations but he distrusted the power which unions might attain.

Walker's Synthesis of Textbook Economics.—Walker's textbook, *Political Economy* (1883), was liberal compared with others then in use, and it was popular. The book follows the same outline as his father's *Science of Wealth* (1866). The first part of Francis A. Walker's book is entitled "Character and Logical Method of Political Economy"; it contains his definitions and concepts. Like practically all his predecessors he says, "Political Economy and Economics is the name of that body of knowledge which relates to wealth," and he further emphasizes the point by saying that it "has to do with no other subject, whatever, than wealth." [6] Value he defines as "the power which an article confers upon its possessor . . . of commanding, in exchange for itself, the

---

[5] It will be recalled that Ricardo held, "There is no other way of keeping profits up, but by keeping wages down." McCulloch, too, held the view that "profits vary inversely with wages." Profits as used here included interest.

[6] *Political Economy*, p. 1.

labor, or the products of labor, of others. Value is power in exchange" (p. 5).

The second part, "Production," treats of land and natural agents, labor, capital, and the productive capacity of a commodity. Land is regarded as one of the three factors of production, along with labor and capital. The principle of diminishing returns is clearly understood as applied to agriculture and to manufacturing industries. The function of labor in production is well stated, and the discussion of the division of labor is accurate and thorough. The third part, "Exchange," contains his views on the theory of value. Since value is the power of one good to command another in exchange, he asks from what source this power comes. He finds that utility is a necessary attribute and "one of the elements of value" (p. 87). It is an inherent property of the good.

Walker denied that labor is the cause of value as stated by classical doctrine. "It is not because an article has cost labor that it possesses value. It is only because it cannot now be obtained without labor" (p. 89). He held a theory of value which makes freely reproducible goods, or goods the supply of which can be replaced, depend "not so much on cost of production as cost of reproduction." Exchange would then take place not on the basis of the labor required in original production but on the basis of the amount of labor which would be required to replace the stock.

Walker took a bold step in stating that "value is not always determined by the cost of reproduction." This point he undertook to prove by recourse to exceptions such as rare, irreplaceable objects or items that acquire antique value. He asked whether there is "any principle of universal application on which value rests?" To this he replied, "Value depends wholly on the relation between demand and supply" (p. 92). Demand he defined in a demand-schedule sense as "the quantity of an article which would be taken at a given price. Supply means the quantity of that article which could be had at that price." He saw the interrelationships of supply, demand, and price, and recognized the importance of price to "bring them together," which is done in the market. One price for a commodity is thus established in the market. In the market the price which is established is known as market price and reflects the supply of, and the demand for, the commodity. The market price, "which always measures the final utility of a commodity" may "differ more or less widely from normal price," which "closely corresponds to the cost of production" (p. 106).

Walker's development shows considerable originality. He recognized an interdependence of supply, demand, and price. He followed Jevons in distinguishing total from marginal utility and also in his own use of final utility. He distinguished between the supply of and the stock of a good, using the former in connection with the price at which a given quantity is offered, whereas the latter referred to the total amount in existence. He also recognized the importance of substitutes as influencing the final price of a commodity. These tools of analysis recall similar ones in the works of Alfred Marshall. Walker's value theory was vastly superior to that developed by any earlier American economist.

In the same part on "Exchange" he gives his views on money and banks. After considering the functions of money and the history of coins used as money, he examines the value of money. He holds that "the value of money, like the value of anything else, is purely a question of demand and supply" (p. 133). The demand for money depends upon the amount of "money-work to be done," by which he means the amount of exchanges of goods and services in a community. This in turn depends upon and "varies with the industrial organization of communities, with seasons, and with circumstances innumerable" (p. 135). He argues that goods are offered for money; if the supply of money is limited, "the more goods are so offered, the higher will be the value of money—that is, prices will rise. The fewer goods offered, the lower will be the value of money, hence prices will fall" (ibid.). Here, he treats price as the money value of goods, a power-in-exchange for another article; or the price of an article is its value in terms of money. He defines supply of money as the "money-force" available to do the "money-work" which the demand for money requires in a community at a given time. His terms appear somewhat strange, but his analysis shows that he knew the functions of money and its behavior under certain conditions affecting both its supply and demand.

On paper money issues Walker was aligned with those who feared the dangers of an overissue of inconvertible paper money. However, if inconvertible paper money is not inflated, it will "serve as the general medium of exchange . . . as satisfactorily as the coin itself" (p. 170). In fact, Walker preferred that paper money supplant metal coins in ordinary exchange. He strongly favored paper money but recognized the need for careful regulation of the amount issued.

In Part IV, "Distribution," the returns to the factors of production were treated in a manner distinctly characteristic of Walker. Rent, which went to the landlord, was treated in a Ricardian sense. It arose from "differences existing in the productiveness of different soils under cultivation at the time, for the purpose of supplying the market" (p. 207). The amount of rent reflected the differences in soils. Land values reflected the productivity of the land. He regarded rent as a result, not a cause, of price. Walker was a staunch defender of the Ricardian rent concept and was severely critical of Carey and others who used "perverted ingenuity" in their attempts to refute this doctrine. He was especially critical of the doctrines of Henry George, whose single tax on the "unearned increment" was "steeped in infamy." The first claimant of the product of industry was therefore the landlord. He not only could demand rent from land, buildings, or mines but he was entitled to it.

The next claimant was the capitalist, to whom interest must be paid, not for the use of money, but for the use of capital. Capital was created by saving and interest was the "reward of abstinence" (p. 232). Thus the strength of the motive for saving will vary with the reward for abstinence. The higher the reward (interest), the more capital will be saved. Walker viewed any attempt to depress the rate of interest—for example, by "force of law"—as a step to retard progress by which capital is supplied; thus the whole of society would suffer. Yet he admitted that, "with the progress of years," wealth (used in a capital-goods sense) had increased and the interest rate had tended to decline. Allowance was made in the analysis for high and low rates which tended to reflect the hazards of the loan, the supply of and the demand for loan capital, and the imperfections in the market. The discussion points toward a productivity theory of capital similar to the productivity element in land rent.

In his treatment of profits, Walker glorified the entrepreneur class in a manner not done heretofore. He observed that the entrepreneur function had not been "adequately treated, indeed it has been in the smallest degree recognized." "The entrepreneur," Walker said, "performs a function which is indispensable to a large and varied production of wealth, and for doing so he receives a remuneration out of the product of industry, which we call profits" (ibid., p. 245). He treated the returns to the entrepreneur as a "specie of the same genus as rent" and governed by the same laws as rent. They "do not form a part of the price of the products of industry, and do not cause any diminution of the wages of labor" (p. 248). The responsibility for successful operation of business, Walker said, depended upon the abilities of this class and their reward would or would not be exceptional in accordance with their ability. This is a differential treatment similar to that of superior versus inferior land. He also provided for a "no-profits class of entrepreneurs" as a quasi-parasitic class who eke out a meager subsistence which is a bare minimum upon which they live. He remarked "from this low point upwards, we measure profits" (p. 252).

Walker finds the existence of the entrepreneur economically justified because "he performs services to laborers and capitalists which they are not able to perform for themselves." That he performs these services is the excuse for his receiving profits. If labor and capital could combine their productive powers themselves, they could dispense with the services of the entrepreneur. This, Walker pointed out, had been tried, but he expressed the feeling that the function of the entrepreneur would always be needed and that his reward would reflect superior ability and productivity, much as superior land yields greater returns in production.

The wage theory developed by Walker has long been known as the "residual claimant" theory. "It has not been by accident, or whim, or from any notion respecting the comparative dignity of the several claimants to the product of industry, that rents, interest, and profits have been discussed before wages" (p. 262). The positive reason for this order of analysis is that "wages equal the product of industry *minus* the three parts already determined in their nature and amount" (p. 263). Rent is first deducted, then interest followed by profits, and the laborer is the residual claimant to what remains of the product of industry. This is the property of the laboring class. The amount of the residue which labor may claim rests upon the "energy in work," the "economy in the use of materials," and the "care in dealing with the finished product"; since the value of the product is increased, the increase will go to the laborers "by purely natural laws" (p. 266). The three first claimants are not expected to take more than their normal share. Therefore wages would be the entire residual after normal rents, interest, and profits were paid. He depended upon competition to regulate the return to each factor and expressed complete confidence that if competition was unhindered, it would bring equitable returns in each case.

The subject of consumption (Part V) is treated in three long chapters in which he analyzes wants in relation to capacity to satisfy them, population tendencies in this and other lands, overproduction and underconsumption as related to consumption. These last terms he regards as "a mere jangle of words" which are but different terms for the same thing. He uses Bastiat's famous "broken pane" to show the futility of any "make-work" panacea and finally treats the methods which the government may use to provide work; he concedes that there are expenditures—largely in the nature of public works such as building roads, bridges, streets, harbors, and so on—which would constitute justifiable expenditures. However, he concludes by saying that "government is only a policeman, to keep people from breaking each other's heads or picking each other's pockets" (p. 334). Part VI is given to some applications of economic principles. This part records his views on some of the pressing problems of his day, notably banks, usury laws, trade unions and strikes, taxation, and so on. They are of little or no interest today.

Walker was bold in expressing and in defending his views. Some of his views were attacked—notably the wage theory—as vigorously as he had attacked the wages-fund theory. His theory of profits was called one of "the wildest creations of nineteenth century economic thought." [7] Despite the criticisms of his theories he stubbornly held to his own views. His views, when compared with earlier writers, were generally liberal. Both his public service and the accomplishments of his private life show him to have been a great American, yet he displayed no narrow views comparable to earlier nationalists. Economics was treated as a cosmopolitan science, and both history and the theories of earlier times were drawn upon to prove or to illustrate the universality of principles. The work, *Political Economy*, rightly deserved first rank among the books which appeared in the last quarter of the century.

The contributions of Francis A. Walker to economics were greater than those of his father. The son's ties with the past were less binding. Francis A. Walker attempted to create his own theories and apply them. Through his efforts in helping to found the American Economic Association he was also an organizer of the economists of his time into a vocal body. Walker was well acquainted with both English theory and German historicism. He had a wide acquaintance with his own American contemporaries and with Europeans as well. He attended congresses in Europe and received decorations from Spain and Sweden.[8]

For many years Walker's *Political Economy* was the standard college text in economics. His contributions to theory appear meager as viewed almost three quarters of a century later. His attack on the wages-fund doctrine, already badly mutilated, was a signal achievement. The theory he proposed would make it possible for labor, under free competition, to get its productivity which, with advances in production, could be an increasing quantity. The entrepreneurial class was defended as necessary in the productive process; and its reward, profits, would serve to augment the employment of labor. The employer-entrepreneur was therefore a benefactor, not an exploiter, of labor. He justified all factors sharing to a greater extent in the fruits of industry. Walker did not engage in the tariff issue as did some of his predecessors; however, he is known to have supported a moderate tariff. He also stood for restriction on immigration mainly because of uncertainties concerning the absorption of immigrant workers and their effect on the labor movement. His contributions, however great, served to raise the level of economic theorizing on American soil, but they fell short of establishing a school of economics.

[7] Edwin Cannan, *A Review of Economic Theory* (London, 1929), p. 358.
[8] See J. P. Munroe, *A Life of Francis Amasa Walker* (New York, 1923).

Henry George

In the last quarter of the century there appeared a writer whose works fall within the general grouping of economics; yet the author was not an economist in the strictest sense. His works place strong social and political emphasis on issues which are distinctly economic in character. Throughout his pages and in his speeches there is a strong argumentative appeal and a propaganda element not found in any writer (except Marx) thus far considered.[9] His *Progress and Poverty* and Edward Bellamy's [10] book, *Looking Backward* (1888), were two publications

[9] Henry George (1839-1897) spent the early years of his life in Philadelphia. His formal education was meager and entirely self-acquired from reading books obtained from the free libraries. He went to sea for two years, and when the gold rush began he headed for California. He was not successful in his quest for gold and ended as a printer in San Francisco. Poverty beset him most of the years of his life, but he never ceased to try to ascertain what caused poverty such as he had seen in the great cities of the world. He became convinced that it was the private appropriation of land that was detrimental to society and a cause of poverty. His life was spent in developing this thesis.

His first published pamphlet was entitled, *Our Land Policy* (San Francisco, 1871). The work which brought him fame was *Progress and Poverty* (San Francisco, 1879). After great difficulty in finding a publisher the book, when finally printed, was a sensation at home and abroad. Millions of copies have been sold throughout the world.

George entered politics in New York City as a candidate of labor and socialist groups for the office of mayor in 1886. He was unsuccessful; however, he had such a large following that it took the best efforts of a coalition of parties to beat him. He was again a candidate in 1897 but died during the campaign. During the peak of his career he was extremely popular both at home and abroad. In later years he traveled in Europe, where he was well received. He debated with Alfred Marshall the "single tax" issues.

Besides *Progress and Poverty*, the one work that made him famous, he wrote numerous other books and essays, among which are *Social Problems* (1883), *Protection or Free Trade* (1886), and *The Science of Political Economy* (1898). The last, unfinished at his death, was completed and published by his son. George was a devout believer in the need for greater social justice and to this end he devoted his efforts. His early training left him with strong religious convictions. These are reflected in the missionary zeal with which he sought to bring about social reforms. The strong logical appeal of his work and the simplicity of composition characterize his writings.

The book, *Progress and Poverty*, was translated into many languages and was also published serially in newspapers. Henry George's son estimated that by 1905 more than two million copies had been sold. The Robert Schalkenbach Foundation of New York and the Henry George School of Social Science are devoted to the subsidization and teaching of the fundamental economics of George.

[10] Edward Bellamy (1850-1898) was a novelist and social theorist who wrote *Looking Backward, 2000-1887*, as a utopian romance. He portrayed a utopian society of A.D. 2000, devoid of private monopolies, waste, competitive profit-seeking production, and great concentration of wealth in the hands of a few. He portrayed the state as a socialistic structure with complete ownership of all resources and all agents of production. There would be complete social, political, and economic equality. The work had a terrific appeal as it pointed out inequalities of the times

which created great disturbance among economists and gave new impetus to socialistic movements of the day.

In a very real sense *Progress and Poverty* was a product of the social conditions of the day as Henry George saw them. This was a period of rapid growth and expansion and many kinds of excesses were common. The corporate form of organization, which was so widely used, was susceptible to practices which many held were antithetical to the best social interests. The railroads were given large land grants which made them land monopolists. The oil, coal, and timber companies were gaining control of great amounts of natural resources, and so on. The laws which might have exerted some control were few and laxly enforced and some courts were not above bribery and graft. Public apathy prevailed. The writings of George and Bellamy called attention to what many already knew, but did nothing about, and at the same time offered a cure for the most flagrant of the evils. The public response was immediate. Nor did the interest sputter out. The doctrines of George have outlived those of Bellamy, and the so-called single tax movement, initiated by Henry George, is still a very potent force both here and abroad.

Progress and Poverty.—The first views of George, which were ultimately incorporated into *Progress and Poverty*, appeared in a booklet of 48 pages entitled *Our Land and Land Policy*, written in 1871. In this work, which was hastily and poorly done, he proposed an end to monopoly in land ownership by shifting all taxes from labor and the products of labor and concentrating them in one tax on the value of land, regardless of improvements. A thousand copies were sold but the author realized he had to produce a more thorough, analytical work if he was to command attention. Thus the major work was begun and completed in a year and seven months of hard work. The preface of the fourth edition (1880) sets the pattern of the inquiry. He proceeds to examine why "in spite of the increase in productive power, wages tend to the minimum of a bare living." What causes an advance in rent? What are the laws of interest and wages? The question of justice arises next. He finds that "private property in land always has and always must . . . lead to the enslavement of the laboring class" (p. x). Also, that private property in land "stands in the way of improvement and use, and entails an enormous waste of production forces." The simple solution is the "abolition of all taxation save that upon land

---

and stimulated many to think in terms of the romantic objectives—called "Nationalism"—as he saw them. The book was translated into many languages. Over a half-million copies were sold within a few years. He enlisted many followers and at one time the group had considerable political power. They finally gave their support to the People's Party.

values" (p. xvi). George expressed the hope that he had been able "to unite the truth perceived by the school of Smith and Ricardo to the truth perceived by the school of Proudhon and Lassalle; to show that *laissez-faire* (in its full, true meaning) opens the way to a realization of the noble dreams of socialism" (p. xvii).

George presents "The Problem," as he calls the introductory part, by calling attention to the tremendous advances that have been made in wealth-producing power in the century. The bounteous material developments in every field should have made for greater abundance and fuller lives for all. But all these things "have neither lessened the toil of those who most need respite, nor brought plenty to the poor" (p. 5). He found that great distress appeared along with material progress. "When the conditions to which material progress everywhere tends are most fully realized—that is to say, where population is densest, wealth greatest, and machinery of production and exchange most highly developed—we find the deepest poverty, the sharpest struggle of existence, and the most of enforced idleness" (p. 6).

The several pages which set forth the problem emphasize the question of how can there be poverty in the midst of plenty. He remarks, "This association of poverty with progress is the great enigma of our times. . . . So long as all the increased wealth which modern progress brings goes to build up great fortunes, to increase luxury and make sharper the contrast between the House of Have and the House of Want, progress is not real and cannot be permanent" (p. 10). He promised to seek the answer to the "law which associates poverty with progress, and increases want with advancing wealth."

The answer is sought by a reconsideration of current doctrines. Wages, he said, were not "drawn from capital" but from the product of labor. He denied that wages of labor are paid and maintained out of the existing capital before final production. Likewise, he did not believe those "vulgar theories" which made the sum to be paid in wages a fixed amount. Capital, he maintained, "consists of wealth used for the procurement of more wealth, as distinguished from wealth used for the direct satisfaction of desire" (p. 80). It enables labor power to produce wealth. It does not advance wages to workers; it assists labor in production, and labor really creates its own fund from which its wages are paid, or its wages are paid from its productivity. This, he thought, was a complete refutation of earlier wage and capital theories.

Henry George would have none of the Malthusian theory. He held it to be completely disproved. Poverty was not a result of overpopulation, for in countries where poverty was greatest the forces of production if fully employed, would "provide for the lowest not merely comfort but luxury" (p. 150). He did not deny that multiplication of the population could bring about misery. But this misery was caused by a maldistribution of wealth which showed up in minimum wages and maximum production. In an economy where productive factors were fully utilized misery would not exist.

In providing a solution for the problem George turned to land, the first great natural resource, and examined its part in production. He used the Ricardian concept that the rent of land is the excess product yielded by better grades of land over those grades which yield no surplus over cost. It accrues to the owner of the land, who as the owner is in a monopoly position and can demand the surplus product—an unearned increment. The owner may contribute nothing to the productivity, but he may enjoy the exclusive return simply because he is the owner of the land which is productive. Labor is paid wages and capital receives interest as a result of the working of natural tendencies under conditions of free competition. However, rent, which accrues to private ownership, is the result of all factors which provide the demand for the product; all the owner has to do is collect and enjoy his monopoly return. Land is a gift of nature, and George finds no justification for private ownership of this natural resource which is not a product of man's labor. "Private property in land . . . cannot be defended on the score of justice" (p. 338). He further contends that "the recognition of individual proprietorship of land is the denial of the natural rights of other individuals—it is a wrong which *must* show itself in the inequitable division of wealth" (p. 341).

The basic cause of all economic and social troubles centered in the private ownership of land. The solution then, as George saw it, was to take away the rent of land from the private owners and give it to the community which really earned it. He did not propose to dispossess owners of land but only to take, by a single tax, the full annual rental value of the land. Land owners would retain their titles to land but speculation in land values would cease mainly because the unearned increment, which generally brought about the speculation, would become society's income. By removing the cause of speculation, in agricultural and mineral land as well, exploitation would end and inequality and poverty would cease.

Every student associates the "single tax" with Henry George. He proposed to have one tax which would rest solely upon land rent. This tax could not be shifted; it would be easy to collect and would really be no burden, for it was socially created and not the result of anyone's sacrifice. The community would enjoy greater income, for as production increased as a result of the growth in the social demand, or for any reason whatsoever, the land values or "socially earned increment" would increase. There could not be unemployment, and depressions would not occur, since the common cause of each was removed. The revenues of the state would increase, as the weight of taxation on productive industry was removed. Both capital and labor would be relieved of taxation, either direct or indirect, and the burden would be placed on rent. If this were done, taxation, "instead of causing inequality, as now, would promote equality" (p. 440), or so Henry George contended. No one would be impoverished if land rents were taken away from the present owners of land. The owner of buildings would be permitted the income from them and no penalty would be attached to anyone who made such productive improvements. "Wealth would not only be enormously increased; it would be equally distributed" (p. 452). If inequalities did exist they would be "those of nature, not the artificial inequalities produced by denial of natural law. The non-producer would no longer roll in luxury while the producer got but the barest necessities of animal existence" (p. 453).

He believed that the changes brought about in social life would be impressive. All the great cost entailed in collection of the many taxes would be gone; total governmental cost would be less; the costs of administration of criminal law "with all its paraphernalia of policemen, detectives, prisons" and the like, would be unnecessary. Society would approach an ideal democracy. Progress would be unimpeded. The revenues which arose from the common source would be applied to public benefit and make possible the establishment of "museums, libraries, gardens, lecture rooms, music and dancing halls, theatres, universities, technical schools, etc. Heat, light and motive power, as well as water, might be conducted through our streets at public expense . . . discoverers and inventors rewarded, scientific investigations supported . . . and in a thousand ways the public revenues made to foster efforts for the public benefit" (p. 456).

Enough has been presented to show that Henry George envisioned a complete change for the better in social and economic life. He saw no obstacles of any nature in the path of human betterment and equal opportunity to all. Inequalities, which to him were the basic cause of misery, would be wiped out and the entire level of society would be raised to a higher plane than ever before. Under his plan there would be a wider ownership of land and many small landholders. Vacant land would be forced into use by the tax and the improvements would earn the owner an income which would not be taxed. He argued that if idle or unused land now held for appreciation were forced into productive use, the monopoly element enjoyed at that time by the landlords would cease and rents would fall for those who must pay rents; everyone would

518 A HISTORY OF ECONOMIC THOUGHT

be better off. Henry George observed that rents were the first thing to rise in a new frontier city. Wages and interest were set by natural laws in which competition played an active part; but land was taken up first, buildings erected, and the exorbitant prices charged by the landlord were passed along to the consumer who was robbed of his wages because of the monopoly in land ownership which permitted such practices. George would have none of this. Society could better itself and be free from this scourge only by removing the cause.

The plan, as George conceived it, was never carried out. It never had sufficient support to make it effective. This does not imply that the single tax movement lacked supporters. On the contrary, both George and the movement enlisted many ardent followers at home and abroad, a following which continues today. In several places in the United States and in Europe there sprang up "Single Tax Colonies," which adopted the George principles with some success.[11]

The greater contribution of Henry George was in pointing to the need for political, social, and economic reform. His followers were so numerous that they were a very effective pressure group for many years.

Henry George's theories drew sharp criticism. At first most of the academic economists ignored him or dismissed him as an uneducated radical. In fact he was, along with Bellamy, a radical thinker. Finally, when the criticism started it was severe. Francis A. Walker, R. T. Ely, E. R. A. Seligman, F. W. Taussig, J. L. Laughlin, and J. B. Clark in the United States and Alfred Marshall in England were unsparing in their criticisms which were directed at the basic assumptions. German writers were more interested and more sympathetic with the doctrines, for the problem of land reform was a pressing one in that nation. While the critics were busily disproving the economics of Henry George's doctrines, the man in the street was reading the George books and pressing for badly needed reforms. George's influence was much greater than contemporary students can possibly realize. "This influence of Henry George has been much greater than professional economists are generally willing to admit . . . He has done more in America to popularize the science of political economy than any other economist."[12]

[11] See *Enclaves of Economic Rent* for the year 1933, a publication begun in 1919. Enclave is defined as "an area of land where, under the terms of the leases, the economic rent is collected, as contrasted with the surrounding region, or exclave, where it is not collected, such economic rent being used for communal purposes" (p. 25). A few of the "enclaves" reported upon were in Fairhope, Alabama; Arden, Delaware; Tahanto, Massachusetts; Free Acres, New Jersey; and Halidon, Maine. These experiments met with varying success over the years but it appears that they were obliged to depend upon other revenues in addition to the economic rent.

[12] Sidney Sherwood, *Tendencies in American Economic Thought* (Baltimore, 1897), p. 41.

Henry George was a keen observer and great student of the expanding American frontier. He saw the economic and political excesses caused by rapid expansion when laws were either unwritten or when, if written, they were unenforced. The boundless national resources were subjected to merciless exploitation. Many of the excesses were brought under legal control by subsequent laws; however, for many years both before and after George wrote, many antisocial economic practices were engaged in about which no one could be proud. It was against the abuses that Henry George protested, not as a socialist, for he was not one, but as a man deeply concerned about the practices which could bring poverty instead of plenty and stifle progress. His writings caused a great ferment from which came many far-reaching national reforms.

Simon Nelson Patten

Simon N. Patten deserves attention as a leading economist of the last fifteen years of the nineteenth century and an equivalent number of years in the twentieth. He lacked the public service experience of Walker and the popular appeal of Henry George. However, Patten deserves a place with the near-great, if not the great, American economists.[13]

[13] Simon Nelson Patten (1852-1922), economist and social philosopher, gained his early education in this country but, like many others, went to Germany and studied at the University of Halle, where he took an A.M. and a Ph.D. degree. He studied there from 1875 to 1878 with Johannes Conrad and was considerably influenced by the German historical school throughout his life. Upon his return to this country he taught in the lower schools at first and finally abandoned that work and studied law. His defective eyesight remained a handicap throughout his life. He soon quit the study of law and later became Professor of Political Economy at the University of Pennsylvania in 1888, holding that post until his retirement in 1917.

He wrote numerous monographs and special articles for the journals. His chief books were: *Premises of Political Economy* (Philadelphia, 1885); *Consumption of Wealth* (Boston, 1889); *Economic Basis of Protection* (Philadelphia, 1890); *Theory of Dynamic Economics* (Philadelphia, 1892); *Theory of Social Forces* (Philadelphia, 1896); *Development of English Thought* (New York, 1899); *Theory of Prosperity* (New York, 1902); *Reconstruction of Economic Theory* (Philadelphia, 1912).

Patten was a keen student of classical economics, especially the writings of John Stuart Mill, of whom he admitted he was a disciple. Yet he accepted little of classical doctrines mainly because he did not find them applicable in this country. He became known therefore as a critic of and dissenter from many accepted principles. His outlook was optimistic and free from the gloomy forebodings of classical economics. In this respect he followed H. C. Carey. He was a staunch defender of protective tariff and also an ardent nationalist. He believed firmly that social change, an all-pervading economic law, produced different social conditions which required new readjustments, a redefining of old principles, and a regrouping of objectives. He placed great emphasis upon consumption economics.

Patten left no scientific treatise despite his many writings. He remained a critic and an unorthodox thinker to the end. He had great originality and was fearless

Patten knew classical economics well but departed from most of its tenets. He did not subscribe to the belief that competition was an automatic regulator of trade or anything else. He did not accept the Ricardian rent theory or the law of diminishing returns. The Malthusian principle he rejected, for it, together with most of the classical doctrines, belonged to a "deficit" economy, not to a "surplus" economy such as is found in this country.

It is somewhat difficult to set forth Patten's views on economics since they are found widely dispersed throughout his writings and at times appear more sociological than economic in nature. However, enough will be presented to show wherein he departed from the orthodox pattern.

His book, *Premises of Political Economy (1885)*, sought to recast the economics of John Stuart Mill in the light of his training in German economics and his Middle West background. In this work he broke with the generally accepted premises of classical tradition. He held that the premises were too narrow and avoided the social nature of the problem. For example, he denied that rent arose solely because of differences in the soil; he insisted that the main causes of rent and of the rise in agricultural prices were social in nature, not physical,[14] nor would he admit that rents will rise with the lapse of time and the increase in population. Social distress was largely a result of social consumption habits which called for certain products to be supplied when other less costly ones would do as well. Here he was calling attention to consumption habits as being to blame for much of the maldistribution of wealth, not the niggardliness of nature, as Ricardo stated. A better adjustment of society to natural conditions he regarded as the only cure for social ills. He used this theory with telling effect in his arguments on land use and rent.

To accomplish greater social benefits Patten would subscribe to some social planning to be undertaken by the government in the interest of the common welfare. This would insure to a growing population higher living standards and increasing profits. Protective tariffs could likewise be defended as measures assuring greater social benefits. He did not believe in the Malthusian population theory and denied any tendency

---

in defending his views, which were distinctly American in treatment and in their application. See R. G. Tugwell, *Essays in Economic Theory* (New York, 1924); J. L. Boswell, *The Economics of Simon Nelson Patten* (Philadelphia, 1933). The American Economic Association devoted a memorial meeting to Patten; see Supplement, *American Economic Review*, XIII, No. 1 (March, 1923), pp. 259-93. A similar meeting was held by the American Academy of Political and Social Science; see *Annals of the American Academy of Political and Social Science* (May, 1923), No. 196. See also R. G. Tugwell, "Notes on the Life of Simon Nelson Patten," *Journal of Political Economy*, XXXI, No. 2 (April, 1923), pp. 153-208.

[14] See *Premises of Political Economy*, chaps. i-v.

of population to outrun food supply. He thought that the tendency characterized a static society, as did many of the classical doctrines, and was inapplicable to society in the Western world in general, and the United States in particular.

Patten was not especially interested in value theory either constructively or critically. The Mill influence appears, since he agrees that in exchange the quantities of goods offered and the quantities taken are equal. He did not subscribe to a cost of production or a cost of reproduction theory, but held that in society the value of goods is far in excess of their cost; as society progresses the surplus increases. Basically, however, labor costs are the sole and only costs; but on this he did not build a value-price theory, as did Ricardo. Being German-trained, he held that there was a strong subjective element in value theory. Marginal utility was a very important factor in evaluating both producers' and consumers' goods, which got their value from the utility imputed to them. No well-defined theory of value can be developed from his writing. He recognized both cost and utility as factors but his theory of value also included the social element which, as a factor, is used both as a cause and as a result.

The returns to each of the factors of production in Patten's distribution theory are subject to the same explanation. The social aspect of rent—or the relationship between land and man's needs was a vital force which would affect the trend of rents. The rent reflects man's needs, and it is his needs rather than the niggardliness of nature that affects the productivity and use of land and the rent that is paid for its use. Wages, he held were paid neither in accordance with the Ricardian subsistence-level theory nor with the wages-fund theory. He held a modified productivity theory which allowed labor, as well as other factors, to share in the growing surplus which was a gradually increasing amount. The same principle applied to capital and interest; the amount of capital reflected society's willingness to save and its interest return reflected the extent to which it was productively employed. All the factors shared in the increasing surplus in a harmonious relationship and in a cooperative society.

Patten supported protective tariffs for the United States. He argued that this was a dynamic nation with an increasing population, and protection was necessary to insure employment.[15] Also, protection was necessary to permit permanent adjustments to be made within this dynamic society. He was more concerned with national prosperity than with world prosperity, maintaining that prosperity within this nation would lead toward world prosperity. He contended that free trade did

[15] *The Economic Basis of Protection*, p. 11.

not lead to the production of commodities for which each nation was best suited, as was commonly argued. Free trade also was detrimental to specialization, and cheapness of goods was no test of efficiency in production; productive power as developed by the nation, was the reason for lower-priced goods. Professor Patten remained a staunch defender of protection, as well as one of the last to hold tenaciously to these views. His belief was an honest conviction and not a defense of any special, vested interests. He believed it was the right policy for this nation to pursue and he defended this conviction.

Patten's influence as an economist, although significant, is not great. He started no economic movements and founded no school. His considerable following was due more to his dynamic teaching than to any credo for which he was responsible. His writings, though extensive in number, are not shaped around any central core. His views were not always clear, nor was his position on issues certain—except on the one issue of free trade versus protection. As a disciple of social change he could never develop a static analysis; hence his ideas changed to the point of inconsistency. As one writer put it, "Consistency demanded that he be inconsistent." [16] He was, as a scholar, a mosaic of a social welfare economist, a practitioner of applied historicism, an Austrian in the subjective aspect of practically all his economics, and an optimist in national outlook, with a strong bias toward evolutionary change. Yet he was not an eclectic. The treatment and the interpretation of the writers and topics were distinctly his own. In this respect he was an extremely independent thinker.[17] As a critic of doctrinal economics and economists, he was reserved and unemotional as compared with some others. In his criticism he never failed to join the issue and enlisted both his broad learning and the current application of the problem in an appealing manner. As one of the original founders of the American Economic Association (and President in 1908) he had a part in shaping the early policies of the organization. The scope of his writings, the catholicity of his views, and his attempt to fit economics into the American setting lead one to agree with his former student, Henry R. Seager, that he "was the most original and suggestive economist that America has yet produced." [18] Another of his students wrote:

His most characteristic contributions to economics were the evidence he presented in support of the economic interpretation of history, his distinc-

---

[16] Boswell, *op. cit.*, p. 140.

[17] This is especially noticeable in his *The Theory of Dynamic Economics* (1892), which contains a bit of the history of economic thought, some graphic theoretical analysis, and an attempt to reduce the theories to laws. See R. G. Tugwell, *Essays in Economic Theory*, pp. 36-136.

[18] *Ibid.*, p. xi.

tion between the pain-deficit and pleasure-surplus stage of human progress, his insistence that there are no natural limitations on progress but that productive power is subject to the law of increasing rather than decreasing returns, his recognition that improvements in consumption may contribute to further progress quite as much as improvements in production, his emphasis on dynamic economics, his confidence in programs calling for the aggressive interference of government with the free play of economic forces varying all the way from protection to prohibition and the economic emancipation of women, and his distrust of competition as a regulator of economic relations and confidence in cooperation and other forms of socialization.[19]

An Evaluation of Walker, George, and Patten

The persons thus far considered in this chapter present three different courses which economic thought took in the last years of the nineteenth century. Each one was significant, but for different reasons. Walker and Patten appealed to an academic audience, whereas George appealed to the layman and generally irritated the academic economists. Walker began his teaching of political economy and history at Yale in 1874, fifty years after courses in economics were first offered in that institution. Patten began to teach at Pennsylvania in 1888, or thirty-three years after the first courses were offered by Vethake. The subject of economics was becoming a part of college offerings, although it was frequently combined with moral philosophy and other subjects, depending upon the training and interests of the teacher. The first professorship of political economy in America was held by John McVickar at Columbia (1818-1857); however, the subject was first taught at the College of William and Mary in 1801. In subsequent years professorships and chairs of political economy were established in practically all the eastern and southern schools. Yet it was not until the last quarter of the century that moral philosophy was divorced from political economy. Walker, in his teaching at Yale, and Patten at Pennsylvania were but two who occupied independent chairs at their respective institutions, which pattern was followed by all leading universities.[20] Walker not only wrote his own text on the principles of political economy, but participated in great national issues as an academician and as a citizen. Patten preferred to remain a critic of former doctrines, and to develop his own. Neither was a reformer despite his keen interest and partici-

[19] R. G. Tugwell, "Notes on the Life of Simon Nelson Patten," *Journal of Political Economy*, XXXI, No. 2 (April, 1923), p. 208.

[20] See Edwin R. A. Seligman, "The Early Teaching of Economics in the United States" in *Economic Essays in Honor of John Bates Clark* (New York, 1927), pp. 283-320.

pation in many of the pressing national issues such as the labor question, silver and banking controversies, corporation problems, and the like.

Henry George shared in none of these experiences. He was not an academician. His appeal was not made to the same groups nor at the same level. His interest was in bringing about basic reforms so that poverty and inequality might be abolished. His views were targets for the academic economists, who generally held them to be quite untenable and unreal. Despite the fact that the academic economists won the argument, no fine-spun theory would explain away the inequalities and economic abuses which the man on the street found to be real. It was argued that the natural rights doctrines of Henry George were unrealistic attempts to revive the social philosophy of the eighteenth century. Also, the unearned increment idea, if applied, would bring about untold hardships and the whole scheme had only a "rabble-rousing" appeal and was completely devoid of scientific foundation.

George, however, believed he had developed a great work in political economy. He had a strong belief that political economy had been "degraded and shackled; her truths dislocated; her harmonies ignored." He declared that political economy is "radiant with hope. It is not a set of dogmas. It is the explanation of a certain set of facts" (*op. cit.*, p. 559). These facts he believed he had discovered. They held the key to crises, poverty, and injustice. His fundamental doctrines were not inspired by any theories, especially of European origin, but by his own environment. He believed he was building a concept of political economy larger than any yet conceived. For calling public attention to certain monopoly abuses in land, he may be credited indirectly with land and tax reforms. George lives on, rather firmly established as a great pioneer whose influence penetrated deeply into the development of America at the close of the nineteenth century.

These men participated in current issues but each in a different way. There can be no doubt that all had something to offer. They contributed their own strong views on certain issues but—even more important—they influenced and stimulated many others in the great issues of political economy.

John Bates Clark

For reasons which are obvious, the first three authors are summarized together. John Bates Clark was a different type of economist whose interests were more in developing fine-spun theory than engaging in controversial issues. It appears necessary therefore to discuss and evaluate his work separately.

The fourth person considered in this chapter is generally regarded as the greatest American theorist. For the most part, earlier American writers were concerned with specific, current economic problems and with social reforms. Price theory and analysis were of less importance than economic and political problems. But John Bates Clark was one whose work was primarily in the realm of theory; for originality, he ranks among the foremost theoreticians.[21]

Clark's best theorizing is found in the *Distribution of Wealth* (1899); however, his earlier views demand attention, for they represent both theories and points of view abandoned in the later and more mature works. His first articles dealt with problems of theory and contemporary business organization and practices. The essays were published in a small one-volume work, *The Philosophy of Wealth* (1885). In this book Clark first criticized classical doctrines, his main objection to them being the lack of utility analysis; next, he analyzed the defects of the economic system and held that they might be corrected if an organic view of society were adopted.

In his criticism of classical doctrine he denied that man's economic activity is motivated by self-interest, that labor is the originator of value, and that labor is the sole producer of wealth. He contended that "man toils, not because labor always produces wealth, but because wealth naturally follows labor. . . . Nature subjected and appropriated is wealth; man's subjection of Nature is labor." [22]

In this same work appears his theory of value. Utility is at the core of his explanation; it is a quality or an attribute of a good and "value

---

[21] John Bates Clark (1847-1938) was educated at Brown and Amherst (A.B., 1872). The next three years were spent at Heidelberg where he studied with Professor Knies, a distinguished member of the historical school. He was also in attendance for a short time at Zurich, Switzerland. Upon his return he served on the teaching staff first at Carleton College, then at Smith and Amherst; in 1895 he went to Columbia University, where he remained until his retirement in 1923. He was one of the founders of the American Economic Association (and third President in 1894-95), and throughout his long career he was highly respected as a teacher and a writer.

His first writings appeared in the magazine *New Englander*. These and other articles were published in 1885 as *The Philosophy of Wealth*. His reputation rests largely upon his second book, *The Distribution of Wealth* (New York, 1899). In his last book, *Essentials of Economic Theory* (New York, 1907) he dealt with "social economic dynamics"; the earlier and better known work dealt with "static economics." While Clark was always interested in social betterment, his work dealt primarily with theoretical economics. For biographical details see Alvin Johnson, "John Bates Clark (1847-1938)," *American Economic Review*, XXVIII (1938), pp. 427-29; also Paul T. Homan, *Contemporary Economic Thought* (New York, 1928), pp. 15-105; George J. Stigler, *Value and Distribution Theories* (New York, 1941), chap. xi, pp. 296-319; Joseph Dorfman, *The Economic Mind in American Civilization, 1865-1918* (New York, 1949), Vol. III, pp. 188-205; and *Economic Essays Contributed in Honor of John Bates Clark* (New York, 1927).

[22] *Philosophy of Wealth*, p. 25.

is the quantitative measure of utility." [23]   Value and utility are inseparable, yet he says, "Utility is never identical with value, either in use or
in exchange." Price is only a mode of expressing value. A conventional
unit must be developed for expressing the utility of a good; this conventional unit is price, which is but a measure of utility. Clark avoided
the expression "value in exchange" and remarked that it had been used
to signify something apart from the kind of value in which he was interested. To him it signified "the measure of the utility of a good to
the purchaser and nothing more" (p. 88). His theory of value was
therefore, as a measure of the quality of things, a utility attribute of a
good.

Clark devotes a chapter to the law of demand and supply, with emphasis upon free competition as a significant factor in attaining a balance between them. After careful analysis of the factors influencing
both demand and supply, he insists that competition has gone beyond
the equilibrating stage and has become a type of "begotten lawlessness."
He had lost faith in competition. He found that it had been lessened
by combinations in industry, by unions, by capital combinations, by
business agreements, and so on. However, he admitted that some competition did still exist among groups "not in combination. . . . Yet the
fact remains that, in the field where its work is most important, in the
division of the products of industry between groups, sub-groups and
classes, competition of the individualistic type is rapidly passing out of
existence" (p. 147). He deplored the fact that labor used "injurious"
methods when dealing with capital and that capital likewise employed
injurious methods when dealing with society. Thus, "individual competition has, in important fields, practically disappeared." This view is
especially important here, for it was reversed in his later writing. His
value theory was somewhat inconsistent with his postulates in that he
depended upon competition to bring about "normal" prices, which
would tend to equal cost of production including a normal profit. Yet
he had grave doubts that competition could be relied upon to bring this
about. However, he did depart from beaten paths in his analysis.
Homan remarks, "The analysis of value is original in two respects—in
the place attributed to the social organism in the valuation process, and
in the treatment of utility in relation to value." [24]

It is neither possible nor necessary to discuss all the ideas developed
by Clark in this first publication. Yet two things stand out which fit
into the later development of his work: first, his break with earlier theory
and development and the launching into his own uncharted seas of

theoretical analysis; second, the originality of his theoretical analysis. He was not acquainted with the work of the early marginalists, Jevons, Menger, and Walras. Evidence based upon lectures and published articles establishes the proof that Clark was one of the early developers of the marginal utility concept. As Homan remarked, "The ideas expressed in the *Philosophy of Wealth* lack unity, if they are not at times flatly self-contradictory" (*op. cit.*, p. 33). However, his subsequent and more mature work saw many of the ideas developed into logical, finely turned tools for analysis.

Clark's Greatest Theoretical Work—The *Distribution of Wealth*.— The *Distribution of Wealth* came out in 1899, fourteen years after his first book and many more years after some of his early articles, the first of which had appeared in January, 1877.[25] This publication was really the first American work in pure theory; it proved that American scholarship could be productive in the field of theory as well as in applied economics. It remains as one of the greatest works in pure theory yet produced in any language.

The preface to *Distribution of Wealth* outlines its general plan. "It is the purpose of this work to show that the distribution of the income of society is controlled by a natural law, and that this law, if it worked without friction, would give to every agent of production the amount of wealth which that agent creates" (p. v). He contends that the classical economists used the term "natural" unconsciously as an equivalent of "static," and adds that "it is such natural or static standards that this volume undertakes to present" (p. vi). He aims to show, by logical deduction, how market prices, wages of labor, and interest on capital would conform, if the changes that are going on in the industrial world would cease. He sought to isolate the static from the dynamic forces for the purpose of analyzing their part in production and their returns. What would be the rates of return to labor and to capital if the amount of labor and capital remained the same, if improvements in the techniques of production remained the same, if consumption levels were unchanged and competition remained perfectly unobstructed? The answer, which is subsequently developed, Clark believes can be scientifically derived from the analysis of returns under the condition of a static state, the concept he uses for explanatory purposes. Clark puts his reader at ease at the very beginning of the book by stating that its purpose is to establish the theory that final productivity is at the basis of the law of wages, interest, and profits. The work then is focused upon the distribution of wealth, not production. The subtitle reads, "A Theory of Wages, Interest and Profits."

[25] See *Economic Essays*, pp. 339-351, for a complete list of his publications.

Clark develops his theories against the backdrop of a capitalistic economy. He assumes freedom of enterprise, private property, the profits motive, and a minimum of government activity, with that activity confined to the protection of the individual under established law. Labor and capital are the only factors of production, and man's efforts are directed to satisfaction of his own wants, not to wealth-getting activity per se. The postulate of pure competition is vital to the complete development of distributive justice, which will reward each factor for what it produces. Monopolies, trusts, unions—in fact, all activities antithetical to pure competition—work as a "friction" and thereby affect the working out of the theory of distribution. In the light of this setting he asks, "Is there a natural law according to which the income of society is divided into wages, interest and profits? If so, what is that law? This is the problem which demands solution." [26]

In the first chapters he discusses the issues and the traditional place of distribution theory. He views the income of all society which is to be distributed as, in reality, concrete articles all having some use. Many groups and sub-groups share in this production and each of them shares in the income. Price and exchange are social attributes which make distribution possible. In exchange, therefore, a lump sum of the net social income is to be apportioned among various claimants within the social unit. Therefore, if "natural laws are unperverted, labor tends to get, as its share, what it separately produces; and capital does the same. . . . Unravel the web of social product, tracing each thread to its source, and you have solved the problem of distribution" (p. 21).

The Static State.—Reference has been made to Clark's use of static analysis in an attempt to analyze the distribution of income. In a static state, in which present economic relationships were unchanged, all wages, rents, and profits, which have been called "natural" or "normal," would be static rates. Perfect mobility of the factors of production would make all returns natural returns and all values, natural values. Thus, under such a state the terms "natural," "normal," and "static" would be synonymous. No factors would disturb the returns to any factor of production and natural values would prevail everywhere.

But a static state is only imaginary. Society is highly dynamic and change is constantly affecting all elements in the economy. Changes occur in production, in the factors of production, and so on. Yet change does not invalidate static analysis and "static laws are nevertheless real laws" (p. 30). In order to arrive at his analysis, the distinction between static and dynamic forces is necessary. In the markets of the world where competition rules, "the standards about which prices fluctuate

---

[26] *Distribution of Wealth*, p. 1.

are set by static forces, and the fluctuations are accounted for by dynamic ones" (p. 32). He believes that the oscillations which constantly take place in market prices about a long-run average, can be measured if we knew the nature of the static forces which establish the norm about which the oscillations occur. In his words, "Static forces set the standards, dynamic forces produce the variations" (p. 32).

Having established the technique for his analysis, Clark identified "universal economic laws" which apply, such as the law of diminishing returns, the law of diminishing utility, the law of final utility, and so on. The values of all things are fixed, so Clark thought, by the principle of final utility, which is universal in scope. The income of a group is likewise governed by a distinct principle; namely—specific productivity. Thus he was able to state, "The specific productivity of labor fixes wages. . . . In like manner does specific productivity of capital fix the rate of interest" (p. 47). This, he believed, is a universal law which operates in all stages of economic life.

In applying the specific productivity explanation to wages, Clark held that it was possible to identify and measure the final increment of labor, whether in agriculture or industry. An entrepreneur will add another employee if that addition increases total productivity and the employee's wage will equal his specific addition to the total. This implies that the employees are interchangeable, in which case the effective importance to the employer of any of the interchangeable workers is measured in terms of the one who does the least necessary work. This is then the product of the marginal laborer. The employer operates in what Clark calls a "zone of indifference," in which he is "indifferent" to the addition or to the loss of any particular employee. The loss of one would be the loss of the marginal unit only, just as the addition of another would not materially affect total production. His conclusion is: "Wages tend to equal the product of marginal labor; and that part of the working force which occupies a zone of indifference is thus marginal" (p. 106). In other words, his theory makes wages conform to the specific product of the marginal employee, under the assumptions of free competition.[27]

Capital and the Capital Goods Concept.—Clark developed an explanation of capital and capital goods which ranks, along with his treatment

---

[27] Clark gives credit to Henry George for first calling this idea to his attention. He says, "It was the claim advanced by Henry George, that wages are fixed by the product which a man can create by tilling rentless land, that first led me to seek a method by which the product of labor everywhere may be disentangled from the product of cooperating agents and separately identified; and it was this quest which led to the attainment of the law that is here presented, according to which the wages of labor tend, under perfectly free competition, to equal the product that is separately attributable to labor." *Distribution of Wealth*, p. viii.

of wages, as the best of his theory. The distinction between the two is basic to his analysis. "Capital," according to him, "consists of instruments of production, and these are always concrete and material" (p. 116). "It is a sum of productive wealth" (p. 119). Then he treats the basic attributes of capital, the first and most distinctive one being its permanence. He emphatically declares that capital

. . . must last if industry is to be successful. Trench upon it—destroy any of it, and you have suffered a disaster. Destroy all that you have of it, and you must begin empty-handed to earn a living, as best you can, by labor alone. Yet you must destroy *capital-goods* in order not to fail. Try to preserve capital-goods from destruction, and you bring on yourself the same disaster that you suffer when you allow a bit of capital to be destroyed. Stop the machines in your mill that they may not wear out, wrap and box them in order that they may not rust out, and the productive action of your capital stops. . . . Capital-goods, then, not only *may* go to destruction, but *must* be destroyed, if industry is to be successful (p. 117).

Thus he drives home his basic arguments which distinguish capital from capital goods.

He further emphasizes the permanence of capital by a second attribute which makes capital "perfectly mobile." This is quickly seen when one considers how specialized capital goods can, as a rule, be used only for the specific purpose for which they were created. For example, he uses ships and cotton mills as forms of capital goods which have no possible interchange in use. Capital "lives, as it were, by transmigration" (p. 120), whereas capital goods surrender their life in the products they create. Thus capital as a fund, or a sum of productive wealth, lives on. He held the view that "capital is completely mobile: it can go anywhere" (p. 258). Since it has these basic attributes, it will also be homogeneous; as a fund, it can flow to any place in the world where it will be profitably employed. Thus capital may be defined in its attributes, as a permanent, mobile, homogeneous fund.

Land—A Special Kind of Capital.—Another factor of production, which from earliest times was treated as basic, is land. Clark made labor and capital the fundamental agents of production, but land was treated as only a special kind of capital goods in which capital is embodied. In fact, land is "the only kind of capital-goods that does not need to be destroyed, in order that the fund of wealth embodied in it may continue" (p. 118). The return to land—rent—is not expressed in a percentage, but is "the aggregate of the lump sums earned by capital-goods; while interest is the fraction of itself that is earned by the permanent fund of capital" (p. 124). Clark explains that capital is created by "abstinence," which means "the relinquishment, once for all, of a certain pleasure from consumption and the acquisition of a wholly new increment of capital" (p. 134). Interest is then the reward for abstinence. Once the capital fund is created it may be regarded as permanent and self-sustaining even though capital goods, which embody capital, may wear out in production. Land, since it is regarded as a form of capital goods, is not a product of abstinence. This apparent confusion is resolved in his static analysis by regarding what he calls "artificial" capital as fixed in amount, just as the amount of land (natural capital) is a fixed quantity. They may therefore be treated as one without undue confusion.

It should be observed that the creation of capital is a dynamic process and belongs in his dynamic analysis. In a static state there would be no abstinence or creation of new capital. Thus in a static condition the absence of change in the rate of interest implies no changes in either the saving or the spending motives or in the earning capacity of society. Therefore, the interest rate would be unchanged as would be also the wage return. Each and every unit of capital would get the exact equivalent of what it produced as its share of total product.

Specific Productivity Theory.—The basic assumptions on which the theory of specific productivity rests include the principle of diminishing productivity, universally applied to each of the factors. The labor force is made up of "units." The employer of labor will add "units" to his force as long as each added man creates for the employer a physical product, the value of which is equal to, or greater than, the amount he pays out in wages. Under the principle of diminishing productivity, each successive "unit" adds less to the total product than the former one. Finally, a point is reached where the marginal product added merely equals the wage; to go beyond this point would mean an entrepreneurial loss. Implicit in this assumption is pure competition, which forces the employer to add men up to the point of marginal product. Among employees the same forces of competition will make the marginal worker accept a marginal wage. The same explanation applies to the extent to which capital will be utilized. A "zone of indifference" exists in the "field of employment that each entrepreneur controls," in which the employer is indifferent to the addition of, or loss of, additional units of labor (p. 102). Additional units add no product or create no surplus over what they are paid; in other words, they are paid their marginal productivity in the form of a marginal wage, and the employer will gain nothing from their labor.

The same "zone of indifference" is found in the employment of capital. On marginal land there is no surplus created such as appears on better land. There is also an intensive marginal use of industrial equipment which yields no surplus.   In each case the marginal man using the marginal land or industrial equipment gets only what he produces under competition.   Marginal returns, under competition, would have the effect of equating all returns to the level of the marginal producer; otherwise, an employee could change occupations and employers would not be affected one way or another by the gain or loss in workers. Great dependence was placed by Clark in the efficacy of competition to make the theory work and to bring about the static relationships. He repeatedly emphasizes that "the earnings of men are fixed by the law of final productivity," which means, in reality, that "every laborer gets what would be lost to the employer if any one man now in the force would stop working" (p. 165).   Again the universal law of final productivity applies in just the same way to capital.   He states, "These incomes (wages and interest) are fixed by the final productivity of labor and capital, as permanent agents of production" (p. 160).

It must be borne in mind that Clark does not indicate any single unit as the marginal one which can be identified and separated from others.   Nor is any one unit the last in time.   Any one unit may be marginal.   Men are employed up to the point where the last one just pays for his wages in the product he creates.   Hence, no matter whether the unit is a single workman or a body of many men who function as a unit, the productivity of the last unit employed sets the rate of wage return or, in the case of capital, the interest return, under full static conditions.

The following diagram illustrates the effect of "setting men at work in succession" which Clark admits is "a bit of imaginary dynamics, but

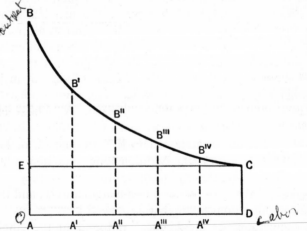

what it reveals is a static law" (p. 181).   The number of units of labor is measured along the line AD.   What the first unit of labor produces, with the aid of capital, is measured by AB. The second unit adds to the product the amount indicated by $A'B'$; the third unit adds product $A''B''$ and so on. The line CD measures the effective productivity of any unit of labor and also fixes the general rate of pay. If the first unit demands more than CD, the employer will let it withdraw and substitute for it the last unit. Should any one of the entire labor unit withdraw, all that would be lost would be CD. The same diagram may be used to arrive at Clark's law of interest: the labor factor would be constant and capital applied in successive units. Thus the sum of the series of surpluses above the line EC would be the earnings of all labor, which could be computed by multiplying the product of the final unit of labor by the number of units. The area below the line EC would be interest. The same illustration is used to show the surplus in the form of interest, in which case, wages would amount to the area below the line EC, or the total area $ECAD$. The sum total of wages and interest together make up the whole static income of society as determined by the one universal law of final productivity.[28]

Since land was treated as a special kind of capital, rent would presumably be identical with interest. He regards rent as a return to concrete instruments of production, paid to the owner of the instruments in either an explicit or implicit amount. The exact amounts would, as in the former case, be determined by competition as prescribed under static conditions. Thus his treatment of rent as "an aggregate of lump sums earned by capital goods" would appear to be quite different from interest, which he defined as "the fraction of itself earned by the permanent fund of capital" (p. 124). The returns are therefore not the same. He abandons the conventional meaning of rent as a differential return to better grades of land over marginal grades. Also, he avoids the abstinence explanation of the way land is created. He does not regard land as having mobility except in the sense that it will "flow" into the most productive uses, but not in the sense in which capital is regarded as so completely mobile.

We must prepare ourselves for a rude awakening to the fact that this extremely logical story is untrue. The whole process is imaginary, as the static state is imaginary. Clark's analysis is designed to show how forces would work out under his own assumed conditions. For the wage theory he argues that "two principles together control the fortunes of laboring humanity: (1) at any one time wages tend to equal the product of the final unit of labor; and (2) this product becomes smaller or larger as, other things remaining the same, the force becomes larger or smaller. The former principle is static, and governs the wages for each period;

[28] See *The Distribution of Wealth*, chap. xiii, pp. 188-205.

while the latter is dynamic, and, with other dynamic principles, controls the future of the laboring class. Mere growth of population without further change, is an impoverishing influence" (pp. 166-67). The same general principle applies to capital. "Capital is completely transmutable in form. . . . Capital-goods are interchangeable, and while this is so, no increment of capital can ever secure for its owner more than the final increment produces" (p. 186).

Dynamic Analysis.—In the dynamic world of society, change is everywhere present. Changes in the supply of and demand for labor and capital are incessant. Technical methods of production are constantly changing. Both static and dynamic forces affect every phase of economic activity. The dynamic forces tend to oscillate about the static ones, and it was Clark's conviction that the dynamic forces could be measured, once the static relationships were known. Again, "Static forces set the standards, and dynamic forces produce the variations" (p. 32). The logic of the method is unassailable. The concept of *ceteris paribus*, which is so indispensable in economic analysis, is static in nature. The economist must assume a static or stationary level of existing forces in order to make an approximation of a trend. The exact scientist conducts his experiments under perfectly controlled conditions of heat, pressure, light, and so on. Clark's attempt to be "heroically theoretical" is his method of approaching the subject of distribution scientifically. No fault is found with his method; only the bold assumptions appear unrealistic.

A very realistic element is injected into the dynamic analysis in his use of "frictions," "perversions of economic laws," or "disturbing influences" which run counter to the action of pure economic laws. No friction exists in a static state but it is a very common characteristic of a dynamic state. Frictions obstruct the free movement of labor and of capital to areas and to occupations which would afford greater remunerative returns. Inertia, which is regarded as a friction, prevents labor from gravitating to more profitable employment and tends to keep the actual rate of wages from reaching a theoretical standard. All this points up the fact that in a dynamic society strong forces prevail, which obstruct the complete working of forces which would tend to make the returns to the two factors of production—labor and capital—equal to their final product.

Clark recognized that basic changes take place in society which are practically continuous. Population is increasing. The capital fund is increasing. Technical changes in production methods occur at a fairly constant rate. Labor and capital, as factors of production, tend to increase in efficiency. Finally, human wants continue to increase along with population, but they become qualitative as well as quantitative. The wants of mankind, in Clark's view, are subject to laws; however, he made no attempt to formulate those laws since he regarded that work as beyond his thesis and as a task for future generations. He was content to present enough of the dynamic changes to permit fairly accurate generalizations.

Summary and Evaluation of John Bates Clark.—The many refinements in economic theory of the half-century since John Bates Clark wrote have tended to make his work, like that of many others, less significant. Marginal utility analysis, under Clark's deft handling, attained its highest level of perfection and its widest acceptance. Marginal utility had been developed as a value theory, but Clark broadened its application to explain the returns to the factors of production—a fully developed distribution theory. He believed that both value and distribution problems were subject to the same analysis and that one central core of truth prevailed which, if applied, would be universal in its explanation of economic problems. He sought to establish natural laws, universally applicable to the economy, and scientifically valid. If one grants the validity of his assumptions, he achieved his objectives.

Basic to the entire analysis is the doctrine of harmonies. Competition is relied upon to bring about conditions which assure each factor of production its just reward. Inequalities and injustices cannot exist, since the all-prevailing, pain-versus-pleasure calculus will automatically eliminate the originating causes. Society, treated as an organism, will function as a harmonious unit in which each factor is assured its own specific contribution to production.

Many of Clark's assumptions are subject to question and criticism.[29] His implicit faith in competition as the harmonizing force which insures the working of natural laws in the economy has elements of both unreality and mysticism. Pure competition, which is necessary for the theories to work, exists only as an assumption; and "natural laws" have long since lost their logical appeal. Static and dynamic concepts, however, are indispensable analysis techniques. The social concept of the state is held. Total social returns accrue to the two factors of production—"social capital," consisting of land and capital which are considered as an abstract mobile fund; and "social labor," likewise regarded

[29] The economic journals around the turn of the century carried many articles which dealt with Clark's marginal utility analysis. Among them are: T. N. Carver, "The Marginal Theory of Distribution," *Journal of Political Economy*, XIII (1904-5), pp. 257-66; J. A. Hobson, "The Marginal Theory of Distribution," *Journal of Political Economy*, XIII (1904-5), pp. 587-90; T. N. Carver, *Quarterly Journal of Economics*, August, 1891; C. W. MacFarlane, *American Economic Association Publications*, 3d Series, Vol. IV, No. 1, pp. 154-65.

as a homogeneous agent. This arbitrary division of the factors of production, together with the concepts of social utility and social value, has not been accepted in subsequent analysis.

Clark treated both labor and capital as homogeneous factors of production. The gain or loss in final product would be the gain or loss of the last productive unit added; yet, he never specifically described or identified the units. They were not reduced to such levels as an hour of labor of one particular type or an acre of land of a given level of productivity. The marginal productivity theory of wages, however, has been generally accepted and, with current modifications, remains as the central core of wage theory. Land is treated as a special form of capital, not as a separate factor of production; thus the controversial relationship of rent to price is avoided, and land rent is of little significance in his analysis. Prior treatments of land made it distinct from capital and characterized by its limitation in supply and by differences in quality. These characteristics were qualities of all capital goods and not solely characteristics of land, in Clark's opinion. Quality differences of land were no different from those which might be found in any capital good. Therefore any differential (in the Ricardian use of the word) in the returns to land was not a peculiarity of land but a common attribute of all forms of capital. Since capital and labor are the only two factors of production, the returns of interest and wages constitute the core of the analysis.

The differences between capital and capital goods are basic in his analysis and possess a reality in his treatment but an unreality in practice. Capital is a fund created by abstinence—that is, by abstaining from present consumption in favor of creating wealth in the future. Concrete capital goods are used up in production, but capital is perpetual and serves in both production and consumption. The interest rate is fixed by the marginal productivity of capital, not capital goods. However, the marginal productivity of capital is affected by the addition or withdrawal of units of capital goods. Since capital is regarded as a permanent fund and capital goods as used up in the production process, interest would logically accrue to the larger item. The treatment of capital is superior to that accorded to capital goods, and constitutes one of his major contributions to economic theory. It is a theoretical analysis of a factor of production and its return is entirely free from any ethical implications. The chief criticism of Clark's analysis rests with his attempt to distinguish between the two and to define them in terms of permanence and impermanence. Despite imperfections in the distinctions and use of the terms, the capital-interest analysis shows his original thinking and clear insight.

If the over-all objective of Clark's analysis is kept in mind, his terminology is less objectionable. He was seeking to examine the economic system analytically and ethically. The analytical device of the static state, in which all factors of production were held constant, was designed to show what each factor produces and how the sum total of social product is divided. Any analysis of the distribution of wealth is bewildering unless it is reduced to simplest terms. This was attempted in the static analysis by holding the productive elements constant. Under conditions of perfect competition, every agent would get, as its reward for participation in the productive process, the equivalent to the value attributed to its own service. The chief contribution of the analysis is that, under Clark's assumptions of static conditions, each factor is rewarded on the basis of its specific productivity, and the price obtained by each factor will equal its specific marginal productivity. The "frictions" found in a dynamic state interfere with the working out of the "natural" forces. The dynamic forces, discussed in his less known volume, *Essentials of Economic Theory*, show that he made some progress in treating the economy realistically.

There is a metaphysical tone in much of Clark's writings which some have characterized as "mystical." The natural laws which would prevail if things worked in perfect harmony are reminiscent of the natural laws of classical writers. The ethical and moral issues which are found throughout his writings are sincere and remind one of the same virtues in Alfred Marshall's writings. Marshall and Clark had much in common. Each used static analysis, but Marshall was more realistic and included many more problems of dynamics and change.

Clark raised marginal utility analysis to its highest level of perfection and set the pattern for teaching and research for many years. He was the founder of the so-called "marginalist school," which enlisted the best of American scholarship. The hedonistic pleasure-pain explanation was further refined by Professor Frank A. Fetter (1863-1949), whose emphasis on psychological analysis was highly developed. In pure theoretical economic analysis John Bates Clark achieved a greatness exceeded by no other American scholar. The words of Jacob Hollander spoken on the occasion of Clark's eightieth birthday (January 26, 1927) are a fitting characterization of the esteem in which he was held by his fellow economists.

Clark's work as an economist has been both the creative activity of a philosopher and the specific service of a scholar. But it ranges wider. For more than a generation he has been a teacher to students, a master to disciples, a critic to fellow craftsmen. In all of these relations he has shown a serenity of mind, a sweetness of manner, a gentleness of spirit that make up "eine schöne Seele." No other among American economists has come so near to founding a "school." But over and above the impress which sheer intellectuality and rare originality have imparted, has been the contagion of mental tolerance and scientific generosity. It is in this spirit that the whole fraternity of political economists, far beyond the small company who here in homage lay before him their offerings, find it a delight to do him honor.[30]

[30] *Economic Essays in Honor of John Bates Clark* (1927), p. 5.

23

Thorstein Veblen and Institutional Economics:
W. C. Mitchell and J. R. Commons

The half-century from 1875 to 1925 was extremely fruitful and eventful in nearly every phase of human endeavor. At no time in history had nations made such strides in raising the levels of both production and consumption of goods. The United States led all other nations in the expansion of business techniques and the development of natural resources. Even the wars which interrupted the tempo on several occasions within this period did not change the course of events. An awareness of the interdependence of nations was forced upon peoples; trade and commerce were not the monopoly of any one nation.

Narrowing our perspective to the subject of economics, there appeared the great European developments as found in the work of the English and the Austrian scholars. The work of many American writers was also extremely significant in both theoretical and applied economics. So rapid was the tempo of business expansion that it seemed to "run away" from the traditional framework of "economic laws and principles" which had had long, if not always distinguished, tenure. Economic practices, as well as economic growth, forced an acid test of theories in a crucible of new proportions.

Thorstein Veblen

Throughout the period there were many who challenged all or parts of the accepted doctrines, but the one who was by far the most critical and challenging in this or any other nation was Thorstein Veblen—philosopher, iconoclast, economist, psychologist, sociologist, social anthropologist, seer, and soothsayer extraordinary. Whether he was more or less—or even none—of one or the other matters little now. His extensive writings have elements of each of these disciplines. His span of active intellectual and academic years is identical with the years of greatest national business activity and corporate growth.

Veblen's first creative writing began in the 1880's and reached a crescendo in the next decade when his contributions to the learned journals reached its peak; in the final year of the decade his most significant book appeared. These were the years of great business and financial growth, when laissez faire practically ran wild and the laws designed to curb corporate excesses were passed. These were the years of great labor unrest which, together with ill-tempered management, led to performances that shocked most people into an awareness of hitherto unknown social and economic problems. The crosscurrents of a dynamic, growing state were probably seen more clearly by Veblen than by any other thinker of the period. Certainly no man so clearly pin-pointed the good and the bad characteristics as did Veblen, and no one else dared criticize practically every phase of life with the invective of this man. Through all his writings there was also a prophetic strain which unfolds its astounding accuracy as the years roll by. He was somewhat of a mystic while he lived; in the years subsequent to his death (in 1929) the mystic concept has tended to give way and reveal a man who may in time be regarded as the greatest prophet of economic change in the century.[1]

---

[1] Thorstein Bunde Veblen (1857-1929) was born of Norwegian parents in Wisconsin. When he was eight his parents moved to Minnesota to a larger farm on what was then almost the frontier. His knowledge of English was very limited at first, since his life up to the age of about seventeen had been spent entirely in Norwegian settlements. In 1874 he was sent to Carleton College Academy, Northfield, Minnesota, and at the end of three years entered Carleton College. The college was founded as a Congregational school and placed greatest emphasis upon theology and religious teaching.

One of the teachers, and the one who influenced Veblen most, was John Bates Clark, professor of political economy and history and also librarian. The text in economics was Reverend Francis Wayland's popular book which had been revised by another Congregational minister, thus giving the book a double dose of theology. Clark's influence on Veblen was such that as a teacher he directed his skeptical student through the theological maze to new ideas in economics which were germinating in Clark's mind. Veblen gained special permission of the faculty to take the junior and senior years in one, which he accomplished by passing prescribed examinations. He graduated with the class of 1880. In college his interests and his reading were in the fields of philosophy, natural history, classical philology, and anthropology.

Veblen entered Johns Hopkins University in the fall of 1880 but because of failure to receive a scholarship and disappointment in the academic offerings, he left before the end of the term and entered Yale where he could study philosophy under the President, the Reverend Noah Porter, an outstanding scholar. He earned the Ph.D. degree in 1884, his thesis being "Ethical Grounds of a Doctrine of Retribution." At Yale he studied deeply in the fields of philosophy, metaphysics, and psychology. His readings in Kant and Spencer, together with the influence of some of his teachers, notably Porter and William Graham Sumner, made deep and lasting impressions upon him.

He was unable to get a position after he left Yale and this fact, together with ill health, accounts for the subsequent six or seven years of more or less idleness. Those years were spent not in productive labor but in intensive reading in practically

Before examining his writings it is necessary to examine briefly the many influences which in part or in whole account for some of the many strange elements in his makeup. His mentality, vastly superior to that of the average student to begin with, was nourished on Spencer, Hume, Kant, whose influence gave him inquisitive, speculative, and critical views applicable to practically everything. Clark whetted his interest in economics and its development. His long years of idleness and illness were given to extensive reading in practically every discipline. He became interested in biology, anthropology, folklore, philology; he was a capable translator and critic of his own old Norse and Icelandic languages, German, and French. In his university contacts, especially in the University of Chicago, he was afforded the opportunity of an encounter with many keen minds on many subjects. He was in the laboratory of a great city where he saw great capital concentrations and corporate growth. The clash of a rapidly growing world was all about him. Labor strife, the Haymarket riots, trusts, monopolies, panics and depressions, wars and peace, and the endless list of changes wrought in this eventful fifty years, were all being enacted on the stage at which he had a ringside seat. No man ever saw these changes so clearly and

---

every field. He was married in 1888 to a Carleton College classmate whose interests were, in general, the same as his own. His unemployment (or possibly even idleness) continued until 1890 when he entered Cornell as a graduate student. Professor J. Laurence Laughlin was impressed with Veblen's possibilities in the field of economics, and through him Veblen obtained a fellowship. When Laughlin went to the newly founded University of Chicago as head of the department of economics in 1892, he took Veblen with him. Veblen had a teaching fellowship which paid $520 per annum. He taught courses in socialism, agricultural economics, and history of economic doctrines. The University had some eminent men on its staff, notably John Dewey in philosophy, Albion W. Small in sociology, von Holst in history, and Judson in political science.

The *Journal of Political Economy* was started at this time (1892) and Veblen served as its editor for almost ten years; he contributed articles to this and other journals on numerous subjects. His career at Chicago was discouraging in an academic sense, but fruitful in a productive sense; he was made an instructor at the age of thirty-nine; he was forty-three before he was made an assistant professor in 1900; and he never held a full professorship. By all standards of evaluation he was not a successful teacher, and this fact plus his many eccentricities led to his dismissal in 1904. He was appointed to an associate professorship at Stanford in 1906 and remained there until 1909. In Chicago he taught graduate students but at Stanford his students were undergraduates. Students and professor bored each other to an impossible degree and his tenure ended. Next he was given an appointment at the University of Missouri by Professor H. J. Davenport; there he remained from February, 1911, until 1918. In the fall of 1918 he moved to New York City where he was to become one of the editors of *The Dial*, a magazine of high literary quality in the field of social science. His career as an editor of *The Dial* came to an end within a few months. His next connection was with the New School of Social Research, established in the fall of 1919, with a very distinguished faculty. His salary was $6,000, $4,500 of which was contributed by a former University of Chicago student. His tenure at the New School ended in 1922. The next few years were spent in New York and in 1927 he returned to California. He died

no one described certain elements so scathingly as did this quiet, reserved, taciturn man who saw change in an evolutionary light which could do nothing but outmode all former, albeit sacred, fundamental doctrines.

Veblen's Critique of the Postulates of Economics.—The sweep of Veblen's thinking can only be sketched in a work such as this. That he has earned a niche in shaping the trend of economic thought cannot be doubted. No other critic, not even Marx, has forced such a re-examination of the postulates of political economy. In attacking the basic assumptions he was more challenging than if he had attacked the theories in final form. His own assumptions may likewise be challenged, for he too set up premises designed to prove his own case.

Veblen held strong critical views on the postulates of economics as it had developed over the years. In an essay entitled "Why Is Economics Not an Evolutionary Science?" written in 1898,[2] he attempted to analyze what was behind the thinking of the classical economists, the historical school, the utilitarians, and others. In general he found many things not to his liking. In the first place, economics is not an evolutionary science. Economists, he thought, were not "modern" but were "still content to occupy themselves with repairing a structure and doctrines and maxims resting from natural rights, utilitarianism, and administrative expediency." He admitted that this criticism was a bit

there on August 3, 1929; in accordance with his will, his ashes were scattered over the Pacific Ocean.

Beginning with the *Theory of the Leisure Class* (1899; new ed. 1918), Veblen published a succession of remarkable books on a wide range of topics. *The Theory of Business Enterprise* (1904); *The Instinct of Workmanship and the State of the Industrial Arts* (1914; new ed. 1918); *Imperial Germany and the Industrial Revolution* (1915); *An Inquiry into the Nature of Peace and Its Perpetuation* (1917; new ed. 1919); *The Higher Learning in America* (1918); *The Vested Interests and the State of the Industrial Arts* (1919); title changed to *The Vested Interests and the Common Man* (1920); *The Place of Science in Modern Civilization and Other Essays* (1919); *The Engineers and the Price System* (1921); *Absentee Ownership and Business Enterprise in Recent Times; The Case of America* (1923); *The Laxdaela Saga* (1925), translated from the Icelandic; *Essays in Our Changing Order* (1934), edited by Leon Ardzrooni.

The best work yet done on Veblen is Joseph Dorfman's *Thorstein Veblen and His America* (1934). This shows clearly the political, social, economic, and other forces that influenced Veblen. See also Richard V. Taggart, *Thorstein Veblen*, University of California, Publications in Economics, Vol. IX, No. 1 (Berkeley, 1932); Paul T. Homan, *Contemporary Economic Thought* (1929); Allan G. Gruchy, *Modern Economic Thought* (1947). R. L. Duffus, *The Innocents at Cedro* (1944) gives an intimate glimpse of Veblen at Stanford. See also *The Portable Veblen*, Introduction by Max Lerner, ed. An obituary appears in *The American Economic Review*, XIX, No. 4 (Dec., 1929).

[2] Originally in the *Quarterly Journal of Economics*, XII (July, 1898). Reprinted in *The Place of Science in Modern Civilization*, pp. 56 *et sqq.*

severe but it was "near enough to the mark to carry a sting." [3] He also admitted that many pertinent facts had been gathered, "often in a painstaking way," but that the facts when gathered failed to provide a "theory of anything or to elaborate their results into a consistent body of knowledge." Economics did not present a theory of process such as is a prime requisite of an evolutionary science. It held too many old concepts such as "natural," "normal," "tendencies," "controlling principles," and the like to be classed as an evolutionary science. The classical economists formulated laws and principles of the normal and natural; their standpoint "in their higher or definite syntheses and generalizations, may not inaptly be called the standpoint of ceremonial adequacy." [4] Economists have given narrative surveys of facts and data; but they have been factual, not an account of an unfolding process of life and society. Even the Austrian economists who worked with the subjective value analysis really made no advance in rehabilitating economic theory as a whole since they were "unable to break with the classical tradition that economics is a taxonomic science." [5] Veblen held no brief for the hedonistic doctrines which supported the subjective analysis. He also found that metaphysical concepts were mingled with ethical norms which were totally impossible. In analyzing the trend of economics in the preceding years, he found "two main canons of truth on which the science proceeded, (a) a hedonistic-associational psychology, and (b) an uncritical conviction that there is a meliorative trend in the course of events, apart from the conscious ends of the individual members of the community." [6]

On the first point he argued that hedonism was outmoded and impossible in that "the hedonistic conception of man is that of a lightning calculator of pleasures and pains, who oscillates like a homogeneous globule of desire of happiness under the impulse of stimuli that shift him about the area, but leave him intact." [7] Later psychology, Veblen argued, disproved this theory. Man is "not a bundle of desires" but rather is made up of "propensities and habits which seek realization and expression in an unfolding activity." [8] This view affords a necessary clue to his own concept of economic behavior, which is but an unfolding of human activity. "All economic change is a change in the economic community . . . The change is always in the last resort a change in the habits of thought." This is true even in the mechanical processes of industry. Veblen placed great reliance on the behavior of the group and in support of this he drew heavily upon his knowledge

[3] *The Place of Science in Modern Civilization* (1919), p. 57.
[4] *Ibid.,* p. 65. [7] *Ibid.,* p. 73.
[5] *Ibid.,* p. 73. [8] *Ibid.,* p. 74.
[6] *Ibid.,* p. 150.

of anthropology and social behavior. Group behavior was of greater significance than theory or logical method of analysis.

Veblen's views on how men behave, which were in a sense an attack on the generally accepted economic theories, was broadened into his system of social theory. In developing the social theory he used anthropology to show how racial traits developed and how they finally became culture patterns. Man was endowed both by his heredity and by his environment with certain characteristics which showed themselves in many ways; instincts had developed which manifest themselves in both peaceful and warlike traits. In addition to his instincts, man had cultivated certain distinct propensities and habits. One of these propensities is man's tendency to emulate or even outdo others in certain social levels.

It was Veblen's belief that man's behavior showed a definite trend which became an accepted pattern for the entire group and developed, in time, into what he called an institution. While he made great use of the concept of an institution, he defined it rather vaguely as a cluster of habits and customs, ways of doing things, and ways of thinking about things, all of which are sanctioned by long practice and by the approval of the community. "They are settled habits of thought common to the generality of men." [9] In fact Veblen saw the whole of material civilization as "a scheme of institutions." They were the outgrowth of habit. That institutions prevail is a result of deeply ingrained habits of thought and action.

Even though institutions owe their origins to habitual action, it is not implied that they are permanent. Human behavior may remain relatively fixed and stable within limits, but the institutions, which afford means for human expression, are transient and subject to change. Since they reflect social habits, change from either external or internal causes is but a normal unfolding and manifestation of social growth. Thus, institutions are habits of thought which change as habits of thought change. The gradual unfolding process of social evolution demands a constancy of change. In treating social behavior and habits in this manner Veblen held that his method was strictly scientific and followed the post-Darwinian pattern of evolution, of which biology was the best example. He was merely avoiding the pre-Darwinian brand of organizing cause and effect, of rigid classifications, natural laws, and the tendency toward equilibrium. These faults of earlier economists made their work unscientific and obsolete. It was only when the evolutionary nature of society was recognized, with its group habits and

[9] "The Limitations of Marginal Utility," reprinted in *The Place of Science in Modern Civilization*, p. 239.

its institutions, that a full understanding of the economic system could be developed.

The Pecuniary Element in Modern Society.—It has been pointed out that Veblen draws heavily upon the past to outline behavior patterns of the present. The basic idea is that all institutions developed by man represent processes of cumulative change in which the only stable elements are certain human traits. To prove this point Veblen examines anthropology, psychology, and indeed most elements of the cultures of many peoples to prove that the present level of man and his institutions was but one stage in cultural development. In this development, two institutions are predominant: private property which has a pecuniary connotation; and technological methods of production which provide the goods to satisfy wants. These two theses in one form or another run throughout his work. In fact, the whole of capitalism was regarded as "our pecuniary culture."

Veblen's strong conviction of the pecuniary element in our culture is dealt with in his first and possibly his best work, *The Theory of the Leisure Class*. This book, written in an ironic style and with sharp criticism, showed not only the author's interest in psychology and anthropology but also his ability to use these disciplines to illustrate social behavior. He maintains in his inimitable way that the so-called leisure class is motivated in its behavior by pecuniary considerations alone. People whose scale of living is above subsistence levels do not use the surpluses, which technological methods have developed, for purposes of their own material betterment but to impress others that they have surpluses. Members of this group resort to "conspicuous consumption" to impress others. Time, money, and effort are spent in an unproductive manner in "pecuniary emulation" to inflate their own egos and impress others. Much consumption is nonproductive; time is spent in "conspicuous leisure" as an evidence of pecuniary ability to afford a life of idleness. Veblen makes the pecuniary motive the dominant and honorific factor in standards of living, taste, and dress; in fact, it is the hallmark of society.

The Theory of the Leisure Class, which has come to be the best known of Veblen's many writings, has little economic theory in it and practically no relevance to economic problems. It is a critique of the pecuniary behavior of peoples mirrored against this cultural background of inherited traits. The analysis is very penetrating and the treatment of the leisure class is scathing. However, one is left with a feeling that the polemic leads to no end. The surplus product which presumably has resulted from technological advancement is not considered in an economic sense, but only as an item by which the cultural identity of a class is maintained. The book provides a picture of the behavior of a group which is but one phase of the exfoliation in economic development.

Another pecuniary aspect of society, apart from the one just described, is the manner in which technological knowledge is given over to pecuniary pursuits. The instinct of workmanship and technological changes in methods of production led to all the great changes associated with the industrial revolution, the factory system, the large-scale production of capitalism, a money and credit economy, and so on. Machine production has supplanted handicraft methods and become a highly complex process with great interdependence among the various branches which now make up an industry. A precise balance must be maintained to keep in operation such an industry which, when functioning at its optimum, will produce in abundance.

The ownership of the productive capital is in the hands of absentees whose sole interest is in the profit or the pecuniary gain they may get from the system, and not in maximizing the production of useful goods for society. The businessmen manage the system with the object of maximizing pecuniary gain for themselves and their absentee owners, while the goods they produce are but by-products of that effort. Around this point, namely, the difference between "business" and "industry," Veblen builds much of his theory and analysis.

Veblen was given to a dualistic analysis, which stands in sharp relief in his views of the cleavage between business and industry, between the making of money and the making of goods, between ownership and technology, between pecuniary and industrial employment, and finally between those who perform social functions and those whose behavior leads to social waste. He aligned scientists, technicians, engineers, or those concerned with the production process on one side and the owners and managers on the other. The never-ending conflict between these groups led to dire effects on society. A conflict arose between the so-called engineer, whose duty it was to devise newer and more efficient means of production, and the entrepreneur, whose problem was to amortize the original capital investment and at the same time earn a profit for the owner.

Veblen on Price and Business Cycles.—The price system is the leading economic institution in the pecuniary economy. Modern industry, Veblen contended, is a complex, interdependent series of units, each of which is a potential profit-making unit, controlled by the businessman. The price system ties the units together and adjusts their interrelationships; it also forces production for profit. This implies continuous purchase and sale of goods and creates in the minds of the businessmen (and others) an accounting-for-profit scale of values rather than a production-for-use concept. Money gain provides the supreme drive in Veblen's concept of pecuniary society.

The price for which goods are sold in this society is not determined by the forces of competition but by "what the traffic will bear." Veblen did not subscribe to competition as an effective force in leveling profits to a minimum. On the contrary, he found that over the years the tendency was for small concerns to be eliminated by merger with larger firms, which finally combined into great trusts exerting monopolistic power. As small concerns are eliminated and become parts of a larger industrial system, the actual management likewise becomes monopolistic and is centered in the hands of "businesslike technicians" or experts who are more concerned with the pecuniary aspects of business than with the production of goods. The captain of industry,[10] as formerly known, now becomes a captain of business, which is a way of making management the function of a business technician. The manager is therefore identified as a technical expert distinct from the businessman in the generally accepted sense.

It was Veblen's belief that not only could prices be controlled by corporate management but that output, production costs, and final prices could all be controlled for maximizing net profits. Industry is under skilled management, and as a result of technological advances is capable of turning out virtually unlimited quantities of goods. If this process is permitted to continue, more goods will be produced, which must sell for less, thus possibly impairing the net profits. Thus business "equilibrium" has been disturbed by increased productivity and subsequent lowering of prices. "So the continued progress of the industrial arts has become a continued menace to the equilibrium of business . . . And the remedy by which this inordinate productivity of the industrial arts is to be defeated or minimized is always businesslike sabotage, a prudent measure of unemployment and a curtailment of output, such as will keep prices running above that salary minimum that is required to pay fixed charges on the funded make-believe and allow a 'reasonable profit' on investments." [11] The vast business enterprises represent vested interests, each struggling with other vested interests for a larger share of profits, with the result that the economy operates with only "partial employment of equipment and man-power." However, boom periods are possible when full employment and full industrial utilization

---

[10] Veblen defined the captain of industry or "Captain of solvency," as he liked to call him, as "the personal upshot of that mobilization of business enterprise that arose out of the industrial use of the machine process." *Absentee Ownership and Business Enterprise in Recent Times* (New York, 1923), p. 102.

[11] Thorstein Veblen, *Absentee Ownership*, p. 97.

may prevail. But the results are always the same. Productive industry is speeded up to meet the accentuated market demands and "for a time the industrial equipment and man power may be allowed at something approaching full capacity." [12] Prosperity leads, as it has in the past, to "overproduction," gluts, depression, and crisis with disastrous liquidation. Thus, because of the many contributing factors most of which are inherent in the system, business is constantly in a state of semidepression.

The inherent reasons for this condition are to be found in the institutional structure of the capitalistic economy. Veblen argued that there was no relation between the physical equipment used in production and the value of the pecuniary capital supplied by the absentee owner of the enterprise. His argument was that the values of the capital were capitalized on the basis of their ability to earn an income for the owner of the capital. These values were obviously intangible and unrelated to physical productivity. This explains, in a brief manner, his theory of business cycles. They were manifestations of excessive inflation or deflation of the capital values as reflected in the profits or losses which subsequently accrued. Liquidation and scaling down of the values followed, which, after a time, might start a revival of business, mainly because of a readjustment of the values.

The future of business behavior was impossibly hopeless in Veblen's analysis. There were the clashes of technological advance which would produce at lower costs more goods that might be sold at lower prices and the interests of the absentee capitalists, who looked only to profits and who resisted any move which endangered their sheltered position. The tendencies toward monopoly in industry and in finance capital were growing and setting the stage for bigger conflicts. As he remarked, "custodians of absentee-credit" were certain to engage in "capitalistic sabotage." [13] And as the production units grew and amassed more economic strength their practices ceased to be merely competitive and assumed warlike proportions. Both positive and negative economic powers were held by the large corporate units. They could manipulate prices for products sold, determine who produces what and who enters industry, and in a real sense control the entire economy. On the negative side, they might control the supply of goods placed on the market, curb production, or even determine the extent to which technological advances may be introduced into industry. Such was the economic power over industry as seen by Veblen.

Control over economic power was not confined to capitalists; labor was given to the same practices with the same objective in mind.

[12] *Ibid.*, p. 91.
[13] *Absentee Ownership*, p. 97.

Through the strength of its organizations, it controls the flow of skilled workers and the amount of work done, and dictates to some extent the wages paid. The organizations have deliberately planned to match their own power against that of the industry. In this struggle for economic advantages for their own vested interests, the actions again follow a reprehensible pattern of "conscious withdrawal of efficiency" by both parties.

Veblen's analysis creates an impasse for the pecuniary society which he does not resolve. A constant warfare between the vested interests would lead, at least in the Marxian analysis, to the end of capitalism and the establishment of a new society. Not so with Veblen. He did not predict a decay of the capitalistic system nor did he visualize what form economic society would ultimately take. Veblen was too much of a social scientist to use crystal-ball gazing in predicting the future of economic society. It is better to view socioeconomic changes as but part of a perpetual unfolding of society which goes on virtually uninterrupted in its long-run evolution.

This brief account may serve to highlight some of the main points of emphasis in Veblen's treatment of the all-pervading pecuniary aspects of society. What he lacked in theoretical analysis he adequately compensated for in describing the broad sweep of the many social forces which were, and still remain, conditioning factors in contemporary society. The Marshallian emphasis on the value-price analysis of an individual has no place in Veblen's analysis, nor has the "economic man" of classical tradition. On the contrary, it is the whole of the cultural behavior of contemporary society that matters, for individual behavior is but group behavior. Thus Veblen's contributions in theoretical refinements are few, if any; his contributions lie rather in applying the concepts of cultural anthropology and group behavior to a broad phase of society which he chose to regard as the one motivated by pecuniary culture.

Veblen's Contribution to the Development of Institutional Economics.—It is generally (and somewhat loosely) said that Thorstein Veblen was the founder of institutional economics. The phrase "institutional economics" is not Veblen's; had he been called upon to suggest a name, it would probably have been "evolutionary economics." Veblen was concerned with the earliest beginnings of human behavior and its subsequent evolutionary development. In this respect he was more interested in method than in content. Over the centuries gradual changes in man's way of doing things and in his habits of thought are responsible for the present level of his culture. Man has certain inborn instincts which, when developed under varying circumstances, become common, habitual types of behavior; these in turn take on greater or lesser degrees of permanency yet allow for changes within the framework of the behavior pattern. This is a Darwinian concept of evolutionary change which Veblen applied to economic society. In order to understand economic society and its problems and in order to develop scientific economics as a discipline, the first thing is to examine and explain the particular group habits of thought which prevail in any given period. Veblen called the habits of thought and the practices which prevail at any given time "institutions," or, to rephrase the definition, "widespread social habit." Thus the economist must examine in their cultural setting institutions which are but passing group habits of behavior in an agelong evolutionary development. Veblen was constantly aware of evolutionary change in all the institutions which man had set up. He was unperturbed by evolutionary change, for indeed he considered it the most common and certain thing in the whole of human existence. This evolutionary concept of society was what he regarded as his own greatest as well as most distinctive contribution.

It has been pointed out that Veblen made extensive use of instincts (tropisms, as he called them) as they manifested themselves in a pecuniary culture. Two of the greatest of the institutions which had evolved in this pecuniary culture were "business" and "industry." Veblen found that the larger share of economic activity centered around these two institutions and that as a result certain patterns of group behavior had developed. The "widespread social habit," or the way of doing things in a complex economic society, has been embodied in institutions that symbolize the group habits and establish the cultural level of that society. The price system, the payment for the use of the factors of production, private property, competition, the profit motive, the money and credit media, the banks, the numerous forms of doing business, and so on are institutionalized group habits, or institutions. Veblen was not concerned with explaining how the prevailing institutions work; the gyrations of the price system and the great mass of problems falling in the category of economic theory scarcely interested him. His concern was with finding out how any given institution evolved: how it got started in society; through what changes it has passed; how it has been changed by society; how it has, in turn, changed society; what light it throws on other group behavior, and so on. The orthodox economic theorist was concerned with the cause and the effect of economic problems in their setting and with an eye to future controls. Veblen was mainly concerned with finding out how the institutions of capitalism (around or about which problems arose) evolved.

Veblen's emphasis on the evolutionary aspect of institutions naturally poses the question: To what does this endless process of change lead?

Since he made the evolution of economic institutions the center of his brand of economics, what does the future hold for society? The answer to this may be more effectively given by briefly comparing Veblen's theories on the future of society with those of Marx, another student of historical evolution.

It will be recalled that Marx was interested in the evolution of institutions. He, like Veblen, was a severe critic of the accepted economic practices. From history Marx drew facts to prove his dialectic, which he learned from Hegel, that social institutions were basically at war with one another and that out of this conflict would come a new synthesis—a society representing the acme of perfection, the socialist state. That was the end of institutional change as he saw it. This new state, which would harbor none of the "bad" institutions which man in his planlessness had evolved, was the final consummation and as such would last forever. This was the ultimate.

Veblen, on the contrary, was a Darwinian evolutionist who believed that the evolution of institutions was the rule and that this process knew no stopping point. He did not envisage a static, utopian social state free from change. He expected the dynamics of change to continue: as social habits changed so would social institutions change. New frontiers would be opened as a result of technological advance; refinements in institutions would follow in a pattern which was traceable to the earliest of times.

This view carried with it a dynamism far more appealing and vital than that offered by orthodox theories, especially classical economics. The staid characteristics of laws based upon *ceteris paribus*, the deductive logic of theory resting upon generalized observations, the induction of the historicists, the impossible psychology of Benthamic origin that man acts rationally to avoid pain and achieve happiness—all these suddenly lost any appeal for many who had long sought a new shrine for worship. Economics patterned on Veblenian lines freed many from the fear of becoming mere theorists, and offered new worlds to conquer. A new cult appeared which attempted to explain the elements of the economy in their proper setting and let the theoretical aspects shift for themselves.

The full impact of Veblen's economics on subsequent writers will perhaps always defy accurate evaluation. By introducing his broad, cultural analysis of the economic behavior of society he avoided all narrow, individual, entrepreneurial behavior of the Marshallian type. Value and price analysis under given conditions of neoclassical economics was lost in a larger collective emphasis and analysis of social evolution. On this point a contemporary student remarks, "His evolutionary economics presents a body of economic theories which are more relevant to the problems and issues of the twentieth century than are the economic theories of the equilibrium economists. This greater relevance of Veblen's institutional economics is derived from its central theories of economic conflict and change. Besides closing the gap between theory and practice, Veblen's evolutionary economics gives a futuristic slant to economic thought." [14]

No one should expect to find in any one of Veblen's books a concise description of man's behavior in the culture in which he finds himself. Apparently he was not interested in such a task: therefore the full weight of the Veblenian diagnosis requires a careful excerpting from all his works. Certain disappointments beset the undertaking. Many of Veblen's highly suggestive economic ideas on such things as monopoly price, corporate practices, technological change, managerial functions, public policy, and so on have no empirical support. Severe criticism has been leveled at his emphasis on the importance of the "instinct" as the important determining factor in behavior and his lack of emphasis on the psychology of class behavior. Statistical analysis is conspicuously absent. He placed too much dependence upon evolutionary change to satisfy everyone completely. But it must not be forgotten that Veblen probably cared very little who, if any, were in agreement or, to say the least, satisfied with what he had to say. To have cared would not have been like Veblen.

The years take their toll of both critics and defenders of all faiths. The new ideas put forth by Veblen enlisted followers and elicited criticism as well. While Veblen did not found a "school" in any strict sense of the term, he did influence both directly and indirectly more American economists than any other American author. Not many American economists would admit direct kinship to the dour Norwegian, but few are the economists who have not rechecked their premises and their conclusions either in line with Veblenian analysis or in deference to his criticisms. Yet there are still others who have followed their own bent in theory and analysis, completely oblivious to the devastating attacks of Veblen on all orthodoxy. In any event, "Veblen has helped to create a new intellectual climate." [15] Those who found the climate more "embracing" have made significant contributions, and some of the men and their works will be discussed in this chapter. Many have followed an "institutional approach" in establishing a background and setting for their researches without any espe-

[14] Allen G. Gruchy, *Modern Economic Thought: The American Contribution* (New York, 1947), p. 123.
[15] Gruchy, *op. cit.*, p. 131.

cial awareness of being "institutionalists," just as others are unaware of being "historical" economists.

Wesley C. Mitchell

The person usually regarded as the leading exponent of institutional economics is Wesley Clair Mitchell.[16] Along with many others, he was a student and an heir of Veblen. It was Mitchell's good fortune

[16] Wesley Clair Mitchell (1874-1948) was born in Rushville, Illinois. He received the A.B. degree from the University of Chicago in 1896 and the Ph.D. in 1899. One year was spent at Halle and Vienna, where he attended lectures by Johannes Conrad and Carl Menger. He joined the Columbia University faculty in 1913 and remained there, except for a three-year interlude at the New School of Social Research, until he retired from active teaching duties in 1944. He served as a member of the staff of the United States Census in 1899-1900, and of the War Industries Board of World War I. For a short time he was an editorial writer on the *Chicago Tribune*. He was an organizer of the National Bureau of Economic Research in 1920, and he was outstanding both as a contributor and later as a director of this organization. He was always active in the Social Science Research Council and the Bureau of Educational Experiments. During the years 1929-1933 he was chairman of President Hoover's Research Committee on Social Trends. President Roosevelt appointed him to the National Planning Board in 1933. He was a member of the National Resources Board in 1934-1935, and special adviser to Secretary Morgenthau in 1937. In 1944 he prepared a report for the President's Committee on the Cost of Living which helped to end the dispute over the accuracy of the official index numbers for changes in the cost of living.

Mitchell was signally honored during his lifetime by learned societies and academic institutions. He was a President of the American Association for the Advancement of Science. The National Institute of Social Sciences awarded him a gold medal for his contributions to economic science and public affairs. He was elected a Fellow of the American Statistical Association, the Econometric Society, and an Honorary Fellow of the Royal Statistical Society. He was president, at one time or another, of the American Statistical Association, the Econometric Society, the Academy of Political Science and of the American Economic Association. In the academic year of 1930-1931 he was a visiting professor at the University of Oxford, in 1934 at the University of California, and in 1935 at Cornell University. Honorary degrees were conferred upon him by the Universities of Paris, Chicago, Columbia, California, Princeton, Harvard, Pennsylvania, and the New School of Social Research. In 1947 the American Economic Association bestowed upon him the highest honor it can confer, when he became the first holder of the Francis A. Walker medal, which is awarded not more often than once every five years to an American who "in the course of his life made a contribution of the highest distinction to economics." On his sixtieth birthday (1934) his former students presented him with a volume of their writings entitled, *Economic Essays in Honor of Wesley Clair Mitchell*.

The best known of his volumes are *History of the Greenbacks, with Special Reference to the Economic Consequences of their Issue, 1862-65*, published in 1903. (This was originally his Ph.D. thesis.) A companion and statistical volume on the greenbacks appeared in 1908 entitled, *Gold, Prices, and Wages under the Greenback Standard*. *Business Cycles* appeared in 1913. The best known and most influential of all his writings is *Business Cycles: the Problem and its Setting* (1927) which was a revision and an expansion of the 1913 edition. While director of research he was co-author of several National Bureau of Economic Research publications such as *Income in the United States*, Vol. I (1921); *Business Cycles and Un-*

to be a student at the University of Chicago when John Dewey was doing his great work in pragmatic psychology and philosophy, and J. Laurence Laughlin and Thorstein Veblen were teaching economics. Dewey was concerned with men's actions as clues to their thoughts; Veblen was concerned with economic behavior; Laughlin, a rugged individualist who held to orthodox, traditional principles and laws of economics, money, and finance, gave direction to Mitchell's thinking. Dorfman maintains that Laughlin's emphasis tended to make Mitchell more receptive to Veblen's type of analysis.

Mitchell showed this influence in the researches incident to his *History of the Greenbacks.* That study was designed to show objectively just what happened to the nation during the years when the greenbacks were used as the common currency. Such an inquiry required empirical research into the whole structure of economic life, for in some fashion or another every segment of the economy was involved. In a sense, Mitchell used Veblen's theory of business enterprise as a starting point and set out to make a study of the price system and its place in modern economic society. Even though he had no special training in statistics and though statistical data were not available in any very usable form at that time, he used the information that was obtainable to gain new insight into price movements and economic fluctuations. He made both a qualitative and a quantitative study of this emergency currency. He examined the reasons why it was issued by the federal government and then considered the broad consequences. The confusion in all phases of life which resulted from the issue was studied as a pecuniary disturbance. The rise in commodity prices at both wholesale and retail levels, the premium on gold, the loss of equities as well as the decline in corporate earnings, and the general confusion and lack of faith in money and financial institutions were treated as interrelated problems. The interdependence of wages and prices was shown to be a cause-and-effect relationship, not a problem in value and distribution.

employment (1933); *Business Annals* (with W. L. Thorp, 1926); *Recent Economic Changes* (1929); *Measuring Business Cycles* (with A. F. Burns, 1946); *Economic Research and the Development of Economic Science and Public Policy* (1946). He contributed articles to the learned journals on many subjects. The best of his articles appear in a collection edited by Joseph Dorfman, *The Backward Art of Spending Money* (1937).

For significant studies of Mitchell see Paul T. Homan, *Contemporary Economic Thought* (New York, 1928), pp. 377-436; Allen G. Gruchy, *Modern Economic Thought: The American Contribution* (New York, 1947), chap. 4; Joseph Dorfman, *The Economic Mind in American Civilization* (1949), Vol. III, chap. xx; Arthur F. Burns, *Wesley Mitchell and the National Bureau*, Twenty-ninth Annual Report of the National Bureau (May, 1949), pp. 3-55. A memorial appears in the June, 1949, issue of the *American Economic Review*.

Mitchell examined the military as well as the business annals of the period and found that the premium on gold shifted regularly with the success or failure of the Northern armies, thus reflecting public confidence in the issuing agency to make good on its promises to redeem the greenbacks in gold. He also found that profits were made at the expense of the community and that the rate of interest did not rise with the rate of profit. This discrepancy he attributed to the uncertainty connected with the fortunes of war and the inability to foresee price changes. The unevenness in the adjustments of commodity prices, the lead and lag of wages and prices, and the economic consequences of slow adjustment, were all presented as interdependent problems of a social economy. The pecuniary aspects of all the elements in the situation went far beyond a price analysis. All the forces that were at work concerned him. As Burns remarked, "Mitchell's prodigious industry was revealed for the first time in his *History,* as was his superb skill in organizing a great mass of factual material and extracting from it significant generalizations. He made extensive new calculations, set out the statistical methods in full, explained their derivation, and noted their shortcomings . . . So gracefully did Mitchell move back and forth between theoretical reasoning and factual documentation that the need for whatever statistical detail he presented was hardly ever left in doubt." [17] *Gold, Prices, and Wages* in 1908 was a second volume on the greenbacks.

Business Cycles—Mitchell's Lifework.—His skill and craftsmanship, together with his approach and analysis, are even more clearly discernible in his *Business Cycles* (1913), which, in its several editions, was probably his greatest research work. *Business Cycles* was an outcome of his plan to write a book with the tentative title, "Theory of the Money Economy," which never was written. No definitive work had been done previously on money and price inflation. He had observed the major booms and depressions toward the close of the century and the Panic of 1907. The behavior of prices and the concurrent and subsequent price readjustments led him to inquire into the uncharted area of business cycles. It was a stupendous task, largely because of inadequate data. He studied the data on the United States, Great Britain, Germany, and France for 1890 to 1911—he wanted figures on commodity prices, wages, bond yields and prices, money in circulation and its velocity, most of which were not usable in their original form. In the amazingly short space of three years he was able to assemble the needed materials, and as Burns says: "Mitchell had worked out one of the masterpieces in the world's economic literature . . . No other work

[17] A. F. Burns, *Wesley Mitchell and the National Bureau,* p. 13.

between Marshall's *Principles* and Keynes' *General Theory* has had as big an influence on economic thought of the Western World." [18] While this might be an exaggerated statement of a single opinion, one would be hard put to name another work which had an equal impact on economic research and analysis. In the 600 pages there appears a staggering quantity of materials dealing with a historical recounting of business cycle theories, the economic organizations of the day, the pecuniary aspects of the economy, and the statistical data necessary to compute trends in each of the four countries. Part III, "The Rhythm of Business Activity," shows his grasp of the integration of the forces in the economy and their responses to causal factors. The work is undeniably a masterpiece in a new type of economic analysis.

Some of the reasons for the high esteem in which the work is held are as follows. The method of analysis does not start from simple assumptions and descriptions of business at a particular stage or date, anticipate that if new factors were introduced a change would ensue, and follow this with an explanation of subsequent adjustment to the change. Such was the more or less common way of dealing with business fluctuation. Theories purporting to "explain" business fluctuation were numerous, but Mitchell would have none of them. He states in the opening line of the preface of *Business Cycles* (1913) that his work "offers an analytic description of the complicated process by which seasons of business prosperity, crisis, depression, and revival come about in the modern world." His "analytic description" is indeed a contribution. Under his method he provides an effective tool for analysis of the subject at hand. It makes something usable out of masses of statistical data and historical evidence. Mitchell has remarked, "A systematic account of cyclical fluctuations, taken seriously, becomes an analytical description of the processes by which a given phase of business activity presently turns into another phase. The obvious framework for such a description is provided by the successive phases of the cycle." [19] He abandons earlier deductive analyses and depends upon empirical data and systematic observations. This enables an explanation based in largest possible measure on facts and not on nicely reasoned logic. An even greater advantage is that his analysis shows what economic activity actually is and how economic society works. Mitchell's treatment is vastly more than a study of the "ups and downs" of business; it is an explanation of our complex economic structure.

The Veblenian influence and teaching is apparent in the emphasis placed upon the pecuniary aspect of society. Mitchell deals with a

---

[18] *Ibid.*, p. 23.
[19] "Business Cycles," *Encyclopaedia of the Social Sciences*, II, p. 100.

money economy. In the early chapters of Book II he shows that "the money economy subordinates the industrial process of making goods and the commercial process of distributing them to the business process of making money. Accordingly, the ebb and flow of economic activity is brought into dependence upon the profits of business enterprise. Upon this basic fact the whole investigation rests. Profits, in their turn, depend upon the margins between buying and selling prices, and upon the volume of transactions." [20] He emphasizes that the "crucial problem" of business profits, prices, the volume of trade, and the behavior of institutions of capitalism such as banks, money, investments, and business failures, constitutes the core of the study. The monetary aspect of the study and the emphasis are described as follows:

The present theory of business cycles deals almost wholly with the pecuniary phases of economic activity. The processes described are concerned with changes in prices, investments of funds, margins of profits, market capitalization of business enterprises, credits, maintenance of solvency, and the like—all relating to the making of money, rather than to the making of goods or to the satisfaction of wants. Only two pecuniary factors command much attention—changes in the physical volume of trade and in the efficiency of labor—and even these two are treated with reference to their bearing upon present and prospective profits (pp. 596-97).

While the emphasis is upon pecuniary phases and physical output, the motivating causes are not overlooked. Business fluctuations are treated as manifestations of originating causes which are themselves a part of contemporary culture. Since the economic fluctuations are generated by causes within the society, the results are recorded in the behavior of its own institutions. The originating causes could be altered by changes in the evolutionary culture of society. Hence each phase of economic activity sets up forces which in turn bring about a succeeding phase in an endless process of economic change. This view is, like many others of Mitchell, cast in a Veblenian mold, who also saw society in an endless evolution.

Mitchell's brilliant analysis was not only a masterpiece in itself but a most revealing work: revealing, in that it opened new vistas on the causes and effects of all economic activity. It provided new techniques of approach for almost every institution of capitalism. The National Bureau of Economic Research, of which Mitchell was research director, has made signal contributions by its studies on segments of the economy. As the years elapsed after 1913, when *Business Cycles* was published, Mitchell wished to continue the inquiry in the light of improved techniques and new developments and also to expand it to

[20] *Business Cycles* (1913), p. 92.

include other nations. This was done in his volume, *Business Cycles, the Problem and its Setting,* which appeared in 1927. This volume of 479 pages is, really, an expansion of the first three chapters of the 1913 volume. It is much better known to students of economics than the original volume; the later work has had wide acceptance at home and abroad and for many years served as the nearest thing to a textbook on business cycles.

In the 1927 edition he reviewed the theories then extant and re-examined the mechanism of capitalism and the money-making aspects of society. Business data from 1790 of the United States and England and of fifteen additional countries are introduced. Again the author presents an unrivaled description of the functioning of the economy with its multifarious tensions, cross-tensions, stresses, and strains. In Chapter V, "Results and Plans," he presents some of the accomplishments as of 1927 and offers tentative working plans for future study. His definition of a business cycle avoids rigid delimitations and offers more of a description: "Following the lines of the analysis, we indicate both the generic features and the distinguishing characteristics of business cycles by saying that they are recurrences of rise and decline in activity, affecting most of the economic processes of communities with well-developed business organization . . ." (p. 468). Further along he says:

Whatever causal connections we may work into our account of business cycles, that account will remain an analytical description of interrelated processes. Of necessity, the causal relationships will appear most complicated. A phenomenon which crops up first as an effect turns presently into a cause, and since we shall be following a continuous process we must treat it first as the one and then as the other . . . in truth every factor in the situation at every moment is being influenced by, and is influencing, other factors—it is not first cause and then effect, but both cause and effect all the time (p. 471).

On the basis of such definitive statements it has been a common practice to say that Mitchell's theory of business cycles was a "self-generating" theory—a statement which he did not use at any time. His analysis and description of mutual interdependence of cause and effect would permit such a characterization, but the term understates and unduly simplifies the all-inclusiveness of his description.[21] The

---

[21] The last volume dealing with business cycles, which carried the Mitchell thesis to its final stage of analysis, was *Measuring Business Cycles* (1946). Arthur F. Burns, Director of the National Bureau, is co-author. "This volume shows how business cycles may be identified, describes the range of observations needed to bring out what happens in modern society during a business cycle, tests the assumptions underlying the general plan of measurement, and explores the funda-

volume ends with a fitting remark that "no group of workers in the present generation can hope to cover the field marked out by these suggestions." Almost a quarter century has passed since he made this statement and, although great progress has been made in scientific inquiry into the behavior of the economy which has made forecasting and control mechanisms reasonably accurate and sure, no one would argue that the great field of study outlined by Mitchell has been encompassed. What success has been attained and what hope men entertain for future controls are in large measure attributable to the pioneering work of Wesley Clair Mitchell.

John Rogers Commons

John R. Commons is another whose work and emphasis fit him into the institutional pattern. He, like Veblen, was born in the Civil War years, and enjoyed a life span which cut across some of the most turbulent years of American history.[22] Commons outlived Veblen by sixteen

---

mental question whether business cycles have been subject to substantial secular, structural or rhythmic variations. The basic features of the plan of measurement described in this volume are Mitchell's inventions." *Twenty-ninth Annual Report of the National Bureau of Economic Research* (New York, 1949), p. 41.

[22] John R. Commons (1862-1945) spent most of his academic life at the University of Wisconsin. His institutional interests are not traceable to a series of teachers, as is true in the case of Wesley C. Mitchell, but to his own convictions and observations of the economic world. He wrote in the fields of value and distribution, public utilities, immigration, housing, labor legislation, social insurance, trade unionism, industrial government, labor history, monopoly, tariff, economic thought, and index numbers. In addition, he contributed significant work in civil service, municipal government and administration, proportional representation, and politics. Few American economists had broader interests. Besides his writing he served both the state of Wisconsin and the national government on many commissions. His life was a busy one. He kept in close touch with the pulse of American life, not only of the industrial worker, but of the industrialist and the statesman as well.

Commons is best known for his writings in the field of labor and is generally regarded as a labor economist. His works include *The Distribution of Wealth* (1893); *Proportional Representation* (1896); *Races and Immigrants in America* (1907); *Trade Unionism and Labor Problems* (1905); the 10-volume study, prepared with associates, entitled A *Documentary History of American Industrial Society* (1910); *Labor and Administration* (with J. B. Andrews, 1913); *Principles of Labor Legislation, History of Labor in the United States* (2 vols., 1918); *Industrial Goodwill* (1919); *Industrial Government* (1921); *Legal Foundations of Capitalism* (1924); *Institutional Economics* (1934); an autobiography, *Myself* (1934). *The Economics of Collective Action* (New York, 1950) was published posthumously. In addition to his books he lists an extensive number of articles in the leading journals.

The best summarization of Commons appears in A. G. Gruchy, *Modern Economic Thought* (1947); Joseph Dorfman, *The Economic Mind in American Civilization*, Vol. III, chap. xiii. See also the autobiography, *Myself*, and the memorial "John Rogers Commons" by Selig Pearlman in the *American Economic Review*, XXXV, No. 4 (September, 1945), pp. 782-86.

years which were certainly among the most crucial. Indeed, Commons lived to see the occurrence of some of the things Veblen foretold. Commons was closer to the firing line of significant events than Veblen, for he made a point of trying to get to the originating causes and of attempting to find what was on people's minds more than did Veblen, who depended rather on his great erudition. However, Commons was just as heterodox as Veblen in his views on current economic analysis; his outlook was more optimistic; he believed that the institutions of the economic system could be reshaped and made to conform to social change. His was not the disturbing voice of Veblen, but rather a dissenting voice of one intellectually honest in his belief that social change would lead to human betterment without the dire consequences of a Marxian revolution and a new order of things.

Commons made his greatest contributions in the fields of labor and public utility economics. In the field of labor economics he taught and wrote in hitherto untouched areas, and his writings have been recognized as both pioneering and encyclopedic. Moreover, he was a realist; he knew what was on the workers' minds and, at the same time, he knew the workings of corporate management. In practice, he always worked to reduce industrial strife—even favoring compulsory arbitration but with voluntary acceptance. Workmen's compensation, social insurance, reduction of industrial hazards, and labor law reforms were among the many improvements he was, in large part, instrumental in bringing about. The state of Wisconsin has been extremely progressive in labor and industrial reforms, public utility regulation, state civil service, taxation, corporate regulation, and so on—many of which are monuments to Commons' farsighted and creative efforts. The liberal leadership of Governor Robert M. LaFollette carried out the recommendations, most of which were enacted into law.

Neither time nor space permits an extended discussion of the many interests of John R. Commons. However, enough will be presented to show how he fits into the category of "institutionalists." Indeed, whether he fits into this category or none but his own is largely a matter of definition of terms. He was a deeply inquisitive investigator, a social theorist, a seeker of deep-seated causes reminiscent of the historical school researchers, a critic, and a social reformer. Yet withal he was an economist with traces of classicism, marginalism, and socialism intermingled. So diverse are the crosscurrents in his economics that there would be substantial agreement that Commons was a "bewildering person," as Mitchell characterized him.[23] Less "bewilderment" and

[23] See Wesley C. Mitchell's review of *The Legal Foundations of Capitalism* in the *American Economic Review*, XIV (June, 1924), p. 240.

more clarity appears in his writings on labor economics than in the other fields in which he worked. This is due to some extent to his intimate experience and acquaintance with labor and its problems. (He was at first a printer by trade and retained membership in that union.) His familiarity with these problems, coupled with a deeply inquisitive mind, led him into hitherto unexplored areas in the broad subject of labor, where he made his greatest scholarly contribution.

Capitalism and the Courts.—In 1924 the publication of *The Legal Foundations of Capitalism* cast the author in a different role. In that book he presented a theoretical treatment different from anything before attempted. The close contact he had had with law courts when drafting social legislation, his work with commissions, and his firsthand acquaintance of how the economic world operated were to provide the background and setting for the work. He began his theoretical analysis with what he termed "Reasonable Value" and proceeded with an analysis of the capitalistic system. The emphasis was upon the role of law and the courts as determining elements in the economic system. In this book he devoted a large part to a historical survey of the development of the concept of private property from the days of William the Conqueror to the present time. The method of the treatment is reminiscent of the historical school. He found scarcely any difference between the concepts of sovereignty and property at the time of this English king. They were one and the same. However, over the many intervening years the courts had clearly brought out the differences between private property in land and sovereignty over the land. Commons made the concept of private property an all-inclusive one extending to rights and privileges as well as tangibles. Laws and courts assure the permanence of the institution of private property and form a center around which the whole of economic activity revolves. The rules of action also become institutionalized, and within this framework economic science dwells. Likewise a framework is provided for cultural behavior. The evolutionary development which led to present levels of institutionalized society explains the setting for the study of modern institutions. He defined institutions as "collective action in control of individual action." Thus, normal economic activity is carried on within a framework of former behavior according to rules made legal by the state and enforceable by the courts. The courts thus exert collective action over individual action.

Commons found that legal history showed certain well-defined tendencies on the part of the courts to eliminate the destructive practices of capitalistic institutions. As final arbiters they sought to ascertain "reasonable" policies which should be followed by competitive elements in economic society, each seeking a larger share of the total product. Thus, "reasonable values" could be used in effecting compromises in labor disputes, public utility rate-making, taxation, pricing, and so on. His belief was that compromise should be used in order to keep the economy in smooth operation. Temporary difficulties which arose between contending parties should not be permitted to drag on and jeopardize the working of the whole economy. He was a pragmatist whose views embraced all of economic society, wherein compromise for the good of collective action was paramount. The flexibility which was so necessary in a changing order was thus provided within the framework of capitalism. He defined "reasonable value," as "the evolutionary collective determination of what is reasonable in view of all the changing political, moral, and economic circumstances and the personalities that arise therefrom to the Supreme Bench." [24] The courts have indeed made extensive use of the concept of "reasonable" in decisions which have involved the ever-present changes in capitalism.

Collective Action.—The last of Commons' books on economics to appear in his lifetime was *Institutional Economics*, published in 1934. The author was in his seventy-second year and the work represented, as he says, "the end" of "much of his personal experiences of the past forty years." [25] The book is a formidable one (903 pages), which, despite the title, can be identified as "institutional economics" only if one is familiar with his approach. In the opening lines of the first chapter he says, "My point of view is based on my participation in collective action in control of individual action. The view may or may not fit other people's ideas of institutional economics." He begins the study with John Locke and ends with the world ideologies and "isms" of 1934. In a sense, the work is a bringing together of elements of collective action which have interested him and in which he had a part, from the time when he became interested in economics as a result of reading *Progress and Poverty*. The many activities and interests of a busy life are enlisted as background materials, along with materials presented in *The Legal Foundations of Capitalism*; from these sources

[24] *Institutional Economics*, pp. 683-84. It is also defined in *Legal Foundations of Capitalism* (1924) as follows: "Every transaction has three aspects of valuing. It is a meeting of will, a transfer of commodities, a determination of their prices. A transaction is thus a compendium of psychological value, real value, and nominal value. The courts, in their decisions, endeavor, by means of common rules, to make a nominal value or price represent, as nearly as practicable, the psychological value, or anticipation, and the real value, or quantity, of commodities and services; their goal is a scheme of reasonable value." *See Institutional Economics*, chap. x, "Reasonable Value," pp. 649-876.
[25] *Myself*, p. 5.

he wrote his last book which he regarded as a "related study of the theories of economists" (p. 3).

It may add to a clarification and understanding of *Institutional Economics* if one bears in mind that Commons' entire life was devoted to studying the conflict of economic, political, and social interests. He contends that it was not until "the heterodox writers of the middle nineteenth century, such as Marx, Proudhon, Carey, Bastiat, McLeod, pointed out that ownership and materials were not the same thing," that the beginnings were laid for institutional economics. Furthermore, one must go back to the court decisions of several hundred years and examine them from the time of John Locke to the present to discover collective action. The problem then is "not to create a different kind of economics—'institutional economics'—divorced from preceding schools, but how to give collective action, in all its varieties, its due place throughout economic theory" (p. 5). "Institutional economics takes its place as the proprietary economics of rights, duties, liberties, and exposures, which, as I shall endeavor to show throughout, give to collective action its due place in economic theorizing" (p. 8).

Commons was critical of classical economics and what he calls the "hedonic" theories of Jevons and the Austrians. The earlier writers were concerned with value and price as determined by two bargaining parties. They failed to see the importance of collective action as determinants of price nor did they recognize the importance of private property or the impact of courts of law as enforcing agencies of collective action. The same criticism applies to the hedonists, who did not distinguish corporate and collective action, but only pleasures and pains as determinants of economic conduct. None of this fits into his thinking. Theory, in the generally accepted sense, is not developed in this work. After his extended treatment of the work of early writers on collective action, he turns to the subject of efficiency and scarcity, wherein efficiency is considered as a means of overcoming scarcity. The subject of futurity which deals largely with debts, interest, and profit margins is treated in detail. Next comes a thorough analysis of reasonable value as it is interpreted in court decisions under capitalism. Finally, the future of capitalism is questioned in the light of other authoritarian "isms."

This briefly describes Commons' concept of institutional economics. The central theme running throughout Veblen's works was behavior in a pecuniary society. Commons also emphasizes behavior with stress upon private property under institutions, laws, and events. This, too, has a pecuniary aspect. Mitchell looked to the pecuniary profit motive. These men found in this element the core of their investigations. It was the collective behavior of man-made institutions as they functioned around the institution of private property, codified laws, and court decisions, that Commons held to be the objective of economic study.

Some Others Who Used an Institutional Approach

There are many writers both before and after Veblen whose researches and writings fall within the general category of "institutional economics." It should not be inferred that describing economic institutions or analyzing economic processes of "man in his effort to make a living" makes one an institutionalist. If this were the basis for the definition of an "institutional economist" then indeed all, or nearly all economists, would be "institutionalists." While much, or possibly even most, of so-called institutional economics as developed in this country stems from Veblen, the tap roots extend back to Sismondi, Fourier, Marx, Max Weber, Sombart, and others. Nor is the development entirely American: the works of Tawney, the Webbs, John A. Hobson, Toynbee, and others in England are not unlike those of certain Americans. Marshall and Smith, but not Ricardo nor Jevons, offered institutional settings, but they would not qualify as institutionalists by any definition.

In any event, and for the time being forgetting any attempt to define (and thus confine) institutionalism, the high priest was Veblen with Mitchell and Commons each equally high in his own chosen discipline. The foregoing pages emphasize these claims. In addition the splendid work of R. F. Hoxie (1868-1916) in labor economics, F. W. Taussig's tariff studies, Ripley's railroad studies, W. H. Hamilton's *The Case of Bituminous Coal* (1925), J. M. Clark's *The Economics of Overhead Costs* (1923) or his *Social Control of Business* (1926), A. A. Berle and Gardiner Mean's *The Modern Corporation and Private Property* (1933), B. M. Anderson's *Social Value* (1911), and Carter Goodrich's *The Miners Freedom* (1925), to mention but a few, are just as good examples of the institutional approach as Mitchell's *Business Cycles* or Commons' *Legal Foundations*. Atkins, McConnell, and others wrote a college text that made use of the institutional approach, entitled *Economic Behavior*; in it the emphasis was upon the institutions of economic development with value and price theory de-emphasized. Sumner Slichter's *Modern Economic Society* was likewise an institutional approach.

The heyday of institutional economics was in the 1920's and early 1930's. The *Trend of Economics*, edited by R. G. Tugwell, received much attention; its articles were contributed by "the younger generation" no one of whom had, at that time, "published a book of the traditional sort called *Principles of Economics*." So-called institutional economics was popular at that time; papers were read before the

American Economic Association which emphasized the new approach. Orthodox economic theory was on the run, or at least it appeared to be. There was public denial that value theory, which rested upon discredited hedonistic psychology and questionable cost data, each of which was unmeasurable, served any useful analytical purpose; that competition and a laissez-faire philosophy could be trusted; that, while some analytical tools could be salvaged, the true picture of economics could only be gotten by examining the behavior of economic institutions in their setting; that institutions reflected the level of social achievement, which was of greater importance than any theoretical analysis of how or why a price system operated.

Many joined the ranks: institutionalism offered a badge of distinction and membership to some who were either not theorists or for some reason wished to avoid such a stigma. Two events seem to have ushered in its perhaps untimely demise. Paul T. Homan's "An Appraisal of Institutional Economics," a paper delivered before the American Economic Association in 1931, stated, "I may as well bluntly state my opinion that an institutional economics, differentiated from other economics by discoverable criteria, is largely an intellectual fiction, substantially devoid of content." [26] Homan's paper was devastating and showed that no such brand of economics existed, except by definition. Next, the publication in 1933 of E. H. Chamberlin, *The Economics of Monopolistic Competition* and of Joan Robinson's *The Economics of Imperfect Competition* brought significant changes in value analysis. Then J. M. Keynes's *General Theory of Employment, Interest and Money* in 1936 showed that there still were worlds to conquer. In the face of these onslaughts, together with the great changes in the national economy brought about by the depression of the '30's, the voice of institutionalism was virtually silenced.

In an interesting little book, John S. Gambs asserts that "institutionalists have taken economics out of the realm of pseudo-physical science, which is where standard theory seems to want to put it, and have placed it squarely into the biological sciences"; [27] also that "method rather than content" is a second fundamental principle of institutionalism. The principle he provisionally names the "doctrine of organic unity" (p. 24). Roughly, he says that "individual behavior, economic action, and social behavior move together." Any disturbing influence on one affects the other.

Almost everyone would agree on the soundness of this thesis. Equilibrium economics demonstrates the general interdependence of factors

[26] *American Economic Review*, XXII, No. 1 (March, 1932), pp. 10-17.
[27] *Beyond Supply and Demand, A Reappraisal of Institutional Economics* (New York, 1946), p. 10.

and factor pricing, as well as final product prices. The principle of organic unity and mutuality is acknowledged in national income analysis, input and output theory. It is fairly certain, too, that institutional economics contributed in no small measure to this development.

Summary and Evaluation

A statement that Veblen was the most challenging writer in economics since Marx and before Keynes would elicit general agreement. No economist and no theory enjoyed immunity of criticism after Veblen. But Veblen still remains a great unknown to many, largely because of the nature and style of his writings. No one has dared rewrite Veblen as Mill rewrote classical doctrines. Yet it may be contended that within the fastnesses of Veblen's writings may be found all that is good and great in economics. He founded no "school"—not even an "institutional school"—for by standard methods of evaluation the movement never attained the stature of a "school." His "evolutionary" economics, with its consideration of so many elements and the mutual interdependence of institutions operating within a framework of a pecuniary society, shed new light upon the larger dependence of institutions and the money economy.

Subsequent writers by the score have examined or re-examined these over-all relationships, and economic literature is richly endowed with many examples of this type of research done by individuals and organized research agencies alike. It does appear that for a brief time at least theory did suffer but criticism flourished. In the long run, however (that priceless escape-hatch of the economist), the goal-less "evolutionary" economics ascribed to Veblen and institutionalism becomes lost in the Marshallian evolutionary concept of "continuity" which knows no time limitations or "schools," per se. That hardy race of individuals known as economists will live on and work as true pragmatists, drawing freely and without inhibition from every font of learning where truth may lie. The larger mark of greatness comes as a result of creative effort in a chosen field rather than in an alignment with any group. Mitchell's work in business cycles and Commons' work in labor economics are cases in point. The creative work lives on in spite of any group alignment, not because of it. Institutionalism has run its course; its heterodoxy, criticism, and emphasis on group behavior bore fruit; nor has the evolution of economics ceased: today such expressions as "welfare," "experimental," "social," and "holistic" identify both treatment and emphasis in presenting the subject. A fundamental fact remains that irrespective of the name or names applied, economics is basically a study of man and the use he makes of his environment in satisfying his wants. He thinks in terms of producing a surplus and consuming it and possibly the surplus of others. Money makes this act possible. Whether he lives under the sun of capitalism or of socialism, the problems confronting him are essentially the same; they result from the same causes—man, his wants, and the limited means at his disposal for satisfying his wants. All economics, regardless of the adjective which is used to describe it, is just that. New emphasis, new interpretations, new theories reflect the dynamics of change and remove economics from mere dogma. Institutionalism, like historicism, marginalism, socialism, and a host of others has served useful purposes.

PART VII

---

*The Main Currents of
Economic Thought in the
Twentieth Century*

PART VII

The Main Currents of
Economic Thought in the
Twentieth Century

24

Alfred Marshall and Neoclassical Economics

The development of subjective or marginal utility economics took place in the two decades after 1871. During these years and subsequently, the theories of marginal utility were criticized, defended, elucidated, explained, accepted by some, rejected by others. Many followers were enlisted, some of whom accepted the theories in part or with modifications. In any event, the development has continued through the years.

However, there arose concurrently in England a school which had a stronger logical appeal and greater staying powers than that begun by the famous Viennese, previously discussed. The school is familiarly known to all students of economics as the neoclassical school. The founder of the school, Alfred Marshall, who published his *Principles of Economics* in 1890, deserves full credit as the founder. He had no intention of founding a "school," but the impact of his development and analysis of economic materials enlisted a following greater perhaps than that of any previous school. Sixty years have passed since the masterwork came out. Great changes, which always come with the passage of time, have tended to make some of the doctrines obsolete, as the author himself had forecast. However, the house which Marshall built so carefully remains more than a relic of the Victorian age. Like all houses built on firm foundations and of sound materials, it has been capable of both repair and refurbishing, and over the six decades a goodly number of academic folk have dwelt therein. True it is that some have moved out into the cyclone cellars intended to offer greater protection from the economic storms caused by war's disorders and the social, political, and economic nostrums which are always proposed afterwards. Few students fully realize or appreciate the extent to which their basic economics (the pre-national-income variety) is Marshallian in origin. They were brought up in the neoclassical tradition without being aware of it. Marshall wanted to develop a body of economic theories which would have universal application and some degree of permanence. Yet he would be the first to admit that, in time, his theories and analyses would be changed—possibly even abandoned. If he were living in the middle of the twentieth century, he would see even more change in the emphasis on theory, but he would find much of his work retained.

Marshall's Life.—Alfred Marshall was born in Clapham, a section of London, July 26, 1842.[1] His father, a cashier in the Bank of England, was moderately well to do. At nine years of age young Marshall was sent to Merchant Taylor's School, where he was trained in the classics with the aim of taking orders in the Anglican church, according to his father's plan. His interests, however, were in mathematics. In 1861 he was eligible for a scholarship at St. John's College, Oxford, which would have led to ordination in the church. He declined the scholarship and entered St. John's College, Cambridge, where he graduated with high honors in mathematics. At one time he considered becoming a physicist but instead turned to the study of metaphysics, then ethics, and finally political economy, a term which he later discarded for "economics." He taught mathematics at Cambridge for nine years, but upon marrying in 1877 he was obliged to resign and became the first principal of University College, Bristol, a position he held until 1881. He spent about a year in Italy for reasons of health. Upon the death of Arnold Toynbee, he became his successor at Balliol College, Oxford, from 1883 to 1885. He held this position until the death of Henry Fawcett made vacant the chair of political economy at Cambridge, which Marshall accepted in 1885, and held until he resigned in 1908 at the age of sixty-six. He continued to write after retirement, and died in 1924.

Marshall's serious study of economic theory began in 1867. By 1875 his own doctrines were far developed and by 1883 they were in almost final form. However, it was not until 1890 that he permitted his *Principles of Economics* to be published. In 1879 there appeared *The Economics of Industry*, written jointly with his wife Mary Paley Marshall. His last two books were *Industry and Trade*, 1919 (5th ed., 1923), and *Money, Credit and Commerce* (1923).[2] Marshall served on

[1] Only the high points of Alfred Marshall's life are presented here. Certain elements of his life are so intertwined with his economics that they will be covered in the general discussion of this chapter. Every student of economics should read J. M. Keynes's "Alfred Marshall, 1842-1924," first published in the *Economic Journal*, No. 34 (1924), pp. 311-73. The sketch has been reprinted in *Memorials of Alfred Marshall*, edited by A. C. Pigou (London, 1925), and again in J. M. Keynes, *Essays in Biography* (New York, 1933). This is a masterpiece in biographical literature. The biographical details herewith presented come mainly from this source.

[2] For a complete list of Marshall's writings see "Biographical List of the Writings of Alfred Marshall," by J. M. Keynes in *Memorials of Alfred Marshall* (London, 1925), pp. 500-8.

the Royal Commission on Labour, 1891-1894, and appeared before many additional committees. He is credited with the first steps that led to the founding of the British Economic Association (now the Royal Economic Society), the sponsor of the *Economic Journal*. He is the undisputed founder of the Cambridge school of economics, through which, and through his students even more than by his own writings, his influence and fame became widespread. Every standard of evaluation of the man and his work supports the statement made by his pupil, John Maynard Keynes, in 1924 that, "as a scientist he was, within his own field, the greatest in the world in a hundred years." [3] Perhaps the author of these words is a likely challenger of the rank of greatest. Time alone will decide.

The Background of His Work.—Marshall was formally trained in the classics and in mathematics. His introduction to political economy he describes as follows: "My acquaintance with economics commenced with the reading of Mill, while I was still earning my living by teaching mathematics at Cambridge; and translating the doctrines into differential equations as far as they would go; and, as a rule, rejecting those which would not go . . . that was principally in 1867-68." [4]

Thus he describes the beginning of his own economic studies. The *Principles* of John Stuart Mill was the leading textbook in the middle of the nineteenth century wherever economics was taught and was regarded by most as the last word. Marshall's statement gives the clue to the genesis of his own *Principles*, which was a further development with the aid of mathematical functions of the Ricardian theories of value and distribution, as expounded by Mill. The direct line of descent, therefore, is clear; from Smith to Ricardo, to Mill, to Marshall. [5] John Stuart Mill, it will be recalled, was brought up as an original Benthamite and throughout his lifetime he was more or less intimately aligned with almost every humanitarian and social reform movement of any significance. In time, however, he became less of a Benthamite and more of a political liberal of his own fashioning. Even though Mill furnished the link with the Smith-Malthus-Ricardo trio of classical economics fame, which was in turn used by Marshall as the anchorage for his own theories, Marshall was not a utilitarian in the Benthamite sense nor a liberal political and social reformer in the Mill sense.

Marshall's political views are not significant here. He believed in the prevailing form of government and its institutions; these he considered

[3] *Memorials of Alfred Marshall*, p. 12.
[4] *Ibid.*, p. 412.
[5] Marshall did not have a high opinion of J. S. Mill as an economist. In a letter to James Bonar he wrote, "I incline to regard Petty and Hermann and von Thünen and Jevons as classical, but not Mill." *Ibid.*, p. 374.

capable of reform within the structural framework. His life was dedicated to the task of alleviating the misery and suffering of the poor, a problem which had indeed disturbed Smith, Ricardo, Malthus, Mill, and Senior.[6] His belief that this could possibly be accomplished through political economy rather than through science was one reason why he chose the former area for his life's work. The numerous facets of his character show a man of deep feelings and sympathies, who believed that man had both the duty and the responsibility to improve his lot. He had no doubts about the vitality of man or his civilization. As Professor Schumpeter remarked, "To serve his nation and his time and to teach what would be immediately helpful, that was what he himself wanted to do more than anything else. He had no objection to the commonplaces about human values and loved to preach the gospel of the Noble Life." [7]

The influence on Alfred Marshall of writers other than those already mentioned is of significance in attempting to trace the germinal ideas and in deciding whether or not his work was a synthesis of prevailing ideas, as is so commonly stated. While still a student at Cambridge he not only came in touch with stimulating personalities, but by his own admission, Darwin's *Origin of Species*, Spencer's *First Principles*, Hegel's *Philosophy of History*, and the philosophy of Kant all had a part, however indeterminable, in turning his interests from science to metaphysics and ethics. Having lived and studied for a brief time in Germany he was familiar with the works of the German historical school, especially those of Roscher. In fact, Marshall showed a great knowledge of historical facts and method, which he generously used in his writings. In the preface of his *Principles* he records that the influences of Herbert Spencer (biological) and Hegel (historical and philosophical) were significant. "These two kinds of influences have affected, more than any other, the substance of the views expressed in the present book; but their form has been most affected by mathematical conceptions of continuity, as represented by Cournot's *Principes mathématiques de la théorie des richesses*. . . . Under the guidance of Cournot, and in a less degree of von Thünen, I was led to attach great importance to the fact that our observations of nature . . . relate not so much to aggregate quantities, as to increments of quantities" (p. x).

---

[6] "I have devoted myself for the last twenty-five years to the problem of poverty, and . . . very little of my work has been devoted to any inquiry which does not bear on that." Alfred Marshall, "Minutes of Evidence taken before the Royal Commission on the Aged Poor, June 5, 1893," in J. M. Keynes (ed.), *Official Papers by Alfred Marshall* (London, 1926), p. 205.

[7] Joseph Schumpeter, "Marshall's Principles: a Semi-Centennial Appraisal," *American Economic Review*, XXXI, no. 2 (June, 1941), p. 244.

Marshall was a contemporary of Jevons (1835-1882) and of the Austrian economists. It may be contended that Marshall's ideas on demand and utility were arrived at quite independently of Jevons or the Austrians, since his work on economics dates from 1867-1868, before either Jevons' or Menger's writings appeared. Certain elements of his own system of economics are discernible in his review of Jevons' *Theory of Political Economy*, which appeared in *Academy*, April 1, 1872. (Reprinted in *Memorials*, pp. 93-100.) Likewise the *Economics of Industry*, with Mrs. Marshall as co-author (1879), and monographs, *Pure Theory of Domestic Values* and *Pure Theory of Foreign Trade*, which were written in the same year at the suggestion of Henry Sidgwick, show his general plan. The context of the last two papers was incorporated into the *Principles* and into Appendix J of *Money, Credit and Commerce*. In a letter to John Bates Clark dated March, 1908, he stated, ". . . my main position as to the theory of value and distribution was practically completed in the years 1867 to 1870; when I translated Mill's version of Ricardo's or Smith's doctrines into mathematics; and that, when Jevons' book appeared, I knew at once how far I agreed with him and how far I did not" (*Memorials*, p. 416).

In the first edition of the *Principles* he makes several references to those who shared in the marginal utility-demand analysis, even saying that, "there are indeed few thinkers whose claims on our gratitude are as high and as various as those of Jevons," and he cautions, "but that must not lead us to accept as hastily his criticisms of his great predecessors" (p. 820). Jevons is mentioned many more times in the *Principles* than are the names of the Austrian writers, but no part of the book is developed on the theories of either, and his debt to them is not clearly discernible. Professor G. F. Shove remarks, "The external evidence is all against the view that Marshall drew anything of importance from the marginal-utility school." [8] There appears to be no reason why one should doubt Marshall's word. In a comment on his own review of Jevons' *Theory* he wrote that, "the kernel of the theory of distribution which I hold to-day . . . is based in the first instance on Adam Smith, Malthus, Ricardo and in the second on von Thünen as regards substance, and Cournot as regards the form of the thought. On many aspects of economics I have learnt more from Jevons than any one else. But the obligations which I had to acknowledge in the Preface to my *Principles* were to Cournot and von Thünen and not to Jevons." J. M. Keynes adds that, "Marshall owed little or nothing to Jevons." [9] One must conclude therefore that if it is true that he owed little or

[8] "Marshall's *Principles* in Economic Theory," *Economic Journal*, LII (1942), pp. 301-2.
[9] *Memorials*, pp. 100, 22. Also *Essays in Biography*, p. 186.

nothing to Jevons, his own compatriot, he was unlikely to be in debt to the Austrians. Any direct or indirect obligation to either virtually defies proof.

If one accepts the independence of the original ideas and their development in the fundamentals of Alfred Marshall's economics, it should not then be regarded as a mechanical synthesis, as it has been for many years. He undertook to rewrite and rehabilitate the economics of Smith, Malthus, Ricardo, and Mill. He was hardly a critic of classical economics in the strict sense of the term, for he saw in the classical doctrines more that was basically good than was basically bad, and, in the light of new truths, very useful. Under his treatment, the cost theory of the classicists took on new life and truth. But this was only half of the picture. Demand analysis was likewise important, as the Austrians had shown. Marshall showed that it had an equivalent part to play in value theory along with cost. Thus, since each group—classical and Austrian—had one of the halves which are necessary to make a whole, it has been the easy thing to say that Marshall synthesized classical and Austrian theories into a new or neoclassical economics. That a synthesis of these two elements was made by Marshall is unquestionably true, but it should be regarded as his own logical, analytical development, not an eclectic synthesis, as some have believed. In a letter to John Bates Clark (loc. cit.) he remarked, "One thing alone in American criticism irritates me, though it is not unkindly meant. It is the suggestion that I try to 'compromise between' or 'reconcile' divergent schools of thought. Such work seems to me trumpery. Truth is the only thing worth having; not peace." Perhaps it is only an "academic indulgence" to try to defend Marshall's work as original and owing no debt to the Viennese, much the same as the spilling of ink over Smith's indebtedness, if any, to the physiocrats. It remains this writer's view that the *Principles* were not written solely to show supply and demand relationships but to attain a larger objective for economics, as described in his own words: "It [economics] is not a body of concrete truth but an engine for discovery of concrete truth," [10] not a synthesis of two theoretical developments, each of which was developed under remotely different time and place circumstances.[11] Supply and demand are coordinates in value and price analysis, but the treatment of each is the author's, not the classical or the Austrian. The analysis of the *Principles* reveals this.

[10] *Memorials*, p. 34. Also *Essays in Biography*, p. 208.

[11] The following are among those who speak of Marshall as synthesizing the utility theory of the Austrians and the cost theory of the classicists. L. H. Haney, *History of Economic Thought* (4th ed., 1949), p. 637; Alexander Gray, *Development of Economic Doctrines* (1934), p. 364; E. Whittaker, A *History of Economic Ideas* (1940), p. 453.

The *Principles of Economics.*—A book as significant as the *Principles* deserves more attention than can possibly be given to it here. Suffice it to say that the economics contained in the *Principles* has had wider acceptance over the past sixty years than any half-dozen books in the field. Neither the pre-eminence of the book nor that of its author is challenged. It should be remembered that at the time Marshall wrote, the economics of the classical group as reshaped by John Stuart Mill was in disrepute as a result of the severe criticisms. The historical school in Germany and its followers in England, the socialists, and later the Austrians uncovered vulnerable spots in the prevailing doctrines. And why not? Some of the doctrines had been propounded more than a hundred years before, and Mill's restatement, although the most recent, was completely beyond repair and ill-adapted to the conditions at the end of the nineteenth century. The inapplicability of the current economic thinking to the complexity of economic life proved a challenge to Marshall. This problem and his genuine desire to help improve the lot of his fellowmen were two of the greatest stimuli that led him to write the *Principles*.[12]

In the preface to the first edition of his *Principles of Economics* Marshall described his aim as follows: "The present treatise is an attempt to present a modern version of old doctrines with the aid of the new work, and with reference to the new problems, of our own age."[13] The old doctrines were those of the classical school. He believed that many had severely criticized the old doctrines, supplemented, extended, developed, and corrected them and had often given them a "different

[12] The *Principles of Economics* was published in July, 1890, by Macmillan & Company, London. Volume I passed through eight editions: second, 1891; third, 1895; fourth, 1898; fifth, 1907; sixth, 1910; seventh, 1916; eighth and last, 1920. The most changes were made in the third and fifth editions; the sixth edition was the first in which the designation, Volume I, was dropped. In the eight editions no changes of major importance were made, primarily because of the thoroughness with which the first edition was thought out. The first edition was divided into seven books, which number was reduced to six in the second edition of 1891 by combining Books V and VI. The fifth edition (1907) had some rearrangement and some rewritten materials. In the sixth edition the term, *An Introductory Volume*, was used as a subtitle and the designation, Volume I, dropped from the title page. The seventh (1916) and eighth (1920) editions were almost identical with the sixth edition. For details see C. W. Guillebaud, "The Evolution of Marshall's Principles," *Economic Journal*, No. 52 (December, 1942), pp. 330-49. The *Principles* had large sales both in England and in the United States. The total sales in England to the end of 1942 amounted to 41,230 and in the United States to 24,151, or a total of 65,381. The greatest sale was in the decade of the 20's (21,991) followed by that of the 30's (16,261). Peak sales were not reached until the fourth decade after its publication and its sales today, in the sixth decade after publication, are greater than at any period before its thirtieth year. See Daniel Macmillan, "The Principles of Economics—a Biographical Note," *ibid.*, pp. 290-93.

[13] Alfred Marshall, *Principles of Economics* (8th ed., 1920), p. v. All references hereafter are from the eighth edition.

tone by a new distribution of emphasis; but seldom have subverted them" (p. v). In taking into account these changes, he held that "if the book has any special character of its own, that may perhaps be said to lie in the prominence which it gives to this and other applications of the Principle of Continuity" (p. vi). This so-called "principle" is not described in detail or in formal terms, but it is clear what he is seeking to develop. He believed that men are motivated by ethical purposes, sagacity, energy, and the enterprise to pursue their ends. "The normal willingness to save . . . to undergo exertion for a certain pecuniary reward, or the normal alertness to seek the best markets in which to buy and sell, or to search out the most advantageous occupation for one's self . . . are relative to the members of a particular class at a given time and place" (p. vii). Likewise he maintained that there are "no sharp lines of division between conduct which is normal" and that which is "abnormal" or between "current," "market" or "occasional values."

They shade into one another by continuous gradations. . . . The values which may be regarded as normal if we are thinking of the changes from hour to hour on a Produce Exchange, do but indicate current variations with regard to the year's history; and the normal values with reference to the year's history are but current values with reference to the history of the century. For the element of Time, which is the center of the chief difficulty of almost every economic problem, is itself absolutely continuous; nature knows no absolute partition of time into long periods and short; but the two shade into one another by imperceptible gradations, and what is a short period for one problem, is a long period for another (p. vii).

The whole trend of economics is one of continuous growth. Temporary interruptions lose their force in the "chain of causation" which makes all the elements in the economy mutually determining, and time-periods lose their significance. It might be compared to the secular growth of a nation, a growth which encompasses all short-run fluctuations. As was pointed out at the beginning of this chapter, Marshall believed that the irresistible forces of change would in time invalidate his own principles.

In Book I, which he calls a "Preliminary Survey," he begins the introductory chapter by defining economics as follows: "Political Economy or Economics is a study of mankind in the ordinary business of life; it examines that part of individual and social action which is most closely connected with the attainment and with the use of the material requisites of well-being." The definition is in sharp contrast with some earlier definitions which made it a study of wealth. Marshall says, "on one side it is a study of wealth," but on the more important side, it is a study of man, who is influenced by multifarious factors among which the "two great forming agencies of the world's history have been the religious and the economic" (p. 1). Almost immediately he grapples with the matter he regarded as the greatest problem of his day—poverty. He expresses the hope and belief that it may gradually be extinguished, the level of education be raised, and a fuller life be made available for all. Economic science can help and it is this "which gives to economic studies their chief and highest interest" (p. 4).

In Chapter II, "The Substance of Economics," he reshapes the earlier definition and emphasizes that economics "concerns itself chiefly with those motives which affect . . . man's conduct in the business part of his life" (p. 14). It is this activity that his economics points up. In the realm of economics Marshall found certain "laws or statements of tendencies" at work; economic laws were, therefore, "statements of economic tendencies . . . which relate to branches of conduct in which the strength of the motives chiefly concerned can be measured in money price" (p. 33). It is also implied that, for analytical reasons, the so-called laws would require the hypothesis of "other things being equal," which would permit cause-and-result relationships to be worked out undisturbed.

In Book II, "Some Fundamental Notions," he discusses general economic concepts, in chapters dealing with such subjects as wealth, production, consumption and labor, income and capital. The treatment is, in general, similar to that found in most elementary texts on principles and will therefore not be discussed in any detail.

Demand and Supply Price.—The materials of Book III deal with wants and their satisfaction, or demand and consumption. Here Marshall points out that "until recently the subject of demand or consumption has been somewhat neglected" (p. 84). He introduces his own phrasing of the concept of the law of diminishing utility:

> . . . the additional benefit which a person derives from a given increase of his stock of a thing, diminishes with every increase in the stock that he already has. . . . The part of the thing which he is only just induced to purchase may be called his marginal purchase because he is on the margin of doubt whether it is worth his while to incur the outlay required to obtain it. The utility of his marginal purchase may be called the *marginal utility* of the thing to him (p. 93).

Thus Marshall has set up the conditions necessary to translate demand into price; specifically, *demand price*, which then applied to the last item purchased, becomes the *marginal demand* price. This is significant to bear in mind, for the same reasoning is encountered under *supply price* later. He is thereby able to construct the familiar demand schedule which relates quantities and amounts a person would be willing to pay for a good. Hence, when Marshall speaks of an increase or a decrease in demand he means an "increase (or decrease) throughout the whole list of prices" at which one is willing to purchase different amounts of a commodity. This then produces his one general law of demand—"the greater the amount to be sold, the smaller must be the price at which it is offered in order that it may find purchasers; or, in other words, the amount demanded increases with a fall in price, and diminishes with a rise in price" (p. 99). This is the familiar *inverse* relationship between the amount offered and the price of the good, familiar to most sophomore students of theory.

Marshall was the first economist to relate elasticity of purchase to price. Here he makes use of the diagrams, so familiar in theory, which show variations in price and quantity at different levels all the way from goods with little elasticity to goods with great elasticity. In connection with the price-utility relationship he introduces the concept of consumer's surplus. It is defined as, "The excess of the price which he [the consumer] would be willing to pay rather than go without a thing, over that which he actually does pay, is the economic measure of this surplus satisfaction. It may be called *consumer's surplus*" (p. 124). He illustrates this by examples such as salt, matches, and other items the price of which is usually far below the price people would pay rather than do without. It is a useful concept in explaining the difference between the marginal utility of a good which yields no consumer's surplus and the utility of all units consumed before the marginal unit. The concept will be used again in connection with his concept of producer's surplus.

Book IV deals with the agents of production: land, labor, capital, and organization. Here he introduces the concept of *supply price* which, like demand price, has a technical meaning. "As the price required to attract purchasers for any given amount of a commodity, was called demand price for that amount during a year or any other given time; so the price required to call forth the exertion necessary for producing any given amount of a commodity, may be called the *supply price* for that amount during the same time" (p. 142). Further on in Book V he says that the expenses of production make the supply price (p. 339). Marshall recognizes "some difficulties ahead" when considering the supply price of some goods and factors of production. The time element, however, is helpful and necessary in explaining a fixed versus an elastic supply of goods. Yet land, the supply of which is fixed, is one factor over which man has no control. It has no cost of production or at least an unattainable one; hence "there is no supply price at which it can be produced" (p. 145). Marshall recognized the "Law or statement of tendency to Diminishing Return" which reads, "An increase in the capital and labor applied in the cultivation of land causes *in general* a less than proportionate increase in the amount of produce raised" (p. 150). The principle is poorly stated in terms of proportionate changes, which will be considered in the discussion on rent. The remaining chapters in Book IV are taken up with discussions of growth of population and its problems, health and strength of the people, food, industrial training, growth of wealth, industrial organization, large-scale production, and so on. In the thirteenth and last chapter of the book he introduces the concept of the "representative firm." [14]

The "representative firm" is a concept for analyzing the supply price of a commodity. The problem is to analyze the normal cost of production of a commodity in relation to the aggregate volume of production of that commodity. To do this the representative firm is set up as a "representative producer" at that volume. Obviously this could not be a new firm just entering or "struggling to enter" business, which possibly operates without profit for some time. Nor is it an old firm with a "vast business, and huge well-ordered workshops that give it a superiority over almost all its rivals." He describes his representative firm as "one which has had a fairly long life, and fair success, which is managed with normal ability, and which has normal access to economies, external and internal, which belong to that aggregate volume of production" (*ibid.*, p. 317). Later on he says the "representative firm remains about the same size, as does the representative tree in a virgin forest, and that the economies resulting from its own resources are constant" (p. 367). Again he stated that "the expenses of a representative firm managed with normal ability and having normal access to the internal and external economies of production on a large scale, may be taken as a standard for estimating normal expenses of production" (p. 497).

The concept is the author's own way of identifying a firm, by first getting to the costs incurred in production of a commodity by but one firm of an industry. In a sense, then, it is an average firm which has been able to make better than normal use of internal and external economies (savings) and from its experience, he reasons as to what extent the economies apply throughout all firms composing the industry. The internal and external economies refer to the measures which the concern will naturally adopt for the purpose of decreasing production costs; improved techniques within, and better credit terms and the like with-

[14] The concept was first introduced in the second edition, 1891.

out, would presumably bring lower net costs. The entire scheme—both the representative firm and the so-called economies—has been severely criticized as a concept. It would indeed be difficult to identify such firms, and the so-called economies sooner or later are common property of all producers. Thus the time element alone tends to invalidate the concept for any practical purpose. Marshall thought the tendency toward any standard performance by representative firms would more or less counterbalance the tendencies toward diminishing returns, as shown in the part nature plays in production, and the increasing return which man has a tendency to produce. Further criticism appears at the end of this chapter.

Equilibrium Analysis.—Marshall's best theorizing is found in Book V, which contains the kernel of Marshallian equilibrium analysis. It was in the second edition of 1891 that Book V was expanded to include Book VI. In the preface of this edition he wrote: "To myself personally the chief interest in the volume centres in Book V; it contains more of my life's work than any other part; and it is there, more than anywhere else, that I have tried to deal with unsettled questions of the science."

The book is entitled "General Relations of Demand, Supply and Value." The first item in the analysis is a description of a market in the then modern sense, not as a local place as in earlier days, but as a highly organized arrangement where both supply and demand are active and a price is set. The market may be local or world-wide as a result of newer methods of communication. In the market, therefore, where and when goods exchange, supply and demand are in temporary equilibrium. Marshall used a corn market for an illustration in which buyers and sellers would use different degrees of "higgling and bargaining" and thus "the price may be tossed hither and thither like a shuttlecock" (p. 333). If the sides are evenly matched one price prevails; if unevenly, another. In any event, a price will result which temporarily equates the existing supply and demand for that market under given conditions and for one day. The time period was assumed to be so short that the price would be applicable to the stock of goods already on hand, no time being allowed for any significant increase in supply.

In Chapter III, "Equilibrium of Normal Demand and Supply," Marshall again brings in the supply price and the demand price. In the supply price he includes "exertions of all the different kinds of labour . . . together with the abstinences or rather the waitings required for saving the capital used in making it . . . will be called the *real cost of production* of the commodity, or for shortness—*expenses of production*"

(p. 339). Supply price, then, is a sum total of the cost of the factors of production for the amount of a commodity in the market at a given time.

At this juncture he introduces his well-known *principle of substitution*, which points up the fact that producers will, whenever possible, substitute a less expensive factor or method for more expensive ones. Therefore the extent to which substitutes are available for a factor tends to make the supply of that factor more elastic. He remarks that "the application of this principle extends over almost every field of economic inquiry" (p. 341).

A fact familiar to students of Adam Smith is that he assumed free competition. Marshall also assumed that the forces of supply and demand had free play and that no close combinations existed on either the buyers' or sellers' side; sufficient knowledge of price exists on both sides so that the resulting price will be neither high nor low but in equilibrium, in which case only one price can prevail in the market at one time. Demand price and supply price would be in equilibrium "when the amount produced has no tendency either to be increased or to be diminished" (p. 345). A balance would exist between the amount produced, which he called the *equilibrium amount,* and the price at which the thing is sold, called the *equilibrium price.* When such a condition prevails, equilibrium is *stable.*

But "stable" is not static. If the demand price for a thing is greater than its supply price, the amount produced tends to increase. This in turn will, sooner or later, cause a new equilibrium price to be established. In other words, when anything disturbs the equilibrium-amount produced, forces are immediately set into operation which tend to restore equilibriums of amount and of price. The forces tending to restore equilibrium are "seldom rhythmical" but uneven in strength and endurance. Here, then, the time element is important in permitting the forces which basically affect both demand and supply schedules to change; this, in turn, permits a new equilibrium price. Both market price and normal price are equilibrium prices and represent, respectively, short-run and long-run factors. At this point, Marshall introduces his familiar scissors analogy.

We might as reasonably dispute whether it is the upper or the under blade of a pair of scissors that cuts a piece of paper, as whether value is governed by utility or cost of production. It is true that when one blade is held still, and the cutting is effected by moving the other, we may say with careless brevity that the cutting is done by the second; but the statement is not strictly accurate, and it is to be excused only so long as it claims to be merely a popular and not a strictly scientific account of what happens (p. 348).

While it is true that the blades conjointly operate to cut the paper, as do supply and demand in establishing price, the time element again gives a greater significance to one than to the other.

Marshall shows that when goods have once been produced and are awaiting sale, the price paid for them will be governed by consumers' desires, together with the amount they can afford to spend for them, or the consumers' effective demand. If the demand price is below the expected price or below the cost of producing the good, or the supply price, it is unfortunate for the seller. In this case production costs play little or no part in the price. If this price should prevail and goods not sell for at least their costs of production, the goods would not be produced. After considering several hypothetical combinations, he concludes that *"as a general rule,* the shorter the period which we are considering, the greater must be the share of our attention which is given to the influence of demand on value; and the longer the period, the more important will be the influence of the cost of production on value" (p. 349). Actual market values or prices are subject to causes which may be of short duration, whereas in the long periods the "fitful and irregular" causes in large measure offset one another and "persistent causes dominate value completely" (p. 350). The truth of the short-run as against the long-run forces and adjustments is apparent. Likewise, in the market at a given time, consumers' effective demand plays the leading part in price. Should this price prevail and the producer fail to cover costs, he will sooner or later be forced to suspend production. This may, then, as the result of a shortage of supply, raise the demand price and ultimately bring about production of goods which will yield a return above cost. This might induce further production by one or many producers and again create a disequilibrium which would only be remedied by new adjustments of both supply-price and demand-price factors. In the long periods, however, price tends to oscillate within a narrow limit generally called normal or natural price, which, as is so commonly said, tends to equal cost of production. This equilibrium of Marshall is generally called "partial" equilibrium; it assumes a constant purchasing power of money and the prices of "other things being equal." Criticism of the theory appears at the end of this chapter.

Marshall made use of what he called the "fiction of a Stationary state," in which the time element and the general conditions of demand and supply would have little effect. Production, consumption, and exchange would remain stationary, as would total population. Firms, especially the "representative firm," would remain at the same size with constant economies and so on. In this state, cost of production would govern value; demand, since it was constant, would have no significant effect; there would be no slack times or sharp upswing of business, and normal supply price would always remain the same. But "nothing of this is true in the world in which we live"; nothing is constant or normal except change. Thus changes in the volume of production, in methods, costs, and demand are always mutually influencing one another and "no two influences move at equal pace" (p. 368). The changes constantly taking place make the economist's problem more complex. Marshall warns, "In this world therefore every plain and simple doctrine as to the relations between cost of production, demand and value is necessarily false; and the greater the appearance of lucidity which is given to it by skilful exposition, the more mischievous it is. A man is likely to be a better economist if he trusts to his common sense, and practical instincts, than if he professes to study the theory of value and is resolved to find it easy" (p. 368).

Chapters VI and VII of Book V deal with joint and composite demand and joint and composite supply, prime and total cost in relation to joint products, and cost of reproduction. The treatment, while important technically, hardly advances the general value analysis. The definitions of the terms are similar to those found in almost any text on principles. It was Marshall's belief that he had treated adequately the general conditions affecting demand and supply and price in the chapters up to this point. He suggests (p. 402) that the reader "pass at once to Chapter XV" unless "experienced in economic analysis." It appears, however, that some of Marshall's best economic theorizing is found in the chapters which he thought might be passed over. Some of this work is now discussed.

After warning the reader that the ground to be covered "is thickly strewn with pitfalls and stumbling blocks," he develops the influence of marginal costs in relation to value. He reminds his reader of the interdependence of demand factors as he developed them in Chapter VI, showing that the demand for commodities which contribute to the making of another commodity affects the supplies of other things used in making the commodity.

The production of any commodity requires varying amounts of the factors of production. The exact amount of each factor will depend upon the extent to which substitutes (the principle of substitution) are available and usable. The sum of the prices which the producer pays for making the commodity is presumed to be the lowest possible. When applied to specific units of the commodity, it is possible to arrive at a net cost for each of the factors employed in production and finally to obtain a net cost for each unit produced. Marshall then asserts that the producer "endeavours to employ each agent up to that margin at which its net product would no longer exceed the price he would have to pay for it" (p. 406). In other words, the value of the net product at this point and the cost of the net product would be the same.

The treatment accorded to "the margin" in the *Principles* deserves especial emphasis. Marshall was concerned with the "general conditions" lying behind both demand and supply; these conditions were equally significant when viewed as a whole, but not specifically important until brought into sharp focus, as could be done only at the margin of production. Total supply and total demand, representing the general conditions, were indispensable conditions to value and price; but final value or price depended upon the net, marginal conditions, which reflected the final, net cost (marginal supply price) of all the factors used in production, as well as the marginal demand price for the commodity. In Marshall's words,

The part played by the net product at the margin of production in the modern doctrine of Distribution is apt to be misunderstood. In particular many able writers have supposed that it represents the marginal use of a thing as *governing* the value of the whole. It is not so; the doctrine says we must go to the margin *to study the action of those forces which govern* the value of the whole; and that is a very different affair. Of course the withdrawal of (say) iron from any of its necessary uses would have just the same influence on its value as its withdrawal from its marginal uses; in the same way as the pressure in a boiler for cooking under high pressure would be affected by the escape of any other steam just as it would by the escape of the steam in one of the safety valves; but in fact the steam does not escape except through the safety valves. In like manner iron, or any other agent of production, is not (under ordinary circumstances) thrown out of use except at points at which its use yields no clear surplus of profit; that is, it is thrown out from its marginal uses only (p. 410).

He argues that "marginal uses [of factors of production] do not govern value; because they, together with value, are themselves governed by those general relations" (p. 411).

The same analysis is found in Chapter X of Book V in connection with his discussion of marginal costs in relation to agricultural values. He argues that the amount of produce raised and the margin of cultivation (i.e., the margin of the profitable application of capital and labor to good and bad land alike) are "both governed by the general conditions of demand and supply." Demand reflects the numbers of population who consume the produce, the intensity of their desires, their ability to pay, and so on. Supply refers to the "extent and fertility of the available land, and the numbers and resources of those ready to cultivate it. . . . Thus cost of production, eagerness of demand, margin of production, and the price of the product mutually govern one another; and no circular reasoning is involved in speaking of any one as in part governed by the others" (p. 427). He drives hard on the point that "the cost of production of the marginal produce can be ascertained without reasoning in a circle. The cost of production of other parts of the produce cannot. The cost of production in the margin of profitable application of capital and labor is that to which the price of the whole produce tends, under the control of the general conditions of demand and supply; it does not govern price, but it focuses the causes which do govern price." [15]

From the foregoing it is certain that Marshall depended upon the marginal cost on the supply side, and the marginal utility on the demand side, to bring the price of the product into sharp focus; the cost of the marginal unit and the revenue from its sale would be equal and thus the general conditions lying behind each would be in focus. It would be at or around this point that the interdependent factors of supply, demand, and price would be centered. Each being mutually determined, it would be just as accurate to maintain that supply and demand determine price as to say that price determines the amount supplied and the amount demanded. In both long- and short-run equilibrium the three elements are at work, however little or much they may be affected by changing conditions. Thus Marshall's theory makes use of cost of production analysis as developed by the classical economists, but not in a strict labor-cost sense as they had done. Nor was demand the sole determinant of value, as the Austrians would have one believe. He recognized that both were coordinate factors in the valuation process and around this principle he built the most fundamental of the elements of the Marshallian or neoclassical school.

Distribution Theory.—Book VI, "Distribution of National Income," sets forth his theory of distribution. Marshall was seeking a universal law of value or price which could be applied not only to a commodity but to pricing the factors of production. Each factor of production except land was assumed to have both a demand schedule and a supply schedule. Land, it was shown, had no supply price, except possibly in new countries, therefore no supply schedule in the sense applicable to other factors. He regarded land as a form of capital to the individual producer; from that viewpoint, the return to land, when regarded as

[15] P. 428. It should be observed here that Marshall uses the Ricardian concept of rent as a price-determined, not price-determining, concept. He remarked, "The amount of rent is not a governing cause; but is itself governed by the fertility of the land, the price of the produce and the position of the margin; it is the excess of the value of the total returns which capital and labor applied to land do obtain, over those which they would have obtained under circumstances as favorable as those on the margin of cultivation" (p. 427).

capital, would enter into cost of production (see pp. 411-12; also, 430). This treatment would be applicable to what is currently identified as contract rent, not economic rent; the latter is the surplus accruing to better land compared with marginal land which yields only normal returns on capital and labor expended in production. Marshall also developed a quasi-rent doctrine which follows this discussion of distribution.

Marshall's general theory of distribution follows. Many of the details in supply-and-demand analysis which are largely historical in their development are omitted.

Each of the agents of production—land, labor, capital, and organization or the entrepreneur, has both a demand and a supply side. Every agent in production tends to be used to the extent that it is profitable. The uses of the agents are governed by the general conditions of demand in relation to the supply of that agent, assuming that each one is used up to the point when its marginal productivity equals its marginal cost. Each factor or agent has its demand price which is set by its marginal productivity; against this is its supply price set by its marginal cost. The wages of labor, the interest on capital, and the rent of land (contract or explicit rent) are all determined in the same general manner. Profits are not susceptible to the same analysis as the returns to the other factors of production. Profits fluctuate with price changes and depend in their amount upon many causes, not the least of which is the "rare natural faculties" of the manager or businessman. Nor are profits an assured income to the entrepreneur. They may or may not appear in the short period as a result of a number of factors. Capital is invested in enterprise largely as a result of the "prospective gains" which draw one toward an undertaking. There must be a likelihood of profits which the entrepreneur expects in the long run for his venture. Hence the earnings of management, which is "the excess of profits over interest" will in the long run "enter into the true long-period supply price" (p. 619). In current parlance, necessary or minimum profits (the amount equal to that which could have been earned by the factors in other employment) do enter into production cost, while pure profits represent any excess above this item. Marshall's treatment also makes so-called necessary profits a part of the long-period supply price.

Marshall pointed out that land, labor, and capital, as factors of production, served a double function. They were both competitive and complementary; at times they were rivals for employment—assuming limited substitutability—and again they constituted the field of employment for each other. There is little use for labor without capital, and vice versa. The total national dividend (or income) is the joint product of all the factors and increases with an increase in the supply of the factors and "is also the sole source of demand for each of them" (p. 665).

Thus the principle of continuity, first mentioned in the preface, was traced through the general theory of equilibrium of supply and demand to different periods of time. In short periods, cost of production exercised little direct influence on value, but in long periods the cost of production tended to exert the greatest influence on price with demand becoming fairly constant. Demand assumed larger proportions than cost in the short periods only. The study of distribution produced another thread of continuity "which lies transversely to the thread connecting different periods of time" (p. 660). The "thread" connected the various agents of production, material and human, and established a fundamental unity between them "in spite of their important differences of outward feature." Factors of production (including labor) were found to have a real cost of production reflected in their supply price. The demand price reflected the marginal productivity. The theory that was advanced to explain value was applicable to each factor of production: the net product of each factor at the margin of its utilization would, as in the case of the theory of value or price, bring into focus the general forces of demand and supply which govern its value. The amounts of the commodity in question and its price and the amounts of the factors of production used in making the commodity are all mutually self-determining. Disturbances or change of any sort in the demand or supply of the commodity would cause a change in the factors. Thus, the distribution theory is but an extension of the general theory of value.

The Quasi-Rent Concept.—The concept of quasi-rent is treated after the discussion on distribution, for the reason that it may be applied to the returns of any of the production factors. Marshall first used the term "quasi-rent" (the prefix means "as if," or "in the manner of," rent) in the preface of the *Principles* in which his discussion of the time element led him to remark that, "the greater part, though not the whole, of the distinction between Rent and Interest on Capital turns on the length of the period which we have in view. That which is rightly regarded as interest on 'free' or 'floating' capital, or on new investments of capital, is more properly treated as a sort of rent—a Quasi-rent it is called below—on old investments of capital" (p. viii). When his principle of continuity is applied, any differentiation between floating capital and that which has been "sunk" for a special branch of production or between old and new investments of capital disappears. They shade into one another by "imperceptible gradations." Even land rent ceases to be different from other returns and becomes "the leading species of a large genus." His purpose is to extend the rent concept and make it applicable to the return from all fixed factors, from which group land is excluded. In Book II (Chapter IV, p. 74) he says that he prefers to reserve "the term Rent for the income derived from the free gifts of nature . . . when the discussion of business affairs passes from the point of view of the individual to that of society at large." Then the term quasi-rent "will be used in the present volume for the income derived from machines and other appliances for production made by man. That is to say, any particular machine may yield an income which is of the nature of a rent, and which is sometimes called a Rent; though on the whole there seems to be some advantage in calling it a *Quasi-Rent*." He warns that when one speaks of interest yielded by a machine, it must be "in relation not to the machine itself, but to its money *value*."

The emphasis should be placed on the word "new" in the first statement. New capital possesses a short-period, temporary advantage. Its yield in value product is presumed to be in excess of the interest payable on it as a price of physical capital. This surplus yield over normal interest is "like" rent on superior grades of land compared with that on marginal grades. Capital once invested will remain invested, presumably, throughout the time period of its depreciation or amortization, and in some instances beyond this ascribed life. Thus, in short periods only variable costs (Marshall calls them prime costs) are price-determining (pp. 374-77), whereas the earnings on the fixed capital investments are price-determined. In the long period, however, price should cover both "general or supplementary costs" and "prime costs," otherwise "an industry will be driven out of existence in the long run as certainly by failing to return even a moderate interest on capital invested in steam engines; as by failing to replace the price of the coal or raw materials used up from day to day" (p. 420). In other words, capital will leave the industry.

Quasi-rent, therefore, refers to the short-run net income accruing to fixed capital. It is purely a price-determined income and has no connection with historical or replacement cost of the capital. Quasi-rent should not be confused with profits. It is explained as a factor return, whereas profits (except normal profits) are, generally speaking, a fortuitous income resulting from a failure of the competitive process or an accident of price in which all factors of production cooperate. They are quite different in origin from quasi-rent.

Marshall would admit that a rent-like element appears in wages which resembles "a producer's surplus or rent resulting from the possession of rare natural gifts" (p. 577) and in the "exceptionally high earnings of successful men" (p. 578). However, in the long run these differentials tend to disappear, and normal wages and normal entrepreneurial earnings tend to prevail.

The quasi-rent concept was developed to explain a return to fixed factors of production in short periods, an explanation which did not quite conform to the accepted terminology. The concept has not proved very helpful and cannot be applied with equal success to each factor. It must not be confused with rent, which is a net return to a permanent asset; whereas quasi-rent is a net return to an asset of limited life, that limitation generally being prescribed in its amortization plans. Also it must not be forgotten that rent is a return in distribution and therefore a problem in value. In the final analysis, quasi-rent is more unlike rent than like it.[16]

It appears that the concept is more useful when confined to capital than when applied to all the factors. What Marshall intends to say is something like this: The return to new additions or accumulations of capital which are being diverted to capital uses, instead of being consumed, is interest. The return to existing capital goods brought into existence by past activities and saving he would regard as quasi-rent. Suppose that a year ago a certain amount of the net money income of the nation was saved and devoted to the production of machines and other kinds of capital goods. Again this year a certain amount of the net money income will be saved and used in the same way. The rate of interest which borrowers will pay will depend upon the amount of such savings and the demand by those who use the savings. Now the machines which were produced a year ago and are, presumably, still in use will yield a quasi-rent in this second year of their life, which may be more or less than their yield in the first year. Because of this fact more (or less) new income may have been invested in the creation of new capital goods, and the rate of interest may have gone down. The capital goods created last year will be revalued in accordance with the new rate of interest which has resulted from a new equilibrium of supply and demand. The revaluation of the capital goods then will be a question of the value of the products they may turn out. These products will be capitalized at a certain rate of interest, which will then give the capital value of the capital goods already in existence. Thus, Marshall regarded the return to new capital as interest, whereas he considered the return to old investments as in the nature of rent, or quasi-rent, as he preferred to call it.

The problem of evaluating old capital is largely a matter of capitalizing the value of its service or product at a current rate of interest. This

[16] See R. S. Meriam, "Quasi-Rents," in *Explorations in Economics* (New York, 1936), pp. 317-25.

value, then, is really the rent from it. There is not much difference between the rent (or return) from such capital as an old ship, or an old piece of machinery, and the rent of a piece of land. Likewise, there is not much difference between the nature of the rent one gets for a building, which is a relatively permanent investment, and that from the land on which the building stands. The greatest difference is that the land is indestructible whereas the building or the old ship is not. This seems to be the main reason for classifying the gifts of nature (land and its return) separately from other physical instruments of production. However, when it comes to the valuation of old capital, such as ships or machines, it is their services or income which is capitalized at their current rate of interest; this is the same as the way in which land is valued. Thus, when Marshall speaks of the return on old investments he does not call it rent, but says it is in the nature of rent, while new investments bring an interest return. This appears to be what he had in mind when he referred in his original definition to "new" and "old" investments of capital." He pointed out, however, that in time all differences would cease and differentials between new capital and old capital would have no significance. Interest on capital would tend to equate the marginal cost and marginal productivity of capital as a factor in production; thus the general conditions of supply and demand would become the ultimate determinants.

An Evaluation of Marshall's *Principles*.—Marshall set out to present a "modern version of old doctrines with the aid of the new work, and with reference to the new problems of our own age" (p. v). In this he succeeded. However, Marshall would be the first to admit that the age he referred to did not imply permanence. He recognized that change was the only thing that was normal in the economic world and that some or many of his principles would be invalidated. In any event he developed tools of analysis and an "engine for the discovery of truth," which have had great staying properties. The high purpose of Marshall and the "dominant aim" of his economics were to "contribute to the solution of social problems." He was a great humanitarian, who tried to deal with problems of a real world.

It was his belief that the forces at work in the real world could be treated as having elements of laws which carried cause-and-effect relationships. He made allowance for changes in economic institutions and phenomena and held that the changes tended to fall within a more or less discernible pattern. One could, by following the pattern of his analysis, find the causes which made for, as well as those which disturbed, economic equilibrium. He avoided the half-analysis, as we now believe, which characterized the two major groups concerned with value analysis before he wrote—the classical writers and the Austrians. He "invented" many of the terms and developed much of the best of the analysis found in current economics, both in theory and in mathematical techniques of presentation. He dealt with man and wealth, but his emphasis on the latter was for the purpose of making it a servant of man, thereby improving his well-being. His work, however exquisitely scientific and thorough, is not faultless. A few of the most cogent criticisms should be noted.[17]

Since his value and distribution theories are the two most fundamental and original developments, criticism has centered around them. In the first place, Marshall believed in the powers of free competition as forces which would tend to smooth out irregularities in both demand and supply. While he admitted the existence of monopoly, he believed that competition was the most characteristic condition of production. It is hardly likely that Marshall, with all his sagacity, could have foreseen the trend toward monopoly or guessed at the extent to which monopoly, more or less complete, was to characterize production of goods. However, it may be argued with considerable accuracy that he relied too heavily on the classical belief in the efficacy of competition as a regulator as well as a leveler, and overlooked monopolistic conditions in his own time.

Even though Marshall placed great reliance on competition, a classical heirloom, he pointed out that competition would not always maximize output. Industries might restrict output, even though they were not monopolies, when it appeared to their own best interests to do so. But, according to his reasoning, this would be a short-run policy. Marshall believed that all forces in the entire economy were mutually determining. Every influencing factor was mutually, not singly, determined. The catena or causal chain such as was used by Jevons and the Austrians was absent from his analysis. Demand factors were equally as important as supply factors. All values, "market" or "natural," whether under pure competition or monopoly, whether produced under increasing, constant, or decreasing cost conditions, all returns to factors of production —rent, wages, interest, and profit—were mutually determined; they were not special problems to which different laws applied. The principle of substitution made certain that no production factor, no price, or no

---

[17] For a critical treatment see George J. Stigler, *Production and Distribution Theories* (1941), chap. iv, "Alfred Marshall." H. J. Davenport, *The Economics of Alfred Marshall* (1935). Also Paul T. Homan, *Contemporary Economic Thought* (1928), pp. 193-280. Jacob Viner's "Marshall's Economics, the Man and his Times," and Joseph Schumpeter's "Marshall's Principles: a Sesqui-centennial Appraisal," *American Economic Review*, XXXI, No. 2 (June, 1941), are excellent reappraisals. Most texts of the commentary type have critical discussions.

product would obtain an undue advantage. Thus his value theory is one of general, not partial equilibrium, especially in its outlook.

However, in his actual analysis Marshall departs from this outlook. He makes extensive use of the assumption of "other things remaining the same" in his analysis. He offers wage and capital theories and treats rent as a surplus. These are rather compartmentalized treatments of the factors and their returns, in the partial equilibrium sense. J. M. Keynes remarked, "The general idea, underlying the proposition that Value is determined at the equilibrium point of Demand and Supply, was extended so as to discover the whole Copernican system, by which all the elements of the economic universe are kept in their places by mutual counterpoise and interaction." [18] It seems that Marshall understood the idea of general equilibrium and at times used it in the *Principles*.[19] However, in this "engine for the discovery of concrete truth" he made use of "tools" which made his analysis easier but his result a "partial" equilibrium. For example, the representative firm was a tool adaptable to partial equilibrium analysis; the theory of capital was better adapted to supply and demand equilibrium analysis than to either rent or wages. Compared with the Walrasian general equilibrium analysis, Marshall's analysis, although general in outlook, should more appropriately be regarded as "partial" or even "particular." In any event, regardless of what it should be properly called, it was far removed from the theories of Ricardo or Mill. It was his own handiwork.

Marshall made effective use of the time element in all of his theoretical analysis. It served him well as it has the whole body of economic theory ever since. However, it has been used as an escape valve when the analysis became somewhat ticklish. Most economic activity is dynamic and decisions must be made now; the decisions generally cannot await the working out of fine-spun theories. It is true that the long-run tendencies do conform to a set of static relations. But as his most distinguished pupil, Lord Keynes, remarked, "In the long run we are all dead." The emphasis on time as a significant force in economics has led to much fine work in short-run economic analysis. Marshall's concept of dynamic growth and change was organic in nature—even biological. Time would permit great changes marked by organic growth. Adjustments in methods of analysis had to be made in accordance with the changes. As he remarked in the preface to the eighth edition, "The Mecca of the economist lies in economic biology rather than in economic dynamics" (p. xiv). But he adds that biological concepts are more complex than those of mechanics, though analogies from the lat-

[18] *Memorials*, p. 42.
[19] See especially the mathematical Appendix.

ter must be used. He is concerned that his use of "equilibrium" be not interpreted as "static" analysis. The repeated attention which he states that he has given to "the normal conditions of life in the modern age," might be interpreted as "static" rather than "dynamic"; however, he reiterates that he is concerned throughout the *Principles* "with the forces that cause movement; and its keynote is that of dynamics, rather than statics" (p. xiv). Thus the manner in which Marshall enlisted the time element and made it a most significant factor in economic analysis is both logical and justifiable. His treatment somewhat bridges a gap between the timeless analysis as used by the classical economists and later dynamic analysis. However, he was not always consistent in shifting from the social point of view, with emphasis on the long run, and the individual producer's point of view which, of necessity, is short run.

It has been pointed out that Marshall placed great faith in competition as an equalizing force. By this, as the *Principles* clearly shows, he did not mean unrestricted laissez-faire. Even though a "rugged individualist" he was not a defender of the social and economic inequalities of existing society. On the contrary, he would support measures which had as their long-run objectives reduction in the inequalities of wealth, so long as they were measures "which would not sap the springs of free initiative and strength of character"(p. 714). He could see "no moral justification for extreme poverty side by side with great wealth." He objected to the socialistic movement, which was "by far the greatest present danger to human well-being," [20] mainly because of its tendency to substitute public for private management and stigmatize individual enterprise. On the other hand he distrusted monopoly for almost the same reason—the stifling of initiative and potential expansive capacity for growth.

The man should not be criticized for failing to appraise fully the growth of these two great economic tendencies. In line with the pattern suggested by his own theorizing on the dynamics of growth, both monopoly and socialism (in one form or another) have grown apace. The "atomic" competition in which he trusted has given way to monopoly elements and opened the new field of economics in monopolistic competition and oligopoly. Likewise, socialistic thought (more or less academic when he wrote) has become an economic as well as a socio-political study, and "welfare economics," the "welfare state," "cooperative movement," "government control," and similar subjects have moved toward the center of the stage.

Marshall's distribution theories do not quite measure up to the value theory. It was pointed out that he gave more of his life's work to

---

[20] *Memorials*, p. 462.

Book V, which contains the value theory, than to any other part of his work. The distribution theories are more vulnerable to criticism and therefore have received more. The main difficulty centers about the application of supply-and-demand analysis to the factors. The forces behind supply, marginal costs and behind demand, marginal productivity, do not pertain equally to all factors. The analysis is perhaps more applicable to capital and less applicable to wages and rent; in the case of profits it is completely unsatisfactory.

The entire theory of distribution rests upon the theory of joint demand and joint supply. In fact, all demand is joint demand just as all demand may be said to be a derived demand. If this is true, the problem of analyzing any one factor would require a set of simultaneous analyses for all factors, which would present a virtually impossible problem. Now to consider specific factors: the supply of land, in the strictest sense, is beyond man's control. The fact that its attributes are far different from those of the other factors makes generalizations similar to those on capital or labor impossible. It has no supply price in the same sense as capital, and it seems virtually impossible to try to reduce labor, with its many grades and degrees of skill and proficiency, to a marginal money cost. It is easier to consider the marginal productivity side of each of the factors, for here productivity brings them into use and determines, in large measure, their remuneration. The entrepreneur and "organization" do not receive equal attention with other factors; yet profit, as distinguished from interest, is a productivity factor which must be recognized and evaluated. Normal profits are a necessary production cost, from the individual point of view; excess profits, then, apparently result from the failure of the competitive system.

It may be argued that the principle of diminishing returns to land and the principle of diminishing productivity to other factors did not receive adequate treatment. Also, that it is impossible to reduce all costs to "money costs," especially since Marshall regarded the value of money as being constant. Criticism may also be directed at the use he made of the "representative firm," not because it was "unrepresentative" but because of the impossible assumptions on which it rested. Many conflicting elements are obvious in the conditions necessary for the existence of such a concern; the economies, both internal and external, under his own time assumptions cease to be the property of any one concern but are adopted by all.

It is entirely possible, in the light of the developments of the last half-century in economic analysis, to find some fault with nearly all of the Marshallian concepts. Nor would Marshall object to this even though he was, for many years at least, very "thin-skinned" when his

works and theories were criticized. He was, at least in later years, prepared for new analytical tools of economic analysis. He wrote Professor
C. R. Fay in February, 1915, "A thousand years hence, 1920-1970 will,
I expect, be *the* time for historians. It drives me wild to think of it.
I believe it will make my poor *Principles*, with a lot of poor comrades,
into waste paper. The more I think of it, the less I can guess what
the world will be like fifty years hence." [21] The world is filled with
many who would make the same statement today. In any event, there
is more than enough of the Marshallian neoclassical edifice remaining
to permit its outlines to be clearly identifiable throughout the whole
body of contemporary economic literature. It does not seem likely that
Marshall's contribution will pass away as did Smith's and Mill's; it may
become merged, but surely not completely lost, so long as any semblance
of capitalism remains.

In some respects, however, Marshallian economics has passed away.
Economic science, like the physical and chemical sciences, has made
great strides. As the physicist has had to admit obsolescence in theoretical analyses in his science, so has the economist. No one could claim
an "atomic age" in economic analysis, but certainly the refinements in
economic analysis have made tremendous strides. We know more
about ourselves, our habits, our incomes and expenditures, our production and distribution processes, economic causes and effects, and many
other things, than ever before. Irrespective of changes in political attitudes, statistical techniques and mathematical adaptations would in
themselves have advanced the science of economic analysis. Marshall's
share in new developments is indisputably large. His book, the *Principles of Economics*, was undoubtedly one of the greatest works in economics in a hundred years; it has earned its place as a classic. It has
had, and in all probability it will continue to have, a very great influence
on economic thought and analysis.

[21] *Memorials*, p. 489.

25

John Maynard Keynes, the Architect of National Economic Policies

In the foregoing chapters attention has been directed to the development of many economic theories, wherein some economists held leading roles while others were less important. Some were originators of ideas; others were critics. Loose fragments of economic thought and theory, some of which scarcely deserved the name of economics, were, in some instances, assembled and shaped into "schools" of thought. Not all the theories lived, nor were all groups of theories graced with the distinction of being "schools." Classical economics held sway from 1776 until the Austrians wrote in the 1870's and 1880's—one hundred years later. Neoclassical economics dates from Marshall in 1890. The Marxian development, which made use of selected portions of classical economics, followed after 1867. Other groups and schools have had less influence on either economic theory or policy and less staying power. In any event, the doctrines which identify earlier schools are well known and the extent to which they were instrumental, if at all, in shaping national policy is a matter of record. The stage is therefore set for the economic thought of our age.

Keynes and Macroeconomics.—By far the most important economist in the first half of the twentieth century was John Maynard Keynes.[1]

[1] John Maynard Keynes was born in Cambridge, England, on June 5, 1883, and died on April 21, 1946. He was the eldest son of Florence Ada Keynes and John Neville Keynes (1852-1951). His mother, a woman of exceptional ability, was once mayor of Cambridge. His father was a writer (*Scope and Method of Political Economy*, 1890) and teacher in political economy and logic and was for many years Registrary of Cambridge University.

Keynes attended the preparatory school of Eton (1897-1902) and then entered King's College, Cambridge. In 1905 he was elected President of the Cambridge Union, a signal honor among undergraduates, resting largely upon general intellectual talents and forensic ability. He graduated in 1905 from Cambridge as twelfth wrangler (twelfth in academic standing) in the Mathematical Tripos. He was also interested in philosophy and economics, and studied deeply in these subjects as well as in mathematics. He was brought up in the intellectual society of

598

Certainly no man in the whole of economic literature (with the possible exception of Marx) has created such furor in both economic theory and policy. A knowledge of his theories is mandatory both for the student and for the statesman. While Keynes might have earned a significant niche in economic literature by his first writings alone, it was his later work which won for him most of the superlatives, not only as an economic theorist but as a national policymaker second to none. It is an almost impossible task to show within the confines of one chapter the impact his work has had upon the economic thought and policy formation of nearly every capitalistic nation; and his most significant work is not two decades old.

His last and by far the most important of his writings in economic theory—*The General Theory of Employment, Interest and Money*—came out in 1936, ten years before the author's death. (His very last

Cambridge and was influenced by Alfred Marshall, Sidgwick, Whitehead, W. E. Johnson, G. E. Moore, and others.

In 1906 he entered the Civil Service in the India Office and remained in this position until 1908. He next returned to Cambridge and accepted a fellowship at King's College (1909), where he lectured until 1915 on money and taught economics in the Marshallian tradition. In 1912 he became editor of the *Economic Journal* succeeding Edgeworth, the first editor of this publication; he remained in this important position as editor until the spring of 1945.

He served in the Indian Currency and Finance Commission (1913-1914), in the Treasury (1915-1919), and as a representative of the Treasury at the Paris Peace Conference. After that he served on the Macmillan Committee on Finance and Industry and at one time or another he held important advisory posts in British finance. He was also a director of the Bank of England. He was active in the management of insurance companies and other business ventures and in addition he was a patron of the arts and the theatre. His government made him Lord Keynes of Tilton in 1942.

Keynes led the British delegation at the monetary conference of the United Nations at Bretton Woods in 1944 and was the main negotiator of the British loan agreement in 1945. He also served as Governor of the International Monetary Fund and the International Bank for Reconstruction and Development. In his many government appointments he had the privilege of serving his nation well in the troubled years since 1914.

His published works include: *Indian Currency and Finance* (1913); *The Economic Consequences of the Peace* (1919); *A Treatise on Probability* (1921); *A Revision of the Treaty* (1922); *A Tract on Monetary Reform* (1923); *A Short View of Russia* (1925); *The Economic Consequences of Mr. Churchill* (1925); *The End of Laissez Faire* (1926); *A Treatise on Money* (1930); *Essays in Persuasion* (1931); *Essays in Biography* (1933); *The General Theory of Employment, Interest and Money* (1936); and *How to Pay for the War* (1940).

For an excellent, brief sketch of Lord Keynes and his work, see Austin Robinson, "John Maynard Keynes, 1883-1946," *The Economic Journal*, LVII, No. 225 (March, 1947). See also *John Maynard Keynes, 1883-1946*, a memoir prepared by direction of the Council of King's College, Cambridge, in 1949. Also, Joseph Schumpeter, "John Maynard Keynes, 1883-1946," *American Economic Review*, XXXVI, No. 4 (September, 1946), reprinted in *Ten Great Economists*, pp. 260 et sqq. Roy F. Harrod's *The Life of John Maynard Keynes* (1951) is the standard biographical work.

work, *How to Pay for the War,* an 88-page booklet appearing in 1940, dealt with taxation and forced saving to curb inflation.) It is safe to say that no book, even including Smith's *Wealth of Nations* and Marx's *Kapital,* has had in such a brief time so much influence on economic thought and public policy. Likewise, no economist has had so much written on and about what he said and what some thought that he said. He has elicited anthems of praise from some and bitter criticism from others. He has been praised for most of the good things and blamed for much of the bad that has become part of national policy in the last two decades. The dynamics of his theories has enlisted a strong pro-Keynes group, while the vulnerable points in the theories, together with what they express or imply in government action, have produced a strong anti-Keynes group. There still remain, however, a goodly number who prefer to remain eclectic and less conspicuous by adopting what they regard as good and dismissing the rest. They are simply post-Keynesians. Directly or indirectly, no economist has influenced the trend of economic thought or public policy as has this man. Although his economics is relatively new and many changes have been made in the basic analysis, enough remains to permit its identification as the "new economics," thereby implying that all else is "old" and either outmoded or tottering.

The preceding chapters have dealt with the origin and development of particular economic theories and problems. Theories of value and price as well as distribution theories were developed by earlier writers and applied to particular cases. Specific theories of rent, wages, and interest were treated as special problems in value analysis. In modern terms, this is "microeconomics" (from a Greek term meaning small or little). It assumes that the forces of supply and demand will automatically bring equilibrium adjustments in all prices and values, full utilization of the factors of production, and an equilibrium price for the use of each. Deviations from these levels caused by cyclical disturbances were regarded as temporary. In general, earlier price and value analysis rested upon assumptions of laissez faire and the application of such theory implied a laissez-faire policy and perfect mobility of factors within a self-regulating economy. Specific cases in the study of microeconomics would be, for example, the demand for wheat, or the wage level of a given industry.

On the other hand, "macroeconomics," also a modern economic term (from a Greek term meaning large or great), is concerned with totals or aggregates. It deals with total national income as it is affected by total saving and spending. It encompasses microeconomics. It views the behavior of the total economy and recognizes that damage to one part is detrimental to all. The idea of flow is of utmost importance in that total national income of society must be maintained at certain levels to insure desired levels of investment, savings, and employment. It is a sort of general equilibrium concept in which every element in the economy is dependent upon every other element. In contrast with microeconomics it does not depend upon laissez faire—in fact it regards this as a completely untrustworthy philosophy, and one which may be held largely responsible for violent disturbances in the level of business activity and subsequent unemployment.

Macroeconomics, however, antedates Keynes. Business cycle theory, whether monetary or nonmonetary in its approach, is primarily concerned with problems of fluctuating income and employment; these problems have concerned economists for many years. Early business cycle studies seldom employed empirical evidence, but at least in the United States empirical macroanalysis had been going on for a half century.[2] Keynes placed the emphasis entirely upon the levels of income as affecting levels of employment, which is, of course, a different emphasis from that found in earlier studies. It is probably true that the whole of Keynesian theoretical economics, at least the two major works, namely A Treatise on Money and The General Theory of Employment, Interest and Money, were primarily intended, albeit each in somewhat different manner, to find causes and cures for periodical unemployment. Indeed, one may ask what nobler project could there be in any economy at any time. Economic annals are replete with records of damaging swings in business activity with their concomitant miseries. Keynes found no answer to the problem in any works on political economy then extant, and his own efforts were therefore exploratory. In the course of charting his approach he was able to make use of some earlier work, but in a larger measure both the course of the analysis and the findings are his own. He deviated sharply from most of the earlier economics, even from that of his former teacher, Alfred Marshall, whose economics was held by most scholars to be almost sacrosanct. It is true that many of his ideas may be found in numerous early writers, such as Lauderdale, Malthus, Rae, Sismondi, Say, Quesnay, and others. However, to pursue such ideas at this point would not be very fruitful. It is sufficient to say here that John Maynard Keynes significantly combined his own theories and earlier developments into an analysis which has effected changes in accepted economics bordering on a revolution. A brief development of some of the theories as found in his three best-known works appears in the following pages.

Development of the Main Keynesian Doctrines.—The deviation from traditional economic theory, with its emphasis on value and distribu-

---

[2] See Chapter 23, especially the work of W. C. Mitchell.

tion, reached a peak in the Keynesian development of economic analysis or macroeconomics. Traditional economic theory placed greatest emphasis on the analysis of individual desires and transactions, as influenced by and also influencing value and price. Keynesian theory, on the contrary, is primarily concerned with the operation of the whole economy; emphasis is placed on problems of employment, investment, and savings, as well as on problems of inflation. In his opinion economic ills arise from institutional forces which, in some aspects, lend themselves to monetary remedies by maintaining a demand consistent with high levels of employment, or, measures which will maintain aggregate demand within the institutional framework. Keynes should be considered as the sole developer of this so-called "new economics"; he did, however, borrow from other writers on economic subjects and his original theories have since been extended and refined by many economists. This discussion is concerned primarily with only a small portion of his economics for the purpose of showing, first, the points of emphasis in his general analysis, and next, the impact his work has had upon economic thought. It disclaims any attempt to present the whole of Keynesian economics.

Of his many works only three will be examined briefly. The first of the three, *The Economic Consequences of the Peace*, was written after his resignation from the Paris Peace Conference, where he had served as official representative of the British Treasury. He resigned in protest against the terms of the treaty then being written which, he held, was economically unsound and irrational. In the book he dealt with monetary and related problems connected with the payment of German reparations. His argument was that payment of the reparations would reduce Germany to servitude for a generation or more and would also cause immeasurable problems for the nations receiving the payments. He said that ultimately it might "sow the decay of the whole civilized life of Europe." [3] His analysis of the problem and the arguments he marshaled were devastating. The English and the French representatives, Lloyd George and Georges Clemenceau, were mainly concerned with reparations, which they considered "from every point of view except that of the future of the States whose destiny they were handling." [4] Keynes argued that the recovery of Europe depended upon the restoration of every state—including Germany—and he forecast a breakdown of the whole scheme if the treaty were drawn according to original plans. His words have proved prophetic. Likewise it should be noted how, at the end of a second world war, his *Economic Consequences of*

[3] Keynes, *Economic Consequences of the Peace*, p. 225.
[4] *Ibid.*, p. 227. President Woodrow Wilson was more interested in the League of Nations than in reparations.

the Peace has been reread with a fresh interest and a genuine desire to avoid some of the errors of the first peace treaty.

Keynes was thinking even at that time about savings and investment as affecting employment. He spoke of the earlier attitude toward saving and capital creation and stated that income was largely going to "the class least likely to consume it." [5] The saving of earlier generations had created capital, but great inequalities in wealth existed and consumption was very uneven. "The population was outstripping accumulation and our self-denials promote not happiness but numbers. . . . The war has disclosed the possibility of consumption to all and the vanity of abstinence to many." [6] While the germs of his later theories were clearly in his mind, they were not developed; reparations and postwar settlements were his main concerns. Despite Keynes's germane treatment of reparations, the greatest importance of the book was to reveal his keen analysis of problems of international importance, whereby he was introduced to the world.

A Treatise on Money.—It has been pointed out that he was primarily a monetary economist. He had implicit faith that the causes and the cures for most economic ills could be found in the monetary aspects of a nation's economy. This belief is evidenced by the views propounded in an early publication, *Indian Currency and Finance* (1913), which followed his appointment in 1906 to the India Office, where he worked on the monetary problems of India. His greatest work on monetary theory, in the estimation of some, was the two-volume *A Treatise on Money*, published in 1930. This study, the second of the three works treated here, was by far his most comprehensive one. It was written in the years when England and other nations were passing through or recovering from severe depressions caused by problems which stemmed mainly from postwar disturbances.

The *Treatise on Money* is not as comprehensive as the title suggests, for it is not a complete treatise on money. However, monetary aspects run through the work; business cycle theory, which occupies a central position, is a monetary theory in which central bank control of the monetary factor is vital. He resembled two writers already considered, Veblen and Mitchell, in that he tended to make money the central theme around which the whole national economy revolved. Veblen saw pecuniary behavior as motivating the individual in practically every phase of life; Mitchell looked to pecuniary rewards as stimulants to economic activity. Keynes, following English tradition, had faith in the ability of the central bank to exercise controls over the quantity of

[5] *Ibid.*, p. 18.
[6] *Ibid.*, pp. 21, 23.

money in circulation (mainly bank deposits) and through them to regulate economic activity. Each of the three regarded money as extremely
significant in the economy, but there are wide extremes of differences
in their theories as to its purpose and functions.

The *Treatise* was orthodox in the sense that it dealt with generally
accepted monetary control mechanisms of the bank rate, bank credit,
quantity of money and its velocity, price levels, and so on. He considers
(Vol. I, Bk. III, chap. ix of the *Treatise*) such terms as income, savings,
and investment, as significant but they acquire their full significance
only in the *General Theory*. He states that his "object has been to
find a method which is useful in describing not merely the characteristics of stable equilibrium, but also those of disequilibrium, and to discover the dynamical laws governing the passage of a monetary system
from one position of equilibrium to another." [7] The work was written
at a period which now appears to have been one of transition in his
ideas—he was still working within the framework of accepted analysis
but he was striving to enter the field of economic dynamics. He argued
that static analysis, which then prevailed, fell short of coming to grips
with new problems. Marshall's *Principles*, which had been published
forty years and thought out fifty years or more earlier, was outmoded.
"For thirty years after its publication the progress of economic theory
was very slight." The partial equilibrium theory of Marshall had been
absorbed but not materially improved; however, Marshall did seek to
make his economics "regain contact with the real world," but Keynes
says he was "disposed sometimes to camouflage the essentially static
character of his equilibrium theory with many wise and penetrating
obiter dicta on dynamical problems." [8] Keynes felt that he himself had
made definite progress toward dynamic analysis. He remarked, "But
now at last we are, I think, on the eve of a new step forward, which,
if it is made successfully, will enormously increase the applicability of
theory to practice;—namely, an advance to an understanding of the detailed behaviour of an economic system which is not in static equilibrium. This treatise, in contrast to most older work on monetary theory,
is intended to be a contribution to this phase of economic science." [9]

It is doubtful whether he accomplished his objectives. His own
qualms are stated in the Preface, where he says,

As I read through the page proofs of this book I am acutely conscious of
its defects. It has occupied me for several years . . . during which my
ideas have been developing and changing, with the result that its parts are
not entirely harmonious with one another. The ideas with which I have

[7] *Treatise on Money*, Vol. I, p. v.
[8] *Ibid.*, Vol. II, p. 406.
[9] *Ibid.*, p. 407.

finished up are widely different from those with which I began. The result is, I am afraid, that there is a good deal in this book which represents the process of getting rid of the ideas which I used to have and of finding my way to those which I now have. There are many skins which I have sloughed still littering these pages. It follows that I could do it better and much shorter if I were to start over again.[10]

This long quotation is prophetic of what was to follow from his pen. The high expectancy of fellow economists suffered a blow. The *Treatise* failed, despite the prodigious efforts of the author, to make any significant change in either economic or monetary theory or policy. It is true, as he stated in the preface, that he was on "the eve of a new step forward" but the step was not taken in this work but from it. The dissatisfaction with the work which the author voiced, even before the public had an opportunity to express disapproval, was in large measure responsible for his assuming the task of rewriting his own thoughts, but along different lines of emphasis. Economic dynamics had to be developed with greater finesse than had been accomplished in the two-volume work. Furthermore, he had not completely "sloughed off" all the "skins" of earlier doctrines. This he succeeded in doing, at least to his own satisfaction, in the subsequent work for which he is best known.

The General Theory of Employment, Interest and Money.—In 1936 this work appeared as his attempt to accomplish some of the things he had hoped for in the *Treatise*. He did this, and more. The work has been acclaimed by many economists as the most important contribution to economic theory since Marshall's *Principles*, and among works which influenced policy it is probably without an equal. No work had such impact on both economic theory and policy within so few years as this book. It was the product of a scholar who was seeking to attain emancipation from traditional doctrines which he was convinced were obsolete and, at the same time, seeking to help a sick capitalistic world back to a modicum of health. In a sense, Keynes's work was a product of economic desperation, for no country had been spared the ravages of the great depression of the thirties. His nation—as perhaps all capitalistic nations—was at the economic crossroads: one way pointed to a new type of totalitarian state; the other to the much-traveled, albeit rough, road to capitalism. Keynes believed the latter could be repaired and so would continue to be the best of all possible routes for mankind to travel.

It has been emphasized that Keynes was trained in the neoclassical economics of his teacher, Alfred Marshall. It, in turn, had its roots deep

[10] *Ibid.*, pp. v-vi.

in the teachings of Smith and Ricardo. Marshall had talked in terms of equilibrium, but it was special, or partial, not general equilibrium and rested on assumptions of questionable reality. For many years it had been assumed that full utilization of resources and full employment of labor would automatically come as a result of forces inherent in the price system. Economic processes were held to be both self-regulating and self-perpetuating. But things were not working out well in the real world. At the very peak of business activity there was unemployment; and with the recurrence of the depression phase of the business cycle, unemployment increased and economic disorders were greatly amplified. There were many who sensed the inadequacy of the economic theory in the early 1930's, and some who were predicting the end of capitalism. It was then that Keynes produced a work which recorded his diagnosis of the ills and prescribed the general nature of the cures which could be accomplished while still retaining the system.

The first step taken by Keynes in the *General Theory* was to sever his economic ties with the past with perhaps more flourish than thoroughness. This he attempted to do in the first few chapters. In the famous first chapter of eighteen lines, he states that his object is to contrast his arguments with those of

. . . the classical theory of the subject upon which I was brought up and which dominates the economic thought, both practical and theoretical, of the governing and academic classes of this generation, as it has for a hundred years past. I shall argue that the postulates of the classical theory are applicable to a special case only and not to the general case, the situation which it assumes being a limiting point of the possible positions of equilibrium. Moreover, the characteristics of the special case assumed by the classical theory happen not to be those of the economic society in which we actually live, with the result that its teaching is misleading and disastrous if we attempt to apply it to the facts of experience.[11]

This statement partly explains why he was interested in determining the forces underlying the "general" case, and indicates why emphasis should be placed on the first word in the title of the book.

Keynes used the term "classical economics" to refer to the principles developed by Smith and Ricardo and restated by J. S. Mill. To these he would add the theories of his father, John Neville Keynes, Marshall, and the latter's successor, A. C. Pigou. In general, the term embraces the leading men and theories before him, whose ideas had been rather commonly accepted and were therefore labeled "classical."[12] In gen-

[11] *General Theory of Employment, Interest and Money*, p. 3.
[12] See *General Theory*, p. 3 n.; and chap. ii, "The Postulates of the Classical Economics."

eral, classical doctrine held that full employment of labor and full utilization of the factors of production would automatically result if there were no government or monopolistic interference. It postulated an economy with a large number of small producing units, each striving to maximize its own gains and minimize its losses. Under this assumption a high level of stable employment would be automatically attained with maximum efficiency and utilization of resources. Supply, demand, and price were mutually self-determining, and each production factor would be rewarded in accordance with its marginal product. Classical analysis tended to be nonempirical and to ignore the way in which things actually worked. The classical model rested upon the automatic balancing powers of forces at work under competition. Hence, if it could be shown that the automatic elements had failed and that no possibility of economic prediction existed, the whole scheme could be relegated to the economic junk heap. Keynes was able to arrive at this pessimistic conclusion on the basis of (1) an assumed consumption function, (2) the alleged fixity of prices, and (3) on a liquidity preference theory of interest. Keynes contended that the capitalistic system could not run itself automatically and maintain full employment. He found that the capitalistic system, if left to its own devices, could find an equilibrium at a level of less than full employment of men and resources. Thus there devolved upon the government a responsibility to enter the realm of economic policy-making with planned objectives devised to correct the inequalities and imbalances caused by failure of the self-regulating system. Theoretically it would be possible for the government to assume some or even many of the functions formerly ascribed to private savers and investors; and by carefully planned revenue and expenditure policies, desired levels of employment might be attained.

The cardinal objective of the theory is to explain the relationship of national income, or employment, to investment, aggregate consumption, money, and the rate of interest. Since employment or national income is usually the dependent variable he attempts to explain "Why, in any given circumstances, employment is what it is." [13] Classical theory, which dealt with optimum factor combinations, admitted short-run economic fluctuations, which would cause temporary less-than-full employment; in the long run, however, the forces would automatically restore the economy to levels of full employment. Keynes repudiated the classical doctrine of self-adjustment and also the classical policy of laissez faire. His doctrine is interventionist; if maintenance of full employment becomes an objective of national policy, then certain elements of the national economy must be controlled. The government must provide

[13] J. M. Keynes, "The General Theory of Employment," *Quarterly Journal of Economics*, LI (February, 1937), p. 221.

for any deficiency in the deflationary gap caused by the failure of the factors responsible for full employment. It must also take measures designed to reduce the inflationary gap.

The essentials of the analysis, briefly stated, are these. Effective demand is the starting point; in simplest economic parlance, effective demand represents desire to buy plus ability to pay. When broken down, this means that demand has economic significance only when the persons possessing the demand have money (income) and a willingness to spend it for the goods they desire. This is the meaning generally attached to the term "effective demand." However, Keynes gives it a somewhat different emphasis. Aggregate demand and aggregate supply refer not to schedules of goods produced and sold by firms or industries as used in the ordinary sense of supply and demand schedules, but to a broader concept embracing the entire economy. Supply, demand, and price have always been treated as mutually determining and applicable to specific measurable units such as a pound, ton, bushel, yard, and so on; but no relationship exists between the old and the Keynesian use of the term.

In the Keynesian analysis it is impossible to reduce total output of the economy to any measurable physical unit, and so he uses the amount of labor employed as the measure of the total output. Therefore the aggregate demand "price," aggregate demand curve ("aggregate demand function" as he calls it), and aggregate supply curve ("aggregate supply function") intersect at a point identified as "the point of effective demand." The "point of effective demand," at which aggregate supply and aggregate demand are equal, determines the amount of employment at a given time.[14] Thus when aggregate demand is at certain levels, employment will also be at certain levels. Total demand, therefore, determines total employment, which is to say that unemployment results from any failure in the total demand. Effective demand is manifest in money expenditure. Money, or income used in expenditure, is obtained by employment; hence, as employment increases income increases, and vice versa. The mutual interdependence is at once apparent.

The levels of expenditure do not always equal the levels of income. As income increases, consumption will also increase, but by an amount less than the increase in the income. Hence a "gap" results which is the difference between the income and the expenditures. Therefore, in order to increase the level of effective demand which will result in an increase in employment, there must be an increase in investment equal to the "gap" between aggregate income and consumption. Investment

[14] See Dudley Dillard, The Economics of John Maynard Keynes (New York, 1948), chap. iii.

is the key factor in determining the level of employment. Employment, in the final analysis, depends upon both aggregate consumer demand and new investment.

Whether or not an increase in private investment is made depends upon the marginal efficiency of capital, a term used to mean the expected profitability of an investment. If the businessman believes he can make a return or profit on productive capital investment above the rate of interest on loan capital, he will continue to invest his capital in production. Thus, expenditures for factories, machinery, and production goods will continue so long as the expected rate of return exceeds the rate of interest. Obviously, the rate of interest is a very important factor in the analysis, for a high rate tends to lessen investment (which leads to unemployment) and a low rate encourages investment. Here again institutional forces tend to make rates "sticky"; they do not change fast enough for a frictionless adjustment to be made. Expectations and uncertainties of investors as well as savers are significant. These are dynamic factors of both present and future significance. So dynamic is the marginal efficiency of capital in the economy that Keynes regarded fluctuations in the marginal efficiency of capital as the basic cause of business cycles.[15] This sequence may be seen when a rapid capital goods expansion, which reflects the investors' expectations of large returns, leads to an expansion greater than is needed. The optimism is reversed and an oversupply of capital goods forces marginal efficiency below the rate of interest. Subsequent declines in investment and consumption lead to unemployment, business collapse, and depression.

Since the rate of interest and the marginal efficiency of capital are related and determining factors as well, they deserve further consideration. The older theories which made the supply of capital, the demand for it, and the rate of interest mutually determining were no longer tenable. The rate of interest did not reflect the individual's "time preference" but his "liquidity preference" (a term coined to express people's desire to hold their assets in monetary form) and the quantity of money. The former is a factor on the demand side and the latter is obviously a supply factor. Here again the uncertainty element is significant, for the anticipated rate will materially influence the extent to which money is held or spent. In general, the higher the rate of interest, the less investment there will be. In other words, low interest rates and high marginal efficiency of capital are conditions favorable to capital investment and full employment.[16] The factors determining

15 *General Theory*, chap. xxii, "Notes of the Trade Cycle," p. 315.
16 The student is referred to Dudley Dillard, *op. cit.*, chap. iii, for an excellent treatment of this subject.

the rate of interest, namely, the supply of money and the liquidity preference function, are not the only independent variables; they, together with the marginal efficiency of capital and the marginal propensity to consume, determine the level of income and employment. The dependent variables, which are the ones to be explained in terms of the relationship of the independent variables, are the volume of employment and the national income.

The Keynesian thesis is one of underinvestment. The level of employment (and output), as was pointed out before, is partially but strategically dependent on the amount of investment. Oversaving and underconsumption (if modern terms may be used) were points of emphasis and of criticism in the theories of Mandeville, Lauderdale, Malthus, Sismondi, Marx, and others. These men thought the total demand, for various reasons, would not support a full level of employment of labor or resources, and history records the accuracy of their views. Keynes, however, emphasizes underinvestment. Since the propensity to consume is fairly stable, and since there can be no oversaving (only underinvestment), for, *ex hypothesi*, savings (the surplus over consumption) equal investment, the emphasis must lie in underinvestment. Thus, the curative is investment. By carefully regulating the factors affecting investment, desired levels of income and employment may be attained. The automatically self-regulating elements of the economy are to be controlled by the established institutions, such as banks, whose function it is to perform regulatory measures within a framework prescribed by a central planning agency, and the government, whose duty it is to see that a desired level of employment obtains. In brief, this would be accomplished by measures designed to increase effective demand.

It was Keynes's belief that money, when spent, had a "multiplier effect" amounting to several times the total amount originally spent.[17] Increased expenditure, being of prime importance in determining employment and income, would stimulate consumption. The multiplier would then be the ratio of an increase in income to a given increase in new investment. Simply stated, the theory is that national income will increase not merely by the amount of the investment but by some multiple of it. While he did not hold that the exact amount of the increase could be predicted, mainly because of the inability to determine with exactness the marginal propensity to consume, he did believe that the multiplier would be about 3.[18] Clearly this figure would

[17] Keynes credits the idea of the multiplier to R. F. Kahn. *General Theory*, pp. 118-19.
[18] See *General Theory*, pp. 122-23, for the multiplier in Great Britain and pp. 127-28 for that in the United States.

vary with several factors but mainly with the phase of the business cycle in which the expenditure (investment) took place.[19] If a given amount of new money is spent in the economy, its influence is not limited to that amount alone, but the economic effects created are spread widely over large segments of the total economy and are somewhat analogous to ripples caused by dropping a pebble into a pool; waves of economic activity are set up which encompass wide areas. While the general effect of the expenditures on the total economy is recognized, the exact amount of the multiplier is not certain. The multitude of influencing forces must be considered under the given circumstances.

The Issue of a "Mature Economy."—The question of whether or not the capitalistic system has reached "full maturity," a term which implies that its growth is ended, has evoked violent controversy. It was believed by some that the attainment of "economic maturity" was characterized by (1) a decline in the growth of population; (2) the disappearance of frontiers; (3) the absence of great new industries; and (4) the increasing importance of depreciation reserves.[20] Keynes did not develop the idea fully but it is certainly implicit in his theories. The proponents of this view hold that because of insufficient private investment outlets for savings, economic stagnation will result. Since savings tend to increase and investment opportunity tends to decline, it might follow that the marginal efficiency of capital would fall so that with a given interest rate the rate of investment would fall. In fact, Keynes strongly believed that the tendency is for the marginal efficiency of capital to fall—in other words, that the tendency of the rate of profit is to fall. This theory was also held by Smith, Ricardo, J. S. Mill, and Marx, but for different reasons. Smith attributed the phenomenon to the capacity of a progressive economy to create capital; Malthus and Ricardo attributed it to the failure of resources to keep up with the demand for them, or, in Ricardo's term, to the niggardliness of nature. Keynes's theory, which was more like that of Marx, made the decline rest upon a shrinking yield due primarily to an inordinately great increase in the supply of capital assets which could, and probably would, produce goods at a more rapid rate than they would be consumed at prices yielding a profit to the producer. This was a long-run and not a short-run tendency which made secular (or long-run) stagnation a certainty. It would naturally follow the slowing down of dynamic

[19] See Arthur Smithies, "Keynesian Economics: the Propensity to Consume and the Multiplier," *American Economic Review*, XXXVIII, No. 2 (May, 1948), for views on the "multiplier effect" in this country.
[20] See A. H. Hansen, *Fiscal Policy and Business Cycles* (New York, 1942), pp. 363-65.

factors, thus leaving the economy to continue at an attained level with no expansive or growth capacity.

At this juncture government intervention would then be necessary, mainly to prevent oversaving and to encourage investment spending. Reverting to his emphasis on monetary controls, Keynes would bring this about by government control of the bank credit and money interest rates, manipulation of the deficit, and by taxation. These would be necessary measures to insure the economy against recurrence of the static levels which were responsible for the original troubles.

The critics of the theory of secular stagnation deny most of its general premises and emphasize the argument that the frontiers of capital expansion are boundless since technological change and development know no moratorium. Profits can and will continue to be made and, though disturbances of even major proportion may slow the secular trend, it is upward and will continue so. No fatalism toward the capitalistic future is admitted. Suffice it to say that neither view rests on adequate empirical evidence. It is probable that interest in this general subject is directly correlated with the level of general business activity. At least it does not appear to be a major issue in the trend of economic thought.[21]

Reaction to the *General Theory*.—The *General Theory* came out in 1936. The book did not have instantaneous acceptance. It was a baffling work which was not understood at first. Many of the early reviews were very critical and none were genuinely friendly. It was not long, however, until the work became gospel for an ardent group of followers, notwithstanding the unfriendly reviews. Likewise, within a short time a new "school" of economic thought developed both at home and abroad, which in its scope and influence has equaled or even exceeded any earlier "school." The basic concepts, many of which were known before 1936, were incorporated into national policies of the New Deal and subsequent administrations. The "timing" of the work no doubt had a great deal to do with its general acceptance, since the ravages of the depression of the 1930's had left deep scars on the economy and caused some doubt about the permanence, as well as the adaptability, of laissez-faire capitalism. It offered a plan which might be used to retain capitalism and, by careful governmental or social planning, make that system work.

[21] Cf. George Terborgh, *The Bogey of Economic Maturity* (Chicago, 1945); A. H. Hansen, *Fiscal Policy and Business Cycles* (New York, 1942). Also Hansen, "Some Notes on Terborgh's *The Bogey of Economic Maturity*," *Review of Economic Statistics*, XXVIII, No. 1 (February, 1946). Also, Benjamin Higgins, "The Doctrine of Economic Maturity," *American Economic Review*, XXXVI, No. 1 (March, 1946), pp. 133-41.

It is true that the interest in Keynesian economics was less during the prosperity and high level of employment induced by World War II; however, as the nation faced lower levels of employment after the war, interest in its basic theories again arose. Concurrently a rash of texts on economic principles has appeared which present the "national income" approach, while older works have been rewritten to include this subject, much as was done in the texts which were rewritten after 1933 as a result of the pioneering work of Chamberlin and Robinson in monopolistic or imperfect competition.[22] Courses that deal with the economics of employment theory and national income economics are offered in most of the colleges. Equally implicit in courses on welfare economics, social and economic planning, and government regulation of business activity is the economics of control, used in its broadest sense. Courses dealing with money, credit, and banking must also deal with policies affecting savings, investment, and monetary policies as affecting national welfare, rather than solely with individual bank management and its profit and loss, national or state affiliation issues, and so on. The economics of the aggregative approach is becoming standard equipment in most theoretical economics. While much of the present analysis is a far cry from the *General Theory*, it is from that source that the inspiration comes. The extent to which it will ultimately be carried is as unpredictable as is the economy with which it is concerned. Certainly its influence has attained great importance and there are no indications that it will become less significant over the years.

The Impact of Keynesian Economics on Theoretical Analysis in the United States.—The foregoing presentation of some of the main elements in the Keynesian analysis was not intended to be either comprehensive or critical. As has been indicated, no one man ever touched off with a single work such a barrage of economic writings in such a short time as did Lord Keynes. It may be contended that Marx stirred up a controversy in which his own and subsequent writings far exceed the Keynesian works in volume. This may well be true, for over one hundred years have elapsed since the publication of the *Manifesto*, whereas major interest in the Keynesian thesis is considerably less than two decades old. Dismissing further fruitless comparisons, let us examine the impact that Keynes has had on the trend of economic thinking, considering first his impact on theoretical analysis and next on national economic policy.

[22] A few of the current texts on principles include L. Tarshis, *The Elements of Economics* (New York, 1947); P. A. Samuelson, *Economics* (New York, 1948); Theodore Morgan, *Introduction to Economics* (New York, 1950). R. T. Bye, Bowman and Bach, A. L. Meyers, and others have included chapters on national income economics.

It is too soon for anyone to offer final judgment or appraisal of the work of Lord Keynes; however, some there are who have presumed to do so. In this case, as in the case of many others in the history of economic thought, considerable time must elapse before the final truth and error are revealed. Since Keynes was essentially a money economist, the full force of his doctrines cannot be more than estimated since many years are necessary for the diverse elements in the business cycle to work themselves out. Theory and policy are inseparable in the Keynesian analysis. Lacking full application of the policy on a national scale, results may fall short of the desired objective.

Keynes declared that he was breaking with earlier economics, and in many respects he did. This does not imply that he completely repudiated or disavowed all that had been done in earlier economics; he rejected only those elements which assumed that the economy was self-regulating and automatic in effecting national adjustments. These theories rested upon assumptions, as does the Keynesian analysis, none of which is entirely suspect or entirely circumspect. The pioneering approach outlined in the *General Theory* like that of many predecessors, did not put the analysis in final form.[23] It has been shown by many that there is really little that is new in his speculations, inasmuch as the main elements in his analysis had been touched upon by earlier writers. Nevertheless, he made a new synthesis of old ideas which gave new direction to both emphasis and analysis in economics. Attention is now directed not to the manner in which the wealth of nations is acquired and distributed on an individual basis, but to how it is created, assembled, maintained, and finally divided in the aggregate. How is a high level of employment of men and materials to be attained, since the automatic working of the whole economy has proved to be untrustworthy?

The challenge of the Keynesian ideas has brought forth many studies and much empirical evidence both in defense and in criticism of the fundamentals. These works have gone far beyond the framework of the *General Theory*. In fact very little of the *General Theory* is rigidly adhered to today. It has been a departure point, much the same as was the *Wealth of Nations*. Defects in the basic analysis were bound to appear; that they have been improved upon is only a normal expectancy of scholarly acumen. It appears that contemporary scholarship is on its way toward developing a more advanced general theory in which Keynes's theory would be but a "special" case. This view was developed

[23] See D. H. Macgregor, *Economic Thought and Policy* (London, 1949), for a lucid work which puts the Keynesian doctrines in their historical and evolutionary setting and shows that they have a long history in economic thought.

by Arthur Smithies,[24] who has stressed, as have many others, the limitations of the general theory of employment. He remarks that, "Great though it is, the *General Theory* is not the last work in economics. . . . The *General Theory* is a most constructive tool for those who are aware of its limitations, but a dangerous one for those who ignore them." [25] It is not yet apparent that the "dangers" are generally recognized and the "inflationary bias" still remains.

Keynes's Influence on Our National Economic Policies.—The Keynesian thesis depends upon the government to expedite national policies as complements to the theories if full employment is to be attained. Neither can be effective without the other. It is common knowledge that policy proposals have been severely criticized: this could hardly be avoided since in some capacity Keynes dealt with policies affecting problems in reparations, exchange ratios, central banking and monetary controls, international equilibrium, interest rates, inflation, deflation, and employment. These are interrelated problems, solutions of which have plagued many able theorists, and none has been finally solved to the complete satisfaction of everyone.

A more incisive view may be gotten if attention is directed to national policy as developed in the United States during and after the depression of the 1930's. Keynes had gained firsthand experience with economic depression in his own country before its worst effects were felt here. His first attempts toward solving the problem centered around money and the interest rate, both at home and in international trade. In the latter instance his concern was mainly with international trade balances as affecting the balances of payment, interest rates, and the supply of money. The same general views appear in his theorizing in the *Treatise*.[26] He continually stresses the economic necessity for lower interest rates.[27] However, his views were expanded after the publication of the *General Theory* to include other factors. He emphasized the marginal efficiency of capital, the propensities to consume, saving and spending. He also reckoned with institutional rigidities, and the likelihood that lowering interest rates alone would not insure investment; he believed that fiscal problems and policies would exert great influence on the whole scheme of things. That more than the interest rate is involved is shown in the following:

[24] See "Effective Demand and Employment," chap. xxxix, in *The New Economics*. Also, John H. Williams, "An Appraisal of Keynesian Economics," *American Economic Review*, XXXVIII, No. 2 (May, 1948), pp. 273-90.

[25] *Op. cit.*, p. 569.

[26] *Treatise on Money*, Vol. II, pp. 196-97.

[27] See his "Open Letter to President Roosevelt," *New York Times*, December 31, 1933. Here he advocated lowering the interest rates on long-term United States indebtedness from 4 percent to 2½ percent, and a program of loan expenditure.

The State will have to exercise a guiding influence on the propensity to consume partly through its scheme of taxation, partly by fixing the rate of interest, and partly, perhaps, in other ways. Furthermore, it seems unlikely that the influence of banking policy on the rate of interest will be sufficient by itself to determine the optimum rate of interest. I conceive, therefore, that a somewhat comprehensive socialization of investment will prove the only means of securing an approximation to full employment; though this need not exclude all manner of compromises and of devices by which public authority will cooperate with private initiative.[28]

This shows a change from earlier thinking. Here he enlists the aid of many institutions in attempting to insure a level of investment that will provide a desired level of employment. The state is given the responsibility of a "comprehensive socialization of investment." It was his belief that capitalism could be preserved if the necessary changes were made and the responsibilities of the state for its preservation were recognized and initiated.

It is generally held that many, or perhaps most, of the measures instituted during the so-called New Deal years of 1930-1940 were Keynesian in origin. There can be no doubt that New Deal policies followed the Keynesian model closely, even more perhaps than in Britain. Both countries made significant changes in the function and use of gold; exchange controls were used extensively in Britain. Heavy national expenditures in an effort to "prime the economic pump" were being made long before the *General Theory* appeared. The economic effects of expenditures were generally known, even if not generally understood, years before the book was published. The work provided a scriptural verification for what had been done and called for a larger dosage of the same medicines.

The deficit financing and loan-expenditure policies employed were thoroughly Keynesian. The growth of public debt incurred by local, state, and federal governments is a matter of record. The sky seemed to be the limit to which the national debt could mount, and with each increase there were some who felt little or no alarm and others who feared its economic implications and urged that spending be curbed. Keynes held that the general policies being followed were correct but complained that the expenditures were inadequate. It is true that many of the New Deal policies should have provided a laboratory for observing and testing the theories at work; however, there were many inconsistencies which worked at cross-purposes with a well-ordered Keynesian model.

While it is true that Keynes approved of some New Deal policies, he did not approve of all. In both monetary controls and fiscal measures

[28] *General Theory*, p. 378.

there were many inconsistencies. He never liked the instability of the dollar, and the creation of artificial scarcity for the purpose of getting price and wages increases was not in line with his policies. Monetary policies were not used effectively, nor was aggregate demand increased as a result of loan-expenditures, which were held to be insufficient in amount. Inflationary measures (intended to raise price levels, usually in terms of the 1926 level) were frequently offset by deflationary ones; popular complaint about the mounting budget, which was almost perennially unbalanced despite warnings, tended to affect both the entire economy and the individual's own propensities to save and invest.

Despite the inherent contradictions of the economic policies in the 1930's and despite the fact that it is almost impossible to attribute measures directly to Keynes, much of the general scheme or pattern of the New Deal was traceable to him. It is probable that New Deal fiscal policy fitted more closely the Keynesian mold than any other pattern. The main fiscal policy recommendations were:

1. Pursue a policy of low interest rates
2. Supplement private investments by public outlays
3. Devise a progressive tax system that falls more heavily on the portion of income that is saved than on the portion that is spent and thereby counteract the decline of the propensity to consume [29]

These three fiscal policies tended to prevail. It would be difficult to prove, however, that the lower trend in interest rates, for example, was due to any deliberate measures taken with that end in view. During the depression years many billions were spent for many purposes, while the tax policy was directed toward reaching unused funds.

In 1938 a sharp, albeit brief, recession led the President to adopt fiscal policies and propose government intervention along Keynesian lines.[30] When the nation began the rearmament program in 1939 the heavy spending and investing of the government led to economic shortages of many kinds and subsequent rises in prices: this fact, coupled with the growth of the armed forces after the outbreak of the war, brought about a level of employment never before attained. In the past decade a very high level of employment was maintained. The budget and fiscal policy outlined by the President in January, 1940, which was perhaps the closest to the Keynesian pattern, indicates its general acceptance.

---

[29] Gerhard Colm, "Fiscal Policy," chap. xxxiv in *The New Economics*, p. 455.

[30] See Arthur Smithies, "The American Economy in the Thirties," *American Economic Association Proceedings* (1946). Smithies argues that this is the first time that the planned use of deficit finance for recovery purposes was employed.

However, with the outbreak of the war and the subsequent economic dislocations, the plan, per se, was no longer identifiable.

It is difficult or even virtually impossible to trace directly the Keynesian influence on New Deal policies in the 1930's. Indirectly, however, it may be argued that the over-all policies were Keynesian in origin. All the techniques employed by the government in an effort to bring about a semblance of recovery are parts of or show a recourse to the Keynesian model. But these techniques were not employed by this nation alone; all nations were faced with essentially the same problems created in the worldwide depression; that the techniques were used to a greater or less extent in this country than in others does not imply any especial degree of acceptance. The fact remains that it was the common desire of all nations to raise the levels of their own industrial activity; therefore the techniques were varied to suit the problem.

In recent years more attention has been directed to factors influencing the levels of national income than to other variables identifiable in the Keynesian model. The nation has experienced the highest levels of national income in its history and also the highest levels of employment. The government is apparently committed to a policy of keeping income at highest levels and in so doing has spent freely and evidenced no fears of mounting deficits. It is not at all certain that this process can go on indefinitely. The policy has enlisted both critics [31] and defenders. Great advances appear to have been made in diagnosing the stresses and strains within the economic system as they develop under different stimuli. The recurrent swings in business cycles have many originating causes and call for many comprehensive, simultaneous, corrective measures. This development has left Keynes far behind, for he was not primarily a business cycle theorist. Future use of the Keynesian model in national economic planning falls in the realm of the dangerous sphere of prophecy. Suffice it to say that adaptations of the policies recommended in his general theory have become such a large part of the national economic policy in all its segments that they are as unidentifiable as they are inseparable from it. As an over-all policy affecting the whole economy at all times, the Keynes general theories are here to stay. Final evaluation will come many years hence.

The Influence of Keynes on British Economic Thought.—The foregoing treatment emphasized some of the points in Keynes's works and touched upon his influence in this country. His theories and applied economics are now the property of everyone; they are no more British

[31] See Henry C. Simons, *Economic Policy for a Free Society* (Chicago, 1948), and Harold G. Moulton, *The New Philosophy of Public Debt* (Washington, 1943).

than American, and they have enriched all nations. It is certain, however, that the larger share of enrichment which Keynes bestowed upon
both theory and applied economics rests with Britain, and rightly so.
The following, which is sketched with some temerity, is an attempt to
evaluate briefly Keynes's impact on theory and policy in his native land.

It is both relatively easy and rather commonplace to evaluate or
compare the theories of one man with those of another. In this instance it is Marshall, Keynes's former teacher, who is usually the
one with whom comparisons are made. One point of sharp contrast
appears early in the theories of each; Marshall leaned heavily—in fact,
admitted his dependence—upon earlier writers, even to the extent of
finding things that probably were not there. Keynes prided himself on
his own independence even to the extent of overdrawing the contrast
between his own and that of earlier writers. It will be recalled that
Keynes went to extremes in the *General Theory* to break away from
the past. Both men, like many of their predecessors, left great technical
equipment for use in economic analysis. Marshall referred to his own
work as "an engine for the discovery of concrete truth"; he was a tool-
maker. So also was Keynes—especially after the *General Theory* appeared, in which he presented terms that have enriched our conceptual
equipment. But neither of them should be remembered or judged
solely for his skill and craftsmanship in this particular. The tools made
theoretical analysis and expression more complete. They were but a
verbal shorthand, which is now the property of all economists.

After Marshall's *Principles* was published, economic thought leveled
off both in England and America. No single publication caused any
stir in the smooth-flowing surface of equilibrium economics; both countries experienced a quiet amounting to complacency, undisturbed by
minor currents of a Veblen or Hobson variety. The excitement over
imperfections in competition was small when compared with the shock
of the *General Theory*, which resoundingly broke the dogmatic slumber.
The brotherhood of economists, whether in agreement or in disagreement with him, arose and entered into the discussion and controversy.
Economics and economists were alive again. Then ensued a period of
creative thought, credit for which goes to Keynes. Should all his ideas
be rejected—which is indeed unlikely—he will remain among the foremost of theoreticians in the entire history of economic thought.

In England, even more than in this country, Keynesian issues were
heatedly joined in books and journals. Nor is the end in sight. His
direct contributions to economic thought are therefore harder to evaluate. Differences in opinion still remain on fundamental issues; but
those who disagreed, in whole or in part, have been obliged so to modify

their own thinking that it becomes difficult to judge what are the main points at issue. Professor Pigou remarks, "Not a little of what we now believe ourselves to have known all along, it may well be we really owe to him. Subject to this caveat, my personal impression is that what he did was not chiefly to discover new truths, but to bring into the centre of the picture and illuminate with strong light aspects of economic analysis whose vital significance for practice has not been seen before." [32]

Austin Robinson, a co-editor of the *Economic Journal* and intimate of Lord Keynes, says Keynes has "three independent claims to greatness." First, "he re-linked the analytical studies of academic economics to the administrative problems of economic government at a moment when they were, in Britain at least, tending to drift apart. . . . Second, we owe to Keynes more than to any of his contemporaries in England the integration of the analytical and the statistical approaches to economics. . . . Third, and most important, Keynes insisted, both with himself and with his pupils, in making us search out the assumptions which underlay our argument." [33] Most students of Keynes would agree with these views and would likely add to the list.

Keynes and British Economic Policy.—The influence of Keynes on economic theory and analysis is universal. His influence on British policy can best be told by an Englishman many years hence. It is common knowledge, however, that he was a chief policy-adviser if not policy-maker in the national and the international sphere for many years. In fact, he had a part in shaping every major financial policy, both domestic and foreign, until his death. In the first World War he held positions of heavy administrative responsibility and possibly made his greatest contributions to policy matters. Harrod remarks, "He occupied the key positions in what was without challenge the center of the interallied effort, he thought out the policy, and in effect bore the ultimate responsibility for the decision and carried the business forward with a success that was universally acclaimed. There have been men of ripe judgment who affirmed that Keynes contributed more than any other person in civil life to winning the first World War." [34]

He was a lone expert in the British Treasury in the first World War; in the second World War he returned as a figure of enormous prestige, surrounded by many who knew most of the principles for which Keynes stood. Again he performed signal duties for his government. Even though he worked under the handicap of failing health, his over-all

---

[32] A. C. Pigou, "The Economist," in *John Maynard Keynes, 1883-1946*, a memoir prepared by direction of The Council of King's College, Cambridge (1949), p. 22.

[33] "John Maynard Keynes, 1883-1946," *Economic Journal*, LVII, No. 225 (March, 1947), pp. 43-44.

[34] *The Life of John Maynard Keynes*, p. 206.

efforts were great and their returns most rewarding for his government. Again he was in on major policy decisions of his own country, and he was consulted on numerous occasions by persons of the inner circles at Washington.

The views of Lord Keynes on the British gold standard issues and central bank policy, national indebtedness, wage levels, and other national issues are well known. His four years with the British Treasury (1940-1946), his work at Bretton Woods, the Loan Agreement— all bear an indelible Keynesian stamp. His many years as a public servant are heavily underscored on the credit side of the British ledger of public service. A peerage was conferred on him as but one testament to this service. One of the objectives he sought to accomplish was workable international economic relationships for the postwar years. No doubt many of his suggestions for postwar economic measures stemmed from the experiences that led to his writing the *Economic Consequences*. The sense of international cooperation, the fear of economic dislocations, the awareness of interdependence of states, the hopes for a new world order remained a significant part of his thinking until the end. He will surely be always ranked high in the long list of distinguished British statesmen.[35]

Epilogue.—The foregoing touches only a few of the high points of the life and work of Lord Keynes. It is obvious that this cannot be a summary, for only a fraction of his work can be considered. In addition to those qualities of mind which account for his greatness as an economist and statesman, he was a fine humanist with wide-ranging interests: He has been referred to as "a man of peerless intellect," [36] and indeed he was. Through his use of this intellect he has become a symbol which stands for and reinforces the belief that man, by taking thought, can predict future economic behavior and hence avoid economic chaos, relieve hardship, reduce poverty, and improve the lot of mankind. It is true that there are some who would contend that the policies of Keynes, if adopted, would lead to the opposite extremes. The years ahead may point out a middle way somewhere between the extremes.

In the past it has been easy to point to the limitations, defects, errors, and shortcomings of the Keynesian system. They are real; yet, notwithstanding this fact, many elements of the Keynesian system have been adopted in theory and policy. No one knows what present theory and

[35] See Arthur Smithies, "Reflections on the Work and Influence of John Maynard Keynes," *Quarterly Journal of Economics*, LXV, No. 4 (November, 1951), pp. 578, *et seq.*
[36] *Listener*, May 3, 1951, p. 703.

both domestic and foreign policy would have been like without the Keynesian revolution.

Perhaps in another fifty years the final estimates will be made. By then the Keynesian tenets will have been given a thorough test; the success of a planned capitalism, the equalizing of incomes, the control mechanisms when applied to a trade cycle, and deficit financing will either be economic facts or cruel fictions. It will be a period in which not only the theories of economics, but also their interdependence with political and social forces, will be tested. At the present time it is doubtful whether we "can see the forest for the trees."

26

Some Post-Marshallian Developments:
English, Swedish and American

It has been shown that chairs of political economy were established in many universities throughout Europe. Some of the occupants were creative while others carried on established tradition. It should also be noted that many contributors to economic thought were not academicians in the strict sense. Among this group in England are Walter Bagehot, Beatrice and Sidney Webb, John A. Hobson, James Bonar, R. G. Hawtrey, and others.

The economic doctrines of Alfred Marshall, who occupied the chair of political economy at King's College, Cambridge, became the most famous. He succeeded in developing a following greater than any of his predecessors had been able to do. Marshall was the founder of the "Cambridge School." Numerous refinements and departures from his original treatise have been made since 1890, until today, after sixty years, it is probable that no such school exists, except in an "equivocal sense," as he himself might put it. Marshall's work, like that of Adam Smith, provided a point of departure for later work which has proved extremely fruitful in many fields of economics. It is possible, however, that a tradition will continue to live around Alfred Marshall and Cambridge University much the same as the tradition associated with Walras, Pareto, and the University of Lausanne.

The purpose of this chapter is to explore briefly a few of the areas of economics as developed by more recent "schools" when and where they exist, and by persons who may or may not be affiliated with any group or "school." More emphasis will be placed on the contributions than on the affiliations. This attempt is made with the full knowledge that grave injustice, however unintentional, may be done both to the ones who are included as well as to those who are omitted.

The Cambridge School.—In spite of the chairs of political economy and the distinguished occupants, none of them changed the course and general tenor of economics until Alfred Marshall laid the general pattern for neoclassical economics. The details of the Marshallian economics appear in Chapter 24. In general, however, the emphasis is on equilibrium of supply and demand and price as mutually self-determining. Marshall's concept of equilibrium, it will be recalled, is known as particular (or partial) equilibrium, not general equilibrium, as developed by the Lausanne economists. He held that tendencies exist in the economic system many of which have the force of "laws," and that all forces work toward an equilibrium. The economic world is assumed to be competitive with only minor state interference and little concern that monopolies will disturb the equilibrium. Economic welfare is of concern to economic endeavor but not its central objective; under the normal, self-regulative scheme, welfare would be maximized. Mathematical techniques were widely used: Marshall, however, fearful that that they might frighten the reader, placed them in footnotes and in appendixes. Although F. Y. Edgeworth (1845-1926) was a pioneer in the use of mathematics,[1] and also made some contributions in utility theory, his influence in shaping the school was not comparable with Marshall's, even though he became, in a sense, the leader of the school after Marshall's death.

It will be recalled that the classical economists used the deductive method in arriving at their generalizations, whereas the historical school used induction. Marshall employed both methods. He recognized the merits as well as the disadvantages of using either method exclusively. Skillful analysis of the economic factors and synthesis of his own and earlier contributions characterize his presentation. In general, it is the economics of Alfred Marshall as developed in his *Principles of Economics* (1890) that provides the original pattern which identifies the Cambridge school. Some further refinements of Marshall's views, as well as the departures from the original, will now be discussed.

Marshall's successor was his former student, Arthur Cecil Pigou (b. 1877-   ), who carried on largely in the Marshallian tradition and ranked as the leading British economist until challenged by J. M. Keynes. Pigou has a formidable list of publications dealing with many more subjects than were ever examined by Marshall.[2] Pigou's work

---

[1] *Mathematical Psychics* (London, 1881). See J. M. Keynes, *Essays in Biography* (1933), pp. 267-93. Edgeworth was the first editor of the *Economic Journal*, the official publication of the Royal Economic Society, founded in 1890, and served in that capacity until his death in 1926. As editor he made significant contributions to English economic literature. His own work in theory dealt with price under monopoly conditions.

[2] Among his better known publications are: *Wealth and Welfare* (1912), later published as *The Economics of Welfare* (1920; 4th ed., 1932), *The Political Economy of War* (1921), *Essays in Applied Economics* (1923), *Industrial Fluctuations*

centered largely on welfare economics. His conception of welfare economics, however, is quite different from that of John A. Hobson (1858-1940)—not a member of the Cambridge School—whose work was highly critical of classical economics and the industrial system.[3] While Hobson never exactly defined what he meant by welfare economics, it appears that his was a "good life" concept which made the state responsible for bringing about a more equitable distribution of wealth. He proposed a social control of practically all economic activity which would insure full employment, good wages, health, education, and recreation; the other amenities of life would then achieve their fullest expression. Thus he believed that the state could end poverty and extremes of wealth, idleness, and insecurity and establish a scheme of things in which human happiness would be the greatest. His ideas tend to fall within the category of utopian socialism, a grouping which cannot be imputed to Pigou.

Professor Pigou's *The Economics of Welfare* is a monumental work. It represents a sort of culmination of the welfare aspects of neoclassical tradition yet it goes beyond; basically, it contains all the elements of his predecessors and at the same time it conveys an optimistic outlook for the entire economy.

His concept of social welfare makes it the sum total of individual welfares. Economic welfare, which is basic to social welfare, is treated subjectively as quantities of satisfactions which can be attained with the measuring rod of money. He contends that "economic causes act on economic welfare of any country, not directly, but through the making and using of that objective counterpart of economic welfare which the economists call the national dividend or national income. Just as economic welfare is that part of total welfare which can be brought directly or indirectly into relation with a money measure, so the national dividend . . . is that part of the objective income of a community that can be measured in money." [4] The Marshallian influence is apparent here since "national dividend" is a term used by Marshall and the productivity concept is both classical and neoclassical.

Pigou departs from neoclassical doctrines in at least two particulars. Marshall was inclined to use a consumers'-surplus concept (See especially, *Principles*, pp. 204 *et sqq.*); this Pigou discards and in its place substitutes a marginal concept which is an attempt to balance the

---

(1927), *A Study in Public Finance* (1928), *The Theory of Unemployment* (1933), *The Economics of Stationary States* (1935), *Employment and Equilibrium* (1941), *Lapses from Full Employment* (1945), *Keynes' General Theory: a Retrospect* (1950).

[3] His best known books are: *The Evolution of Modern Capitalism* (London, 1894) and *Work and Wealth* (London, 1914).

[4] Pigou, *The Economics of Welfare* (4th ed., 1932), chap. iii, p. 30.

advantages and disadvantages of variations in industrial output as affecting total welfare. Next, Pigou recognizes but disregards all particular frictions which may develop under laissez faire and which were usually treated as special cases or exceptions by most neoclassical writers; instead, he treats all conflicts that might conceivably arise under a generalized concept called marginal social product.[5] He thereby avoids any special-case analysis and creates a general welfare analysis built around a concept of a national optimum which requires that the marginal social product be equal throughout the whole economy. The value of the marginal social net product of any volume of resources is both defined and measured by "the money value of the difference made by the marginal increment of those resources so employed to the sum total of economic welfare." In other words, the products and services used are multiplied by their market prices. The value of the marginal social product is, in reality, the money value of economic satisfaction due to it. The sum of such services in terms of money is taken as the size of the marginal social product. Like Marshall he treats the marginal utility of money as constant, and free competition as the prevailing form of business within the economy; however, he does recognize the deviations caused by monopoly and imperfect competition.[6]

Although Pigou builds his analysis on a free play of self-interest and generally free competition, he makes allowances for deviations from a perfect balance of marginal products—marginal returns, due to imperfections in competition, labor disorders, inefficiency in production, inflexible contractual agreements, and the like. Most of Part IV, "The Variability of the National Dividend," is devoted to dynamic influences.

Many criticisms have been directed at Pigou's work. It was a pioneering attempt to carry out Marshall's desire to use economic science as a means of improving the lot of mankind. "The misery and squalor that surround us, the dying fires of hope in many millions of European homes . . . the terrible uncertainty overshadowing many families . . . are evils too plain to be ignored. By the knowledge that our science seeks it is possible that this may be restrained."[7] Objectively, Pigou seeks to examine the elements in the economy which make for inequality. National income occupies his attention but only as it affects the levels of economic welfare. The Pigovian marginal social product, as it is frequently called, emphasizes a general welfare concept, whereas Marshall's analysis was based on partial welfare, with major emphasis

---

[5] Pigou defines the marginal social product as "the total net product of physical things and objective services due to the marginal increment of resources in any given use or place, no matter to whom it may accrue" (p. 132).

[6] *Ibid.*, Part II, chap. xiv-xvii.

[7] *Ibid.*, Preface, p. vii.

resting upon an economic surplus. After 953 pages of prolix discussion a reader may find himself hard put to find specific recommendations which have current application.[8] In any event, and despite germane criticisms, the work has served to stimulate many others to investigate all elements of the economy with the same ultimate objective in mind.

In contrast with his predecessor Alfred Marshall, Pigou is not greatly concerned with developing a universal theory of value, yet he belongs with the neoclassical group. Throughout his writings there is evident a strong desire to improve economic welfare. He is not a socialist—not even a Fabian socialist—yet the problem of effecting a more equitable distribution of wealth concerns him even to the point where he would advocate limited government intervention. The British Labor government probably went further than Pigou would like if one may judge from his analysis of welfare economics, published first in 1912 and later in 1920. He has never advocated absolute equality of national income distribution, but has regarded it as the duty of the state to coordinate all economic, fiscal, and social policies toward bringing about a greater equality of incomes. Only in this manner can social welfare be maximized.

In business cycle theory and analysis Pigou's work is noteworthy. His impressive work, *Industrial Fluctuations* (1927), presents an empirical study of the many complex influencing factors responsible for variations in business activity. Unlike many theorists, he holds that there are many originating causes. He therefore attempts to investigate the influence of agricultural crop production on business and on credit, changes in consumers' habits, technological improvements, and development of natural resources. He also stresses the possibility that booms and depressions are, to some extent, caused by psychological factors leading to miscalculations by businessmen, which bring cumulative errors of extremes of optimism and pessimism. The automatic readjustment of economic forces under classical theory is brought under close examination.

It is not feasible to develop in similar detail all the economic views of Professor Pigou. His many writings indicate the scope of his interests and his willingness to deal with controversial issues. In every respect he remains the dean of British economists.

Imperfect Competition.—The persons responsible for the simultaneous development in 1933 of the concept of imperfect competition

[8] See Hla Myint, *Theories of Welfare Economics* (1948), for a splendid discussion of welfare economics. He remarks, "*The Economics of Welfare* has reigned supreme as the book on the subject and there are few economists who would hesitate to accept most of Professor Pigou's practical conclusions" (p. 197).

(the English term) or monopolistic competition (the American term) are associated with Cambridge and Harvard universities, respectively. Economists after Adam Smith had accepted the assumption that competition was virtually unhampered, and that monopoly, custom, or long-standing trade practices would not materially affect the long-run tendencies. However, few of the writers assumed completely perfect competition. The French economist and mathematician Antoine Augustin Cournot (1801-1877) had argued that the natural tendency for unit costs was to fall with increased production thereby giving a monopoly to the producer. Accordingly he argued that monopoly, not competition, was the common characteristic of economic society.[9] No attention was paid to his theories for years. In 1926 a former student of Marshall, Piero Sraffa, wrote an article for the *Economic Journal* entitled, "The Laws of Returns Under Competitive Conditions," in which he, following Cournot, emphasized the monopoly element in economic society. This was a very original and challenging point of view.

Quite independently and unknown to each other, Edward H. Chamberlin of Harvard published *The Theory of Monopolistic Competition* and Mrs. Joan Robinson of Cambridge published *The Theory of Imperfect Competition*. Each work bears the copyright date of 1933. The next year a German economist, Heinrich von Stackelberg, published a less pretentious analysis of the same type.[10] These works challenged the assumptions of perfect (pure) competition and equilibrium price in the Marshallian sense. In general the monopolistic, or imperfect competition, theory held that the economy is neither entirely competitive nor completely monopolistic but that it is in reality a combination of both. There are many sellers but not an infinite number as implied in pure competition; products are not standardized but differentiated to some degree. Each producer who can continue to produce and sell his product has, by virtue of that very fact, a near monopoly; however, his protected position is always threatened by substitutes and by competition from the many (though not infinite) producers. The individual producer finds his position influenced materially by the actions of his competitors. Therefore, the slope of the demand curve for his product (considered as a producing firm) and the slope of the demand curve for all producers (considered as an industry) will be less elastic than under pure competition, which assumes perfect elasticity of the demand curve. While the elasticity

---

[9] *Recherches sur les principes mathématiques de la théorie des richesses* (1838). English trans. *Researches into the Mathematical Principles of the Theory of Wealth* (1897).
[10] *Marketform und Gleichgewicht* (1934).

of demand under monopolistic competition is less than under pure competition, it is greater than under monopoly, or under "oligopoly," a term which implies "few" producers—"few" obviously being more than one (monopoly) but less than under monopolistic competition.

The economic analysis supporting this explanation is familiar to students, since it was hastily incorporated into texts on economic principles after 1933. Mrs. Robinson's theory and analysis are not significantly different from Chamberlin's, except in emphasis. She uses a single firm and its attempt to adjust output in order to maximize profit. In her analysis, the interrelationships of marginal revenue and marginal costs [the revenue (MR) obtained from the sale of the last unit as related to the cost (MC) of the last unit produced], are emphasized, whereas Chamberlin is mainly concerned with the product and with the manner in which the producer's own decisions affect the actions of competitors.[11] Chamberlin emphasizes the process of differentiation, whereas Robinson stresses positions of equilibrium rather than the processes which bring it about.

The theory of monopolistic competition brought a needed re-examination of the effectiveness of competition in value and price analysis. Subsequent to the publication of the two pioneer works, the literature in economic theory was enriched with many studies which carried the analysis and its refinements farther. The present emphasis has left monopolistic competition behind and considers the price and production policies of a really small number of concerns (oligopoly, from a Greek term *oligos*, meaning small) rather than of many. It is recognized that in very few instances, if at all, does only one firm (which could conceivably also be the industry) have a clear, nonlegal, or pure economic, monopoly. However, there are many instances in which an industry consists of only a few firms. A possibility therefore exists for these firms, by collusive agreements, to control both price and output. New analytical skills have been developed not only in the mechanics of presentation in which mathematical analysis has a large share, but also in new emphasis on all economic relationships. Likewise, new policy issues have been raised which are social in nature; these involve the public attitude toward monopolistic tendencies and finally the attitude of the courts toward combinations and consolidations, which may lead to trusts, monopolies, and tendencies toward monopoly.[12]

The present type of theoretical analysis in monopolistic competition falls in the category of microeconomics. Problems of the firm and of

[11] See Robert Triffin, *Monopolistic Competition and General Equilibrium Theory* (Cambridge, Mass., 1940).

[12] See Howard S. Ellis (ed.), *A Survey of Contemporary Economics* (Philadelphia, 1948), chap. i.

the industry are treated in a manner designed to show how, by taking adequate steps, some effective control is maintained over the amount of goods offered; this in turn would permit control of production schedules and cost. Enlisted in the analysis is an impressive array of average and marginal revenue curves on the demand side and an equally impressive array of cost curves on the supply side. These are far cries from the Marshallian development, which deals with both short- and long-run normal equilibrium analysis in purely competitive situations, which he believed had almost the force of laws. It is possible that economists have been too prone to center their analysis on the behavior of a small number of firms and thus produce case studies rather than comprehensive principles. In any event, the present-day refinements have carried far beyond the neoclassical fundamentals as found in Marshall's *Principles*. To this development many economists have contributed independently of their affiliations with any "school." Neoclassicism, which is the all-embracing body of economic theories, has long since ceased to be the property of any one group. No claim should be made that it is or was the ultimate in theory; it should rather be recognized as providing the framework in which changes may be made to accommodate new emphasis and new developments.

The changes that have taken place in the value theory, together with the departures that have been made into related fields, leave the impression that the Cambridge school no longer exists.[18] This is true in only a doubtful sense. The Marshallian concept of competition has been severely challenged, and admittedly it is true only as a long-run tendency. Depressions, with their many disorders, have brought business cycle studies to the forefront. Disequilibrium in trade balances has brought new interest in both the theory and the policy of gold and exchange rates. Central bank control of money and credit, problems of devaluation, foreign balances, and the socialization of great elements in the economy are but a few of the many problems which have tested the old and challenged the new theories and policies. Many of those trained in the Cambridge tradition have made distinctive contributions to these several fields. There are few, if any, who cling to the strict orthodox economics of Marshall, but many have surpassed the founder and carried economic science to higher levels of exactness.

Departures from the Marshallian tradition, it should be noted, were not caused by any "failure" or lack of truth in the theory of the founder, but by the inadequacy of certain parts of his theory. The great depression after World War I highlighted the inadequacy of Marshall's treat-

---

[18] L. H. Haney, *History of Economic Thought* (New York, 1949), p. 869, refers to "The Disintegration of the Cambridge School."

ment of business cycles and of money and credit as determining factors in the economy. Imperfections, rather than perfections which had been shown to be the main characteristics in the competitive forces, brought damage to the self-adjusting mechanisms in his theory of value. Concurrent with this development came the so-called "Keynesian economics" which emphasized the "monetary aspect" of economics, with savings, investments, interest, employment and levels of consumption, thus "stealing the show" from value theory.

Some Contemporary Cambridge and Oxford Economists.—Perhaps the most noteworthy group of economists in the British Isles are those at Cambridge University. Indeed, the richest traditions stem from Cambridge, with the possible exception of Glasgow University. The Sidgwick, Marshall, Edgeworth, Pigou, and Keynes tradition is indeed outstanding and difficult to match. The senior member of the Cambridge group is A. C. Pigou. D. H. Robertson, R. F. Kahn, N. Kaldor, C. W. Guillebaud, Austin Robinson, Piero Sraffa, Mrs. Joan Robinson —these are a few of the distinguished staff. The pioneering work of J. M. Keynes is still carried on with different degrees of emphasis by an avowed Keynesian group consisting of Pigou, Kahn, the Robinsons, Sraffa, Kaldor and others; D. H. Robertson comes nearest to being an anti-Keynesian in the group. The Keynes tradition is very strong in this university and many continue to hold strictly to what he said; some prefer their own interpretation of what they think he said. In this respect Keynes had suffered from his friends, however well-intentioned their purpose. Keynes had a distinctive capacity for changing his views as conditions changed or as new evidence appeared. In an economy charged with many static and dynamic factors, it is futile to anticipate (or defend) what Keynes would have said, thought, or done; he would examine the issues as they existed and probably arrive at an answer based on the immediate circumstances, not on a former diagnosis.

It is not to be inferred that Cambridge University has had a monopoly on the development of economics in England for the past fifty years. Oxford, too, has had a long list of distinguished economists. However, lacking a genius of Marshall's stature, that university has not enjoyed the wide reputation in the field of political economy accorded to the younger institution. Despite its distinguished economists, it has been in recent years somewhat eclipsed as a center of study in economics by the work of Pigou, Keynes, and others at Cambridge. However, of the many who have served at Oxford, the work of Roy F. Harrod [14] has

[14] *International Economics* (New York, 1933), *The Trade Cycle* (Oxford, 1936), *Toward a Dynamic Economics* (London, 1948); *The Life of John Maynard Keynes* (London, 1951).

been noteworthy, especially in marginal cost and marginal revenue theory and refinements, in developing modern tools for monopoly analysis, in international trade, and in presenting a splendid biography of Lord Keynes. As for theoretical affiliation, it is likely that Harrod is more a Keynesian than a Marshallian neoclassicist.

J. R. Hicks,[15] also at Oxford, has made significant contributions to value and wage theory, general equilibrium analysis, and welfare economics. In his *Value and Capital* Hicks develops a dynamic theory of prices and production. He starts with subjective value and develops a static theory of general equilibrium along Walrasian lines. For purposes of analysis he uses a timeless, static theory as a point of departure. In his dynamic analysis he uses a price and production system with many markets, the time element, interest rates, variations in demand and supply for commodities, securities, and money. With these items as the main elements he develops a dynamic theory of temporary general equilibrium. In the first chapters of the work he incorporates an improved version of Pareto's indifference curves and other analytical tools which are effectively used in developing the dynamic theory.

The starting point in production analysis is the individual firm: What are the conditions necessary for its equilibrium and for maintaining its stability? Perfect competition is assumed throughout the analysis, which, together with no government interference and no uncertainties in time, makes possible the conditions of stable equilibrium. However, the uncertainties of saving and investment, speculation in future values, and entrepreneurial decisions inject dynamic elements. The analysis then deals with the elements of stability and those of instability in the economy.

His capital and interest theories, which are superior to those developed by Wicksell, are presented as a part of the dynamic approach. He regards the rate of interest as determined by either the supply and demand for loanable funds or the supply and demand for money. An opportunity cost idea is implied when he holds that money has most general acceptability, but securities, which also bring an interest return, are subjects for investment. All things considered, money is the most satisfactory form of "security," and interest must be paid to induce savers to lend—a sort of "liquidity preference" in the Keynesian sense. The work is an attempt to present a dynamic system with an equilibrium resulting not only from present market prices, but also from former prices which are factors influencing the present equilibrium.

[15] *The Theory of Wages* (London, 1932), *Value and Capital* (London, 1939), *The Taxation of War Wealth* (Oxford, 1941), *A Contribution to the Theory of the Trade Cycle* (Oxford, 1950).

It is not possible even to attempt a discussion of the work which has been done and which is still being done by economists in the many universities and colleges of the British Isles. Economic literature has been enriched by their contributions in many fields.

The London School of Economics and Political Science.—The London School of Economics was started in 1895 by the Fabian Socialists, Sidney Webb, Graham Wallas, and G. B. Shaw. Of the three, Webb's influence was by far the greatest. These men were dissatisfied with both the inadequacy of the offerings in the social sciences and the lack of facilities for research offered in London by the two colleges—King's and University.[16] They assumed active responsibility for securing funds, wherein Webb was especially successful. (The original funds came as a bequest, and the London Chamber of Commerce helped by making some funds available at the beginning stages.) The first director was a young Oxonian named W. A. S. Hewins, who served with distinction in the formative years (1895-1903). In 1900-1901 the School was made one of the units of the University of London, along with King's College and University College; before that time it was organized as a private body sponsored almost entirely by Sidney Webb. When it became affiliated with the other colleges, it was given power to grant the B.Sc. (Econ.) degree, the first degree in the social sciences offered by any English institution.

The next two decades were years of steady growth both in number of students and in breadth of academic offerings. Especially notable was the establishment of a "School of Sociology and Social Economics" in 1912-1913 for the special purpose of training social workers and administrators.

The first lecturer in political economy in the School was Edwin Cannan (1861-1935), who began his work in 1897.[17] In 1907 a professorship in political economy was created and Cannan held this chair until his retirement in 1926. His successor was Allyn A. Young of Harvard, who died suddenly at the end of the second year after his appointment.

It was Cannan who, more than any other person, created the intellectual climate which characterized the school. Fabian socialism received no greater emphasis than any other subject. One of the ob-

---

[16] F. A. Hayek, "The London School of Economics, 1895-1945," *Economica*, New Series, XIII (1946), pp. 1-31.

[17] His best known publications are: *The Economic Outlook* (London, 1922), *An Economist's Protest* (London, 1927), *A History of Theories of Production and Distribution in English Political Economy from 1776 to 1848* (London, 1894, 1903, 1924), *A Review of Economic Theory* (London, 1929), *Wealth: A Brief Explanation of Wealth and Welfare* (London, 1914).

jectives of the school was to counteract the dominant teachings of Ricardo and Mill, which had long prevailed. Cannan, although a close follower of classical tradition, was an individual thinker and a rather severe critic of some of the classical positions. He also had a clear historical perspective and a keen interest in institutional developments as well. His teachings were therefore a departure from earlier emphasis.

From the time of Cannan's appointment the work in political economy expanded rapidly. The offerings were increased and many distinguished scholars lectured in the School for periods of varying lengths of time during the first half-century of its existence. Among them may be mentioned F. Y. Edgeworth, H. S. Foxwell, Edwin Cannan, A. L. Bowley, Sidney Webb, G. B. Shaw, Bertrand Russell, James Bonar, R. H. Tawney, Harold Laski, L. C. Robbins, F. A. Hayek, J. B. Condliffe, D. H. Robertson, J. R. Hicks, and many others. Even though the School was originally sponsored by Fabian socialists it presented other phases of economics and never showed any particular bias even in its early days; it has prided itself upon the broad list of offerings which contain all shades of economic and political convictions.[18]

The great expansion of the School came in the 1920's and 1930's when substantial grants were made by the Rockefeller Foundation [19] and by the Carnegie United Kingdom Trust. This assistance permitted substantial expansion not only in the physical equipment but in academic staff and library facilities. The war interrupted the School's activities; all of the physical plant but the library was taken over by the government and the academic work from 1939 to 1945 was moved to Cambridge University. At the end of the war the School returned to its former location in the center of London.

The library, known as The British Library of Political and Economic Science, is peculiar among British libraries in that it is the working library for the London School of Economics and a research library as well. It has one of the largest collections in the world devoted exclusively to the social sciences. It is also particularly rich in material on international law, social, economic, and international aspects of history and in government publications. The quarterly journal of the

[18] The School is by no means limited to the teaching of economics. While its teaching and research are concentrated on the social sciences, they embrace the following broad list of subjects: economics, commerce, banking; industry and transport; statistics; political science and public administration; sociology; social anthropology; social and economic history; law in all its aspects; criminology; international relations; international history; geography; psychology; demography; logic, scientific method; and modern languages.

[19] By 1935 the Rockefeller Foundation had given a total of £430,000.

School, *Economica* (first issue in 1921), ranks among the best journals in the field of economics.[20]

The London School of Economics has earned an international reputation as shown by its students who come from all nations. While the Webbs and Harold Laski were alive, it was an active leader in socialistic theory and practice. Since then, however, work in this area is not so outstanding. In theoretical economics no particular school of thought or bias is admitted. Professor Lionel Robbins, who was associated with the late Lord Keynes, occupies with distinction the chair first held by Cannan. Many members of the staff have done significant work with the various bureaus of the government, as well as in their chosen fields of academic specialization.

Some Developments in Swedish Economics.—The Swedish economists are sometimes known as the Swedish school or the Stockholm school; their contributions to pure theory and to econometrics are distinctly noteworthy.[21] The first to attract wide attention was Knut Wicksell.[22]

[20] From 1934 the field covered by the original *Economica* was divided between *Economica* (new series), which covered economics, economic history, and statistics, and a new journal, *Politica*, which was discontinued at the outbreak of the war in 1939.

[21] The rise of the Stockholm school, 1927-1935, is related in an article by B. Ohlin, "Some Notes on the Stockholm Theory of Saving and Investments," *Economic Journal*, XLVII (March, 1937), reprinted in *Readings in Business Cycle Theory* (1944), pp. 87-130.

[22] Johann Gustaf Knut Wicksell (1851-1926) graduated (1885) with a degree in mathematics and philosophy at the University of Uppsala, after which he spent another five years (1885-1890) of study in England, France, Germany, and Austria. His Ph.D. degree was earned in 1895 at the University of Uppsala. He served as a professor at the University of Lund from 1910 to 1916. He was a contemporary of Böhm-Bawerk, Pareto, and Alfred Marshall. Wicksell followed Walras closely, especially in price theory and in its mathematical expression; his indebtedness to Böhm-Bawerk, especially in his capital theory, and to the Austrian explanation of production and distribution is apparent. He drew heavily upon the English economists Wicksteed and Edgeworth. In addition, he knew classical theory and Marshallian doctrines extremely well. His work was largely a fusion of the best elements of the above-named economists: in this eclectic work he succeeded more effectively than any other writer in presenting a finely integrated, clear, and exact synthesis.

His first important work was *Über Wert, Kapital und Rente* (*Value, Capital and Rent*, Jena, 1893), reprinted by the London School of Economics as No. 15, in the series of Reprints of Scarce Tracts (London, 1933); followed by *Finanztheoreticshe Untersuchungen* (*Studies in Finance Theory*, 1896), and *Geldzins und Güterpreise* (*Interest and Prices*, 1898; English ed., 1936). *Vorlesungen über Nationalökonomie* was first published in Swedish in two parts, 1901 and 1906 (German ed., Jena, 1913); this work has been translated into English and published as *Lectures in Political Economy*, edited by Lionel Robbins; Vol. I, *General Theory* (1934), Vol. II, *Money and Credit* (1935). In addition to his books he published many journal articles. See B. Ohlin's article, "Knut Wicksell (1851-1926)," *Economic Journal*, XXXVI, pp. 503-12; also Professor Robbins' Introduction to the English edition of *Lectures on Political Economy* (1934), I, vii-xxiii. Carl G. Uhr presents a comprehensive

It is difficult to evaluate Wicksell properly for the reason that he was both eclectic and original in his work. He had an almost perfect grasp of the theories then extant and an extraordinary ability to blend and systematize them into a logical and consistent body. In addition, his originality appears in the treatment of the marginal productivity theory, for which he should be regarded as a discoverer. "This statement of the marginal productivity theory is one of the most satisfactory available." [23]

The best elements of Wicksell's theories are found in his *Lectures on Political Economy, Vol. I, General Theory*. The work is divided into the theory of value, the theory of productivity and distribution, and capital accumulation. This volume contains his lucid views on the marginal utility explanation of value and price determination in competition, and on objections and exceptions to marginal utility theory. Here the Austrian influence appears, although in price theory he generally followed the Walrasian system. He carried the marginal utility theory into the explanation of production and made use of the marginal concept in explaining the returns to land, labor, and capital. In this work he was a pioneer. Many of the ideas which are presented in the *Lectures* date back to his first publication in 1892, *Über Wert, Kapital und Rente*. While they were changed somewhat in later years, they were among the first to be developed by him.

Wicksell followed Böhm-Bawerk closely in his own theory of capital and interest. He accepted the Austrian definition of capital as "produced means of production" and held that interest, as the return to capital, has the peculiarity of being the same kind of thing as capital itself; "interest is an organic growth out of capital, a certain percentage. . . ." [24] However, he went further in defining the concepts, "Capital is saved-up labor and saved-up land. Interest is the difference between the marginal productivity of saved-up labor and land and of current labor and land." [25] Capital may be regarded then as stored-up subsistence owned by capitalists. He also considered the life of capital, its technical renewal year by year, as well as its accumulation and maintenance. Therefore, the "saved-up labor and the saved-up land," or capital, of one year is augmented by the saved-up capital of the preceding year. Not all capital is used up in production; a part is carried over into the subsequent years and so on. A permanence of capital is im-

---

treatment of the Wicksellian theories in "Knut Wicksell—A Centennial Evaluation," *American Economic Review*, XLI, No. 5 (December, 1951).

[23] Lionel Robbins, Introduction to *Lectures on Political Economy*, Vol. I, *General Theory*, p. xii.

[24] *Lectures*, Vol. I, p. 145.

[25] *Ibid.*, p. 154.

plied and the time element is especially significant in interest. Time is the essence of the capital theory.

The interest theory is basically a marginal productivity explanation which is the difference between (1) "current labor and land [which] must, from technical necessity, be employed in their original form" and (2) the marginal productivity of "stored-up productive power" (land and labor).[26] He held that the marginal productivity of stored-up productive power is greater, because current land and labor exist in relative abundance for the purposes for which they can be employed. On the other hand, saved-up labor and land are not adequate in the same degree for the many purposes in which they have an advantage. There is an "opportunity cost" element involved in that interest, within a time-period (say, one year), must be the same in all enterprises and in all kinds of employment and also in saved-up land as related to current land, and saved-up labor as related to current labor. This identity will then assure a constant amount of saving of both land and labor.

It is necessary that these relationships be maintained over the years; otherwise interest might disappear. However, this tendency for interest to sink to zero would change the investment period and also change the values of the capital goods and their relation to consumption goods. The tendency is that "interest rates for both long and short periods tend to be equal."[27] In time, therefore, a full equilibrium will be restored between the amount of capital and the interest rates on the marginal productivity principle.[28]

Wicksell followed Walras in stressing the mutual interdependence of all elements in the determination of price. His interest theory is a part of the equilibrium system of mutual dependence. In this general equilibrium pattern appears his greatest contribution, namely, his theory of the relations between money and natural rates of interest and movements in the general level of prices. He recognizes a "natural" rate of interest and a bank rate or market rate; the interrelationships of these two rates have important bearings upon prices.[29] The "natural" rate of interest on capital, although not defined, is that rate which tends to equate the savings and investment and tends to equal, in amount, the anticipated yield on the capital. The bank or market rate is what is charged by institutional lenders; it may, at least in the short run, be "lower or higher from that which corresponds to the current value of the natural rate of interest on capital."[30] If banks or lenders

[26] *Ibid.*, p. 155.

[27] *Ibid.*, p. 161.

[28] See G. J. Stigler, *Production and Distribution Theories* (New York, 1941), chap. x, for presentation and criticism of the theories.

[29] See *Lectures*, Vol. II, *Money*, chaps. vii and viii.

[30] *Ibid.*, p. 105.

loan at rates above or below the natural rate, economic equilibrium is disturbed and must be finally restored. The chain of relationships that brings the disturbance is, briefly, this. Assuming a fall in interest rates below the natural rate, savings decrease and expenditures increase; entrepreneurs move in to take advantage of increased expenditures by expanding production, with a resulting increase in investment capital; increased capital outlay, together with increased expenditures on consumption, lead to a rise in the level of prices. A reverse pattern follows a rise in interest rates. The conclusion is, therefore, that "at any moment and in every economic situation there is a certain level of the average rate of interest which is such that the general level of prices has no tendency to move other than upwards or downwards. This we call the *normal* rate of interest." [31] The magnitude of the natural rate of interest is not fixed or unalterable. Likewise, the magnitude of the *normal* rate is "determined by the current level of the natural capital rate, and rises or falls with it." [32] If, for any reason, the average rate of interest is below the normal level, prices will rise or go on rising. Wicksell contends that, even if the prices are already in the process of falling, the trend will be reversed and eventually begin to rise. Also, the opposite holds: interest maintained above the current level of the natural rate will lead to a fall in prices "without limit." His theory is a synthesis of Austrian marginal productivity and the general equilibrium of Walras.

While this theory is a blending of the two elements, Austrian and Walrasian, it is, nevertheless, a new and challenging approach. Likewise, it is purely theoretical and designed to explain long-run price movements. This theory is undoubtedly rejected by Wicksell's followers, Ohlin, Myrdal, and Lindahl. Ohlin remarks, "Moreover, he always regarded his own contribution as a doubtful hypothesis and never became convinced of its tenability as did some of his pupils." [33] Wicksell was interested in this analysis mainly because of the controversy which arose over the reasons for a gradually falling level of prices during the period, 1873-1895, prior to the publication of the book, *Geldzins und Güterpreise*, in 1898. The paradoxical behavior of prices and interest rates challenged him. Why should there be a fall in prices accompanied by a low discount rate when theoretically the low rate would indicate an abundance of money that should make prices rise? After an examination of existing explanations, including the quantity theory of which he was an adherent, he arrived at his theory of the discrepancies of rates as a cause. Despite his careful analysis, it lacks the

[31] *Ibid.*, p. 120.
[32] *Ibid.*
[33] *Interest and Prices* (London, 1936), p. viii.

possibility of verification since the "natural" rate of interest is hypothetical and does not exist on any market.

In addition to Wicksell's views thus far presented, brief mention should be made of his population studies which were developed along neo-Malthusian lines, a subject which first interested him and was responsible for a brief jail sentence. His works in public finance and the incidence of taxation were among the earliest and best in the field. In addition to the major writings listed above, he participated in the controversial issues of the day and published his views in the scientific journals of Sweden and elsewhere.

Wicksell's influence was great. He was the founder of a "school" of economic theory and has enlisted a group of Wicksellian followers.[34] The followers do not hold to all the theories as he drafted them, especially the "natural" interest explanation, but his influence on general economic equilibrium analysis, the relationship of savings, investment, interest, and price levels, has been recorded not only in the works of his fellow economists in Sweden but also in those of J. M. Keynes. He carried the general economic equilibrium of Walras to higher levels of refinement, especially in mathematical technique. Few scholars have had a grasp of economic literature even approaching that of Wicksell. In original contributions, especially in value theory, he is probably not comparable with some. However, his ability to blend the best of the theories into a clear and concise restatement is unequaled. His craftsmanship is at its best in the clarity of expression, in showing the interdependence of economic factors, and in the general high level of attainment reached in the *General Theory*, Volume I of the *Lectures*.

Gustav Cassel.—Next in chronological order (but not necessarily in general significance) is Gustav Cassel, who served for many years as professor at the University of Stockholm.[35] Cassel should not be

[34] See Gide and Rist, *A History of Economic Doctrines* (2d ed., 1948), pp. 725 *et sqq.*

[35] **Gustav Cassel** (1866-1945) was educated at Uppsala University and the University of Stockholm, where he earned the Ph.D. degree. In 1904 he became professor of economics at Stockholm, serving there until 1933. Cassel earned great fame as an international monetary expert; he served as adviser to many European states on financial matters which arose as a result of World War I and was a delegate to numerous international conferences. He was invited by the League of Nations, in 1921, to present a paper on world monetary problems before that body. He was the financial adviser to his own nation for many years. In 1922 he was financial adviser to the Soviet Union on the newly created Russian State Bank. In 1928 he was invited by the Banking Commission of the United States House of Representatives to give his opinions on the stabilization of the dollar. Among his many publications the best known are: *Outline of an Elementary Theory of Prices* (1899); *The Nature and Necessity of Interest* (London, 1903); *Theory of Social Economy* (German ed., 1918; English ed. London, 1923); *World's Monetary Prob-*

regarded as a follower of Wicksell. In a review of Cassel's *Theory of Social Economy*, Wicksell was devastating in charging inaccuracies, lack of anything new, vagueness, and even a failure to recognize the author's indebtedness to earlier writers. The last part of Cassel's work, which deals with the theory of trade cycles, Wicksell regards as "incomparably the best part of his work"; however, he does not regard it as being of a very high level.[36]

Cassel's contribution was in monetary theory rather than in pure economic theory. He rejected the value theories, and marginal utility especially, declaring that psychological phenomena underlying price did not fall within the economist's domain. This critical view of economic theory was held throughout his life. As late as 1935 he stated:

Economic theory stands out as having been singularly incapable of that form of renaissance which in other sciences manifests itself in an incessant clearance of what is no longer of value. Loose and dim concepts, falsely stated problems, confused reasonings, representations not in touch with reality—in short, all sorts of dogmatic rubbish inherited from earlier epochs and accumulated for more than a century—continue largely to determine the problems which economic science sets itself to study, and entangle fresh and constructive work in a mess of unnecessary difficulties.[37]

His view is that quantitative analysis had to supplant all earlier psychological and metaphysical concepts, yet he regarded "the principle of scarcity" as the basic reason of price; he remarks, "thus the whole process of price-fixing is based on the principle of scarcity." [38] This idea, first introduced by him in *The Theory of Social Economy*, is fundamentally the same as marginal utility. Walras used the same idea in his *rareté*, a term which he used to signify both scarcity and rareness. Cassel also used scarcity to explain what he called the "Equilibrium Theory of Prices," in which total demand and total sup-

---

lems (London, 1921); *Money and Foreign Exchange after 1914* (New York, 1922); *On Quantitative Thinking in Economics* (Oxford, 1935); *The Downfall of the Gold Standard* (Oxford, 1936). In addition to his books he wrote hundreds of newspaper articles and contributed to the scientific journals of Sweden and other countries. For twenty-five years (1920-1945) he was a regular contributor to nearly every issue of the quarterly publication (*Skandinaviska Banken*) of the Bank of Sweden. Few economists have achieved an international recognition approaching that of Gustav Cassel.

[36] Wicksell's review originally appeared in *Ekonomisk Tidsskrift*, 1919, No. 9, and in Schmoller's *Jahrbuch*, Vol. LII, No. 5 (1928). The review appears as an appendix in *Lectures on Political Economy*, Vol. I, *General Theory*, pp. 219-57.

[37] Gustav Cassel, *On Quantitative Thinking in Economics* (1935), p. 3. The book is really not a systematic treatment of the use of quantitative methods in economics, but a series of essays covering methodology, production, money, income, prices—in which quantitative methods as a supplement to theoretical analysis are illustrated.

[38] *Ibid.*, p. 155.

ply are responsible for determining all prices at the same time. This idea, which is also Walrasian, calls for the use of simultaneous equations which he regards as necessary when dealing even with "the most elementary case of price fixing." Despite his own contentions, it is doubtful that he achieved anything approaching an explanation of value and prices, nor was he able to divorce his reasoning from the concept of margins and the principle of substitution. Cassel held no brief for any narrow cost-of-production theories as proposed by the classical economists, or for strictly subjective explanations as developed by the Austrians.

In his work, *Money and Foreign Exchange after 1914* (1922), he studied the contemporary problem of unbalanced exchanges and offered his purchasing-power-parity explanation of exchange rates. Briefly stated, it meant that "when two currencies have undergone inflation, the normal rate of exchange will be equal to the old [pre-inflation] rate multiplied by the quotient of the degree of inflation in the one country and in the other." [39] He thought that exchange rates when calculated by this method would provide a new parity between the currencies and provide a balance toward which exchange rates would tend, in spite of all temporary fluctuations. Because of its many technicalities and variables, this theory did not gain any very general acceptance. It is statistically unmanageable but provocative of further research.

His monetary theories gained wide publicity, especially in the 1920's when world currencies were badly disturbed by causes stemming from World War I. He favored a return of the prewar gold standard; this proved to be bad advice, especially in Great Britain. He argued at length that the reason for the fall in prices at the end of the 1920's and in the early 1930's was the failure of the world's gold supply to keep up with the general increase in production and trade. He argued in *The Crisis in the World's Monetary System* (1932) for a permanently managed currency system, even to the extent that there should be a managed currency inflation for countries on the gold standard.

Cassel was always interested in having his monetary and economic reforms put into practice as a means to social betterment. In the Cobden lectures delivered in London in 1934, he expressed apprehension of the planned economies being introduced in the United States, Russia, and Germany and warned that "they tend to develop political as well as economic dictatorship." In this respect, he was prophetic. However, the long-run monetary policies which were highly respected in the 1920's have not proved their staying qualities. Nevertheless, it

[39] P. 140.

is probable that the success of a managed currency system in his native land is attributable in part to Professor Cassel.

From the foregoing treatment it is apparent that both Wicksell and Cassel went their separate ways. Cassel was not a follower of the "Wicksellian school" in any respect. Indeed, a "school" can be identified among the Swedish economists only in a qualified sense. Wicksell proposed theories dealing with the general level of prices as related to income analysis but without any cyclical implications (*Interest and Prices*, 1898). His emphasis was on the relationship of income and consumption, saving and investment, but not in the present accepted meaning. These early views were further developed and reinterpreted by G. Myrdal, E. Lindahl, B. Ohlin, and others who are frequently referred to as members of the school.

Their work has been, for the most part, in the fields of general equilibrium analysis with considerable emphasis on period analysis; macroeconomics, developed by use of econometrics, and a generally realistic approach have ranked them high among modern economists. Ohlin, who applied Cassel's system of simultaneous equations to international trade by using an equilibrium theory of prices, raised it to a high level of refinement.[40] The foundation of his analysis is the Walras-Pareto-Cassel mutual interdependence theory of prices. He uses the general price theory to cover world markets and thereby makes the theory of international prices an integral and consistent part of a general system of mutual interdependence of prices. Provision is therefore made for all the complex international factors, such as capital movements, changes in demand, tariffs, duties, quotas, and similar factors which nations use; they become elements in an extremely complex but interdependent system of prices established and balanced on a worldwide scale. This is a marked advance over classical trade doctrines stemming from the Ricardian doctrine of comparative costs, which was basically a labor-cost theory.

Ohlin reckons with the fact that trade rests on the cheapness or dearness of production costs, or price differences as they exist between producing areas. These differences in turn rest upon the limitations in the supply of factors of production. These cost and supply differences also account for the location as well as the development of industries and for the course of international trade. Ohlin's analysis was a successful attempt to explain trade on a realistic basis and consistent with general equilibrium theory.

Gunnar Myrdal's *Pricing and the Change Factor* (1927) was a criticism of the Wicksellian interest theory and an attempt at dynamic

[40] Bertil Ohlin, *Interregional and International Trade* (1933).

analysis. His *Monetary Equilibrium* (1931, translated from the German in 1939) also contained criticisms of Wicksell's interest theory and emphasized an interest and price theory of his own. The academic interest had shifted from the Wicksellian emphasis to money and employment theory, with the result that Myrdal's work received less attention than it would otherwise have achieved.[41]

The Swedish group has done splendid work, especially in the general field of monetary theory. Likewise, employment theory, period analysis, econometrics, and national income analysis have been materially improved by their researches and writings. Some of their finest contributions are in journal articles (often unavailable in English) in which contemporary issues have been fairly joined in the best of tradition. The permanent, lasting contributions of the Swedish economists, like those of economists of other nations, will be evaluated many years hence. They are still too recent to be history.

Some Recent American Writers and Their Contributions.—The development of early economic thought in the United States was treated in earlier chapters. The most significant writers from the time of Alexander Hamilton, Franklin, and Raymond up to and including W. C. Mitchell, together with their contributions, were given considerable attention. At this juncture only brief reference will be made to a few of the many distinguished economists who have made significant contributions. The calculated risk of inclusion and exclusion, fairness, and thoroughness is just as great as that encountered in reporting on current British economists.[42]

The American contributions have served, like many of the British, to enrich the whole of economic literature. After the American Economic Association was organized in 1885 many economists found an outlet for their views.[43] In the same decade the following journals also appeared: *Political Science Quarterly* (1886-   ), sponsored by Columbia University; *Quarterly Journal of Economics* (also, 1886-   ), Har-

[41] The study of the Negro problem in the United States, directed by Myrdal, is outstanding.

[42] Detailed treatment has been accorded many American and British economists by the following authors: Paul T. Homan, *Contemporary Economic Thought* (1928); George J. Stigler, *Production and Distribution Theories* (1941); Allan G. Gruchy, *Modern Economic Thought* (1947); Joseph Dorfman's monumental work, *The Economic Mind in American Civilization*, Vols. I and II (1946), Vol. III (1949). Joseph Schumpeter, *Ten Great Economists* (1951), treats Marshall and Keynes of England and F. W. Taussig, W. C. Mitchell, and Irving Fisher of the United States.

[43] For details on the Association see R. T. Ely, *American Economic Association Quarterly*, XI, pp. 46 ff. The first publication of the American Economic Association was known as *Publications*; from March 1886 to April 1908 it was known as the *Bulletin*. In March 1911 the name of *American Economic Review* was adopted and is still used.

vard University; *The Annals of the Academy of Political and Social Science* (1890-), a University of Pennsylvania publication. Since 1892 the University of Chicago has sponsored the *Journal of Political Economy*. Later the Econometric Society began sponsoring *Econometrica* (1933-); the Economics History Association publishes the *Journal of Economic History* (1941-). The Southern Economic Association publishes the *Southern Economic Journal* (1933-), and the Department of Economics of Harvard University sponsors the *Review of Economics and Statistics* (1948-) (originally published as the *Review of Economic Statistics*, 1919-1948). These are but a few of the many journals in the general field of economics; the list would be greatly extended if it included all the publications in the field of the social sciences published in the English language in the United States, Great Britain, Canada, and Australia, not to mention the publications in languages of other countries.

In the field of theoretical economics the work of John Bates Clark was outstanding (cf. Chapter 22). Among others whose work was almost as noteworthy the following familiar names appear: Richard T. Ely (1854-1943), wrote a book on principles, which originally bore the title *An Introduction to Political Economy* (1889) and was used more widely and for a longer period of time (in the original and several revisions) than any other principles text. His work in labor economics, monopoly and trusts, land economics, and public utilities was also outstanding. Edwin R. A. Seligman (1861-1939) also wrote a text, *Principles of Economics* (1905), which had wide acceptance. The major part of his work was in the field of public finance and taxation rather than in pure theory. F. W. Taussig (1859-1940) enjoyed a wide reputation for his work in the fields of international trade and finance and the tariff question, as well as for his authorship of a widely used *Principles of Economics* (1911). Frank A. Fetter (1859-1949) came near to being the founder of a "school" which emphasized the subjective and psychological aspect of value theory along lines somewhat the same as those followed by the Austrian economists. In his *Economic Principles* (1915) he emphasized welfare economics over price economics and criticized marginal utility. Professor Fetter enjoyed great prestige as an original thinker and critic in the field of general economics. Edwin W. Kemmerer (1875-1945) was one of the leading monetary theorists of his day; in addition, he was known as the "Money Doctor" for his services in restoring the money and banking systems of many nations. The work of Frank H. Knight (1885-) has been both constructive and critical. His *Risk, Uncertainty and Profit* (1921) cast new light on entrepreneurial returns in the economy. The *Ethics of Competition and Other Essays* (1935) present many economic subjects in both a philosophical and a psychological setting. He has earned wide acclaim as a teacher and writer in the realm of economic theory.

In the field of statistics, monetary theory, interest, and capital, Irving Fisher (1867-1947) earned an international reputation second to that of no other American economist. Fisher dealt with controversial issues in theory and in addition advanced many new ones in the general field of interest rates, capital, quantity theory of money, price levels, index numbers, and many related subjects. In the general field of economic statistics the work of H. L. Moore (1869-) and Henry Schultz (1893-1938), to mention only two, has been outstanding.

Schumpeter and His Contributions to Economics.—One of the most famous of economists in the past half century was Joseph Alois Schumpeter. Indeed, one of his biographers calls him "one of the great economists of all time. His claim to that rare title rests as much on the fact that he was far more than an economist as on his achievements in the economic field itself." [44] He was an extremely erudite person, versed in mathematics and statistics, history of economic doctrines, political and social history, and social philosophy and institutions. While there have been some writers who excelled in knowledge of certain special fields, there are few, if any, who held such complete mastery over all fields of economics.[45]

Only a few of Schumpeter's leading contributions are here presented. It is obviously too soon for anyone to attempt a detailed evaluation of

---

[44] G. Haberler, "Joseph Alois Schumpeter," *Quarterly Journal of Economics,* LXIV (August, 1950), p. 333 *et sqq.* See also the issue, "Schumpeter, Social Scientist," of the *Review of Economics and Statistics,* XXXIII (May, 1951).

[45] **Joseph Alois Schumpeter** (1883-1950) was born in the Austrian province of Moravia (now Czechoslovakia). His doctor of laws degree was obtained at the University of Vienna in 1906. He attended the seminars of von Wieser, Böhm-Bawerk, and von Philipovich while at Vienna, which was still enjoying the great fame of its distinguished triumvirate. He served for a few months as Minister of Finance of the Austrian Republic in 1919. His early teaching experience was gained at the University of Czernowitz (now in Russian territory), Graz in Austria, and Bonn in Germany. He came to Harvard University in 1927-28, again for the autumn term of 1930, and permanently in 1932. There he spent the remainder of his academic career of eighteen years. His work as a teacher and lecturer was outstanding. He was very widely known both at home and abroad and highly respected for his scholarly achievements. He was one of the founders of the Econometric Society and its president from 1937 to 1941. He was president of the American Economic Association in 1949. A full list of his publications (eleven pages) appears at the end of Professor Haberler's article. Of his many books the best known are: *Theorie der Wirtschaftlichen Entwicklung* (Leipzig, 1911) translated as *The Theory of Economic Development* (Harvard University Press, 1934); *Business Cycles: A Theoretical Historical and Statistical Analysis of the Capitalistic Process* (2 vols., New York, 1939); *Capitalism, Socialism and Democracy* (New York, 1942); *Ten Great Economists* (New York, 1951, essays on ten economists which formerly appeared as journal articles); *History of Economic Analysis,* a two-volume work as yet unpublished.

his work and his achievement amongst economists who have shaped the direction of economic thought. One of his works, on which he spent many years, has not yet been published; many of his articles and a few of his books are in German and not readily accessible. It is certain, however, that when a final evaluation of his scientific achievements is made, he will rank with the finest economists in any land in the past half-century.

The following discussion is intended to recount briefly some of the leading doctrines presented in his best known books. Even this is a difficult task because of the sweep and complications of the analysis, the interdependence of forces, and the general dynamics of the treatment of the subject. Schumpeter had a tremendous grasp of the whole framework of the economy with its multifarious forces; add to this an uncompromising thoroughness in the analysis and an end product results which is anything but simple.

His first major work was produced in 1911 when Schumpeter was twenty-eight years old; it bore the German title of *Theorie der Wirtschaftlichen Entwicklung*. The English translation was made from the 1926 German edition and published in 1934 under the title of *The Theory of Economic Development*. This work contains the basic ideas of his conception of the whole economic process. Certain elements contained in this work are further developed in subsequent books, *Business Cycles* (1939) and *Capitalism, Socialism and Democracy* (1942).

In Chapter I of his *Theory of Economic Development* the author traces the circular flow of economic life as conditioned by given circumstances. A clue to what follows is given in the first line which states, "The social process is really one indivisible whole." He sets up a series of relationships, admittedly modeled on the Walrasian general equilibrium concept, in which goods or commodities, money and credit, factors of production, all fit into a constant stream which circulates throughout economic life as naturally as blood circulates in "an animal organism." Goods flow in one direction as a stream to the consumers, while money flows in the opposite direction from the consumer back to the producer, who employs it again in production. This process keeps up year after year. Prices, which are necessary in facilitating the exchange of commodities, are "the results of processes which work under the pressure of many individual evaluations." [46] There is always a constant tendency toward an equilibrium position "which tendency gives us the means of determining prices and quantities of

[46] *Theory of Economic Development*, p. 56.

goods, and may be described as an adaptation to data existing at any time." [47]

The idea of a circular flow does not mean that the same things happen year after year. He makes ample allowances for changes within the socioeconomic structure which permit the forces to work continuously towards an equilibrium position, but not necessarily towards the same one. Growth is normal and arises from within the structure; population is not assumed to be static in the model but, like wealth, grows in the process of the economic development. Every new element of growth rests upon a preceding one and this in turn sets up conditions for subsequent development. Development is therefore a continuous process of growth; a dynamic movement "which forever alters and displaces the equilibrium state previously existing. Our theory of development is nothing but a treatment of this phenomenon and the processes incident to it." [48]

Provision is made for the entrepreneur who carries out the new combinations in production. This may be made on either a small or a large scale; hence a leadership function is assumed which is important. The entrepreneur becomes an innovator.

Next Schumpeter considers entrepreneurial profit—a surplus over costs—which goes to the entrepreneur. Profit is essential to economic development, and vice versa. Without profit there would be no accumulation of wealth which is normal in economic development and necessary in the circular flow. It should be observed that Schumpeter emphasized the importance of money in the circular flow. Monetary theory, with all its implications, must of necessity be a part of the analysis and explanation not only of prices, but also of capital and interest. His interest theory, briefly stated, is as follows.

In a static economy, in which there were no inventions, new processes or innovations, only consumption loans would be made and the rate of interest would be at a minimum or even zero. In this stationary economy (a term he finally adopted in place of static), which does not change of its own initiative, there would be no reason for the rate to be above zero; there would be no (or very little) uncertainty; the supply of, and demand for, capital would always be in perfect equilibrium; and borrowers could obtain any amount of money at current rates. These unreal assumptions, which were made purely for establishing a concept, are virtually reversed in his treatment of interest in a dynamic economy. Here he treats interest largely as a result of economic dynamics. Entrepreneurs or innovators introduce innovations which bring in returns above their cost, thus creating an income out of which in-

[47] *Ibid.*, p. 62.
[48] *Ibid.*, p. 64.

terest can be paid. The rates which prevail reflect the intensity of demand for capital; this demand in turn reflects the availability for profitable investment opportunity. In other words, interest is a result of economic progress, and the interest rate tends to reflect the level of that progress in a dynamic economic society.

The extreme assumptions of the static or zero rate are really not necessary, nor are they sufficiently realistic to be defended.[49] The theory of interest, although important in his model, is in reality only a minor part of his concept of economic dynamics. Economic activity will force interest rates above the zero level; at the same time there are dynamic forces which tend to work in the other direction, i.e., to keep it from rising. Bank credit and voluntary and involuntary savings, which may result from extremely large incomes, would tend to augment supply and hold rates down. Interest is therefore a result of dynamic economic progress which is both a creator and a regulator of the amount and the rate.[50]

Schumpeter's Business Cycle Theory.—Chapter VI, the last one in the *Theory of Economic Development*, deals with the business cycle. Thus Schumpeter recognized the importance of cyclical economic behavior long before his comprehensive two-volume work, *Business Cycles*, appeared in 1939. The latter book covered in great detail the vast historical and analytical literature on the subject of business cycles, but only for supplemental and illustrative purposes in developing the fundamentals laid down in the business cycle chapter of the earlier work. The subsequent discussion is applicable to Schumpeter's views on business cycles as such, not specifically to either one of the two sources.[51]

The first assumption must necessarily be general economic equilibrium, a repetitive process which is the circular flow of economic life.

Every firm in the system is in perfect competitive equilibrium, with its costs, consisting of wages and rents, exactly equal to its receipts. Prices everywhere are equated to average costs; profits are zero; profit opportunities are nonexistent; interest rates are zero; and there is no involuntary unemploy-

---

[49] Schumpeter himself defended his views vigorously in a famous controversy with Böhm-Bawerk, reminiscent of the Menger-Schmoller "Methodenstreit" polemics. For the Böhm-Bawerk controversy see *Zeitschrift für Volkswirtschaft*, XXII (1913).

[50] For further treatment see Arthur Marget's monumental work, *The Theory of Prices*, 2 vols.; also Gottfried Haberler's article, "Schumpeter's Theory of Interest" in the "Schumpeter, Social Scientist" issue of the *Review of Economics and Statistics*, XXXIII (May, 1951), pp. 122 *et sqq.*; also Marget's article in the same issue, "The Monetary Aspects of the Schumpeterian System," pp. 112, *et sqq.*

[51] Professor Schumpeter was one of the pioneer Continental European business cycle theorists. The others were Wicksell in Sweden, Aftalion in France, Tugan-Baranowsky in Russia, and Spiethoff in Germany.

ment of resources. Every household, like every firm, is in full long-run equilibrium, with receipts equal to expenditures, and with a budgetary pattern that cannot, under the existing circumstances, be advantageously altered.[52]

It is this fine adjustment which is disturbed by what he termed "innovations."

An innovation is defined as "the setting up of a new production function,"[53] or the introduction into the economy of a combination of production factors that could not have been made or introduced before. It is something which is introduced as an internal factor, influences the economy, and becomes responsible for the process of economic evolution.[54] Broadly speaking, an innovation may be regarded as a historic and irreversible change in the way of doing things. He does not regard an innovation as resulting from any changes in the production factors, but only as a change in the production function. This would permit new techniques of production, new markets, new products, and new forms of organization. In general these are exogenous factors. Next comes Professor Schumpeter's belief that there is a tendency for innovations to appear in groups or clusters. This is explained by the fact that even though inventions and discoveries are continually being made they are not always commercially profitable at the time they are developed. When an entrepreneur believes that he can safely take the risk of introducing an innovation, he will do so. If he is successful other entrepreneurs will do likewise, not only because he has shown the way but because of his success in the venture. Thus, other innovations follow and more funds are made available for additional innovations, which in turn produce more goods; thus there ensues an acceleration effect of an inflationary nature. Scarcities begin to appear in the factors of production that tend to raise their price, which fact together with the group behavior of all innovators leads to a boom. These actions set up wave-like motions in the levels of economic activity.

As the boom continues disorders begin to appear in the economy. The former innovations, now firmly established as a part of the productive equipment, turn out at lower prices an ever-increasing supply of goods which tends to flood the market. This affects all producers, those who introduced the innovations as well as those who did not adopt them; profits tend to fall and become uncertain; in fact, the whole

[52] Richard V. Clemence and Francis S. Doody, The Schumpeterian System (Cambridge, 1950), p. 9. This is a brief but excellent exposition of Professor Schumpeter's concept of economic dynamics.
[53] Business Cycles, p. 87.
[54] Ibid., p. 86.

future becomes doubtful. Thus it becomes extremely difficult for the entrepreneur to plan and he is increasingly wary in taking risks. If production continues at the new rate, prices fall and the future of present or prospective innovations becomes uncertain. The new as well as the old innovators move to pay off their debts; this means a contraction of credit, reduction of loans, absence of venture capital, and subsequent economic conditions amounting to a collapse. The extent to which this is a completely true picture of dynamic forces at work in economic society depends upon the accuracy with which the effects of innovations are calculated. Errors or miscalculations with respect to the success of the innovation and its impact on the economy will influence the general direction, as well as the speed, of the economic cycle. The foregoing is a brief outline of the generating force of an innovation in business activity.

The business cycle was, in Schumpeter's analysis, an ebb and flow of innovations and subsequent repercussions. When innovations are introduced "entrepreneurs appear en masse" as do their products, which are placed on the markets simultaneously; likewise capital investment "appears en masse at intervals." Hence the innovators, as well as the innovational activity appear "swarmlike" or in "clusters,"[55] and they act as a flood which sets up a wavelike, yet discontinuous, movement in economic life. These actions are endogenous, having as their origin the dynamic forces within the system. The wavelike pulsation may, as a result of innovational activity, pull away from an equilibrium level, but the counter forces, which are also dynamic, will tend to produce a new equilibrium which may be higher than the former level. The theory may be interpreted as a self-perpetuating one, having its origin in the dynamics of the economic society.[56]

Starting, therefore, from a condition of equilibrium, the innovators are responsible for the two primary waves, or a two-phase cycle of prosperity and recession without any definite periodicity. It is possible, however, that the forces will react in such a manner that they will not restore a two-phase pattern, but a secondary wave may follow which will add two more phases—depression and revival—thus making a four-phase cycle. Again no definite periodicity or time interval is assigned to each, and only an examination of the levels of economic activity can determine its extent and presence.

[55] *Theory of Economic Development*, pp. 214, 228, 230, 231.

[56] Whether the theory is purely endogenous or exogenous, or a combination, is a controversial and unsettled issue which is not especially germane to the development of business cycle theory. For further discussion see Professor A. H. Hansen's article, "Schumpeter's Contribution to Business Cycle Theory," *The Review of Economics and Statistics*, *op. cit.*, p. 127.

Schumpeter's business cycle theory, with its emphasis on innovations, has had perhaps more than its fair share of criticism.[57] It seems more important, however, that business cycles (which Schumpeter nowhere defines) should be treated as but a part of his concept of the capitalistic process and system of circular flow. He held to a theory of capitalistic development in which both qualitative and quantitative adjustments in the circular flow are necessary and normal. Schumpeter's contribution to business cycle theory has been great; it ranks even higher when viewed as a contribution to the general understanding of economic behavior.

Schumpeter's last major work was *Capitalism, Socialism and Democracy* (1942), an extremely provocative treatment of political motivation and aspects. This work exhibits all the fine points of Schumpeterian composition: profuse historical references, finely turned phrases, suggestive chapter headings, impelling argumentation, mild invective, popular appeal, and above all a challenge to twentieth-century students of the political and economic future.

The first part deals with Marxian doctrine as a preface "to bear witness to this non-Marxist's belief in the unique importance of that message, an importance which is completely independent of acceptance or rejection" (p. ix). The four brief chapters of the first part treat Marx as a sociologist, an economist, and as a teacher. The next part raises the question, "Can capitalism survive?" To which Schumpeter bluntly answers, "No." The important thing for the student of economics is not the conclusion but the arguments which lead to this conclusion. Schumpeter uses a historical approach in considering the rate of total output over the years and expresses alarm that, despite the rapid increase in total output, unemployment remains a great tragedy; this condition may impair economic development and lead to a situation in which public opinion would support irrational economic methods of financing and administration.

He recognizes that the capitalistic system has served the human race well, and that it has raised the level of output and the standard of living of many people, but he believes that it is engaged in the process of "creative destruction." The glaring inequalities could be removed without impairing the system or reducing over-all productivity; yet despite this, he believes that capitalism is doomed because the very success it has attained is bound to destroy the structure which supports it.

In Part II he asks: "Can socialism work?" to which he answers, "of course it can. . . . There is nothing wrong with the pure logic of so-

---

[57] See Clemence and Doody, *op. cit.*, especially chaps. vi and vii, which treat of the many criticisms of innovations and their impact.

cialism" (p. 172). He contends that a socialist form of society will emerge in time as a result of an inevitable "decomposition" of capitalistic society. He presents these views as a part of his general concept of social dynamics, not as his own hopes or desires. Few accept his paradoxical conclusion that "capitalism is being killed by its achievements," mainly as a result of "vanishing investment opportunity" (p. 112), nor are these views essential to his theories of circular flow. They do, however, offer challenging materials, and highlight the interrelationship of socioeconomic forces so characteristic of his doctrines of economic dynamics.[58]

Reasons Why There Is No Schumpeter School.—One who enjoyed international prestige for so many years, as a result of his original and pioneering work, might well be expected to have a following which would assume the proportions of a school. But such is not the case. There are not Schumpeterians, in the sense that there are Marshallians and Keynesians. His works have been read and studied by hundreds of economists in all countries yet there is no "school" named for him. Many reasons might be cited for this,[59] some of which appear to be germane whereas others border on prejudice or jealousy. Some of the reasons, however, may be traced to his work and its timeliness, and others to the nature of the man himself.

His first work, written in German in 1911, although known to many, was not made accessible to the majority of English scholars until 1934. In the meantime the work and the author as well had been buffeted about as one result of a great war and an aftermath which was uncompromisingly cruel to the writings of many European scholars (notably some of the writings of the Austrian School, Brentano, and others). The economic views of Schumpeter were competing with both theoretical and applied economic doctrines which dealt with world problems in currency and banking, tariffs, inflation, depression, and similar warbred issues.

It may also be argued that while Schumpeter's major writings were highly regarded, they provided no real challenge nor did they offer a focal rallying point. The *Theory of Economic Development* put the circular flow of economic life and general economic equilibrium on a very high level of perfection, but the model had been first developed by Walras and further expanded by Pareto. There was no *cause célèbre* in his theory. It remained comfortably situated in the realm of pure theory. Little relief for a sick world was found in the theory of inno-

[58] See W. J. Baumol, *Economic Dynamics* (1951), chap. iii, "The Dynamics of Marx and Schumpeter."

[59] See Professor Haberler's obituary article, "Joseph Alois Schumpeter," *loc. cit.*, pp. 370-72.

vations; no answer to the pressing world problems was forthcoming. The business cycle study came out in 1939, when a rearmament program was rapidly lifting national income and production to new levels. The book did not gain the recognition warranted by its scholarship.

Schumpeter has, no doubt, suffered from the timing of his publications. Both academic and public interest in Keynes's *General Theory* far surpassed that accorded the Schumpeterian thesis; in fact, the interest in national income analysis completely eclipsed the economics of business cycles. Had Schumpeter, who was an anti-Keynesian, allowed some of the Keynesian views to enter his business cycle discussion it could well have been "required reading," for what student would not have enjoyed a skirmish if not a battle of the giants.[60] Schumpeter's *Business Cycles* did not offer a positive program, whereas Keynes not only had a program but even predicted the final outcome. Apparently, there was little room for any other economics in the decade after the publication of the *General Theory* in 1936.

It may also be observed that Schumpeter was not a staunch defender of any "ism" or cause. He was a critic of socialist doctrines, yet he found truth in them; he hated Marxism yet he acknowledged the brilliance of "the great teacher of the socialist creed"; he was not a staunch advocate of capitalism, yet he was critical of New Dealism, which attempted to plan the next move of capitalism. He was probably a conservative with a penchant for open-minded political views and an unwillingness to show a reformer's zeal or an enthusiasm for any particular dogma. His objective scholarship made close affiliation an impossibility. Despite his criticisms of doctrines and his unwillingness to join any particular camp, he was held in high esteem by defenders of all shades of political and economic doctrine. There can be no doubt that scholarship has suffered a loss from the indifference shown by Keynes and Schumpeter to each other, especially when the Keynesian and the Schumpeterian theories could easily have been made complementary.[61]

The definite Schumpeterian characteristics could be further expanded. Enough have been presented to identify them and to show that there is no "Schumpeterian School." While he will, no doubt, always claim highest respect as an original thinker, it is unlikely that a generation will sometime arise and call him blessed.

It is not to Schumpeter's discredit that no "school" bears his name. Few have earned this honor. He left a rich heritage of original con-

[60] There is no reference to Schumpeter in the *General Theory* or in the *Treatise on Money*. Keynes refers only to a summary of the innovation theory made by W. C. Mitchell.

[61] See Arthur Smithies, "Schumpeter and Keynes," *The Review of Economics and Statistics, op. cit.,* p. 163 *et sqq.*

tributions that will forever bear witness to his greatness. At present, it appears that his greatest contribution will remain his explanation of the process of capitalistic development. Into the explanation of the circular flow (*Kreislauf*) of economic life is woven a vast array of qualitative and historical materials drawn from all the social sciences. The reasons he assigned for the wave-like behavior of the economic data, whether one subscribes to the innovation concept or not, are a great aid in understanding business cycles. His emphasis on the tendency of capital investment to be made in clusters is a very significant contribution, especially when investment is considered as affecting the whole economy. All these points are highlights of a Schumpeterian model of economic development drawn in broad strokes by a firm hand. Future critics will decide whether it is economic art.

Summary.—The foregoing treatment is admittedly not intended to be exhaustive or all-inclusive. One must be eclectic both in the choice of personalities and as to the points of emphasis. The persons considered in this chapter have had important parts in developing and shaping the general direction of basic economic thought. In specific fields, such as monopolies and trusts, transportation, currency and banking, econometrics, government regulation, international economics, business cycles, fiscal policy, wage theory, and so on—a most expansive list —splendid work has been done by many in both Europe and America. The occupational specialization made famous by Smith in his pinmaking example has been practised in *academia*, as in the medical profession, until it is nearly impossible to find a "general practitioner" in either field. Few, if any, would undertake today a complete treatise that would embrace the whole of social economy. The choice of emphasis rests with the writer himself. Pigou chose to highlight the welfare aspect of political economy, which Marshall wished to do, but in which he probably never succeeded. The Swedish economists likewise chose their own fields of emphasis; Wicksell carried on in an improved Walrasian pattern whereas Cassel advocated quantitative measurements but gave more attention to monetary theory. Schumpeter regarded economic development as basic and overlooked monopoly and monopolistic competition, or at least they were allotted smaller dimensions by him. The post-Marshallian writers, like those of every other period, tend to mirror the issues and interests of their own day. Only after time has tested and mellowed their work will it be known what endures.

27

Retrospect and Prospect

The foregoing chapters sketched in some detail the highlights in the development of economic thought. Schools and individual writers were considered in their setting, and their contributions to economic thought were presented. Much of the early doctrine has been retained and is now a part of economic thought and language, and equally much has been forgotten. Economics is, relatively speaking, a new science. Even though certain economic practices are as old as any recorded history, economics, as it is known today, is a new discipline. It is well to recall that the first works in the field, which today are regarded as noteworthy and original, were not written by professional economists. Cantillon was a banker, Quesnay was a physician, Adam Smith was a professor of moral philosophy, Ricardo was a successful stockbroker, Malthus was both a preacher and a teacher, and John Stuart Mill was a logician and philosopher as well as an employee of the East India Company. Others were doctors, landlords, journalists, politicians, reformers, traders, and so on.

In the nineteenth century only a few universities taught the subject of political economy as such, and likewise only a few had chairs of political economy. The high point in the teaching of economics in England came with Marshall's work at Cambridge University in the years after 1890. The teaching of economics in American universities generally followed the same pattern. The works of J. B. Say and J. S. Mill, together with some books on principles written at an elementary level for the purpose of presenting a simplified classical version, were used as texts in both English and American universities in the era before the writings of Alfred Marshall and J. B. Clark. It is not implied that economic scholarship was unaware of the developments—such as they were —but there was little popular demand for the subject.

The best of the theories associated with the classical and the Austrian "schools" were used by Alfred Marshall in conjunction with his own theories to produce a work which set a new level of attainment. The

655

theories of Marshall became gospel and their presentation, terminology, organization, and emphasis set the standard for subsequent work. Economics had by now become an accepted discipline and claimed a place with other social sciences.

The paths which led to the Marshallian synthesis were long and tortuous. Many minds had a part in developing the theories, a goodly number of which grew and survived criticism. Economic change has always had a part in shaping doctrines, and in many instances it was the doctrine which brought about change in economic practices. In general, however, political policies tended to reflect national aims and objectives rather than finespun economic theory. It was many years before theories of economics played a dominant role in national policy.

The role of criticism in the development of economic thought must not be overlooked. Smith's theories were attacked, as were those of all the classical school. The most telling of all criticisms was made by the socialists, especially, in Marx's *Das Kapital* (1867). This work had a profound effect not only upon accepted doctrine but upon the entire world. It was more than an attack on doctrines; it was basically an attack on the socioeconomic structure of capitalism. Even though Marx added little or nothing to the broad development of economic thought, he must be regarded as responsible for the highest level of criticism yet reached. Attacks by others usually were directed at institutional deficiencies and shortcomings within the framework of a capitalistic society. Indeed, criticism appears to have been a favorite diversion of most writers in political economy.

If one may regard the Marshallian principles as a high point—or better still, the starting point of modern economics—the years since its inception in 1890 have been strewn with economic wreckage and marked by violent criticism as well. These were also years of "model building" —a term in great current use. Taking the cue from the exact sciences it was observed by later students that classical economics actually used a model, although no writer used the term. Classical writers were disposed to think in terms of a large number of small economic units: each person strove to maximize his own gain, with the result that the whole of economic society automatically reached high levels of efficiency and utilization of resources. This schema permitted simple assumptions from which deductions could be made concerning supply, demand, price, and so on. Hence it could be said that, barring abnormalities, an end result could be deduced. This was the world of microscopic analysis. Individual elements of the economy were examined without any special relationship to the whole.

The equilibrium theory of Marshall was temporarily abandoned by some who deserted to the ranks of the "institutionalists" in the 1920's;

theory was abandoned rather than attacked critically at this time. Greater interest was centered in producing particular studies than in developing theoretical refinements.

The first significant advance in economic analysis for forty years came in 1933 with the studies in monopolistic or imperfect competition. Chamberlin and Robinson analyzed market situations and found that industrial production and markets were neither purely competitive nor purely monopolistic but a hybrid with elements of both monopoly and competition. Economic analysis should therefore be readjusted to accommodate this more realistic approach.

The new theories were less than enthusiastically accepted by the orthodox equilibrium economists. They held that the classical model was sufficiently flexible to accommodate the extremes which were, after all, only exceptions. The original model of a large number of small producing units, and a possible second model of one producer with a monopoly control over the amount supplied, were challenged from the standpoint of reality. The new doctrines were received gradually and became a part of price theory. Empirical studies followed which not only supported the theory but had telling effects on government policies of regulation and on antitrust legislation. Further studies have been made in the matter of oligopoly, in which an even smaller number of producers may exercise control over prices by actions short of collusion. Price theory at present has made adjustments to accommodate the less-than-purely-competitive market conditions. It is probable that economists are seeking "representative" conditions which Marshall also sought but never quite found.

The Keynesian proposals in 1936 drew attention away from price theory. Monopolistic competition theories, although challenging, were of little help in curing or even relieving the problems caused by the great depression. The almost complete change of emphasis from price economics to an aggregative approach revolutionized not only theoretical analysis but national policy as well. The influence of the Keynesian doctrines on teaching, on individual careers in public service, and on policies in both war and peace in practically every government is a matter of record. The Keynesian influence has proved to be the dominant one in the first half of the twentieth century.

The Keynesian theories touched off a great pyrotechnical display of polemics which for a time threatened to split the economists into sharp groups, pro and con: economists tended to group themselves behind new fiscal-income theorists versus old classical money-price theorists; old classicists versus new Keynesians; interventionists versus noninterventionists; or even age versus youth. The polemics have subsided and each side has given some ground.

The furor created in the first few years after the Keynesian theses were proposed has proved to be more like a rebellion than a revolution. Economists are more or less reconciled to the government's having a larger share in economic activity than ever before but not to the extent of complete surrender to government. In a sense, economists have re-examined the classical theories to find what is responsible for the wealth of nations. Micro-studies of wealth, such as occupied the attention of early writers for many years, gave way to macro-examinations of how wealth was created, assembled, maintained, and distributed in the aggregate. Microscopic studies of firms, markets, consumer choice, and the like still occupy a prominent place. In fact, there are many who hold that the scientific approach to macro-studies is through micro-analysis.

Schools of Economic Thought.—It is a dangerous and somewhat un-profitable pastime to attempt to classify economists or place them in "schools." Extreme difficulty is encountered in defining a "school" in accurate terms and the only criterion for including someone in a school seems to be the nature of his writings. The lines of demarcation for delineating groups or schools have grown dim. It appears, however, that economists fit into fairly well-defined generic groups: first, theoretical economists, subdivided into the classical theorists and those who emphasize the aggregate analysis; second, the institutionalists.

The first subdivision of the theoretical group—here identified as classicists—is thought of as those who hold with some tenacity to the money-price analysis of the economy. The analysis makes use of supply, demand, and price as mutually determining forces operating under some degree of laissez faire. This does not imply adherence to an eighteenth-century laissez-faire economy with all its evils. Rather it implies a capitalistic economy with the profit motive, with competition somewhat less than perfect, and with individual initiative, cooperation, private property, and freedom of choice all operating within a friendly but nonpaternal government. This grouping admits neoclassicists, welfarists, and all those whose emphasis has been on micro-studies of the economy. Those who emphasize the aggregative approach are concerned with the macro factors which influence, and in turn are influenced by, the whole economy. National income, levels of investment and employment, savings and consumption, fiscal policy—all are viewed as being of greater importance than pricing of goods and services. This division includes Keynesians, post-Keynesians, and national income theorists of all shades of conviction. Such a scheme of grouping does not force anyone to be a pro or con with respect to any particular creed, issue, dogma, or "ism." It permits those who went overboard in embracing Keynesian doctrines without qualifications to return to the fold of price theorists.

The second generic grouping is identified as institutionalists. This term is not defined or used in the narrow sense that it had when first introduced in the 1920's. It is intended to include all those who seek to explain economic behavior and economic institutions within the present socio-economic order. Again two subdivisions may be identified: those interested in describing institutional arrangements within the economy; the other group mainly concerned with changes within the institutional framework of society. The differences in emphasis involve mainly the place and the importance of a particular institution in society. The former is a historical approach; the latter implies social objectives. Both are interested in objective appraisals of end results as affecting public policy. Both micro- and macro-studies have been produced by the institutionalists in trade unionism, price policy, taxation and public debt, national income, farm subsidies, monopoly, small business, and in many other segments of the national economy.

The two so-called schools are not antithetical to one another, nor is the grouping especially significant since neither group shows any great missionary spirit for its own cause. There seems to be a tendency toward fusion of ideas; the classicists become less model-minded and use empirical research, and the institutionalists become less behavior-conscious and more quantitative and specific.

Some Present-Day Trends.—The most outstanding feature of modern economics is the use of mathematics in analysis and exposition. Ever since Cournot's work in 1838, mathematics in some form has been used by many economists, notably Jevons, Walras, Pareto, Wicksell, Edgeworth, Marshall, and Fisher. It has now attained levels of perfection far in advance of the original, simple presentations. The interest in mathematics and statistics is indicated to some extent by the growth of membership in the Econometric Society, which has about 1,500 members. This is an international group of scholars interested in a theoretical-mathematical-statistical approach to economic data. They have developed a highly complex language which is difficult for the non-mathematical economists to follow. The theory of games and probability analysis has attracted much attention and offers distinct possibilities. It is applicable to model building and may be made to simulate human actions under different circumstances. Additional areas of research may be opened up by the complex computing machines which make possible the solutions of many simultaneous equations. A danger lies in eliminating the human element from economic analysis and thus removing economics from the social sciences where it belongs. In any event, mathematics and statistics have widened the horizon of empirical research into both micro- and aggregate economics.

The areas of micro- and macroeconomics apparently offer the most challenging questions in the future. They may develop into joint, rather than competitive, areas of study. World conditions, more than anything else, are responsible for the attention given to macroeconomics. Mutual interdependence of nations is a reality and a definite factor influencing national policy. The power centered in the government of most states has forced the use of economic measures on both national and international levels. Economists, who have had a large part in developing the measures, have used many new tools for measurement of economic data as they have learned more and more about economic behavior under different stimuli. They are also responsible in large part for carrying out the economic measures. It is at this point that micro-analysis is enlisted to ascertain how given institutions will function under different stimuli. For example, it is well to know, not only that price control is desirable from the point of view of consumers' real income, but also how price control will affect production in a free economy. National income economics, business cycle theory, and price economics can all be accommodated in the sphere of economic theorizing and research, with much room to spare. Perhaps, in time, all the significant empiric data of the many fields of economics will be brought together and coordinated with a high degree of perfection which will achieve the goal of accurate economic prediction.

The extent to which that goal is attained will depend on the success achieved in isolating originating causes and applying effective controls. For many years the recurring ups and downs of business activity, or the business cycle, were regarded as temporary deviations from equilibrium which would automatically readjust themselves in accordance with an economy regulated by price. Problems of mass employment and mass unemployment were nonexistent prior to the advent of the machine age, or until about the last quarter of the eighteenth century. Employment and unemployment have always been problems, but since the last quarter of the nineteenth century they have been major economic problems. Even the charges of Marx that depressions were characteristic of a capitalistic economy did not force any significant re-examination of the original laissez-faire attitudes. War-induced unemployment and the depressions of the past thirty or more years led to realistic study of business cycles. No longer is the study of business cycles approached as a simple exercise in logic but with great realism and technical refinement, since they constitute a grave economic problem which threatens national existence. Great efforts have been made to isolate the causes of business cycles both by private researchers and by agencies set up for that purpose. There has been a merging of business cycle theory with national income analysis, for in the final analysis both are only different aspects of the problem of how to keep men and resources employed. The economic interdependence of nations is such that researchers must look for world-wide influencing factors, which contribute to produce an economic balance or imbalance and force governments to take corrective measures.

There can be no doubt that the first fifty years of the present century have seen more government participation in economic activity than any time in the past. Nor is the end in sight. The trend is irreversible. Government interference is widening, and controls have materially changed the whole structure of economic activity and restricted economic freedom. The activities of the fascist states of Europe, while they lasted, were probably extreme examples. The controls exercised by a strong central government over every phase of life in the Soviet Union represent the present-day extreme, whereas the measures adopted by the Labor Government in Great Britain represent less stringent controls applied with some degree of popular consent. Under the guise—or disguise—of economic planning, there is no limit to which a government may not go in assuming economic functions. In every case thus far known in the recorded history of governmental planning it has meant a loss of economic freedom. However, in a world in which states are living in fear of other states the choice no longer seems to be either freedom or security. Most states have accepted security—largely as a result of violence or a threat of violence—and have foregone freedom. If the present clash of ideologies continues, the likelihood of ever attaining both freedom and security becomes less. Extreme nationalism has developed economic weapons less spectacular than those used in warfare but equally devastating. An atmosphere supercharged with defense (or war) ideologies is not conducive to such freedom of thought and speculation as was present during previous periods when great economic thoughts were developed.

The role of government appears in practically every page of the development of economic thought. Extreme views have characterized economic thinking ever since the beginning and are equally applicable to the opposed groups today. Many, perhaps even most, theoretical price-economists would prefer to see production, distribution, exchange, and consumption of goods controlled by economic forces operating under conditions of so-called "free" private economy without legal restrictions superimposed by a government. This does not mean anything even remotely resembling the excesses which characterized the unbridled laissez faire immediately following the industrial revolution. No extremist would defend this. There is, however, a sphere in which competition can be effective and a price-and-profit structure can prevail; scientific developments leading to greater output and efficiency will reach high levels of perfection and incentives will remain which the system rewards. It was under such a system that the high levels of industrial output of the Western World were achieved. Despite all propaganda arguments to the contrary, there is no substitute for the profit incentive. Such a system of competitive capitalism is, admittedly, wasteful. Men and resources may have periods of idleness. Regrettable as this is, it seems preferable to complete surrender to government, no matter what form that may take. Perfect freedom from government controls and complete government regulation are extremes—at least in theory, if not always in practice. They are the extremes of early eighteenth-century conditions in England versus the twentieth-century Soviet dictatorship.

The trend toward greater governmental regulation is both a cause and a result of present world conditions. The political philosophies of authoritarian control, such as fascism, communism, and socialism, demand strong central government control of every phase of economic life. As a result of the ravages of two world wars, together with several years of depression, every nation has been obliged to adopt control measures of different degrees of severity. Every nation has applied controls designed to further the war or defense efforts and in most instances these nations were unable to abandon the controls at the end of hostilities. Judging from the control measures alone, the wars seem to have continued and peace has not been and may not be restored. In the opinion of many, the problem is no longer a matter of control versus noncontrol in the economic system. The question is how much control should the state assume and how little is to be left to free enterprise.

The prevailing economic thought for the past twenty years has tended to support a larger share of government planning, regulation, and control of economic activity. National planning, a large share of which has been done by economists, has brought theory and practice together on a national scale. There is a strong indication that we are returning to "political economy," since political considerations play such a predominant role in "economics." In other words, we may be tending to accept political economy in the eighteenth-century sense of the term, which implies a study of measures designed to be helpful to the state, rather than specific theories dealing with wealth, income distribution, taxes, tariffs, and the like. This view is not expressed as a prediction but as a tendency which might be reversed, to some degree at least, if world conditions should change. So long as nations continue to gird for war and to live under a constant threat of war one may expect the efforts of everyone, including economists, to be pointed in one general direction. Total war demands the total effort of all. Complete economic freedom of both thought and action does not flourish in an unfree climate, such as looms at the middle of this century.

What Can Be Learned From the History of Economic Thought?— We might all cherish the pious hope that the familiar remark, "All we learn from history is that we learn nothing from history," is untrue when applied to economic thought. Unfortunately, however, this statement seems to apply to the history of economics as well as to political history. Many of the causes of strife and conflict which are economic in character remain with us. The world has seen a recrudescence of mercantilism with its many measures of control. International trade follows opportunistic principles, not the laws of comparative cost. Prejudices, biases, and ulterior motives which found their way into early economic doctrines are, lamentably, still with us. There also seems to be just as much interest in nostrums as in the days of John Law. The English public relief which was denounced so vigorously by Malthus and Ricardo as a socioeconomic evil, has become an accepted practice (admittedly with some changes) in most nations, in slightly different form for social and economic purposes but with political overtones. Pressure groups and special interests are far more effective today than at any time when the guilds were most powerful. Writers on economic subjects have always reflected the prevailing attitudes and practices of the times; the most objective efforts to find the truth have been colored by the environmental factors of the period. Indeed it is possible that, allowing for a range of circumstances which prevailed at a given time, many or even most of the early writers were recording truth as it appeared to them. A change in the circumstances would then invalidate the doctrines.

Thus it seems that the few doctrines which have survived to this day are universal economic truths. Doubtless one is obliged to say that few have survived. Economists, like statesmen, have not been clothed with omniscience; this lack accounts to some extent for their inability and even unwillingness to forecast. The forces which affect economic behavior in the present century are so varied and complex that the economist must recognize with humility that precious little is known about them. It is only in this spirit that the problem of diagnosis and analysis of the forces which determine the course of economic affairs can be approached.

The most hopeful development in the direction of building a workable body of economic thought comes as a result of the many exploratory studies of the economy. We know more about ourselves, statistically at least, than ever before. The extent to which this knowledge can be put to use in directing the course of economic events remains to be seen. Contemporary measures, even though almost a quarter-century old, are not yet matters of history. Time has its own peculiar methods of selecting what shall become permanent additions to the history of economic thought, just as it does with all knowledge.

Bibliography

The following bibliography is a selected list from the many works which deal with economic materials. It is intended only as a representative, not an inclusive, list. Economic literature in the past fifty years has been enriched by materials which appear in the numerous journals. References appearing in the footnotes have not, as a rule, been included with the chapter bibliography.

I. General References

ASHLEY, W. J. *An Introduction to English Economic History and Theory.* London: Longmans, Green & Co., 1893.

BLANQUI, J. H. *History of Political Economy in Europe.* Translated from the 4th French edition by E. I. Leonard. New York: G. P. Putnam's Sons, 1880.

BONAR, JAMES. *Philosophy and Political Economy*, 2d ed. London: George Allen & Unwin, 1909.

BOUCKE, O. F. *The Development of Economics, 1750-1921.* New York: The Macmillan Co., 1921.

COSSA, L. *Introduction to the Study of Political Economy.* (3d ed., Milan, 1892). Translated by L. Dyer. London: The Macmillan Co., 1893.

FERGUSON, J. M. *Landmarks of Economic Thought*, 2d ed. New York: Longmans, Green & Co., 1950.

FRASER, L. M. *Economic Thought and Language.* London: A. & C. Black, 1937.

GIDE, CHARLES, and RIST, CHARLES. *History of Economic Doctrines*, 2d ed. Translated from the French by R. Richards. New York: D. C. Heath & Co., 1949.

GRAY, ALEXANDER. *The Development of Economic Doctrines.* New York: Longmans, Green & Co., 1933.

GRUCHY, A. G. *Modern Economic Thought; the American Contribution.* New York: Prentice-Hall, Inc., 1947.

HANEY, L. H. *History of Economic Thought*, 4th ed. New York: The Macmillan Co., 1949.

HEIMANN, E. *History of Economic Doctrines.* New York: Oxford University Press, 1945.

HOMAN, P. T. *Contemporary Economic Thought.* New York: Harper & Bros., 1928.

INGRAM, J. K. *A History of Political Economy.* London: A. & C. Black, 1888; enlarged edition, 1915.

NORMANO, J. F. *The Spirit of American Economics.* New York: John Day Co., 1943.

PECK, HARVEY. *Economic Thought and its Institutional Background.* New York: Rinehart & Co., 1935.

PRICE, L. L. *Short History of Political Economy in England from Adam Smith to Alfred Marshall.* London: Methuen & Co., 1891.

ROLL, ERIC. *A History of Economic Thought*, rev. ed. New York: Prentice-Hall, Inc., 1942.

SCOTT, W. A. *The Development of Economics.* New York: Appleton-Century-Crofts, Inc., 1933.

SPANN, O. *The History of Economics.* Translated from the 19th German edition. New York: W. W. Norton & Co., 1930.

SURANGI-UNGER, E. T. *Economics of the Twentieth Century.* Translated from the German edition, Jena, 1926. New York: W. W. Norton & Co., 1931.

WHITTAKER, E. *A History of Economic Ideas.* New York: Longmans, Green & Co., 1940.

ZWEIG, F. *Economic Ideas: A Study of Historical Perspectives.* New York: Prentice-Hall, Inc., 1950.

II. Readings

ABBOTT, L. D. (ed.). *Masterworks of Economics.* New York: Doubleday & Co., 1947.

BURTT, E. A. (ed.). *The English Philosophers from Bacon to Mill.* New York: Modern Library, 1939.

JOHNSON, E. A. J. *Predecessors of Adam Smith.* New York: Prentice-Hall, Inc., 1937.

McCONNELL, JOHN W. *Basic Teachings of the Great Economists.* New York: Barnes & Noble, 1943.

MONROE, A. E. *Early Economic Thought.* Cambridge: Harvard University Press, 1924.

———. *Monetary Theories Before Adam Smith.* Cambridge: Harvard University Press, 1923.

PATTERSON, S. H. *Readings in the History of Economic Thought.* New York: McGraw-Hill Book Co., Inc., 1932.

III. Periodicals

English:
American Economic Review, American Economic Association, 1911- . (1887-1910 as *Publications.*)
American Journal of Economics and Sociology, Lancaster, Pa. 1941-
American Journal of Sociology, University of Chicago, 1895- .
American Political Science Review, American Political Science Association, 1906- .
Annals of American Academy of Political and Social Science, 1890-
Canadian Journal of Economics and Political Science, Canadian Political Science Association, 1935- .
Econometrica, Economic Society, 1933- .
Economic History, Royal Economic Society, 1926- . (Vols. 1-4 as *Economic History Series.*)
Economic Journal, Royal Economic Society, 1891- .
Economica, London School of Economics and Political Science, Vols. 1-13, 1921-33; n.s., Vol. 1, 1934- .
Journal of American Statistical Association, 1888/89- .
Journal of Economic History, Economic History Association, 1941- .
Journal of Political Economy, University of Chicago, 1892- .
Manchester School, Victoria University of Manchester, 1930- .
Political Science Quarterly, Columbia University, 1886- .
Quarterly Journal of Economics, Harvard University, 1886- .
Review of Economic Statistics, Committee on Economic Research, Harvard University, 1919-47; superseded by *Review of Economics and Statistics,* 1948- .
Review of Economic Studies, London School of Economics Studies, 1933- .

Social Research, New School for Social Research, 1934- .
Southern Economic Journal, Southern Economic Association, 1933- .

German:
Archiv für Sozialwissenschaft und Sozialpolitik, Berlin, Tübingen u. Leipzig, 1888-1933. (B. 1-18 als *Archiv für soziale Gesetzgebung und Statistik.*)
Jahrbuch für Gesetzebung, Verwaltung und Volkswirtschaft im deutschen Reich, see *Schmollers Jahrbuch.*
Jahrbuch für Nationalökonomie und Statistik, Jena, 1863- .
Schmollers Jahrbuch, Leipzig, 1877- .
Schriften des Vereins für Sozialpolitik, Munich, Leipzig, 1873-1939.
Zeitschrift für Nationalökonomie, Vienna, 1929- .
Zeitschrift für Sozialwissenschaft, Berlin, Leipzig, B. 1-12, 1898-1909; n. F. B. 1-12, 1910-21.
Zeitschrift für Staats- und Volkswirtschaft, Vienna, 1890-1924.

French:
Journal des économistes, Paris, 1841- .
Revue d'économie politique, Paris, 1887-1940.
Revue d'histoire économique et sociale, Paris, 1908-
Revue des sciences économiques, Liége, 1926- .

Other foreign languages:
Economia, Trieste & Rome, 1-13, 1923-27; n.s., 1928- .
Ekonomisk Tidsskrift, Stockholm, 1921- . (English ed. also.)
Giornale degli economisti e annali di economia, Bologna & Rome, 1939-
Nationalökonomisk Tidsskrift, Copenhagen, 1873- .
Tijdschrift voor Economie en Sociologie, Ghent & Louvain, 1935- .

Chapter 2

BEWER, J. A. *The Literature of the Old Testament.* New York: Columbia University Press, 1933.
The Biblical Encyclopedia. 3 vols. Edited by J. C. GRAY and G. M. ADAMS. Cleveland: F. M. Barton Co., 1910.
CLEMEN, CARL. *Religions of the World.* New York: Harcourt, Brace & Co., 1931.
CONDER, C. R. *Judas Maccabaeus.* New York: G. P. Putnam's Sons, 1883.
——. *The Survey of Western Palestine.* London: The Committee of the Palestine Exploration Fund, 1881.
——. *The Survey of Eastern Palestine.* London: The Committee of the Palestine Exploration Fund, 1889.
DUMMELOW, J. R. *A Commentary on the Holy Bible.* New York: The Macmillan Co., 1917.
FOAKES-JACKSON, F. J. *The Biblical History of the Hebrews to the Christian Era.* Cambridge, Eng.: W. Heffner & Sons Ltd., 1921.
——. *A Brief Biblical History.* New York: George H. Doran Co., 1923.
HOSKYNS, E. C. *The Epistle to the Romans.* London: Oxford University Press, 1938.
The Jewish Encyclopedia. New York: Funk & Wagnalls Co., 1901-06.
The Jewish People, Past and Present. New York: Central Yiddish Culture Organization, 1946.
KAUTILYA. *Arthasâstra.* Translated by R. Shamasastry. Bangalore: The Government Press, 1915.
KUMAR, SANTOSH. *The Economic History of Ancient India.* Calcutta: Mita Press, 1925.

MULLER, MAX (ed.). *The Sacred Books of the East.* 50 vols. Oxford: Clarendon Press, 1879-1910.
RENAN, ERNEST. *A History of the People of Israel.* Boston: Roberts Bros., 1889-95.
———. *The History of the Origins of Christianity.* London: Mathieson & Co., 18??.
SANDERS, H. K., and H. T. FOWLER. *Biblical History and Literature.* New York: Charles Scribner's Sons, 1907.
TERRY, MILTON S. *Biblical Dogmatics.* New York: Eaton & Marius, 1907.

Chapter 3

BARKER, ERNEST. *Greek Political Theory.* London: Methuen & Co., 1918.
———. *The Political Thought of Plato and Aristotle.* New York: G. P. Putnam's Sons, 1906.
CORNFORD, F. M. *The Republic of Plato.* New York: Oxford University Press, 1945.
DEMOS, RAPHAEL (ed.). *The Philosophy of Plato.* New York: Charles Scribner's Sons, 1939.
ELLWOOD, C. A. *The Story of Social Philosophy.* New York: Prentice-Hall, Inc., 1938.
———. *The History of Social Philosophy.* New York: Prentice-Hall, Inc., 1939.
GETTELL, R. G. *History of Political Thought.* New York: Appleton-Century-Crofts, Inc., 1925.
GONNARD, RENÉ. *Histoire des Doctrines Economiques.* Paris, 1921-22.
JOWETT, BENJAMIN (trans. and ed.). *The Dialogues of Plato.* 4 vols. New York: Scribner, Armstrong & Co., 1876.
LAIDLER, H. W. *A History of Socialist Thought.* (1927); Revised as *Social-Economic Movements.* New York: The Thomas Y. Crowell Co., 1945.
LICHTENBERGER, J. P. *The Development of Social Theory.* New York: Appleton-Century-Crofts, Inc., 1923.
McKEON, RICHARD. *Introduction to Aristotle.* New York: Modern Library, 1947.
ROGERS, A. K. *A Student's History of Philosophy.* New York: The Macmillan Co., 1902; 3d ed., 1933.
TAYLOR, A. E. *Plato, the Man and His Work,* 3d ed. London: Methuen & Co., 1929.
———. *Aristotle.* London: T. Nelson & Sons, 1943.
WALFORD, EDWARD. *Aristotle's Politics and Economics.* London: Bohn's Classical Library, 1853.
WHEELWRIGHT, PHILIP. *Aristotle.* New York: The Odyssey Press, 1935.
ZIMMERN, A. E. *The Greek Commonwealth.* New York: Oxford University Press, 1924.

Chapter 4

ANDREADES, A. M. *A History of Greek Public Finance.* Cambridge: Harvard University Press, 1933.
BEER, MAX. *Social Struggles in Antiquity.* New York: International Publishers, 1929.
BOTSFORD, G. W. *Hellenic History.* New York: The Macmillan Co., 1922.
ELLWOOD, C. A. *The History of Social Philosophy.* New York: Prentice-Hall, Inc., 1939.
GETTELL, R. G. *History of Political Thought.* New York: Appleton-Century-Crofts, Inc., 1924.
LICHTENBERGER, J. P. *The Development of Social Theory.* New York: Appleton-Century-Crofts, Inc., 1923.
LOT, FERDINAND. *The End of the Ancient World.* New York: Alfred A. Knopf, 1931.

LOUIS, PAUL. *Ancient Rome at Work.* New York: Alfred A. Knopf, 1927.
OLIVER, E. H. *Roman Economic Conditions at the Close of the Republic.* Toronto: University of Toronto Library, 1907.
ROSTOVZEV, M. I. *Social and Economic History of the Roman Empire.* New York: Oxford University Press, 1926.
SABINE, G. H. *A History of Political Theory,* rev. ed. New York: Henry Holt & Co., 1950.
TENNY, FRANK. *Economic History of Rome.* Baltimore: Johns Hopkins University Press, 1933.
———. *An Economic Survey of Ancient Rome.* Baltimore: Johns Hopkins University Press, 1933.

Chapter 5

AQUINAS, THOMAS. *Summa Theologica.* 20 vols. Translated by the English Dominican Fathers. London, 1911-1925.
BEER, MAX. *Early British Economics.* London: George Allen & Unwin, 1938.
BRAUER, THEODORE, et al. *Thomistic Principles in a Catholic School.* St. Louis: B. Herder Book Co., 1943.
CHESTERTON, G. K. *Saint Thomas Aquinas.* London: Hodder & Stoughton, 1933.
COULTON, G. C. *Medieval Panorama.* New York: The Macmillan Co., 1938.
D'ARCY, M. C. *Thomas Aquinas: Selected Writings.* (Everyman's Library.) New York: E. P. Dutton Co., 1939.
ELLWOOD, C. A. *The History of Social Philosophy.* New York: Prentice-Hall, Inc., 1939.
FLUBACHER, JOSEPH F. *The Concept of Ethics in the History of Economics.* New York: Vantage Press, Inc., 1950.
GILSON, ETIENNE. *The Philosophy of St. Thomas Aquinas.* St. Louis: B. Herder Book Co., 1939.
GONNARD, RENÉ. *Histoire des Doctrines Economiques.* Paris, 1921-22.
HEARNSHAW, F. J. C. *Medieval Contributions to Modern Civilization.* London: G. G. Harrap & Co., 1921.
———. *The Social and Political Ideas of Some Great Medieval Thinkers.* London: G. G. Harrap & Co., 1923.
O'BRIEN, GEORGE. *An Essay on Medieval Economic Teaching.* New York: Longmans, Green & Co., 1920.
PIRENNE, H. *Medieval Cities.* Princeton: Princeton University Press, 1925.
RAMBAUD, JOSEPH. *Histoire des Doctrines Economiques.* Paris: L. Larousse, 1899.
TAWNEY, R. H. *Religion and the Rise of Capitalism.* New York: Harcourt, Brace & Co., 1947.

Chapter 6

ANGELL, J. W. *The Theory of International Prices.* Cambridge: Harvard University Press, 1926.
BEER, MAX. *Early British Economics from the XIIIth to the Middle of the XVIIIth Century.* London: George Allen & Unwin, 1938.
BUCK, P. W. *The Politics of Mercantilism.* New York: Henry Holt & Co., 1942.
CHILD, JOSIAH. *A New Discourse Upon Trade.* London, 1690.
CLAPHAM, J. H. *A Concise Economic History of Britain from the Earliest Times to 1750.* Cambridge: Cambridge University Press, 1949.
CUNNINGHAM, WM. *The Growth of English Industry and Commerce.* Cambridge: Cambridge University Press, 1882.
FORTREY, SAMUEL. *England's Interest Considered.* Cambridge, 1663.
GREW, NEHEMIAH. *The Means of a Most Ample Increase of the Wealth and Strength of England.* London, 1707.
HALES, JOHN. *A Discourse of Common Weal.* London, 1548.

HECKSCHER, E. F. *Mercantilism.* 2 vols. London: George Allen & Unwin, 1935.
JOHNSON, E. A. J. *Predecessors of Adam Smith.* New York: Prentice-Hall, Inc., 1937.
LIPSON, EPHRAIM. *The Economic History of England.* London: A. & C. Black, 1915.
LODGE, E. C. *Sully, Colbert, and Turgot.* London: Methuen & Co., 1931.
MONROE, A. E. *Monetary Theory Before Adam Smith.* Cambridge: Harvard University Press, 1923.
MUN, THOMAS. *Englands Treasure by Forraign Trade.* London, 1664.
NORTH, SIR DUDLEY. *Discourses on Trade.* London, 1691.
PETTY, SIR WILLIAM. *Discourse on Political Arithmetick.* London, 1691.
STEUART, SIR JAMES. *An Inquiry into the Principles of Political Economy.* 2 vols. London, 1767.
VINER, JACOB. "English Theories of Foreign Trade before Adam Smith," *Journal of Political Economy*, XXXVIII (1930), pp. 249-301, 404-57.

Chapter 7

BRIDGES, J. H. *France Under Richelieu and Colbert.* London, 1912.
CLÉMENT, PIERRE. *Histoire de Colbert et de son Administration.* Paris: Perrin et cie, 1892.
COLE, CHARLES W. *Colbert and a Century of French Mercantilism.* 2 vols. New York: Columbia University Press, 1939.
———. *French Mercantilism, 1683-1700.* New York: Columbia University Press, 1943.
———. *French Mercantilist Policy Before Colbert.* New York: R. R. Smith, 1931.
HEURLE, VICTOR DE. *Essai sur Colbert et Turgot.* Troyes, 1878(?).
JOUBLEAU, FELIX. *Etudes sur Colbert, ou Exposition du système d'économie politique suivi en France de 1661 à 1683.* Paris: Guillaumin, 1856.
MAZAN, J. *Les doctrines économiques de Colbert.* Paris, 1900.
SERGEANT, A. C. *The Economic Policy of Colbert.* London, 1899.
SMALL, ALBION W. *The Cameralists.* Chicago: University of Chicago Press, 1909.

Chapter 8

BARBON, NICHOLAS. *A Discourse on Trade.* (London, 1690.) London: G. Allen & Unwin, 1938.
BEER, MAX. *An Inquiry into Physiocracy.* London: George Allen & Unwin, 1939.
———. *Early British Economics.* London: George Allen & Unwin, 1938.
BLOOMFIELD, A. I. "Foreign-Trade Doctrines of the Physiocrats," *American Economic Review*, XXVII, No. 4 (December, 1938), pp. 716-35.
BODIN, JEAN. *Les Six Livres de la République.* Translated by R. Knolles. London: G. Bishop, 1906.
BOUCKE, O. F. *A Critique of Economics, Doctrinal and Methodological.* New York: The Macmillan Co., 1922.
CHINARD, GILBERT. "Jefferson and the Physiocrats," *University of California Chronicle*, XXXIII (1931), pp. 18 ff.
FEILBOGEN, S. *Smith and Turgot.* Vienna: A. Hölder, 1892.
HIGGS, HENRY. *The Physiocrats.* London: Macmillan & Co., 1897.
———. "Cantillon's Place in Economics." *Quarterly Journal of Economics*, VI (July, 1892), pp. 455-91.
———. *The Life and Work of Richard Cantillon.* London: Macmillan & Co., 1931.
JEVONS, W. S. "Richard Cantillon and the Nationality of Political Economy," *Contemporary Review*, January, 1881.

LASKI, HAROLD J. *The Rise of European Liberalism.* London: G. Allen & Unwin, 1936.
LAVERGNE, L. DE. *Les Economistes français du 18 siècle.* Paris: Guillaumin, 1860.
LEWINSKI, JAN ST. *The Founders of Political Economy.* London: P. S. King and Son, 1922.
PUFENDORF, SAMUEL VON. *De Jure Naturae et Gentium.* Translated by B. Kennett *et al.* London: J. & J. Bonwicke, 1749.
SCHELLE, G. *Du Pont de Nemours et l'école physiocratique.* Paris: Guillaumin, 1888.
SMITH, ADAM. *Wealth of Nations.* 2 vols. ed. Edwin Cannan. London: Methuen & Co., 1904.
VINER, JACOB. *Studies in the Theory of International Trade.* New York: Harper & Bros., 1937.

Chapters 9 and 10

BAGEHOT, WALTER. *Economic Studies.* London: R. H. Hutton, 1898.
BONAR, JAMES. *Philosophy and Political Economy.* London: George Allen & Unwin, 1893; 3d ed., 1922.
———. *Catalogue of the Library of Adam Smith.* London: Macmillan & Co., 1932.
COSSA, LUIGI. *Introduction to the Study of Political Economy.* (3d ed., Milan, 1892.) Translated by Louis Dyer. London: Macmillan & Co., 1893.
FEILBOGEN, S. *Smith and Turgot.* Vienna: A. Hölder, 1892.
GINZBERG, ELI. *The House of Adam Smith.* New York: Columbia University Press, 1934.
HALDANE, R. B. *Life of Adam Smith.* London: W. Scott, 1887.
HIRST, F. W. *Adam Smith.* London: Macmillan & Co., 1904.
HOLLANDER, J. H., *et al. Adam Smith, 1776-1926.* Chicago: University of Chicago Press, 1928.
LESLIE, T. E. CLIFFE. *Essays in Political and Moral Philosophy.* Dublin: Hodges, Foster & Figgis, 1879.
———. "Political Economy of Adam Smith," *Fortnightly Review,* I (1870).
MORROW, G. R. *Ethical and Economic Theories of Adam Smith.* New York: Longmans, Green & Co., 1923.
PRICE, L. L. *A Short History of Political Economy in England.* London: Methuen & Co., 1896.
———. *Economic Science and Practice.* London: Methuen & Co., 1896.
RAE, JOHN. *Life of Adam Smith.* New York: The Macmillan Co., 1895.
STEWART, DUGALD. *The Collected Works of Dugald Stewart.* 2 vols.: 1st ed., Cambridge, 1829; 2d ed., Edinburgh: Constable & Co., 1854-60.
TOYNBEE, ARNOLD. *Lectures on the Industrial Revolution.* New York: Longmans, Green & Co., 1908.
VINER, JACOB. "Adam Smith and Laissez Faire." *Journal of Political Economy,* XXXV (April, 1927), pp. 198-232.
WAGNER, D. O. *Social Reformers.* New York: The Macmillan Co., 1934.

Chapter 11

BAGEHOT, WALTER. *Economic Studies.* London: R. H. Hutton, 1898.
BONAR, JAMES (ed.). *Letters of David Ricardo to Thomas Robert Malthus.* Oxford: Oxford University Press, 1887.
———. *Malthus and His Work.* London: Macmillan & Co., 1885; 2d ed., 1924.
———. *Philosophy and Political Economy.* London: George Allen & Unwin, 1893; 2d ed., 1909.

CAIRNES, J. E. *The Character and Logical Method of Political Economy.* London: Macmillan & Co., 1875.

CARR-SAUNDERS, A. M. *The Population Problem; A Study in Human Evolution.* Oxford: Clarendon Press, 1922.

——. *World Population—Past Growth and Present Trends.* Oxford: Clarendon Press, 1936.

ENSOR, GEORGE. *An inquiry concerning the population of nations, containing a refutation of Mr. Malthus's essay on population.* London: E. Wilson, 1818.

GODWIN, WILLIAM. *Essay on Population.* London: Longman, Hurst, Rees, Orme & Brown, 1820.

GRIFFITH, G. T. *Population Problems of the Age of Malthus.* Cambridge: Cambridge University Press, 1926.

KEYNES, J. M. *Essays in Biography.* London: Rupert Hart-Davis, 1951.

LLOYD, W. F. *Two Lectures on the Checks of Population.* Oxford, 1833.

MALTHUS, THOMAS ROBERT. *Essay on the Principle of Population.* London; 1798; 2d ed., T. Bensley, 1803.

——. *Principles of Political Economy.* London: J. Murray, 1820.

——. *Definitions of Political Economy.* London: J. Murray, 1827.

OWEN, ROBERT D. *Moral Physiology, A Brief and Plain Treatise on the Population Question.* London: E. Truelove, 1832.

SADLER, M. T. *The Law of Population; a Treatise in Six Books; in Disproof of the superfecundity of human beings, and developing the real principle of their increase.* London: J. Murray, 1830.

SENIOR, N. W. *Two Lectures on Population.* London: J. Murray, 1831.

STEPHEN, LESLIE. *The English Utilitarians.* 3 vols. New York: G. P. Putnam's Sons, 1900.

Chapter 12

BAGEHOT, WALTER. *Economic Studies.* London: R. H. Hutton, 1888.

CANNAN, EDWIN. *A History of the Theories of Production and Distribution in English Political Economy.* London: P. S. King & Son, 1903.

HOLLANDER, JACOB H. *David Ricardo; A Centenary Estimate.* Baltimore: Johns Hopkins University Press, 1910.

——. "Development of Ricardo's Theory of Value," *Quarterly Journal of Economics,* XVIII (August, 1904).

MARSHALL, ALFRED. "Ricardo's Theory of Value," Appendix I in *Principles of Economics.* New York: The Macmillan Co., 1920.

McCULLOCH, J. R. *The Works of David Ricardo.* London: J. Murray, 1846.

RICARDO, DAVID. *Principles of Political Economy and Taxation.* London: J. Murray, 1817.

SRAFFA, P. *The Works and Correspondence of David Ricardo.* 9 vols. Cambridge: Cambridge University Press, 1951 and 1952.

Chapter 13

BAIN, ALEXANDER. *James Mill.* London: Longmans, Green & Co., 1882.

——. *John Stuart Mill.* London: Longmans, Green & Co., 1882.

BOWLEY, MARIAN. *Nassau Senior and Classical Economics.* London: George Allen & Unwin, 1937.

COURTNEY, W. L. *Life of John Stuart Mill.* London: W. Scott, 1889.

HAYEK, F. A. *John Stuart Mill and Harriet Taylor.* London: Routledge and Kegan Paul, Ltd., 1951.

LEVY, S. LEON. *Industrial Efficiency and Social Economy.* 2 vols. New York: Henry Holt & Co., 1928.

Levy, S. Leon. "Nassau W. Senior, British Economist in the Light of Recent Researches," *Journal of Political Economy*, XXVI (1918), pp. 347-65, 509-35.
——. *Nassau W. Senior: Prophet of Modern Capitalism.* Boston: B. Humphries, 1943.
Marshall, Alfred. "On Mr. Mill's Theory of Value," *Fortnightly Review*, XXV (1876).
Mill, John Stuart. *Autobiography.* ed. by John Jacob Coss. New York: Columbia University Press, 1924.
——. *Principles of Political Economy.* 2 vols. Boston: Little, Brown & Co., 1848.
——. *Utilitarianism.* London: J. M. Dent & Sons, 1912.
Murray, R. H. *Studies in the English Social and Political Theories of the Nineteenth Century.* Cambridge: Cambridge University Press, 1921.
Neff, Emery E. *Carlyle and Mill—An Introduction to Victorian Thought.* New York: Columbia University Press, 1926.
See, Henri. "Stuart Mill et la propriété foncière," *Revue internationale de sociologie*, XXXII (1924), pp. 606-19.
Stephen, Leslie. *The English Utilitarians.* London: G. P. Putnam's Sons, 1900.
Taussig, F. W. *Wages and Capital* New York: Appleton-Century-Crofts, Inc., 1896.

Chapter 14

Hasek, C. W. *The Introduction of Adam Smith's Doctrines into Germany.* New York: Columbia University Press, 1925.
Hermann, Wilhelm von. *Staatswissenschaftliche Untersuchungen.* Berlin, 1832.
Kuhn, E. *Der Staatswirtschaftslehrer Christian Jakob Kraus und seine Beziehungen zu Adam Smith.* Königsberg, 1902.
Lueder, A. F. *Ueber Nationalindustrie und Staatswirtschaft. Nach Adam Smith bearbeitet von August Ferdinand Lueder.* 2 vols. Berlin, 1800-2.
Paulsen, F. *Geschichte des gelehrten Unterrichts.* 2 vols. Berlin, 1921.
Roscher, W. *Geschichte der National-Oekonomik.* Munich, 1874.
Sartorius, G. *Von den Elementen des National-Reichthums und von der Staatswirtschaft, nach Adam Smith. Zum Gebrauche bey akademischen Vorlesungen und beym Privat-Studio ausgearbeitet.* Göttingen, 1806.
Say, J. B. *Treatise on Political Economy.* Translated by C. R. Prinsep. Boston: Wells & Lilly, 1821.
Small, A. W. *The Cameralists.* Chicago: University of Chicago Press, 1909.
Teilhac, E. *L'oeuvre économique de Jean-Baptiste Say.* Paris: F. Alcan, 1927.

Chapter 15

Carey, H. C. *The Harmony of Interests, Agricultural, Manufacturing, and Commercial.* Philadelphia: H. C. Baird & Co., 1865.
——. *The Past, the Present, and the Future.* Philadelphia: H. C. Baird & Co., 1869.
——. *Principles of Political Economy.* 3 vols. Philadelphia: Carey, Lea & Blanchard, 1837-1840.
——. *Principles of Social Science.* Condensed as *Manual of Social Sciences* by Kate McKean. 3 vols. Philadelphia: J. B. Lippincott & Co., 1858-1860.
Hausser, Ludwig (ed.) *List's Gesammelte Schriften.* 3 vols. Stuttgart, 1850.
Hirst, Margaret E. *Life of Friedrich List and Selections from his Writings.* New York: C. Scribner's Sons, 1909.
Levermore, C. H. "Henry C. Carey and his Social System," *Political Science Quarterly*, V (1890), pp. 553-82.
List, Friedrich. *The National System of Political Economy.* Translated by S. S. Lloyd. New York: Longmans, Green & Co., 1904.

NEILL, C. P. *Daniel Raymond; an Early Chapter in the History of Economic Theory in the United States.* Baltimore: Johns Hopkins University Press, 1897.

NOTZ, WILLIAM F. "Friedrich List in America," *American Economic Review,* XVI (1926), pp. 249-65.

RAYMOND, DANIEL. *Thoughts on Political Economy.* Baltimore: F. Lucas & E. J. Coale, 1820.

———. *Elements of Political Economy.* Baltimore: F. Lucas & E. J. Coale, 1820.

TEILHAC, ERNEST. *Histoire de la pensée économique aux Etats-Unis au dix-neuvième siècle.* Paris: 1928. Translated by E. A. J. Johnson as *Pioneers of American Economic Thought in the Nineteenth Century.* New York: The Macmillan Co., 1936.

TURNER, JOHN ROSCOE. *The Ricardian Theory in Early American Economics.* New York: New York University Press, 1921.

Chapter 16

ASHLEY, W. J. "On the Study of Economic History," *Quarterly Journal of Economics,* VII (January, 1893).

———. "Thorold Rogers," *Political Science Quarterly,* IV (1889).

BAGEHOT, WALTER. *Works and Life of Walter Bagehot,* ed. Mrs. Russell Barrington. 10 vols. London: Longmans, Green & Co., 1915.

BELOW, GEORG VON. "Zur Würdigung der historischen Schule der Nationalökonomie," *Zeitschrift für Sozialwissenschaft,* VII (1904).

BÜCHER, KARL. "Roscher, Wilhelm," *Allgemeine deutsche Biographie.* Supplementary Vol. LIII. Leipzig, 1907; and "Wilhelm Roscher," *Preussische Jahrbücher,* LXXVII (1894).

DEFOURNY, M. "Karl Knies," *Revue d'économie politique,* XX (1906).

FALKINER, C. L. "A Memoir of the Late John Kells Ingram," *Journal* (Statistical and Social Inquiry Society of Ireland). XII (1906-12).

FRANZ, GOTTFRIED. *Studien über Bruno Hildebrand.* Marburg, 1928.

GEHRIG, HANS. "Bruno Hildebrand Gedenkworte," *Jahrbücher für Nationalökonomie und Statistik,* 3d Series, XLIII (1912).

HUTER, M. *Die Methodologie der Wirtschaftswissenschaft bei Roscher und Knies.* Jena, 1928.

KEYNES, J. M. *The Scope and Method of Political Economy,* 3d ed. London, Macmillan & Co., 1904.

LESLIE, T. E. CLIFFE. *On the Philosophical Method of Political Economy.* Dublin: Hodges, Foster & Figgis, 1876.

LIFSCHITZ, F. *Die Historische Schule der Wirtschaftswissenschaft.* Bern, 1914.

LOOS, I. A. "Historical Approach to Economics," *American Economic Review,* VIII (1918).

MONTAGUE, F. C. *Arnold Toynbee.* ("Johns Hopkins University, Studies in Historical and Political Science," VII, No. I.) Baltimore, 1889.

SCHUMPETER, JOSEPH. "Gustav v. Schmoller und die Probleme von heute," *Schmoller's Jahrbuch,* I (1926).

Chapter 17

ADAMS, HENRY. *Karl Marx and His Earlier Writings.* London: George Allen & Unwin, 1940.

BEER, MAX. *The Life and Teaching of Karl Marx.* London: National Labor Press, 1921.

BLODGETT, R. H. *Comparative Economic Systems.* New York: The Macmillan Co., 1949.

BOBER, M. M. *Karl Marx's Interpretation of History.* Cambridge, Mass.: Harvard University Press, 1947.
BÖHM-BAWERK, E. VON. *Karl Marx and the Close of His System.* London: T. Fisher Unwin, 1898.
COLE, G. D. H. *The Meaning of Marxism.* London: V. Gollancz, 1948.
——. *What Marx Really Meant.* London: V. Gollancz, 1934.
DOBB, MAURICE. *Capitalist Enterprise and Social Progress.* London: G. Routledge & Sons, 1925.
GONNER, E. C. K. *The Social Philosophy of Rodbertus.* London: Macmillan & Co., 1899.
GRAY, ALEXANDER. *The Socialist Tradition.* New York: Longmans, Green & Co., 1946.
HOOK, SIDNEY. *Towards the Understanding of Karl Marx.* New York: John Day Co., 1933.
KAUTSKY, KARL. *The Economic Doctrines of Karl Marx.* London: A. & C. Black, 1925.
LAIDLER, H. W. *Socio-Economic Movements.* New York: The Thos. Y. Crowell Co., 1945.
LASKI, HAROLD. *Karl Marx: An Essay.* London: George Allen & Unwin, 1922.
——. *Karl Marx with the Communist Manifesto.* New York: League for Industrial Democracy, 1933.
LIEBKNECHT, WILHELM. *Karl Marx, Biographical Memoirs.* Chicago: Charles H. Kerr, 1901.
MARX, KARL. *Capital.* 3 vols. Chicago: Charles H. Kerr, 1907-09.
——. *Value, Price, and Profit.* Chicago: Charles H. Kerr, 1913.
MEHRING, F. *Karl Marx: the Story of His Life.* New York: Covici, Friede, Inc., 1935.
RÜHLE, OTTO. *Karl Marx: His Life and Work.* New York: The Viking Press, 1929.
RUSSELL, BERTRAND, DEWEY, JOHN, et al. *The Meaning of Marx.* New York: Farrar & Rinehart, 1934.
SCHWARZCHILD, LEOPOLD. *The Red Prussian, the Life and Legend of Karl Marx.* New York: Chas. Scribner's Sons, 1947.
SHAW, GEORGE BERNARD. *The Intelligent Woman's Guide to Socialism and Capitalism.* New York: Brentano's, 1928.
SWEEZY, PAUL M. *The Theory of Capitalist Development.* New York: Oxford University Press, 1942.

Chapter 18

ECKARD, E. W. *Economics of W. S. Jevons.* Washington, D. C.: American Council on Public Affairs, 1940.
EDGEWORTH, F. Y. "William Stanley Jevons," *The Academy,* XXII, pp. 151 ff.
FRASER, L. M. *Economic Thought and Language.* London: A. & C. Black, 1937.
HAYEK, F. A. VON. Introduction to the 3d edition of Gossen's *Entwickelung der Gesetze des menschlichen Verkehrs und der daraus fliessenden Regeln für menschliches Handeln.* Berlin, 1927.
HIGGINS, B. H. "W. S. Jevons—a Centenary Estimate," *The Manchester School,* VI (1935).
JEVONS, W. S. *The Theory of Political Economy,* 2d ed. London: Macmillan & Co., 1879.
KEYNES, J. M. "William Stanley Jevons," *Journal of the Royal Statistical Society,* XCIX (1936), pp. 516-48.
Letters and Journal of W. Stanley Jevons. Edited by his wife. London: Macmillan & Co., 1886.
LIEFMANN, R. "Gossen, Hermann Heinrich," *Handwörterbuch der Staatswissenschaften,* IV. Vienna, 1927.

LIEFMANN, R. "H. H. Gossen und seine Lehre." *Jahrbücher für Nationalökonomie,* XL (1910), pp. 483-98.
MARSHALL, A. "Mr. Jevons' *Theory of Political Economy*," *The Academy,* April 1, 1872. Reprinted in *Memorials,* ed. A. C. Pigou, London: Macmillan & Co., 1925.
MEITZEL, C. "H. H. Gossen," *Handwörterbuch der Staatswissenschaften,* V, p. 45.
ROBBINS, L. "The Place of Jevons in the History of Economic Thought," *The Manchester School,* VII (1935), pp. 1-17.
WEINBERGER, O. "Hermann Heinrich Gossen," *Schmollers Jahrbuch,* LI (1927).
WICKSTEED, P. H. "On Certain Passages in Jevons' Theory of Political Economy," *Quarterly Journal of Economics,* III (1889), pp. 293-314.
YOUNG, A. A. "Jevons' Theory of Political Economy," *American Economic Review,* II (1912), pp. 576-89.

Chapter 19

BLOCK, HENRI-SIMON. "Karl Menger, the Founder of the Austrian School," *Journal of Political Economy,* XLVIII (January, 1940).
CLARK, JOHN BATES. *The Distribution of Wealth.* New York: The Macmillan Co., 1899.
DAVENPORT, H. J. *Value and Distribution.* Chicago: The University of Chicago Press, 1908.
HAYEK, F. A. VON. "Karl Menger," *Collected Works,* Vol. I. ("The London School of Economics, Reprints of Scarce Tracts, No. 19.") London, 1934.
HOLLANDER, J. H. (ed.). *Economic Essays, Contributed in Honor of John Bates Clark.* New York: The Macmillan Co., 1927.
KNIGHT, FRANK H. *Ethics of Competition.* New York: Harper & Bros., 1935.
MACFARLANE, CHAS. W. *Value and Distribution.* Philadelphia: J. P. Lippincott & Co., 1898.
MENGER, KARL. *Grundsätze der Volkswirthschaftslehre.* Vienna, 1891.
MITCHELL, W. C. "Wieser's Theory of Social Economics," *Political Science Quarterly,* XXXII (1917), pp. 95-118.
ROBBINS, LIONEL. *An Essay on the Nature and Significance of Economic Science.* London: Macmillan & Co., 1935.
SELIGMANN, E. R. A. *Essays in Economics.* New York: The Macmillan Co., 1925.
SMART, WILLIAM. *An Introduction to the Theory of Value.* London: Macmillan & Co., 1920.
STIGLER, G. J. "The Economics of Karl Menger," *Journal of Political Economy,* XLV (April, 1937), pp. 229-50.
———. *Production and Distribution Theories—The Formative Period.* New York: The Macmillan Co., 1941.
VINER, JACOB. "The Utility Concept in Value Theory and Its Critics," *Journal of Political Economy,* XXXIII (1925), pp. 369-87, 638-59.

Chapter 20

ALLEN, R. G. D. *Mathematical Analysis for Economists.* London: Macmillan & Co., 1938.
ANTONELLI, E. "Walras," *Revue d'histoire des doctrines économiques et sociales,* II (1910), pp. 169-90.
BORTKIEWICZ, L. VON. "Léon Walras, éléments d'économie politique pure," *Revue d'économie politique,* IV (1890), pp. 80-86.
BOUSQUET, G. H. *Introduction à l'étude du Manuele de V. Pareto.* Paris: Payot, 1927.

Bousquet, G. H. "Léon Walras et son temps, 1834-1934," *Journal des économistes,* CIV (1934), pp. 806-10.

——. *Vilfredo Pareto.* Paris: Payot, 1928.

Boven, R. *Les applications mathématiques à l'économie politique.* Lausanne, 1912.

Cournot, A. *Recherches sur les principes mathématiques de la théorie des richesses.* Paris, 1838.

Edgeworth, F. Y. *Mathematical Psychics.* London: C. Kegan Paul & Co., 1881.

Hicks, J. R. "Léon Walras," *Econometrica,* II (1934), pp. 338 ff.

Jaffé, W. "Unpublished Papers and Letters of Léon Walras," *Journal of Political Economy,* XXXXIII (1935), pp. 187-207.

Jevons, W. S. *Theory of Political Economy.* London: Macmillan & Co., 1871. "Léon Walras et sa correspondance avec Augustin Cournot et Stanley Jevons, avec une note d'Etienne Antonelli," *Econometrica,* III (1935), pp. 119-27.

Marget, A. W. "Léon Walras and the 'Cash-Balance Approach' to the Problem of the Value of Money," *Journal of Political Economy,* XXXIX (1931), pp. 569-600.

——. "Monetary aspects of the Walrasian System," *Journal of Political Economy,* XLIII (1935), pp. 145-86.

Pantaleoni, M. "Autobiografia di Leone Walras." *Giornale degli economisti,* Series 2, XXXVII (1908), pp. 603-10.

Pareto, V. *Cours d'Economie Politique.* Lausanne: F. Rouge, 1896.

——. *Manuel d'Economie Politique.* Paris: V. Giard & E. Brière, 1909.

——. "Walras," *Economic Journal,* XX (1910), pp. 137-40.

Schumpeter, J. "Marie Esprit Léon Walras," *Zeitschrift für Volkswirtschaft Sozialpolitik und Verwaltung,* XIX (1910), pp. 397-402.

Wicksell, K. *Lectures on Political Economy.* Vol. I. New York: The Macmillan Co., 1934.

Chapters 21 and 22

Dorfman, Joseph. *The Economic Mind in American Civilization.* 3 vols. New York: The Viking Press, 1949.

Ely, R. T. *Ground Under Our Feet, An Autobiography.* New York: The Macmillan Co., 1938.

Essays contributed in honor of John Bates Clark. New York: The Macmillan Co., 1927.

Fetter, F. A. "The Early History of Political Economy in the United States," *Proceedings of the American Philosophical Society,* XXCVII, No. 1 (1943).

George, Henry. *Progress and Poverty.* New York: Appleton-Century-Crofts, Inc., 1882.

Gruchy, A. G. *Modern Economic Thought; The American Contribution.* New York: Prentice-Hall, Inc., 1947.

Homan, P. T. *Contemporary Economic Thought.* New York: Harper & Bros., 1928.

Normano, J. F. *The Spirit of American Economics.* New York: John Day Co., 1943.

Chapter 23

W. C. Mitchell

Clark, J. M. "Wesley C. Mitchell's Contribution to the Theory of Business Cycles," *Methods in the Social Sciences,* ed. S. A. Rice. Chicago: University of Chicago Press, 1931.

Mitchell, W. C. *The Backward Art of Spending Money.* New York: McGraw-Hill Book Co., 1937.

MITCHELL, W. C. *Business Cycles.* Berkeley: University of California Press, 1913.
———. *Business Cycles, the Problem and its Setting.* New York: National Bureau of Economic Research, 1927.
———. *Gold, Prices and Wages under the Greenback Standard.* Berkeley: University of California Press, 1903.
———. *A History of the Greenbacks.* Chicago: University of Chicago Press, 1903.
——— and BURNS, A. F. *Measuring Business Cycles.* New York: National Bureau of Economic Research, 1946.
SCHUMPETER, J. A. "Mitchell's Business Cycles," *Quarterly Journal of Economics,* XLV (1931), pp. 150-72.

THORSTEIN VEBLEN

DORFMAN, JOSEPH. *Thorstein Veblen and his America.* New York: The Viking Press, 1934.
DUFFUS, R. L. *The Innocents at Cedro.* New York: The Macmillan Co., 1944.
The Higher Learning in America, a Memorandum on the Conduct of Universities by Business Men. New York: The Viking Press, 1918.
HOBSON, J. A. *Veblen.* New York: J. Wiley & Sons, 1937.
TUGWELL, REXFORD G. *The Trend of Economics.* New York: Alfred A. Knopf, 1924.
VEBLEN, THORSTEIN. *The Theory of Business Enterprise.* New York: Chas. Scribner's Sons, 1904.
———. *The Theory of the Leisure Class.* New York: The Macmillan Co., 1912.
———. *The Vested Interests and the State of the Industrial Arts.* New York: B. W. Huebsch, 1919.

JOHN R. COMMONS

American Economic Review, IX (1919), Supplement.
ATKINS, W. E., *et al. Economic Behavior.* Boston: Houghton Mifflin Co., 1931.
BURNS, E. M. "Institutionalism and Orthodox Economics," *American Economic Review,* XXI (1931), pp. 80 ff.
COMMONS, J. R. *Institutional Economics.* New York: The Macmillan Co., 1934.
———. "Institutional Economics," *American Economic Review,* XXI (1931), pp. 648-57; XXVI (1936), pp. 236-54.
———. *Legal Foundations of Capitalism.* New York: The Macmillan Co., 1924.
———. *Myself.* New York: The Macmillan Co., 1934.
COMMONS, J. R., *et al. History of Labor in the United States.* New York: The Macmillan Co., 1918.
———. *Industrial Government.* New York: The Macmillan Co., 1921.
HAMILTON, W. H. *Current Economic Problems.* Chicago: University of Chicago Press, 1925.
HOMAN, P. T. "Appraisal of Institutional Economics," *American Economic Review,* XXII (1932), pp. 10-17.
———. "Institutionalism: What It Is and What It Hopes to Become," *American Economic Review,* XXI (1931), pp. 134-41.
THORP, W. L. *Economic Institutions.* New York: The Macmillan Co., 1928.

Chapter 24

DAVENPORT, H. J. *The Economics of Alfred Marshall.* Ithaca: Cornell University Press, 1935.
KEYNES, J. M. "Alfred Marshall, 1842-1924," *Economic Journal,* XXXIV (1924), pp. 311-72.
———. *Essays in Biography.* London: Rupert Hart-Davis, 1951.
MARSHALL, ALFRED. *Principles of Economics.* New York: The Macmillan Co., 1890.

Pigou, A. G. *Memorials of Alfred Marshall.* London: Macmillan & Co., 1925.
Stigler, George J. *Production and Distribution Theories.* New York: The Macmillan Co., 1941.
Taussig, F. W. "Alfred Marshall," *Quarterly Journal of Economics,* XXXIX, pp. 1-14.

Chapter 25

Dillard, Dudley. *The Economics of John Maynard Keynes.* New York: Prentice-Hall, Inc., 1948.
Harris, Seymour. *The New Economics.* New York: Alfred A. Knopf, 1947.
Harrod, R. F. *The Life of John Maynard Keynes.* London: Macmillan & Co., 1951.
Keynes, J. M. *Indian Currency and Finance.* London: Macmillan & Co., 1913.
———. *The Economic Consequences of the Peace.* New York: Harcourt, Brace and Co., 1920.
———. *A Treatise on Probability.* London: Macmillan & Co., 1921.
———. *A Revision of the Treaty.* New York: Harcourt, Brace & Co., 1922.
———. *A Treatise on Money.* 2 vols. London: Macmillan & Co., 1930.
———. *Essays in Persuasion.* New York: Harcourt, Brace & Co., 1932.
———. *Essays in Biography.* London: Macmillan & Co., 1933.
———. *The General Theory of Employment, Interest and Money.* New York: Harcourt, Brace & Co., 1936.
———. *How to Pay for the War.* New York: Harcourt, Brace & Co., 1940.
"Lord Keynes," *Fortune,* April, 1944.
Marget, A. W. *The Theory of Prices.* 2 vols. New York: Prentice-Hall, Inc., 1938-42.
Mantoux, E. *Carthaginian Peace; or the Economic Consequences of J. M. Keynes.* London: Oxford University Press, 1946.
Pigou, A. C. "Mr. J. M. Keynes' General Theory of Employment, Interest and Money," *Economica,* III (1936), pp. 115-32.
Robertson, D. H. *Essays in Monetary Theory.* London: P. S. King & Son, Ltd., 1940.
———. "Mr. Keynes' Theory of Money." *Economic Journal,* XLI (1931), pp. 395-411.
Robinson, Joan. *Essays in the Theory of Unemployment.* London: Macmillan & Co., 1937.
Sauliner, R. J. *Contemporary Monetary Theory.* New York: Columbia University Press, 1938.
Schumpeter, J. "John Maynard Keynes, 1883-1946," *American Economic Review,* XXXIX, No. 4 (September, 1946).
Tarshis, Lorie. *The Elements of Economics.* Boston: Houghton Mifflin Co., 1947.
Timlin, M. F. *Keynesian Economics.* Toronto: University of Toronto Press, 1942.

Chapter 26

Cassels, J. M. "Excess Capacity and Monopolistic Competition," *Quarterly Journal of Economics,* LI (1937), pp. 426 ff.
Harrod, R. F. *The Trade Cycle.* New York: Oxford University Press, 1936.
Kaldor, N. "The Equilibrium of the Firm," *Economic Journal,* XLIV (1934), pp. 60 ff.
Lerner, A. P. "Evaluation of the Practical Significance of the Theory of Monopolistic Competition," *American Economic Review,* XXIX (1939), pp. 227 ff.
Robinson, E. A. G. *Monopoly.* Cambridge: The University Press, 1941.

ROBINSON, JOAN. *The Economics of Imperfect Competition*. London: Macmillan & Co., 1933.

——. "What is Perfect Competition?" *Quarterly Journal of Economics*, XLIX (1934), pp. 104 ff.

SRAFFA, P. "The Laws of Returns under Competitive Conditions," *Economic Journal*, XXXVI (1926), pp. 535 ff.

STACKELBERG, H. VON. *Grundlagen einer reinen kostentheorie*. Vienna: J. Springer, 1932.

——. *Marktform und Gleichgewicht*. Vienna: J. Springer, 1934.

TRIFFIN, R. *Monopolistic Competition and General Equilibrium Theory*. Cambridge: Harvard University Press, 1940.

INDEX

(Biographical references appear in boldface type.)

INDEX